Start-Up!

An Entrepreneur's Guide to a Successful Small Business

**Everything You Need To
Know, But Didn't Know To
Ask**

Ronald K.
Ferguson

Start-Up! An Entrepreneur's Guide to a Successful Small Business

First edition, May, 2016

Second edition, November, 2017

ISBN: 0-9974846-1-6

turning-ip101.com publishes books that promote small business success.

www.turning-ip101.com

<u>Disclaimer</u>

The information in this book is intended to provide helpful information on a wide variety of topics related to planning, starting up, and successfully operating a small business. It is provided and sold with the knowledge that the publisher and author do not offer any legal or other professional advice. If you need such expertise, consult with the appropriate professional. While this book has tried to be comprehensive, it does not contain all information available on each subject that it covers. Therefore, it should serve only as a guide, and not as the ultimate source of subject information. Every effort has been made to make this book as accurate as possible. However, there may be typographical and or content errors. This book has not been created to be specific to any individual's or organization's situation or needs. References are provided for informational purposes only and do not constitute endorsement of any websites or other sources. Readers should be aware that the websites listed in this book may change. The author and publisher shall have no liability or responsibility to any person or entity regarding any loss or damage incurred, or alleged to have incurred, directly or indirectly, by the information contained in this book. You hereby agree to be bound by this disclaimer or you may return this book directly to the publisher for a full refund.

Contents – What's Inside

Contents

Contents

As a first-time entrepreneur who wants to start a small business, you won't know one very important detail ... *what you don't know* ... until it's too late.

This little-known fact (shall we call it an unknown fact?) will repeat itself dozens of times throughout the life of your small business, potentially biting you in the patoot each time. The resulting mistakes, and the costs to correct them, can be large, painful, and damaging, not only to your business, but to you as the owner, your employees, your product success, and possibly your customers.

Start-Up! An *Entrepreneur's Guide to a Successful Small Business* was written to address that dilemma. Written in an easily-readable style, it's the ideal book to read from cover-to-cover when you are first bitten by the start-up bug, hopefully showing you that starting a successful small business is eminently do-able – provided it's done right. And keep the book at your fingertips as you work through everything necessary to bring your new small business to the big opening day ... and beyond.

This book wasn't written for the Mark Zuckerberg's of the world – the high-flying college guy who fleshes out the Facebook idea in his dorm room and then has several million venture capital dollars lined up before the business opens its doors. Even an entrepreneur with that much instant money will still face all of the business challenges discussed in this book, but with so much money to speed up the process, he'll have dozens on staff to handle the challenges as they arise.

Instead, this book is written for the other 99.9% of the first-time entrepreneurs who want to start a small business. And being a first-timer, you'll have the luxury of a business idea in your head, with a pitfall of little knowledge how to actually achieve a *successful* business start-up. Today's small business failure rate hovers around 50% – yes, that's 1 out of every 2 small businesses are likely to fail *before the end of their 5th year*. The challenge is, what kinds of things can go wrong to cause a business failure, and *what do you need to know – before it happens*?

Here's what makes this book so special. Much of the reference information this book contains can be found on the internet. But a huge amount of that information is not focused to the correct perspective. Or it's from a website that's primarily trying to sell you something. Or worse, information that is simply wrong. The problem is, when you don't know what you don't know, there's no way to make the correct internet search to find the right answers – *before you need it*. With this book in your back pocket (or on your iPad), you'll have a detailed guidebook that can steer you through the labyrinth of small business areas – *just in time*.

How does this book solve the dilemma? The first two chapters walk you through answers to many questions you need to ask very early in the process – and I'd be the first to admit that these two chapters are pretty lightweight, but pretty important. It helps you answer the questions:

- Is the entrepreneur's life really for you?
- Do you have a sound business idea?
- Do you have a personal level of commitment required to make this work?
- Do you have enough sheer will power and drive to succeed?
- Do you have the necessary family support?
- Are you comfortable with the level of risk you're taking?
- Are you good at turning opportunities into reality?
- Should you have co-founders, and if you do, how should you divide up the ownership and responsibilities?

Then the book gets down to real brass tacks, with a step-by-step resource and information guide that takes you through the hundred (or so) business tasks you need to accomplish as you work towards your magic Grand Opening. It provides insight to the importance of your company name, including how it looks, sounds, and spells. What if you can't get the website domain name you want for your business – and how important is it to be twinned with your company name? How much thought have you given to your company branding and out-of-the-box sales and marketing that will see you through the initial start-up?

When it's time to formulate the business, what is the difference between a sole proprietorship, a general partnership, an LLC, and a corporation? What are their costs, filing differences, and what are your liabilities and tax consequences for each? What are your state's requirements for business licensing? You'll need to select your professional services consultants – a good business attorney, a good tax advisor, and a business banker – so how do you go through the search process when you have little idea of the optimum criteria for each area?

Do you have enough money in the bank to get you through the initial start-up, plus the inevitable slow sales/revenue period after your Grand Opening hype dies down? The Small Business Administration (SBA) and your small community banks are eager to lend to new start-up businesses, but do you know the ins and outs of successfully applying for a start-up loan – *and winning it*? What's the best business plan to present to your desired SBA-preferred bank? How do you develop *believable* financial projections for your business plan – when you really have no idea how much business you'll have in the first six months, and what will be required to reach profitability? This book will show you, step-by-step, how to create a Cash Flow/Budget spreadsheet, the single most important financial tool you can have, giving you profit/loss projections for the entire next year, plus actual numbers for the previous months. The spreadsheet shows you which products are creating a profit, and which are losses, and how to play what-if scenarios to determine if higher/lower sales, lower expenses, or different pricing will yield the necessary results to meet your expectations.

There's a major section on day-to-day financial management of your business. This includes your day-to-day cash management – such as pricing your products and services, getting paid and collecting the money, and paying your bills. Beyond an SBA-guaranteed loan to get started, we'll look at financing options for working capital, including a revolving line of credit with your business bank, and ask whether you should consider alternative forms of credit that are available to small businesses – some are OK, but many are incredibly risky and expensive.

As a business owner, you _must_ know enough about small business financial statements to maintain a handle on the financial health of your company. Internet searches on how to read a Balance Sheet and Income Statement pull up nothing but information on how to read financial statements for very large publicly-traded companies – which are a totally different kettle of fish from small business financial statements. For example, to see whether your numbers are good or bad, the typical suggestion is to "compare your numbers with others in your industry". For a small business owner, this recommendation is complete rubbish. Your small business numbers simply _won't compare_ to a publicly-traded company. Worse, there's no way to get the financial numbers from your competitors down the street, who aren't about to let you see their financial statements. This book solves the dilemma, and provides advice for comparing your numbers _against your own numbers_, often and consistently, so that you can learn what _good_ numbers are for your business.

Employees, corporate policies, regulatory oversight, and all that stuff. Most new small business entrepreneurs never think of it ahead of time, but adding employees represents one of the single biggest challenges you'll face as a new owner. Even if you've hired (and fired) employees in a past life, doing it for your brand new start-up will be _entirely_ different – where _you_ have to create the rules (and policies) that establish a huge part of the framework of your company. The challenges begin with the initial job postings, résumé reading and fact-checking, job interviews (including questions you cannot and should not ask), salary negotiations, reference and background checks, and finally, successfully making the job offer. But it doesn't end there. Employees will require the appropriate level of a personnel system, a payroll system, and a management system for your fledgling company. Employees require benefit packages, such as vacation time, sick leave, maternity leave, holidays, health care, 401(k) plans, stock option plans – _stuff_ that each entrepreneur might be familiar with from a previous job, but with no past experience for deciding which ones are right and affordable for _your_ new start-up – nor how to set them up. How will you establish your work rules – such as telecommuting, flex time, job sharing? Will you purchase computers and cell phones, or will you let each employee use their personal equipment – including answering their cell phone as if it's a private phone, and a personal computer that isn't secure.

And then there's government oversight of your company. There won't be, you say, because your business is a small mom and pop shop, or a tiny lifestyle company that just sells on Amazon.com or ebay, or a small consulting company that advises clients on innocuous topics. Well, think again – there's an alphabet soup bowl of city, county, state, and federal regulatory agencies ... enough to make your head spin. And it's amazing how even the tiniest business is overseen by the government. First you have to know who they are – the NLRB, the FLSA, the EEOC, OSHA, and ADA to name just a few – why they are important to you, and how everything you do fits into their purview. If an employee (or ex-employee, or even an employment candidate interviewing for a job) files a discrimination or harassment claim to the EEOC, you'll wish you'd paid attention to the regulatory oversight sections of this book.

Lastly, whether you have employees or not, your small business needs a Mission Statement, a Code of Conduct, and company policy rules. Customers won't flock to your door unless they feel good about what you're selling and how you operate, so having some or all of this on your website is important. You won't attract – and keep – good employees unless they believe in the company they're working for – which is why a *corporate culture* is so important. But how does a small business create a culture if you can't even state what that culture should be?

And lastly, how does a small business protect its critical business information – such as proprietary information, trade secrets, and copyrights? Do you have unique processes or products that you've developed that should be protected by a patent, and how much value can they create for your business? Should all of your employees be required to sign non-disclosure statements to protect your proprietary information?

Conclusion. It needs to be said again and again – typical small business entrepreneurs often *don't know what they don't know – until it's too late*. You've just hired your first employee, made gushing statements during the interview that your company's culture will keep new employees around forever – and guess what! – with that one innocuous-sounding statement "keep new employees around forever", you've just thrown your company's at-will employer rights out the window ... without even knowing what "at-will" means to you. Or, you've taken in two partners on your new business deal, keeping 45% ownership each for you and your main partner, and another 10% for a junior partner, only to figure out later that these other two can combine forces to oust you from your company.

There are gotcha's lurking around every corner when you're a small business owner, particularly at a time when you don't have lots of HR infrastructure to keep you out of trouble. Do a search on "*small business harassment stories*", or "*small business hiring mistakes*", or "*small business wrong business structure*". The problem is, these are just three areas that can get you into trouble – there are dozens more – and once you plop a foot into it, the damage is done. This book is designed to keep you out of trouble in the first place.

Hyperlinks – access to them in the printed version. This book is essentially a reference work, providing hundreds of links to internet sites and suggested browser search terms that will get you to the information necessary to achieve your small business success. As exhaustive as it is, the information in this book can only scratch the surface, so the reference sources not only provide backup information to that which is given in the book, but it may help with more complete or alternative opinions and factual information.

In the Kindle version of the book, the Hyperlinks are active. Provided you are connected to the internet when you click on a blue-font Hyperlink, it will take you directly to the internet page being referenced (the link opens in a browser-like page within Kindle). (If you wish to use the links outside of Kindle, use the Hyperlink list via PDF or Word that is described in the next paragraph.)

In the print-on-demand version, though, these Hyperlinks obviously aren't active, and the very last thing you'd want to do is type a 20, 30, or 40 character URL address into your browser. To make life easier for you, all of the Hyperlinks are available in a PDF or Word document (sorted by chapter) that is one of the files you can download – and information on how to request the download is given in the Preface to Chapter 5.

A word about footnotes. As you'll see when you read this book – there are lots (!) of footnotes – and some readers might find them intrusive. In the eBook version they are reformatted as endnotes – since an eBook doesn't have the concept of pages, it's not possible to have bottom-of-page footnotes – so each endnote reference in the text is a link to the appropriate note in the endnote section just before the index. In the printed version, footnotes are placed as normal at the bottom of each page. Sometimes the footnotes provide clarifying information about a topic, but more often they are one of the bibliographical sources for the information being discussed. More importantly, because many topics have more detail than can be covered in this book, the footnotes serve as a description and link to where more information can be found. Many authors use a bibliography for this, but in my lifetime of reading I rarely use a bibliography entry to find out more about a topic – it's just too difficult to determine specifically which bibliography entry is associated with a given topic. For this book, I elected to "pin" a footnote reference to the specific topic where more information can be found. My hope is that this will allow the reader to more easily and fully study up on a topic that interests or concerns them.

Ron Ferguson

Seattle, Washington

Second Edition, October, 2017

Chapter 1   Do You Have What It Takes To Be An Entrepreneur?

> *"My son is now an entrepreneur. That's what you're called when you*
> *don't have a job."*
> Ted Turner, founder of CNN, Turner Classic Movies, former owner
> of the Atlanta Braves, and winner of the America's Cup, 1977

Can anyone be successful at a small business start-up?

Absolutely!

In this first chapter, we'll explore a lot of things to *think about* before making the decision to start a small business – ideas that might help you actually decide if it's right for you. After that, we'll get down to serious details about the many tasks you face in starting your small business, and the gotcha's to watch for in running your new company.

This book is not intended to be a rah-rah motivational book, but rather, a practical book that focuses on the nuts and bolts of starting a new small business, plus a wealth of information on how to keep it running. The bookstore shelves (and Amazon.com) are lined with motivational and inspirational books on what it takes to be a successful small business entrepreneur – but very few (maybe none) are in-depth, totally practical books on the actual mechanics of all that is necessary to hang out your shingle.

> *"Some people dream of success ... while others wake up*
> *and work hard at it."*
> Unknown

Should you start your own business?

"*Are you nuts?*" You're likely to get that response from friends and relatives when you mention you're planning to leave a secure paycheck and start a business. The ones who'll ask are usually the rock-solid, cautious type, who work for someone else and can't imagine why anyone would want the risks, hard work, and sacrifices required of owning your own business.

Actually, a better question to ask is, "Can you afford to fail?" That's not to suggest everyone is automatically doomed to failure, but the grim reality is that the odds of success are not exactly stacked in your favor. If you fail, will your life savings or retirement nest egg go out the window with that failure? If that happens, where does it leave you? Can you recover your life savings? Can you get back into the work force to start earning a salary once again? Do you have other assets – assets that weren't lost in the business failure – that you can liquidate to recover? If you're not comfortable with the answers to those questions, maybe you can't afford to fail – and it's time to rethink your plan.[1]

Here's a story to illustrate the point. In her recent book,[2] *A Fighting Chance*, Elizabeth Warren, U.S. Senator from Massachusetts, relates a story about a student who dropped by her office (when she was a professor of bankruptcy law), and confided, "My parents are bankrupt." To quote Ms. Warren, "They had a small business. It went under, but not until after her parents had cashed out their retirement savings and lost the house." That's an example of a small business entrepreneur going beyond the *afford to fail* point, and it's not the place you want to be with your dream. That situation is hard to bounce back from – at any age.

> *"Whether you think you can, or you think you can't, you're right."*
> Henry Ford

An entrepreneur must be an optimist

If viewed simply from statistical assumptions, common sense would tell you that it's futile to even try starting a new business. The most recent statistics from the Small Business Administration indicate that approximately 66% of new small businesses survive the first two years of operation – and that roughly 50% are still alive and well after five years. With around 500,000 new small businesses started each year, that's approximately 250,000 that succeed. Obviously that means an equal number won't succeed, but the numbers are certainly better than the 30-90% failure rate that's often bandied about. Not surprisingly, the most common reason for failure is lack of experience – and that can easily be chalked up to simply making too many mistakes and falling into too many pitfalls.

If you worry too much about being in the failing half of the statistics, or that you're not experienced in running a business, those worries can cloud your drive and ambition to succeed. And it means you've lessened your chances to succeed – which is exactly Henry Ford's point in the above quote – that good entrepreneurs are optimists.

As an entrepreneur myself, having started my own business when I felt I could still afford to fail, working my tail off for 30 years – and then selling it to retire just before I turned 60 years old – I'm here to say emphatically that if you can afford to fail, you should definitely give it a go! Throughout the journey, there will be times when you feel at the point of failure and ready to throw in the towel. I distinctly remember waking up one morning in a hotel room on the other side of the world, getting ready to head out for a client meeting, and feeling a terrible sense of dread. I'd received an overnight message from my internal accountant of the dire financial straits we'd be in if a promised customer payment didn't arrive *that day*. My primary thought was, "we're heading into bankruptcy by the time I get home". Another time, an entire day was spent

---

[1] Jay Goltz, *Is Starting a Business Brave, Smart, Stupid or Nuts?* New York Times blog, You're The Boss, September 11, 2009, http://boss.blogs.nytimes.com/2009/09/11/is-starting-a-business-brave-smart-stupid-or-nuts/
[2] Elizabeth Warren, *A Fighting Chance,* Metropolitan Books, Henry Holt & Company, 2014

with our corporate attorney discussing how to *flush* the company through bankruptcy as the last resort to an alliance partner who was squeezing us into financial oblivion due to an ill-advised royalty payment contract I'd agreed to – and I knew the bankruptcy wouldn't have a happy ending. At least a dozen scenes like this stick in my mind – maybe none of them as vivid as these two. But nevertheless, at the end of almost 30 years we were still standing ... and financially stable, ready to sell the company and retire.

Are you sufficiently capitalized for that first year? Another impediment to starting a business is the attitude of only jumping in as soon as you have enough capital raised. Granted, it can spell disaster if you jump in with too little capital, but at some point you either need to get your priorities right – or back away from dreaming. The fact of the matter is, the vast majority of new business ventures raise their initial seed money from their own bank accounts, 401(k) account, the Bank of Family and Friends, or anyone else they can convince to help them. Generally speaking, it's difficult to get banks to lend to start-ups, so if you go that route you'll likely need a Small Business Administration (SBA) loan guarantee, which requires sufficient personal assets to be able to meet the collateral requirements for a loan (we'll see a lot more about SBA-guaranteed loans for start-ups in Chapter 4).

As we go through the following chapters, we'll explore many questions to determine if you have what it takes to succeed with a start-up business. Obviously, none of them will specifically tell you if your own business will succeed. – which largely depends on choices you make along the way – choices that you might call good or bad luck. It could be choices in timing ... choices in products or services you're offering ... choices in location ... choices in how you respond to business decisions. In short, you'll be forced to make hundreds of choices.

One good thing about running your own business is that you get to have the final say in many of these choices, so it's very much a case of "the buck stops here".

The good, the bad, and the ugly

Everyone dreams of working for himself or herself. It starts with visions of being your own boss, with no one telling you what to do ... working your own hours ... charting your own destiny ... finally having all the money in the world ... taking vacations whenever and wherever you wish ... in other words, running with the ball, and the ball is all yours.

Aaaaahhhh, yes, life would be easy-peasy if any of this was reality.

And yes, dreaming is great ... but reality is hard. All of these often-stated reasons are, in fact, the biggest fallacies for people dreaming to start their own business.

You've undoubtedly heard the old expression, "chief cook and bottle-washer". Well, nowhere is it more true than someone starting out to run their own business. Whether it's a 1-person operation, a small business with just a few employees, or even a small-to-medium business of fifty employees – you, the business owner and founder, will have to wear many hats, including founder, owner, chief executive, finance officer, production manager, marketing manager, sales manager, chief morale manager, chief communicator, and chief wage earner.

The reality is, when you're working for yourself, 12-, 14-, even 16-hour days might well be the norm, not the exception. Taking weekends off might be de rigueur when you're working for someone else, but it's damned hard to take a full weekend, let alone the luxury of a 1-2 week vacation when you're working for yourself. In many small businesses, when you're not working, you're not bringing in revenue either – making time off and vacations very expensive. At your old 9-to-5 job, working for someone else, a vacation meant you were getting paid a regular salary for the time you're on holiday. When you're working for yourself, if you pay your regular salary while on vacation – and you don't bring in revenue during that vacation – the overall cost of the vacation time doubles – the loss of revenue _and_ the outlay in salary to you.

If you're going to succeed with your new start-up, a critical decision will be to get your priorities right – the choice _now_ that you need to work hard ... and _maybe_ you'll be able to play hard later. That means long hours each day; 6-7 day workweeks are standard, and annual vacations are often bypassed, at least for the first few years. Even family planning might have to take a backseat. I know ... in my case, my wife and I consciously evaluated the question every year, asking ourselves if we should scale back the business development to start a family, knowing that biological clocks were ticking away.

If you're lucky and grow to have employees, you'll find that office and company politics begin as soon as you have three employees (just you and two others). Much of the time, the other two will be positioning to _their_ best advantage, and not necessarily yours (or the company's). That often saps energy and productivity, not only from you and the parties involved, but also from every other employee affected by it.

As soon as you have employees, you have payroll to meet – which is different than when you're just a 1-person company. In your company's early days (or even later), you can always forego your own salary if there isn't enough money in the bank. Try telling that to employees who are expecting a regular payday. And if they don't get that regular paycheck – even missing it once – their new focus could be on job hunting. You've sown the seeds of doubt and contention about the viability of your business, and that makes employees nervous.

You'll also find that with employees, you're now working _for them_ in many ways, and not so much the other way around. Employees require a lot of hard work, managing and communicating with them, finding work for them – particularly work that brings in revenue, resolving employee issues, setting up benefit plans (just try to keep employees if you don't offer any benefits!), establishing work rules, creating work space and good working conditions. The simple fact is, you're now a manager, and with it comes all the responsibilities of being a manager. If you haven't any prior experience as a manager, you're in even deeper doo-doo, as you also now have the opportunity to make all the mistakes of an inexperienced manager, which, if you aren't careful, can sink your ship in the blink of an eye.

While all this is going on, try dredging up new business when you're already putting in more hours than you did at your old job working for someone else. Worse, watch and see what happens if you slough off on new business searches because you already have enough current business. Or see what happens when times get tough and customers stop buying your products or services, or competitors steal some of your customers away.

If you work to keep it a 1-person company, you'll probably be a lot happier – until you get to the age where you'd like to think about an "exit strategy" – a fancy-schmancy pair of words that mean you want to retire to actually live the good life. As a general rule, most 1-person start-ups won't be able to build up enough equity to retire on, or create a product base that can be sold as a viable business without you at the helm. The problem is worse if your skill and service requires hard physical labor – such as many of the building construction trades – as your body will likely wear out earlier than you want it to, and you might not have any business to sell.

Sorry. This is beginning to sound like nothing but arguments for _not_ starting your own business. Au contraire. Starting your own business can be the best idea in the world – but only if you go into it with your eyes open, knowing what you're up against, and knowing what it takes for the long term. Only then, if you still want to tackle it, have you climbed a giant step above naïveté.

In this rest of this chapter we'll explore what it takes to be an entrepreneur. None of it is hard and fast, and not all of it applies to every situation. Much of it is food for thought. It's also geared to anyone who currently works for a living, and who thinks they have a good idea for starting a small business. It's not really intended for someone fresh out of business school, or someone with connections to the elite venture capitalist world. Rather, it's intended for the budding first-time entrepreneur who knows in his or her heart that life's more than just working for a paycheck; someone who is willing to make tremendous sacrifices to break out on their own.

"Starting a business is a lot like jumping out of an airplane and assembling the parachute on the way down."
Unknown

Do you have what it takes to be an entrepreneur?

I'm not suggesting that everyone is cut out to be an entrepreneur. I certainly didn't know that when I started my company. At the time, I didn't have a fully thought-out business plan for my business, or the slightest idea of how to start – and then run – a small business. I didn't have the overall strategic knowledge for fleshing out a full business plan, and I had no idea how to get beyond the first customer I was chasing. I tended towards rather shallow planning, and didn't have any previous experience in business management (except for watching my mother run her small restaurant in my high school years). What I had, though, was an unshakeable belief that whatever I set my mind to, I could do – and I'd work out how to do it along the way. My initial thinking – that I could succeed – fit Henry Ford's quote almost perfectly, and my execution of it was exactly like assembling my parachute on the way down.

Later, after my own company was successfully up and running, I often wondered why more of my employees didn't jump ship and start their own company. There were employees throughout the three major phases of my company who saw what we did, exactly how we did it, and I'm sure they learned lessons from it. Interestingly, though, not a single employee left of their own accord to start their own small business. I could only conclude that none were of the mindset to be an entrepreneur on their own, preferring instead to let me be the entrepreneur they followed, letting me take the risks and losing nights of sleep. In short, assembling the parachute on the way down wasn't in _their_ life's plan.

I recently ran across an article in The New York Times about President Abraham Lincoln and the difficulties he faced as he charted his course through the Civil War.[3] It was very interesting to read how a case study of Lincoln's experiences can inspire someone who has a small business. Here's an excerpt from the article, written by Nancy F. Koehn:

> *The ability to experience negative emotions without falling through the floorboards is vital to entrepreneurs and business leaders. Ari Bloom, a strategic adviser to consumer-related companies and a former student of mine, put it this way: "Nothing prepares you for the emotional ups and downs that come with starting a business. There will be obstacles, big and small, that come at you every day, from personnel issues to supplier delays, to late payments or even hurricanes. Throughout, entrepreneurs must maintain their professional composure while staying true to their vision and their integrity."*

> *"Lincoln is striking because he did all this under extremely difficult circumstances," Mr. Bloom said. "Some of his ability to navigate such difficult terrain was about emotional intelligence and the deep faith he nurtured about his vision. But some of it was also about how he gathered advice and information from a wide range of people, including those who did not agree with him. This is important in building a business because you have to listen to customers, employees, suppliers and investors, including those who are critical of what you are doing."*

> *When I discuss my Lincoln case study with executives, that is one of the most powerful lessons they take away. As Kelly Close, founder and president of Close Concerns, a health care information firm, said in an e-mail, "Being responsible for even a small company and all the people and issues involved in such management forces you to come to terms with yourself and whether you can rise to the challenge — not once but many times." Lincoln, she added, "was able to do this in a way that amazes and inspires me."*

Not everyone is cut out to be an entrepreneur, or to run their own company, but if you choose that path, a quick study of the "Lincoln school of management" emotional intelligence, listening to advice of others, maintaining your vision and faith, isn't a bad idea.

So, the important thing is, no one but you (or a spouse who knows you very well) can judge whether you have what it takes to be an entrepreneur. If you believe enough that you can – a belief in your own vision – you're further along on the path to success than someone who doesn't have it. After that, all it takes is _everything else_ necessary to succeed.

---

[3] Nancy F. Koehn, excerpted from *Lincoln's School of Management*. The New York Times, January 28, 2013, http://www.nytimes.com/2013/01/27/business/abraham-lincoln-as-management-guru.html

"I never took a day off in my twenties. Not one."
Bill Gates, Co-Founder, Microsoft

Are you up for the work level necessary to start a company?

What is your level of commitment to the effort in starting and managing your own company? Are you a self-starter? Do you prefer initiating things to work on, or do you prefer hiding in the corner until a manager selects you for a task? You'd better be the former if you're going to run your own company. By the time they're out of the shower each morning, good entrepreneurs are already thinking about the day's tasks, planning new products or services to develop, plotting new ways to bring in new customers or keep old ones, or figuring out how to manage revenue and expenses. These pesky problems, plus a gazillion others, will fill the remainder of the day. And they'd better be things you either enjoy doing, or are willing to do to achieve your end goal. If not, maybe you should be working for someone else.

Has your family bought into this idea? The old adage "don't take your work home at night" doesn't apply to entrepreneurs – if you don't take your work home at night, you won't stay in business for long. There just aren't enough hours in a workday to allow you *not* to take work home – unless, of course, your typical workday at work is already a lot longer.[4]

The question really is, how will it affect your family life if your all-consuming passion is the founding and managing of your new company – at least for a few years? Will they put up with it and support it, or will you be in divorce court in a short time? How many kid's school plays, music recitals, soccer matches, and kid's birthday parties can you afford to miss as your dream of running your own company plays out? If you don't think about all of this ahead of time, you can easily become so wrapped up in your new venture that you forget about it later – until it's too late.

What about the outside activities you're involved in? By the time most of us are ready to start a company, we already have activities and hobbies outside of work that interest us a lot. It might be the President of the local PTA, it might be weekend dog shows, it might be several-nights-a-week softball – whatever it is, there probably won't be enough time for your outside activities, and there almost certainly won't be the necessary mental effort to continue with them.

Lastly on the topic of commitment, don't forget that life's ambitions don't always stay on track – so you have to be ready for the serendipitous events that come along when least expected. Depending on how you react, these events could derail you into the ditch, or they could strengthen your commitment.

---

[4] There's an old story from the early days of Microsoft about a manager (at the time, managers at Microsoft were entrepreneurs with lots of stock options on the line, even though they were working for salary) who sent a message to Bill Gates at the end of a 12-hour day saying he was going home. Bill shot back, "Working half days again, huh?"

> *"The difference between a boss and a leader:*
> *a boss says 'Go!' – a leader says, 'Let's go!'"*
> E.M. Kelly, U.S. Army

Are you a leader or a manager?

There is a difference, you know.[5] Good entrepreneurs are good leaders, but often good entrepreneurs don't make good managers. In fact, many first-time entrepreneurs fail at getting their company from its initial stage to the viable business stage – where good leadership is required – because they aren't good leaders.

By the time a small business has employees, and maybe the beginnings of its own management team, the first-time entrepreneur also has to be a good manager – but the business starts to fizzle and problems develop because the entrepreneur isn't a good manager.

As a would-be entrepreneur, if you aren't born with both skills, you'll hopefully acquire them when the appropriate time comes.

Much has been written on the subject of leadership versus management. Let's have a brief look at the differences.[6 and 7]

Leaders	... develop the vision of where they want to go
	... have followers
	... are good communicators and can rally the troops around their vision (a corollary is that leaders persuade)
	... empower the people who are following, and encourage innovation
	... are capable and willing to take risk
Managers	... are inserted into an organization to execute a vision
	... have employees
	... can translate the vision into executable actions (a corollary is that managers communicate and get things done by the book)
	... tend to be risk-averse

Suffice it to say that the two skill sets are very different. Many people say that you can't be both a leader and a manager – actually you can be both, but it's crucial to display the appropriate skills *at the appropriate time*. If you're capable of doing that, you can be a leader when you're starting your company, and both a leader and a manager as you transition to a more mature company.

---

[5] Curt Richardson, *Are You a Leader or a Manager? There's a Difference*, Inc. guest blog, undated, http://www.inc.com/curt-richardson/are-you-a-leader-or-a-manager-theres-a-difference.html
[6] Mark Sanborn, *9 Differences Between Managers and Leaders*, Mark Sanborn leadership blog, undated, http://www.marksanborn.com/blog/9-differences-between-managers-and-leaders/
[7] Warren Blank, *The 108 Skills of Natural Born Leaders*, available from amazon.com, http://www.amazon.com/gp/product/B000SARM4O/ref=dp-kindle-redirect?ie=UTF8&btkr=1

As a leader, your primary task will be to carve out and understand the big picture of where your company is heading, and how you'll get there. You must then articulate that vision to everyone in the company, and enable them to carry out your vision.

Unfortunately, in a small business, particularly one that's just starting up, you're wearing so many hats that you can lose sight of the forest for the trees. With everything else you're trying to juggle, it's easy to find that you're being more of a manager and less of a leader. The key is to get your head above the fray as often as you can and make your primary task that of a leader.

What exacerbates this is the part that got you to be an entrepreneur – dreaming up and designing the product or service that enabled you to start your business – can now be your downfall. Tinkering with it, improving it, and seeing that it gets out the door exactly the way you want it could steer you away from other challenges in growing your business.

This aspect of the problem reminds me of Steve Jobs – the guy who was a fanatic micromanager of incredible minutiae of corporate details, not only of product design, but even the design of the famous glass stairs in the Apple stores (which he had a patent for).[8] Others can make this work (I'm sure Bill Gates did it too), but it can just as easily be your downfall.

As often as possible, and just for brief periods of time, get your head out of the nitty-gritty details of running your business, and step back to focus on your *business goals* for the next quarter, or the next year. Most of us don't have the luxury, but I've always been impressed with the twice-a-year, week-long sabbatical getaways that Bill Gates treats himself to, called Think Week.[9] Obviously, the concept as Gates does it is far more elaborate than us mere mortals could afford – his plan requires that a personal assistant spend two months searching through Microsoft to find dozens of concept papers that have been written about all sorts of potential projects, plus culling dozens of publications specifically to get Gates' juices flowing.

Think about the concept – carve out some time, on a regular basis and maybe even regularly scheduled, to just sit back and think about the overall state of your company. It could be a certain place in the world where you're able to do your best thinking, without distractions and other pressures – such as a vacation on the beach, or hiking. It could be just a couple of hours once a month in your office, where you don't take calls, you don't look at e-mails, and you don't sneak a peek at any of the day-to-day details of what's going on with the company.

However you do it, remember that how you balance your thoughts and actions between leadership and management is critical. These two parts of your task as founder and CEO complement each other, and getting it right can be of immense importance to you and your company.

---

[8] Chunka Mui, *Five Dangerous Lessons to Learn From Steve Jobs*, Forbes blog, October 17, 2011, http://www.forbes.com/sites/chunkamui/2011/10/17/five-dangerous-lessons-to-learn-from-steve-jobs/1/
[9] Robert A. Guth, *In Secret Hideaway, Bill Gates Ponders Microsoft's Future*, The Wall Street Journal, March 28, 2005, http://www.wsj.com/articles/SB111196625830690477.

"Be nimble as a cat and build like the ants."
Adarsh Manpuria, start-up advisor

Who is the better entrepreneur – young, old, or tweens?

Today's attitude on the street suggests that the entrepreneur most likely to succeed is one who has nothing to lose – typically thought of as the young 20-somethings, fresh out of college, or even abandoning their degree work to jump into a start-up that was dreamed about in their dorm room.

Surprising, though, there's almost equal data suggesting that more *long-lasting* start-ups are created by older entrepreneurs – the 50+ crowd who are often thought to have *everything* to lose.

Not surprisingly, another study finds that the "tweens" – between the ages of 30 and 50 – are the most typical at creating successful start-ups.

In other words, who's to say that age is really that much of a factor in whether your start-up succeeds. In fact, each group might have age-related, circumstance-related, or attitude-related factors favoring their unique situation.

The 20-something crowd. When you have nothing to lose, you have everything to gain (or so the theory goes). When you're young, have few responsibilities and few commitments, little or no debt, no kids forcing you to save for college tuition – if a wildly risky entrepreneurial venture fails, it's much easier to pick up the pieces and get on with life. If someone in this category even *thinks* about failure risk, it will be minor thoughts that will soon pass. This person isn't bridled with the already-known reasons why he or she would fail. Their enthusiasm and confidence of success, not to mention their knowledge that they already know everything, overrides all other thoughts.

While all this might be true, the audacity of this next pronouncement is stunning. A blog post[10] on TechCrunch, a popular high-tech news blog, quoted this argument by a venture capitalist about a 30-something prospect searching for seed money: "They [entrepreneurs] peak at 25, by 30 they're usually done". The VC went on to say, this is "not a guess, this is a data driven observation". With incredibly ill-reasoned arguments as this, who needs real facts? To be fair, the blog continued "… this only applies to consumer internet entrepreneurs. Enterprise and hardware startups tend to do better with older founders, where experience (and direct sales experience) matters a lot". Duh, why not say that up front, rather than a bold-faced statement that implies you're pond scum as an entrepreneur if you're older than 25?

The corollary to the argument usually goes like this: If you're 50, with a job that already eats up your 9-to-5 day, a big mortgage payment each month, kids to put through college, and a retirement you're struggling to fund, everything about the startup is more difficult. In other words, you have everything to lose, so your risk aversion worries take hold and paralyze you. The argument concludes that this makes you a poor candidate for success as an entrepreneur, so why bother?

---

[10] Michael Arrington, *Internet Entrepreneurs Are Like Professional Athletes, They Peak Around 25,* TechCrunch blog, April 30, 2011, http://techcrunch.com/2011/04/30/internet-entrepreneurs-are-like-professional-athletes-they-peak-around-25/. This blog focuses on information technology companies.

Here's another factor that supposedly favors the young.[11] Big corporations often won't give an inexperienced 20-something a chance, mainly because they don't yet have the experience and a successful track record – not to mention the worldly experience for conservative decision making that is a hallmark of corporate thinking. Yet, being young can be the perfect time to start an earth-shaking small company. You're hip with the times, you have a totally fresh perspective – rather than the drilled-in lessons from the corporate world on how things are *supposed* to be done. Plus, you have all the energy in the world. While this might be true, you can also argue that someone older, wiser to the world, with more assets to help fund the venture, has the better chance to create something lasting ... not to mention more useful for the world at large.

To look at this anecdotally, here are a few examples of well-known and wildly successful start-ups that support the theory of the young crowd being good entrepreneurs (all ages are at time of start-up):

- Apple: Steve Jobs (age 21) and Steve Wozniak (age 26), founded in 1976, recent company valuation $723B
- Microsoft: Bill Gates (age 20) and Paul Allen (age 22), founded in 1975, recent company valuation $383B
- Google: Sergey Brin and Larry Page (both age 25), founded in 1998, recent company valuation $364B
- Facebook: Mark Zuckerberg (age 20), founded in 2004, recent company valuation $230B
- Pinterest: Ben Silbermann and Evan Sharp (both age 27), founded in 2010, recent company valuation $7.7B

Of course, these are all tech software/hardware companies – and all male founders to boot, which we're learning is the norm in the gender-biased world of tech. But take heart, there are successful women entrepreneurs in this age group too, as well as non-tech computer companies, including:

- Spanx: Sarah Blakely (age 29), founded in 2000, the company is still privately owned by Blakely, so there isn't a public valuation of its stock, but Forbes magazine estimates her net worth over $1B.
- Airbnb: Nathan Blecharczyk, Joe Gebbia, and Brian Chesky (all three age 25-26), founded in 2008, recent company valuation $10B
- LearnVest: Alexa von Tobel (age 22), was an investment trader at Morgan Stanley in 2006. Realizing that she – and most of her friends – had never had any serious training in how to manage their personal finances, she founded LearnVest. Over a short span of 7-8 years, she pulled in $78M in venture capital funds, selling the company to Northwestern Mutual Life Insurance Co. in 2015 for an undisclosed amount. She is still the CEO of LearnVest, and her net worth is reportedly $100M. She is also the author of The New York Times best seller, *Financially Fearless*.

The list could go on and on – and these are just some of the high-flyers in the "billion dollar club". In every city across the country you could find dozens more that operate out of the spotlight, but are turning successful for their founders. Think small-time pizza chains that have

---

[11] Brock Blake, *Why 20-Somethings Are the Most Successful Entrepreneurs*, Forbes online, November 12, 2013, http://www.forbes.com/sites/brockblake/2012/11/30/why-20-somethings-are-the-most-successful-entrepreneurs/.

the potential for going national, software start-ups who are writing apps that catch on quickly, craft breweries that are riding a high in people's taste buds.

The Tweens. For every start-up founded by a 20-something, there's almost certainly one or more that are created by the tween-crowd – those in the 30-49 age group – whose age at start-up isn't a news story so it tends to go unreported. If you don't believe that, consider these well-known and wildly successful start-ups:

- Twitter: Jack Dorsey (age 30), Evan Williams (age 34), and Biz Stone (age 32) – with Dorsey supposedly the primary idea guy behind the idea after first spending a few years developing a small company that dispatched couriers, taxis, and emergency services through the internet. Founded in 2006 after lots of growing pains, Twitter now has over 300M users, revenues of $1.4B, and Jack Dorsey has a reported net worth of $2.7B.
- Uber: Travis Kalanick (age 33) and Garrett Camp (age 31) – with Kalanick being the primary founder, who was a serial entrepreneur with earlier start-ups Scour (music file sharing that ran into lots of copyright problems) and Red Swoosh that netted him $16M when he sold it. With the money, he founded Uber in 2009. Kalanick is reported by Forbes to be one of the 400 richest Americans at $6B.
- Amazon: Jeff Bezos (age 31) got his start in IT back office programming in areas related to high-speed internet trading and internet-enabled business opportunities. With this background he pulled up stakes on Wall Street, moved to Seattle (supposedly writing his business plan for Amazon during the road trip from New York). His net worth is over $49B, and his company now leases almost one-quarter of Seattle's best office space (10 million square feet).
- LinkedIn: Reid Hoffman (et al, average age 36), founded LinkedIn in 2002, from early roots working on an Apple product in the 1990s called eWorld (it was an early bulletin board system), then going on to found an internet dating site called socialnet.com (the URL now takes you to spark.net, "a fun site for serious daters"), ending up at PayPal as COO. This circuitous route led to the idea of a business-oriented social network, now with over 380M users, revenue of $2.21B (2014). Microsoft acquired LinkedIn in 2016 for $26B in cash. Hoffman is now on the Microsoft Board of Directors and reportedly has a net worth of $3B.
- Zara: Amancio Ortega (age 30), now 76 years old and the fourth richest person in the world according to Forbes Magazine at $64B, he was the son of a railway worker in Spain. In his early teens he started his work life as a shirt shop helper. Ortega and his wife opened the first Zara store in 1975, sewing many of his earlier designs in his living room. The chain grew exponentially in the 1980s, with upwards of 8,000 stores around the world.
- Gap: Doris Fisher (age 37), now 83 years old and named one of the 100 Most Powerful Women in America by Forbes Magazine, co-founded the Gap (which denoted the "generation gap") in 1969 with her husband, Donald, when he was unable to find a pair of jeans that fit him. Her forte was merchandising, and she was still active in the company until 2009. The Gap also has store brands that include Old Navy, Banana Republic, and Athleta. Her net worth is listed in Forbes at $2.9B.
- Intel: Gordon Moore and Robert Noyce (age 39 and 41), were the co-founders of Intel Corporation in 1968 (they were also co-founders of Fairchild Semiconductor in 1957). Their goal at Intel was to successfully bring the world's first integrated circuit (microchip)

to the commercialized market – and it soon fueled the personal computer revolution. Intel is the largest computer chip manufacturer in the world. Moore's personal net worth is $4.6B.

- Skype: Niklas Zennström (age 37) is a Swedish entrepreneur who has created several successful high-tech and communications businesses, the most notable being Skype. He led Skype until its acquisition by eBay in 2005 for $3.1B. Through an investor consortium, he repurchased Skype and subsequently sold it to Microsoft. Zennström's personal net worth is reportedly $1.3B.
- Mary Kay Inc. (cosmetics): Mary Kay Ash sold books and home goods door-to-door – and founded the firm named after her in 1963 when she was 45, with an investment of $5,000. The impetus to quit her previous job? A protest after watching several males that she had trained get promoted over her, earning a much higher salary than hers. The company she founded now has worldwide annual sales of over $2.5B.
- Southwest Airlines: Herb Kelleher (age 40) is the co-founder of Southwest Airlines – based on a business plan sketched on the back of a cocktail napkin with a law client. A top-notch business executive (named "perhaps the best CEO in America by Fortune Magazine), Kelleher's biggest claim to fame could be the unstoppable corporate culture that he instilled with employees of the airline. And how did he do it? "Well, the people did it. I just stayed out of their way. Be there when they're having problems, and stay out of their way when things are going well". Now retired from Southwest Airlines, Kelleher's net worth is listed at $2.5B.
- Comcast: Ralph Roberts was 43 when he founded Comcast, building it into the nation's largest TV cable company. Before Comcast, Mr. Roberts sold golf clubs, worked for Muzak, and owned a suspenders company. When he was 95 years old he was still chairman emeritus of Comcast's board of directors, while his son, Robert, was the chief executive. Roberts died in 2015, at 95 years of age.
- Lululemon Athletica, Inc.: Chip Wilson was 42 in 1998 when he founded Lululemon, an apparel maker of yoga stretch pants. His net worth is estimated by Forbes at $2.2B, and the company is listed on the NASDAQ with a recent valuation of $9.27B. As a result of various disputes with the company's Board of Directors, founder Wilson has sold all but 13% of his shares in the company and has gone on to other ventures.

Or consider these very successful people in other endeavors that aren't strictly considered start-ups, but are basically dynamos, and their "work" has made each individual rather wealthy:

- Harry Potter author J. K. Rowling was a single mom on welfare until she was 31. After rejection slips from eight publishers for the first Potter book, *Philosopher's Stone*, she went on to create a set of seven Harry Potter books between 1997 and 2007. The collection has sold over 450 million copies, and the movies it spawned have become the highest-grossing series ever created. The brand value of Harry Potter is over $15B, and J.K. Rowling's estimated net worth is around $1B.
- Harrison Ford was a carpenter until his 30s. Although he played around with acting in college (which he never finished), plus moving to Hollywood to see if acting was really for him, Hollywood wasn't ready for him and he wound up becoming a carpenter to pay the bills. He'd probably still be pounding nails except that some of his carpentry work was for the likes of George Lucas and Francis Ford Cuppola, who both gave him acting roles in

feature films such as American Graffiti and Apocalypse Now, followed by the Star Wars series. The big break came when Steven Spielberg cast Ford in the Indiana Jones series. Ford's estimated net worth is around $210M.

- Stan Lee created his first comic book hit when he was 39, then went on to create (or co-create) legendary comic characters, such as Spider Man, and The Hulk, while working for Marvel Comics. While he's certainly not in the super-rich category – rating his own net worth at $50M – he receives an annual salary (*for life)* of $1M from Marvel Comics.

The over-50 crowd. This demographic usually draws the most votes for Least Likely To Succeed as an entrepreneur ... which is just plain wrong. There's little question this group often suffers the greatest angst in pulling the plug on a steady paycheck when mulling over the uncertainty of a start-up. But by this point in life, most people have seen all the reasons why things *can* go wrong, and the natural tendency automatically cranks in for risk aversion as they get older.

The flip side is, this group has all of the attributes that point towards success: experience in how to make things work right, more financial resources at their fingertips – credit, retirement savings accounts and pensions, friends and family who have some money to burn, contacts from years of networking, and maybe most importantly, some common sense.

To lend a bit of credibility to this argument, Dane Stangler, Vice President of Research and Policy at the Kauffman Foundation,[12] in recent testimony to a U.S. Senate committee stated that in 2013 "businesses started by those ages 55 to 64 accounted for nearly one-quarter of all new businesses started", arguing that the rate this group is starting businesses is *higher* than for entrepreneurs in their twenties and thirties. His testimony suggested that some of this entrepreneurial aggression from the older crowd might be due to joblessness as a result of the global recession in 2007-2009. He also cited many of the reasons given in the preceding paragraphs.

Interestingly, in another study Kauffman is working on, research on 5,000 start-ups launched in 2004 showing how they have fared over time is even more interesting. Initial data indicates firms still in business after five years are much more likely to have primary owners older than age 45, and his conclusion so far is, "previous industry experience and start-up experience had less impact on firm survival prospects than did owner age".

The challenge is, the Over 50 Crowd doesn't get the press coverage that the 20-40 year old entrepreneurs get. Oftentimes, the businesses that older entrepreneurs start just aren't as sexy, and likely won't become shooting stars that explode to $100M success in a short time – with products that grab the instant gratification needs of the younger buying crowd. Instead, it might be a business geared towards a more mundane result.

Are there good examples from the 50+ crowd? You bet, and here are some examples:

---

[12] Dane Stangler, *In Search of a Second Act: The Challenges and Advantages of Senior Entrepreneurship*, Testimony Before the U.S. Senate Special Committee on Aging & the Senate Committee on Small Business and Entrepreneurship, February 12, 2014, http://www.kauffman.org/what-we-do/research/2014/02/the-challenges-and-advantages-of-senior-entrepreneurship

- McDonalds. Hmmm, how many people in the world *haven't* heard of McDonalds, or recently ate a Quarter Pounder with Cheese? Well, this restaurant chain currently has 34,480 restaurants across 119 countries[13] – and since there are around 196 countries in the world, there are actually quite a few that don't have a McDonalds. Nevertheless, there aren't many companies with such a widespread market, and with the brand recognition that McDonalds has. So, who started McDonalds? Ray Croc, who sold soda fountain equipment in his early days, until the mid-1950s *when he was 52 years old*, founded the McDonalds as we know it today. To be more precise, the original McDonalds was earlier an 8-restaurant chain in San Bernardino, CA, owned by two brothers named McDonald. Liking their concept, Ray Croc opened a McDonalds franchise in Des Moines (Iowa), quickly building it up to dozens more franchises, and in the early 1960s bought out the McDonald brothers. The rest is history.
- The Huffington Post. Founder Arianna Huffington was a writer and journalist – not to mention a staunch conservative opponent to liberal Al Franken on Comedy Central's *Strange Bedfellows* segments during the 1996 U.S. Presidential campaign. By 2004, various national and international events had turned her into a serious liberal, and along the way she founded The Huffington Post in 2005 – *when she was 55 years old*. While it's likely she didn't start the online blog to become rich, she has since sold it to AOL in 2011 for $315M – and however you make that kind of money in six short years, it has to be called entrepreneurial, even if it's by accident.
- Coca-Cola. John Pemberton was a pharmacist and physician who started out to create an alternative to morphine, first creating a concoction called Pemberton's French Wine Coca (with the last word referring to cocaine being an ingredient) to treat an infection that he suffered from a Civil War saber slash. But in 1886, when Pemberton was 55 years old, local temperance laws forced him to alter this to a non-alcoholic version, and one day after accidentally mixing it with carbonated water and finding it made a pleasant soda fountain drink, Coca-Cola as we know it today was born.
- Kentucky Fried Chicken: Harlan Sanders (known as The Colonel, although that was an honorary title from the governor of Kentucky for outstanding service to the community) worked various jobs throughout much of his life, including railroad laborer, life insurance salesman, ferry boat captain, tire salesman, and gas station operator (the last, selling chicken dishes out of his house next door, which is where he got his real start). In 1939 he moved on to a motel, and next door to it he built a sit-down restaurant that served his soon-to-be-famous "Secret Recipe" for cooking chicken in a pressure cooker. By 1952, when he was 62 years old, Sanders was ready for franchising his Kentucky Fried Chicken restaurants, which grew to become the now-worldwide restaurant chain that bears his image. He sold his entire stake in the chain in 1964 for $2.5M (and when he died in 1980, his estate was worth almost nothing). Sanders was certainly an entrepreneur, but not a good businessman.
- Zagat Restaurant Guides: Tim and Nina Zagat were both successful corporate attorneys until they quit their day jobs. Tim was 51 when he quit for good to join the entrepreneurial

---

[13] *Countries Without McDonalds*, Fox News.com, August 8, 2013, http://www.foxnews.com/leisure/2013/08/08/countries-without-mcdonald/

world. In 2004 they sold their company to Google for a reported $151M.[14] The majority of the price ($102M) was goodwill, and the rest was for the trade name, customer relationships, patents, and technology.

Even the Small Business Administration (SBA) has a page on their website titled "50+ Entrepreneurs", offering tidbits of advice and resource information, presumably to get the idea across that being an entrepreneur isn't just for the younger set.[15]

My example. At 30, I was pushing the upper limit of "young" in this context. But I was still at the point of having nothing to lose. Sure, I was newly married, had a solid job that I'd have to give up, but I had almost zero expenses, no mortgage, no kids on the horizon, and a retirement that seemed so far in the future that I figured I'd never get there. And after 13 years in the mainframe software industry, I also was getting less and less satisfaction from my current job – little chance of advancement, slow pay increases, one of 105 guys (almost all mainframe operating system programmers were male in those days) in the huge corporate mainframe computer center of a major Fortune 25 corporation.

The biggest problem was lack of money – with almost zero in a savings account and a meager $20 of disposable income at the end of each month (no, I didn't leave off any zeroes on that number), there wasn't much left over for new business start-up development. In 1977, it wasn't yet the time for finding investors – the go-go days of venture capitalists throwing money at wild-eyed entrepreneurs was a decade and a half in the future. The situation argued for a no-frills, ultra-low-cost start-up – service-based, with little cost of entry, almost no development costs, and a quick revenue stream (assuming I could find one or two customers before I ran out of the little cash I had).

All this was the perfect incubator for a start-up to succeed: nothing to lose; everything to gain. I was young enough and motivated enough to pull out the stops. I had the energy to do everything required to make it succeed, and most importantly, I had a supportive wife who understood that I'd have to work 16+ hour days for the foreseeable future.

> *"You don't have to be a genius or a visionary or even a college graduate to be successful. You just need a framework and a dream."*
> Michael Dell, founder and CEO of Dell, Inc.

Is a college degree necessary for success?

That's a really good question – how beneficial is a college degree for success at starting a small business? But a parallel question: is life experience and street smarts better than a college degree? The answer is ... it depends. Obviously, in some professions a college degree is an absolute requirement – lawyer, architect, professor, scientist, to name a few – as they typically

---

[14] *Google Paid $151 Million To Get Zagat, Ditch Yelp*, Forbes/Intelligent Investing, October 27, 2011, http://www.forbes.com/sites/chrisbarth/2011/10/27/google-paid-151-million-to-get-zagat-ditch-yelp/
[15] *50+ Entrepreneurs*, Small Business Administration, https://www.sba.gov/content/50-entrepreneurs and https://www.sba.gov/blogs/over-50-and-ready-start-business-free-resources-inspire-you-make-it-happen

have state certification boards that require a degree. But in other situations, on-the-job experience and self-training may be the best way to get there.

Strictly speaking, a college degree isn't necessary for success in a wide variety of business types as a start-up entrepreneur. Just look around you at the myriad small businesses and ask yourself, is there any aspect of this business that would require a college degree?

As we've already seen, some of the hottest and wealthiest founders in today's exploding growth companies never graduated college. And in most cases, they started businesses that didn't require a college degree in the first place (many are in the software industry, and while a college degree might be useful there, it certainly isn't required). All of us probably know people from our everyday lives who have started a small business. They are friends and associates whose products and services we use or read about. What it shows is that anyone can be a success in starting a small business – what you need is a unique idea or talent, the desire and commitment to start your own business, and the stick-to-it-iveness to make it a success. A college education is absolutely wonderful, but it isn't always necessary to be successful.

> *"I'm convinced that about half of what separates the successful entrepreneurs from the non-successful ones is pure perseverance."*
> Steve Jobs

Can you make it on sheer will power and drive?

It's said that Bill Gates worked 90-hour weeks in the early days of Microsoft. At the time, Bill was very young, a bachelor, totally driven, and purportedly eating junk food at his desk so it would take up less time. There's no question, Bill had nothing to lose, and he certainly had the sheer will power and drive.

Many of today's well-known start-up entrepreneurs fit this same mold – driven to succeed at all costs, and often leaving a trail of destruction behind them, but ending up with a pile of success to show for it. But it doesn't have to be that way. For 99.9% of small business start-ups, the goal isn't to become an Amazon.com, Facebook, Google, Microsoft, or Apple – but instead, a lifestyle-*supporting* business, as opposed to an all-consuming, 90-hour workweek, people-eating monster (that's not to say the .1% aren't enjoying what they're doing – it's just that they're unusual in enjoying such an all-consuming way of life).

No doubt, starting a small business will require a huge amount of will power and drive, including a level of work that far exceeds what you'd be doing if you're working for someone else. Friday night happy hours can still be OK, but those fun times often become expendable if there's a product glitch, or a customer needs tending to. Time-consuming hobbies might have to be given up, as running your new business will almost have to become your new hobby – one that you take home with you each and every night, and still think about when you're heading off to sleep.

Let's see an example of fire in the belly of Bill Gates at the time Microsoft was founded.[16] Microsoft in its early days was well-known as a soul-crushing place to work.[17] Stories abound of

---

[16] James Wallace & Jim Erickson, *Hard Drive – Bill Gates and the Making of the Microsoft Empire*, Harper Business, 1992.

employees working such long days that they never even went home, and instead slept on cots in their offices.

To see where this level of work pressure came from, let's look at the crushing workload Bill and Paul worked under in the early start-up days of Microsoft. Early in 1975, they wrote the first-ever program language compiler[18] for the world's first microcomputer, the MITS Altair. Ed Roberts, creator of the Altair and owner of MITS, desperately needed a BASIC compiler for the Altair if he was going to make it a truly usable microcomputer. After seeing an article on the Altair in the January, 1975, issue of Popular Electronics, Gates and Allen initiated a phone conversation with Roberts, and Gates glibly offered that they had such a compiler. This was a bald-faced lie because they had no such compiler. Suspecting they were lying, Roberts challenged them to produce it, and promised that if and when they did, he'd be agreeable to discuss licensing it from them, with the compiler packaged inside every Altair sold.

This task, in itself, was monumental (particularly for two kids not long out of high school), but adding to it was the incredibly tiny storage size of the Altair – a miniscule 256 _bytes_ of memory, and even with all 18 additional memory slots filled it would only have 4096 bytes (4K). There was no keyboard, no screen, no peripheral devices (i.e., no disks or cassettes). So the compiler had to be designed to fit within that limitation – and with enough memory space left over to run a program from the output of the compiler. To pile onto the challenges, engineers from Intel, maker of the 8080 chip at the heart of the Altair, stated that it couldn't be done. (That last challenge alone probably spurred Gates along.)

Working secretly in the Harvard computer center, Gates and Allen worked night and day for eight weeks on the impossible. Gates stopped going to classes. They worked for days at a time, sleeping as little as 2-3 hours a day, most times just grabbing a nap on a table in the computer room.

They didn't even have an Altair to test their code; instead Gates and Allen worked from a set of schematic drawings of the 8080 circuit board design. The duo had to jimmy the Harvard PDP-10 to emulate the Altair before they could even begin to test their compiler code.

Eight weeks later, Allen flew to Albuquerque to test the new compiler, and according to legend, it worked right out of the box. When Allen typed (on a teletype that was specially connected to it) the command "print 2 + 2", it whirred away and typed back the answer, "4". This compiler would later be known as Microsoft BASIC.

The success of the Altair was staggering, from the moment the Popular Electronics article came out. With Gates still at Harvard, Allen signed on as the Director of Software for MITS in Albuquerque, at a time when the company was struggling to keep up with demand for the Altair. From this, Gates and Allen knew they had a future in the software business. They also had their first-ever software licensing agreement – in addition to a $300 signing fee, they would receive

---

[17] Julie Bort, _Microsoft Is Filled With Abusive Managers And Overworked Employees, Says Tell-All Book_, Business Insider blog, May 23, 2012, http://www.businessinsider.com/microsoft-is-filled-with-abusive-managers-and-overworked-employees-says-tell-all-book-2012-5?op=1.

[18] A compiler is a program that transforms source code statements (written by an external human) into an executable program for a computer.

$30 for every copy of BASIC that was licensed as part of an Altair sale. This licensing concept was to be their modus operandi from that point on

If you think luck played a big role in this ... well, as we'll see in the next section, it didn't. Bill and Paul later handled the question of MS/DOS for the IBM PC almost exactly the same way – with Bill saying, sure, we have it, when in fact, they didn't. What they did have, though, were the cojones to say it in the first place, and then the sheer will and drive (and audacity) to produce it and make good on their word.

Sometimes (and maybe many times), you just have to do stuff like this to make a success of a brand new start-up. As so often happens, when you introduce the first edition of your first product to the marketplace, all you hear is, "looks good, but what I really want is this variation of it". The *non*-entrepreneur will say, "sorry bub, but this is what I created", whereas the entrepreneur will say, "hmmm, that's really interesting ... I think we can do that". The trick is to know which response is best for each situation.

> *"The harder I work, the luckier I get."*
> Samuel Goldwyn, co-founder of MGM Studios

Is luck a big factor?

An aspect of plain old luck does play a part – and maybe a significant part – in the success of a small start-up business. I'm a strong believer, though, that (a) "lucky" people create a lot of their own luck, and (b), more importantly, how they _handle_ luck plays an even bigger role.

Rather than luck, I prefer to use the word "opportunity". Many opportunities that come along might be called luck – whether it's good timing, or just being in the right place at the right time, or with the right product or service at the right time – and if you take advantage of those opportunities, you can call that good luck. If you don't, it's usually called bad luck. In other words – and to paraphrase the song lyrics – if you don't have any opportunities, good or bad, you won't have any luck at all. Put another way, lucky breaks aren't the exception with successful people, they're the rule.

Several opportunity factors gave Bill Gates an edge on his future success – born into a well-to-do family, sent to the exclusive and private Lakeside High School in Seattle, spending a gazillion hours programming in Basic while at the school, and getting a chance phone call from his old friend Paul Allen after seeing the Popular Science computer article.

But let's look at an even more significant opportunity _that just happened_ to come along for Bill – the story of how he was linked up with IBM and how he got MS/DOS – the basic operating system software that became the guts of millions of IBM personal computers and clones. In 1980, Bill's mother, Mary Gates, was on the national United Way Board of Director's executive committee. In an interesting twist of fate that you rarely hear about, during a coffee break at a United Way Board meeting, Mary had a chance conversation about her son's newly formed business, Microsoft, with another Board member, John Opel, who also happened to be Chairman of the Board of IBM. Later, Opel mentioned what he'd heard about Bill Gates' microcomputer software business to a few other IBM executives. Shortly after that, IBM reached out to Microsoft.[19]

When IBM came knocking on Microsoft's door in 1980, their first discussions were about the possibility of Microsoft writing a version of Basic for a proposed PC that IBM planned to introduce – similar to what Bill and Paul Allen had done earlier for the Altair personal computer. IBM, in a major miscalculation, figured the PC business was small potatoes and decided it should be built with off-the-shelf parts and software – and so they hoped to get the operating system from Microsoft.

At that first meeting, Gates reportedly advised IBM to talk with a guy named Gary Kildall of Digital Research in Pacific Grove, CA, about 60 miles south of the soon-to-be-famous Silicon Valley. Kildall had written a successful operating system called CP/M that was currently running on 500,000 personal computers that used Intel chips (which the IBM PC was planning to use).

Not surprisingly, given the quirkiness of Gary Kildall, an initial deal struck between IBM and Kildall about licensing CP/M didn't go well,[20] and after some jostling back and forth, IBM settled on a promised MS/DOS from Microsoft. The quirky part is, at the time, *Microsoft didn't actually have such an operating system*, but Gates and Allen were aware of a CPM-like operating system called QDOS (Quick and Dirty Operating System), written by Tim Paterson, owner of the tiny Seattle Computer Products. They hastily purchased it, lock, stock, and barrel from Paterson for $50,000, apparently not telling him of their plans for it with IBM.[21] In an incredibly shrewd deal, Microsoft licensed the newly renamed MS/DOS (as in <u>M</u>icro<u>s</u>oft DOS) to IBM, with a royalty to Microsoft for every PC sold that was loaded with MS/DOS – and the stroke of genius, Microsoft retained ownership rights that enabled them to license it to anyone else who came along.

Now, if that isn't a silver spoon-in-the-mouth moment, first getting IBM talking to Microsoft, followed by an incredible coincidence that laid MS/DOS in Gates' and Allen's lap, I don't know what is. Throughout 20 years of doing business with IBM with my own software company, I'd have cut off my right arm to have had a parent who could put a bug in the ear at that stratospheric level of IBM – and then to have IBM come calling like they did on Microsoft.

Significantly, though, Microsoft's success really derived from Bill and Paul having the good business sense to capitalize on the situation. Some might call that luck, when in fact it's more a case of seeing an *opportunity*, and then acting on it like a good entrepreneur should – with guts, accepting a lot of risk, and then going balls out.[22]

---

[19] *Mary Gates, 64; Helped Her Son Start Microsoft*, The New York Times, Obituaries, June 11, 1994, http://www.nytimes.com/1994/06/11/obituaries/mary-gates-64-helped-her-son-start-microsoft.html

[20] There are several legends surrounding this, including one that Kildall was off flying his airplane on the day IBM arrived to discuss a deal. There's a version that he was off visiting another – more important – customer and felt IBM was small potatoes. Still another says that IBM's offer to Kildall wasn't enough to turn his head. What actually happened isn't important to our story at hand – suffice it to say that Kildall didn't end up being the guy who supplied a PC operating system to IBM.

[21] Paterson subsequently went to work three different times for Microsoft.

[22] If you're thinking this expression is too crude for the situation, consider this: (a) old steam engines had a governor rod with ball-shaped spinning weights on the ends – when the engine was running at maximum speed centrifugal force moved the balls all the way out; (b) in the game of rugby, when the ball is pulled

For many would-be entrepreneurs, finding serendipitous situations like that staring them in the face, might have blinked, or made a choice that turned it into bad luck, or simply didn't have the entrepreneurial flair to turn the opportunity into good luck.

But that's just one example – does it make a rule? To answer, let's look at an article in The New York Times that studied the effects of luck (good or bad) on business success over a nine-year period.[23] Calling the outperforming companies "10xers" (for 10 times success), as opposed to the average companies (1x–2x success), they found that both groups had equal measures of good and bad luck. They concluded that luck itself doesn't cause the 10x success, but rather, whether the 10xers turned their luck into a very high "return on luck" (or ROL).

Naturally, their study included Bill Gates and his incredible ROL, coupled with his advantageous positions in life. They also observed that "had he been born 10 years later, or even just five years later, he would have missed the moment" – the point being that an entrepreneur's timing might play a significant role in opportunities.

The article's second example focused on Progressive Insurance. They relate how Progressive's CEO Peter Lewis reacted when California voters passed Proposition 103 in 1988, requiring a jaw-dropping 20% premium reduction, and including givebacks of premiums to current customers. Not long after, Lewis heard from his old college chum and friend Ralph Nader, the consumer rights activist, that "people simply hated dealing with insurance companies, so they revolted, screaming with their votes."

Now, your typical insurance CEO would probably have reacted with something drastic, such as pulling out of the state entirely, whereas Lewis (obviously after thinking it through very carefully) took it as an opportunity "to create a better company". From that revelation, Lewis and his team created their "immediate response" claims service, making claims adjusters available 24 hours a day, every day, driving right to the customer's home, or to the scene of an accident.

The year before Proposition 103 was passed, Progressive ranked 13th nationwide in the private car insurance business; fifteen years later they were 4th. Peter Lewis called Proposition 103 "the best thing that ever happened to this company."

As the study described it, this 10x-type of achievement was the result of major setback and luck (this time bad luck), making it "a catalyst to deepen purpose, recommit to values, increase discipline, respond with creativity and heighten productive paranoia — translating fear into extensive preparation and calm, clearheaded action. Resilience, not luck, is the signature of greatness". In other words, they took bad luck, turned it around, and used it to their advantage.

My example. Nine years after starting my company (as a 1-person mainframe software education company), I now had 14 instructors roaming the world. A third of our classes were taught, onsite, in contracts that were direct to our customers. Another two-thirds were under contract to Amdahl

---

from the scrum by the scrum half, the fly half yells "balls out!" so the forwards and the pack can begin pursuit and support. Which one do you think it is? Source: http://www.letsrun.com/forum/flat_read.php?thread=1816691

[23] Jim Collins and Morten T. Hansen, *What's Luck Got to Do With It?*, The New York Times – Business Day, October 29, 2011, http://www.nytimes.com/2011/10/30/business/luck-is-just-the-spark-for-business-giants.html?pagewanted=all&_r=1&

Education, the education services of the IBM lookalike mainframe computer manufacturer, Amdahl Corporation. At Amdahl, we taught all of our regular courses – same title, same material, same instructors – but Amdahl printed the material for us, adding their corporate logo to the material, and we acted as if we were Amdahl Education instructors.

Each October, Amdahl would send us the course schedule for the following calendar year, so managers at customer sites could plan their training budgets. This advance notice was great for my company, as it gave us a schedule well in advance for two-thirds of our business for the entire year. This schedule typically had 350 5-day courses in it, and represented almost $2 million in annual revenue for us.

When October, 1987 arrived, I eagerly awaited the Amdahl class schedule for 1988. Without advance warning, it was _down 85%_ from what I expected – only 50 classes, when I expected over 350!

Since we relied so heavily on this one customer, and our other business was either repeat customers or word-of-mouth customers, we didn't have a single sales person on staff, and any marketing we did was almost entirely by accident.

Luckily, we had three months – the remainder of 1987 – to cushion the blow. Then out of the blue, we got a call from an IT manager at a major American airline. She had just attended a class on a highly technical disk storage management concept that we had taught the previous week in Phoenix. Returning to work after the class, she recognized that implementing this storage management concept was far too large a task for just one person. She then talked her manager into bringing personnel in from my company on a consulting basis to assist with the implementation. I got a phone call out of the blue.

None of our people were technical consultants, and we'd never before had a consulting contract, but with a bleak 1988 staring us in the face, we pitched several presentations to the airline's IT center about our technical services capabilities. We won the contract. Over the next several years, we had as many as seven technical staff onsite at the airline for this project, and it turned out to be our largest-ever customer.

With this new business model under our belts, it wasn't long before 40% of our annual revenue was from similar consulting services, and even better, this contract with the airline helped us produce two of our biggest selling software products, which subsequently launched us into the third phase of our company ... a true software development company.

Getting the axe from Amdahl was the catalyst that began our turnaround. The serendipitous phone call from the airline got us going in two very different (and more profitable) directions. When the dust finally settled and my company was sold a few years later, it had truly become a 10xer.

Chapter 2   Behind-the-Scenes Decisions

"All great deeds and thoughts have a ridiculous beginning. Great works are often born on a street corner or in a restaurant's revolving door."
Albert Camus

What are your reasons for starting a company?

The reasons most often heard for starting a company are: (a) to be your own boss ... (b) to earn bagsful of money ... and (c) to take control of your life.

Three goals that all sound wonderful, and if true would make almost *anyone* interested in starting a business.

The reality is, you rarely get to be your own boss. Instead, you find yourself working more for your customers and less for yourself. And if you don't, you might not stay in business very long. If you always have too many other things you'd rather do than call a customer back, or fail to get a product built or shipped because your personal life was too important – well, that customer just may decide he's not important enough to you. Once you lose that customer, chances are you won't see him back.

Once you have employees, you start to work a lot *for them* and less for yourself. And if you don't, they go someplace else where they might feel more appreciated – i.e., more pay, better benefits, more opportunity for growth, more say in how things are run ... and a dozen more things that employees want.

Ahhhh, and bagsful of money. What a thought ... *and what a myth*! In my own case, I seemingly had bagsful of money at one time in my company's life – *when I was the only employee*, and therefore, the only one with my hand in the bag grabbing money. The trouble is, at that stage in a business, if growing your business is in your plans, that bagful will be necessary. And at each successive stage in your company, the next bagful – no matter how large – will be necessary. You'll soon realize that what seemed like a bagful isn't that much after all – certainly not enough to retire and head for a paradise island to relax. If you choose to remain a 1-person company, you can only produce whatever the sweat of your own body (or mind) can produce, and that has its drawbacks. I can't think of a 1-person company that sold for a retirement-level amount. So that leaves you stuck – you either keep doing what you're doing until you can't do it anymore. Or, you plow profits back in to grow your company ... and there goes your bagful of money.

Take control of your life – mostly hooey! When I left the big corporate world to start my own company, sure, it was to take control of my life – and to get it back from the doldrums of being in a large corporation that seemed to suck my ambitions dry. I didn't like my management, I didn't like my odds of ever being able to step into the manager's shoes, and I certainly didn't like being low man on the salary totem pole. I wanted to be in control of my destiny! This reason is the only one of the three most-heard reasons that may actually become a bit real – but only a bit. As a business owner, you get to make a lot of decisions – whether to accept business on terms the customer wants, or to turn it down, or whether to forego your personal vacation this year so that company revenue can meet expenses.

So far I've made this sound pretty dismal, and if true, why would anyone want to start a business? Well, it's because these aren't the actual reasons a person *should* start a small business. Sure, each of the three has elements of truth behind them, but there are several other, significantly better, reasons to become an entrepreneur. We'll see lots more about them throughout this book.

> *"A business is simply an idea to make other people's lives better."*
> Sir Richard Branson, founder of the Virgin Group

What sort of business are you trying to start?

Many start-up business owners don't give a lot of thought to the specifics of this question. They're just so enamored with the idea of starting a company or producing a product – or as I was, to escape a current life – they jump in to get it started, and then worry later about whether it's really an idea whose time has come or whether they can make it profitable. Or they know of a product or service that could launch a business, but don't know exactly how to execute on that idea. The problem is, heading in the wrong direction without properly thinking things through can result in a dog-leg course, wasting energy and money and time and resources ... and worse, increasing the chance of failure.

The big questions you need to have solid answers for *in advance* boil down to:
- What are your reasons for starting a company? (apart from the ones just discarded)
- Will your company be service-oriented or product-oriented?
- Are you planning to start a company that requires real "brick-and-mortar" facilities, or can it operate at first from the proverbial spare bedroom?
- What are your start-up expenses, and do you have enough money in the bank to cover the almost-certain lean times during start-up?
- What are your sources of capitalization?
- Realistically, what are your revenue, *expense*, and profitability expectations in the early days? (Months?) (First Year?)
- Do you want a company whose revenue goal is steady and even – and is your primary goal for the company to pay you a regular and steady wage as long as you continue to operate it?
- Do you want a company with high growth potential – one that could grow into a large company, possibly with an IPO as your exit strategy, or an M&A?
- How good is your ability to execute on your idea?
- What is your level of commitment to the effort required to start (and then manage) your own company? Has your family bought into this idea? Can you adjust your outside activities for this? Are you here for the long haul?

You should have clarity on lots of other questions before you actually start your company, but these are some good ones to begin with. Let's look at each in turn.

"Many people just want to start a business but don't think of all the pieces that accompany it."

Buck Stinson, Capital One

What will your company do? What is your business idea?

Many would-be entrepreneurs think they have to create the world's "new thing."[24] Sure, the fabulously successful businesses you read about tend to be the latest new thing that's never been done before (particularly in the technology and online industry), such as coming from nowhere to create the concept of crowdfunding, or Jeff Bezos starting Amazon.com, or the four guys who developed the concept of Twitter.

At the same time, though, just as many really successful start-ups were just a new twist on an old industry – but such a unique twist that it took off like wildfire. Uber is revolutionizing the taxi industry, mostly in the way you "hail" a taxi and pay for it, but nevertheless, it's still just a taxi business. For that matter, Amazon.com is just another way of selling books and other stuff – online, rather than from a brick-and-mortar storefront.

As we saw in example after example in the last chapter, few ideas were truly revolutionary or new – they just had a new twist, or found a market where their idea wasn't being covered already, and they jumped on it. Most of these people weren't serial entrepreneurs, learning from previous business how to succeed, and few had made a gazillion dollars from a previous start-up that gave them a financial leg up on the success ladder.

It should go without saying: the only successful business idea is one that has products or services that will sell. And sell in enough volume, and with sufficient profit margins, to remain in business – enough to pay all of your bills, pay you (and your staff) a salary, and of course, repay investors if you have them.

Your business idea has to be something your customers want to buy, at a price they're willing to pay, and with a sustainable market that isn't just a flash in the pan. The proverbial "pet rock" product from 1975, Beanie Babies from the early '90s, or whatever the latest fad is, will hopefully not be part of your chosen business plan – although both of them made millions before they flashed in the pan.

In short, is your business idea one that will sell? A New York Times article lists the #1 reason businesses fail as "*The math just doesn't work. There is not enough demand for the product or service at a price that will produce a profit for the company. This, for example, would include a start-up trying to compete against Best Buy and its economies of scale.*"[25]

Here's a suggestion that might help while you're still in the early dreaming stages of starting your business – when you have just a fleeting kernel of a vision of the start-up you'd like to try. Keep

---

[24] Jay Goltz, *Eight Fallacies of Entrepreneurship*, The New York Times – You're The Boss blog, March 23, 2011, http://boss.blogs.nytimes.com/2011/03/23/eight-fallacies-of-entrepreneurship/?_r=0
[25] Jay Goltz, *Top 10 Reasons Why Businesses Fail,* The New York Times – You're The Boss Blog, January 5, 2011, http://boss.blogs.nytimes.com/2011/01/05/top-10-reasons-small-businesses-fail/

your eyes open to every new start-up you see around you, particularly ones that aren't too dissimilar from what you're thinking about. Take note of how well capitalized they seem to be. Did they choose a business location (or place to sell) that would give you confidence if you were in their shoes? Over time, watch to see how well they're doing. Are lots of customers hanging around? Are their products or services beginning to look stale or is everything looking pretty innovative? Is there any buzz – online reviews, newspaper articles, friends talking about them? How many are still around a year from when they opened their doors?

When I recently saw a 15-flavor popcorn store go into a local mall, my first thought was: this is another bad business plan going into action with almost no chance for success. Worse, I figured the founders were about three months away from losing their life savings. Sure enough, it didn't even last until the next time I visited the mall. When I did an online Google search for "popcorn buy online", I got 34 million hits – obviously, that's a bogus number, as there are not 34 million places to buy popcorn online, but when you look at the actual entries that come up, it would make one wonder how anyone can succeed at a small dollar volume business when they're paying shopping mall rates for a brick-and-mortar location.

> *"Everyone has an idea, but it's really about <u>executing</u> the idea and attracting other people to help you with the idea."*
> Jack Dorsey, Entrepreneur, Co-Founder of Twitter

Does your idea make business sense?

Shortly after my software education business began to turn a profit – to the point of finally having a bit of extra cash in the bank – my first office manager suggested I invest in a mailbox franchise, which were becoming popular. At least six of them were already in town, and I felt the last thing the area needed was a seventh. In fact, at the time I couldn't imagine why the world needed this type of business in the first place. Without saying much, I discarded the advice. One by one these franchises fell by the wayside, and the ones that succeeded likely paid little more than the owner's salary and that of an assistant.

The sage business advice has always been to start a business in something that you know – and hopefully, this will give you a good idea whether it's the type of business the world needs. This seems obvious, but a lot of people use their nest egg to jump into a franchise, or some hot new business fad, selling services or products they know absolutely nothing about. Coupled with a basic lack of business knowledge, succeeding in those scenarios can be difficult.

But just because you have great personal knowledge that could translate to a viable business, it doesn't mean it is viable for *where* or *when* you start it. Sure, if you intend to sell primarily on the internet, you can possibly succeed from just about anywhere (assuming you have a good internet server, good inventory and production sourcing, and good shipping capability). But if you need local or regional customers to make a go of it, you'd better know a lot about your area marketplace. For both situations, you need to research that marketplace. For internet sales, you need to know how many other online competitors you have, what their strengths and weaknesses are, and how your products will fare against them. The same goes for local sales, but your research also needs to focus on your ability to attract sales in the location you've chosen, and –

this is an important "and" – whether you can succeed selling locally if existing online competitors can beat you down in price and selection (for example, a small boutique book store in a strip mall may have too much competition from a nearby Barnes & Noble, not to mention Amazon.com).

My example. Shortly after selling my software company, I decided that dabbling as an angel investor for tiny, low-funded start-ups might be a good way to invest – and also a way to help fledgling start-ups. I joined two angel investor groups in the Seattle area, and once a month I attended entrepreneur sessions, where 25 or 30 potential angel investors listened as, one by one, several would-be (or even serial) entrepreneurs pitched their business idea in hopes of getting a few hundred thousand dollars to get started. While a few of the business ideas sounded good, many were destined to never see the light of day. Even for the good ones, it was extremely difficult to gauge whether the start-up management could succeed in getting it off the ground. Sure enough, of seven or eight companies that survived the vetting process (including several that I invested in), over half were out of business in less than two years – obviously taking our individual angel investments with them.

Timing is critical. One entrepreneur who pitched to our group – an attractive and articulate young British woman who now lives in Seattle – presented an engaging argument why the world not only needed a high-class nail, pedicure, and massage kiosk near the departure lounges at major airports, but also needed cosmetic products that were less toxic. The 9/11 terrorist attack had struck several years earlier, forcing air travelers to arrive at the airport earlier to get through security, and once at the departure gate they had time on their hands. Another plus, air travelers were flush with cash more than ever before.

Even her business name – Butter London – had an exotic air about it, and while "butter" and "London" made absolutely no sense to me in this context, it somehow had a poshness that was appealing. Frankly, I was intrigued with the whole concept, particularly since I had just finished a 30-year stint as a serious air traveler, and knew as well as anyone what life is like waiting at the airport. But, not only did I have absolutely zero knowledge of this type of business – never really being the manicure, pedicure, or massage kind of guy – I had no interest in the actual business operation. I passed.

Within months, the Great Recession of 2007–2008 struck, and along with almost every other business in America, air travel took a nosedive. By then, a Butter London kiosk had opened at Sea-Tac Airport in Seattle, plus several more around the country, but before long it had dwindled to just the original start-up. Who knows how this interesting idea might have fared if her timing had been better.

Nevertheless, Butter London has since survived, not because her original airport kiosk idea was so great, but because her business model proved flexible and durable. The airport kiosk concept is no longer their main focus (in fact, the one at Sea-Tac Airport is the only one left). Now they focus on online sales, plus partnering with hundreds of upscale specialty retail stores making their products available around the world. It's nice to see they're still around.[26]

---

[26] www.butterlondon.com

Should you write a business plan?

Yes and no.

By all means, as you are beginning to develop your thoughts for jumping into the entrepreneurial world, write down as much as you can about your plans for starting your business. It's the best way to initially formulate, and then to coalesce, your thoughts into a serious plan of action. At this stage, though, it should not be the formal business plan that all the business books and internet sites promote.

But before going into the details of what to put in your business plan, and how to use it, let's first explain the "no" side of the advice.

An internet search on "*should you write a business plan*" brings up overwhelming responses that indicate yes. Some of the listed arguments[27 and 28] for creating a business plan are:
- it's the single most important thing you'll ever do for your business
- it's absolutely crucial for the success of your business
- it will show you know where your company will be in five years
- it is the antidote for businesses that fail due to poor planning
- it will keep you from straying too far off your original idea
- it will provide the rationale for hiring new employees, or renting new business space, or acquiring new assets
- it provides the explanation of your business objectives to your management team
- it gives a roadmap to your outside professional advisors (such as attorney, accountants)
- it will eventually help you sell your business

Of these nine reasons, (in my opinion) *only* the next to last bullet has even a modicum of truth and good business sense to it. The rest are all gibberish, and represent the kind of advice that will likely cause an unsuspecting entrepreneur to blow tens, maybe hundreds of hours writing something *that should not be written*. Advice like this usually comes from people who are primarily in business to sell you a business plan template. Beyond using a *brief* business plan to get you up and running – one that very possibly only you (and maybe your banker) will ever see – the exorbitant time it takes to write the type of business plan that most gurus suggest is far better spent elsewhere.

There's no question a business plan will be necessary if you're looking for outside capital or investors, but that's a very targeted (and brief) document, and written specifically with that purpose in mind.

These same gurus also say (or imply) that a business plan should be such a fluid and updateable document that you live and breathe by it. My feeling is, if you're spending that much time

---

[27] Jason Cohen, *Don't write a business plan*, A Smart Bear Blog, December 14, 2009, https://blog.asmartbear.com/business-plan.html. Jason's "take" on this is spot on, and in his blog post he debunks all of the reasons I've listed here.

[28] I'm not making this up. All of it is actually the thrust of an online article from Entrepreneur, *15 Reasons You Need a Business Plan*, at http://www.entrepreneur.com/article/83818. I'm sure the author believes everything he's written, but he's also an "entrepreneur" with a vested interest – in the sense that he develops and sells business planning software.

writing and maintaining a comprehensive business plan, you aren't paying enough attention to your business. Sure, some of the people who swear by business plans might have such a precisionist personality that this is how they choose to manage their business planning, but I'll bet the percentage in this camp is quite low.

To be more specific, consider the first bullet above – that a business plan is the single most important thing you'll ever do for your business. Can the person who believes this be for real? In the case of Jeff Bezos (founder of Amazon.com), who supposedly wrote his business plan while driving from New York to Seattle to start the business he'd already planned in his head. Was his business plan _the_ most important thing he did ... more important, say, than the creation of his basic website that actually became Amazon.com?

I don't know if Bill Gates ever wrote a business plan for the early runaway success of Microsoft. I have a hunch he didn't, as so much of the company's real success seemed to stem from out-of-the-blue opportunities that he wisely took advantage of – and then worked like the devil to succeed with. For example, I have a feeling that the follow-up he did after his mother's United Way board meeting chat with IBM's John Open, by purchasing a rudimentary version of MS-DOS after IBM approached him, was _the single most important thing he did_ – and considering that was so serendipitous, it would be impossible to imagine it as part of his business plan.

In my case, transitioning my company from a services-oriented business to a product-oriented business was the single most important thing I did with my company. Since I didn't have the slightest clue that was going to happen, it's just ludicrous to think it was the result of following a business plan.

Which brings us to: will a business plan tell you where your business will be in five years? And will it keep the company from straying too far off course? It's just pathetic (and 50 years behind the times) to suggest that you'll know where your business will be in five years! If you seriously think you'll know where your business will be in five years – and then live by those predictions – you're just too narrowly focused.

And second, if you use a business plan to keep from straying, you can easily miss any of the serendipitous or unexpected paths that could blow the doors off anything you might do intentionally. As argued in A Smart Bear Blog, "business plans are just guesses, and they're almost always wrong." What if you had written a business plan at the beginning of 2007, projecting where you'd be in five years, plus not planning to stray from your current course – where would you be now after the Global Financial Crisis of 2007–2009?

As the blog post goes on to say: _"At the beginning you don't know_ anything _about what your business will look like. Your product will evolve to fit the market. You'll test marketing messages on AdWords and make unexpected discoveries about what works. Good and bad luck shape your company. You have no answers, no predictive power. Nor should you artificially pin yourself down! Even a "plan" buried in a drawer makes you less likely to consider the radical new idea that changes everything and makes you successful."_

And if you think it's just the opinion of a few, consider this collage of opinions from a bunch of business venture blogs:[29] Don't send a business plan to investors ... nobody reads them and nobody executes them … document your detailed plans on a napkin ... nothing slows down a VC as much as a comprehensive business plan ... five-year plans aren't worth the ink they're printed with ... the only plan you should make is a plan to improvise. (That last quote is an absolute gem.)

Having said that, what should you do about a business plan, when should you create something, and how much? For your early planning purposes, write down enough in a brief version of a business plan so that you have a very clear idea how your business will hopefully start out. At this stage, the only person looking at it is you, but if you can, see if you can get a business advisor to review it and give you an opinion. As your plans begin to gel, and if you're considering an SBA loan to get the venture off the ground, you'll need to polish this up, modify it a bit, and prepare to submit it to a banker (or three or four, depending on how many it takes to get a "yes"). For this version of a business plan, keep it to no more than 15 pages, and written very precise, to the point, and for the specific purpose of your banker reading it to approve your loan.

Include:

- a list of the detailed steps needed to getting the business up and running – as discussed in the following chapters
- detailed descriptions of your products/services – this could very well become the basis of your initial marketing campaign
- establish estimates of your product/service pricing – this will be crucial for Cash Flow/Budget projections
- a detailed list of the sales volume for your products/services, breaking out month-by-month how much you hope/plan to sell in the first year – this helps you develop revenue projections that will be the foundation of your Cash Flow/Budget
- a detailed list of every expense required to produce the sales volume you've forecast – this will also go into your Cash Flow/Budget projection
- a highly detailed Cash Flow/Budget projection – this could easily be one of the single most important thing you create in the planning and execution phases of your business (we'll cover this in detail in Chapter 5)

Once you've completed this, you'll essentially have a business plan, but it doesn't have to be in a professional format, it doesn't have to be bound and ready to distribute to every new employee you hire, and it certainly isn't intended to be the living and breathing document that drives your business life for the next five years.

As the business starts out, and on a weekly/monthly basis, pay close attention to your Cash Flow/Budget projection spreadsheet to see if sales and expenses are on target, and update the projections as necessary. And rather than fixate on sticking with your business plan, keep your

---

[29] Nivi, *What should I send investors? Part 3: Business Plans, NDAs, and Traction*, Venture Hacks blog, November 8, 2007 ... and ...
David Cowan, *How To NOT Write A Business Plan*, Who Has Time For This? blog, November 17, 2005 ... and . .
Mike Moritz, Fireside Chat: Money and passion video, building43 website, August 7, 2009

eyes and ears to the ground for any serendipitous whisperings that come along, study and analyze each one very carefully to see if it suggests a wise course change, and then follow your instincts (and hopefully they're good).

> *"Fit no stereotypes. Don't chase the latest management fads. The situation dictates which approach best accomplishes the team's mission."*
> Colin Powell, Chairman Joint Chiefs of Staff, 1989-1993, and U.S. Secretary of State, 2001-2005.

Be wary of business fads

Stay away from the latest business fads or new-fangled business methodologies that don't fit your style and mode of operation – and especially, those that don't fit your current business and financial situation. They can be a drag on your resources and finances, and worse, derail your corporate goals.

Most fads or methodologies that you get talked into will likely result in endless meetings to trumpet the new fad and get everyone on board, plus cause extra work that a start-up crew just doesn't have time for. If unchecked, and if someone in management doesn't come to their senses, fads can snuff out your business and drive you bankrupt. Many are the result of outside consultants getting their claws into you, most likely from an employee who has bought into them (thinking they know how to run your business better than you do), and they will put no end of pressure on you to succumb. *Resist.*

Particularly in the early stages of a start-up, and stretching well into your go-go growth period(s), a lot of things about your management of the company might seem helter-skelter, unplanned, and even lacking specific direction in the eyes of your management team and employees. This seemingly chaotic style you're operating in might seem foreign (and maybe even dangerous) to your employees who worked in large corporate organizations before you brought them in. Many may have never worked for a small company before, particularly not a start-up, and they don't feel comfortable if your day-to-day management seems a bit scattershot – which is exactly what it needs to be in a small start-up that is struggling to survive and grow.

But keep one thing in mind – you are the entrepreneur of the company, not them. You are the one who created the vision for the company. You are the one who has bottom-line financial responsibility – and to put it more bluntly, *you have the responsibility to meet payroll and pay bills.*

Always keep in mind that as soon as you have more than one employee, other employees are bound to have a different perspective on every aspect of how the company is run. They will think the company's focus should fit their plan. Unless you – as the company's Chief Communications Officer – successfully get your vision across, they may often work at cross purposes with you. They will think the company's resources and finances should be spent on projects and directions they would take in their own company. And it's highly likely some might push for the company to adopt a management style that fits how _they_ believe it should be run. In my situation, and in a slightly veiled version of this, one of my employees said over and over again when he disagreed with something we were doing, "well, we did it this way at *my old company*" – and it got old very fast

Depending on your staff, you might be bombarded – well, OK, that's a bit strong ... you might be steered – to consider proposals for change, and you're going to become the company Grinch when you turn them down. But turn them down you should, as many won't be appropriate for your company at its current stage, and could actually be downright harmful due to the amount of diversion and resources required; which you can scarcely afford in an early stage company.

How can you tell if a management practice that's being pushed at you (or that you're thinking about on your own) is a fad or a truly effective classic methodology? There are several very good papers about this on the internet, and here's a quote from an opening paragraph:

> *"Many popular administrative ideas are epitomized by a search for the quick fix—a simple solution that all organizations can embrace to make employees more productive, customers happier, or profits greater. Although some companies are profoundly transformed by these ideas, many are merely grazed by them. The notions do not serve the core business, or are embraced ritualistically without having any profound effect on performance or any other desired outcomes. Before long, the fad is forgotten and the firm is left with the human costs of disappointment and the financial costs of fruitless implementation. Frequently, fads can have a lasting destructive influence as a practice is embraced that alienates employees or triggers an abortive reorganization."* [30]

If you have the time to read the entire paper, you should. By analyzing the rapid rise and fall from grace of a half-dozen management practices (which is a good definition of a business fad), and developing several common-sense warning signs to look for, it provides a fairly good way to tell if the latest whiz-bang theory is here to stay, or just a waste of your time and resources.

My list of business fads that you should be wary of includes:
- Business plans – at least, formal business plans that you spend months preparing, holding meetings to discuss with any and all within the company, and countless hours keeping up to date
- ISO 9000 quality management systems (http://en.wikipedia.org/wiki/ISO_9000 for more details)
- Outsourcing
- Stephen Covey's *7 Habits of Highly Successful People*
- *Who Moved My Cheese*, the small parable book by Spencer Johnson, with its frequent mass distribution to employees. This also includes his earlier work, *The One Minute Manager*
- Six Sigma by Motorola, process re-engineering[31]
- Hiring outside consultants to tell you how to run your business (an example: the contract CFO who almost ran our company out of business, and then pressed to be hired full time as

---

[30] Danny Miller, Jon Hartwick, Isebelle Le Beton-Miller, *How To Detect A Management Fad – And Distinguish It From A Classic*, Business Horizons, Issue 47/4, July/August 2004, https://www.researchgate.net/publication/4885139_How_to_detect_a_management_fad_-_And_distinguish_it_from_a_classic

[31] *The Stupidest Management Fads of all Time*, Business Management Leaders, http://businessmanagementleaders.com/business/management-fads/

an in-house CFO, wanting a huge salary _and 35% of the company's stock as a signing bonus_).

While implementing a management fad might have advantages – for example, provoking thought and discussion about current management orthodoxies that might be out of date, or creating excitement with the staff – too often they do just the opposite, resulting in countless meetings and time wasted that could be spent otherwise.

Frankly, in a start-up company, if you (and your staff, assuming you have any) had the spare time on your hands to be implementing business fads, you'd be far better off using that time to work on core concepts of your company – jazzing up the marketing and sales efforts to potential customers, making your products better, making sure your existing customers are 1,000% happy with your product or service, or for that matter, getting more product or service ready to go out the door.

"Done is better than perfect."
Sheryl Sandberg, COO of Facebook

How good are you at executing on your idea?

Unless your goal is raising a pile of cash – enough start-up cash that you can hire specialists for the many business areas you'll need for getting your business off the ground – you're going to be the company's "chief cook and bottle washer" during the start-up phase. You might have dreamed up the world's greatest-ever widget as your business idea, but if you can't bring it to market, and then take it through the entire sales cycle, your odds of success aren't very good. Even if you can tackle all of these widely disparate areas, they will fragment your time and energies (not to mention your financial resources).

From the start, you have to be the one bringing in business. And before the first actual day of business, you'd better have a good idea where that business will be coming from, and _how you're going to find more of it_. No matter what the business plan is, just hanging out the proverbial shingle won't cut it, even if your new business is a retail storefront and you're planning on walk-by traffic for customers. If you stumble at this, you could starve before you even get started, so you'd better figure out how to create "the buzz". It's surprising how many hits you'll get when you Google "creating start-up buzz" – one of the best is a Forbes article on just that – how to inexpensively create new company buzz.[32] In fact, the entire first page of hits was spot-on the topic, and provided a wealth of good ideas. My experience is, good entrepreneurs tend to be good at bringing in the business – it must be in the genes, or a strong marketing sense is one of the factors that lead to being an entrepreneur. Whatever it is, you need it, and if you don't have it already, you need to figure out how to develop it.

You have to be the one who creates the initial processes under which your company will operate. That too needs to be underway by the first actual business day. If you're selling to other businesses (B2B), you have to figure out how the sales process will actually work – including

---

[32]David Teten, _How To Create Buzz Around Your Startup At No Cost_, Forbes online, July 13, 2013, http://www.forbes.com/sites/davidteten/2013/07/12/how-to-create-free-buzz-around-your-startup/

contracting, invoicing, receiving payments, fulfilling orders, and a myriad other things. If you're selling to the general public, most of the same stuff applies, but it revolves around how you'll accept business from individuals, how they'll pay you, and again, a myriad of other business-related details. If you rely on vendors to produce your product(s) and services, how will you order from them, how will you protect your company intellectual property, how will you pay them and what terms will they accept, how much inventory do you need, and a dozen other things you'll have to learn along the way. Very soon after you open your doors, you'll also have to create some level of after-sale support – because no matter how well you design and build your products, things will go wrong – quality control slips, sub-par vendor material, the customer thought they bought something other than what you sold them, and a dozen other things you haven't yet thought up.

<u>You're in charge of profit/loss management.</u> Most importantly, you'll be the one who has to manage the business finances – not so much in actually keeping the books (you can always hire an outside bookkeeper right from the start). No, I'm talking about understanding the difference between profit and loss, and what you're going to do when either one of them happens (hope for the former, but expect the latter). You'll need to create the financial controls to know, as far as possible in advance, what to expect from a profit/loss standpoint – and that means having an operating budget. In business, *cash in the bank is king* – and if you aren't keeping your eye on it virtually every day you're in business, you can very well <u>not</u> be in business in the blink of an eye. We'll spend a lot of time on several financial management spreadsheets in Chapter 5, the most important of which is a very powerful Cash Flow/Budget spreadsheet (there are also several examples you can cadge from the SBA website (but not as good as the one used with this book).[33] Whichever you use, these will be your week-by-week and month-by-month tools to manage your business health. If you can't (or won't), it will be your first big sign you aren't cut out to be an entrepreneur.

Where will your company operate from?

The easiest and least expensive company to start is one that doesn't require real bricks and mortar. If it does, though, look closely for ways that you can reduce early start-up costs. Carefully search for that perfect brick-and-mortar location, as well as how you outfit the new digs – and don't settle on anything until you have confidence you can really afford it.

As an example, a guy I knew was retired from IBM – the definitive big company – and had risen to Branch Manager by the end of his career. That type of background can be dangerous for a newbie entrepreneur, as the former perks, office style and location, salary requirements, and not understanding the whole concept of cash preservation can all spell doom for even a well-capitalized start-up. When this guy first started his small business, he rented high-rise office space just like he was familiar with at IBM, with a corner office that had a view, and expensive office furniture. Those three items alone would probably have funded a year's worth of entire

---

[33] Caron Beasley, *Projecting Your Business Cash Flow, Made Simple*, SBA Blogs on Financing, https://www.sba.gov/blogs/projecting-your-business-cash-flow-made-simple, read down to What Does A Cash Flow Statement Look Like, then click on the link that takes you to cash flow projection spreadsheet template, and look for the next link that says cash flow statement (12 months).

business expenses in a well-run start-up, and sure enough, he was out of business before his new company could even get off the ground.

Unless there's a compelling reason, for example, to impress potential customers with your high-end digs, head for the suburbs and decorate accordingly, or better yet, operate from the proverbial spare bedroom or garage until you have good revenue coming in. Granted, if you're forced to start off with employees on the payroll, having them work out of your spare bedroom isn't cool, so if you do need to rent space, make it appropriate for your *affordable* cash burn.

My experience. For the first two years – as a 1-person company that customers never visited – I operated from a spare bedroom where I had a desk set up in the corner. Later, when I was forced to hire an office manager to take care of administrative tasks, we rented a 900 sq/ft two-room office above a steakhouse in a small office park. The beauty of it was, over the next 12 years as we expanded to larger and larger offices, we moved from one office space to another *within the same business park*. All the while, we kept our official mailing address as a U.S. Post Office box, and that way we didn't have to change anything with our stationary or customer records. (A secondary benefit – the frugality of our office environment was instrumental in developing our corporate culture, keeping our employees well-grounded in the concept of spending money wisely.)

As we added employees, we needed office furniture, an expense that can break the bank in a hurry if you aren't careful. We found a local auction company specializing in surplus office furniture – like-new stuff that was sold when companies went out of business, or moved up in the world. A couple of times we ended up with lots more than we needed, but that came in handy later on when we needed more – and in doing it that way, we'd have a consistent look and feel to our office.

The long road to revenue

Whether you're lean or whole-hog on your start-up costs, in all likelihood you need to plan carefully to get that long-awaited first bit of revenue in the door. One of the biggest causes of start-up business failure is running out of cash before sufficient revenue flows in to cover costs.

By nature, entrepreneurs are optimists, and we think our business idea is the greatest thing since sliced bread. We also think customers will stream through the door the minute the business opens, beating it down to buy whatever we're selling, and waving huge fistfuls of cash. The unfortunate fact is, even the most conservative new business owner falls prey to under-estimating how long it will take for cash flow to equal or exceed expenses. So, keep this mantra in mind: *running out of cash is the single most frequent reason for the failure of new businesses.*[34]

This might seem intuitive, but if your business is running on the edge of a cash flow squeeze, all it takes is one misstep – a glitch in the sales cycle, one contract or business deal failing to hit the doorstep when expected, or one customer payment that's delayed, a blizzard shutting down the town for several days, or some problem with your production ability – and you can find yourself squeezed out of business. At the risk of explaining the obvious, I'll delve a bit into each of these.

---

[34] Jay Goltz, *Top 10 Reasons Small Businesses Fail*, New York Times, You're The Boss, January 5, 2011, http://boss.blogs.nytimes.com/2011/01/05/top-10-reasons-small-businesses-fail/

Plan on a longer-than-expected sales cycle. As an entrepreneur with a new start-up business, it almost goes without saying that you'll have little experience with the initial sales and revenue cycle for your new small business. However long you *think* it will be, it will most likely be longer. If your product or service is new to the world, factor in the extra time required to convince potential customers they can't live without this new product or service – and maybe a product or service they didn't even know they needed until you came along. Even if other competitors are already in the marketplace, it'll take longer than expected to win over converts to why yours is better.

Delayed business. Every business runs the risk of this. In any business, it's easy for a customer's head to be turned and decide to buy something else, buy from a competitor, or decide not to buy at all. A customer could be right on the cusp of saying yes to your product or service, and out of the blue something interrupts that decision.

You should soon learn what your business cycle is, what your sales cycle is, and those two will tell you a lot about how to handle delayed business in your cash flow planning. If your sales pipeline is made up of a relatively large number of sales and for relatively small dollar amounts (so the loss of one sale isn't likely to impact your cash flow), you can afford to have a few sales go south. If, at the opposite end, you have few sales – but each is a relatively large revenue item – the loss or delay of one sale can seriously impact your cash position. In the latter instance, you should account for that in your Cash Flow/Budget, and operate assuming that the risky business won't come in as planned. Or, better yet, you could have a worst/best case scenario in your Cash Flow/Budget spreadsheet, which gives you visibility of your cash position in either situation.

Delayed payments. Every business relies on money coming in the door, knows how much to expect, and plans for when to expected it. If your business operates on a cash-on-delivery basis, there shouldn't be any delayed payments, unless of course, you opt to give credit terms to a customer. If the amount of that credit is significant, then you need to figure it into your Cash Flow/Budget.

If your payments are typically on credit terms, it's imperative that you implement controls to ensure payments are received on time (we'll discuss this in Chapter 4 in much greater detail). But to just touch on it in a simple sense, it isn't unusual for a customer, even a good customer, to delay payments to you for reasons totally outside your control. That customer might have their own cash flow problems and intentionally decide to slow down their payments.

In either case, you should allow for this in your Cash Flow/Budget, including an allowance for delayed or uncollectible accounts on your financial statements. Again, your budgeting could have a worst/best case scenario, which gives you a better feel for the impact on your ability to survive.

Failure to deliver. Whatever you produce, whether it's a product or service, if you can't deliver on promises or expectations of your customers, it's going to hit your bottom line (which can result in running out of cash). If you're constantly apologizing to customers for your failure to deliver, word will get around, published reviews will be read, and you'll find yourself taking your lumps.

For product-based businesses, it's knowing *everything* about your production cycle, including the ordering time for raw materials, the time required for the actual production process, and details of product delivery. Staffing vagaries must be taken into account, including holidays, sick days, vacations, and work stoppages and slowdowns. Consider every imaginable obstacle outside of your control – particularly outside vendors and the scheduling problems they might have to deal with.

For service businesses, staff scheduling is of paramount importance, including what's required to have the necessary staff at the right place at the right time.

Having a software background, I learned more and more about this problem with every software product we created – because developing software code, particularly challenging software code, is inherently difficult to build an accurate schedule. Oftentimes, the software developers might not even know what it's going to take to solve a gnarly design problem, or won't have a good feel for how many cycles of logic changes or bug-fixes will be needed during testing. At the same time, though, the sales and marketing side of the house is waiting anxiously for this code to be delivered to early customers where it's been promised for real-life testing, and knowledge of the new feature/product has been slipped into marketing material that's beginning to raise some buzz. If customers really want this new software, they might even be building their own plans around when they'll get it. All of this is leading you, ever the optimist, to add the expected revenue for it into your budgeting plans. Then, horror of horrors, some basic premise in the code design is proven wrong, or a bit of testing produces some niggly problems – and the product delivery delays begin.

Almost every business is prone to this problem, and the reasons are too many to even contemplate. In your case, you need to identify the specific problems that could jump out and bite you, and then develop an idea for how long the delays might be. In all of these situations, planning for the worst/best case scenario can be a good exercise, adjusting as you gain experience. At the start, though, take the most conservative approach possible. Optimism is the basis for what keeps an entrepreneur going, but keeping a positive cash flow is still the golden rule.

Creative credit. Unless you're extremely careful about this, it can also be *destructive credit*. We'll discuss this in detail in Chapter 4, but here are a few tips for now:

- There are a dozen ways to obtain credit in creative ways – some easier than others. But one thing will almost certainly be true ... it will be more expensive than the standard types of credit. If you need creative credit, it's probably because you can't get any other credit, and knowing that, the providers of it demand a higher price for it.

- It's riskier than standard credit. The consequences when/if you default on repayment will likely be more swift and more severe than standard credit. If that happens, it may feel like you're dealing with Guido and begin to fear for your kneecaps.

- If customers learn you're under pressure from creative credit, they may assume you're having financial difficulties, which can scare them away from buying from you.

- Because of the above realities, dealing with creative credit can generate a lot of extra worry and effort, adding to your regular day-to-day tasks of growing the business – and the last thing you need is something more to worry about.

If there's ever a time in your business life to have a detailed budget to live by, going after credit is just that time– and a budget that you watch on a daily, weekly, monthly basis, *with factors built in for contingencies.*

Revenue goals

Do you want a company whose revenue goal is *steady as she goes* – where your primary interest is a regular and steady paycheck as long as you continue to operate the business? And at the same time, a steady growth plan, where you aren't betting the farm every day, and where you're living the lifestyle that you want right now, rather than foregoing it to fund more rapid growth.

Or do you want a company with high growth potential – one that could grow into a large company, possibly with an IPO as your exit strategy, or an M&A for a good multiple of your annual revenue? In this mode, you're likely facing more sleepless nights, longer workdays, fewer vacations to relax now and enjoy life – and plowing every penny of profit to fuel the growth.

Either of these goals is realistic, but usually mutually exclusive for any given business plan. Oftentimes, the business itself will dictate which it will be, as lots of businesses just don't fit into an unrealistic mold – in which case, you need to recognize it and plan accordingly. Other times it will be your capitalization (or lack of) that will dictate your realistic revenue goals. Still other times it will be how much creativity you (and your team) put into the success of the business.

Getting a realistic *handle* on how your business will operate – and the money you'll deposit in the bank as a result of that operation – is crucial to the accuracy of your business planning. As we just saw, accurately projecting revenue, first for your beginning days, and then monthly and yearly, is important for short and long term planning of your company. For the typical entrepreneur, it's easy to project optimistic numbers, expecting that they'll look good to investors and banks you might borrow from. The reality is that your actual numbers (no matter how conservative) most likely won't reach your projections. Most humans tend to be optimistic, and even when we try to be realistic, some amount of optimism creeps in. That's why it's important to have multiple projections in your spreadsheet – best case, worst case, and most-likely scenario.

Revenue goals go hand-in-hand with your cash flow projections, but they need to be kept separate. Cash flow is most useful for your short term planning; revenue projection is for longer term planning. With good revenue goals and careful cash flow management, you can plan on how to reach your longer range objectives. For example, it can show you the long term viability of your business plan. It helps with the advance planning necessary for new products you want to develop, hiring additional production staff, both of which can have many ramifications – production facilities, office space and additional furniture, additional staff in other areas to support them, or more IT equipment and software. It can give you the confidence for making capital equipment expenditures, and whether the expenditures can be paid for from available cash on hand or the ability to pay down loans used to finance these expenditures. And ultimately, it helps you decide if your exit plans really have legs.

In my own business, I was prone to overly optimistic revenue projections. I had a line of credit from our bank that I used for day-to-day operating expenses, and being a software company I was constantly outside of the bank covenants that kept my credit line from being called (which would have forced my company into bankruptcy – but more about this later). In addition, many times it was difficult to maintain *my own level of confidence* in the company's future without highly optimistic revenue projections. By being optimistic, we achieved business goals that might otherwise wouldn't be attained, or in far greater timeframes. It resulted in substantial risk, but it was risk I felt comfortable with, and managing risks is one of the most important things an entrepreneur has to do.

Every single angel investor who presented at the monthly seminars I attended painted a rosy picture about their projected revenue stream. Of the ones I ultimately invested in, not a single one even came close to their projections – and those revenue projections were vetted by each investor committee doing due diligence – but we invested on what we believed in, and that's what an entrepreneur has to do as well.

> *"... contradictory personality traits of a good founder ... someone who is stubborn yet open-minded and dedicated ... [but] when they get new data is able to change their mind — but not too often."*
> Sam Altman, serial entrepreneur, founder of Y Combinator

How many arrows are in your entrepreneurial quiver?

Virtually every business, large or small, has ups and downs in the business cycle. If you don't, you're probably cooking the books – in terms of *smoothing* the business cycle across quarterly reporting periods, which, in the big league business world is frowned upon by regulatory agencies and investors, and under some circumstances is illegal (think GE and the $50M penalty they paid in 2009 for "accounting shenanigans"[35]). As a small business owner, your business cycle is a fact of life, but to be successful, you need to do everything possible to mitigate it. Here are some examples from my own situation, intended to spark your thinking about how you can do similar things for your business.

- Think about developing business opportunities to provide additional revenue sources when you might otherwise be going through a slowdown.

  In my own software education business, I initially had 3- or 4-day courses, often because that's what the customer requested, or because that fit the timeframe of my topic knowledge (i.e., I didn't know enough to teach longer about a topic). That always left non-revenue days in my work schedule, with little opportunity to fill out a week with revenue. Several customers were reluctant to increase course length. I soon found a solution – lecturing about a topic taught me more than I ever thought possible, allowing me to pack more and more highly valuable teaching material into the class (at its current length) – and feedback from the students to the training coordinator soon resulted in *requests from the customer* to increase the number of class days. I also concentrated on ways to increase student interest in the classes, resulting in a large number of repeat classes.

  After a couple of years' experience in the business, I could readily see that during some seasonal periods business wasn't so strong – such as the summer months when everyone was on holiday. The solution was to focus marketing efforts on places in the world where I

---

[35] Dan Fisher, *Accounting Tricks Catch Up With GE*, Forbes online, August 4, 2009, http://www.forbes.com/2009/08/04/ge-immelt-sec-earnings-business-beltway-ge.html

could teach when things were slow in the U.S. – the Southern Hemisphere has reversed seasons from my home base, so when it's summer vacation time in the U.S., it's the middle of the winter in Australia and New Zealand. Sure enough, the broader I made my customer base, the more revenue increased – *and smoothed out*.

Another twist that worked was scheduling around holidays. Since most of my business soon grew to 5-day teaching assignments, any week that had a holiday in it was automatically a low revenue week (more likely, a no revenue week). We have several major holidays in the U.S. that other countries around the world don't have (e.g., 4th of July, Memorial Day, Labor Day, plus several more that some customers observe and others don't). Throughout the year, whenever a class request came in from anywhere outside the U.S., I pushed it towards a time when everyone was at work in the destination country, and away from holiday weeks, or typical vacation times in the U.S.

- Another way to smooth out the business cycle is to build a more robust source of revenue. If you're a one product or one service company, put as much effort as you can into developing a second, third, fourth (or more) product/service line. Not only will this help even out your current revenue stream, but when your customers turn fickle and forsake you for the next popular thing, you'll have longer legs to ensure your long-term success. In my case, I continued to add new class titles to my curriculum, which then enabled me to more quickly add instructors to the staff, ultimately adding to my bottom line.

Maybe your slowdown is due to days that *you* experience slowdowns. For example, you might already be satisfying customers Monday–Friday, and your work/life balance just can't handle any additional days – and so you're missing some weekend opportunities. Maybe a part-time new hire is in order, allowing you to hand off some workload to balance your workdays out. Maybe your slowdown is due to material sourcing vagaries, or vendor breakdowns – and you could fill in with other revenue products or services whenever that occurs.

The key here is that you need to be resourceful if situations beyond your control make it difficult to predict – or increase – revenue streams. This resourcefulness can make the difference between profits that grow your business and cash shortfalls that cause your business to fail or stagnate.

What level of risk are you comfortable with?

Until you've been there and done that, it's almost impossible to understand what's on the line almost every day of your life as an entrepreneur. If one of your big comforts is the security of payday coming around regularly, and knowing that you always have enough money in the bank to cover any eventuality ... well, your risk level doesn't sound good for being an entrepreneur. If, on the other hand, you feel you can live with taking *calculated* risks, maybe the life *is* for you.

You'll soon find that banks *pierce the corporate veil* – in fact, they *force* you to allow them to do that – in exchange for any level of credit they extend to you (such as a revolving line of credit).[36] In so doing, *every personal asset you own* may be required to collateralize the credit, which

---

[36] The term "piercing the corporate veil" technically refers to how this applies to a corporate business structure. When you have an LLC, the equivalent term is "piercing the limited liability shield", but the former term is so well known that it can be equally applied to the corporate or LLC situation.

means your house, your personal bank account, your car ... in short, all of your assets up to the credit amount will be at risk (but not your retirement accounts such as 401(k) or an IRA).

Once you have employees, you'll also discover the challenges of "making payroll" ... on time, and with a full bank account balance to cover it. In 30+ years, we never missed a payroll – but came extremely close more times than I can count. One time, we had to delay the payroll by three days – with the cockamamie story that our bank had made a mistake (and I know several employees guessed at our subterfuge, and knowing they knew didn't make me very comfortable or happy with myself).

Due to occasional cash shortages, we also had to stretch out our accounts payable more than was comfortable. Several times my wife (who also worked in the company) and I took our paychecks on time, but quietly arranged with our bookkeeper to immediately loan the money back to the company – in exchange for promissory notes to pay us back as soon as the company could afford it. At one point, we did this for six straight months – almost wiping out our personal savings.

We never *cooked the books* – i.e., we always maintained our financial books according to GAAP ... well, most of the time, but since we owned the company, it wasn't as if we were deceiving investors. We held the books *open* a few times past the end of the month in order to report revenue that we'd promised to the bank to maintain the covenants on our line of credit. Our VP of Sales, as well as our bookkeeper, knew of these situations, and we also had a high degree of certainty that a customer would sign a sales agreement in the next few days – otherwise we wouldn't have done it.

When considering all of this, keep in mind that everyone faces risks these days. Gone are the days of guaranteed lifetime employment (as many large corporations offered 50 years ago). Today's merger and acquisition mania, not to mention outsourcing, downsizing, global financial crises ... you name it! ... force the risk levels high for employees, as well as for small business owners. It's important to keep it in perspective, though.

Here's an interesting example. At one time during the mid-life of my company, a highly valued senior manager came to me and asked that he be given (yes, *given,* at no cost to him) a substantial stake in the company – meaning he was asking for actual shareholding, otherwise known as part-ownership – to the tune of 20%. At the time, he was a highly compensated employee, and was overseeing a division that was bringing in 40% of our annual revenue. He argued that I was taking too much money out of the company in my own compensation (he knew nothing of the fact that I often loaned the money right back to the company to keep us afloat), and stated that I was doing this "*on the backs of the employees*".

I was so taken aback at this notion that I hardly knew how to craft a response. One argument I gave him was the difference in the level of actual risk that I was at, versus his situation, explaining that even my house was on the line as collateral for our corporate bank line of credit, *and every day I risked losing that.* He retorted that he too faced the same level of risk – that if the company went under, he'd be out of a job, he'd no longer be able to make his house payments, and he too would lose his house.

My next response took the wind out of his sails – I explained the big difference was that the moment (yes, the *moment!*) I defaulted on our bank line of credit, the bank had the right to invoke their collateral (my house, my bank accounts, and all of my other assets), and along with my company I could lose all of those assets *in a heartbeat*. Sure, if he lost his job because I also lost the company and his position was terminated, he'd be at risk that he couldn't pay his mortgage. But assuming he could cover his mortgage payment from savings for a few months, or by borrowing from his IRA, or by waltzing over to a new job, he'd still be able to keep his house. Yes, he finally agreed that I had a totally different level of risk with respect to my company, and the discussion that I *owed* him a share of the company was ended.

I have a hunch this is a fairly common perspective with a sizable number of employees.

Will your company be service-oriented or product-oriented?

While this seems like a duh!-type of question at first, it really isn't – and it could help you decide on a planned multi-phase start-up launch that provides a better chance for success.
The question deals with two important aspects: upfront capitalization and scalability. Both should be considered from the get-go, but the first helps identify your odds of running out of money almost before you get started, and the second is related to low or high growth potential.

Service-oriented. At the risk of sounding obvious, a service-oriented business will have (in most cases) a requirement for lower upfront capitalization. You'll still have some aspect of product development time and costs to create whatever service you'll be providing, as it's hardly likely you'll step right off the curb and bring in revenue immediately. To ease yourself into the service aspects of your new business, you may decide to keep your day job initially.

Oftentimes, banks won't loan to a service-based business, so an option is to create a business plan that details exactly what is needed to help you create your service capability, then try for an SBA-backed loan, as small business loans to start a business are much more available. Friends and family may not be able to loan to you, and your idea might not be appropriate for a crowdfunding campaign.

The benefit of a service business, though, is that an ordinary, everyday person, with skills that can be hired out, can start a company with almost no capitalization. Your product is in your brain, in your muscles and physical talent, your communication skills, and your knack for identifying ways that your knowledge and experience can help another person or business.

Downsides are that you could be one step away from homelessness in the blink of an eye. Just lose one customer, get sick, require major surgery, get hit by a bus, or make just one bad business mistake and everything could be down the drain.

Because of its low capitalization, though, service-oriented businesses have a low barrier to entry – meaning that competitors can start up at the drop of a hat and you're left scrambling. The more you can differentiate yourself, the better your odds of success.

Because I barely had a month's salary in the bank when I started my company (the epitome of being under-capitalized), a service business was my only option. In simplest terms, that meant the number of billable hours in the day (week, month, year) determined the extent of my business revenue. Other than working more billable hours, there was no way to increase revenue. And without increasing revenue, there's little opportunity to grow the business.

Product-oriented. Depending on the product itself – how much money the product requires to produce, how the product is built or created, and how quickly it gains traction in the marketplace – starting a product-oriented business typically requires more upfront capital to build the initial sellable products.

It's not unusual for a new small business trying to break into an established product area (where you think you have a better product than currently on the market) to require multiple years working on design and development before they start to turn the sales and profitability corner. In the process, you can hit very high barriers of entry, including customer lethargy in changing over to new methodologies. You can hit production snags; you can hit management and investor roadblocks. Throughout this time, other small companies might have zoomed to stardom, due heavily to sexier product niches, and maybe the ability to dazzle potential investors. The point is, being a product-oriented business – and depending on where you are in the product world – can have huge barriers to entry, and the costs along the way can swallow you up.

That generalization isn't always true. If, for example, you decide to start up a fancy cake decoration business, the upfront start-up costs might not be any higher than a service-oriented business (in fact, the business itself is sort of a service business, but with a product that you build to order and then sell). I once worked with a guy who was a software engineer by day, and a fancy cake decorator by night at his home. His business was all word of mouth (weddings, anniversaries, birthdays, office parties), and his only start-up costs were supplies and the utensils. Once he worked out his business kinks, he quit the day job and turned his cake business into full time. At first he worked out of his own kitchen, but when his orders overflowed his capacity, he had to rent a facility to operate from.

Multi-phase start-up. There's nothing wrong with planning a two-prong approach from the beginning for getting your new business up and running.

Let's say your new business idea doesn't have a tremendous time-urgency, and maybe there's a year during which you can gain your foothold in the industry with a service approach, and using the profitability from that, you then use the money earned through service contracts to capitalize your business. I did exactly that when I started my business – I just didn't realize that's what I was doing at the time, with the result that it delayed my second phase *by about a decade*.

In my example, I founded my company with just a few dollars in the bank (hardly enough to pay a month's worth of bills). It wasn't totally stupid, though, as I had some contract teaching assignments already lined up. I parlayed each teaching assignment into several more, until I had some money in the bank. If I'd had the focus (and the software development idea) at the time, I could have fairly easily converted my services company into a product company by beginning an earnest software development project in my company's early days, paying all of my costs from the profits of my teaching contracts.

To do this, you need the cleverness (in other words, the ideas and the moxie) to develop a service offering that is a business idea in itself – one that customers will buy – all the while having your eye on the real end goal ... getting the product side of the business up and running as quickly as you can. The service business that you start with doesn't even need to be in the same area of expertise as your eventual product business – although it can help by building name recognition and marketplace access that makes life easier when it's time to introduce your product.

Many people in this world today lead such busy lives, or they simply lack the time, the desire, or the ability to learn about something they need to accomplish – and this is where your service business can come in. For example, I'm a computer guy, but I don't have any real technical background in PC-based systems, particularly home networks. Rather than spend the hours and hours necessary to learn all of that stuff, I'll gladly pay someone with that knowledge to do my setup work for me. Likewise, I don't have the time or the inclination to keep the windows on my house spotless, and whenever window washing is needed, I'll pick up the phone before I'll pick up a bucket and sponge. If the thought occurs, let's do a dinner party for six friends next month, my first thought is, "Gee that would be fun to cook for!", but my second thought is, let's look online for local caterers. I'm sure this happens to lots of other people – the list just goes on and on. Any of these areas are possibilities for near-term service businesses that can be turned into cash cows for what you really want to do later with your life.

Are you primarily focused on a lifestyle-sustaining business?

For the sake of discussion, let's call this an LSB. As the name implies, with this type of model you are not focused on a meteoric business growth, but rather, one that you can work with indefinitely (maybe until retirement). More specifically, though, is the idea that your goal is to provide you – and your employees if you grow to that level – with sufficient profit to pay a salary that enables the lifestyle you've chosen, for as long as you're working.

Important for you is that the business is also sufficiently profitable and sustainable to create a *retirement* lifestyle that you want to have. Hopefully, your LSB will be the type that is sellable when you reach the end of your working days. If it isn't, or if it can't be sold for enough money to retire on, you'd better have 401(k) plan contributions to your retirement plan to sustain you. Because the contribution amount to a 401(k) plan is limited, make sure you salt away enough after-tax dollars to fund the retirement lifestyle that you're working towards.

Don't _overestimate_ the value of your LSB – and don't _underestimate_ the challenges you'll face in successfully selling your LSB. What it's worth to you may be very different from what it's worth to a potential buyer, and because of the nature of the business, you can get badly tangled up in the sale. Keep in mind that an individual (or your employees) interested in buying an LSB might not have the upfront cash to buy your business. In this case, you might have to consider being the finance bank.

Four examples might help illustrate the difficulties of LSBs. Though none of these are explosive growth businesses, each provides a lifestyle-sustaining profitability – and they are real businesses (not hobbies), paying real salaries, and several with real employees.

Owner #1. A friend owned a wine bottle label printing company – a highly specialized printing business. As the company founder, he had built it from inception into a successful and respected business, largely the result of his associations within the wine industry. With a keen knowledge of the business, he was able to run a very tight ship, even though on slim profit margins. With that, he created a very nice lifestyle for his family – a home in the country, a well-stocked wine cellar (mostly purchased from his business associates at good deals), a small single-engine airplane that he flew recreationally, and membership in a private club in the city where he could entertain friends and business associates.

As he neared retirement age, and after quite a long search, he found a buyer for his company – but one that didn't have the upfront cash to fund the entire sale. So my friend decided to carry the purchase contract himself, meaning that he took a down payment in cash, with the new owner expected to pay the remainder of the note from future earnings. Unfortunately, because of the increased debt load, or from a less-tight ship that the new owner ran, the venture didn't succeed. My friend was forced to foreclose on the deal two years later, taking over the business again. By now, though, the struggling new owner had seriously damaged the businesses' client base, the employee situation was in disarray, and the company's physical equipment wasn't in good shape – in short, he now had his old business back, but it was a mess.

Luckily, my friend hadn't jumped into conspicuous consumption with the original down payment he'd received, and that gave him a bit of cushion to begin the rebuilding process. The downside was, it wasn't what he wanted to be doing at this stage in his life.

It took over two years to rebuild the business, and he then found another buyer. But this one too wasn't able to raise the necessary capital to buy his company outright. With no other options, my friend again carried the purchase contract ... *and the same thing happened.* The new owner wasn't successful, and my friend now owned his old business for the third time.

Finally, after bailing the company out once more, on the third sale he found a buyer with sufficient capital to buy him outright – and who was able to successfully run the business. The whole process cost him several years of his retirement time, not to mention a lot of grey hair.

Owner #2. As of this writing, the LSB owner I'm next describing hasn't yet sold her business, but is in the planning stages, and she's thinking through the obstacles to selling. This particular business is a canine therapy swimming center.

Obviously, your local civic swimming center won't allow dogs to swim in a pool where humans also swim, so my friend has a small, private, enclosed, above-ground pool in a dedicated business area of her rural residential property. Think of a heated pool about the size of your living room, maybe 4´ deep all around, and enclosed so that it can be used in all kinds of weather conditions.

My friend spends her entire working day _in_ the pool, usually with a single dog that she leads by a leash. From her earlier days as a dog trainer for show and agility rings, she can instantly spot under-developed fore and hind muscles, and shoulder and back muscles that require exercise – and she leads the dog in swimming exercises that build those specific muscles. She works a lot with injured dogs, mostly dogs with back injuries, arthritis, and other pain situations. My friend is really good at what she does, and over the years she's built up a loyal clientele who return with each new iteration of family pet or show dog – many just for sheer exercise.

At $40/half-hour pool session for one dog, this is obviously not a high-growth, IPO-type of business, but rather, one that sustains the lifestyle my friend has chosen (she used to be a postal clerk, and this was her way out of it). It's a real business, and one that requires her to officially treat it as a business – pay taxes, be licensed as a business, keep official business records, and in all other ways run it like a business. Being a 1-person business, she doesn't have the option for a 401(k) plan, so she contributes the maximum amount to a Roth-type self-employed retirement fund, plus any savings and investment plans she can afford.

The challenge will be when she tries to sell her business – which is her ultimate goal. Having a steady and longtime client base, it has *going concern* aspects that are attractive. But since it's physically located on her property, it's unlikely she'd want to sell it and let operations continue there (but that might have to be an option, although it has lots of drawbacks, not the least of which is liability). Her preference would be to have the buyer move her existing swimming pool to a new location or construct one from scratch. This gives the business a definite barrier of entry, as not everyone will be able to create the facilities she has without a considerable equipment investment. Like Owner #1, it's also unlikely that a prospective buyer is going to have tens of thousands of upfront dollars to buy the business, and it's unknown if the buyer would be able to get a loan to buy – so she may be faced with carrying the contract, which we've already seen is risky, and in fact, even more risky for her, as the business would now be operating from a new location.

A likely conclusion is, this LSB is one that obviously can sustain a current lifestyle, but it's questionable if it's a business that can be sold for enough money to fund a long-term retirement. One solution is to squeeze as much of the profit as she can out of the business while she still operates it.

Owner #3. This small business owner used to work in my own software company but was unfortunately laid off after its purchase, when the buyer consolidated many back-office functions into the parent company HQ. After being let go, she elected not to stay in the wage-earning workforce, and with a very young family, decided to be a stay-at-home mom while the kids were young. She had recently married into a young family – an existing family of two boys – plus she had three more children of her own after the marriage. With this, she very rapidly experienced, first-hand, the challenges of clothing so many quickly-growing children. More to the point, she saw how quickly children outgrow clothes, and therefore need replacement clothing – clothing they'll then soon outgrow before it wears out. That gave her the idea for a secondhand consignment clothing store in the small island community she lives in. With less than $5,000 that she borrowed from family and friends, she opened her store, specializing in infant to toddler clothing.

The venture turned into a business that began to pay her a small salary after a while – and therefore could only be described as an LSB for a limited financial lifestyle return. Importantly, it also returned a far greater sense of community worth. Her comment about the accomplishment five years after she founded the business: "Every day someone comes in and tells us how much they like the shop and are so happy we are here for them".

Recently, my friend opened a second retail space, another consignment clothing store and next door to her original store, but this time for adult clothing.

Given the type of business this is, it will be hard to replicate the success in order to grow much larger. It's been successful enough, though, to repay – on time – every one of her friends and family that she borrowed from to start the business.

> *"Stay self-funded as long as possible."*
> Garrett Camp, Co-Founder of Uber

Higher-growth potential businesses

What is a *higher-growth potential business*, and is it something you're looking for in starting a small business? Only you can answer that.

For the sake of discussion, let's assume there are two categories of higher-growth potential businesses:

- **Moderate.** This type of business can be the result of many entrepreneur and product choices, and the business environment, where the business provides *pretty good* (but not spectacular) growth. It could be 35%, 40%, or even 50% annual growth, which over a few years' time gets the business to the point where a buyer with a serious money offer is likely to enter the picture if that's what the owner wants. This business can provide a fun and profitable ride along the way, and a nice payout at the exit.

   This category of company usually doesn't have the financial firepower to propel it into the next category, often because the owner lacks the knowledge, vision, or focus to achieve beyond this level, but it may be that timing or the right product mix holds it back.

- **Fast (or high growth).** In today's world, this company is most often the brainchild of a high-powered person who dreams up an idea like Facebook or Uber, and while the product idea is critical to success, the founder's vision and focus aimed squarely at big-money investors, is the key to high-growth success.

   A tiny percentage of entrepreneurs who start the business of their dreams ever achieve the 10-bagger success story,[37] even if that's their stated goal at start-up. And there's nothing wrong with dreaming – but don't let the bright lights of Broadway derail you to the point of implosion (unless, of course, you have the wherewithal to pick up the pieces to start over).

   Chasing venture capital money can eat up inordinate amounts of time and resources – and unless you're hell-bent on your start-up being very high growth, the time might be better spent tending to down-to-earth business development.

As I detailed in the previous section, my own company spent its first few years in the slow-growth mode – and we seemed to be stuck in the doldrums of slow growth, medium-sized profits, and aging employees who were getting within a few short years of retirement age. Luckily, a life-changing event came along (a massive, almost immediate downturn in our business, all outside of our control), and if it wasn't for recognizing that as an opportunity, we'd have been lucky to even remain in business.

---

[37] In his writing, Peter S. Lynch coined the term *10-bagger* to describe companies to invest in that return 10 times their original purchase price. The term derives from baseball, where 'bags' refer to the number of bases a batter reaches from a hit ball – so a double is a 2-bagger, and a triple is a 3-bagger. Baseball obviously never had a 10 bagger, as it would be equal to two home runs plus a double – in a single at-bat. Peter Lynch was famous in the 1990s as the Magellan Fund manager at Fidelity Investments who achieved an astonishing 29% average annual return over a 20-year period, from 1977–1990 – the best return ever made by a stock fund.

At one point I began the hunt for some angel investment money, which could give us a jumpstart to larger venture capital money.[38] Once a month I attended a half-day breakfast meeting, hosted by a local start-up investment group whose mission was to help entrepreneurs link up with potential investors. Each meeting began with an hour or so to chit-chat with potential investors and other entrepreneurs. After breakfast, some already-successful local entrepreneur or one of the investors would give a presentation, and then we'd get a briefing on some topical aspect of how to pitch our company to investors. The idea was to gradually bring entrepreneurs up to speed on how to attract investment money. At the end of each meeting, any entrepreneur who felt ready was then funneled into a series of outside sessions to help them develop the presentation pitch to use with potential investors. When the entrepreneur was ready for prime time, a special meeting would be set up for the entrepreneur to give the pitch to a group who might be potential investors in the company. After that, if there was actual investment interest, a formal due diligence process began, reviewing the start-up's financial data, their business plan, and any other aspect of their company the investors felt necessary.

I could see this was going to take a huge amount of time and personal commitment from me, just to get to the point where I could make my investor pitch – and if that panned out, it would require further effort that could be orders of magnitude greater as we went through due diligence. Having heard stories of how small business founders could easily lose control of their company in this type of process, I was also very leery of that aspect. Besides, it would take me away from pressing and immediate needs to keep my company afloat.

It didn't take long to figure out the process was a non-starter – at least for me. In the late 1990s, mainframe computers were being called dinosaurs, and the marketplace sizzle of the day was about the PC revolution (it didn't help that Bill Gates proclaimed the PC would cause the total demise of the mainframe world). It was also when the dot-com bubble was sucking all of the air out of the room, attracting huge bundles of money towards the PC and network environment. College kids in dorm rooms (with nothing more than a business plan, no actual product, and no revenue whatsoever) were getting millions of dollars thrown at them by gullible investors.[39] It's no wonder the mainframe software world was considered a backwater – and slow growth.

In fact, my company's annual revenue growth was in the 25–35% range – pretty darn good by any other industry measure – but compared to the wildly inflated expectations in the PC software

---

[38] Angel investors and venture capitalists are two different breeds of investors, and provide two different type of investment to small businesses that need capital. Angel investors are typically small investors – someone who wants to invest $25,000–$100,000 in a small business start-up. They get in on the ground floor of the start-up, and typically become the first outside investors for the company. Usually, when angel investing is done with a group, each investment might bring $300K–$500K to the start-up, hopefully giving it the *legs* to grow to the next level. For that money, the angel investors typically get a small stake in the company, maybe a total of 5%–15%. Venture capitalists (single, or in a group) may come in with an investment at the beginning of life for a start-up, or further down the road – but for a much larger dollar volume ($1M–$10M), and will want to grab at least 51% of the company's stock – in order to control their investment and direct the company for their own goals (i.e., huge profit).

[39] And all of this came crashing down in the last half of 2000 when the dot-com bubble burst, causing a 46% drop in the NASDAQ – the securities exchange where most of the dot-com public companies were listed.

world, it just couldn't turn the head of an investor. I never got past the initial hobnobbing breakfast stage of the angel/VC investor get-togethers.

What it did teach me, though, was to come to grips with the reality of my company's future. Turning my back on this outside money allowed me to knuckle down and return my focus to maximum effort on growing my company *organically* – plowing all of our profits back into the business and bootstrapping ourselves from within. It was actually a rather satisfying result, as it freed me up from the angst of having half my mind distracted by the lure of fast growth – the thought of, "if only I had a million bucks from a venture capitalist".

100% ownership versus partial ownership

Obviously, if you own 100% of your company, the only way you can lose it is by defaulting on some type of financial obligation that uses your company as collateral. But outside of that, no one within your company can override anything you do with your business, take control of it, or oust you from it. Even if you bring in a high-level executive, such as CEO or President, and give them authority to do as they wish with the company (within reason, obviously), that person is just an employee, works for you, and you can boot them out the door any time you wish (this is still true if you own 51% or more of your company).

The moment you dilute your ownership to the point where any one individual – or any group of aligned individuals – manages to have a controlling ownership larger than yours, you no longer have that level of control. This group can now out-vote you on company directions, even to the point of firing you. In this situation, you might still own some part of your company, but you've essentially been ousted from any active participation. It's happened time and again, and it's always sad to hear of it, even if warranted.

Sure, you might say, Bill Gates (as one example) essentially had full control of Microsoft with only 11% stock ownership, so why can't that work for you? Well, it could ... if your company reaches an IPO stage, followed by a feeding frenzy of widely disparate investors buying your stock ... with the ultimate result that you are still the single largest shareholder – *and* if you can swing those disparate investors to your way of thinking to become a large voting block if another investor chooses to challenge you.

Losing control is always a primary concern with bringing in outside capital, and it should give you significant pause when you feel it's your only choice for funding. Keep this truism in mind: if someone else has the money, and you want that money badly enough, they'll ask for a larger percentage of the ownership than the dollar amount warrants. And if you want the money badly enough, you'll give it to them – and from that point on, they have you by the short hairs.

Here's a simple example. You start your business with a few thousand dollars, and you work your butt off for the first two years to get it going. You have a bit of profitability and some growth, but it's still a slow slog. You create a growth plan, determining that you need $100,000 to really grow the company. You find an investor with that amount of money to invest – but the kicker is, the investor wants a 51% shareholding in your company as part of the deal. The investor's argument is that only with that level of ownership will the investor be able to help guide the company to its new level of growth, and still manage the risks associated with investing $100,000 in your business. They'll use the word *guide*; and you should think *control*.

Another scenario might be an outside investor offering to invest $500,000 (even if you aren't asking for that much), on the condition they get controlling ownership. Or, they might just invest the amount you need ($100,000), but force you to accept some kind of super-voting power, where their 25% ownership weighted vote outweighs your 75% non-weighted ownership votes.

Once you agree in any of these situations, you've basically sold your soul to the devil, as you are now beholden to the outside investors. This is known as the *founder's dilemma*,[40] and afflicts an astonishing percentage of founders with growth ambitions that outrun their ability to generate *internal* capital to fund the growth. In a study for the Harvard Business Review,[41] Noam Wasserman found that fewer than 50% of original founders still had control of their companies by the time the company was three years old – and by the time these companies made it to an IPO, fewer than 25% were still run by the original founder. In most cases, the founder doesn't choose to go, but rather, is forced out by the investor group (by stacking the Board votes). *The amazing part is, for those founders who were forced out, the amount of money they ultimately made for their efforts was no more than they could have made as an employee.* Let that last word sink in.

But hey, you think, this still might work. You give in because you see it as the only way to achieve your goals – and besides, you really trust everything this investor says to you. After all, you and the investor are now *almost* 50/50 partners, so both you and the investor have equal goals in the future direction of your company.

Sorry, Charlie, that just isn't the way it works – and the absolute last thing you *ever* want to believe is anything an outside investor tells you (this may sound really cynical, but you should heed it). Odds are, the investor's goal is very different from yours. You had a dream that resulted in the company's founding – some product that you feel passionate about, or your goal to own your own business, or whatever the reason was. The investor, on the other hand, has one goal – to earn a maximum return on the investment. The moment your two goals clash or diverge, the investor is going to win any arguments, and he's going to take the company in whatever direction he wants – even to the point of firing you, locking the doors behind you, and keeping you from ever setting foot in it again. And worse, even trashing the product(s) you founded the company for, as maybe there were other parts of your company that the investor really wanted. It's their right to do it if they have controlling interest in the company.

But, let's say you stay on with the company – and being the eternal optimist, you still think the odds are in your favor. This investor wants to make a gazillion bucks, and since you still own 49% of the company, you too will make a gazillion bucks right along with him. That could be true, but actually you're at even more risk of getting shut out. If that investor decides the company truly has legs (i.e., maybe a really good product idea), but needs even more money to reach success, the investor may decide to bring in *more* outside capital, diluting your shareholding with every further investment of outside money.[42]

---

[40] Noam Wasserman, *The Founder's Dilemma*, Harvard Business Review, February 2008, https://hbr.org/2008/02/the-founders-dilemma

[41] IPO – an acronym for Initial Public Offering – is a company's first sale of shares to the public. When a company goes public, the shares are listed on a stock exchange, such as the NY Stock Exchange (NYSE) or the National Association of Securities Dealers Automated Quotations (NASDAQ).

[42] Matt Cavallaro, *The Danger of Share Dilution*, Investopedia, undated, http://www.investopedia.com/articles/stocks/11/dangers-of-stock-dilution.asp.

You might still end up with shares worth a lot more than you ever put into the company, but you could also end up with a check for $25. It just depends on how things play out.

So, the advice is, any time the urge strikes you to bring outside capital into your company, slap yourself up the side of the head a dozen times until the urge goes away. Only if you have really sound advice and counsel, and you really know what you're doing, and what marketplace you're playing in in doing, should you consider bringing in outside capital – particularly outside capital that could override your ownership stake in the company. Otherwise, do absolutely everything possible to finance your growth another way, or change your goals and dreams.

Below are some examples that illustrate this, both the upside and the downside.

- ***Men's Warehouse.*** When was the last time you saw the ad-pitchman, George Zimmer, tell you he'd "gare-ohn-tee" the way you look in the suit you bought from Men's Warehouse – he's the man who founded the company in 1973 and owned 100% of it until he brought in outside investors to expand). Yup, he was given the boot by the Board of Directors representing others who subsequently owned a lot more of Men's Warehouse than Zimmer. When he was ousted, he owned a mere 3½ % of the company, and while it was worth tens of millions of dollars, the ousting was because Zimmer and the Board had a different idea of where the company should be taken in the future.

- ***Tesla.*** Almost everyone who lusts after a super-sexy Tesla all-electric car, whether it's the hot Roadster or the fast but more sedate-looking Model S or X, will immediately agree that Elon Musk was the company's founder. But in fact, actually two co-founders, Martin Eberhard and Marc Tarpenning, started Tesla in 2003, and it was only when the company obtained Series A venture capital financing from Elon Musk that he entered the picture. Along the way, both co-founders were effectively shoved out of the company.

- ***Groupon.*** Andrew Mason may not be a household name for many people, but the company he co-founded with financial backer Eric Lefkofsky is. It's Groupon. Now, Groupon reported revenues of $800M in 2010, and not long after, Mason supposedly rejected an acquisition offer from Google for $6 billion. For that decision, Mason was subsequently named the "worst CEO of the year" by CNBC journalist, Herb Greenberg. Mason was fired as CEO by the Board of Directors in early 2013, for missing analyst's revenue projections and falling far short on the profit projections.[43] But the story doesn't end there. If you believe the news,[44] and can follow your way through a labyrinth with as many twisty turns as the Paris sewer system, indications are that a bunch of well-heeled mezzanine-level investors were given a haircut to the tune of hundreds of millions of dollars, but Mason himself now sits on a couple hundred million dollars. The odds of a situation like this turning out as it did are higher than winning a Powerball lottery, and it's not for the faint of heart.

- ***Balcones distillery.*** Unless you're from Texas, or are heavily into prime-time whiskey, you may never have heard of the artisanal corn-and-malt whiskey from this small business

---

[43] Wikipedia article on Andrew Mason, http://en.wikipedia.org/wiki/Andrew_Mason
[44] Joan Lappin, *Don't Cry For Groupon's Andrew Mason*, Forbes online, March 5, 2013, http://www.forbes.com/sites/joanlappin/2013/03/05/dont-cry-for-groupons-andrew-mason/

in Waco.[45] Founded in 2008 by Chip Tate, the phenomenally successful company needed to expand to keep up with customer demand. Who wouldn't want that problem? The trouble was, upgrading a whiskey-producing still to meet demand is capital-intensive, and Tate needed funding – to the tune of $4M. He found it in a well-heeled investor in Virginia, Gregory S. Allen. At first they were partners on the same mission, but along the way, perspectives changed, as did the amount needed to build the new custom still – increasing first to $8M, and recently reaching a whopping $12M. With the new investor now controlling the majority shareholding, founder Tate was told in no uncertain terms that the additional money was forthcoming, but only if the founder himself departed – and with terms that didn't allow him to compete in the same business for a specified time. After becoming increasingly ugly (purported threats, calls to the police, law suits, and lots of rancor) the split was inevitable. Chip Tate is completely out of the company – but has waited out the no-compete time and is reportedly back in the business with a new brand of whiskey.

So, what's the point? The point is, if it's your desire to keep control of your company, you should make a conscious decision about that early on – maybe even as early as when you decide what your company will do, and what it will cost to get there – as you run a very high risk of eventually losing your company later when your ownership share drops below 51% (the low point where you still have majority control).

> *"If it doesn't feel right, keep looking. If you're compromising, keep looking.*
> *A company's DNA is set by the founders, and its culture is an extension of*
> *the founders' personalities."*
> Naval Ravikant, Co-founder of Epinions, AngelList, and Vast

Thinking of co-founders? – get it right

Having a second, or even a third (or more), person involved in the start-up of your new company can be a good idea – or it can be a really bad idea. Not everyone has the skills – let alone the interest – to manage and oversee the myriad details necessary to make a new company succeed. A co-founder, particularly one that fits in really well and fills in the skill sets, might increase your odds of success (notice I said *might*). If you're going to read this next section, make sure you read both the pros and the cons.

So let's start with the pros. Consider this: would Microsoft or Apple be the companies they are today without the teamwork in the early stages of Gates and Allen, or Jobs and Wozniak? Or how about the five co-founders of Facebook – Eduardo Saverin, Mark Zuckerberg, Dustin Moskovitz, Chris Hughes, and Andrew McCollum? Or Google's Sergey Brin and Larry Page? All are successful companies, and all had co-founders whose strengths balanced each other's weaknesses – to a point. Intel (the computer chip maker) had co-founders – Bill Hewlett and Dave Packard, both engineers – were also close enough to share management responsibilities.

---

[45] Clay Risen, *How Dreams and Money Didn't Mix at a Texas Distillery*, The New York Times, December 27, 2014, http://www.nytimes.com/2014/12/28/business/how-dreams-and-money-didnt-mix-at-a-texas-distillery.html?_r=0

How to determine if you should have one or more co-founders? Almost by definition, a co-founder is going to be a co-owner in the company, meaning there's an owner's split between the co-owners (or shareholding split if it's a corporation). While this obviously means there's an expectation of shared workload and commitment to the business, it also means more than one mouth to feed when profits and dividends are taken from the company, or when the company is sold. Getting the co-founder ownership percentage right is paramount from the start. If you take in a 50/50 partner, but you created the idea and you put in 75% of the work to make it successful, yet both of you share equally in dividends and later when you sell the company, well, you might have been screwed (unless, of course, the other co-founder put up the money in the first place).

So, some of the big questions you need to ask yourself revolve around these ideas:
- Are you ready and capable to take on this new company all by yourself?
- Are you the sole originator of the product/service ideas behind the company?
- Do you have the skill set to be Chief of Everything?
- Do you have the capital – both in real money and sweat – to go it alone?
- Do you have the personality and temperament to work with a partner, to put up with their differences in opinion/work ethic/skills/foibles in a business venture?
- Is your potential co-founder compatible enough with you to share ownership of something as important in your life as a business?

And the most important question might be: Is this someone who brings enough to the table that you'd want as a co-founder and partner, or would you be better served to hire the person as an employee?

Keep in mind that an awful lot of people you might be considering as a partner or co-founder, down deep really don't want to start or run a business – but would rather have the security of working for you and just taking a nice, steady paycheck. They might be daydreamers about owning their own business, but when the rubber hits the road, aren't entrepreneurial after all. Or there might be antagonisms and personality quirks that make you incompatible. None of these situations work for a successful co-founder or partner situation.

Let's assume you've decided to have a co-founder or shareholding partner. How do you determine an equity split between you? There's a significant body of opinion on this topic, with lots to think about – and should be! – as this could be one of the most important decisions made in the early days of your company's founding.

As for the actual split numbers, a 50/50 split isn't the only way to do it – and in fact, an exact 50/50 split could be the worst decision you could make, unless there are clear and concise policies and guidelines (in your **_written_** partnership or operating agreement) on who's running the show and how to resolve conflict. A 33/33/33 split, or 25/25/25/25 split can be a slightly better situation, although neither give any one individual the ability to effect important changes unless a coalition is built – and it can work against you if the other co-owners align *against* you.

Finding the right percentage is a negotiating process, and considering how important it may be in the future, a process you should discuss at length. If the negotiations don't go well, it might indicate it wouldn't have been a good partnership after all.

Assuming the ball is in your court to influence the founding decisions, here are some factors to consider: (a) if you want or need a co-founder, and if so, (b) how to create the equity split, and (c) how to manage the equity positions.

- Who came up with the foundation idea for the company? Oftentimes, ideas have an ambiguous beginning point. You may be two college buddies who kick an initial idea around in your dorm room (think Mark Zuckerberg with Facebook), and both of you are feeding off each other in coming up with all the reasons you should do this. The details of this need to be worked out *and set down in agreed-upon writing* before the company is ever founded, as this could be a serious basis for a later dispute.

- Which of you is capable of executing on the idea? If your idea is to create the latest concept in how to brew an artisanal beer, and you've developed the crucial know-how, it might justify your stake being higher than your proposed co-founder, whose biggest input might be as your production manager or hotshot salesperson. On the other hand, if your buddy is the one with all the brewing knowledge and you're the hotshot salesperson (and your buddy isn't), it might argue for a more even split.

- Who is putting in the bucks, and who is putting in the sweat equity for the new venture? If someone happens along with $100,000 and you're penniless (or maybe your dorm room partner is a rich kid with dollars to spend), it could very well be that no amount of work on your part could ever get this venture off the ground. In that case, the person with the cash-in-hand at the start-up stage could reasonably argue for a larger stake.

- Which of you will play a bigger role in actually starting and running the business? And which of you is taking the bigger risk in making it successful? If you are quitting your day job, but your sidekick is sticking with his day job until the success is assured, you'd better be taking the lion's share of the equity stake (unless, of course, your co-founder is funneling money from the salary of his current day job to fund the start-up). Also, if you're going to be the CEO, President, Chief of Everything, but your co-founder is taking on lesser duties and responsibilities, it might warrant less a bigger split for you.

- Vesting the equity stake ensures that people who come into the business to get it started actually stick around and do their part to make it happen. Vesting can be tied to a timetable, or to performance goals being achieved. For example, shares could vest over a four-year period, 25% vesting after one year and the remainder in equal monthly or annual installments over the next three years. Or, if one of your primary responsibilities is to increase sales, reaching (or exceeding) pre-established revenue goals could trigger vesting (or any other measurable performance metric also works).

- Before your company issues stock grants or stock options (either to co-founders or subsequent employees), make sure you (and your corporate tax accountant) study up on a relatively new (2006) concept called restricted stock,[46] or restricted stock units (RSUs). RSUs can have significant (favorable) effects on your company's balance sheet, as well as being significantly less expensive to set up than stock option plans.

---

[46] A good layman's discussion of restricted stock can be found in the tax booklet, *Restricted stock: the tax impact on employers and employees*, by G. Edgar Adkins, Jr., and Jeffrey A. Martin, of Grant Thornton LLP, https://www.grantthornton.com/~/media/content-page-files/tax/pdfs/white-papers-survey-reports-articles/2013/Restricted-stock-tax-impact.ashx

- Stock ownership/selling restrictions. This is different from the bullet above – in this case it refers to restrictions on disposition of stock once it gets distributed. These restrictions ensure that stock options or restricted stock disappear if an employee (or founder) departs. Your best bet is to create the strongest possible restrictions with your stock so that it remains in the hands of people who can do the most for your company – i.e., current employees. Include clauses that force first right of refusal to the company to purchase any stock that's up for sale, *with clear rules on how the stock is to be valued* (which is important for a privately held company, as valuations are not easy to get).

Now for the cons of having a co-founder or partners. There's a wide body of opinion that having a root canal is much less painful than having co-founders or partners – and many opinions are from entrepreneurs who have been down that road in the past.

The simple fact is, life doesn't always work out as planned. People who seemingly work together during the idea stage often don't work well later. People who promise to do things once the new company gets off the ground don't come through when needed on those promises. People who are thought to have the skill set necessary for the task prove that they actually don't. The reasons are manifold, and you need to be on the lookout for any and all of them.

If you decide to go with one or more co-founders, or take in partners in the future, and one or more of the partners don't work out, be prepared to fire the person (for lack of a better term). The difficult task is ... how to do it.

The best solution is to have the equivalent of a pre-nuptial agreement – an ahead-of-time agreement that spells out the mechanism for parting company. Like a marriage situation, though, in the early days when everything looks rosy, who is rational enough to stick a poker in the fire (or in the eye) to discuss how to pre-arrange a split-up? Obviously, the one with the most to lose should be the one to initiate the agreement and push it through.

Barring a pre-nup, the second best thing in the event of a split is to do it quickly and cleanly. Get an attorney to draft a separation agreement that spells out the exact terms of the termination. Suggested ideas include "give them slightly more than what they are entitled to – perhaps some vesting acceleration or a few weeks' pay", and have them sign a release promising they will not later sue the company.[47]

- **Apple Computer.** Here's an easy example – and a situation you may have never heard of before. Ronald Wayne was Apple Computer's (now Apple Inc.) third co-founder. With Steve Wozniak and Steve Jobs as the nerdy guys creating the now-famous Apple I computer, Wayne's role was to provide the administrative capability that the other founders didn't have (or didn't want to be involved with). He joined the new company at the outset with a 10% stake, with the goal of getting it properly incorporated, developing the original logo (depicting Sir Isaac Newton sitting under a tree), and writing the documentation for the Apple 1 computer. A few weeks after the founding, Wayne sold his shareholding to Jobs and Wozniak – because he was worried that being the only one of the three with any assets, they might be seized by creditors if anything went wrong with the new venture. He

---

[47] Andre Gharakhanian, *How to Fire Your Co-Founder*, Inc. guest blog, undated, http://www.inc.com/andre-gharakhanian/how-to-fire-your-co-founder.html

voluntarily sold his 10% share back to Apple, and took an additional $1,500 to agree not to make any future claims against Apple. Eliminating an incompatible co-founder couldn't have been easier or simpler – and to this day Wayne says he has no regrets.[48]

- **Facebook.** Here's a more difficult example. Consider the primary co-founders of Facebook, dorm room friends at Harvard who linked up, starting their venture off with the following split: Zuckerberg 65%, Saverin 30%, and Moskovitz 5%. (Chris Hughes and Andrew McCollum were also co-founders, but their roles were considerably smaller, and most likely their split was less than 1% each – if any at all at the actual company founding). Here was their stated basis for this share split: Zuckerberg had the idea and ability to execute, Saverin had the money (a mere $15,000) and supposed business sense, and Moskovitz was a software guy.[49]

  Saverin was also supposed to get the company incorporated, build the company's business plan, and scrape up heavyweight funding for the company – but instead headed off to New York for an internship at a large investment bank. It was soon apparent that Saverin should be squeezed out of the new venture. With the company already set up and the shareholding split a done deal, Zuckerberg got a bright idea (from someone else) to secretly form a new company and have it buy the original company, with Zuckerberg in total control. A major VC (Peter Thiel) came in with a $500K infusion of cash; a boatload of new shares were issued (but no new shares to Saverin), and when the dust settled, Saverin's shares were diluted to something like 5%. A few weeks later, Saverin was formally fired from the new company, and he moved to Singapore to escape U.S. taxes on the *paltry* $2B he received from the company's later IPO – and sued Facebook, settling out of court.

- **And then there's Microsoft.** When Bill Gates and Paul Allen incorporated Micro-Soft in late 1976 in Albuquerque (NM) – yes, it was two words and hyphenated in the original filing, then changed to today's name in 1979 – they agreed to a 60/40 shareholding in Gates' favor. Bill had successfully argued these percentages to be fair since he'd done more of the independent development work on the BASIC language when he was still at Harvard and Paul was working at another job. Sometime later, Bill and Paul changed the shareholding to a 64/36 split, again in Gates' favor, but little has ever been said about that.

  Adding mystery to the Microsoft split, there was a third vital person on the BASIC compiler development. This third co-founder never even got paid for his efforts, let alone a share in the co-founder split (or even a bit of gift stock).[50] In their frenzied eight-week development of the BASIC compiler, one critical and necessary aspect of it was a series of floating point routines that enable the machine to handle basic arithmetic, such as addition, subtraction, multiplication, and division. To help out, a guy they met at their Harvard dorm lunch room, Monte Davidoff, dropped his classes to spend every waking hour writing these routines. Later, when the Altair took off as a result of the BASIC compiler within it,

---

[48] Kerima Greene, *Apple's Third Co-Founder and the $35 Billion He Left Behind*, CNBC blog, September 14, 2011, http://www.cnbc.com/id/44505957#
[49] Nicholas Carlson, *How Mark Zuckerberg Booted His Co-Founder Out Of The Company*, Business Insider, May 15, 2012, http://www.businessinsider.com/how-mark-zuckerberg-booted-his-co-founder-out-of-the-company-2012-5?op=1
[50] James Wallace & Jim Erickson, ibid.

Davidoff was never even mentioned as a co-developer of the arithmetic code, and has never shared in any of the subsequent success from it. Talk about leaving someone at the altar! The moral is, in situations like this you can be a straight-up person, or you can be a scoundrel – and where money is concerned, it can cause a lot of problems later. In this case, it didn't, as Davidoff just walked away.

Nevertheless, Bill and Paul certainly made out very well, although there's been a lot of speculation over the years that tempers flared and Allen's exit from Microsoft wasn't as rosy as most people believe.

- **<u>Snapchat.</u>** And be prepared to go to court, as illustrated in this example, where one of the original idea guys gets ousted before the company is even formed.[51 and 52] An entrepreneur named Reggie Brown claimed that he came up with the original idea for the now-successful app, Snapchat, with (among others) his Stanford University fraternity brother, Evan Spiegel. Brown was squeezed out of the company as a co-founder when it was subsequently being formed to execute on the idea, with Brown claiming he should have at least 20% shareholding. It created a long-running, loud, and expensive argument in Silicon Valley, culminating in a lawsuit resolution in late 2014, when the two company co-founders settled out of court for an undisclosed amount. (You can see just how expensive this demand for 20% would have been when Snapchat went public in early 2017 with a total market valuation of $22 billion.)

The moral of these examples is, when you're in on the ground floor – even if it's just an idea you're kicking around in the dorm room – and you're putting effort into it, or even just an idea you're discussing with your friends and potential co-founders – get something formalized ASAP, either an LLC operating agreement, or an intellectual property (IP) agreement, listing you as a co-founder that clearly states your involvement in it. If you don't, you may have a he-said/she-said situation as your only defense. You could be squeezed out before you ever get in – and it may have been your idea to begin with, and you may have put in a good chunk of sweat equity.

> *"Your exit strategy entails a choice between two options: close the doors, or sell your business. The former is generally the result of failing to plan."*
> anonymous

Should you have outside advisors?

Yes! That's an easy question to answer, but not always an easy suggestion to <u>correctly</u> fulfill. In the last section we discussed co-founders, illustrating their ability to round out your skill set and provide another voice in decision-making. Whether you have co-founders or not, having a trusted advisor is a really good idea. This person (or multiple people) can be as close to you as you want,

---

[51] Sapna Maheshwari, *Snapchat Concedes In Settlement: Ousted Co-Founder Came Up With App Idea*, BuzzFeed, September 9, 2014, http://www.buzzfeed.com/sapna/snapchat-concedes-in-settlement-ousted-co-founder-came-up-wi#.yg2N95qL2

[52] Laura Entis, *5 Facts About Evan Spiegel, Snapchat's Often Controversial Co-Founder*, Entrepreneur online, July 9, 2015, http://www.entrepreneur.com/slideshow/248136

even attending meetings and accompanying you on trips to meet customers and alliance partners, hearing conversations and formulating opinions in a different way than you are. He or she can be as formal or informal as you want, including on your payroll or in a strictly outside advisory role (for the new start-up entrepreneur, I strongly favor the latter, as you need to be as lean as possible at this point). There can be as many advisors as you want, covering as many topic areas about your company as you feel comfortable with.

Areas where an outside advisor might be of value:

- **Financial management.** Chances are you have no experience in the many aspects of small business financial management, and will stare blankly the first time your bookkeeper presents your company's financial statements to you for review. Sure, you can (and should) read up on it in books such as this one, but having a person experienced in it at your elbow can significantly shorten your learning curve.

- **Strategic planning and business growth.** In the early stages of your start-up (not to mention at any point in your growth cycle), you might be too focused on the trees to see the forest. Having a trusted advisor who can talk with you about bigger picture items might be very good. But not just the big picture – but rather, small sideline pictures that might be hitting your radar screen but aren't registering in your thought or planning process.

  For example, while you're focused on getting every detail of current products just right, employees in customer or technical support might be grumbling that there isn't enough management attention being given to those areas.

- **Building CEO skills.** This advisory can usually be filled with a local small business organization in your area. They can be found with an internet search on "*yourcity* small business ceo peer advisory group". There might be a small fee to join, and their get-togethers might be once a month over lunch, or longer scheduled meetings.

  For example, the Las Vegas area has one called Catapult Groups (www.catapultgroups.com), which meet once a month, in groups of 12-14 members *from non-competing industries*.

  You can also try national organizations, such as Vistage (www.vistage.com) or the Peer Advisory Council (www.peeradvisorcouncil.com). The SBA has an organization called Score, and while this service isn't specifically for CEO skill building, you can probably get it to achieve just that if you want.

- **Employee benefit plans.** Wait! Wait! Don't skip this one by just because you're just a 1-person company right now. There are several employee benefits just for you, the business owner, if you know about them. When I started my company, I stumbled on some of these quite by accident. If I'd known about them earlier I could have taken advantage of them, plus benefited from the tax deductions they provide. Having an employee benefit advisor who is knowledgeable in this specific area is someone you should have in your back pocket from the start.

Once you have additional employees, this advisor (or a replacement) can advise you on the pros and cons of various employee benefit plans that you might want to consider.

It might be of interest to know that Jeff Bezos, founder and CEO of Amazon.com has used multiple advisors since 2003, "shadowing" Bezos in meetings and on trips, and offers advice for building this ever-expanding empire. In the case of Amazon, the advisors were hired as company employees specifically for this role, and most have now gone on to head major divisions of the company.[53]

Planning an exit strategy

For any type of business, you should have an exit strategy in mind, or start laying one out when you first open your doors. It doesn't have to be a fixed-in-stone exit strategy, but it needs to be something to give you a goal to work towards. None of us can work forever (and most of us don't want to), and when the time comes to move on to another phase of life, having an exit strategy can really help that transition.

While an exit strategy is a way for you to transition away from day-to-day running of your business, more importantly it's a way for you to get _your_ money out of _your_ company. That could be money for your retirement, it could be money for the next business phase of your life, it could be for estate planning purposes if you know in advance your kids can't/won't run the business the way it needs to be run ... or any number of reasons. It's your choice.

Thinking about this in the formative days of your company seems counter-intuitive, since the last thing you'd like to think about as you're racing around starting your business is how you'll eventually get out of it. Early decisions that you make, even as early as when you begin the start-up phase, can have a significant impact on the success of your exit strategy, so you really need to think about it early on.

Here are several ideas to get you thinking, based on a very interesting Entrepreneur online article titled _Exit Strategies for Your Business._[54] It's very informative to read in its entirety, but here are a few gems from the five strategies that are discussed:

- **The Nike maneuver.** Take the money and run ... starting early! The technique is simply "to bleed the company dry" on a regular basis. If your company was created primarily to be a lifestyle-sustaining business, a good way to get your money out (and you don't have other investors to worry about) is to pay yourself a huge salary and bonuses, rather than using the money to grow the company. The idea has lots of pros (remember, it's identified

---

[53] Casey Coombs, _Amazon CEO Jeff Bezos' shadow advisors have gone on to big things_, Puget Sound Business Journal, March, 17, 2017, http://www.bizjournals.com/seattle/news/2017/03/17/amazon-ceo-jeff-bezos-shadow-advisors-big-things.html?ana=e_ph_prem&u=ZjsyWY2Pva46UGJhB%2FG%2BwQ08ea75f4&t=1489768538&j=77674741.

[54] Steven Robbins, _Exit Strategies for Your Business_, Entrepreneur blog, at http://www.entrepreneur.com/article/78512. This list is taken from this blog post, with supporting information on each list item supplied by me.

as a lifestyle-sustaining business), but also several cons (serious tax implications, or you may pull out too much, too soon).

- **Liquidate.** Just close it down, lock the doors, and walk away. Actually, the term *liquidate* sounds a lot like Chapter 7 bankruptcy, but that isn't what's meant in this context. It could very well be that you've simply decided to liquidate while you still have assets left – assets that you can squeeze money from as your just desserts.

  At first, liquidation on your own terms seems like a simple, straightforward way to extricate yourself from business life. The downside is, you might not get full value for your assets – such as customer lists, or equipment the company owns – so if this is your planned route, explore every other avenue before you just shutter the company and move on to the next stage of life.

  Depending on the situation, liquidation might be the only alternative. You might have been searching to no avail for years to find a buyer, but without anyone stepping in. You might have unforeseen health issues (or family issues, or whatever) waltz into your life, making it impossible to continue running the business on your own – and it may be the type of business where there's realistically no one to take it over. We often think of this as *going out of business*, which it is, but the more precise term for it is liquidation.

- **Selling to a friendly buyer.** If a strategic buyer can't be found, maybe a friendly buyer can. You may not get as much money from a friendly buyer as you would from a strategic buyer, but hey, it might be better than liquidation. Friendly buyers come in many forms – a customer who loves your product(s) so much they just can't stand the thought of you going out of business, or a customer who needs your product and its updates/upgrades so much they're willing to buy the company to keep it going. It could be a competitor down the street who might see opportunities that benefit their own business.

  A friendly buyer could even be your employees, who want to see both the products and their jobs continue. Be very careful of this, particularly if you're required to carry the contract while they earn enough profit to buy you out – they might want the company to remain in business, but they might not know how to run it. There's even an IRS-approved employee benefit plan, called an Employee Stock Ownership Plan (ESOP)[55] that facilitates this. An ESOP is designed to invest in the stock of your company, with the ownership of that stock in the hands of the company's employees. It's a complicated and expensive plan to set up, but in the past 20+ years it's become more and more popular.

  Another possibility is passing the business down to family, either in a giveaway or in a nominal purchase. This too is fraught with problems, as no one else in the family might be as good, or as knowledgeable, as you in what makes the company tick, and how to make it succeed in the future. It might be more advantageous to sell the company outright for as much as you can get, then pass the return on to the family in the form of cash or a trust.

---

[55] An ESOP is a qualified, defined contribution employee benefit plan, controlled by rules established under the Employee Retirement Income Security Act of 1974 (known as ERISA, and discussed in Chapter 7). An ESOP is a special version of a defined contribution plan, and can be a way for a company's owner to pass ownership to employees. Do a simple internet search on ESOP and you'll get a dozen good hits.

- **Acquisition.** Get as much as you can, and get on with your next stage in life. If you can find the right buyer, at the right price, this option could be the most profitable. The word "if" at the beginning of the sentence, though, is key – you could search until you're blue in the face, and still not find an acceptable buyer.

   (In my case, it took over five years to find the buyer that I finally closed the deal with – and this was after four other deals went right down to the 11th hour and then fell through. And I wasn't fiddle-fritzing about – I had a very successful investment banker representing me throughout this time, and he specialized in my type of company and knew the marketplace very well.)

- **IPO.** This is the carrot many budding entrepreneurs dream about. Unfortunately, an IPO is the least likely of all small business exit strategies ... unless, of course, you'd tried to start your company in the late 1990s dot-com era, with access to venture capital financiers who were throwing money at any harebrained idea that came along. Nowadays, though, the chances of your company making it to an IPO are so slim that, typically, only serial entrepreneurs or the lucky 1-in-10,000 start-ups (or worse) have even the slightest odds in their favor. It's good stuff to dream about, but keeping yourself grounded in the real world makes more sense. In the U.S. in 2013, there were only 178 successful IPOs, in 2014 a mere 244, 2015 had an even fewer 169, and 2016 was a dismal 102 – and that's nationwide.

Chapter 3   Setting Up the Business ... Very Important Details

Hyacinth gave herself airs of good breeding, correcting people who mispronounce her last name – spelled Bucket. "It's boo-kay'" she exclaims in exasperation when they pronounce it "buck'-et".

BBC comedy sitcom on PBS, *Keeping Up Appearances* (1990-1995), Hyacinth played by Patricia Routledge

Naming your new business (and starting your branding process)

Actually, this isn't mundane at all. In fact, finding the right name for your business is one of the most important things you'll do at this early stage, as it will help establish your professionalism – and your brand identity – not only in the general marketplace, but also in the online world.[56] Interestingly, given some of the company names one sees, it's pretty obvious a lot of would-be entrepreneurs haven't felt the same degree of importance about this.

Since your company name is a primary part of your marketing brand emphasis, there are quite a few factors to consider in settling on a name, including:

- Can your customers pronounce it? Will they pronounce it the way *you* want them to pronounce it? Givenchy probably doesn't really care how you pronounce their brand name, so long as you spend big bucks with them. But if you're just building your brand, resist the urge to be overly cutesy in your company name, particularly if it leads to mispronunciations, or worse, being unpronounceable.

  For example, Sony introduced their music streaming service with the name Qriocity, assuming everyone would intuitively pronounce it like "curiosity". Duh! When that didn't work, they smartened up and – are you ready for this? – rereleased it as the incredibly boring and unexciting name, but very descriptive name, "Sony Entertainment Network".

- And just to show that this isn't uncommon (even with big, well-known brands), Pentax has introduced a line of cameras called *ist. It's certainly catchy, but why would anyone think it is brand-effective for your potential customers to have no idea how to ask for it at the store counter? (Answer: according to Pentax, it's simply "ist".) How will it appear visually and psychologically? Consider all the places you'll see it: stationery, business cards, signs on your storefront (if you have one), marketing literature, website and social media pages, your tradeshow booth, Yellow Pages listings, and product packaging.

---

[56] Marianne Bickle, *The Power of a Name: Branding Your Company for the Future*, Forbes online, January 10, 2011, http://www.forbes.com/sites/prospernow/2011/01/10/the-power-of-a-name-branding-your-company-for-the-future/

Visual appeal of your company name is very important, with respect to your location, your target market, and the subsequent names of your products or services.

An *eeeuuu!* example: Pocari Sweat … a non-carbonated drink from Japan, created as a sports drink, where the name was derived from what it was supposed to supply to the drinker (and not what it was supposed to taste like) – and in a culture where English words are used differently than in the U.S. Now bring that drink to the U.S., and you can see the challenges of this name.

A *don't get it* example: oooooc.com … supposedly pronounced "five-o-C", a social marketplace website that is the "easiest and safest way to sell your content and files over the internet and achieve economic independence, without a risk." Not only is the pronunciation not intuitive, but the name doesn't have any connections to the business description found on the site's home page.

- How it will sound, not only when you introduce it to your customers, but also in little-thought-of ways – such as answering the phone, or saying it repeatedly in business conversation. If it's a mouthful, or doesn't sound good, you'll probably shorten it to something that does sound good – and that defeats the purpose. Why not start off with a name that already sounds good – *and one that you'll be proud of saying*. Keep in mind that you and your employees (particularly anyone who answers a company phone) will use this name quite a few times each day, not only face-to-face, but in your phone greetings, and as part of the first impression about your company. (Who knows, maybe you'll eventually even hear it in a local TV commercial jingle, but that's probably not something you'll be thinking of at start-up time.) Best recommendation: keep it short.

- Does it convey your business purpose, or will you have to explain it every time the name is used? Will it appeal to your marketplace? Will it reflect the business culture that you hope to instill throughout your company? Your company name should be *obviously meaningful* to your customers – and your potential customers.[57] Not being meaningful can result from trying to be too cutesy or clever, or for that matter, too obtuse. For example, if you named your company Qwerty Corp and you were in the keyboard business, everyone would probably get it instantly, but if you tried for Poiuyt Corp, it would just be a head-scratcher (not to mention unpronounceable), and you'd have to explain it to everyone who looked at it – destroying any message you were trying to make (if you hadn't guessed, it's the other side of the keyboard, running right to left).

- Will the name stand up to your growth stages? A name that conveys a sense of fun surrounding your first (and maybe only) product, may begin to look really silly when your company is older, more established, and has other products. Unless the basic idea of your company is surrounded by silliness, or you're honestly trying to mimic some of the latest naming trends, stay away from something that sounds good when you're sitting around having a beer. Think about it several times (over several days) before deciding.[58]

---

[57] Geoffrey James, *The 1 Essential Rule For Naming Start-Ups*, Inc. online, undated, http://www.inc.com/geoffrey-james/the-1-essential-rule-for-naming-startups.html?cid=readmore
[58] Eliana Dockternam, *7 Silly Tech Company Naming Trends*, Time Magazine online, April 21, 2014, http://time.com/70206/silly-tech-company-naming-trends/. Their article also has a link to an hilarious video that brings out several points about this in an HBO sitcom, Silicon Valley, surrounding the choice of

- Is the name you're thinking of *web-ready*? Does the business name correlate with the visual style and tone of website you want for your company? You may want a domain name that's associated with your business name – which means you'll want to get the best possible domain name reserved even before you register the business name.

    It's not conducive to your business success if the business name you really want happens to exactly match a domain name already in use, particularly if it's a competitor, and every time someone searches for your business they land on your competitor's site. If possible, you'd like to have a domain name that matches how people pronounce your business name, so factor that in when selecting a name.

    Try a Google search on "inappropriate domain names" and you'll find several to illustrate the point. For example, a supposedly legitimate custom pen crafting company with the name of Pen Island – has a domain name of www.penisland.net (given the logo on the website, it's obvious someone is having fun with this one – although www.penisland.com is a legitimate pen company).[59]

    Think beyond the domain name – is your company name *social media ready*? Check Facebook and Twitter, plus other social media sites, to ensure no similar brands are operating in the social media sphere. Even if you don't intend to use these social media sites, controversy or defamation of another name that matches yours can potentially cause problems for you.

    Is your company domain name conducive to e-mail addresses? For professionalism in your business dealings, you should establish an e-mail hosting service for your domain. That way, all e-mail addresses used within your company can match your domain name. For example, if your domain name is "sb101brewery.com", every e-mail address in your company would have an address of "*name*@sb101brewery.com". As you can see from this example, our domain name is 12 characters long, which is definitely more cumbersome than typing …@ibm.com. It also includes both alphabetic and numeric characters, which on mobile device keyboards will require switching from the alpha to numeric page. When selecting your company and domain names, factor this in, and if possible keep the name as short as possible.

- Give some thought to a business logo that goes well with your company name. In combination, the name and logo should evoke the overall image you'd like to express – and that's the start of your overall branding process.

    Your logo is an important enough factor in your branding that you really should hire a graphic designer (unless you already have this skill). Your logo is the *face* of your company, and as such it allows customers and potential customers to instantly recognize you, and provides a shorthand way of referring to the company in advertising and marketing materials.

---

name and logo for a fictitious company called Pied Piper, at http://techcrunch.com/video/silicon-valley-a-name-defines-a-company/518197690/

[59] Alyson Shontell, *21 Domain Names That Sound Totally Inappropriate*, Business Insider online, March 3, 2013, http://www.businessinsider.com/21-domain-names-that-sound-really-inappropriate-2013-3?op=1.

For example, if you see a Microsoft or Apple logo, you instantly recognize it even without the company name next to it. On Facebook and Twitter, the logo is all that one ever sees these days. Domino's Pizza incorporates their company name right into the domino tile logo, but you'd probably recognize it even if the name was omitted.

Bad idea. A women's clothing company, Catwear, at one time floated this logo:

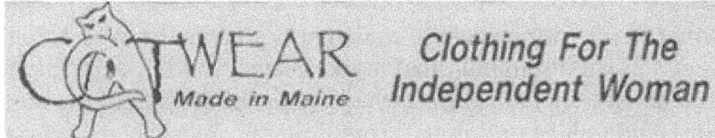

but then thought better of it. They now use just their stylized company name as their trademarked logo, leaving out the questionable image of the cat – a much better idea.

- Along with your name and logo, create a tagline for your company that shows your customers and potential customers what you can do for them – what one writer calls a "unique advantage point" that differentiates you from your competitors.[60]

  When you hear the phrase, *Melts in your mouth, not in your hands*, is there any question of the product it's meant to invoke? Of course not, and I'll bet when you pick up a package of M&Ms at the store counter, the jingle automatically plays through your head. Now that's a good tagline!

  Other examples. *Can you hear me now?* If you didn't instantly think Verizon Wireless when you read that question, well, you've been under a rock for a decade or two. For us old-timers, the Yellow Pages, *Let your fingers do the walking* instantly conjures up a quick search through the ad pages of the phone book. Interestingly, for today's equivalent of the Yellow Pages – that's Google if you hadn't guessed – they don't have a tagline ... but then, they have something better – their name and what they do is known so well that it's been turned into a verb by the users, *Google it*.

  But, you can also blow it with your tagline, so be careful of what you come up with. The worst mistake you can make is to settle on the catchiest, cutest, and memorable tagline, splash it on your website, your stationary, your tradeshow booth, your product packaging ... and then find out it's already in use by another company and readily recognizable. And worse, that you then receive a cease and desist letter to stop using it. The moral – vet your tagline by doing an internet search on it, and if you find someone else also using it, check to see if it has a trademark symbol next to it. Search the U.S. Patent and Trademark Office to see if it's already been legally taken.

- Is your name and logo *print-ready*? You might come up with the snazziest CMYK (color process) name and logo, and it's easy to render on your website in those colors. But if you'll need printed letterhead, printed business cards, and product packaging that have that name and logo emblazoned on it in full color . . . well, you need to check into the cost of 4-color process printing before you settle on it – the price is outrageous at a print shop. You

---

[60] Charles Gaudet, *How To Craft A Powerful Tagline For Your Business*, Forbes online, June 18, 2014, http://www.forbes.com/sites/theyec/2014/06/18/how-to-craft-a-powerful-tagline-for-your-business/

can never get full color printing down to the cost of black-and-white printing, but at least 1-2 color is more in the affordable range.

Be sure to design a grayscale version of your logo because you'll almost always have something that needs that option. In this day and age you might wonder where and why, but consider that most newspapers are in black and white (as just one example), and it will look better when used with a black and white printer or copier.

- Very importantly, is the name *clean* with respect to trademarks? Consider where you'll be doing business, and ensure it's clean throughout that marketplace. It will be terrible for you to find your business name already in use somewhere on the other side of the country (or in some foreign location), and you're prohibited from doing business there under your own name because you've been blocked by the earlier use. It's worth it to run a trademark search, and don't cheap out on just an internet search – instead, have an attorney's office do it for you. They have access to subscriber-only databases that you probably don't have – such as LexisNexis. As soon as you settle on a name and logo, check into whether you should trademark them, and if so, how broadly the trademark needs to be filed (i.e., domestic, internationally).

It's almost a certainty that every dictionary-listed name you think up *will not* come up clean on a nationwide search. There are only so many words, and so many ways to put those words together, that some company, somewhere in the country, will already have the name in use – or a name similar to it in use. Or, they'll have a website domain that's already locked up. Odds are, you'll be forced to seriously consider a made-up name, perhaps a play on words, a contraction of multiple words (think: Microsoft), or a real word that's spelled phonetically (one of my favorites that's really simple: Gardenworkz).

- Begin your brand-building with your name. With a name that really says something about your company, use the name in everything you do, *and be consistent*.

Wal-Mart example. It's amazing to me that a company as large as Wal-Mart – one of the largest corporations in the world – can't seem to get their company name consistent. Spend an hour on the road, any day of the week, and you're likely to see at least a half-dozen Wal-Mart semi-trucks. The side and back end of the trailer will be emblazoned with the Wal-Mart name in 5´ high letters, and just take note of inconsistencies from truck to truck: Walmart, or Walmart*, or Wal-Mart, or Wal-mart, or Wal*Mart, or wal*mart, or WAL*MART. The legal corporate name is Wal-Mart, Inc, but it's *never* consistent on their website, their advertising, their huge store signs at the parking lot, or their trucks rolling down the highway.[61]

With the marketing clout of Wal-Mart, they could spell their name anyway they darn well please and it wouldn't matter much – you'd still know who they are.   But let's look at a very small business – one that's isn't a household name – and you can readily see how inconsistency can be a problem. What if your registered company name is Yardworkz, but on your Facebook page it's shown as Yard-workz, then Yard*workz is on the side of

---

[61] Merrill Perlman, *Wal-Mart. Walmart. wal*mart*, April 7, 2014, Columbia Journalism Review, http://www.cjr.org/language_corner/language_corner_040714.php

company vehicles, and Yard Workz is on the company's tradeshow booth. If a potential customer is searching the internet to find this company, could they find it?

There's a legal term, trade dress, that generally means "all of the various elements that are used to promote a product or service" – and this includes not only consistency of how the business name is used, but also the detailed and overall look and feel of the company logo, colors used in branding, tagline, marketing materials, and a host of others. All of these factors of trade dress will determine whether your company's visual definition can be protected as part of your trademark, registered or not.

- Lastly, your business name will be automatically registered with your state's regulatory agency when you register your business – so no other process is required with regard to that. That's where you will hit a roadblock if the regulatory agency determines that the name is close enough to another business to be confusing, or if your name matches any other registered business name *within your state*. Be aware that registering your name in your state only assures no conflict in your state, but does not consider other states at all. Your state agency will also deny names that include any restricted words, such as "bank", "insurance", "federal" to name a few. Some states, such as California,[62] have downloadable documents that clearly spell out what is (and isn't) allowed in your choice of business name. In many states, you can also search a corporation-name database to look up registration information on business entities of all types (check for a link to this search within the internet pages for business registration in your state).

My business naming example. When I started my company, I realized at the last minute that I needed a company name for the incorporation. One evening, I went through the phone book business listings (this was in 1978, before the internet), creating lists of words used in computer and software company names – Computer, Software, Education, Information, Data, Training, Systems, Services ... you name it. For some now-forgotten reason, I specifically wanted a 3-word company name (bad idea, by the way – too long), so I created a matrix of the words I'd compiled, looking at every possible three-word combination. It proved much more difficult than I imagined, and I labored over it for hours to find a name that fit the bill. Finally, I settled on Software Information Services. It turned out to be a name that I was forever embarrassed with – too bland, too nondescript ... nothing about it was cool, crisp, and professional. In later years, we ended up using the acronym SIS for everything but legal documents, just so I didn't have to hear the full corporate name. Finally, we went through a complete company name change.

The moral is, assuming you're successful and your company name stays around for a long time, it's something you have to live with day in and day out, in every answer of a phone call, every introduction to a customer, and in a thousand other ways. Give it your very best shot, as it could very well be a decision that will help your company succeed.

Establishing your business structure

Before you officially open the door for business, you need to decide how you'll legally structure your business. The type of business structure you select impacts the taxes you pay, the liability

---

[62] *Business Entity Name Regulations & Additional Statutory Requirements and Restrictions. To find this PDF document, search with your browser on the full document name.*

you have as a business owner, and the amount of paperwork and rigmarole necessary to maintain your business in good standing with the state and federal government, among other things. Seems simple enough, but ... *don't screw up the decision*! There are other – *really important* – ramifications that we'll get to in a bit.

In this section, we'll look at these types of business structures:

- **Sole Proprietorship**
- **General Partnership**
- **Limited Liability Company (LLC)**
- **Limited Partnership (LP) and Limited Liability Partnership (LLP)**
- **Corporation (S-Corp and C-Corp)**

Once you decide which structure to use, you'll complete the necessary filing and registration with the state. This is officially known as "filing a business application", and doing an internet search on these words (preceded by your state name) will bring up lots of information about it – each state has its own agency and structure for overseeing the business within the state. For example, in the State of Washington where I live and owned a business for many years, business filing is done in the Office of the Secretary of State, Business Licensing Service.[63]

In making your business structure decision, never rely on the first piece of advice you read or hear – some of it is very misleading, and some is just plain wrong. As an example, here's advice from an online site that *perpetuates a serious misimpression that many new entrepreneurs have*: "With a sole proprietorship ... there's no wall between your business and personal assets. S-Corps and LLCs may cost more to set up and maintain *but your business is kept legally separate from personal assets* -- so it's less risky if your company goes under or is the target of a lawsuit".[64] [italics and underlining are mine]

Note the last sentence "your business is kept legally separate from personal assets." This statement may be *mostly* true from a legal perspective, but in reality, it's hardly ever true from a *financial perspective* if you have any bank loans or credit with others. We'll see more about the infamous *piercing the corporate veil* in a bit.

By the way, the silver lining here is that although the business structure you select at the start may not be the best structure for your business as it grows, you can later change your business structure. However, changing requires some effort and cost – re-filing and re-registering with your state agency, and the expense and effort to change the business name (for example, if you've used LLC in all of your marketing collateral), and possibly a whole lot more.

Let's look at the basic differences between the various types of legal business structures. Keep in mind you'll also find legal differences from state to state, as businesses are registered by the state, not federal.

---

[63] Life is easier now than when I started a business in 1978. For example, Washington State has created an online service (http://bls.dor.wa.gov/startbusiness.aspx) that can walk you through quite a bit of the process. The site has information on planning your business, licensing your business with the state, and even city and county licensing requirements. Each state should have something similar.

Sole Proprietorship. Sole Proprietorship is the most common type of small for-profit business entity, and the one we often think of when we use the word *company*. It's also the business structure that most small business owners have when they say they are self-employed.

According to government statistics, there are 28 million small (fewer than 100 employees) businesses in the U.S., and of those, 23 million are sole proprietorships, employing just one person.

Ownership of a Sole Proprietorship is with the individual who is named on and files the business application. Sole control of the business is by that individual – and the implication is that *all* liability – tax liability, debt liability, and legal liability – is carried on the shoulders of that individual. All income the business generates is considered personal income, and is taxed by the state and federal taxing authorities as personal income. While sole proprietorship is the easiest and least expensive way to operate a business, it also exposes the individual to more risk than the others. (Note: all references to "individual" include the option of a married couple filing for a Sole Proprietorship as well.)

A word of caution about liability issues in a sole proprietorship. When it says above that the owner carries all of the tax, debt, and legal liability, the word *all* is the operative word. You've probably heard the term *corporate veil* (see more about this under Corporation below) – which supposedly prevents shareholders (owners) of a corporation from being liable for any of the corporation's obligations – tax, debt, or legal. A sole proprietorship *does not* have such a veil, making the owner completely liable for these three obligations. If the company doesn't pay its taxes, the IRS will immediately drill straight through to the owner to pay the tax; if the company racks up debt that it can't pay, the creditors can come after the owner to pay it – and most worrisome, if you hit legal troubles, particularly a lawsuit, you can be personally sued for everything you're worth, and you have little recourse if you lose. So think this through very carefully when settling on your business structure, and don't just choose a sole proprietorship because it's quickest, cheapest, and easiest. If you're doing anything in the business that creates the slightest possibility of *any* of these liabilities, you might be better off with a bit more expensive (in effort and resources) structure such as an LLC or a corporation.

Liability issues aside, many businesses operate as sole proprietorships, including many storefront businesses that aren't required to be licensed (e.g., privately-owned drive-in restaurants, tattoo parlors, hair salons, small retail stores, and independent auto mechanics). In-home businesses and individual contractors often operate as sole proprietorships, such as ebay.com or Amazon.com sellers, handyman and lawn care services, small general contractors, and the like.

Many entrepreneurs start out as 1-person freelance operations – providing services such as magazine article writing, website design and development, social media consulting, graphic design, photography, tutoring, personal training, and a host of other specialties – that allow them to be their own boss, work their own timeframes and priorities, and maybe even work part-time outside of a regular day job. To be on the right side of things, you need to be structured as a business, either as a sole proprietorship or an LLC. Otherwise, you're inviting legal problems, tax problems, and liability problems.

Business taxes for a sole proprietorship are different from some of the other business structures.[65] Simply put, as far as the IRS (and your state tax office) are concerned, business profits on your business pass directly through the business bookkeeping to you, and are reported directly on your *personal* income tax return. This is known by the IRS as *pass-through* taxation. Here's a very brief explanation of pass-through taxation: you list your business profit or loss on IRS Schedule C (Profit or Loss From a Business), which should be taken directly from your business accounting ledger. You're then taxed on the total profit, regardless of how much salary you actually took from the company during the year, or how much money you left in the company for expenses or future expansion.

In your day-to-day business, you can deduct expenses just as in any other business structure – including operating expenses, your direct cost of sales (i.e., what it costs to make the products you sell), sales and marketing expenses, and travel and entertainment expenses, as well as some start-up costs and equipment costs (but they might have to be depreciated, just like in other structures). If you don't have a tax accountant to advise you, it's important that you read carefully through IRS publication 535, *Business Expenses*. This publication doesn't cover home office expenses, which many owners of sole proprietorships have – check the lengthy IRS publication 587, *Business Use Of Your Home*.[66]

In a sole proprietorship, paying your taxes can be a quarter-end killer if you're not good at planning your finances. When you're working for someone else (or when you work for your own corporation or LLC), federal (and, if appropriate, state) withholding tax is taken out of each paycheck and paid into your *account* with the tax authorities. Depending on how you set up your W-9 as an employee, this could result in little or no tax due on April 15th. It's different for a sole proprietorship. Taxes are not withheld as you achieve profitability or withdraw money from your sole proprietorship, but rather, *are required to be paid when you file your quarterly tax return* – and the money for this has not been withheld and submitted ahead of time (unless, of course, you do it yourself, by planning ahead).

Self-employment taxes (Social Security and Medicare taxes) must also be paid quarterly in a sole proprietorship, at rates equivalent to those paid by any other business structure (*including the portion that is normally paid by your employer when you work for someone else*). This is an important point to remember, as the self-employment tax is paid as a lump sum along with your personal income taxes (most likely quarterly), rather than with each paycheck or profit distribution that you pay to yourself.

For 2017, the self-employment tax is in two parts: Social Security tax (OASD) is 12.4% on the first $127,200 of income (up from $118,500 in 2016); Medicare is 2.9% on all income – for a total of 15.3%. So you'd better plan on that money being in your bank account at each quarter end, in addition to the amount due for your other taxes.[67] As an example, if your 2017 quarterly *net income* is $32,000, your annual self-employment tax adds up to $4,896 (in addition to

[65] *Self-Employed Individuals Tax Center*, irs.gov website, https://www.irs.gov/Individuals/Self-Employed
[66] IRS Publication 587, *Business Use Of Your Home*, http://www.irs.gov/pub/irs-pdf/p587.pdf
[67] A table of current year tax amounts, including a history of these taxes dating back to 1951 can be found online at Bradford Tax Institute, http://bradfordtaxinstitute.com/Free_Resources/Self-Employment-Tax-Rate.aspx

quarterly income tax due to the IRS and the state), and it's something you really need to be aware of on the first day you open your doors for business – otherwise, you can get behind very quickly.

Conclusion on sole proprietorship. It is definitely the easiest, quickest, and least costly way to start a business, particularly one that will always be run as a 1-person business. In the old days (20+ years ago), about the only alternative was a corporation, which was far too costly and cumbersome for this type of situation, so sole proprietorship was the best way to go. In today's world, where every state allows an LLC-type of business structure, at a very low cost to create and maintain, and with the ability to shield you from almost every form of liability, the advantages of an LLC far outweigh a sole proprietorship.

DBA. This well-known acronym is short for *doing business as*, and is often associated with a sole proprietorship, but it can also be used with any other type of business structure. Filing with your state for a DBA is merely a way to legally announce that your business is operating under a different name than you registered for your business license. It's also called a *trade name*, and in some circles, a *fictitious name* (but that sounds devious, which it isn't intended to be).

A DBA is not your legal business name, but rather, a name that you can *hang on the shingle* outside your actual place of business (if you have one). You can also transact online business, open a business banking account, and issue and collect invoice payments under that name – but it's easier to use your DBA name with your customers, and have the DBA name set up as an alias to your legal business name on your bank account). The DBA name never becomes your legal business name (unless you re-register with that name). You can have multiple DBA names listed for the same legal business name. (Corporations and limited liability companies must also file for a DBA if they are operating under a different name than their legal business name.)

In many states, when you register for a sole proprietorship, the _default_ name of your business is the owner's name. It's difficult to cultivate a marketing presence under just your personal name, so registering as a DBA makes sense. For example, a painter named Ralph Quigley might have a sole proprietorship that's officially registered with the state as Ralph Quigley (which is also the default), but could have a DBA of Ralph Quigley Painting, or Quigley and Associates, or Quigley Enterprises.

General Partnership. The definition of a General Partnership (also known as a General Proprietorship in some states) consists of two or more people (usually not a husband and wife) who agree to commit money, skill, and labor in a for-profit business. Like a sole proprietorship, profits are taxed as personal income. **Important note:** a general partnership should not be confused with a limited partnership (LP) or limited liability partnership (LLP) – two very different beasts that will be described later. *And just so you know where we're heading with this discussion, a general partnership is the worst possible type of business structure.*

Where a general partnership differs from a sole proprietor – *and differs dramatically* – is in the liability that each of the general partners has. Simply put, in a general partnership *all partners are individually liable for all business debts and obligations*, including court judgments. This means that if the business can't pay a creditor (such as a supplier, lender, or landlord), the creditor can legally come after _any_ partner's personal possessions, including house, car, or other possessions – for the entire amount. (This is the point where you should be slapping yourself up the side of the head if you're contemplating this type of business structure ... but read on if you're not yet convinced.)

Additionally, an individual partner can sign a contract or close a business deal *without the concurrence of the other partners*. For example, if a partner signs a contract to sell some goods at a price below what it costs to make, or commits to purchasing some inventory that your partnership doesn't have the money for, *you* can be held personally responsible for it.

Let's get down to the nuts and bolts of this. If you are a co-owner of a business, and you have not formally filed with your state's business licensing division to create a corporation, LLC, LLP, or some other type of business structure that limits your liability, you are, *by default*, operating a general partnership. This means that you have *unlimited personal liability* for all of the businesses debts, *including the acts of your other partners, as well as your employees*. Don't underestimate the significance of the words "unlimited personal liability" in the above sentence.

Here's the best advice I've found for a general partnership: "If after reading the above paragraphs and you still want to operate in the form of a general partnership, here is some general advice: ***Don't do it***."[68] (emphasis in the original)

Limited Liability Company (LLC). Throughout the U.S. in the past 40 years, there has been a tsurami in the world of business structures by the Limited Liability Company (LLC), especially in the small business arena. Whereas corporations (both S-Corp and C-Corp) were more prevalent in the past, nowadays LLCs are far and away the most predominant choice of business structure for new companies. (*But before you let that statement sway you, read all the way through to the negative aspects of an LLC – and also, read about corporations.*)

The reasons for choosing an LLC are manifold, but here are the four most important:
- Simplicity and low cost of creating an LLC
- The legal formalities of maintaining an LLC are significantly simpler than for a corporation
- A taxing structure that can be similar to either a sole proprietor or a corporation (your choice)
- As the name implies, the limited liability protection that it offers to the LLC's owners

Compared to a corporation, an LLC provides similar liability limitations to its owners as a corporation. Where an LLC shines, though, is:

- No requirement for a Board of Directors or officers (such as President, Vice President, Secretary, Treasurer)
- No legal requirement for formal meetings of directors and shareholders, or maintaining minutes of these meetings
- Fewer restrictions on how profits are distributed

Conversely, an LLC has limitations and drawbacks that a corporation doesn't have:

- An LLC is automatically dissolved if a member dies or files for bankruptcy

---

[68] Quoted from *Sole Proprietorships and General Partnerships Are Risky Business Forms*, on their website page, Business Owner's Toolkit, by BizFilings, http://www.bizfilings.com/toolkit/sbg/run-a-business/assets/sole-proprietorships-general-partnerships-risky.aspx

- An LLC cannot be taken public, and shares or share options cannot be issued to your employees (if that is your plan, the LLC would need to be converted to a corporation)
- Unless otherwise filed (discussed in a bit), the owner of an LLC is considered by the IRS to be self-employed (and the LLC is known as a *disregarded entity* by the IRS), requiring each owner to pay the full 15.3% self-employment taxes towards Medicare and Social Security, up to the maximum annual limit per employee. With a corporation, you (as the employee) pay half of this tax amount and the corporation pays the other half, but only on the amount of your official salary (the remaining income is either paid to you as a distribution – and taxed at a lower rate – or held in the company as retained earnings).
- Outside investors typically aren't wild about an LLC business structure, and for many professional investors (angel, venture capitalists/funds), an LLC is an absolute show-stopper – they will require you to have a corporation, and preferably a C-Corp.

 Technically, it's legal to have outside investors in an LLC, but since an LLC doesn't have the concept of equity stock (as a corporation does), the only way to bring in an outside investor is to create an agreement with all other LLC members that provides for *membership interest* in your LLC, essentially giving it the look and feel of a partnership. You would also want to have a written Operating Agreement which governs the rights and obligations of members. (The details behind this last bullet are beyond the scope of this book, but much of that detail is covered in a very good blog post on Startup Law Blog, hosted by the Seattle law firm of Davis Wright Tremaine.[69])

- If a friend (or business associate) wants to invest in your company, it's much more complicated than if you had a corporation. First, you'd need to make the friend a member of the LLC. Because a member of an LLC is an owner, and because by default an LLC has no distinctions on majority/minority ownership, you'd need a membership interest agreement that spells out the rights *and limitations* of that owner. After all, if someone put up a small amount of money, you wouldn't want them to have a controlling say in how you run the business, so you'd need to carefully write this agreement and have it clearly understood between all parties. (With a corporation, though, their percentage of shareholding would inherently identify their level of control in the corporation.)

Let's look at an example of that difference between a corporation and an LLC:

- Let's say a friend wants to invest in your corporation. Assume you own all 100,000 shares, and you grant your friend 1,000 shares – it's a meager 1/100th shareholding in your company, and as such the friend only has 1 out of the total 100 voting rights.
- If you add a member to an LLC for that same 1/100th investment amount, the new member – by default – becomes an equal owner to you. To correct for that, you would need to write a *membership rights agreement* to establish the member's ownership percentage, *and that's an agreement you need to pay a lawyer to write*, and you'd better get it right if you don't want problems later.

---

[69] Joe Wallin, *12 Reasons For A Startup Not To Be An LLC*, Startup Law Blog hosted by Davis Wright Tremain, September 30, 2011, http://www.startuplawblog.com/2011/09/30/12-reasons-for-a-startup-not-to-be-an-llc/

Compared to a sole proprietor or partnership business structure, the limited liability aspect of an LLC is huge, shielding the owners from *the debts of and any judgments against the business.*[70] Even more importantly, the LLC operates as a separate legal entity from the owners (owners are typically called *members* in an LLC), including owners who are active in the management of the company and don't lose their limited personal liability protection by doing so. (But don't entirely believe the limitation on legal and financial liability in an LLC to be absolute – make sure you read later about *piercing the corporate veil*, which also applies to an LLC.)

The taxing benefits can be just as compelling. Simply put, the IRS does not recognize an LLC as a type of business entity – so for federal taxing purposes, an LLC will be taxed as if it was any of the *other* types of business entity, based on how you elect (by form to the IRS), or based on circumstances.

Don't take the following as tax or legal advice, but rather, consult your own legal *and* tax advisors for specific rules in your state and situation. *An hour or two spent with both of them on this topic will be well worth the time and money.*

- By default, and unless you file IRS Form 8832 and elect otherwise, your LLC will be taxed like a sole proprietorship (or as a partnership if it has more than one member – although husband and wife are treated as a single member). *As such, you (the owner/member of the LLC) are not considered an employee of the LLC, but rather, as self-employed (like you are with a sole proprietorship).* For some unexplained reason, the IRS uses the term *disregarded entity* for an LLC that is treated as a sole proprietorship or partnership for tax purposes, and because disregarded entity is an official IRS term, you'll probably hear your tax accountant use it a lot in your conversations.

  So, the LLC itself does not pay any taxes, nor does it file a tax return, and the LLC owner(s) pay taxes on their allocated share of profits, or deduct their share of business losses, on their personal tax returns.

- You can elect to have your LLC taxed as a corporation if you file IRS Form 8832 (Entity Classification Election). On the form you can elect to be treated as a regular C-Corp for all taxing purposes, or (as we'll see in the next bullet) you can later elect to be treated as an S-Corp (and you should be getting your advice on this from your tax advisor). *Regardless of C-Corp or S-Corp, you (the owner/member of the LLC) will be considered an employee, and paid and taxed as such.*

  As a C-Corp for taxation purposes, your LLC:
  - files a standalone tax return each year and pays taxes at the corporate level (currently 35%) on the first $75,000 of net income
  - business losses are kept within the LLC and can only be applied against income within the LLC
  - the LLC must pay a fair market salary to all owners/members working for the LLC, and also pay the corporation's 50% share of the required payroll taxes (income tax withholding, Medicare and Social Security) for the employee, and the other 50% share must be withheld from the owner/member's salary

---

[70] David Meier, *The Many Benefits of Forming an LLC*, August 15, 2004, Entrepreneur magazine, http://www.entrepreneur.com/article/72134

- o profit distributions (over and above employee salary) that are subsequently paid to owners/members will be additionally taxed at the individual's tax rate – effectively double taxation, as corporate taxes have already been paid on this money at the corporate level before the distribution, and they will now be paid again at the individual level.
- If you decide to have your LLC taxed as an S-Corp, this election can be made after your LLC is up and running (and after you've already filed an IRS Form 8832 and have been approved by the IRS). The filing must be made within the first 2½ months of the tax year that you wish it to take effect (or at any time during the previous year). With this election, an LLC acting as an S-Corp for taxation purposes:
- o files a tax return each year (on IRS Form 1120S, reporting the business income, deductions, profit, losses, and tax credits for the year, but the profits and losses pass through (via an IRS Form K-1) *to the individual tax return of all owner/members of the LLC* (eliminating the double taxation situation that might be incurred with a C-Corp tax status).
- o this individual tax liability is incurred by the individual owner/members of the LLC regardless of whether the LLC paid out sufficient passive dividend income to cover the taxes (this can be a significant factor, as it means that the LLC owners are on the hook for paying the taxes even if the LLC hasn't shelled out the money to do so).

    The percentage of tax liability of each owner/member is equal to the percentage ownership specified in the LLC Operating Agreement. If an Operating Agreement doesn't exist (and you should always have one), the percentage will be 100% divided by the number of owner/members.

- o if the salary paid out to owner/members is at least fair market value, the LLC must pay the corporation's 50% share of the required payroll taxes (income tax withholding, Medicare and Social Security) on that salary, and the other 50% share must be withheld from the owner/member's salary – but any additional net income distribution to the owner/members is treated as passive dividend income and not subject to additional payroll taxes.[71]
- o you cannot qualify as an LLC with S-Corp tax status if the LLC has more than 100 members, or if any of the members are nonresident aliens.[72]

Registering your LLC. Registration is required by every state in the country. States differ on details for forming an LLC, but basically it requires filing a Certificate of Formation, or Articles of Organization (the terms vary from state to state).[73] In California, for example, you can download a one-page PDF form (LLC-1), fill it out and submit it to the Secretary of State, but as soon as you begin to fill it out, you'll almost certainly realize that – at the very least – consulting

---

[71] Small Business News, *LLC Electing S Corp Status – The Best of Both Worlds*, Business Owner's Toolkit, August 28, 2012, http://www.bizfilings.com/toolkit/news/tax-info/llc-plus-scorp-equal-best-of-both.aspx

[72] Nolo, *Why You Might Choose S Corp Taxation for Your LLC*, http://www.nolo.com/legal-encyclopedia/why-you-might-choose-s-corp-taxation-your-llc.html

[73] The easiest way to find out your state's business registration requirements is to click the link for your state at the Small Business Administration's web page, *Register With State Agencies*, https://www.sba.gov/content/register-with-state-agencies

with legal counsel and a business tax accountant is a good idea. So, plan to have your legal counsel assist you with filling out and filing this form.

Formalities for maintaining an LLC. Creating an Operating Agreement for your LLC is not mandatory, but it is *highly recommended*, especially if you have multiple member/owners who are forming the LLC (remember, a married couple who are both members of an LLC are treated as a single member). The operating agreement does not get filed with your state's regulatory agency for businesses, but instead, serves as an internal document within your LLC that formalizes and legitimatizes the basic rules under which you will operate. Provided you actually operate in accordance with it, the operating agreement can become very valuable if there is any legal challenge to your LLC status.

The operating agreement usually includes your decision on how you will elect to be taxed, lays out the rules on how you will handle accounting and finance practices (such as creating financial statements, no commingling of personal money with LLC money), states percentages of ownership interest by the owner/members, how you will allocate passive dividends, and owner/member rights and responsibilities.

One overarching rule – run your LLC as a business. For example, don't commingle money between your personal accounts and business accounts. If you do, you run the risk of losing its limited liability status by a subsequent court of law. From the start, create an operating agreement that clearly spells out your business' operating terms, your management policies, your tax structure, and possibly your financial controls (including rules against commingling personal money with LLC money).[74]

Oftentimes, commingling is the result of just being lazy. Typical lazy situations are, not establishing a checking account for your LLC, or not bothering to use it for paying the LLC's bills, instead paying the bills out of your personal checking account. It can be obvious that the LLC is a close extension of your personal life, but if you're going to pay LLC bills with personal money, at least maintain a proper paper trail. Create a proper LLC checking account, then actually transfer money into it from your personal account as necessary, and at least write the bill paying checks from the LLC account. If you were doing everything completely right you'd actually document this as a loan, etc, etc, but you're not likely to create a problem for your LLC if you don't.

Document all important decisions in the LLC. Unlike a corporation, where Board of Director resolutions are *required by law* to document decisions, state laws do not require that an LLC do so. Nevertheless, there are many practical business reasons to do so, and it's imperative that you keep them complete and up to date – and they are simply called Resolutions. Since it's not a requirement of law to document your business decisions with a Resolution, there also aren't any rules and guidelines for what to document, so common sense will usually dictate. Some examples of LLC decisions to consider for Resolutions include:

o   changes to the LLC formation paperwork

---

[74] To get you started on an Operating Agreement, samples and templates can be found at http://www.entrepreneur.com/formnet/form/805 and https://www.rocketlawyer.com/article/why-create-llc-operating-agreement.rl

- each member's capital contribution, and member distributions
- designation of managing members, and who can sign contracts that bind the LLC
- adding or removing members
- hiring or terminating members of senior management
- annual budgets
- decisions known to carry substantial risk for the LLC, including members in attendance for the discussion and member votes
- member loans to the LLC
- major changes to business direction
- major banking changes, such as taking out a line of credit, or changing banks
- employee benefit plans (401(k), profit-sharing, health insurance, etc.)
- sale or other distribution of all or substantially all of the assets of the company
- a dissolution or winding up of the company
- entering into any agreements that could be of material importance to the company (intellectual property licenses, customer/vendor contracts, consulting agreements, office leases, equipment leases, etc.)

(Note, there is an LLC member Resolution template in the files that readers of this book can download – at no charge. The preface to Chapter 5, Financial Management, contains complete instructions for requesting this download.)

Hold regular LLC meetings and write up meeting minutes. As stated earlier, the legal formalities of maintaining an LLC are simpler than for a corporation. Corporations are required by state law to hold regular Board of Director meetings (at the least, an annual meeting) and to maintain a Minute Book documenting all decisions made at the meeting. State law does not require an LLC to hold such meetings, and therefore, meeting minutes are also not required. Nevertheless, in a business sense, the Resolutions just discussed are the result of such meetings (though perhaps less formal than a corporate Board meeting) and should be documented as such. It's a small paperwork cost at the time, but can pay huge dividends later, let's say when a serious buyer for your business emerges and hands over a due diligence list that asks for all meetings and minutes. If your answer is, "I don't have any", the potential buyer could easily conclude that you run a lot of other things in your company the same way.

(Note, there is a sample LLC Meeting Minutes template in the files that readers of this book can download – at no charge. The preface to Chapter 5, Financial Management, contains complete instructions for requesting this download.)

Beyond that, why does any of this paperwork and rigmarole matter? Here's one really good reason. You legally structured your business as an LLC – and the reason for doing that was to limit the liability exposure, legally and financially, between the business and your personal assets. So let's say you let any and all of this *stuff* slide by (you're too busy, just can't be bothered, you'll take care of it another day), and you're just plain sloppy about operating your business *as an LLC*. One day your business goes to hell in a handbasket – let's say a customer gets E-coli from improper sanitary practices – and the customer hires a good lawyer to go after your business for all they can get. The lawyer digs and digs into your operation and notes that you've never really managed your business properly as an LLC, you've commingled your personal funds with company funds, or done other things that indicate you aren't really operating the LLC as a separate entity. You run the risk of a court making the determination that you've been treating the LLC as an extension of your personal affairs, rather than as a separate legal entity – and you could lose your liability protection.

Conclusion on LLC. An LLC is almost certainly the way to go for many new small business owners in today's world. It is very inexpensive to set up, there is very low maintenance to keep it in good stead with your state's business overseer, and for your tax treatment by the IRS you can choose between sole proprietorship and a corporation. These features make it the best of all worlds. But make sure you read all of the caveats against shareholding ability or having additional partners or stock option plans, and serious challenges if your exit strategy is an IPO or to investors along the way.

Limited Partnership and Limited Liability Partnership. A Limited Partnership (LP) is a form of business structure that is valuable for business partners who join together to operate a business with more than one owner. Unlike an LLC or General Partnership, an LP has at least one partner who is considered a *general* partner – the person who is making business and management decisions and who also is personally liable for business debts and contract obligations. An LP also has at least one *limited* partner – someone who invests money in the business but has little control over day-to-day business decisions – and therefore is granted limited personal liability protection for business debts.

The general partner can be either an individual or a corporation, often running the business on behalf of the limited partners, who might in fact, be *silent* partners who are providing financing for the venture, but whose assets are protected by limiting their exposure and liability. In this case, the limited partnership is effectively a conduit to pass operating profits and losses to the silent partners.[75]

A Limited Liability Partnership (LLP) is similar to an LP, except that there are no general partners – all LLP partners have limited liability protection for business debts.

Simply put, this limited liability feature that's carved out for an LP or LLP is primarily what distinguishes it from a General Partnership (in a General Partnership, every partner is legally liable for all company debts and obligations, including court judgments).

For tax purposes, an LP and LLP is treated like a General Partnership, in that all partners (general and limited) pay taxes as individuals for their share of the profits within the partnership.

Which brings us to the question – how do limited and general partners get *paid* from an LP or LLP? Here are some basic rules:

- The partnership agreement should spell out exactly how profits and losses within the partnership are to be shared among the partners. Generally speaking, profits and losses from a partnership *pass through* to the individual partners. The amount distributed (or assigned as a loss) to each partner is established in the partnership agreement. Profits can be distributed to each partner on a regular *draw* against the partnership's year-end profit.

---

[75] Entrepreneur staff, *Limited Liability Partnership*, Entrepreneur online, http://www.entrepreneur.com/encyclopedia/limited-liability-partnership

- Partners are responsible for paying any and all taxes on the profit within the partnership. The agreement can state whether the partnership will pay an extra dividend to each member to cover the tax liability, since this dividend is over and above any salaries paid to the partners.
- As a rule, limited partners do not pay self-employment taxes, as their share of the partnership income is not considered earned income.
- The partnership itself does not pay any taxes, although it does file an annual tax return (for the IRS, Form 1065, U.S. Return of Partnership Income), plus each partner receives an IRS Form K-1 to report money received from the partnership.
- To get back to the original question then, any person who performs work inside a partnership is not considered by the IRS to be an employee (either general or limited partner). So, the money generally paid is not considered a wage, a W-2 is not created at year-end for this money, and payroll taxes are not withheld or paid by the partnership for the partner.
- If a general partner performs specific tasks for the partnership (typically spelled out in the partnership agreement) for which there is financial compensation, this compensation must be reported to the IRS as guaranteed payments. Since a guaranteed payment essentially functions as a salary amount, this income might be subject to self-employment taxes – and this is where the partner should seek tax advice.

LP and LLP formation can be more complicated and costly than for a corporation, as most states, in addition to requiring registration with the appropriate agency, also require detailed partnership agreements to be drawn up, and the partnership might even be governed by securities laws. More troubling, if a limited partner isn't careful about the extent of day-to-day management and control exercised within the partnership, the limited partner could be declared a general partner, with the partner suddenly losing all liability protection.

Corporation. Historically, a corporation has been the most popular business structure that provided limited liability protection for the business owner, by creating a legal entity that is recognized as separate from the owner. By the late 1970s, the LLC format became very popular as an alternative to corporations, particularly for small businesses – providing limited liability, and a separate business entity.

For many, the simplicity of managing an LLC over a corporation is important, particularly the requirements for regular Board of Directors meetings and a formal Meeting Minutes book for a corporation, plus keeping Board resolutions for all important decisions made during such meetings.

In some ways, a corporation and an LLC can be similar in operation, particularly when the LLC elects to be taxed as a corporation – in which case, the LLC is a hybrid that might be considered the best of all worlds. Nevertheless, in some situations a corporation is the only way to go (particularly if you have high growth plans, resulting in lots of shareholders, and maybe even a potential future IPO).

There are two types of corporations: the traditional C-Corp, and the specialized Subchapter S Corp (a.k.a., S-Corp), which is a hybrid between a corporation and a partnership for tax purposes.

(It's called a Subchapter S corporation because the tax rules that apply to it are defined in Subchapter S of the Internal Revenue Code).

When you file your corporation papers with the state agency that regulates business entities (typically the Secretary of State), the default is a traditional corporation (a C-Corp). Once registered, if you want to be an S-Corp for special tax status, you then file an IRS Form 2553.

If you have thoughts about being an S-Corp, don't dither, as it can be a lot more complicated if you submit Form 2553 to the IRS more than 75 days after you initially incorporate.

Except for taxing differences, S-Corp and C-Corp corporations are very similar. Here's where they are _alike_:

- All states require you to file incorporation papers to legally document the creation of the corporation. These are called the Articles of Incorporation (or Certificate of Incorporation, or Corporate Charter, depending on which state you file in), and typically contain the firm's name and address, who the *registered agent* is (more about this later), the type and amount of stock to be issued, and the *purpose* of the corporation (which can be as vague as you like).[76] Another important corporate formation document is the Bylaws, which contain backbone information about how the corporation is to be run, the makeup of the Board of Directors and corporate officers and how/when they will be elected. Typically the Bylaws aren't required to be filed with the state, but it's important they are kept with your official corporate documents – and also kept handy in your files, as they are a *living document* that you need to keep up-to-date.

- A corporation is a separate legal business entity from its owners, and must be operated that way to maintain its status. Compared to an LLC, for example, which is automatically dissolved upon the death or bankruptcy of the owner/member, a corporation continues without any legal effect from an event such as this of the shareholder(s).

- Corporations require a much more formal structure than any other type of business entity, including a Board of Directors and officers of the corporation (President, Vice-President, Secretary, and Treasurer). In addition, corporations have *shareholders* who own the corporation (an LLC has members who own it). Officially, the officers of the corporation report to the Board of Directors, and the Board of Directors answer to the shareholders (in a small business, all three of these might be made up mostly – if not all – by the owners).

- The official formalities of day-to-day running of a corporation are very different from any other type of business entity – and they can be the undoing of your corporation if you don't abide by them. Regular and official meetings must be held periodically (usually spelled out in the Bylaws), and minutes of these meetings need to be filed in the corporate Minute Book. Important decisions – such as issuance of stock, decisions to take on debt, decisions to acquire another company, changes in Board of Directors and/or officers – should all be

---

[76] More than half of all corporations in the U.S. are incorporated in Delaware or Las Vegas, primarily because of their attractive state corporate tax provisions, and for favorable and minimal regulatory requirements. To see why, go to https://www.rocketlawyer.com/article/incorporating-in-delaware-or-nevada-whats-the-best-option-for-my-business.rl.

recorded in the extemporaneous minutes filed in the Minute Book. Extemporaneous is the operative word here – it isn't good form to forget about all of this for 5–10 years, then suddenly decide you need to create meeting minutes for events that happened long ago, and for which you now need to back-date paperwork. Failure to do this can be one way to lose your corporation status. (A fairly thorough example of the types of Resolutions you should create for a corporation can be found in the earlier section on LLCs.)

Because of this formal structure and record-keeping, you'd be wise to hire a registered agent (often a paralegal with your outside corporate attorney), to maintain the original of all corporate filing paperwork, your official corporate Minute Book, and who sees to it that annual corporate license renewals are made on time. It might cost you a couple hundred dollars a year, but this attention to detail is invaluable. Twenty years after you launch your start-up and go down the road of merger and acquisitions for your exit strategy, you'll be glad you did this, with everything in order for the buyer's due diligence.

- Limited liability protection is the single biggest benefit of a corporation (and it's similar to that provided in an LLC), shielding your shareholders from personal liability for any of the corporation's business debts, liabilities, and legal and contractual obligations.

  This limited liability protection is often referred to as the *corporate veil* – which you'd be well advised to recognize can be *pierced* in several ways (and can be similarly pierced in an LLC). The most common instance is if you want a bank loan – it's almost a certainty the bank will require you to pledge any and all of your personal assets as collateral for the loan – and that's certainly a sword piercing through the heart of your financial liability protection. A court judgment that you lose can also result in your personal liability – which means you've lost your legal liability protection from the corporation.

And now for the main *differences* between a C-Corp and S-Corp:

- Taxation is the single biggest difference:
  o With a C-Corp, a tax return is filed at the corporate level (IRS Form 1120), tax is based on net profits and losses within the corporation, and tax is paid at the corporate tax rate.

     The challenge with this for a small business is the resulting double taxation, as the corporation has already paid taxes on net profits, and some (or all) of the remaining profits are later distributed to shareholders (owners) as dividends – and the shareholders then pay personal income tax on those dividends. (This double taxation does not occur on salaries (even to shareholder employees) paid inside the corporation, as they are considered valid business expenses, and are therefore a deduction for tax purposes.)

  o With an S-Corp, an *informational* tax return is filed at the corporate level (IRS Form 1120S), but profits and losses are treated as *pass through* income to the shareholders (on a pro rata basis of their shareholding), and personal income tax on it is paid with the shareholder's tax filing, and at the personal tax rate of the shareholder.
  o   For both C-Corp and S-Corp, the individual shareholder pays income tax on any salary drawn from the corporation, as well as on any dividends received from the corporation.

(It's up to the corporation to decide if an additional dividend amount will be paid to the shareholders to cover the tax consequences of any dividends.)

o   Some states do not recognize an S-Corp for *state* tax purposes, instead treating them like a traditional C-Corp (although they are still recognized in those states by the IRS for their special taxing rules for federal taxes).

The states that do not recognize S-Corp state tax status are: New Hampshire, Tennessee, and the District of Columbia. In addition, five states (Arkansas, New Jersey, New York, Ohio, and Wisconsin) recognize S-Corp status only after you comply with additional filing requirements in those states.[77] It's even more weird in Massachusetts, Indiana, Kentucky, Idaho, Maine, Wisconsin, Michigan, California, New Jersey, and New York, as they each play games with companies that elect to be S-Corp, some taxing both the corporation and shareholders also as a C-Corp (the standard double taxation), with special rules on capital gains and passive income. If you live in any of these named states, you really need to obtain good tax advice before making your election.[78]

- Shareholding rules are a bit different. In a C-Corp, there's no limit to the number of shareholders, there's no rule on their citizenship or resident status, and there's no limit to the number of classes (or voting rights) of stock. In an S-Corp, the maximum number of shareholders is 100,[79] there can only be one type of stock class, and shareholders must be U.S. citizens or resident aliens (i.e., have a Green Card) – and the shareholders must be individuals (i.e., stock in the S-Corp cannot be owned by a corporation, an LLC, a partnership, or a trust).

Pros and cons between C-Corp/S-Corp and other business entities.

- Accounting for a corporation is significantly more complicated than any other type of business entity, and particularly so for an S-Corp – so much so that it's hard to imagine any corporation owner doing his/her own taxes, as the time spent could easily be more valuable doing other business things that generate profits and business growth. Not only is the tax filing more complicated, but bookkeeping and accounting are considerably more rigorous.

- If you are as small as a 1-person corporation, you'll have to step up to the business task of handling payroll, as by definition you – the owner and most likely sole shareholder – will also have to be a bona fide employee of the corporation, and you must draw a fair market salary. This means the corporation will have to file quarterly and annual payroll tax returns, submit your withholding income tax, withhold FICA employment taxes (Medicare, Social Security), pay half of the FICA taxes at the corporate level and the other half as deductions from your salary. Of course, if you have other employees anyway, then you are just another employee, so you're already doing this stuff.

---

[77] You can learn more about each of these five state's special requirements at http://eminutes.com/five-states-require-s-corporations-to-jump-through-additional-hoops

[78] Stephen L. Nelson, *S Corporations Explained*, http://www.scorporationsexplained.com/how-do-states-treat-s-corporations.htm

[79] The maximum number of shareholders in an S-Corp is continually increasing. It was originally 10 shareholders (in 1958), then increased to 15, then 32, and most recently to 100 in 2004.

- Dividend or profit distribution is more flexible in an LLC, partnership, and a C-Corp than it is in an S-Corp, where it can only be done on a pro rata basis of shareholding.

- As mentioned earlier, the day-to-day formalities of running a corporation, regardless of whether it's a C-Corp or S-Corp, require more stick-to-it-iveness on the part of the owner, and particularly on the accounting staff. As a start-up business owner, you're probably already wearing at least a half-dozen hats: chief product developer, chief sales person, chief marketing person, chief financial officer, chief contracts officer, chief business development officer, chief communications officer and chief of the company's janitorial service. With a corporation, you (and maybe your spouse or partner) you also get to be Chairman of the Board, Chief Executive Officer, President, Secretary, and Treasurer. To stay on the right side of your state's Secretary of State (who regulates corporations), you'll need to hold regular Board meetings and shareholder meetings (even if all of these meetings are attended by just you and your spouse, significant other, or partner), and you need to keep minutes of these meetings and file them in the corporate Minute Book. The truth is, no one is really going to be watching over your shoulder to make certain you do all this stuff, and it's quite possible you'll actually sit down one day every few months to catch up on all of it, but the risk is, if you stumble in between, or if an out-of-the-blue acquisition for your company comes along, you'll want things to be as up to date as possible.

- Stock options and Restricted Stock Grants are a valuable way to award employees in a corporation (remember, though, that an S-Corp can have a maximum of 100 shareholders). Shareholding of stock is a unique aspect of corporations, and isn't available in an LLC, sole proprietorship, or partnership. If your strategy is to maintain most of your net profit for business growth, rather than pay it out in the form of salary – and assuming your employees are vested in the belief that your business is going to grow to be worth something – some type of stock ownership by employees can be quite useful. If, on the other hand, your employees believe that any stock you award them isn't worth a Starbucks latte and they'd rather have current cash, keep 100% ownership of the corporation and don't bother with the stock plans (in the hopes that it *will be* worth far more than that latte at some point).

- The rights of minority shareholders can be large. As long as you own at least 51% of the shares in a corporation (C-Corp or S-Corp), you might assume that as majority shareholder you can make any and all decisions you like about how the corporation is run. Not necessarily so. State law differs quite a bit on this, plus federal corporation statutes also apply, so this information is generalized, and you need to consult corporate legal counsel in your state. In general, minority shareholders have outsized rights compared to their actual shareholding percentage – sometimes requiring *unanimous* shareholder approval for certain decisions that you wish to make.

  For example, in many states, a corporation's majority shareholders have a fiduciary responsibility to the minority shareholders, prohibiting them from making decisions that favor majority shareholders – such as forcing minority shareholders to sell their shares at less than fair market value, issuing additional shares to majority shareholders at an inadequate price, or reducing the minority shareholder's share value disproportionately.

In some states a minority shareholder can sue a majority shareholder if that shareholder uses the corporation's assets for personal gain – such as paying an unjustified salary to a majority shareholder, when those funds could otherwise be paid as dividends to all shareholders on a pro rata basis.

Do you need a business license, permit, and other start-up documentation?

Most states require business licenses for certain business types to operate, and yours might be one of them. Each state is different, so don't be caught out if your state requires it and you don't have a license. For example, my state (Washington) requires licenses for 41 different types of business operations, including (among others): body piercing and body art, cosmetologists, barbers, manicurists, firearms dealers, landscape architects, limousine services, onsite designers, telephone solicitors, and vehicle and vessel dealers.

Find the requirements for your particular state at: https://www.sba.gov/content/what-state-licenses-and-permits-does-your-business-need. Each type of license might also require a certain level of training that must be met, plus other required permits.

Additionally, several types of business operations require a *federal* license and permit. A rough idea of these can be found at: https://www.sba.gov/content/what-federal-licenses-and-permits-does-your-business-need. In general, the list includes any business that falls in the category of "activities that are supervised or regulated by a federal agency – such as selling alcohol, firearms, commercial fishing", or any activity that involves the operation of aircraft.

Obtaining your Employer Identification Number (EIN). Similar to the requirement for employees to have Social Security Numbers (SSN), essentially all businesses are required to have an Employer Identification Number (EIN) ... one reason for which, logically enough, is a requirement by the IRS if you have employees. You'll also need an EIN just to open a business bank account and for many other financial transactions.

An EIN is an IRS-issued number (also known as a Federal Tax ID Number), which allows the IRS to identify your business' information and tax records. Most importantly, the EIN helps the IRS ensure that every business entity required to file a tax return does indeed file one.

Does your business require you to have an EIN? The IRS website page[80] has a simple YES/NO table that asks you several questions:

- o Do you have Employees?
- o Do you operate your business as a corporation or as a partnership?
- o Do you file any of these tax returns: Employment, Excise, or Alcohol, Tobacco, or Firearms?
- o Do you withhold taxes on income, other than wages, paid to a non-resident alien?
- o Do you have a Keogh plan?
- o Are you involved with any of the following types of organizations?
    - o Trusts, except certain grantor-owned revocable trusts, IRAs, Exempt Organization Business Income Tax Returns

---

[80] *Do You Need An EIN?*, http://www.irs.gov/Businesses/Small-Businesses-&-Self-Employed/Do-You-Need-an-EIN?

- o Estates (yes, you may require an EIN if you are the executor of an estate)
- o Real estate mortgage investment conduits
- o Non-profit organizations
- o Farmer's cooperatives
- o Plan administrators

If you answer YES to any of these, the link (on the website page) will take you directly to an IRS page with specific instructions for applying for an EIN. Don't get suckered by online sites that purport to be a fast-track for getting you an EIN, or sites that charge you to apply – such sites will be a scam, as an EIN is quick and free to obtain.

But wait, there's more! Just as everyone and their uncle requires you to provide your SSN, the same is true for an EIN. Open a bank account in the name of your business and you'll need an EIN. Apply for a credit card in the name of your business and you'll need an EIN. Fill in a business form with almost any state agency that is regulating you, and you'll need an EIN. So, even though a Sole Proprietorship or LLC doesn't require a YES answer in the IRS form, you'll almost certainly need an EIN since you'll likely have a bank account, a company credit card, or employees.

In conclusion: yes, your business will need an EIN, so go ahead and get one. And keep a good record of the EIN number itself (i.e., store the IRS issue letter of the EIN in a safe place. If you lose the EIN number, it's extremely difficult to get anyone at the IRS to provide the number to you, and like a Social Security number, you can't just request a replacement without a lot of rigmarole.

For more information on an EIN, download the IRS publication *Employer Identification Number – Understanding Your EIN*, by searching on IRS Publication 1635. This brief PDF also describes the various tax reporting forms that each business type must file.

Selecting your professional services consultants

> *"The only people who benefit from lawsuits are lawyers.*
> *I think we made a couple of them rich."*
> Gavin Rossdale

Corporate attorney. Don't underestimate the value of getting the best corporate attorney you can find – even if you feel you can't afford it. Not only in working out everyday problems, but if and when the time comes to sell your company, having a good corporate attorney could be the most valuable advice in this book. This is truly one of those situations where you can't afford not to.

Many people tend to scrimp on good legal advice, maybe because finances are tight, maybe it doesn't seem like a necessary time to have the top dollar services, or maybe a good corporate attorney's name and phone number isn't in your speed dial and you haven't a clue how to find the right person. Well, the importance of this is huge, so it's a good idea to allocate the funds and spend some energy and time on it. (Whatever you do, don't use an online referral service – this is too important for that!) Most importantly, *don't use an attorney who isn't a specialist in* _corporate law and small businesses_. As I discovered when incorporating my company, I foolishly selected an old high school chum who now had a law degree – a guy it turned out who didn't have a clue about corporate matters, and the damage could easily have cost me tens of thousands of dollars a few years later when his mistakes came to light.

Particularly if you're creating a corporation, not only is your state incorporation filing important, but you need legal advice to ensure your company is operating legally and properly within the framework of your state's incorporation authority. (In Washington State, for example, the Corporation Division within the Secretary of State's office is the incorporation authority, so it's probably something similarly named in other states). You need an attorney in a law firm with the paralegal staff to maintain and manage your corporate filings with the state, to keep your corporate records up to date (remember, if you're a corporation, you'll need annual meeting records, minutes of Board of Directors meetings where official decisions are made, etc.). These are details that you'll almost certainly not have the bandwidth, interest level, or legal knowledge to handle, and the couple hundred bucks a year the service costs will save your bacon later when due diligence is being carried out by an investor, or for a merger or acquisition. Having these records in perfect order – going all the way back to initial founding – will create lots of confidence for whoever is doing that due diligence, and it can mean real money in your pocket.

In the early days of your company, as well as on a continuing basis, you'll almost certainly need your outside legal counsel to review all contracts, agreements, or understandings that you enter into. Our corporate legal counsel very sternly told me once that he didn't want to _ever_ again hear of me signing a contractual agreement without first running it by him. This was right after we found that a major consulting agreement with a large U.S. airline (one of our biggest customers) turned out to be one of the worst business decisions in our entire history – so bad, in fact, that we seriously discussed the possibility of filing for a disastrous Chapter 11 bankruptcy just to eliminate the partnership agreement with this airline.

In my situation, I certainly didn't run every individual software licensing agreement signed with a customer through our attorney – rather, I made sure that he thoroughly reviewed the standard license agreement, and he advised me on the various terms and conditions within it that I could negotiate. If the customer demanded serious modifications to our standard license agreement terms, I ran it by our attorney.

I also ran software distributorship agreements by him, even though he had written the general agreement, as there were enough modifications to fit the conditions of each that I wanted him to approve from a legal standpoint. All of our distributor agreements were international (we performed all domestic sales from within our own company), and our U.S. attorney's office usually referred us to an attorney in each country where we negotiated distributorship agreements, to ensure compliance with local law and business customs. As an example of the problems this can help with, when we subsequently terminated a distributor in an EU country, the distributor claimed that EU law required us to pay him a large termination fee (about $100,000), but our attorney got us off the hook. In another situation (again, with a distributor in an EU country), the distributor absconded with software license fees that required a royalty be paid to us, and having an attorney already in place to work with was very helpful.

Our outside attorney also proved invaluable when we created an employee stock option plan that allowed us to issue stock options on a discretionary basis as a way to conserve much-needed cash reserves that were necessary for the growth of the company. Creating a legal and effective stock option plan is virtually impossible without the knowledge of a specialist attorney, and again, our outside counsel did an incredible job with that.

Finally, when we found a potential partner to purchase our company, our corporate attorney was brought in from the start, drafting the definitive sales agreement for the deal, and then followed it through due diligence, and to the sale closure. His biggest concern was the possibility of us losing our shirt through some sort of slip-up on what's called the *reps and warranties* of the sales agreement (where you *represent and warrant* that everything about your company is exactly as you say it is). During that process, he identified key Board members and senior management to be in his office for an all-day meeting, where each was asked to look him in the eye in response to each representation and warranty in their area of the company. As a result, none of the several dozen reps and warranties came back to bite us in the warranty period following the close of the sale.

In the end, we almost certainly paid for two of his kids to go to Ivy League colleges, but there's no question about it – he was worth every penny.

One word of caution about attorneys (and this can also be said of accountants and other professional services consultants that you hire) – be wary of any business advice they provide that doesn't relate strictly to legal or accounting matters. These professional service consultants are not entrepreneurs, and tend to have a conservative streak that makes them so risk-averse, any advice they give on how to run your business might not be the best for you.

> *"Management is doing things right; leadership is doing the right things."*
> Peter F. Drucker, management consultant

Human Resources attorney (HR). The minute you have your first employee, you need to know a human resource attorney or specialist you can turn to for advice. Notice I didn't suggest you hire any in-house HR specialists at the initial start-up stage – it's far too early for that. You just need an HR attorney in your back pocket that you can call on in a moment's notice when a situation arises that needs a quick and vital answer.

This might seem like an over-the-top recommendation at the early stage of your company, particularly when you don't have the luxury of an actual personnel or HR department. But when any employee dispute or problem in the HR arena arises, it will pay dividends in spades.

It would be nice to think that every new hire will turn out to be the perfect employee and will stay with you forever – but the odds against that happening are likely worse than winning the Powerball (which is usually about 1 in 175 million).

It would also be nice if human relations had progressed to the point where they are perfect.

No matter how much you keep tabs on what your managers and employees are doing, hiring situations can get sticky, sexual harassment issues may arise, discrimination issues or employee work rule issues crop up, and employees have to be terminated. At some point in your business life, if you have employees, you're bound to have at least one bad apple in the bunch. (The section at the end of Chapter 6 on *at-will* employment spells out the guidelines on your rights as an employer in situations when terminating employees.)

The best advice is to always deal with personnel issues quickly, but only after getting the necessary guidance and advice from an experienced HR person or attorney (my preference is an attorney, given the legal ramifications of the situations mentioned here, but in many cases a trained (non-attorney) HR person that you can consult with will likely be just fine).

In my own company, our corporate attorney was a partner at a large law firm, with several HR specialist attorneys on staff. This gave us access to some very good talent, which served us well in at least a half dozen situations – situations that could easily have cost us more in far more in damages than we paid for the advice.

> *"The difference between tax avoidance and tax evasion is the thickness of a prison wall."*
> Denis Healey, British politician

Corporate tax accountant. When we founded our company many years ago, we approached a friend who was a long-time owner of several small businesses, so we figured she probably had an outside accountant. One day we asked if she could recommend a corporate tax accountant. Her answer surprised us – "*do you want to sleep at night, or do you enjoy living on the edge?*" she asked.

We certainly hadn't thought of it this way. She figured there were already too many aspects of business that could keep her awake at night, and she didn't want dodgy tax issues to give her one more thing to worry about. She opted for a conservative accounting firm specializing in small- to medium-sized businesses, knowing that this firm wouldn't allow her to take tax options that potentially crossed – or were even near – the IRS line. We acted on her advice and worked with that tax firm for at least a dozen years, until we felt we were beyond the limits of support they could offer. In all those years, we didn't face a single IRS tax audit, and nothing we did was ever questioned by the IRS. We had one audit by a state corporate tax auditor, and to our surprise received a $30,000 *refund* for Business and Occupation (B&O) tax we'd overpaid (where they interpreted the tax law more generously than we had).

This accounting firm proved invaluable when it was discovered that we'd been paying taxes based on our company being an S-Corp, when in fact, as we later discovered, the original incorporation papers weren't filed that way. Our tax accountant went to bat for us with the IRS, successfully arguing that the filing was a simple mistake, and the IRS agreed. I believe they could just as easily *have not* agreed, and it might have cost us tens – maybe hundreds – of thousands of dollars in back taxes and penalties if the IRS decision had gone against us. (My instructions to the attorney who created and filed incorporation papers for my company were to elect S-Corp status – after the initial C-Corp filing – for tax reasons. Silly me, even though I personally signed off on the paperwork, I assumed he had done exactly that.)

Most importantly, the support provided over the years by our outside accounting firm, like our legal representation, proved invaluable when it came time to sell our company. They, with the help of our exceptionally good internal accountant, kept our books so spotless that during our buyer's due diligence they developed a huge level of confidence that our company was worth the money they were paying for it. If your books are sloppy, with records filed willy-nilly or difficult to lay your hands on, it can give a negative impression that other aspects of your business aren't so well managed either. This was something I didn't understand when the company was first getting started, and I'm _very_ glad circumstances turned out the way they did.

> *"A bank is a place that will lend you money if you can prove that you*
> *don't need it."*
> Bob Hope

Your bank and your business banker. Your business banker is not a professional services consultant in the strict sense of the word – mainly because you don't pay this person a direct consulting fee, or hire him/her specifically as a consultant. At the time you open your doors for business, though, you'll need to have a business bank account, as a place to deposit revenue from your business sales, to write checks to pay your business bills, and very likely a Line of Credit to smooth over working capital shortfalls. For tax and legal reasons, you also need a *paper trail* of all your financial dealings, and the bank account(s) – and the records you save from it – will serve as that trail. For reasons that both your lawyer and tax accountant will tell you (in no uncertain terms), commingling business and personal finances is a serious no-no, and you should never handle any of this directly from your personal bank account.

Selecting your bank – and your business banker – is another important early decision you're going to make. You cannot open your business banking account until you've legally formed your company, and you must provide your business filing paperwork to the bank when you open your account. For example, if you have an LLC, the business documents you'll need are the Articles of Organization (or whatever it is called in your state), and your Operating Agreement (listing you as the Member who is authorized to open the account).

Once at the bank, and before opening the account, you should ask who your *business banker* will be and set up an interview with that person to ensure it looks like a good fit with you. The teller behind the window isn't your business banker, and hopefully won't be the person in the bank lobby with whom you are opening the business account. Very likely he/she will be in an office environment away from the actual bank branch where you do your banking. As your company grows, this person will become more and more important to you, and along the way you should nurture the relationship at every chance.

In the early stages of your business, and unless you think your business is quickly destined for the big time (in which case, you're probably a dreamer and not an entrepreneur grounded in the real world), this bank could be the same one where your personal bank account is held. The benefit of that is, they will more than likely recognize you – not so much personally, but as an existing customer – and the more business you bring to them (i.e., the more money of yours that they hold), the better they will treat you.

Don't expect this bank, though, to be a ready source of loans, particularly start-up loans, unless it is fully collateralized or guaranteed. The bank can be a source of overdraft protection, and the better customer you are, the larger overdraft amount they'll protect. In my own business, we sometimes took calculated risks that a promised deposit from a customer invoice was due into the bank in one or two days and we issued checks (sometimes payroll checks), knowing that the money technically wasn't in the bank. Sure enough, over the years we were caught out a few times, and because we had a good relationship with our business banker, when she called[81] mid-

---

[81] Our business bankers were almost always women, which I appreciated because for me they were easier to deal with – more understanding and more flexible than the male bankers I sometimes had.

morning and our corporate checking account was in the red, we could hopefully tell her that funds to cover the shortfall would be in the bank by end of day (and, of course, we then had to make good on that).

Later, when our accounts receivable (AR)[82] were solid enough to support it, our bank agreed to a Line of Credit that we could draw on, and that's when a close working relationship with our business banker became all-important. As a condition for the Line of Credit, the bank also began requiring monthly financial statements be submitted to them, specifically a Balance Sheet and a Profit and Loss Statement (typically referred to as a P&L, or Income Statement). Being the conservative type, the banker crunched the financial statement numbers to produce all kinds of ratios that would give her a heads-up if our business was heading south (banks never like surprises, so they want to know this as early in the game as they can).

Something I didn't learn until too late, our business banker didn't understand the software business (which was odd, as we were located in an area where there were thousands of small software businesses). Maybe it's because of that, or because our Line of Credit (LOC) had grown to $350K, or because our financial ratios just weren't looking good, but our bank also added the dreaded *loan covenants* to our LOC agreement, forcing us to live within those covenants (discussed in detail in Chapter 4). Our loan covenants were drafted to stipulate that certain parameters of our financial statements had to remain within guidelines drawn by the bank, even though our loan was fully collateralized by our accounts receivable. The purpose of the covenants was to give the bank better control over our LOC, giving them the right to *call* our LOC note any time we were in covenant default. Try as they might, our banker was never able to draft covenant terms that worked for our particular business, and we were almost always in technical default of our loan terms. The good relationship we had with our business banker saved us, though, and that proved to be the best reason yet to have a good relationship.

As an up-and-coming software business (growing revenues at about 35% per year), when we felt we had outgrown the capabilities of our local hometown bank, we moved our banking relationship to one that specialized in our type of business. That was an extremely advantageous move for us, and one we'd wished we'd done earlier.

Owner salary

Depending on the structure you set up for your company, you might be the first employee in your company – or you might not. This sounds like a wishy-washy consideration, but it is very relevant, and you need to be acutely aware of it from the day you open your business door. For this reason, you should seek the advice and counsel of both <u>an attorney and a tax accountant</u> before actually filing with your state authorities to form your company, and before you pay yourself a salary for the first time from your company. It's complicated, so we'll just scratch the surface of it in this discussion.

For taxing purposes, owner salary in a sole proprietorship and an LLC are treated the same, so we'll discuss them as a group. In a corporation it's very different, so we'll discuss it separately.

---

[82] Accounts receivable (often known simply as AR) can be defined as the money owed to your business as the result of valid invoices that you've issued for services rendered or products sold to customers. This will be discussed in detail in Chapter 4.

If you incorporated (regardless of whether it's an S-Corp or C-Corp), you are an employee of your company. If you have a sole proprietorship or an LLC (and haven't elected to be taxed as a corporation – see the earlier detailed discussion of LLC taxing for this) – you are technically not considered an employee. Whichever you are, it will have a substantial effect on how you pay yourself, and how *and when* you pay your employment taxes.

Corporation and your salary. Simply put, if you have a corporation (or an LLC that's elected to be taxed as a corporation), you (as the founder and owner) are treated exactly like any other employee of the corporation with respect to salary and withheld employment taxes – meaning that you set a salary for yourself, and hopefully, take a regular paycheck. You also withhold federal income taxes, Social Security and Medicare taxes (known collectively as FICA) like any other employee, and the company pays the employer share of FICA, and if required, Federal Unemployment tax (known as FUTA).

Don't forget, if you have an S-Corp (i.e., elected to be a Subchapter S corporation when you filed for incorporation), both you and the corporation are treated as one from the standpoint of taxes. All of the company's profit and expenses at the end of each calendar year *flow directly* (or pass through) to your personal income, and you (as an individual) then pay federal and state taxes based on the combined amount (your salary and the corporation's net profit). (The assumed benefit of this is that you will pay less in overall taxes – and you need to get serious tax advice on this).

If you have a regular C-Corp (which is the default if you don't make the separate filing for S-Corp), the corporation's profit/loss at the end of the year is considered to be completely separate from you as an individual. Any profit/loss within the corporation will be taxed at corporate rates, and will be filed with the IRS and state tax authorities separate from your personal tax filing. For your salary, you will pay federal and state taxes at the individual taxpayer rate. The possible downside of this is that any profit within the company in future years (which was taxed at the time it was earned) that is now paid out to you as a dividend will then be taxed again at your personal tax rate for dividends – and effectively you will have paid tax on it twice.

Sole proprietorship or LLC and your salary. Since you are technically not considered an employee of a sole proprietorship (or an LLC that's elected to be treated as a sole proprietorship for taxes), you do not pay yourself a salary, but rather, you take what's called a *draw*, written on one of your company's business checks – *but the check is technically not a paycheck.* You do not withhold federal income taxes, or FICA, or Medicare. But hold on – you aren't getting a free ride here. Instead of these taxes being withheld as part of your paycheck, you will pay 100% of the employment taxes yourself, on a quarterly basis, based on the total amount of your draws.

To reiterate that (and it's something that surprises many first-time entrepreneurs), you'll actually pay quite a bit more in tax as a self-employed person than you would as an employee of someone else's company. As self-employed, you pay the full amount of your Social Security and Medicare tax, whereas it is typically split between you and your employer in most company situations (but, obviously, your employer has factored that into your salary, so it's not as if you're getting off scot-free).[83]

Another big difference between self-employed taxes and employee taxes is the *how* and *when* you'll pay the taxes. The tax withholding system set up by the IRS and your state and local government has been around since 1943. This system greatly simplified the tax *collection* burden for the various taxing authorities, since without it employees would be paid their entire salary throughout the year and expected to cough up the tax amount as a lump sum at the end of the year – and obviously, not everyone would have the foresight to save the required amount. The burden would then be on the tax authorities to come after the employee for it, which sounds great for the taxpayer, but not so great for the tax authorities. The same is true with self-employed taxes.

Instead, you are generally expected to file your Form SE (the SE means self-employed) and pay your taxes on a quarterly basis. If you don't pay enough, you can be assessed a penalty for underpayment. So the burden is still on you to actually pay your taxes ahead of the standard end-of-year tax time, but it can trip you up if you don't sufficiently manage your finances to have the necessary funds available at the end of each calendar quarter.

How much should you pay yourself? A common question for small business owners is, how much to pay yourself. This seems like a very easy question, but it isn't. What makes it difficult is there are no guidebooks on the subject, and there are few valid opinions to be found – and besides, it's entirely business-specific.

If you do an internet search on "small business owner salary", you find such gems as: "*The Average Salary for Small Business Owners Is $68K*". Ohhhhkkk. But why is that particular amount relevant to me? If my small business can't afford to pay me $68K, this information is not only useless to me, but it makes me feel bad if I'm below average. If I'm pulling in far more profit than $68K, even after allowing for all the growth I can handle, do I care what any other business owner makes? The answer should be an emphatic no to those questions.

To resolve this dilemma, start first with what the IRS will think about your salary when you file your business taxes. This is really a gray area, not to mention an overly broad area, but you can find a pretty good discussion of it in "A Practical How-To Blog For Small Business", by Evergreen Small Business, at https://evergreensmallbusiness.com/s-corporation-reasonable-compensation/#comment-3642, and titled *S Corporation Reasonable Compensation*. This post is specifically for an S-Corp corporation, but the advice holds true for other business structures.

Once you've created a salary range that will keep you out of the "unreasonable compensation clutches" of the IRS and other regulatory agencies, a safe conclusion is, you should pay yourself whatever the company can afford to pay you. But a big caveat to add to that … after all expenses have been paid (including employee salaries, taxes paid or allocated), and after business growth and development plans have been funded. In other words, you're paying yourself only after all

---

[83] For 2017, the Social Security tax rate is 6.1% <u>each</u>, for employee and employer, with a *wage base limit* of $127,200 (which means it's paid only on wages up to that amount, and then is 0% beyond that). The Medicare tax rate is 1.45% <u>each</u>, for employee and employer, with no wage base limit (so you pay that rate on all wages). So the total that you'll be paying is 15.3%.

other obligations have been met. Another way of saying this is, pay yourself whatever you want from your business' _net profit_.

But that still doesn't really answer the question in the way it should. Here are some thoughts you need to work through.

First, and maybe your biggest question is, how much do you want to reinvest in your company (i.e., to grow) versus how much you want to take out of it at present? That's a really tough question, and as Bill D'Alessandro of RebelCEO.com says,[84] _"Every dollar you take out of the business is a dollar you could've spent growing the business. It's very easy to run your business dry in the early days when there's just not much extra money, and it gets even worse if you've got partners, you've got two, three, four people wanting to take money out of the business. It can be really hard. You can end up starving the business in order to pay your salary."_

So, that presents a conundrum: for most entrepreneurs, one of the biggest reasons for starting your company was to have a pile of money and live life the way you wanted to. Now you're faced with the big decision of foregoing the big paycheck now, growing the company now, and hoping you'll be able to take out an even bigger salary in the future. That takes some self-control, plus a lot of confidence and belief that you really can grow the company. It's a real balancing act, and it's something you have to step up to very quickly.

Unless you're independently wealthy and don't need the paycheck (not likely), you'll need to pick the salary/reinvestment point that suits you the best, and then charge ahead.

Second, once you've decided how much to take out as salary, make a decision that you're going to pay yourself that salary, either weekly, bi-weekly, or monthly. Then try to stick to it <u>as much as you can</u>. _This way, you have that number in your operating budget to work towards._ That's the single biggest reason to do this, and while you might not be able to meet that number in difficult times, at least you have that amount in your budget, providing a scale for how you're actually doing, in comparison to what you'd like to be doing. (Your tax accountant will also advise that you to pay yourself a regular salary, for reasons we'll see in a bit.)

But what salary number should you actually settle on? Well, the operative word in the last paragraph was _budget_. Whether you like budgets or not, you should be making a Cash Flow/Budget spreadsheet if you're worth a grain of salt as an entrepreneur. This budget is giving you a measure of whether you _expect_ to have any money left over at the end of the period or not. If you've included the amount you'd like to pay yourself two weeks from now, well, that number is your salary (or, to put it more correctly, it's your distribution of the profits). Once you've done that a few times, maybe averaging your salary amount over some period of time, you'll start to see a number emerging that could become the established salary _that you can afford_.

If, on the other hand, you blindly decide – let's say, from a suggestion you got from that web page about average small business owner salary is $68K, to pay yourself that amount without factoring it into a budget ... well, it's obviously a foolish thing to do, and your business won't be around for very long. So, the moral of that is, don't set a salary number willy-nilly, as it can develop expectations that cause you to spend money you don't have.

---

[84] Andrew Youderian, _The Right Way to Pay Yourself a Salary_ (an interview with Bill D'Alessandro), eCommerceFuel, November 13, 2016, http://www.ecommercefuel.com/paying-yourself-a-salary/

Let's look at the other end of the spectrum. Let's say you set yourself an annual salary of $50K, then plug just over $4K/month into your budget and proceed to pay yourself that amount each month – and the budget indicates you can afford it. As the months go by, you find that your revenue is growing a bit faster than you had projected, or expenses are less than budgeted, and at the end of the year you find your profit exceeds what you expected. If next year's budget gives you the confidence that this trend is continuing, you might decide to increase next year's salary to $60K – or you decide to keep your salary where it is, and invest the money in more business growth.

An annual term is a reasonable length of time to establish (or smooth out) trends. If you tried to make these determinations based on each month's budget (or even a quarter's budget), you'd find the term length is too short to take into account seasonal ups and downs.

So, that's the basic idea for *how* you establish how much of the profit to take out of the business – which most of us would think of as the owner's salary.

It should also be pointed out that the IRS doesn't look kindly on a business owner trying to fiddle the tax structure by going around tax laws on the owner salary issue. For example, as a sole proprietor you might decide it's a great idea to pay yourself a very low salary – thereby reducing the amount of quarterly payroll taxes you are paying. You might get away with it, but tax auditors (if you get audited) may decide that your official salary is unreasonably low, based on the job you're doing and the amount of time and effort you're putting into it (relative to the company's business situation). Believe it or not, tax courts have the right to determine the reasonableness of your salary, based on factors such as your role and effort in the company, the company's financial health, consistency (i.e., are you being paid an outrageous salary only in really good years), and comparable situations from other companies.

To summarize in plain English, compensate yourself regularly, and if at all possible, at an amount from your profit amount that falls within your company budget. As your company grows, so should your compensation.

Lastly, don't worry about whether your compensation is fair ... to the other employees or to anyone else. Unless you have partners or investors that you have to answer to, how much you earn from your company is private and your own business (well, between you and your tax accountant and taxing authorities). As Jay Goltz writes in a New York Times blog,[85] "To some extent, the owner's salary is a false issue. There are all sorts of reasons why an owner might want to take more or less money out of the company in the form of salary. The more complicated, and more important question is, how much an entrepreneur should make in profit". He argues that your company's profitability will tell you how much you should pay yourself. If your profits are too low, maybe you should look at your pricing, maybe your expenses are out of whack, or maybe too much competition is forcing profits downward. The reality is, if your profits are good, pay yourself accordingly; if your profits are low, figure out why and fix it, or adjust your expectations downward. You own the company, so you are the only one who can.

---

[85] Jay Goltz, *How Much Should You Pay Yourself?*, The New York Times, You're The Boss blog contributor, June 29, 2010, http://boss.blogs.nytimes.com/2010/06/29/how-much-should-you-pay-yourself/?module=Search&mabReward=relbias%3Ar%2C{%222%22%3A%22RI%3A13%22}&_r=0

"A small business person has Uncle Sam as a partner, a partner who puts up no money, does no work, and wants 30 or 40 percent."
Irwin Schiff

Paying your taxes

Business Rule #1 should be: Don't mess with the IRS. Rule #2 should be: Don't mess with your state tax authorities. If you have any common sense, you aren't in business to outwit the tax people – you're in business to run a business, pay your bills, make a profit, and take that profit home with you at some point. Every hour you spend fighting with the tax people is an hour you aren't running your business.

Simply put, once you start a business, your taxes are going to become exponentially more complex than what you may be used to, so be sure to pay specific attention to an upcoming section on business record-keeping – and then let your tax advisors advise you on the best ways to mitigate your taxes *within the tax law*.

The previous section contained a recommendation to have an _outside_ tax accountant – and to have that person lined up on (or near) the day you open your doors for business. A rule from the tax authorities is that it's up to you to know _which_ taxes - and how much taxes – your your company must pay. That job goes to the combination of your bookkeeper and your tax accountant. As you undoubtedly know already, claiming ignorance of tax law won't get you anywhere, so don't even attempt it.

Having said that, there's no suggestion you should pay a penny more than you owe, and you should take advantage of every tax deduction the tax code allows. Managing your taxes goes hand-in-hand with managing your business. You need to find the time, at least once a year, to sit down with your tax accountant (and bring along your bookkeeper if you have one), to have a wide-ranging (but informal) discussion about where your business is likely to go in the next year, and what your revenue/expense projections are. Bring along your Cash Flow/Budget projection spreadsheet, have an idea about equipment you'll need to purchase in the coming year, other major expenses you foresee (such as R&D if you have such a thing), and anything else that might have an impact on taxes. From that discussion, you can get an idea if it's better to lease or purchase equipment, what the depreciation schedule should be, whether it's better to obtain new or used equipment, and so on. If your revenue projections for the coming year indicate a sharp rise compared to projected expenses (or income lower and expenses higher), your tax advisor can give you an idea of just how much you have to manage your cash flow to meet tax obligations.

This meeting is also a good time to discuss whether your tax mitigation practices are on rock-solid ground, or if you're walking close to the line that might attract tax audit attention. If a tax audit hits your business, don't (necessarily) expect your tax accountant to be the major resource going to bat for you. If the purpose of the audit is to question what they're calling a tax dodge (which can be legal or illegal) that your tax accountant recommended to you, then yes, you should expect the tax accountant to *be your face* in the audit discussions. If the audit is to question a slew of business deductions that you took – and you've been advised you'll need all of the supporting documentation to back up the deductions ... well, that will involve a lot of time with your bookkeeper – and very possibly, you as well. Your tax accountant is working from business revenue/expenses that your company provided, so the burden will be on you to justify your deductions.

In the next section, whenever you see the word *documentation*, know that it also means that you can lay your hands on any given receipt that's being used as a tax deduction. Most audits will take place at your place of business – usually not sitting in front of the auditor's desk somewhere, but rather, at a desk you've provided when they come knocking on your door.

As a rule, auditors are taught to be very polite and congenial, but reserved. Once the audit begins, one of the things the auditor will be looking for is how well-organized you are. There isn't any law about this – it simply determines whether they'll cut you any slack, or give you the benefit of doubt with some details you might be shaky on. If the auditor asks for a particular receipt or group of receipts and it takes you three hours to produce it (because you're rifling around in a bunch of shoe boxes), the audit won't likely go well for you. If, on the other hand, you (or your bookkeeper) can lay hands on every paper request in a couple of minutes flat, the auditor will be very impressed – and will likely figure that you aren't trying to hide anything.

Hiring a bookkeeper

First, should you hire a bookkeeper? If your business is a sole proprietorship – truly a 1-person business, with only you to worry about, and that's the way it will be for a while – you might be OK to do your own financial bookkeeping. It doesn't take much more business complexity, though, before you find that hiring a part-time bookkeeper – and then a full-time in-house bookkeeper – can actually save you money. After all, unless your business revolves around bookkeeping or accounting, doing it yourself can add a large number of hours, not to mention headaches to your day ... a day when you're supposed to be growing your business.

If nothing else, lack of knowledge and lack of interest can result in your own bookkeeping becoming sloppy, with filing or note-keeping tasks set aside as other pressing business pops to the surface. Who has the time to keep up with the bulletin reading and internet searching required to stay on top of IRS and state guidelines?

A bookkeeper is typically not a CPA-level professional. For small business day-to-day bookkeeping needs, you don't need a CPA, and shouldn't be paying a CPA's rates for your requirements. Whether you have a bookkeeper or not, though, you should have an outside CPA prepare your annual tax filing, and to help analyze your financial statements (see Chapter 5 for more on that topic).

Some entrepreneurs have found that hiring even a part-time bookkeeper saved them enough in monthly late fees due to bills not being paid on time to justify the cost of the bookkeeper. Others find that the additional financial knowledge they now have of their business is a big justification for hiring someone who really knows what they're doing. Here's an example from an article in Entrepreneur online magazine: "If you're thinking of buying a truck or van for your business, did you know that if the vehicle weighs 6,000 pounds or more, it qualifies for the so-called Section 179 expensing election? That means you can deduct up to $24,000 of the cost. A passenger car – that is, one that weighs less than 6,000 pounds – is eligible for a deduction of only about $3,000.

Thus a business owner with the choice of buying a Chevy Suburban, at 5,700 pounds, and a Ford Super Duty Van, at 9,000 pounds, may choose the latter for the tax break".[86]

How to hire the right bookkeeper. This too is a tough question, and a problem you need to think about before actually starting the hiring process. Keep in mind that this is a person who will be handling your company's finances – possibly even handling some of your real money if your business deals in cash transactions, or company credit card access if some of your bills are paid by a card that the bookkeeper has access to (not a wise idea in my mind, but if you do, make certain you carefully check each month's statement of charges). *This person should not have check signing privilege on your checking account.*

Here are several things you need to seriously consider when hiring a bookkeeper (including a contract bookkeeper):[87]

- **What exactly does a bookkeeper do?** Unless you already have small business experience, it's unlikely you'll have a clue what a bookkeeper actually does, and therefore, how you'll define the job, how you'll interview, how you'll vet their qualifications, and how you'll manage the person you hire.

  At the very least, the bookkeeper will:

  o Keep track of sales and expenses from a cash flow/budgeting perspective
  o Process your accounts receivable and accounts payable (i.e., revenue payments coming in and expense payments going out)
  o Post and update journal entries in your software bookkeeping system
  o Reconcile bank and company credit card accounts
  o Prepare payroll, even if just for you and the bookkeeper, but also for additional employees as you grow
  o Prepare financial information critical to your business management
  o Prepare financial information necessary for your tax accountant
  o Create IRS 1099 forms for all contractors who work for you during the year. (Don't underestimate the importance of this – doing it yourself is not trivial.)
  o Understand your internal business processes

  Depending on when this person is hired (i.e., is it your first office staff person?), the bookkeeper might also be your office manager. If that's the case, the bookkeeper will need to have good communications skills to work with other employees (especially you), vendors, and customers. That means the bookkeeper could also become your de facto first-level HR and personnel person.

  Depending on your business needs, the bookkeeper might be in charge of inventory control, as well as product shipping and handling – at least in the very early stages of your business.

---

[86] *Hiring a Bookkeeper or an Accountant*, Entrepreneur online, October 28, 2001, unattributed, http://www.entrepreneur.com/article/45628. Note, the date on the article is from 2001, so don't assume this tax break is still valid. This example is being quoted just to illustrate a point.
[87] *5 Things to Consider When Hiring a Bookkeeper*, Accountemps, https://www.roberthalf.com/accountemps/employers/hiring-tips/hiring-solutions-and-staffing-agencies/5-things-to-consider-when-hiring-a-bookkeeper

While these aren't usually in the job description of a bookkeeper, they are detail-oriented functions within your company, and what you'll be looking for in a bookkeeper is good detail management skills. If this is in your business plans, make sure you bring it up at interview time, as springing it later on a bookkeeper who isn't expecting it might not work out so well.

- **What skills are needed?** It's critical that you search correctly and thoroughly for your bookkeeper, as it can be quite traumatic and time-consuming to hire the wrong person, then have to replace them with someone else who's better suited. Consider these skills:
  - Good understanding of bookkeeping skills that go with how your sales are recorded (i.e., by contract, POS system, cash register).
  - Expertise with the bookkeeping software system to be used (and if you don't already have one, ability to assist with analysis and implementation of a system). If you find a person you want to hire who doesn't have experience with your bookkeeping system, be prepared to provide training.
  - Background in small-business bookkeeping, preferably in businesses that are similar to yours (i.e., it may not be helpful if the person has a background in large corporate or government finance when you're opening a craft brewery).
  - Good problem-solving skills to resolve discrepancies in your financial numbers.
  - Skills in managing your Cash Flow/Budget spreadsheet, plus preparation of financial reports and ratios for you (so good Excel skills).
  - Neat and tidy bookkeeping practices. This is a tough one, but a good bookkeeper will keep your books clean and make it easy for you to review and query the entries; a bad bookkeeper will leave your books in shambles. If the person makes mistakes (and then sweeps those mistakes under the carpet), or makes your bookkeeping impossible to decipher, you've got a mess on your hands.

    One good way to check this is to ask for references from tax accountants the candidate has worked with in the past, and then specifically ask the accountant if financial data was presented that fit this requirement.
  - Honesty and reliability. This is an even tougher requirement. You likely won't get the answers you need if you ask about this outright (but it can't hurt to ask, such as "have you ever been fired for dishonesty or reliability?"). You can also ask it obliquely, with questions such as "Has your trustworthiness ever been challenged? What was your response to the situation?" This is also a good question to ask when checking previous employment references.
  - Professional certifications or memberships – check for certification by the National Association of Certified Public Bookkeepers (NACPB)[88] or the American Institute of Professional Bookkeepers (AIPB).[89] If the candidate belongs to either one, you have a better assurance their skills are up-to-date.

---

[88] National Association of Certified Public Bookkeepers (NACPB), at www.nacpb.org
[89] American Institute of Professional Bookkeepers (AIPB), at www.aipb.org

- **Carefully check references.** This is an area where you need to ask probing questions during the hiring interviews (see my example in Chapter 6, Checking Employee References, for a chilling example in my own company). If you're hiring a part-time outside bookkeeper – one that has other clients – ask for references of their other current clients, and ask all of the questions mentioned above.

- **Establish checks and balances.** This one is vital, so it's imperative that you establish this at the outset. Checks and balances within your accounting and bookkeeping system are also known as *financial controls*. With the bookkeeper operating so closely to your company's bank account and credit, it's essential that you think long and hard –*before* you do any hiring – about setting up checks and balances in your company's bookkeeping practices. With so much else going on in a new business start-up, this can help you sleep at night, with greater assurance that your money isn't being embezzled or misdirected. Establishing the checks and balances before you make the first bookkeeper hiring will make it just a part of the way you do business, rather than afterwards making it seem punitive or suspicious.

  Here's the sobering reason why this is so important to you – by the time you detect fraud, and particularly if you aren't paying attention to these checks and balances or warning signs, a large amount of money might already be out the door, *with no way to recover it.*

  What are some reasonable checks and balances? (Some of these seem over the top, and the list seems overly long, but each one has real world examples of having occurred.) And while we're on the topic, fraud can be carried out by employees other than your bookkeeper, so this list will include other types of fraud to be on the watch for. Pay close attention to warning signs that something fishy is going on, and do this regularly and thoroughly. In addition to the warning signs listed here, keep a copy of *"Top Twenty One Signs Of Bookkeeper Embezzlement"* at the address in the footnote link. [90]

  o Don't give your bookkeeper a reason to embezzle from you. Create the best possible working relationship with your bookkeeper, pay the bookkeeper fairly, and treat the bookkeeper right. Unless you hire a bookkeeper who is patently dishonest, with these suggestions you stand a pretty good chance that your bookkeeper will do right by you. *But don't be lulled into a sense of false security.*

  o Cash and sales recognition. Make certain that all cash/check/credit card sales transactions are recorded, and then reconciled against the money received for those sales. Put yourself in the shoes of the most devious and dishonest person imaginable.

  Inventory control (also covered below) goes hand-in-hand with this. Skimming from cash sales is easier if the person handling the cash can also cover up inventory losses, so make sure that you have some way to reconcile production amounts or inventory on hand against the recorded cash receipts. For example, if you've started a craft brewing operation with a tap room, make sure that the quantity brewed and available for sale is in line with sales receipts while it is being drawn down.

---

[90] *Top Twenty One Signs Of Bookkeeper Embezzlement* , Fast Easy Accounting, September 27, 2016, https://www.fasteasyaccounting.com/bid/129527/top-twenty-one-signs-of-bookkeeper-embezzlement

Here's another example. You own a business building parking garage. When a customer enters, a parking ticket is taken from a machine. On exit, the customer pays at an attendant booth – but your attendant doesn't ring up the transaction and doesn't issue a receipt to the customer unless asked. Unknown to you, the attendant is pocketing some or all of the customer's money. When the cash receipts are sent in to your bookkeeper, parking tickets aren't properly accounted for, cash isn't properly accounted for, maybe there's collusion between the bookkeeper and attendant. This owner's task would be to create a system whereby every transaction is recorded (every ticket issued), time-in stamps and time-out stamps are checked, and the payment amount is reconciled.

Now think about how similar situations could occur in your particular small business circumstances.

o   Checks, bill-paying, and monthly bank statement reconciling.

- Eliminate manually-written checks (or keep them to a bare minimum) and write checks only from your accounting software. Most accounting software products these days have built-in fraud protection features – and you need to be aware of these to ensure they aren't being sidestepped. These features should be one of your important criteria in software selection, and not only save you a lot of time, but also increase your peace of mind.

- Don't even think about giving your bookkeeper check signing authority. This won't be an insult to an experienced bookkeeper. Your bookkeeper will be expecting you to require a batch check signing session on a regular basis so that you (or your spouse or partner) can sign all of them at once.

- Leaving emergency signed checks when you are away – bad idea. It's almost a certainty that you (and your spouse or partner) will be away from the business at times, and that bills need to be paid while you're away. You think, "Gee, what can it hurt to leave behind a couple of signed, but otherwise blank, checks?" Whatever the urge, resist it! By the time you get back and discover it, you could have been looted for all you're worth and your bookkeeper is now living in Brazil. If you're away and your business is still running (which it presumably would be), there's no excuse not to stay in contact, and have some procedure set up for an emergency situation – one that won't put you at financial risk.

- Insist that all checks to be signed are accompanied by two backup documents – the invoice (or whatever supporting documentation) that the check is paying, and a 1-page list of all checks that are being signed, noting vendor name, invoice number, date, check number, and amount. This not only gives the check signer ample evidence that each check is an honest and valid payment, but the list can later be checked against the bank statement when it's reconciled (so the check signer should keep the check list).

  Dishonest bookkeepers are known to create fictitious vendor companies, invoice your company for some made-up amount, and then the bookkeeper writes a check to that vendor. If the vendor and the amount aren't obviously valid, question it. Pay special attention to fictitious vendor names that are just slightly different from a valid vendor. According to the Association of Certified Fraud Examiners (ACFE), one of the five most common fraud schemes for small business with fewer than 100 employees is bill-paying fraud.[91]

- Reconcile the bank statement. There's a gaping hole in your checks and balances if you let the bookkeeper (who is already managing accounts payable) also reconcile each month's checking account statements. Insist that the person authorized to sign checks is also the one who reconciles all bank statements – and does the reconciliation once a month.

  Cross-reference each returned check (or electronic check image) accompanying the statement against the check list provided during the check-signing session. Pay special attention to sequential check numbers and look into any number gaps that are found, as this can indicate bogus checks that you're not seeing (some accounting software has features to guard against this). Also look for check alterations in the vendor name or dollar amount, and particularly in forged signatures. Question all aging checks and deposits that haven't cleared the account.

- Phony bank account(s). Your bookkeeper, acting as a clever forger, can quite easily establish a phony bank account in your company's name. All it will take is the audacity to pose as a company owner at a bank *other than your regular bank*, with the company's Certificate of Formation (if an LLC) and Operating Agreement and EIN number in hand (all three of which are probably in the paper files the bookkeeper can access), and a business account can be opened. After that, a subset of your cash receipts or regular AR payments could be funneled to that account, with you none the wiser.

  To help foil this common fraud trick, it's good if all incoming postal service mail is picked by the check signer – or if electronically-delivered bank statements are sent to the check signer – and after a check on everything to see there's nothing suspicious, forward it to the bookkeeper.

- Online bill pay. A great feature with most of today's bank account setups, but also rife with the possibility of fraud. For example, if the same person sets up the requirement for the bill to pay, then takes it through the payment process, the *bill* could be bogus. Two different people need to handle these two tasks, just as there are for writing and signing checks.

o AR bank deposits. If your accounts receivable payments are received by check (as opposed to online or direct deposits), they should always be matched up with invoices that you've sent – and tracked in a double-entry system within your accounting software. If the invoice and subsequent payment aren't properly cross-referenced, a payment check can be diverted to an outside account under the bookkeeper's control.

If your business operates on daily cash receipts, make sure they aren't presented for deposit to the bank with a request for cash back (where the *Less cash* field on the

---

[91] G. Stevenson Smith and Theresa Hrncir, *Small business fraud and the trusted employee*, ACFE website, January/February 2013, http://www.acfe.com/article.aspx?id=4294976289

deposit ticket is filled in), as an unscrupulous bookkeeper can then skim that cash. So ensure your bank never allows *less cash* transactions on business accounts.

o AR or sales payments made to you by credit card. A monthly audit report, *with sequential transaction numbers*, listing every payment number, the date, and the amount should be prepared. When you set up your merchant banking relationship, make certain you are the one to do it (or at least audit it), to ensure that all payments from this source are going into your company's bank account. Make sure that some of the payments aren't set up to siphon into an outside account.

o Cash payments. This is the easiest place for skimming to occur, particularly once the money gets into your back office.

o Withdrawals of any kind should not be allowed, with the exception of line of credit advances to your company checking account.

o If you have a company credit card and your bookkeeper will use the card (for example, to charge production materials or supplies for the office that are received, or to make reservation deposits, among other things), establish the authorized uses. Just like your bank statement reconciliation, establish a separate person for reconciliation of the credit card statements. If no one is watching what gets charged to this card, it can be very tempting, and no different than having a hand in the company's petty cash.

o Audit your bookkeeper – which is another way of saying, stay closely involved with your bookkeeper. As a small business owner, your bookkeeper will soon become your most trusted confidant (and will know more about you than you think). On a random basis, ask to see exactly how various aspects of the bookkeeping system work. It's your money you are looking after, so don't be shy or embarrassed if it looks like you're checking up. An honest bookkeeper will expect this, and won't resent it.

o Payroll. Regardless of whether your payroll system is manual or contracted with a payroll service, it's easy to scam the system, so ensure you have visibility to it. If your only involvement in this is to see that your own paycheck is cut each period, it wouldn't be hard for an unscrupulous bookkeeper to put a non-existent employee on the payroll, or to pay extra overtime that wasn't worked, or to fiddle vacation and sick leave time. In most cases, your bookkeeper will be keeping track of payroll checks that are mailed out or direct deposited – with the result that you never see any of the detail. There's no shame in setting up oversight, or creating a cross-reference, and that way you know your payroll system is working correctly.

o Inventory shrinkage. Employees might think that taking a bit of the company home on a regular basis is their just desserts – but unless you've specifically allowed it, it's really no different from shoplifting. In fact, one or more employees might be *selling out the back door*, cutting directly into your bottom line. Take a physical inventory at whatever frequency makes sense for your business. If it doesn't make sense, at least make a regular calculation to ensure that your purchased/manufactured supplies and materials reasonably add up to your quantities produced and sold.

o Over-ordering supplies. A scam that's possible is for a bookkeeper or office staff to over-order company supplies. After they are delivered (and while no one is watching), the employee returns the extra amount to the store, exchange it for a gift card, then buy something small with it and pocket the rest in cash. This is a very hard scam to catch, so it's worth the effort to spot-check.

- o   Watch for lower profits. Most likely it's because your sales aren't high enough or your expenses are too high, but it could also be from embezzlement. Spot check for it in your analysis of the Cash Flow/Budget each month, by checking to see if Cost of Goods numbers and G&A salaries are where they should be.

With a list of checks and balances that long, it may seem as if the dishonesty of bookkeepers is rife, but that wouldn't be a fair statement. The problem is, they are inherently placed in a position of trust within your company, and it's in a position where the level of temptation might be high. There's no way to know when outside circumstances change in an otherwise honest bookkeeper's life, pushing the temptation over the line. Your best option is to establish good controls, and then keep an eye on things to ensure bad things don't happen. By the time you find out otherwise, it's probably too late – and your chances of getting the money back are slim.

Recordkeeping – managing company documents

When you're just starting out with your new business, most of your time and energy will be spent getting the business going – *and growing*. Keeping records of everything that happens – not just financial records, but plain old everyday business records – seems like something you can always do tomorrow. And then it doesn't get done tomorrow ... or the next day ... or the next day. Before you know it, you have piles and piles of paperwork scattered all around, commingled with your personal papers, and on your computer you have e-mails and data files scattered willy-nilly. Simply put, you have a mess on your hands.

So you do an internet search on "business record-keeping", hoping to find tips on how to make heads or tails of the mess – and what do you find? Dozens of hits on eDocument software systems that are guaranteed to make your life so simple you'll wonder how you ever lived without it. My recommendation ... close that web search and don't even think about an eDocument software product until your company is far bigger, with a half dozen departments, a couple dozen employees, and an employee who is totally dedicated to making an eDocument system work (unless you already have some experience with such a system, and then only if you have the bandwidth to set one up).

At this early stage in your business life, what you most likely need is some simple help on how to organize your paper and digital mess down to a clean desk and computer. I'm not trying to insult your intelligence with this information, but there are some details about it that aren't intuitive until you've done it once, and they can pay big dividends a few years later when old records need to be produced (IRS or state tax audit, some regulatory agency is nosing around, or a buyer for your company comes knocking on your door and is ready to do due diligence).

Paper or electronic filing system. The electronic world is moving at the speed of light, and one decision you need to make – or at least start thinking about – is whether your new company will be paper-driven, all paperless, or some combination in between (recommended). Several factors help make this decision:

- •   The owner's personal preference. Are you computer-savvy, and do you tend to do all (or most) of your communication via electronic format? Do you prefer that many of your company's important documents are accessible from anywhere? Or, are you essentially a low-tech person, happy to have a traditional company environment where all back-office business management is done with papers, printers, and filing cabinets?

- Does your business better lend itself to a traditional paper-based office management system, or to a fully-computerized, software-driven environment? Software is available to help manage payroll and accounting, personnel management, benefits management, production control, inventory control, sales and marketing, and customer communications. However, you probably don't have a transaction level large enough in each area to warrant purchasing and implementing a software system.
- Are your employees in each of those areas better suited to lower-tech or higher-tech solutions?
- Are you committed to establishing whatever is necessary for either/both systems? This includes allocating physical offices, work space, and equipment (filing cabinets, computers, scanners, printers); establishing a corporate network and security protocols for corporate records, and archival processes for each system.

Even if you are computer-savvy, a combination of paper-based and paperless is almost certainly the best solution. Some documents simply have to be (or should be) in paper format, though you can also keep a scanned copy. Such mandatory paper documents include those with notarized signatures, or those marked as requiring physical paper copies. Otherwise, there aren't any requirements stopping you from implementing a paperless document strategy in any part of your business that you wish. The requirements tend to focus on mandatory retention period, security of the documents, and accessibility. That leaves the decision up to you, and the needs of your business should dictate the direction you go.

For the vast majority of small business start-ups, building a product and everything that's necessary to bring in revenue from that product are the most important efforts you should be making. Spending your time and efforts elsewhere on implementing software solutions can be a real barrier to growth.

Take as an example your sales efforts. When your company is further down the growth path, you might find it valuable to implement a sales management software product such as *salesforce.com* to oversee all aspects of your sales staff's efforts to find and win customers (and to manage all of your sales documents). At the beginning, though, you are probably the company's entire sales force, and you're doing this alongside the ten other critical hats that you're wearing. At this point, *salesforce.com* would be an incredible overkill, and just the effort to implement it for a single sales person could negatively swamp every other effort.

You may also be traveling around a bit on sales calls, purchasing and collecting raw materials for your production process, and perhaps delivering products to your customers. As we'll discuss later, any travel expenses you incur are deductible business expenses – but with just you on the road, does this justify purchasing and implementing an expense reporting software solution? A far simpler system would make much more business sense.

Your product manufacturing might consist of a backroom operation with just a few employees (and maybe just you), receiving raw materials from a handful of vendors, and maybe sales are being made to a few dozen (or few hundred) customers. Does the supply chain and process flow for this level of business activity warrant an Enterprise Resource Planning (ERP) software product to oversee it and document it? An ERP product would certainly provide electronic documentation capability for this business process, but the cost and effort required of such a product far outweighs the benefits for a small business.

All of these situations warrant a resounding *no* to the question of automatic electronic documentation – at least until the business is much larger. In the meantime, a lot of these processes will be handled by seat-of-the-pants methodologies, involving piles of paper. That's not to say that scanning paperwork into electronic format, and systematically filing it in various document folders isn't feasible (it is), but that too is an effort, and if you're scanning just to get rid of the paperwork, you're duplicating a lot of effort.

As an example of this, consider your growing personnel files (assuming you are hiring employees). As we said before, there are no government agencies, state or federal, that dictate the format of your personnel files – but they do dictate how long you need to keep them, and how secure from prying eyes they need to be. If you decide on digital format, every piece of paper that would otherwise go into a series of manila folders in a locked file cabinet must now be appropriately scanned in (if originally in paper format), then stored in a unique file for the individual employee (or group files in some situations). If they are already in electronic format, each document must be squirreled away in an appropriate folder. For some records, there are requirements to keep them separate and distinct from other records, and with different protocols for access. All of the sensitive documents must be sufficiently password-protected or encrypted to satisfy various government agencies and regulations that require safeguards for employee data, such as USCIS (I-9 forms), ERISA (benefits documents), ADA, HIPPA, EEOC, Department of Labor, OSHA, etc. Importantly, since this example assumes a paperless (electronic document) system, the original paper documents that require protection must also be shredded (or equally protected) to preserve confidentiality. Everyone who needs access to this data must also have the protection access keys – and don't forget, when any person in that category terminates employment with you, they now have those keys, even though you might lock them out of your system. Compare this to storing all of the paperwork in a series of manila folders, locked in a locking file cabinet, inside your locked premises, with only appropriate employees having access to it. It's certainly your choice and responsibility, but my recommendation would be to keep it clean and simple – paper in a file cabinet.

Electronic file management. (This discussion assumes you are using a Microsoft Windows-based system. If you use another system – such as Apple Mac – the considerations are similar ... but some details slightly different.)

Obviously, electronic documents take up less physical space to store, can be set up to be accessible quickly and easily from anywhere, are easy to duplicate, and are a very green alternative to paper. It's also true that electronic files require a concerted file management system – one that has parallels to paper file requirements, but also other, totally unique requirements.[92] Here are some considerations:

---

[92] Bridget Miller, *Convenience and Efficiency Considerations of Electronic Employee Files*, HR Daily Advisor, January 27, 2015, http://hrdailyadvisor.blr.com/2015/01/27/can-an-electronic-system-replace-paper-employee-files/

- Understanding, deciding on, and keeping track of data formats, file formats, and media types that raw data and documents are to be stored in. Odds are, the typical small business owner isn't an IT (Information Technology) professional, and isn't up-to-the-minute on the latest and greatest electronic formats, and also isn't familiar with the appropriateness of a wide variety of formats available for the company records at hand. Therefore, that owner might not be the best person to make the final decision governing this (which is important for the *Big Caution* at the end of this section).

- Understanding the complexity and concepts of the raw data formats that proprietary back office software systems use to maintain company data.

- Understanding various governmental agency requirements for security and confidentiality of certain types of company data and records, and subsequent accessibility of that data and records. This also includes a good understanding of how long certain records must be kept and be accessible.[93]

- Determining how to provide (and enforce) limited access to individuals, at the same time keeping other nearby data secure. For example, allowing an employee to see his/her own personnel file, but preventing them from seeing any other employee's records or other data.

- Establishing a planned retention period for certain company records. Regulatory and governmental agency rules dictate how long some records must be kept. After that period has elapsed, you are free to establish your in-house rules for deleting files that you no longer wish to keep.

- Surprisingly, electronic copies of company files can be significantly more difficult to destroy than paper copies. Often, the only copy that exists for many paper files is the original – and when it's destroyed, the document is gone, completely and forever. With an electronic document, the original might be on one computer, but copies of it on a dozen other computers, plus any number of additional backup and archived copies in storage. That can be a real benefit *or a real problem*. When asked to produce a document in a court order by a regulatory official (maybe even one that you'd prefer isn't available), you may think it is deleted, but if someone makes a concerted effort, odds are good that the document can be found … *somewhere*. In an important situation, forensic analysis could turn up data that you haven't seen for a long time.

- A similar problem exists with multiple versions of the same document. The creator of a document might keep several progressive versions as it's being developed, with the final product turned over to someone else. The versions might remain around for a long time – longer, in fact, than the final copy. If that doesn't fit well with your planned document destruction, you need to address it.

- The risks of outside hackers gaining access to the company's most important data.

Big caution – electronic documents and format/obsolescence. In today's world, the big push is to eliminate paper. *Go paperless* is all the rage, and environmentally there are no arguments

---

[93] Tiffani L. McDonough, *Going Paperless? Legal Guidelines & Tips for a Paperless HR Department*, July 29, 2014, http://www.hrlegalist.com/2014/07/going-paperless-legal-guidelines-for-the-electronic-retention-of-personnel-documents/

against it. Here's my big concern: every document you keep electronically today will become unreadable (and therefore, inaccessible) in a relatively short time as software and hardware changes. Since the concept of electronic document storage for small business came along (what, 30 years ago or so?), we've traveled down the road of micro-cassette tapes, 5¼" and 3½" floppy disks and drives, to hard drives, then zip drives, CDs, DVDs, and now cloud storage. Each storage medium had its own software *drivers* to read/write to it. Each type of data had its own software that created it – such as Word for text documents, Excel for spreadsheet data, PowerPoint for presentation documents, accounting software for your financial data, and on and on. Now just think about how quickly our world discards each one for the next new thing to come along – and how little effort is made to ensure that everything created from the previous methodology can still be accessed in the future. Also think about how often a new release or version of a software product *drops* accessibility (or another term for it, compatibility) for files created by earlier releases or versions.

For example, your company's entire financial system will be stored and processed today by, let's say, QuickBooks, a good starter accounting system for small business. But a few years from now your business might outgrow QuickBooks and you decide to convert to, say, Intacct – a top-rated mid-range financial management system.[94] Sounds wonderful, and probably is, and conversion tools are almost certainly available to make it quite easy to transition to the new software. But, unfortunately, the unique data structure for storing application data (i.e., your actual accounting data) in one software product is fundamentally different from any other product. What this means is that backed-up or archived accounting data from your original product can never be looked at again, once you're removed the original software product from your system.

Another example also illustrates this point. Years ago (1980s), I used WordStar almost exclusively for text editing, installed on an ancient Z8080 microprocessor running the CP/M operating system that predates Microsoft's MS/DOS (which predates Windows) (and yes, people today laugh when they just hear the mention of WordStar). I still have hundreds and hundreds of 5¼" floppy disks that contain WordStar files in my company archives, none of which can be successfully opened by today's version of Microsoft Word. Luckily, the DOS prompt is still available on my PC, from which I can start WordStar on my PC. It doesn't happen very often, but every once in a while I have a very great need to look up something from those long-ago days when everything was in WordStar format – and I can still look at it in its primitive format.

So, in this context, the problem with today's world is that it's moving forward too fast for anyone to really pay attention to *backward compatibility* – or the ability to access yesterday's stuff.

Does anyone care? Well, it's worth thinking about. I formed my own small business in those same WordStar days, and if all of my important corporate documents had been only electronically archived, would they be accessible today? If *conscious* decisions had been made along the way to either convert them into new formats with each technological change (which rapidly becomes impractical), or to create archive paper copies, then yes, there's a chance. But *conscious* is the operative word, and the work involved in keeping up with it is significant.

---

[94] QuickBooks and Intacct – two highly popular and well-known accounting packages – were named here strictly for telling the story, and nothing is to be inferred about the benefits or failings of either product. This example is strictly to illustrate a point.

It's hard to think about the future like this, so you should tuck this caution away, and as you begin to add software products to your business management processes, give some thought to how you will archive important business papers – and crucially, how you will retrieve them in future.

The following section discusses methods to store different categories of paper files. If you want to store any of the categories in electronic format, think about how you could accomplish the same goals using digital storage.

Really important papers. This is the category you need to worry about first and foremost. Some papers will remain in your main office filing cabinet(s) for the entire life of your company, as well as being stored electronically on your company's primary computer for business management. Others will remain in the current year's filing cabinet for just this calendar year, and are then moved to secure storage for archive. Others get replaced with next year's current information.

- **Corporate business papers.** All paperwork related to the formation of your business should remain in your main office filing cabinet for the life of your company. This filing cabinet should be kept locked at all times, and only you and your bookkeeper should have access to it (you may prefer to exclude your bookkeeper). This includes your state-level company start-up filing documents, your By-Laws or Operating Agreement(s), and any documents related to major decisions or business alterations taken by your company (such as Board of Director Meeting minutes and corporate resolutions). A copy, or the originals if you prefer, should be stored with your attorney or registered agent.

- **Company policy paperwork.** All paperwork related to your company policies should be filed by category, with current year's policy documents in your main office filing cabinet(s). Replaced policy paperwork and updated (and now outdated) policies should be archived with the end-of-year files, *and kept for the life of your company*. You may have employees (or other aspects relating to your policies) that have been with you the entire life of your company, and having to prove this or that about an out-of-date policy that can no longer be found puts you at risk. This includes all employee and employment policies, papers that describe benefit policies, and original and revisions to your employee handbook policy.

- **Employee personnel files.** Each employee should have his/her own file, and the entire file should remain in your primary office filing cabinets throughout the employee's tenure with the company. This filing cabinet should remain locked at all times, and only you and your bookkeeper (and HR person when you have one) should have access to it – and preferably, whatever office/closet it's kept in should be locked when no one is using it. If an employee departs, the associated personnel file could move to the archive files for the year of departure if necessary to make room (but they still need to be secured).

  Each employee's file should contain all employee hiring documentation, including job posting advertisements, notes from the interview process, and the employee's resume. It should also contain salary information (including salary history), vacation and sick leave (and other types of family leave) records, benefits paperwork relative to the employee, and all employee performance paperwork.

A second personnel file for each employee might be necessary, to include appropriate HIPAA paperwork for that employee – i.e., health and welfare-related benefits information that may be protected under the Health Insurance Portability and Accountability Act (HIPAA).

- **Travel expenses.** Travel expense paperwork should be filed as a separate category, and preferably filed by individual employee (and certainly not in a shoebox!). For each trip by an employee, staple together all receipts with the travel expense report and identify the trip (if you have travel expense software, this should be a feature of it). If travel expense deductions become the focus of a tax audit, how well you file and keep track of this could affect how well your audit proceeds.

  A bit of extra advice might be warranted about travel expenses. You'll find the word *contemporaneous* bandied about in various places where business and travel expenses are explained – as the IRS does not take kindly to expense reports going back several years that are quickly cobbled together when you get the audit notice. Instead, you need to be gathering your expense data at the same time you are traveling.

  For years, my system for each trip has been to simply collect all travel receipts (including my airline ticket, hotel receipt, and car rental receipts), annotated if necessary, place them in an envelope and fill out a paper travel expense form while I'm on my way home from each trip. That way the information is fresh in my mind, it satisfies all of the requirements for contemporaneous, and I can then file the report with the company bookkeeper the next day back at work. The medium is different, but the logic is the same for preparing expense report data through a software app on a mobile device.

- **Deductible business expenses.** This paperwork will not only be important at tax preparation time, but also in case of a future tax audit. All expenses for the current calendar year should be kept in this year's filing system, then archived at the end of each calendar year (or at the end of tax preparation) in a composite filing for that year. If you lease equipment, you might want to have a copy of the paperwork for each piece of equipment kept in the current year's files.

  It should go without saying, but you should also know what are and aren't valid deductible business expenses if you have any hope of staying on the right side of tax law. When you have a struggling (or rapidly growing and demanding) young business, the last thing you can afford is an IRS audit breathing down your neck, killing dozens (maybe hundreds) of hours of time that could be better spent on business growth. And, I'm saying this multiple times – if the tax auditor finds some of your recordkeeping to be sloppy, it'll be a red flag to dig deeper in other areas as well.

  Interestingly, the definition of deductible business expenses is rather vague (and intentionally so, by IRS acknowledgement) – a deductible expense must be *ordinary and necessary* for your business. An entire IRS publication is devoted to it (IRS Pub 535[95]) and it's huge.

---

[95] IRS Pub 535: http://www.irs.gov/publications/p535/index.html.

Here are some examples of what *are and aren't* valid deductible business expenses (and there are many more, so don't stop with this list): [96]

- Your business start-up expenses? No, they are not deductible before you officially start up your business, and even then, *up to a limit* once you're up and running. (Talk to your tax accountant about this.)

- Business use of your home? Yes, but only for the part that is used exclusively and regularly for business, but again, with very strict rules that you must follow. Every advice you'll ever see warns that the IRS considers a home office business to be a notorious red flag for tax audits. It's definitely an allowable deductible expense, but it's so rife with abuse that the IRS watches carefully over it.

- Shared business and personal use of your car? Yes, but only with good documentation.

- Cell phone expenses? Yes, but technically only the business use, and it could get dicey if an auditor decides to look at detail. You'll need to keep the itemized bills in your record keeping, and if asked the percentage of business use must be verifiable.

- Entertainment expenses? Yes, but with very strict rules and documentation that you must keep. For example, it's imperative that *actual business* is discussed immediately before or afterwards.

- Travel expenses? Yes, but you must keep good documentation.

- Bad debts? Yes, but with strict rules attached.

Get used to the idea of collecting receipts and invoices, and don't just throw them in a box for a rainy day. If they're travel receipts, file them with your expense report – yes, you'll need to come up with a written or electronic expense report to file in your recordkeeping system. Ditto for business receipts or invoices. Your monthly credit card statement and your company checkbook are not detailed enough for that purpose, although they provide collaborative backup that you actually paid the expense.

Stop the paperwork clutter. Early on, figure out what paperwork needs to be saved, and get rid of the rest. As it arrives, sort through every piece of paper and decide which need to be saved and which can be tossed – and toss or shred any in the latter category immediately after they've been read. (Similar advice can be developed for electronic clutter.)

- If it's a piece of mail, read it and toss it (unless for some reason it needs to be saved)

- If it's a business expense receipt, separate the day-to-day receipts (lunch with a customer that you paid for) from office supplies (copier paper, software that you downloaded) from capital equipment (a new computer, an office desk) and your regular business receipts (rent, utilities, phone, internet access). At the end of the month, put all of these receipts into an expense folder labeled for the month and year, and get them to your bookkeeper for any necessary accounting. After that, file them in your filing system, where they'll eventually be stored with the paperwork for that year.

---

[96] Caron Beesley, *Business Expenses and Tax Deductions Explained; A 101 for Small Business Owners*, All Business online site, https://www.allbusiness.com/business-expenses-and-tax-deductions-explained-a-101-for-small-business-owners-14771333-1.html. This is a good place to start. For more detail, do an internet search on "allowable small business expenses."

- If you have the time (and inclination), once the accounting usage is complete, a better technique than keeping all of the receipts filed just by month in the permanent file is to have a set of receipt categories – let's say, Office Supplies, Office Equipment, Business Expenses, etc. That way, if ever questioned, you can find them more readily than if they are stored all together.

Paper file management system. This one seems like a no-brainer – just heap everything into file folders that fill a filing cabinet and Bob's your uncle. Well, that can work, but another year down the road and you'll wish you'd done a better job of it at the start. And the same goes for setting up an electronic filing system, rather than just lumping it all together. (You might think this is a trivial topic, but it's a great way to cut down on paperwork and filing clutter in your office, allowing you to more readily locate documents.)

Following are some organization tips[97] (and again, I'm not trying to insult anyone's intelligence with this, but the basic concept of it might not be intuitive):

- Get yourself a metal filing cabinet and keep it separate from all of your personal filing. It doesn't have to be fancy – just a four-drawer letter-sized filing cabinet. I wouldn't bother with a lateral file – it's much bigger and more costly. Later, when you hire dedicated people who shuffle lots of paper – such as accounting staff, personnel staff, or contract management staff – you may need fancy lateral files, but by then you'll have bigger office digs and more money to spend on office equipment. For now you should be able to pick up a basic file cabinet for $200 at your local office supply store, or even buy one used. (If you're really strapped for cash, or tight on space, a couple of plastic filing totes (or the cardboard Bankers Boxes® from Office Depot) can work for a while, but don't rely on them for very long.)

- Decide on a filing system. You don't have to have an accounting degree to do this – just decide how you're going to set up the folders in the filing cabinet drawers – alphabetically, by category, or even chronologically. My preference (and that of many others) is by category.

- From your office supply store, pick up a couple of boxes of hanging file folders – make sure you either get the kind that come with the metal frames to set up the hanging bar on each side of the drawer, or buy separate frames for each file drawer. As time goes on, you'll end up with quite a few pieces of paper and manila folders in these hanging folders, so get the kind that have an expansive *box bottom.*

- Once the hanging frames are in place, fill each drawer with at least a dozen of the hanging folders. *Note: from this point on, you'll never remove these hanging folders.* Once labeled, they'll just be place holders for the actual file folders inside them where you'll file your paperwork for each year.

- Sort your papers into categories. You'll probably have categories for: Banking, Travel Expenses, Personnel, Payroll, Business Expenses, Equipment, Taxes, Customer Contracts,

---

[97] *How To Establish An Office Filing System*, wikiHow, undated, http://www.wikihow.com/Establish-an-Office-Filing-System

and so on. Your business will dictate the categories you have. These will make up the labels that you put on the tab for its associated hanging file.

Arrange the hanging folders in whatever sequence makes the most sense to you – and particularly, the sequence or arrangement that allows you to find them quickly. For example, if Banking is the one you access most often, it could be at the front of the top drawer. Or you could do it alphabetically – whatever allows you to locate any folder quickly.

- Within some categories you'll likely end up with sub-categories, and depending on the size of it, each sub-category could have additional hanging folders behind. For example, under Personnel you'll start with a file for yourself, and when you begin hiring employees you'll add others behind it. Alphabetical by name makes a ton of sense.

- Now fill each hanging folder with an identically-labeled manila folder – and add the current year after the category. You'll now file your paperwork in this folder.

- Keep up with the filing task, or it can quickly get out of hand, but no one says you have to file every single piece as it comes in the door – there's nothing wrong with an unorganized pile for a little while, but keep it under control.

- Throughout the year, you should be able to find anything you need on a moment's notice, and better yet, you'll feel better that you are more organized.

- Now here's the key trick to a long-term filing plan. At the end of each year, as early in January as possible, get one or more Bankers Boxes with lift-off lids from your office supply store.

From your filing cabinet, pull out the manila folder and its contents from *each hanging file that can be archived by year*, and load them into the Bankers Box in the same sequence they were in the filing cabinet (because after a while you'll have that sequence memorized, and then you can find folders just as quickly in the archived Bankers Box as in the filing cabinet). If some paper items in the file cabinet are not year-specific, yet need to remain for easy and quick access for year after year (such as current employee records and customer contracts), by all means leave them in the metal filing cabinet. But all others go into the Bankers Box.

With a marker pen, note the year on the outside of each Bankers Box, and if necessary, the folder contents that are in each box.

Replace all of the manila folders that you put in the Bankers Box with fresh ones, labeled the same as before and with the upcoming year.

- Now your metal filing cabinet is set up for the next calendar year. Keep last year's Bankers Box around as long as you need to (for whatever office needs may exist for that year), and then move the box to your permanent storage area. Considering that much of the records are confidential company information, wherever you archive the box, make certain that it's locked. The last thing you need is an employee (disgruntled or just curious) searching around in the files to dig up something.

- Keep the files for at least four years (that's the required filing time by the IRS), *or longer if you wish* (and I believe longer is better than shorter). Don't forget that some of the records could be very useful (or even very important) when/if it comes time to sell your business and the buyer is ready to do due diligence on your business.[98] For example, company records should be kept forever. Financial statements from past years can be important in showing company growth over time.

Business stationery and business cards

Part of being a real business is having proper business stationery and business cards. You might be primarily an online company, and the bulk of your communications with customers and vendors is by phone and e-mail, but many times you'll need to correspond the old-fashioned way – by snail mail. You need business stationery that looks professional, looks crisp, and expresses the desired image of your company. (The term business stationery usually refers to letterhead paper, containing your company name, address, and logo, as well as envelopes with the same information.) Since much (maybe most) of your business correspondence will be generated electronically and then sent as an e-mail attachment, you should also have a digital stationery file that looks the same as your business stationery.

More importantly – create professional-looking business cards. Every time you meet potential and current clients face-to-face it's customary to exchange business cards. Every time you meet someone on an airplane, at a tradeshow, or even at a social event, the frequent question will be, "Do you have a business card?"

Neither of these cost very much and they go a long way to making you look professional – and they can pay dividends that far exceed the cost. Your first thought might be to drop by the nearest FedEx Office (many of us still call it Kinko's) and have them print some up. Often it's more cost-efficient to locate a small printing company specializing in business stationery. They usually have design services that can help with choosing a font and incorporating your logo. Spending a few dollars on a professional graphics designer can later pay dividends that far exceed the cost. When ordering your stationery from the printer, the more you order, the cheaper it is – so plan on getting one or more reams of letterhead paper, a box of envelopes, and 500 business cards.

It's usually creating your corporate look and feel that makes business stationery expensive – the font used for your company name and the tagline that goes with it, and the design of your company logo. Since today's entrepreneurs likely create their online look and feel first, it may be just a matter of transferring that over to the printer, who will then create your stationery and business cards.

But here's a caution – and an important one. As you're dreaming big dreams about the look and feel of your company, don't forget printing costs. With your imagination running wild about how to make your new company look really cool, with multi-color fonts and logos on your website, when you get the price for that same great look on your *printed* material, you'll probably choke. The difference between a 2-color and a 3-color print job is not only steep ... it can take

---

[98] For a comprehensive buyer's due diligence checklist, see *Buying a Business: Due Diligence Checklist*, http://smallbusiness.findlaw.com/starting-a-business/buying-a-business-due-diligence-checklist.html. This checklist provides a very good list of things you'll likely be asked to produce by your potential buyer. If you can't locate some or any of them, it can be a serious red flag about your prospective buyer.

your breath away, so do everything possible to keep your logo to a 2-color design (or even just black and white – at least at first).

No matter what your products or services are, you'll likely need collateral material, such as product brochures to hand out at tradeshows or give to clients, as well as product packaging materials that will also be printed with your standardized look and feel. If you aren't careful, the added cost of multi-colored printing can have a big effect – or even wipe out – your expected profit margin for each sale.

Creating an internet presence

In this day and age, letting your fingers do the walking no longer means dragging out the Yellow Pages – but rather, doing an internet search.

Just think about the first thing you do when someone tells you about a fantastic restaurant they just visited, or about the latest hot item they just purchased. You whip out your smart phone or tablet, enter a search into the browser, and most likely you then visit the official site for that product or service. Sure, if someone tells you they just had a fantastic meal at Joe's Pulled Pork Palace, you might access Yelp to check out customer reviews, but more than likely you'll first head for www.joespulledporkpalace.com, and find out where it is, and what's on the menu. If you don't find a domain name that matches the business, I'll bet you assume that outfit won't be around long – they just aren't with today's times.

At the beginning of this chapter, we discussed the important aspects of choosing your business name that is web-ready. You should try to get a domain name that closely matches your business, and before registering your business name (before you get your heart set on it too!), you should obtain the domain name that matches it.

There are dozens – maybe hundreds – of internet domain hosting companies that you can turn to for a domain name and website hosting, at prices that won't bust the bank. Because there are so many, you really need a review service to let you comparison-shop. Consumerrankings.com[99] has a Top 10 list, with prices starting around $3.00/month (and even less if you want the absolute cheapest deal). PC Magazine is another good place to look for reviews.[100]

Don't be surprised if your hoped-for domain name isn't available. If you've bandied about your start-up plans, or announced it on Facebook or a crowdfunding site, there are unscrupulous trolls out there who search for those situations, checking them against available domain names. If they're currently available they'll lock them up – hoping to get you to pay them a ransom to hand over the domain name of your dreams. If that happens to you – and you can get it freed up for a hundred bucks (or a few hundred bucks), it might be worth it to you in the long run, as it could be the key to getting potential customers to you once you open your doors for business. If you find yourself in a domain name negotiation, be extremely careful and circumspect in your words and behavior, as a troll can probably spot in a heartbeat how badly you want the domain name.

Obviously, as soon as you register your domain name, the task of designing and creating your company's website must be tackled. If you don't have graphic artist's talent in your bones, this

---

[99] Consumer-Rankings, at www.consumer-rankings.com/hosting/
[100] PC Magazine, at http://www.pcmag.com/article2/0,2817,2424725,00.asp

might be where you have to consider spending at least a few hundred dollars for design advice (more likely, a couple thousand dollars), as your website might be your most important portal to your company's success. When a friend tells a friend about your company and its products, the first thing they'll do is pull up your web site.

Your company's website doesn't have to be a knock-'em-dead killer right out of the box, as you can always fine-tune it later, but it needs to be good enough that potential customers browsing it can _easily and quickly_ learn about you and your products and services, and most importantly, find out how they can purchase them from you. It must be graphically appealing, and it needs to be clean and uncluttered. Most of all, it's going to be your window on the world, and it could be your main source of business leads.

When your website goes live, it will be your main business driver and your main source of branding, so put a lot of effort into your site. As your company is getting off the ground, find out what's working with the website and what isn't. You can say what you want about how important Facebook, Twitter, craigslist, and any other social media sites will be to your success, but having a website that nails your company – and what it does – is a most important part that you _have_ to get right.

There are many other details about how important your internet presence is – such as _analytics_ that let you see how effective your website is. That's outside the scope of this book, and there are hundreds of websites on the topic, plus books you can buy.

Chapter 4   Money in the Bank is (Almost) Everything

"Money is like a sixth sense –
and you can't make use of the other five without it."
William Somerset Maugham, author

Pricing your products or services

One of the most difficult decisions you'll face as a new business owner is the price point for your products or services. Price them too low and you'll have difficulty making a profit; price them too high and customers won't pay for them. It's a real Goldilocks issue – the prices you set should be *just right*.

Large multinational firms have MBA-level staff members who slice and dice statistics, competitive market share numbers, cost of sales analysis, and a dozen other factors to determine the optimum price point for their product. The pharmaceutical industry is an example – they can establish, for every country their drugs are sold in, exactly how to price, right down to the penny – and assuming their pricing specialist gets it right, they'll hit the quarterly numbers the stock market financial analysts are suggesting.

For the rest of us mere mortals (i.e., an entrepreneur with a small start-up business), the process feels more akin to wetting a finger and holding it up to the wind. Here are several ideas to get your thoughts started.[101]

- **Make a profit.** To set your prices correctly for making a profit, it's imperative that you know your cost metrics – *and* make the best possible assumptions on sales numbers that you can. This is where the concept of *cost accounting* comes in (extensively discussed in the next chapter), as well as monitoring your Cash Flow/Budget spreadsheet month-by-month.

  Underestimating costs and overestimating sales are the single biggest underlying factors in small business failure, and it's crucial that you spend lots of effort studying this during your early planning stages. It's equally important to continue this business analysis on a monthly basis for the rest of your business life. As the old adage goes, you can't succeed if you lose a little bit on every widget you sell, but try to make up for it with volume.

---

[101] Caron Beesley, *How to Price Your Small Businesses' Products and Services*, SBA Blog – Starting a Business, September 28, 2016, https://www.sba.gov/blogs/how-price-your-small-business-products-and-services

The big question you have to resolve is how much profit is enough? Is it enough to pay all the bills, plus paying whatever salary you feel is appropriate? Is it enough to give you the financial incentive to concentrate on business growth. Does it help build a cash cushion to get through any lean times that will certainly arise? If not, and you don't change it ... well, you're setting yourself up for a future disaster.

- **Marketplace positioning.** Do you want your company and its products and services to be known as the lowest-cost, absolute best deal around, or do you want your customers to perceive you as the high-end alternative? This is how you begin to build your brand presence and niche in the marketplace, while expanding your marketplace penetration as quickly and thoroughly as possible.

  Branding may not seem like a big deal when you first start up. You may be thinking that just getting the business going is the most important thing, and you'll worry later about the niceties like brand definition. That would be a mistake. Two aspects here:

  o if your business is always going to be the low-cost specialist, your profit margins will likely be lower, and you'll need increased sales to achieve profitability, whereas if you strike for the high-value position, you can charge more and maintain higher margins

  o your business is likely to be an extension of your personality, so you'll want to define your brand in the area you're most comfortable with.

  Lots of bargain hunters are out there, but sometimes when customers see a low price they assume there's a reason – that the low prices come at the expense of quality.

- **Create upselling and cross-selling situations**. Most small businesses spend huge amounts of time, energy, and money acquiring new customers – and they often forget about existing customers. Business owners who recognize this often think of ways to get existing customers to return for future purchases, rather than only looking for new customers. In fact, getting a customer to buy more on the current visit (or opt for an upgrade) is just as important, and the amount of money it can add to your bottom line can be huge. Make upselling and cross-selling a focused part of your sales efforts and you may very well reap dividends far greater than by increasing prices.

  Here are some ideas, across various types of small businesses that might get your own thoughts going on this:

  o A hair salon earns $75 gross profit on a hair color, cut, and style, and then racks up another $15 profit on two high-end hair products at checkout, plus the customer is talked into returning two weeks later for a touch-up and trim.

  o At your start-up craft brewery taproom, a pint of your best brew goes for $4.25, but the bar snacks that make it taste even better can double that amount – and then talking the customer into taking a growler home for another $12 is even better. Everyone these days likes logo merchandise, so a T-shirt or baseball-style cap not only increases the profitability but also helps to spread the word about your new business without increasing your marketing budget.

  o For your fledgling interior design business (where you're paid commissions rather than an hourly fee), you lead a promising customer to an upscale furniture design center where they order an expensive sofa and chair set. Then after the sale is closed, you mention that another design store around the corner has some really nice pieces that would give a wonderful upgrade to the customer's dining room. Cross-selling such as this means you've used an existing customer for another potential purchase, without the expense of gaining another entirely new customer.

o   Your online store is wrapping up a new-customer order, and just before you take them to checkout you pop a special offer on the screen, with a sales pitch that scores an add-on sale 50% of the time. We've all bought items on amazon.com or the iTunes store, and you've likely noticed that you're always returned to a page showing suggestions of related items that others have purchased. How many times has that tactic successfully lured you into further purchases?

o   Your small back-office software product is profitable for you, but you've reached a bit of a plateau, as you'll need to spend a bunch of money to reach new sales levels. Your customers pay a monthly subscription to use the software – but once they achieve their goals with the software they cancel their subscription. By adding an inexpensive new feature to the software that extends the usable lifespan for many customers, you achieve additional revenue that's more profitable than searching out completely new customers.

Each of these ideas might put more money in your pocket than a price increase would – and no matter what your small business is, thinking creatively about how to **_upsell_** and **_cross-sell_** to your existing customers is easier and more profitable than the cost of finding new customers.

- **Pricing based on the competition.** In some situations, your competition will tell you what you can charge. If you go lower than your competitors, you could end up with more business but less overall money in your pocket; if you go higher, you could wind up with less business and also less money.

The problem with competitive pricing is, determining your competitor's behind-the-scenes costs can be very difficult. They might be half of yours – or, looking at it the other way around, yours might be twice what theirs is – as they might have lower production costs, lower employee costs, negotiated a better deal on raw materials than you did, or they might have some sourcing techniques that you can't match. Their location might bring in a higher percentage of walk-in customers (even if it's an online store), possibly giving them a significant advantage.

The reverse of that is a competitor who is simply in a fog, caught up in how they've priced for years, and being more nimble and hungry, you could possibly swoop in and scoop up a chunk of their market share. Your competitor could be sitting fat, dumb, and happy, thinking they have the market all to themselves, and before they know it they've lost it to you.

Nevertheless, the competitor's pricing can give you a good starting point *to your thinking* – provided you then plug their price(s) into your Cash Flow/Budget spreadsheet, with *your* Cost of Sales numbers also plugged in, and you'll be able to tell if your pricing (or your costs) needs to be analyzed further (see the next chapter for more information on the Cash Flow/Budget spreadsheet).

- **Value-based pricing.** For many first-time entrepreneurs, not only is asking for money a very difficult barrier to break through, but it's also where mistakes are made in pricing your products/services fairly – i.e., what it is truly worth – in the mistaken belief that customers won't buy at that level. This usually results from not understanding the value that your products (or service) bring to the customer. For first-time customers, or customers who are used to dealing with a competitor who is undercutting your price, the value might not be obvious, so you need to figure out the best way to communicate this. Articulate it clearly and succinctly if you're making the sales pitch face-to-face; spell it out in big letters (literally and figuratively) if your pitch is being read by the customer. Then live up to your value claims in your customer support and they'll more likely return for future sales. And make sure you suggest to each customer that they tell a friend about the value of your product/service – and if they do it, arrange some kind of deal for them.

- **Discounting can kill your bottom line.** Mattress, furniture, and Persian carpet retailers seem to discount 360 days a year, and the only way to understand their logic is to assume their discounted prices are really their intended price, and they only expect accidental sales on the 5 days they *aren't* discounting. If you're seen as a constant discounter, your customers will assume that you're willing to discount even more, and they'll always expect a bargain. And on the days you're not discounting they'll stay away.

  Sometimes discounts are warranted, such as when you have too much inventory, or when an unexpected situation at the end of the year knocks out your numbers. Discounting *can* produce an increase in sales – which is good if your primary goal is to push goods and services (and maybe increase revenue) – *but it also plays havoc with your bottom line.*

  Discounting can be particularly bad if your primary goal is to increase profitability, but you're mistakenly trying to do so by simply increasing revenue. (You can see this effect by running *what-if* numbers on your Cash Flow/Budget spreadsheet, plugging in discount pricing and then seeing how it affects your Net Profit. It's very possible that a mere 10% discount requires you to sell 50% more goods or services to achieve the same level of profitability.)

  A better gambit is to add *value* to your base product/service, holding your prices at the normal level. The benefit is that you can give away something to your customers without lowering your profitability, and your customer still feels they gained something for free – which can also be a great factor in that customer returning in future.

In summary, once you settle into the sweet spot of your pricing strategy, try to be as firm and strong with it as you can. The end result will be increased confidence in your ability to create and maintain a viable and profitable business.

Example. A situation in this pricing category arose in the early days of my software education company. I frequently ran into an acquaintance who taught similar classes to mine at one of my repeat customers. One day over coffee I asked her if she was willing to tell me her teaching rate. I was astonished that it was *twice* what mine was. In thinking it over, my first reaction was that I'd be shown the door if I tried that price level. Her response? She confided that she'd rather work half as much and get paid twice as much for essentially the same work we were doing. Hmmm, a novel idea and it made sense. It made me think long and hard about the viability of it, but in the end I let it pass as a bad business model. Within a year, I never again saw her around that customer site, and I heard through the grapevine she had folded her business. It forced me to double-down on the idea that finding the right price point is critical to business success ... that building the business is always better than shrinking it or letting it stagnate.

Conserving cash

Managing cash flow is one of the most important – if not _the_ most important – tasks a new business owner must worry about. This is doubly important in a company's early days, when selling products and services is just getting off the ground and the bank account is very low – particularly if the company is poorly capitalized from the start. It's equally true, though, for well-capitalized companies, especially those new owners feeling flush with seemingly lots of cash in the bank, who suddenly begin spending lavishly, in the mistaken belief there will always be plenty of cash.

Stories abound, particularly in go-go start-up days before the dot-com crash, of young companies that leased expensive office space and furniture that drained the bank account, or who doled out lavish employee perks that are unaffordable over the long haul. You might have the naïve perspective that you can't attract and keep qualified employees unless you entice them with expensive perks, but before you head down this path, it's imperative to first have enough money in the bank _for the long haul_. One thing is certain: if the perks prove too costly, you'll have lots more trouble eliminating them later (just think about how successful you'd be in _lowering_ someone's salary).

Instead, from the first day you open for business, your focus should be on conservative spending habits, watching every dollar that goes _out_ the door – and just as importantly, watching every dollar that comes _in_ the door. It's every new business owner's dream that customers will knock down the door the minute word gets out about your products or services, but the reality is almost always very different.

All of this begins with the Cash Flow/Budget, which will be discussed at length in the next chapter. The key element of it is to know if you have sufficient cash in the bank to meet current needs, and just as importantly, to know if that cash will tide you through bumpy times, such as seasonal fluctuations, or times when a big expense outlay is projected. The big problem for almost every new entrepreneur is _over_-projecting sales and _under_-projecting expenses. That can lead to thinking your cash cushion is good, and tempting you to spend more.

To stay on budget, another important task is knowing how to get paid for services you've provided or products you've sold – including how to price your services and products, how to ensure that potential customers understand payment is expected for those services and products, when that payment is expected, and how you'll know that you've been paid – and paid on time – for each of the services or products sold. If you don't have a handle on these tasks, not only will your profitability suffer, but it can drive you out of business.

Agree on the work and price up front

There shouldn't be any surprises in a business transaction – at least not between you and the customer – on scope of work or product, or what the customer is expected to pay. If there are, you haven't done your job right, and you potentially face problems.

- Pricing shouldn't be a factor if your business is online or cash-based, where the customer always pays up front. Assuming you make it a policy not to ship any product or perform any service unless/until full payment has been received, you'll be paid before any product goes out the door. This has two benefits for you: (1) there's no *float* time on your product/service revenue, and (2) except for a bad debt possibility (customer stops payment on a check or credit card, or a check bounces), you know you're getting paid.

- If you're asked to bid for the services or product purchase, make sure you fully explain the pricing issues, exactly what the scope of service or product will be, and lay out payment terms (payment on receipt, 30-day, or a discount for paying early). Include how cost overruns might be handled (if applicable), how scope of work changes will be handled, and how product returns or service disputes are to be handled.

- If your work and pricing is laid out in a verbal, face-to-face meeting, make sure that you document the exact details of everything discussed, adding any that weren't discussed (identifying them as such), and send it to the potential customer – *with an acknowledgment signature block at the end and a requirement to return it before work begins or product is shipped.*

- If appropriate, insist on an upfront deposit – maybe 50% of the final cost. That way, both parties have a clear interest in seeing the transaction through to the end, and there's an incentive for timely completion. Similarly, if the customer offers to pay up front, by all means take it – it gets you paid earlier, and it eliminates the risk that you won't get paid.

- If your quoted price is an estimate, or if the price is based on *time and materials*, make it very clear up front what the limits are and what is expected if a limit is reached. That way, both you and the customer can understand the boundaries you're working within.

How will you accept payment?

Cash is always nice: it's immediately available in your company checking account when deposited, it doesn't carry any costs associated with it, and once received it cannot be stopped (like a check or credit card can). A lot of people don't carry cash like they used to, and you can lose sales if your customer doesn't have cash on hand when they're looking to make a purchase.

There are lots of other ways besides cash to accept payment, including credit card (VISA, MasterCard, American Express, Discover), debit cards, PayPal, Google Wallet, Apple Pay, Samsung Pay, barter, gift cards, and who knows how many other ways.[102]

If you plan to accept payment forms other than cash, consider this:

- Setting up other forms of payment takes time, so make your decision early and give yourself time for this task before opening your doors for business. Run some tests so that you know how the whole process works – it doesn't cost much to charge a few of your services/products on your own card (or whatever), and that way you hopefully won't seem like a total novice on your first real transaction.

- If you're going to accept credit cards, you must have a merchant account that allows you to accept credit cards for payment of services/products. It's imperative that you learn how it

---

[102] There's a blog on many aspects of non-cash payments, at http://www.cardfellow.com/blog/

works, what a customer charge costs you, and how/when you will get paid. With a merchant account, you'll need to enter into an agreement with either a member bank that has a processing relationship with, let's say, VISA and/or MasterCard, or with an authorized agent of the member bank.

At the end of each business day, you send all of your credit cards charges to the merchant bank for processing and settlement, and two days later you receive the funds in your merchant account, either withholding the processing fee or letting it accumulate to an overall payment that you make at the end of the month.

What's the typical processing fee you'll pay? It depends. If you are swiping a credit card in a face-to-face transaction (called a *card-present* transaction), the average fee will be roughly 2% of the total charge amount; if it's a *card-not-present* transaction (such as online or over the phone), plan for upwards of 2.5% of the charge amount (due to the higher risk of fraud). Many factors determine the exact fee(s), and the details are beyond the scope of this book. Gather as much information as you can from online sources before contacting any credit card processors – and that way you'll know better how to negotiate.[103] These charges will add up, so make sure you factor them into your Cash Flow/Budget spreadsheet.

An interesting internet site is CardFellow,[104] which provides "a comparison shopping engine for merchant accounts". Once you enter your new business information, it's submitted to several merchant processors, who then bid to win your business to process your credit card charges. After evaluating their bids, you pick the processor that sounds best for you. It doesn't cost anything, and CardFellow gets its fee from the card processor you select. There's a review of CardFellow in a newsletter called The Merchant Maverick that you'd be wise to look at before signing up with them, as it explains a bit more about how it works, and some good info on whether you should use them, or go it alone on signing up a merchant.[105]

- Do you plan to accept payments from your website? If so, the two most popular methods are by credit card or PayPal. For credit cards, you'll need to set up a *payment gateway*, which is similar to the credit card machine at a retail store, as it captures the credit card info, encrypts it, transmits it to the card processor you've selected, then returns an approval or decline response to you.

To accept PayPal,[106] you'll need to build the necessary online store (or use a third-party storefront) that manages the customer's *shopping cart* and *checkout* processes. You then set up PayPal as your payment processor by linking a PayPal business account to your site (which you do through PayPal). When your customer touches the PayPal button on your

---

[103] PS blog, *How To Set Up A Merchant Account*, PaySimple, September 7, 2011, https://paysimple.com/blog/how-to-set-up-a-merchant-account/.

[104] www.cardfellow.com

[105] http://www.merchantmaverick.com/reviews/cardfellow-review/#comments

[106] https://www.paypal.com/cgi-bin/webscr?cmd=xpt/bizui/IntegrationHub-outside . This site takes you through the entire process of setting up your online storefront, taking payments, and getting paid through Paypal.

site, it transfers the customer to the PayPal site to take the payment. When payment is complete, you then (most likely) return the customer to your site to continue browsing. In your cost analysis, don't forget that PayPal also charges a processing fee for its service, typically between 2–3% of each transaction amount (the percentage is a sliding scale, based on your monthly volume), plus you'll pay a monthly merchant fee of $30. If you're using PayPal exclusively as your payment option, you don't need a separate merchant account with a credit card processor, even if the customer is using a credit card through their PayPal account.

- Do you plan to accept payments from your mobile phone or tablet? Using handy gizmos such as the Square,[107] or the Intuit QuickBooks mobile credit card scanner,[108] you can easily accept credit cards wherever you're selling – at an airport kiosk, at a tradeshow, farmer's market, arts and crafts fairs, mobile food trucks – just about anywhere you might find yourself peddling your products and services.

- International payments. If your products or services are sold over the internet, decide whether you'll accept international orders and payments, and if so, how will you handle those payments and how will you deliver the service or products? Obviously, the rest of the world doesn't use the U.S. dollar, and while many parts of the world use the same credit cards that we have, your merchant account might not be set up to receive payment in another currency, and your site might have to allow for pricing in other world currencies. If you include shipping and handling in your pricing (which you probably shouldn't), costs can quickly get out of hand for international shipping.

- Educate yourself on credit card fraud – how to spot it and how to avoid it. VISA has an internet page[109] that provides a wealth of information on these topics. You should use this, along with other online documentation, to create your own business-specific rules that every employee must adhere to ... and then follow up to make certain they do.

Managing your accounts receivable

Accounts receivable (usually shortened to just *receivables*, or even better, AR) refers to the dollar amount owed to you on invoices sent to your customers.

Since each receivable dollar is owed as a result of a product or service you've already provided to a customer, accounts receivable is a legally enforceable claim for payment by those customers to you (and if for some reason an invoice isn't legally enforceable, it isn't proper to include it in your AR total).

Because it's legally enforceable, the current receivable amount is added to the Current Assets side of your Balance Sheet *as if the money is already in the bank*.[110] From the bank's point of view

---

[107] https://squareup.com/
[108] http://quickbooks.intuit.com/payments/mobile-credit-card-processing/
[109] *Fraud Prevention*, VISA, https://usa.visa.com/support/small-business/fraud-protection.html?ep=v_sym_cisp
[110] Interestingly, your accounts receivable do not show up on your monthly (or whatever period) Income Statement (also known as a Profit and Loss Statement), because it is a revenue *obligation* that is owed to you, and not yet actually in your bank (but it *is* shown on your Balance Sheet. The *revenue* you receive

(and from any investor's perspective looking at your financial statements), *out-of-the-ordinary* movements in your AR balances provide indications of your company's financial health – namely, whether you can pay your bills and pay your employees (including you) *in the near term*.

Just as importantly, your AR balance is a number you should jot down on your wrist every morning, and it will soon become a critical indicator to you of how your business is doing. You should look into variances in AR, and find out why it is occurring. Too high and it can mean you aren't collecting outstanding invoices – or it can mean you're doing better this month than last month. Too low and it could be due to slipping sales – or it could be that one or more customers paid earlier than expected. One way or another, you need to be familiar enough with your typical AR number that it gives you an instant-read of how you're doing – *at that particular moment*.

A business that operates on a cash sale basis doesn't have (or shouldn't have) an accounts receivable balance, because you're getting paid at the time you provide the product or service. Similar to AR, though, knowing your total receipts for the day is the same type of indicator.

Comparing each month-end AR amount to the same period a year ago can be a good indication of how much your business is growing (or shrinking). Comparing it quarter-by-quarter can give you good seasonal indications.

AR credit terms. If your business sends out an invoice with the expectation of receiving payment, the time period between when you send the invoice and when you receive payment is the *term* (otherwise known as *credit term*). It essentially establishes an agreement for the date on which you fully expect to be paid. In a more basic sense, your AR balance represents the amount of money that you've *loaned* to your customers, interest-free, provided they pay by the end of your stated term. The term is typically Net 30 Days, which means you've given the customer 30 days from the invoice date to pay, or Payable on Receipt, which means the customer owes you the money as soon as you've received the invoice and you expect them to pay immediately.

As mentioned above, *out-of-the-ordinary* movements (either up or down) in your AR balance from one period to the next (or in a corresponding period from year to year – let's say January last year compared to January this year) provide a quick indication of your company's financial health – and it's something you should monitor very closely (in my own business, I knew it every week).

Consider this simple example to illustrate the point. If your typical (or average) end of month AR balance is, let's say $25,000, and your net payment terms are 30 days, that means you should have $25,000 coming in the door during the next month. If your expenses (also known as accounts payable (or AP), including business space rent, utilities, salaries, and Cost of Sales (i.e., what it cost to produce the goods you sold, which will be discussed next chapter) that have to be paid within the next month are $20,000, you can feel somewhat comfortable that you're operating *in the black* and will show a slight profit of $5,000 for the month. But don't feel so good about this that you decide to splurge by buying that new conference table you've been wanting for $5,000. As sure as anything, one or more of those customers with an outstanding invoice in your AR list will end up paying late.

---

each month as a result of accounts receivable being actually received does show up on your Income Statement, but not on your Balance Sheet.

To continue the example, let's assume that at the end of next month your receivables balance falls to $15,000 and your expenses remain the same. You're now facing a $5,000 shortfall (loss) for the next month, and that $5,000 profit cushion from the previous month will come in very handy (assuming you didn't spend it on the new conference table).

Obviously, this is a very simplistic example, but it should be instructive as a basic foundation to begin building financial management skills for your new company. If you're going to make it as a small business entrepreneur, you need to know your AR like the back of your hand, along with many other financial metrics that are part of your accounting system.

In my company, and for the entire time I owned it, asking my accountant about AR was easily my most frequent question, usually on a weekly basis. You can fiddle your company's financials in many ways (assuming it's in a legal way, of course) – by stretching out your accounts payable, tightening your belt to reduce expenses, dipping into your company savings or bank line of credit – but there's little you can do if your accounts receivable come up short ... *except doing everything you can to increase your sales revenue – and fast*!

Collecting accounts receivable

It isn't enough to just _know_ your accounts receivable balance at any point in time. _Managing_ your AR means implementing procedures to ensure you're paid on time and within the terms specified in your invoices (or stated in your contracts). If your invoice terms are net 30 days from date of invoice, then you need to do everything you can to ensure this is followed. Many customers know that your invoice to them is a form of credit, and also knowing they are a customer you really want to keep, they'll often take advantage of it to stretch out their payments to you for as long as they feel they can get away with it.

Managing your AR also involves knowing the process and time flow of adding new revenue to your AR. If your sales cycle is typically three months long, by the time you see a dip in your AR number you'd better already have efforts going to build up that AR balance. That means you also need to know your sales *pipeline*, and where every potential customer is in that pipeline. This is where you need to be working very closely with your sales operation, possibly making sales calls yourself, and *working* the customers to bring them to a decision – _and a closing of the sale_.

At my company (which was a very small business), we had an extraordinarily long sales pipeline – sometimes stretching into 1–2 _years_ – but the average was probably six months. It usually involved a dozen or more onsite visits by the sales person assigned to the territory, and it wasn't uncommon at all for me to fly to the customer site to make one or more technical presentations to educate the customer on why they needed our software. It also involved lots of discount negotiation, not to mention *sweetening the pot* deals demanded by the customers, requiring careful customer analysis and strategy going into the potential sale. It was _always_ like pulling teeth, but everyone knew it was the nature of the beast. For me, it created headaches of a monumental magnitude to manage the growth of our AR.

On the other end of a deal, after a sale was closed and we had the value of a new invoice to add to our AR, then we had to constantly deal with the issue of getting paid. _All_ of our customers were large corporations and government agencies, and surprisingly, our government customers were the best behaved, paying on time and within the terms of the invoice. I was surprised to learn that most have strict policies requiring them to pay their bills on time, and are specifically prohibited from abusing small vendors. Banks and other companies in the financial sector were the worst – obviously they know the time value of money, and they often played the game to the hilt.

We tried everything, including stern warnings of late payment penalties, which the customers often ignored, paying us only the original amount even though they might be *very* late in paying. We tried discounts for early paying – and wouldn't you know it, the worst offenders took the discounts (subtracted the discount from the amount owed to us) *and still paid 10, 15, 20 or more days late*!

In the end, the only thing that consistently worked was to have our AR accounting clerk carve out time on a regular basis to call every customer who had reached their invoice payment term but hadn't sent us a payment. I always felt empathy for the clerk, as it was a job I certainly wouldn't have liked doing, but there was just no way around it.

Here's some good advice. If you have payment deadbeats, don't let them off the hook. If your work was honest and fair, and the price to be paid was agreed upon, the customer has a *legal* obligation to pay you. If they don't, you have options. At the very least, continue your collection efforts. By all means, don't accept further business from them until/unless they pay all amounts due. And if they still don't pay, give them one final warning, and then don't be afraid to report them to the credit agencies (Experian, TransUnion, and Equifax) or the Better Business Bureau.

Face-to-face AR situations. Here, the problem is what I call *asking for the money*, and it's due to the timidity factor of many first-time entrepreneurs. Most entrepreneurs have a really strong desire to start a business and work for themselves, but once they get into it, they find they're shy about asking to be paid for their services or products. Don't be. If you've provided a service or product, expect to be paid for it, and paid in a timely fashion. Also, customers *expect* you to be paid, and most of the time they'll ask you what they owe you. If you owned a restaurant and your wait staff was uncomfortable handing the bill to the customer, you'd be pretty irritated – but for some reason, the business owner often feels personally uncomfortable doing it.

Growing up, I worked 30+ hours a week in my parents' hamburger joint all through junior and senior high school. My mother ran the place, mostly working the kitchen, while I waited tables, delivered food, wrote out the customer's tickets, and took the money. I can't remember ever being taught by my mother how to ask for the money – it just seemed second nature to me. Customers paying us was just part of everything we did, but in a detached sort of way – where *asking* was not a verbal exchange with the customer, but rather, the customer saw the prices on the menu before ordering, and later I'd casually lay a coffee or lunch tab down on the table as I walked by to another table, then collected the money when the customer coughed it up ... or simply responded with an amount when the customer asked, "How much do I owe you?" I'm sure if I was forced to actually walk up to a customer and say, "Hey, buddy, it's time to pay up", I'd have considerably more hesitancy. But making it more of an arm's-length transaction is a less direct and in-your-face way of asking for the money. That's where the contract ahead of time and invoice afterwards idea makes the task easier. But you still have to be comfortable with it.

Example #1. One time I had a sizable landscape project going on at my home, with a very talented young landscape designer who was on her first fairly large project. Throughout the project she was getting paid a monthly retainer to design all aspects of the project, selecting and purchasing the planting material, directing where everything should be planted by the landscape contractor, laying out the design of pathways, and spec'ing the pathway material. If her invoice included payment for material she had purchased, she had no problem getting her invoice to me as soon as the plants and material were installed – because she had fronted the material purchase on her company's credit card and wanted to make certain it was paid on time. Yet, if her invoice was just for her own labor and design work, I often had to remind her to send me a bill. She always apologized for those invoices, and I could tell she was flustered if she had to personally hand them to me. The project ran long enough that an increase in her hourly design fee charge was reasonable, yet she hesitated to raise her hourly rate until I almost forced it upon her – for some reason she just didn't feel that her own work was worth more money – and that made her uncomfortable *asking for the money*.

Each monthly invoice she sent specified her payment terms as "Due on Receipt" – which means our *agreement* is that a payment is due the day I receive her invoice. She obviously hoped a return check would immediately go into the mail, but sometimes her invoice would get stuck in a pile of papers or somehow forgotten, and three weeks later she might send me a notice that it hadn't been paid. Sometimes a payment wouldn't be made, and 2–3 months would go by before she'd do an audit of her receivables and notice that it hadn't been paid. Or, maybe she was afraid to be a pain in the butt and would simply hope that I'd finally pay up (which I typically wouldn't, because the invoice was already lost in my clutter).

But the other truth of the matter is, this is her business, and payment for these invoices are paying her bills and putting her kids through college. It was also my fault for not being more conscientious in paying my bills. Several times I'd mention *tightening her receivables* as an important aspect of being a small business owner, and that she really should have a tickler system set up to send out a reminder if an invoice hasn't been paid on time. Many invoicing applications and online invoice services have reminders built into them.

Example #2. Our landscape designer also oversaw the landscape company that was actually doing the heavy lifting on our project. This company was owned by an ex-Marine, but he was very mild mannered, self-assured, and easy to work with. His crew was anywhere from 1–3 people, plus rental equipment – trench diggers, small backhoes, and the like. He had to pay the equipment rental on the spot, and he paid his workers at the end of each work week. So he made it a point to stop by each of his projects at some point every Friday, supposedly to check on how things were going. He also sent an invoice via e-mail a day before the visit, mentioning that he'd be by on Friday and would like to pick up the check while he was there. When he showed up, he also had a printed invoice that he'd hand to me. If I wasn't going to be home, he had no qualms about asking that I leave the check under a mat at the front door.

It was very obvious he expected to have a check in his hand before he departed. Both of us knew the situation – that he was a very small business owner, had employees to pay and equipment rental companies to pay. There was nothing personal about it ... he just needed to get paid, on time, and the full amount. I've never known anyone who understood *ask for the money* better than he did.

Example #3. And then there's the problem of *just getting around to it*, or maybe too tired at the end of a long day. A friend has a 1-person heavy equipment repair business – a small business that's been his livelihood for several years. Because of the recent nasty economy, virtually all of his business has been on projects in Alaska, funded by the Great Recession stimulus money – and since his home is in Seattle, he spends months at a time away from home. While on the job, he's working long days, but what else could you do in Dutch Harbor, halfway out the Aleutian Chain from the Alaskan mainland? He has good internet access in his apartment provided by the construction company he contracts to – but surprisingly, he doesn't use it to invoice his customer, and instead, waits until he returns home, then catches up *2–4 months' worth of invoices* at one time. Who knows why he isn't asking for the money much earlier – effectively losing the use of that hard-earned income for himself all that time, and giving his customers free use of the money.

Example #4. In my own small software company – in the early startup days when it was a software education company and I was its only employee, which meant I was chief instructor, lead course developer, office manager, shipping and handling clerk – and of course, bookkeeper. I had a policy of invoicing the day after each course ended, and I clearly stated payment terms of "Net 30 Days" on every invoice. My customers were mostly large Fortune 500-type companies, or government IT centers. Most were quite good at paying, especially at the city, state, and federal government agencies – as they all have small business *pay on time* requirements. One large city government agency in California, though, seemed to fall off a cliff on paying my invoice, even though I sent follow-up invoices, letters asking for payment, and I made direct phone calls to their accounts payable office. They had the gall to simply ignore me – and for no reason. My invoice wasn't a budget-breaker ... probably no larger than $4,000, and it wasn't in dispute for any reason – and there had been no problems with the course I taught. Someone in their accounts payable department just couldn't get off their duff to write me a check. Finally, three months after the class, I was on another teaching assignment to a customer in a next-door city, and on the morning of my last day of class I called the IT manager who had contracted for the class, telling her that I was in the area, and at 3PM I'd be parked outside their data center, expecting someone there to personally walk out to the street to hand me a check for my invoice. Before I drove there I phoned again to remind them of my visit – and if a check wasn't ready for me I was coming inside to speak directly with someone from their accounting office. On arrival, an AP clerk was waiting at the curb and sheepishly handed me an envelope with the check inside. I have a hunch we were both glad to see each other's back.

Example #5. My company enlisted the aid of a small, privately-owned, 3–4 person distributorship who sold our software products throughout their assigned territory. Our distributorship agreement stipulated that a 50% royalty of each software sale was to be paid to us within 30 days of receipt of payment by the distributor's customer (effectively giving the distributor a 60-day payment term, which allowed for the usual late payments by his own customers). Well, two, three, four months would often go by after a software sale (they were reporting all sales to us on a monthly basis), yet we wouldn't receive a royalty payment. We'd ding the owner of the distributorship, we'd cajole him, we'd threaten him, we'd tack on late payment penalties – but to no avail. In a face-to-face visit to get the situation straightened out, he blurted out that I was being unfair to him ... that he had a primary obligation to first pay his employees and his business expenses, and secondarily, to pay the royalty to my company *after all else was paid*. In other words, he was treating it more like a partnership situation, and not a contractual obligation, even though my company was getting no partnership benefits – such as a share of the end of year profits – or even interest on the late payments. He never did understand the difference. We got a lot of business from that part of the world – business that overall was beneficial to my company – and we just had to accept the fact that getting payment from this distributor would be a continual chore.

Asking for the money isn't always a pleasant task, but getting paid for your work or products is the lifeblood of your company, and it's the reason you're in business. If it isn't, well, maybe you're really running a hobby.

Managing accounts payable

On the Current Liabilities side of your financial statement is the money *you owe* for invoices sent to you for goods and services you've received – collectively called your accounts payable, or AP for short. Just like your invoices to your customers, these represent legal debt obligations you are liable for, and are expected to be paid within the invoice or contract terms that obligated you to them. (We'll see what Current Liabilities on your financial statements are all about in Chapter 5.)

Just like your AR balance, at any given time you should have a pretty good idea about your total AP number. Simply put, it helps you know whether you're living within your means relative to your revenue intake. It's more serious than that, though, as once you've created the obligation for a payable, there's no backing out of it. Cutting back on your *future* expenses won't make the current obligation go away – although, it can help you pay it off late if you have lower payables next month and the money in the bank can cover it.

AP and employee payroll are often the two *between a rock and a hard place* situations that you face. Both are obligations, and if you can't fulfill them, they can seriously damage your business, your business reputation, and your chances of future success. Obviously, the best way out is to generate enough revenue to cover both obligations, plus a profit – and going into debt to resolve it might be a short-term solution, but it can be a slippery slope.

Two ticklish problems with your AP:

- AP often lags behind your revenue (as represented by AR). Your business might be such that you have to purchase raw materials (which generates an AP invoice) early in a production cycle, but you won't see the revenue benefit of these materials until the product cycle is completed, sold, invoiced, and the customer pays. Payroll and other normal expenses for production staff most likely precede the revenue generated from the work. You might have sales staff who are creating expenses in the sales cycle, such as travel expenses and other costs.
- AP includes fixed and recurring expenses that have no correlation to generating revenue. Most of your overhead expenses (facilities, utilities, equipment leases and purchase pay-downs, back-office employee costs) will continue through a slow sales period.

Your job is to use a Cash Flow/Budget spreadsheet to manage these lumps, ensuring that you have sufficient cash-on-hand to cover the slow periods. This is also the main reason for getting a *working capital* line of credit from your bank, which we'll explore in a bit.

The mark of a good accounting staff – your bookkeeper in the early days, and your staff accountant as you grow – is how well that person manages your AP. Just like your customers "manage" their invoice payments to you based on their cash flow needs, your bookkeeper needs to do the same with your AP invoices. Certain payments can't be late, such as payroll and employment tax submissions, and there's probably no reason to pay some of the others until they're actually due. Paying early, though, can have an upside – particularly if the vendor offers early payment discounts. Assuming you actually have cash in the bank to cover it, paying an invoice in 10 days when offered a 2% discount makes a lot of sense (it's usually shown on an invoice as "2/10 net 30"), since cash that's parked in a company checking account is earning almost nil interest for you. If paying early results in a draw against a line of credit that's costing you over 2%, that's another story – as there's no sense paying a higher interest rate on the money in order to pay off a supplier who is asking for 30 day net terms for regular (100%) payment. So don't just set up a single rule for all AP management – and make certain your bookkeeping staff understands what's best for your company.

Stretching AP invoices <u>beyond their due date</u> in cash-tight situations can have negative effects, eroding your supplier goodwill that can result in slower delivery time, with less willingness to fix defects, and more onerous payment terms. Sometimes you have to, simply because you don't have the cash in the bank, or your operating line of credit is fully tapped out. In virtually all situations like that, as the small business owner you should be made aware of it, as it's a serious indication that you need to consider if your business strategies are set correctly.

Managing inventory

This topic seems like it should be a no-brainer – you keep enough inventory on hand to cover what you think you'll sell. The *managing* concept behind it also seems simple –"generate the maximum profit from the least amount of inventory investment, without intruding upon customer satisfaction levels".[111]

Very soon you're bound to discover that your business cycle isn't that straightforward. An unexpected drop in sales can leave you with far too much inventory – which translates to business assets that are tied up and can't quickly and profitably be converted to cash. Or, the seemingly good side of the equation, where many product orders cannot be filled because you can't increase your inventory quickly enough. Managing your inventory can be like pushing a rope uphill. One month it could be the former situation, and you could easily run the company out of cash, and in the worst case, lead you towards bankruptcy. The next month could be the latter, causing you to not only lose immediate business, but also to risk losing customers – permanently – to a competitor.

It's imperative that you develop an inventory management system for your business – one that works for your situation. After implementing it, you need to closely monitor it and learn from it.

The system doesn't have to be complicated or expensive, and you probably don't have to spend a lot of money on a template or software (at least not at the outset when you're small and don't have a lot of money in the bank). Do an internet search on "inventory management template" (or "inventory management software"), and you'll find dozens of sites that will be happy to take your money. Instead, if you're at all handy with Excel, create a spreadsheet that's unique and specific

---

[111] Steven Bragg, *What is inventory control?*, AccountingTools web site,
http://www.accountingtools.com/questions-and-answers/what-is-inventory-control.html

to your business – and it will probably work much better for the vagaries of your business than purchasing something off the shelf.

Here are some ideas for getting your inventory management under control:

- First, create your Cash Flow/Budget projections for each product. You might be wildly inaccurate in your sales numbers the first few months, but since this report should track your actual sales against projections, at the end of every month you can tweak the projections for upcoming months – and they should soon become more accurate.

- Expand your Cash Flow/Budget worksheet for a full year. Later, you'll then have year-over-year comparisons, and you can readily see sales patterns that develop for your particular business, including relevant seasonal variations, such as end-of-year buying sprees, or better sales in the spring than in the fall.

- Since our worksheet is based on full-month projections, you might also develop a separate worksheet to track sales numbers throughout the month, helping illustrate if you have beginning or end of month spikes.

- Track promotions, keeping detailed records of ones that bring in sales, by product, and note how pricing and discounts affect sales. Make certain you create a sales recordkeeping database, allowing you to resurrect the numbers in future. Notes in a simple spreadsheet or workbook are OK, but even better, look to see how much of this recordkeeping can be done within your accounting system software (such as QuickBooks or Peachtree, and this could be a factor in which accounting system you choose for your business).

- Make sure your inventory counts are as accurate as possible, particularly for your popular and fast-selling products. Haphazard inventory accounting can lead to a shortage of products just when you've received a critical order, and it can make or break your financial numbers. *You're going to need these inventory counts for your financial statements and tax calculations.*

- Determine the best time to reorder raw materials or finished products that you sell. If you focus too much on keeping inventory low, thereby keeping better control of your money, you could run short in the middle of a manufacturing process or when trying to fill an order, costing you more money than you saved. Again, you can use your Cash Flow/Budget worksheet to forecast quantities you'll need on hand, helping you to fine-tune your reorder levels.

- Plan for bottlenecks, knowing they're going to happen, rather than simply hoping they won't. When you least expect it, you'll discover a reorder is now on backorder because a supplier can't deliver on time, or a batch of raw materials will prove defective in the middle of a manufacturing process. If you can, create inventory buffers where the most likely bottlenecks will occur.

- Just-in-time (JIT) delivery of inventory is all the rage in many big businesses (such as auto manufacturers), having learned about this many years ago from the Japanese.[112] As noted by Investopedia, this method "requires that producers are able to accurately forecast demand" – which is a tall order for a brand new small business to do. Besides, large companies that rely on this have shifted the burden of having raw materials or finished parts or products on their doorstep right when they need it – and they typically do it by

---

[112] *Just In Time – JIT*, Investopedia, http://www.investopedia.com/terms/j/jit.asp

squeezing their suppliers to the nth degree. It's not likely you'll have this luxury or buying power, so the burden of timing remains with you.

- Prioritize your inventory, paying special attention to inventory of the most important products. Writing in Entrepreneur online magazine,[113] Lisa Girard theorizes that 80% of your sales demand will be generated by 20% of your products, so spending more time and effort on inventory control for these "A-list" products is a better use of your resources.

- If your up-and-coming business is heavily oriented towards distribution-intensive product sales, you might need to consider hiring a dedicated inventory control specialist, sooner rather than later. Someone trained to do this can develop tons of data for you that might otherwise keep you running ragged, with inventory costs and timing out of control. This person can monitor lead times for optimum ordering of material and products, can watch pricing and quantity discounts so that you get the best possible deals, can take advantage of optimum shipping costs, and can oversee the process for moving inventory out the door after sales are complete.

- When the time is right for commercial software to help manage your inventory, you'll find dozens of products on the market.[114] They can either be a boon or bust for your business, saving you huge amounts of money and frustration if you pick the right one, or creating huge nightmares and headaches if the wrong one. Some of the software simply counts widgets on the shelf, cost very little, and can even run on your smartphone or tablet; others – known as Enterprise Resource Planning (or ERP) – oversee and integrate information for broad aspects of your business (such as product planning, manufacturing, sales and marketing, inventory management, shipping and payments), and can cost tens of thousands of dollars.

  Beware of services that help you find the best software solution, as they are often paid by the company whose software you choose. Sometimes these advisors get paid more for pointing you towards one solution over another, even if it isn't the best for you – sort of like product distributors in your grocery store who pay for extra shelf space at eye level, inducing you to purchase their products over the ones that are on the bottom shelf.

Operating line of credit: when you need it and how to use it

Unless you break into the business world with lots of personal savings, a wad of family money, or a really hot product or service that consistently generates revenue, chances are high you'll encounter lean financial times at some point or another. Other times, you'll simply need more money than you have on hand. This need hits virtually every type of business, and every business could have dozens of reasons why it happens.

You could start a retail business with a storefront in the optimum location, only to find that a winter snowstorm six months after you open keeps customers away ... or the city decides to tear up the street in front of you and the hassle of reaching your business shoos customers away. Or, you have an online business and the Black Friday customers you're expecting decide to visit your

---

[113] Lisa Girard, based on our SB101 Brewery operation., Entrepreneur, November 2, 2011, http://www.entrepreneur.com/article/220631

[114] *Top Inventory Management Software Products*, Capterra, http://www.capterra.com/inventory-management-software/

competitor due to an unexpected better deal they're offering. Or, you have a large customer contract in the works, and for whatever reason the customer decides to put off the purchase for a while. Or, you've just sealed the biggest business deal you've ever had, and the customer stiffs you a few extra weeks on payment.

I'm here to warn you – it's going to happen, and you need to be prepared for it. The obvious way is to have plenty of cash reserves. Yup, that's like telling Americans to have emergency savings equal to six months' salary. According to a report in USA Today: "more than a quarter of Americans have *no* emergency savings ... of those who do have savings, 67% have less than six months' worth of expenses ... and those with at least three months [of savings] declined from 45% in 2013 to 40% [in 2014]".[115] Why would we think that typical small business owners would operate their businesses any differently than they operate their personal cash reserves? After all, they're trying to grow the business, they're trying to make enough money to pay the owner's salary, everything costs more than anticipated, customers don't buy or pay when they'd like them to ... and lots of other reasons. So, unless you have a rich patron who slips you lots of cash whenever you need it, odds are your business bank account is running leaner than it should be.

Even if you are sufficiently conservative, you may have perfectly valid business reasons for needing more cash than you have on hand. Maybe you have a one-time need to buy an expensive piece of equipment, or you want to buy a building to house your business. Or maybe you need to hire a new (and expensive) employee, but it will take some time to recoup the upfront costs.

What to do? The best solution is to establish a business line of credit (LOC) with your bank. It's called a working capital line of credit. *But a word of advice – do it before you really need it* (remember the Bob Hope adage about who the banks lend money to....).

The concept of a line of credit (LOC) is easy enough to understand – and it's often like having a business credit card, but without the card. It's a pre-established loan approval, for a set maximum amount, and you *draw* against it with a simple phone or e-mail request to your business banker (or an advance could be activated by you with online banking). Interest is paid monthly on the outstanding balance, and you can usually choose when/if to pay down the principal loan amount.

There are two types of LOC – revolving and non-revolving. With a revolving (which is the kind you most likely want), you're able to make additional draws against whatever remains between the current balance and the maximum LOC amount; with a non-revolving line of credit, once you reach your approved loan limit, further draws against the LOC are not allowed, even if you've paid down some or all of the debt.

Three important aspects to keep in mind:

- The ability to get approval for an LOC will depend heavily on your relationship with your bank, and particularly, your business banker, so make sure you work that relationship to your best advantage

---

[115] Hadley Malcolm, *Americans still don't have enough savings*, USA Today online, June 23, 2014, http://www.usatoday.com/story/money/personalfinance/2014/06/23/americans-emergency-savings/11085869/.

- Once you have an outstanding balance on your LOC, the bank will keep a close eye on your ability to pay it back, through monthly financial statements and other documentation that you must submit.

- Determine ahead of time the valid LOC use types that the bank will allow. Typically, a working capital LOC is intended by the bank to cover short term cash shortfalls in your day-to-day business operations. It's not intended to finance growth projects for your business, or to fund purchase of capital equipment (there are other loans for those purposes).

- Determine what the pay down requirements are on the LOC. Many working capital LOCs require complete pay off at least once a year. This ensures (to the bank) that you aren't using the loan for unauthorized spending (unauthorized by the terms of the loan).

Sometimes a bank other than your current business bank can be a source of a business LOC, but they typically require you to move all (or most) of your business banking to the new bank as a condition – so that (plus better terms) is a possible reason to shop around. Sometimes small community banks are more willing to provide an LOC to a new small business, whereas your large retail bank isn't, usually because the small banks they're trying to build business themselves. In recent years, many of these small community banks have been gobbled up by larger banks, and you can find yourself stuck with a bank you're not wild about (or one that's itself in financial straits).

Collateral. Most LOC approvals will require collateral (the loan is also known as a *secured loan*), unless the maximum amount of the LOC is so low ($5K–$20K, but sometimes more) that it's really an overdraft protection or considered a signature loan (called an *unsecured loan*).

Simply put, collateral is a form of security (assets) that you pledge to the loan, giving the lender the assurance that you have a second source of loan repayment if your business can't repay.

For a secured loan, the type of collateral will depend on your type of business and the assets that you own. If your business owns real estate or valuable equipment, the bank might consider it for collateral – but only up to a bank-determined percentage of your actual owned amount of the asset – and also, what they think of the *liquidity* of the asset if they end up owning it – i.e., how fast they could convert it to cash if they take possession of it.

If you're an invoice-driven business, the most common asset the bank will accept is your current receivables (your AR accounts), because AR is considered to be an asset that will soon be converted into cash and deposited in the bank granting the LOC. To put it plainly, if you were to default on your loan, the individual invoice payments within your AR ledger could be grabbed more easily (and quickly) than any other asset you might pledge.

Assets that aren't typically allowed as collateral include the business itself, autos, office equipment and software, and other rapidly depreciating, intangible, or difficult-to-convert-to-cash things. The bank is not allowed by law to accept money in a 401(k) plan or any other type of pension account. Your inventory might be accepted as collateral, but that opens a whole different can of worms – requiring you to maintain certain levels of inventory, which can add to your cash flow problems in maintaining inventory (which was created specifically to sell).

In my company's experience, even though we owned a half-dozen very profitable (and substantial) software products that we developed internally and actively marketed, they were not considered an assets that we could pledge – and these were the primary revenue generators for our company, collectively worth millions of dollars. It would take a very special bank – one that knows the software industry extremely well – to accept as collateral something they consider as intangible as a software product. I'm sure the same holds true for other products, even tangible ones like (jokingly) pet rocks. The last thing the bank wants to do in the event of a loan default is to run your business or sell these assets, and that's what they'd have to do if they ended up owning your products as a result of a default.

Piercing the corporate veil (a.k.a., personal pledge). Surprisingly (at least to me) was the bank's requirement to *pierce the corporate veil* (that's a commonly used term, and not one that I'm making up here[116]) as a condition for granting my company's working capital line of credit. One of the reasons people set up corporations (C-Corp or S-Corp – it doesn't matter which) or a limited liability company (an LLC) is to ... get ready for this ... *limit your liability*. But limiting your liability won't extend to your financial liability when you get a bank loan or many other types of financial transactions. If you have personal assets (a house, property, or other asset) that qualify as a pledged asset, the bank will almost certainly require those assets *to also be included in the collateral for your LOC*, and you'll be agreeing to that as part of the Terms and Conditions in your LOC agreement (read the terms and conditions carefully to ensure you fully understand this). The lending terms will typically refer to this as "a personal pledge", so watch carefully for it, and make sure you understand what's involved, and ask yourself, is the risk worth the personal assets that I'm pledging here? The simple fact is, if you want the money badly enough, the bank will feel no compunction in requiring you to forego that liability limitation in case you default on the loan. If that's part of the required terms, well, *that's just what you'll have to agree to if you want the money* – either that, or figure out how to pledge other corporate assets (if you have them) that the bank might want.

Receivables as collateral. Your best option for LOC collateral is your accounts receivable. In simple terms, receivables are all of your outstanding invoices to customers. The bank will be picky, though, about your receivables, accepting only *current* receivables (i.e., not past due by a bank-specified amount), and receivables that they feel are legally and reasonably collectible. They won't, for example, accept foreign receivables, as there is little reasonable recourse in law to collect foreign receivables that go bad. Also, the bank will only count a certain percentage of any given receivable towards collateral – for example, 85% – as they figure there's a cost to collect the receivable if it comes to that, and there's a risk that some percentage of receivables will go bad.

Once the bank accepts your receivables as collateral, they will require a monthly report of your *acceptable and current receivables*, listing date of invoice, due date, and other pertinent details of the associated invoices. You can bet your business banker will review this report very carefully (or the banker's butt will be on the line if something goes wrong), and will question you or your bookkeeper about any invoices in doubt.

---

[115] To learn more about the overall concept, go to the Wikipedia article on *Piercing the corporate veil*, at http://en.wikipedia.org/wiki/Piercing_the_corporate_veil.

Financial reports to the bank. Before having a working capital LOC, assuming you don't have outside investors, your monthly financial reports (Balance Sheet and Income Statement) have been entirely your business, in the sense that they are private and not required by anyone outside of your company. As soon as you have a working capital LOC, though, the bank will require a copy of both financial statements on a monthly basis.

Behind the scenes, the bank will run the numbers six ways to Sunday, correlating and tracking financial metrics that you've probably never heard of – all to find out what *they* think is the real financial situation with your company. They'll be calling you to question any number they don't understand, and this is when you'll really be glad you have a bookkeeper they can talk to (as that person should have the necessary numbers and explanations readily at hand).

In addition to the official financial reports, the bank will probably want some words of wisdom from you, the owner, on how you think the business is doing. This is where your ability to write – specifically, writing positive things about how your business is doing – will hopefully provide comfort and satisfaction to the banker that your business outlook is actually better than the financial statement numbers are indicating. I faced this bank requirement at least a dozen times, usually spending a full half-day at my computer banging out a 1-2 page report about the big software sales contracts we were chasing down to completion, the heroic efforts our Accounts Receivable clerk was doing in speeding up payments, and the fact that we didn't lose that big contract last month – it was just postponed for a bit. You certainly can't lie (at least, you can't lie and get away with it) in these missives, but you can definitely write in such a way that it puts the best possible spin on how your company is doing when the numbers aren't looking all that great. This is also where the good relationship with your banker comes in very handy.

Line of credit covenants. The odds are pretty good that your bank will also include special requirements, called *loan covenants*, in your LOC agreement terms and conditions. If they aren't in the agreement when you first take out the LOC, they could become a condition of renewing your LOC if the bank gets nervous about your company's financial stability.

Loan covenants are clauses that outline financial conditions your company must maintain throughout the loan period, giving the bank tighter protection (and not protecting you, the entrepreneur) in case the bank feels there's any chance you could default on your LOC. In more stark terms, loan covenants allow the bank to declare your company in default on the loan agreement, even if you are currently making (and are able to make) your monthly interest payments, simply because you're outside the covenant limits.

A wide range of covenants can be drafted into LOC terms and conditions, mostly based on the type of business you have, how you get paid by customers, how and when you recognize revenue, what your cash flow numbers tend to be, and where your company fits within standard metrics from the numbers in your financial statements (standard metrics by the bank's perspective, and you'll have a hard time finding out exactly what those metrics are).

This may sound like the bank is starting to gang up on you, looking for ways they can force you into default – and therefore, grab your pledged collateral assets – but that is almost certainly not the case. The simple fact is, banks are conservative and they don't like to lose money – and they like even less to be suddenly saddled with assets that are problematic for them. They don't want your equipment, because it would be a pain to convert it into cash; they don't want your house because then they'd have to evict you and sell it to pay off the note; they don't particularly want your receivables, because then they'd be responsible for collecting them in order to get their money. So what the bank is doing is exerting tighter control over you (and your company), giving them additional *advance warning* if it looks like you might be heading into financial trouble ... *but maybe you haven't yet figured it out*. As soon as you're outside of your covenants, you'll certainly be getting a phone call from your business banker to discuss the situation.

If your AR is collateral for your LOC, the most obvious covenant is making sure that your acceptable receivables can cover your current LOC balance on the day your financial statements are prepared and sent to the bank (AR is a line item in your Balance Ssheet) – and along with them you'll have to submit a detailed list of your specific receivables that are current and acceptable (no, you won't be able to just tell the bank, "yes, I have sufficient AR to cover as collateral".) If you typically have plenty of AR headroom as collateral, no problem, but it gets tricky if you've just had to draw a large advance on your LOC, at the same time that expected sales have been slow, or large numbers of customers have paid their invoices – all of which can make it difficult to have enough collateral. This situation can give you sweaty palms, and you definitely don't want to get caught out with cooking the books. This is where a solid morning's effort at writing up some words of wisdom to your banker, or scheduling a face-to-face meeting with your banker to explain your situation. Technically, your financial statements will show you're in default on your line of credit, and if you can't convince the bank to give you some breathing room, they are legally allowed to "call" your line of credit, starting the process to seize your collateral assets, and it could be a path towards forcing you into bankruptcy. That's a terrible situation to face if you're absolutely certain (in your mind) that the situation will correct itself in a few days (or whatever).

Drop-box receivable collection. If the bank begins to suspect that your receivables aren't as solid as you've led them to believe, or if the bank wonders whether you'd resort to paying creditors other than the bank in a financial crunch, they might require you to set up a *drop box* to collect receivables. This is nothing more than a special account within the bank that your receivables are directly mailed to and deposited, and you'd be instructed to list the bank's address as the place for customers to send invoice payments. When a receivable amount is deposited to the drop box, the bank turns the receivable over to you (transferring the money to your company account), or if they feel the need to, they can apply it to the LOC principal or overdue interest amount.

These days it might not be so bad to have a drop box set up for your receivables, as it could be viewed by your customers as just another location to pay you – provided they don't figure out that the reason you have it is because you're getting closer to default on your LOC. Nevertheless, it can be an embarrassing situation to be in, and very possibly damaging to your business, as it can send a clear signal to your customers (at least, that is, to the accounts payable people at your customers) that you're in some sort of financial difficulty.

SBA-guaranteed loans

In years past, the words bank loan, entrepreneur, and start-up in the same sentence would be a serious contradiction in terms (unless, of course, the reference also included the words *never, ever*). With the release of stimulus money in 2009 at the beginning of the Obama administration,[117] the Small Business Administration (SBA) received a whopping $375M in stimulus funds, opening the floodgates for a much-needed increase in SBA-backed bank loans for small business creation and expansion. For fiscal years 2011 and 2012, the SBA reported record years of bank loan guarantees (a bit over $30B total for the two years), followed in 2013 by a loan guarantee amount that set another record at $29B, and with a similar amount in 2014.[118] Fiscal year 2015 was another good one, with over $23B in loan guarantees.

According to a statement in October, 2013 from the Acting SBA Administrator, Jeanne Hulit, *"Under President Obama, SBA lending has reached record levels and we continue to get more capital into the hands of small business owners than ever before. Small businesses are the engine of our economy, and reaching our third highest year of SBA lending in FY 2013 demonstrates the strength and resiliency of America's 28 million small businesses as they continue to recover from the Great Recession and drive our economy forward."*

The amazing statistics of that statement show that the SBA backed 1200 small business loans for capital lines of credit in fiscal years 2011–2013, compared to only 1500 *in the previous 15 total years*. In fiscal year 2013, in a closely-related program known as CDC/504, the SBA also backed over 7.7 million (yes, that's million!) small business loans, providing "small businesses with long-term, fixed-rate financing to acquire real estate and major fixed assets, for a total of more than $11.7 billion".

But enough dry statistics. How does an entrepreneur who needs an SBA loan go about getting one? Do a search on "how to get an SBA loan" and it will bring up quite a few hits that should help you, including one that links to an SBA Loan Program Quick Reference Overview. [119] You definitely want to start there, and use this overview to determine the type of loan that's applicable to your needs. What it doesn't say – and it's very remiss in not doing so – is whether any of the loan types can be granted to start-ups that are in the planning stage and who haven't yet opened their doors for business. Another search (asking that specific question) gets us to a page that clears it up – at Starting and Managing[120] –in the section titled *Starting and Expanding Businesses*.

Step-by step guide to getting an SBA-backed loan. What's really missing, not only from the SBA site, but also from searches you might make, is specific and detailed information on exactly how to go about applying and getting an SBA loan. With that in mind, here's a guide of where you need to start, what you have to do, and what you need to know:

- The first two facts that you must know about an SBA loan are:

---

[117] The stimulus bill was officially called The American Recovery and Reinvestment Act (TARP), or more simply, "the Recovery Act".

[118] *SBA Lending Activity in FY 2013 Shows SBA Continuing to Help Small Businesses Grow and Create Jobs*, https://www.sba.gov/content/sba-applauds-stimulus-bill-planning-underway-broadest-quickest-small-business-impact

[119] *Loan Program Quick Reference Overview*, The U.S. Small Business Administration (SBA), https://www.sba.gov/sites/default/files/articles/Loan_Chart_HQ_February_2017_Version_B_0.pdf.

[120] *Starting and Managing*, The U.S. Small Business Administration (SBA), https://www.sba.gov/starting-business/finance-your-business/loans/sba-loans.

- o The SBA itself doesn't provide any loan money directly to the borrower under any of its loan programs, but rather, guarantees 90% of whatever loan you are granted by the commercial lending institution you select for the loan (i.e., a bank or other alternative lender)
- o You don't apply for an SBA-backed loan through the SBA – instead, you initiate it through your chosen lender (in fact, assuming you don't default on the loan, you may never actually come in direct contact with the SBA throughout the life of your loan).

- To start the process, decide which type of SBA-backed loan you are looking for.[121] Your bank and the SBA might use different terminology for loan types, and you need to become familiar enough to understand the differences (and to then talk intelligently with your banker when you start the process). Your bank might have the following loan types: working capital credit line (what we earlier called a line of credit, or LOC), a term loan, a real estate term loan, an equity credit line, or an investor real estate loan. The SBA has a series of programs that match up with each loan type. For example, a working capital line of credit is an SBA 7(a) program loan; if your loan is to expand or modernize your business, or to purchase real estate, buildings, or long-term equipment, you'd apply for an SBA 504 program; and if your loan is granted through a certified micro-lender, the SBA Microloan program fits the bill.

  The program or loan type you select will have its own set of qualifying criteria, collateral requirement, and repayment terms, so look carefully at the details of each loan type or program to determine which one best fits your needs.

- Then decide how much money you need to start, maintain, or grow your business, and be ready to *intelligently and accurately* articulate how you will use the money. How well you present this to your lender, how well prepared you are, how much you act like you know what you're doing, how much confidence you project in your venture, and how enthusiastic you are about your venture could have a significant effect on whether the lender goes to bat for you in securing the loan approval. Your brief business plan (let's say, 15 pages), plus your Cash Flow/Budget spreadsheet (printed out, of course), will come in very handy for this step.

  According to the SBA blog, they readily admit that there isn't a *typical* loan amount, but the average small business loan is in the range of $130,000–$140,000, and can go as high as $250,000. If you're trying to start a full-fledged brew pub, that amount might be necessary (due to high capital costs), but loans in the $25,000–$100,000 range are also common.

- Be prepared to put your own *skin in the game*, even with an SBA-backed loan. If you have nothing at risk, it's hard to see why a bank (or the SBA for that matter) will put their money at risk.

  Before we get to collateral, you must first recognize that both the lending bank and the SBA will want to see a considerable portion of your business funded by you – also known as *equity in the business*. Equity can be in the form of retained earnings in the business,

---

[12] *SBA Loan Programs*, https://www.sba.gov/loanprograms. This website page is much more detailed than the Quick Guide referenced above.

which implies that the business is already up and running to some degree, and the retained earnings are shown in your Balance Sheet (retained earnings are fully explained in Chapter 5). Equity can also be the amount of cash you've injected into the business, and this is typically to the tune of 20%–40% of the total loan amount you're requesting.

Obviously, the collateral that you pledge is an important indication of your commitment to the business. The collateral isn't pledged to the SBA, but rather to the bank, as they are the source of your loan, although the SBA insists that your lending bank accept your collateral as part of the loan package, as this collateral will be used to pay back both the bank and the SBA in the event of a default. Nevertheless, the value of the collateral that can be applied to your loan isn't necessarily the same between your lending bank and the SBA.

Personal assets that you pledge can be the equity in your personal or secondary residences, or a percentage of value of stocks and bonds that you hold in an investment account, but it cannot be any retirement accounts (such as your IRA or 401(k) money). If you don't meet the collateral requirement, the lending bank and the SBA might require someone else (parents or other family members) to co-sign the loan and put up the collateral pledge.

Behind the scenes, the SBA will likely have different _values_ they'll assign to the collateral than the lending bank. For example, the SBA accepts 80% of the equity in your house (based on appraised value), whereas the bank might only accept 75%. In the other direction, though, the SBA will only accept 50% of your allowable business receivables, and the bank will likely accept 75% or 80%.

Note of caution: Using your business receivables for an SBA-backed loan assumes your business is already up and running (otherwise, you wouldn't yet have any receivables). Your AR is the best form of collateral for a working capital line of credit, which may not be the reason you are applying for an SBA-backed loan. If possible, and assuming your AR is already pledged towards an LOC, or might be in the future, you'll want to be looking at other assets as collateral for the SBA-backed loan.

Important! Additionally, your lending bank (as a requirement of the SBA) will require your _personal guarantee_, also known as a personal pledge, of the loan – which will also be required of any owner of your business who holds a 20% or more stake – which goes way beyond the simple piercing of the corporate veil that you were establishing in setting up an LLC, LLP, or corporation. This is crucial to understand, as it essentially puts the personal assets of others into play in the event of a default, including personal assets that were not part of the collateral pledge – even to the cash value of life insurance policies.

If you aren't able to provide this collateral or guarantee, your chances of getting an SBA-backed loan decrease dramatically, although it doesn't make it impossible.

- Get your credit history as clean as possible – and do it early in your start-up process.

Your lending bank will request your credit history at the outset of your application, and this will be a significant factor in your success. It's important that you review your credit report with all three primary credit bureaus – Experian, TransUnion, and Equifax. (You are authorized by law to receive a free credit report once a year from each of these credit reporting companies – to do so, go to the Federal Trade Commission site, at https://www.ftc.gov/faq/consumer-protection/get-my-free-credit-report. This site is the best one to go to, as it doesn't try to jerk you around in any way, and doesn't make any efforts to sell you something. *Do not get involved with anyone who promises to obtain reports <u>for a fee</u>.*)

On each report, check to make sure that all of your personal information is exactly correct. Then look for any signs of payment problems with any credit that you've established in the past. If it indicates you've been late on a single payment (or something minor like that), it shouldn't affect your credit score, but if any creditor reports that you've been consistently late it will be a red flag. If anything is in error, follow the procedures in the report for requesting corrections; if it isn't in error, have a good explanation ready when you meet with your lending banker.

Since it can take upwards of a month to correct any errors in your credit reports, get this credit history check started several weeks before you plan to meet with your banker.

- Select several potential lending institution (and arrange them in priority sequence for looing into). If your business is already up and running, the obvious first choice is your current bank – the one where your business checking account is maintained and where you have a business banking relationship. If you don't already have a business bank, your first choice might be where you have your personal checking/savings account.

  But don't select that first choice out of hand – it might not be your long-term best bet for a business loan. Many large commercial banks simply aren't set up for small business loans – it costs just as much to analyze, approve, and manage a small loan as it does a medium-sized or large loan, and the larger banks might prefer the large loan environment. It can't hurt to ask, and besides, if you get turned down it can satisfy the requirement necessary to qualify for an SBA loan (which many bankers loudly protest is an urban legend, but it is definitely a requirement for approval of an SBA Rural Loan Program request). Getting turned down can also increase your interest in switching to a bank that's more tuned to your own small business needs, rather than one that caters to the largest employer in your state.

- The smaller community banks tend to have more of a regional or local perspective, and are eager to work with small businesses, with loans that fit within their scope or focus of business. In granting you a loan (either SBA or otherwise), the smaller bank might require you to switch all of your business banking to them (including personal), and if you want the loan badly enough, that could be your only option.

  So, how to identify local banks that are hungry for your small business? An internet search on "*yourcityname* small business best lending banks" should pull up several hits to get you started. One strong caveat when you are analyzing the search results – pay special attention to the posting date that any article or blog has on it, and only look at the ones in the past one or two years. If the date is from 2009–2012, it's probably so far out of date as to be useless, as small business lending has changed dramatically since that time.

  Some searches turn up banks where you can easily tell from the brief link description that they specialize in SBA-backed small business loans. Sample searches for several cities turn up links to local newspaper articles delving into local-area banks that have recently loosened up their loan practices for small business loans (after the 2008–2009 global financial crisis, you almost couldn't get a bank loan if you were Bill Gates or Warren Buffet).[122]

For many cities, a seemingly useful hit references an Entrepreneur.com site[123] where there's a link to the "Business Loan Search Tool" to help identify local banks that loan most to small businesses. Unfortunately, this tool is no longer available, but instead is replaced with a list of "Latest Raising Money Articles", several of which are useful. Another frequent search hit (and often at the top of the list) is headlined "The Best Small Business Banks in *yourcityname* – MultiFunding", and the website is an online commercial site for a It's a paid service where they offer to help you find a bank for a fee.[124] *My suggestion – stay away from it.*

Once you've developed a list of local banks to research, head for their websites and glean as much information as you can about their small business lending practices. If they have a page on SBA lending, that's a good indication of their interest in this type of business. From there, study all the details you can find about their sweet spot for loan size, terms of loans, and the types of business loans they're most interested in (for example, SBA 7a or 504 loans).

- Another route to take in searching for a lending bank is to use the SBA LINC website,[125] where they will walk you through a 3-step process that connects you with potential lenders. It involves an online registration, and a short questionnaire about your business, the loan amount and purpose. Once submitted, lenders (presumably SBA-approved, and maybe even SBA-preferred) will begin contacting you. This may result in short-circuiting some of the following steps, so make certain you have all of them under control before using this step.

- Pull together all of the information and paperwork that you'll need for the loan process, described on the SBA site.[126] It's going to include both personal and business credit history, plus a succinct business plan.

As I've said elsewhere in this book, I'm not a big advocate of business plans, but this is one place where you'll need one – so write it well, keep it brief, polish it, polish it (and polish it again), and specifically focus it towards your loan application. Unless there are factors in your business that make it complex, your business plan shouldn't be longer than 15 pages. If possible, have it reviewed by your small business coach, who can dispassionately look it over, spotting omissions, duplications, faulty or ambiguous financial numbers, and just

---

[122] Joyce M. Rosenberg, *Bank Loans Loosening for Small Businesses*, Seattle Times Business section, March 5, 2014, http://www.seattletimes.com/business/bank-loans-loosening-for-small-businesses/

[123] *Discover Which Banks Loan Most To Small Businesses*, Entrepreneur.com, undated, http://www.entrepreneur.com/bestbanks. This site is no longer available, and the replacement links it provides are of little value for our purposes here.

[124] MultiFunding LLC markets aggressively for their services to help locate local banks that lend to small businesses. For that reason, I hesitate to suggest going down this route, and think you should instead focus on tracking down banks from the search hits that indicate they make loans to small businesses.

[125] *Connecting Borrowers with SBA Approved Lenders*, SBA LINC, https://www.sba.gov/tools/linc

[126] *7(a) Loan Application Checklist*, SBA website, https://www.sba.gov/loans-grants/see-what-sba-offers/sba-loan-programs/general-small-business-loans-7a/7a-loan-application-checklist

plain bad writing. This is an area where writing skills will prove invaluable, so work as hard as you can to make the business plan read as a professional document.

Your presentation of this information will look considerably more professional if you take it to a FedEx Office center, photocopy it into a consistent format, with inside tab pages to make things easier to locate, a title page, a clear plastic front and back page, and a binding to hold it all together. The small cost of doing this will pay big dividends in illustrating that you are professional and know what you are doing. This is also where business cards, business stationery, and a well-designed business logo will show that you're running a business that expects to be around for the long haul, and most importantly, profitable enough to pay back the loan. (Have at least a half dozen copies made. You'll very likely need to make your pitch to multiple banks, and somewhere along the line you'll be asked for a second copy.)

- Once you're comfortable with your plan of attack, it's time to make the first approach to your hoped-for bank or lending institution. You might need to start the process through their website, and you might even need to fill in your basic requirements and request online. If that's the case, after completing the request, you'll want to transition over to a personal, face-to-face meeting with your assigned lender. Don't forget to take all of the required information/documentation listed in the SBA guide to the meeting.

- There's a good possibility you'll need to pitch your loan application to multiple banks before you find one that's receptive – to the point of approving a loan. On that basis, make certain you don't pin your hopes very high on the first bank you select. Instead, select three banks for your preferred list, and work with all three in parallel. It's not a case where you'll play one off against the other – but rather, to short-circuit the process. If one turns you down, you're already moving along towards a second and a third possibility. Besides, having others to turn to is a good way to keep a positive attitude.

- At the meeting, try to be as comfortable and confident as possible (which will be difficult, as you're probably doing something brand-new for you, and you may have your business future riding on the outcome) – but don't be overconfident and cocky. Ask about the bank's approval process, as well as how they work with the SBA.

If the banker asks you for a presentation on exactly how you plan to use the loan money, make sure you have a prepared presentation, created in the format expected by the banker, and only present it after you've practiced it ... *and practiced it*.

If you've already been in business for a while (long enough that you've already had some financial statements created), be ready to present them to the banker, and make certain that you know the numbers behind the statements and can speak to them if queried.

Ask if your lending bank is an SBA-preferred lender – if so, they are authorized by the SBA to grant SBA-backed loans without first getting approval from the SBA. If at all possible, work through a bank that is an SBA-preferred lender (also known as a CLP Lender, or Certified Lender), and all you'll have to do is get your bank to see the value in your loan.

- As you work through the loan application process, do everything possible to make the banker your *business friend* – helping to build empathy for what you're trying to do so he/she will go the extra mile for you. This requires you to be as forthcoming as possible, not only providing all information the banker requests, but also conveying and projecting enthusiasm for what you'll gain from the loan proceeds. If you're not able to create a convincing argument of your project's success potential in your banker's mind, there's little chance the banker will pitch it effectively to the bank loan committee necessary for the approval.

- Following the meeting, a good reason for developing a solid rapport with your banker is to enable a communication link between you to easily convey requests for additional information, as well a way for you to keep in touch with the bank's decision-making.

- The lending bank's loan committee takes the primary lead in analyzing the creditworthiness of the loan request, and will make the initial decision on granting the loan. If they approve it, the loan request is then submitted to the SBA. The SBA's limited involvement is to review the loan application for eligibility and credit standards, and if it meets those standards, the SBA will issue an authorization to the lending bank. Assuming the bank is an SBA-preferred lender, this authorization will be very easy and quick.

- Don't be surprised if the loan committee comes back to you with clarification questions, asking you to more fully explain the basis for your financial projections, or details about the collateral you've pledged. Sometimes this process can take several weeks, hopefully giving you an idea of how positive the bank seems about your loan request. If the vibes you're getting back don't seem positive, it's a good clue that you should be proceeding with the other banks on your preferred list.

- If you're granted the loan, keep in mind that you haven't been granted manna from heaven. It's a business loan – just like any other business loan that you'd get from a bank. You'd better treat it as such, making timely payments and submitting your ongoing financial statements to the bank. The SBA will essentially be out of the picture, and won't come back into it unless the bank notifies them that you're in default on the loan. The bank will likely set up automatic monthly payment deductions from your business checking account and you obviously need to know the exact date and amount of these payments.

- What if your SBA-backed loan application isn't accepted? Try another bank, then another, and another – until you've worked your way through all of the potential lending banks in your list if necessary. Persistence pays off, as there might be reasons outside of your control that were behind the denial. The experience of each failure is valuable, as it helps create insights into how you can improve your application for the next bank.

Defaulting on a bank loan (SBA and non-SBA)

Technically, once you're outside the limits of your loan covenants, or if you've missed an interest or required principal payment on your loan, the bank can declare you in default. At that point they can legally seize your collateral to pay down the loan. This is not something they'll be wild about doing (unless it's your 10th time of being in default, and the bank figures it won't be long before it's the 11th). Clawing their money back from your collateral isn't how banks make money.

If you've maintained a good relationship, your business banker will want to work with you to resolve the default – but you too have to be willing and upfront about working with the banker.

Believe me, when you're behind in a loan payment, or when a payment is coming up and you know you don't have the money, talking to the bank is the very last thing that's high on your "want to do" list. Nevertheless, your best bet is to contact your banker with information when you know you have a problem, and not at the 11th hour when your options are minimal.

If it's a case of being outside covenants, but otherwise your business is a going concern, they might call you in for a discussion. At the first word of this you'll probably have a panic attack, thinking "Oh my gosh, I've just defaulted on the bank loan!", and we've heard all of our lives that it's the end of the world when that happens. While you're technically in default when this happens, it shouldn't be as bad as all that (unless, as I mentioned earlier, this is the 11th time it's happened). Keep in mind that your banker may have no idea how to run a business such as yours, and as we'll see in Chapter 5 on Financial Management, even less of an idea how your financial statement numbers should look – which is the data used in the financial calculations that make up your loan covenants. The best you can hope for is your banker will determine (or you can suggest) the covenants weren't workable from the start, and might work with you to modify them with terms that better suit your particular business. (I have firsthand experience of this, and while the modified covenants didn't make me feel all that much better either, I very much appreciated that the bank would do this for me – and after two attempts at this my company managed to get itself out of the doldrums and we went on.)

If the collateral includes your personal residence, the bank isn't allowed by law to just seize it, unlike the finance company who can repossess your personal automobile in the dead of night if you default on car payments. Rather, the bank would have to initiate formal foreclosure proceedings. The process is lengthy, and it should allow you to continue operating in default, but with an even tighter watch by the bank – and even if you escape from this predicament, it will likely spell the beginning of the end of your loan relationship with that bank.

In the worst possible turn of events, the bank could force you into bankruptcy, or you may decide on your own that it's your only recourse – either Chapter 7 (known as liquidation) or Chapter 11 (reorganization and a potential recovery).   It's important to keep in mind that bankruptcy doesn't remove the personal lender's lien or security interest you may have given on any assets pledged as collateral for the loan. As a result, the lender can still foreclose on your home mortgage or other real property. If this possibility rears its ugly head, consult immediately with your attorney to discuss your options.

In any case, don't hide under a rock when you begin to realize that, financially, things aren't going as you'd have liked. If you see a sudden drop in business that's going to run you out of cash or push you over the edge on the covenants, *talk to your banker as soon as you can*. This isn't an easy thing to do, but the earlier you catch it, the more likely the bank will be agreeable to working it out. Try to discuss if there is any way the loan can be restructured, either the repayment terms or the covenants that you're currently not able to meet.

At the same time, begin serious development of ideas on how to alter your business plan – such as cutting expenses (laying off staff, stop taking a paycheck, foregoing purchases that aren't critical). Do everything possible to conserve cash (inject personal money into the company from any source you may have, stretch out your payments to unsecured creditors, and if you have to, work with your employees to lower payroll and costs). While it may harm longer term profitability, it might be beneficial to cut short term deals with customers to increase sales revenue. As a last resort, you may have to utilize some of the high-cost alternative financing options discussed in the next section – but if you do, go into it with your eyes wide open, as you will have then moved to a much higher level of risk.

One big caution – it's usually not wise to go down a path of total ruin on this. If the realistic outlook for your business isn't good, decide if you should cash in your chips now, in order to live another day. Here's where advice from your attorney and tax accountant, while it may cost you some money, could be the best advice you can get (but keep in mind – they aren't entrepreneurs).

But back to the problem at hand. If the loan is an SBA-backed loan, the process from your perspective isn't much different than with a non-SBA loan. Contrary to popular misconception, at the time of default you won't have federal agents knocking on your door, you won't have bounty hunters pursuing you, and you won't have the SBA hassling you on the phone or in e-mails. Initially, the SBAs involvement is to guarantee a portion of the loan amount to the lender, and your immediate negotiations following the default are entirely between you and the bank. At the same time, you aren't going to get off any easier than if it was a non-SBA-backed loan.

The lenders initial default actions will focus on collecting from your pledged collateral, then possibly forcing an auction of the business assets, and last, going after the borrower's home, and any other real property. Behind the scenes (and at any time in the loan default process when the lender has reached the decision), the lender may notify the SBA of the default and begin collecting their guaranteed loan repayment amount from the SBA (typically 85% on loans up to $150,000 and 75% on loans above that amount, and SBA Express loans are set at 50% guarantee). Once the SBA has presumably paid their guarantee amount to the bank, they will both begin coordinated efforts for recovery of your assets, personal and business, to pay off the default.

The SBA effort starts off with a 60-day demand letter for the loan balance to be paid in full, or asks you to respond with an *Offer in Compromise*. This is an offer from you to settle the debt for less than face value, presumably to save the liquidation costs if going that route is the only alternative.

This offer consists of a number of forms – downloadable from the SBA site[127] – that are submitted to your lending bank, requesting that you be allowed to pay a reduced amount of the debt as a full and final settlement. The lender will review your offer, and may or may not accept it (in which case you start negotiations on this). If it's accepted, the lending bank will then submit the offer to the SBA. It's a long, complicated process, and you might be well advised to have an attorney working with you each step of the way (which is also going to cost you money).

From whatever is collected from you, 75% goes to the SBA to repay the guarantee, and the lending bank keeps the remaining 25%. (And oh, by the way, whatever amount from your loan is forgiven as a result of an Offer in Compromise, you'll likely receive a 1099 for that amount, which signifies taxable income on your next tax return.)

---

[127] Lending Forms, SBA website, https://www.sba.gov/content/offer-compromise-oic-tabs, then follow the link to the Offer In Compromise tabs.

Only if you can't reach a settlement with either the bank or the SBA, the SBA can then turn your case over to the Department of Treasury for further collection. Yes, you read that right – if the SBA should decide to throw in the towel on your debt, federal law now requires the SBA to turn it over to the U.S. Department of Treasury for collection – the arm of the government that we truly call *the Feds*. Just as you'd expect of an agency that also includes the IRS, the Department of Treasury has their own debt collection methods – *outside of any statute of limitations*, and doesn't require a court order – enabling them to intercept your tax refunds, garnish your wages, and even collect federal benefit amounts that are direct deposited into your bank account (i.e., Social Security benefit checks, veterans benefits, federal and military retirement, railroad retirement and other government payments to you).[128] If all this seems rather heavy-handed (especially since several of these repayment sources aren't available to any other creditors than the federal government), don't take it personally – several new laws since 2000 have established the Department of Treasury as the government's big stick for all kinds of federal debt collection, from student loans, to overpaid Social Security benefits, to back taxes. It's the law.

None of these processes are easy, but also, none of it is worth jumping out the window, so take it one day at a time, don't panic, and work through it as best you can.

Alternative financing

UCC filings. Before we get to examples of alternative small business financing, you should be aware of UCC-1 financing statements that creditors file with your state's Secretary of State (or Department of Licensing). A UCC-1 filing is a legal form that creditors file to give notice that they may have a financial interest in your personal or business property as a result of a debt to the creditor. This gives the creditor a relative priority with other creditors. In legal lending documents, this is known as *perfecting the security interest*, so when you see this term in a loan contract, this is what it means. Any item(s) that you pledge as collateral (i.e., your security interest) for a loan will be identified in the UCC filing.

Your state's UCC filing office does not attempt to qualify or quantify the collateral pledged in the filing, or even to determine if the information in the filing is correct, thus *making it important for you double-check its accuracy*.

Your state's Department of Licensing web site will likely have a search capability for UCC-1 filings. Whenever you've paid off a creditor, it's in your best interest to ensure the UCC-1 filing has been removed.

Loading up your personal credit cards. This section isn't included as a suggested way to finance your company, but rather, as a cautionary tale. The truth is, financing your company with personal credit cards is often done (I've done it) – even to the point of taking out multiple additional credit cards just to load them up (I've done that too). It's also incredibly risky, and the cost is very high (although you're going to find that almost any form of alternative financing will be expensive).

---

[128] "What can the Treasury take to satisfy a defaulted SBA loan balance?", Perliski Law Group, July 27, 2014, http://www.perliskilawgroup.com/what-kind-of-collection-power-does-the-u-s-treasury-have-to-collect-my-loan-balance/

The credit limit on many of today's credit cards is the key factor in getting you in trouble. It's oftentimes high, and unlike a piddly $500 credit limit that wouldn't make much difference to your company's survival anyway, if a bank is foolish enough to offer a $10,000+ credit limit, it can be tempting. Just as running up your credit card balances willy-nilly for personal charges without giving much thought to how you're going to pay it back, it's just as easy to do this for your company when it's going through lean times, figuring some really good business income is right around the corner.

The big difference with credit card financing compared to some other forms is that it's _debt financing_. Charging on a credit card is real debt – unsecured debt – that you're taking on, including not only the interest charges but the principal you'll have to pay back – and since you're likely paying down the credit card charges over time, you'll be paying interest charges that are almost certainly _higher than your state's legal usury limits_ (which will be discussed in more detail in a bit). Worse, any time you're late on a payment, even by a single day, the late fees are effectively jacking up the already-high interest and fees you're paying to the stratosphere.

My strong suggestion is, use this form of financing only with your eyes wide open, and only for very short-term situations where you can be absolutely certain you'll have the money to cover the payback – and do the payback ASAP. Credit card borrowing ranks right up there with the riskiest of all alternative financing methods, and you should avoid it.

Small business credit cards. You'll almost certainly need at least one business credit card. Otherwise, there's always a hassle paying small business expenditures, travel expenses, and lots of everyday stuff that your business needs. At the same time, credit card issuers are going after this market in a big way, offering signup perks, cashback rewards, no annual fees, and lower interest rates than with consumer credit cards.

If you need $20K, $25K, even $30K in quick business financing, what's to stop you from signing up for multiple business credit cards, each with the maximum credit limit you can get? Well, nothing actually – except that it might not be the brightest and safest thing in the world to do. Sure, you can pay the minimum each month, but as with using personal credit cards in the same way, the interest charges and late fees can eat you alive – at the very least, eat up any profit that your business had hoped to earn.

Depending on how long you've been in business, and how good your business credit rating is, credit card companies usually require a small business owner to personally guarantee a business credit card. Some credit card companies also report business credit card payment problems on your personal credit report, so again the fallacy of creating a _corporate veil_ of financial liability with an LLC or corporation is gone. Also, since the global financial crisis, recent personal credit protections aren't applied to business credit cards, allowing credit card companies to increase interest rates without warning, and impose exorbitant late fees. (More succinctly, nothing in the Consumer Credit Protection Act of 1968[129] covers small business credit problems, which is ironic

---

[129] Debt.org, _Consumer Credit Protection Act – Laws Protecting Consumer Rights_, https://www.debt.org/credit/your-consumer-rights/protection-act/. This is not to be confused with the Consumer Financial Protection Bureau (CFPB), created in 2012 as part of the Dodd-Frank Wall Street Reform and Consumer Protection Act – which is being hotly contested by Congress and could be on the chopping block. The CFPB also does not cover small business protection.

since over 80% of the 28 million small businesses in the U.S. are single-owner, single-employee businesses, and if these individual consumers need protection for their personal credit cards, they also need it for their small business credit card.)

Whichever type of credit cards you use, keep personal and business expenses separate. If you commingle them, you stand to create serious problems, not only with the IRS if there's an audit, but also with your state business agency (who might even take away your limited liability status if they think you're gaming the system).

Trade credit. This is simply credit extended to you by suppliers who let you buy now and pay later. Rather than paying cash when supplies arrive, receiving goods and services from a vendor and then waiting to pay until a required date is a form of credit. Depending on your relationship with your suppliers, you can sometimes negotiate a longer payment term – possibly with a sweetener if it's required.

Generally, suppliers won't be eager to extend trade credit when you're just up and running – you don't yet have a track record for them to feel comfortable. They'll likely want cash on delivery – at least until they know your business is able to pay its bills.

If you want a longer trade credit period, you might have to divulge some internal financial or business information, such as showing them contracts for products that you'll be using the supplies to create, or maybe giving them a serious look at your current accounts receivable (both so they know you'll have money coming in to pay them). You'll probably need to discuss deals such as this with the business owner or CFO of the supplier, and you'll want to make this approach personally, and with all of the necessary information in hand. One angle to consider is whether the vendor is interested in taking a financial stake in your company in lieu of payment.

Trade credit can be costly. A 30-day payment term at no additional cost might be the norm for the supplier's regular customers, but if they're requesting cash upfront or cash on delivery for you, it might cost you the loss of an early payment discount, or they might insist on some really steep interest terms – perhaps 24%, 30%, 36%, or even more. There are no legal limits on the interest percentage they can demand, and it may be simply up to you to take it or leave it (your state's usury laws will not apply).

Selling assets. You may be tapped out completely on your cash-in-the-bank to fund your new startup idea, but you very well might have an asset or two that could help raise some cash. If you have an old car around (particularly a classic) that you're hoping to give to your kid when old enough to drive, you might find that making the choice to part with it now is a better strategy. Likewise, if you have a boat that's regularly used for weekend waterskiing, well, since you won't have time for that anymore once you start your business, how about selling it?

You don't normally think of it as such, but taking out an equity loan on your home is essentially selling an asset. It's a _very_ risky thing to do, though, and you should only consider it if you have lots of confidence in the success of your new business (or want the start-up badly enough). Given the high percentage of startup business failures, you're adding your most valuable (and probably most hard-earned) asset directly into the mix with your new business risk. Think long and hard about it before making the leap. At the very least, if your business fails and you close it by your own decision, you'll still have the second mortgage to pay down, which can cripple your personal cash flow for a long time. If you put your business into Chapter 11 bankruptcy to _flush_ your outstanding business debt, the second mortgage on your personal residence will not be part of it, as it's considered personal debt (unless, of course, you also file for personal bankruptcy).

Product presales. Often paired with crowdfunding efforts, selling your products to potential new customers before you have manufactured them can help raise capital for your new business. The traditional businesses on the crowdfunding sites promise a reward to anyone who kicks in a bit of money, but that has now evolved to *rewarding* with your product itself. In your crowdfunding pitch, you list your product's price on introduction, as well as your projected shipping date, and hopefully the enthusiastic future customers will provide a source of development funding.

But beware of this from several aspects. Being internet-driven, the response is completely unpredictable, and therefore, the demands on your production capability will also be unpredictable. If initial reaction is wildly successful, you may find yourself in the uncomfortable position of having too much product to produce and ship, with the revenue from it having already been spent. Then, when you actually begin shipping, you'll need additional customers to create new current revenue, but you might already be running at maximum capacity to fulfill the crowdfunding orders. If the helter-skelter situation this creates also lowers your customer service capability, you have some serious problems that could destroy your business before it hardly gets started. For many, it's been a downward spiral.

If you can manage these potential problems, though, and if your newfound customers are so happy with your product that they will purchase more, you've successfully used your presales campaign to kick start some of your ongoing product sales.

The presales gambit is growing so rapidly that it might be more opportune for you to study up online for the latest tactics. Try a browser search on "successful product presales".

Factoring receivables. If your cash flow is in a continual state of tatters and a business line of credit (or more headroom on a current line of credit) isn't in the cards, you might look into *factoring* your receivables (also known as *financing your receivables*). In simplest terms, the process involves selling your accounts receivable to a third-party commercial finance company, allowing you to receive the money owed to you more quickly – usually within 24 hours – rather than waiting the normal payment period from your customers.[130]

Gee, it almost sounds like free money. Well, it isn't, and it also might not be good for the reputation of your company – so you should *consider this only as a last resort*, and in the smallest doses you can afford.[131]

The *factor* company will advance you something like 75%–80% of each invoice amount – typically within 5–10 days of issuing the invoice. The factor then collects your invoice amount from your customer(s), skims off a hefty fee for its efforts, and subsequently forks over any

---

[130] *What is factoring?*, RTS Financial, http://www.rtsfinancial.com/guides/what-factoring. This company's primary business is factoring receivables for companies, so consider all of this information as a sales pitch that tries to convince you that factoring could be the best thing that ever happened to your company.
[131] Tom Taulli, *The Pros and Cons of Factoring*, Bloomberg Business online, October 3, 2008, http://www.bloomberg.com/bw/stories/2008-10-03/the-pros-and-cons-of-factoringbusinessweek-business-news-stock-market-and-financial-advice

remaining money to you. The factoring *advance* percentage could be larger for some receivables than others, depending on the quality of the individual receivable. For example, for an invoice you have outstanding to Wal-Mart, it could be more, but an invoice to Joe's Trucking down the road will be at the lower end of the scale.

If the cost of factoring isn't a concern for you (and speed of getting paid is) – and if you don't care that your customers know you're doing this – there can be some benefits to factoring receivables:

- You get quicker payment for your sales.

- Factoring is effectively a financing scheme, but unlike traditional debt financing, it doesn't appear on your Balance Sheet (which can be good if anyone is scrutinizing it, and if that debt creates a negative effect on your financial health).

- Your <u>customer's</u> credit determines your early payment rate, not your own company's credit rating. To do factoring, your company isn't required to have a credit check, since all the factor wants to know is whether your customers will pay.

- Factoring can be an alternative to a bank-granted line of credit, based on your company's sales, not its financial stability, and has no upper dollar limit (up to the limit of your receivables – and you factor only the invoices that you want, such as large ones, or invoices from late-paying customers).

The downsides of factoring. Reading the advertising hype on factoring, you might get the impression that it's an old and cherished way to run your company's financing, and that it's a panacea for all of your cash flow woes. Factoring definitely has downsides.

- <u>Factoring will likely result in a negative hit to your company's reputation.</u> Many factoring companies require your customers to make their payments payable – and mailed or deposited directly – to the factor, and that's a dead giveaway you're factoring, which is seen in many eyes as a sign of financial instability. If your customers are performing any type of risk assessment about the viability of your company, this could be a significant negative for you in that respect.

- Any receivable that you've factored instantly becomes a receivable that doesn't qualify as collateral for a bank line of credit – makes sense, since you've given up ownership of the receivable to the factor, so it's of no value to the bank.

- True cost of factoring. You need to ask the factor what the real fee cost will be in all circumstances – it could easily wind up costing you 20% of the total invoice amount (which is typically more than your net profit margin). Additionally, factors often don't want the hassle of handling just a few piddling invoices, so they'll require a minimum – sometimes as high as $75,000 (or more) per month.

  Let me explain how the fees add up – and the numbers quoted here can differ from factor to factor, so this is just an example. From the advance dollar amount given to you, the factor will take something like 2%–5% as the service fee (the same thing would be called interest on a bank loan) – and that fee covers the first 30 days the invoice is outstanding. If the invoice isn't paid to the factor by your customer until after 30 days, an additional fee will be somewhere between 1/8th percent to 1/15th percent ***per day***. Yes, that's per day, so you can see how this can very quickly add up, and you'll soon find yourself looking up the word *usurious* in the dictionary – but your state's usury laws will not regulate fees by factoring companies.

Worst of all (and here's where you really need to carefully read the fine print) – if the invoice remains unpaid for some contract-specified number of days, *the factor can come back to you and force you to buy back the invoice*. Whew! That's tough, since you've now paid the fee, plus you've spent the advance money to keep your company going.

A lot to think about before you pick up the phone to call your friendly factoring company. In the dozens of cash flow crunch situations I found myself in with my own company, I never once reached the point where I thought factoring was a good idea. If you do, be ready for the worst, and keep the amounts as small as possible. This one is truly bad news.

Merchant cash advance. If you're in a retail business, or any business where your products and services can be paid by credit card – and if you're nearing the end of your negative cash flow rope – you might find yourself considering the Merchant Cash Advance (MCA) form of business financing. Simply put, an MCA lender advances cash to a business, in return for a percentage of their future credit card sales.

Merchant cash advance is similar to factoring your receivables, but for the situation where a company doesn't have any receivables, and instead, is heavily credit card driven. For example, a restaurant where customers are paying for goods and services with a credit card at the time of purchase. Or it could be for an online business, or any store-front retail business.

Like a factoring provider, the MCA lender is not a regulated bank, and your upfront money from your credit card sales does not work like a bank loan. Because it's not regulated, an MCA is not bound by usury laws that limit the percentage of interest charged. The *annualized cost of an MCA advance might be in the neighborhood of 70% to 90%.*[132] Even though this quote came from the credit-dried-up-times of 2008, credit might be tight at any time for entrepreneurs with less-than-sterling credit, or even for solid businesses who want/need to get their cash faster. Today, rates will more likely be in the 30%–40% range, with 60% being at the high end. Even so, these rates are higher than the *gross* profit margin for a lot of businesses, let alone their net profit, and if you get on this treadmill, it can be a downward spiral that takes your business into the toilet.

The way a merchant credit advance works is, after an advance is paid out to a small business, the MCA "taps into the merchant's credit card terminal and takes a percentage of daily credit and debit card swipes until they recoup their advance and a fee".[133] You almost always have to switch your credit card processing and point of sale (POS) system over to the MCA lender, which is another way they lock you into whatever fees they want to charge for their services.

The heyday for merchant cash advance companies was 2009, when many businesses were in the depths of the global financial blowout – with as many as 50 MCAs cropping up across the U.S.

[132] Maureen Farrell, *Look Who's Making Coin Off The Credit Crisis*, Forbes online, 3/13/2008, http://www.forbes.com/2008/01/31/cash-advance-goldman-ent-fin-cx_mf_0131cashadvance.html
[133] Bryant Ruiz Switzky, *Merchant cash advance industry operates in a regulatory Wild West*, Washington Business Journal, February 23, 2012, http://www.bizjournals.com/washington/stories/2010/07/26/story5.html

almost overnight (actually, the industry had already been around for at least a decade). Incredibly, with all the talk in Washington about bank and consumer credit reform – even the start of regulation for payday loan shops – there is little talk about regulating the MCA industry.

Like subprime lenders and payday loan merchants who prey on the most fragile customers, MCA lenders go after the small businesses who are already on shaky financial ground and make it even worse for them. I mention this type of alternative financing only to warn against it.

Small business loan stacking. A term that only recently came into existence, loan stacking is now becoming a business model for unscrupulous credit providers in the alternative financing industry.

And here's a negative aspect where your UCC filings come into play. At some time in the past, let's say you took out a secured loan (i.e., one with collateral pledged). Your creditor made a UCC filing with your state licensing agency, listing your debt and collateral. Sometime later, a second lender – most likely one you've never done business with before – searches the UCC database and sees your UCC-1 record and sends you a letter or calls you on the phone. Their pitch seems too good to be true – can we give you a bit more financing? – suckering you into easy money that you may not be able to afford. This gambit is to stack one or more loans on top of the original loan – in an environment where you've found financing to be quite difficult. You're thinking, "Gee, I've never found credit this easy before ... I must be a good credit risk" – and you're suckered in.

Interestingly, many of us use the general concept of credit stacking all the time – with multiple credit cards in our wallets. In fact, credit card issuers might actually be using their knowledge of your existing credit cards to tailor their junk mail pitches at you.

But credit stacking in a small business can be very problematic, not only for the business owner, but for the first-in-line lender too. According to a recent Forbes/Entrepreneur article,[134] when a business owner stacks another piece of debt on top of existing debt, it puts the original lender at greater risk of loan default – and the original lender likely doesn't even know about it (and not likely to go back to check for additional UCC-1 debt filings). It's worse for everyone if other stacking lenders talk the business owner into one or two additional loans, saddling the business with too much debt and causing it to fail.

Setting up a ROBS plan. This alternative financing option is an even riskier funding method, and you'd better have a strong stomach for the level of risk, as doing it involves using your retirement funds as investment money in your new venture. But life is full of choices, and this is one that you might choose to look at.

ROBS is an acronym created by the IRS for something they call *Rollovers as Business Start-ups* (interesting choice of acronym, wouldn't you say?). A ROBS plan allows you to "use the money in your IRA or 401(k) to start a business (or buy an existing one) without paying taxes on the withdrawn funds or getting hit with an early withdrawal penalty".[135] While this sounds exciting,

---

[134] Brock Blake, *Small Business Loan Stacking -- Friend or Foe?*, Forbes/Entrepreneur, December 9, 2014, http://www.forbes.com/sites/brockblake/2014/12/09/small-business-loan-stacking-friend-or-foe/

[135] Parija Kavilanz, *Should you drain your 401(k) to start a business?*, CNNMoney, Small Business Resource Guide, June 23, 2014, http://money.cnn.com/2014/06/23/smallbusiness/startup-funding-401k/

it's a lot riskier than you think, and you really need to know what you're doing ... and what you're getting yourself into.

It should also be mentioned at the outset that the IRS doesn't quite know what to think of the ROBS concept, clearly stating in a 2008 internal IRS memorandum that several aspects of a ROBS methodology are "questionable" – and while they haven't yet ruled it a tax-avoidance scheme, they are certainly keeping a watchful eye on virtually everyone who might have set up a ROBS to date. The SBA, though, has a page on it, and it might be a good place to start your detailed research if you're interested.[136] Another good source is a Wikipedia article that translates a lot of the IRS bureaucratese into simple layman's language. [137]

If you decide to explore this route, here are a few of the things you need to know.

- Due to the complexity of properly setting up a ROBS, do one of two things:
  - Sit back and spend a good long day or so researching the IRS communications[138] or some published study results.[139 and 140]
  - Seriously consider hiring a firm that specializes in this. If you ask your current 401(k) plan administrator or personal IRS custodian about it, chances are they'll talk you out of it, so that's why I suggest someone who specializes in ROBS Plans (do an internet search and you'll find several around the country). If you go this route, be prepared for a hefty start-up fee (perhaps $4–$5K), plus the cost for ongoing support (maybe $1.5K/year).
- You're not eligible for a ROBS if you're planning to be an absentee owner of your business (such as a situation where you've just bought a franchise for a McDonalds, and you don't plan to work there, but rather, just want it as an investment.) The reason is that a 401(k) plan in any company is only available to *employees* of that company – so if you're not working there, you're not eligible to have a 401(k) account in your company, even if you own it – so a ROBS is possible only if you're actually a wage-earning employee.
- By the very nature of it, a ROBS *isn't* something a young wage earner can likely benefit from, as it takes a sizeable amount of money within the 401(k) to be worthwhile (and that can take years to build up in your personal retirement account).
- If you're still interested in setting up a ROBS plan, the first requirement is that your new business venture (or the one you're buying) must be a corporation – and these days, many new business owners prefer to be structured as an LLC (which doesn't have shareholder

---

[136] Barbara Weltman, *Can Your Retirement Plan Own Your Business?*, SBA guest blog, August 30, 2013, https://www.sba.gov/blogs/can-your-retirement-plan-own-your-business

[137] *Rollovers as Business Start-Ups*, https://en.wikipedia.org/wiki/Rollovers_as_Business_Start-Ups

[138] *Memorandum for Director(s), Employee Plans Examinations and Rulings & Agreements*, October 1, 2008, http://www.irs.gov/pub/irs-tege/robs_guidelines.pdf

[139] *Employee Plans Compliance Unit (EPCU) - Completed Projects - Project with Summary Reports – Rollovers as Business Start-Ups (ROBS)*, IRS website, December 15, 2014, http://www.irs.gov/Retirement-Plans/Employee-Plans-Compliance-Unit-%28EPCU%29-Completed-Projects-Project-with-Summary-Reports-%E2%80%93-Rollovers-as-Business-Start-Ups-%28ROBS%29

[140] *Rollovers as Business Start-Ups Compliance Project*, Retirement News for Employers, Fall 2010 newsletter, www.irs.gov/pub/irs-tege/rne_fall10.pdf

stock, required by a ROBS). It's unclear from IRS statements whether an S-Corp can participate in a ROBS plan – but it very likely may be able to do so.

- The corporation that you set up to initiate the ROBS plan is essentially a shell corporation (but not necessarily in an offshore, tax-haven sort of connotation, which has an unsavory reputation), in that you don't want any corporate stock to be issued yet (so therefore, no corporate owners yet), and the corporation will have no assets. You'll also want to delay doing any business from this shell company until all aspects of the ROBS plan are completely set up, and you don't want any other employees in the company at this time (for reasons that will become obvious in the next bullet).

- A qualified 401(k) plan is then set up inside your new corporation. The plan documents have to state (or be modified to state) that *all* 401(k) plan participants may invest all or part of their account in employer stock (i.e., the stock that you're about to create). (This is why you don't want any other employees in the company at this stage.)

- You now direct that all or part of your current retirement plan's money is to be invested in your new company's stock. Effectively, your 401(k) account is now the technical owner of this new company, as it holds all of the stock within your 401(k) account.

- You initiate the rollover of funds from your existing 401(k) or IRA (the source plan) to the new 401(k) plan (the target plan) just set up inside your corporation. Since by IRS definition, this is a rollover – and not a plan-to-plan transfer – you have to abide by very strict IRS rules. Such rules include a time limit of 60 days from the date the money leaves the source plan until it's deposited in the target plan, and a restriction to only one rollover (from the aggregate of all your retirement plans) per year. If you err on these rules, the IRS will likely consider the money to be a distribution to you, and you will suffer the tax and penalty consequences.

- The stock valuation in this purchase is tricky. Your shell company is privately held at this point, and therefore, an accurate valuation is almost impossible to make. Therefore, how you allocate shareholding to the 401(k) account, versus other shareholding that you allocate to you and other later investors becomes very difficult. The IRS will probably scrutinize this area carefully during an audit.

- As the managing employer of the company, you transfer this money from your 401(k) account to your company checking account, and from there the money is available for any corporate spending.

- At this point, you would presumably modify the 401(k) plan documents to prohibit further employee investment in company stock. This is where – like the fat cats parking millions in the Cayman Islands to lower their tax rate – you'll have to face the sniff test if word gets around that you've funded your company this way, as some might not think it's fair to use your pre-tax retirement money in this fashion without paying taxes on it. It's also where the IRS might step in and declare your ROBS a tax dodge if you aren't really careful in correctly following the steps.

  Alternatively, you could leave this plan rule in effect. For example, if you have founding partners (or employees) who are also willing and interested in using their retirement funds to cover start-up costs, the rule allows them to do the same thing you've done. Additionally, during the 2008 IRS analysis of ROBS problems, the IRS wasn't favorable to an amendment prohibiting employees from purchasing company stock with their 401(k) accounts, so you now face the challenge of how to appease the IRS, at the same time as you work to control ownership of your company.

- Let's again state something from above – you, the individual employee of the company, don't own the company ... but rather, your 401(k) account owns the company – even though it was your money in the 401(k) account that purchased the company shares.

- Your 401(k) plan must now *annually* file an IRS Form 5500 and all of its schedules (and there are no exemptions). Because your retirement account was used to invest in a ROBS plan, *it* must file the Form 5500.

- Profits – in future years as the company has profits to distribute to shareholders, those profits are paid back into the 401(k) account (remember that your 401(k) account is one of the company's shareholders), not to you personally, unless, of course, you want to pay an early-withdrawal penalty plus the taxes at this time. This means that you aren't able to easily take money out of the company that you consider to be your own. That's just one of the prices you have to pay for using pre-tax money for something like this.

- Losses – if *your* company never pays all of the original investment money back to your 401(k) account, this could be a tax benefit to you, as it will reduce the tax liability by that amount from other profitable investments made through your 401(k) account.

Loaning money from your IRA. The truth of the matter is, you can't loan money from your personal IRA to your company – but with some risky footwork you can *effectively* do that with a technique you might call short-term borrowing from your personal IRA account. There's no specific paper trail of what you're doing with the money while you have it on loan from your IRA, and the IRS doesn't rule this as unacceptable. They are simply silent about whatever you do with the money while it's in transit from one account to the other. It's also extremely risky, as you only have 60 days to pay it back, and if you don't, it's considered a distribution from your IRA, and then you're forced to pay the income taxes on the distribution, plus any early withdrawal penalties.

I've borrowed from my IRA three or four times during some extra lean financial periods with my own company, but only when I was *really* confident that I'd have the money to repay it within 60 days – such as when I knew for certain a sufficient receivable was due to arrive very soon, or when we had a software license agreement just waiting for a sure-fire management signature before we could call it a bona fide sale. In really tough situations this method can be invaluable – but I have to caution, it can lead to very sleepless nights!

Technically, what you're doing is going through the motions of *transferring* an amount of money from one personal IRA custodial account to a new or second IRA account, using that money for your business needs before you actually deposit it in the second account. Keep in mind, this is not considered a rollover, and make sure you don't request anything by that term with your source and target IRA custodian. Here are the specifics of what you do:

- Since the process is technically called a *transfer* of IRA funds from one custodial account (source bank) to another custodial account (target bank), you would normally have an IRA at each of two financial institutions. (I always maintained two self-directed IRA accounts, one at Charles Schwab and the other at Fidelity Investments – and with my wife (who was part-owner of our company) having two accounts at each firm as well, we could double up on this). IRS rules, though, allow you to treat your source custodial account also as your target custodial account, simply putting the money back into the account you took it from.

- Request a transfer (again, don't ever let the term rollover enter into the discussion) of the necessary amount from the IRA at your source custodial account. Be sure to request that the check be made out personally to you and paid directly to you. The only problem with this is, the financial institution won't know whether you're really transferring it to another IRA account, or if this should be considered as a distribution, so they might argue that a 20% tax withholding _has_ to be done – and if they do, it could mess this idea up, as you still have to deposit the full amount in the target IRA, and there's no way you can get the money back except by declaring it as a refund on the year's taxes. To make this work, you need to argue as hard as necessary to have the custodian write the check to you _without withholding_. If you can't, forget this idea.

- You can now deposit the money in your personal bank account, and for 60 days from the date of withdrawal you can do whatever you wish with this money – such as loaning it to your company.

- By no later than the 60th day from date of withdrawal, make certain that you deposit the money in your target IRA account.

- At year-end, the source financial institution will report to the IRS that you've withdrawn x-amount of money on such-and-such date, and the target financial institution will report that you've deposited a like amount on such-and-such date (and you don't report anything). Assuming the two dates match up within 60 days, the IRS will figure out that you've made a transfer, and everything is OK.

It couldn't be simpler ... and like the ROBS plan described above, _it couldn't be more risky with your retirement money_. Don't do this unless you're fully aware of the risks – and accept them with your eyes wide open. The upside to this is, there are no advisor fees; the downside is, it's a 60-day loan at most.

Peer-to-peer lending (P2P). And now we're back to more appropriate alternative lending methods – peer-to-peer lending. It's only been around for a few years (about 2006 to be exact). It's also known as the _social lending business_, and sometimes referred to as person-to-person lending. The basic idea is for a middleman website to match up borrowers with lenders – and hence, the lending is done directly between two people (i.e., peer-to-peer), without going through a traditional financial intermediary such as a bank or other financial institution.[141]

In addition to brokering and managing the loan, a P2P organization also charges a fee (called an origination fee) for the service, which is typically between 1%–6% of the loan amount, based on the borrower's credit score. Loan amounts can be up to $35,000, with terms ranging from 3–5 years, and interest rates currently (2017) ranging between 4.9%–35.9% , again based on the borrower's credit score (ouch, on the high end of the interest rates are murderous!).

---

[141] Peter Renton, _Understanding Peer-to-Peer Lending_, Lend Academy Investments website, 2014, www.lendacademy.com/Understanding-Peer-to-Peer-Lending.pdf

This is a fluid business, and of the six P2P lending sites that were dominate in the market in 2016, only one is still in the list of top lenders (and that's Lending Club):

SoFi (https://www.sofi.com)

Even Financial (www.evenfinancial.com)

Discover Personal Loans (www.discover.com)

GuidetoLenders (www.guidetolenders.com)

24/7LoanPros (www.247lendingpros.com)

LendingClub (www.lendingclub.com)

LightStream (www.lightstream.com)

These additional P2P lenders still exist; they just aren't quite as much the flavor of the month as last year:

Prosper (www.prosper.com)

Funding Circle (www.fundingcircle.com)

Upstart (www.upstart.com)

Kiva (www.kiva.org)

Zopa (www.zopa.com)

The loan money does not originate with any of these brokering sites, but rather, from investors who link up with the borrower through one of the sites, thereby expecting to earn a higher return on money than they can otherwise earn. At least, that's the theory – but since financial institutions rarely miss a trick in how to earn money, nowadays several large banking institutions have essentially replaced the small-time investors and the big money is now lent by the banks – the very outfits that P2P was trying to go around.[142]

Given how difficult traditional lending from commercial banks can often be these days, even with the aid of SBA-guaranteed loans, a Peer-to-Peer loan might be a very attractive option.

Vendor or customer financing. Both of these alternative lending options might seem rather odd, but each can be useful in its own way, when either your supplier or customer sufficiently value enough what you do to give you financial assistance.

I know an owner of a very small software company – with a small customer base of about 75 commercial customers – whose software is heavily custom-tailored specifically for these customers. As a result, the customers are very loyal to this vendor – so much so that one customer is willing to finance the development of a new software enhancement to the tune of several hundred thousand dollars ... and it's likely they wouldn't balk if the money was never repaid. That's how much this customer wants/needs this enhancement, and there's no alternative for it except from this vendor's software.

It's a nice situation if you can get yourself into it, but it can also be a very risky way to run your business. Rather than become indebted to just a few customers, it might be better in the long run

---

[142] Nav Athwal, *The Disappearance Of Peer-To-Peer Lending*, Forbes online, October 14, 2014, http://www.forbes.com/sites/groupthink/2014/10/14/the-disappearance-of-peer-to-peer-lending/

to build your business on a broader customer base, and one that's not so reliant on just a few customers. Customers can turn fickle for the strangest of reasons, and it can leave you holding the bag with a product that can't be sold anywhere else.

An alternative to vendor financing is where a customer lends money (or resources) so that the vendor (you) can then buy products or services from that customer. Another form of it is when the customer takes an equity stake in the vendor in exchange for the money loaned. Both of these are risky business for the customer, as it would typically only happen when you (the vendor) are in a shaky financial condition, which means you may never repay the loan, leaving the customer to write down the loss as a bad debt, or the shares you've pledged to the customer become worthless – and worse, you are no longer buying products from that customer.

This type of financing is quite unusual, except in cases where the vendor and customer have a very solid relationship. But when you can't qualify for loans any other way, it's worth considering.

Bartering. Probably one of the oldest forms of alternative financing, bartering can be a very cost-effective way to preserve capital, not only in the start-up phase, but as you grow the business. Sometimes you have to be quite creative in identifying products and resources that you might offer for barter, pairing them up with vendors or customers whose expertise or products you need.

The items being bartered don't even have to be tangible. An example might be to offer your accountant or CPA firm a valuable introduction to a client they might want to have, in exchange for the cost of a tax filing you need done. Or, if you're a small craft brewing start-up in that same situation, you could offer several kegs of your best beer for their upcoming annual company picnic, or if you have a tasting room , you could offer free use of it for one or more of their late Friday afternoon happy hours.

As described in a 2013 story in The Washington Post,[143] one small start-up, Round Table Companies (www.roundtablecompanies.com), a somewhat non-traditional marketing company in Jacksonville (FL), *"bartered the creation of a full color graphic novel in exchange for a new website design from one of the top companies in the design business. The value of the trade was $50,000. We provided three months of writing services to create the graphic novel storyline (as a marketing vehicle for this company) and then five months of illustration. In exchange, they helped us to define, design, and then program our new website in Expression Engine over the course of six to seven months"*.

In another example from the Post story, a small health information services company with offices in New York and Chicago, called ContextMedia (www.contextmediainc.com, and now Outcome Health) , bartered *"an upfront rent abatement for a long-term lease ... [and also] used one of our equipment provider's logo in our sales material, and we got a pretty neat discount in return"*.

---

[143] J.D. Harrison, *Bartering secrets: Entrepreneurs turn to age-old business strategy when money gets tight*, March 6, 2013, http://www.washingtonpost.com/blogs/on-small-business/post/bartering-secrets-entrepreneurs-turn-to-age-old-business-strategy-when-money-gets-tight/2013/03/05/e50708ba-859b-11e2-93a3-b3db6b9ac586_blog.html.

In addition to bartering one-on-one with vendors you deal with every day, you can also join a bartering organization – look for it under "barter exchange *yourcityname*". For example, for my hometown, I pulled up Seattle Barter Exchange, at www.seattlebarterexchange.com; in San Francisco, it's IMS San Francisco Barter, at https://www.imsbarter.com/san-francisco-barter, and they list 50 other city markets they operate in.[144] Another is U-Exchange, at http://www.u-exchange.com/businessbarter. With many of these online exchanges, even businesses in small- to medium-sized cities can access exchanges that specialize in business services – such as a nationwide network called ITEX – at www.itex.com – where you key in your state and it pulls up a nationwide map of locations.

In most of these exchanges, you can specify what you can give and what you'd like in return, or simply throw out what you're offering and see what kinds of offers you get in return.

Lastly about bartering, if you're going to do it, make sure you know all of the tax implications. The IRS has created a web page for your benefit,[145] listing four very important things you need to know if you barter:

1. If you barter through an exchange, the exchange itself is required by the IRS to issue you a 1099 and file it with the IRS. That ensures the taxman knows the value of your bartering, and you'll be liable for the tax on it.

2. For tax purposes, bartering (including *trade dollars*) is the same as real dollars for tax purposes. Make sure you give your tax accountant the fair market value of your bartered goods and services received.

3. Bartering must be reported in the tax year it occurs.

4. Know the rules for reporting bartering to the IRS (which is something your tax accountant will likely know).

---

[144] Michelle Goodman, *Using Barter To Help A Business Succeed*, January 17, 2012, http://www.entrepreneur.com/article/222478

[145] *Four Things You Should Know If You Barter*, March 8, 2013, http://www.irs.gov/uac/Newsroom/Four-Things-You-Should-Know-if-You-Barter

Chapter 5   Financial Management

"Finance is the art of passing currency from hand to hand until it finally disappears."
Robert W. Sarnoff, former President of NBC and RCA

Preface to this chapter: The small business financial statements discussed in this chapter are too large to be reasonably included inside this book. You can obtain a downloadable sample of each, as well as an Excel spreadsheet template of our recommended Cash Flow/Budget spreadsheet at www.turning-ip101.com/books, and accompanying website for this book. Fill out the brief form and enter the code "CFB2016-1" in the box. It will then download a sample Balance Sheet, P&L Statement, Cash Flow/Budget, and a sample LLC Resolution template in PDF format. It will also download an Excel spreadsheet of a Cash Flow/Budget template that you can modify for use with your small business. With it, you'll also receive instructions for filling out the Cash Flow/Budget with your own small business numbers, as well as several ideas for how to use this spreadsheet in your everyday small business life – particularly for "what-if" planning and running pricing scenarios.

Preparing for financial mechanisms and internal controls

In the last chapter we explored many ways to finance your business operations. Now we need to explore how you gauge your company's success – with financial management that not only tells *you* how your company is doing, but also provides insight on your company's business and financial health to outside banks and investors you might be dealing with (including someone who might be interested in buying your business). The full spread of financial reporting isn't something you must have in place on the day you open your doors, but parts of it are extremely valuable in your start-up planning, and will remain even more valuable as your business grows.

Just as importantly, as other people in your company begin to play a role in managing aspects of your company's finances, you need to know if all the money you're earning from product/service sales is going where it should be going, not being nefariously spent, and not being accounted for incorrectly.

For many first-time entrepreneurs, financial management is a black hole – with terminology that doesn't make intuitive sense to the non-accountant layman, and it's not intuitive in how to apply it to your business operations. Worse, it's difficult to find simple English language explanations of how to financially manage your new small business. It's such a major problem that a New

York Times article ranks it as the 3rd biggest cause of new business failure in the first five years.[146]

The problem is, most of the literature on how to read and understand financial management reporting is written for – and about – large, publically-traded companies, where a huge percentage of the information is irrelevant to a small business. To prove that statement, do an internet search on "reading financial statements" and follow the links to the first dozen (or so) hits that you get. You'll get opening sentences such as "*Knowing how to work with the numbers in a company's financial statements is an essential skill for <u>stock investors</u>*", or you'll see an example of a Consolidated Balance Sheet that's being explained – where the word *consolidated* in this context means that not only is the parent company's financial information included, but also for all of its subsidiaries. How much does any of that apply to you, the first-time sole business owner who is trying to fathom the financial health of your 3-person company? On the other hand, if you specifically search on "financial statements for the small business owner", you'll get some good hits. For our audience here, we need practical information that will benefit a small business owner.

> *"Remind people that profit is the difference between revenue and expense.*
> *This makes you look smart."*
> Scott Adams, creator of the Dilbert comic strip

Cost accounting and cash flow budgeting

Let's start our financial management discussion with cost accounting and cash flow budgeting, as these two terms represent the single most important tool you need for getting your new business started smoothly and for managing <u>day-to-day operations</u> – as opposed to the more traditional financial statements that your bank and other outside sources will ask for, but that you'll also need to learn about.

Most business advisors suggest that you implement a Cash Flow Statement as one of the three primary financial statements for your business, the other two being the Balance Sheet and the Income Statement (a.k.a. the Profit & Loss Statement or P&L). In fact, for publicly-traded companies, the Cash Flow Statement became a legal requirement in 1987. Because of their complexity, we'll leave any further description or discussion of the Balance Sheet and P&L for a separate topic later in this chapter.

In simple terms, a Cash Flow Statement shows actual cash-in (revenue) and cash-out (expenses) of a company during a specific time period (usually the same time period as your P&L). To see what a *standard* Cash Flow Statement looks like, and to read a description of what's in it, review the Investopedia article on Cash Flow Statements.[147]

---

[146] Jay Goltz, *Top 10 Reasons Small Businesses Fail*, The New York Times – You're The Boss, January 5, 2011, http://boss.blogs.nytimes.com/2011/01/05/top-10-reasons-small-businesses-fail/?_r=0
[147] Reem Heakal, *What Is A Cash Flow Statement?*, Investopedia website, http://www.investopedia.com/articles/04/033104.asp?header_alt=b

In this book, we'll use the term Cash Flow/Budget report, which is a variation of the typical Cash Flow Statement, incorporating a budget that we'll live and die by in successfully running our small business.

The format of our Cash Flow/Budget report has an extensive Excel spreadsheet behind it and is designed to be a full year report of cash flows (cash in and cash out), with side-by-side monthly columns starting in January. It's also a budget, because there are three columns for each month's numbers – including a Budget column, allowing you to forecast ahead of time what each revenue and expense line will be in future months. Then as each month ends, an Actual column is filled in for each revenue and expense line, and a Variance column is automatically computed that shows the positive/negative difference between the budget number and actual number. Our Cash Flow/Budget also encourages you to be as detailed as you can, down to the detail of each product/service that you sell (or if you sell lots of different products, grouping them into categories). Just as importantly, it includes a Cost of Sales section with each category of products, giving you a Gross Profit Margin for each. With these additions, our Cash Flow/Budget is transformed into a type of cost accounting tool that lets you see extremely valuable profitability numbers at the individual product level.

The real beauty of the Cash Flow/Budget is that it starts off as your single best tool *during the planning stages for starting your company*, giving you a template for testing and proving your numbers for your initial business plan. Without it, most first-time small business entrepreneurs are stumbling in the dark to put together revenue numbers. From these numbers, you can determine product pricing strategy, individual profit margins by product/category, determine if chopping expenses is mandatory, and view overall company profit/loss by month. With the cash flow information plugged in, you can see how each month's operations flow to your business checking account. Best of all, incorporating a copy of it at the pre-start-up stage into your SBA bank loan application can be very beneficial for your banker.

Similar level of detail is recommended for all of the expense numbers, forcing you to think carefully through all of the expenses that you anticipate in the next year, plugging them into the budget in the specific months you expect them to occur (for example, business insurance will probably be due every six months, various product resources and raw materials will hopefully be purchased at appropriate times, etc.).

What I've just described for the Cash Flow/Budget report is essentially what cost accounting is all about. By definition, cost accounting is:[148]

- determining the costs of products, processes, projects, etc. in order to report the correct amounts on the financial statements, and
- assisting management in making decisions and in the planning and control of an organization.

Your cash flow budgeting principles are especially important in your company's early days, when the bank account is very low, your ability to project levels of sales versus expenses isn't yet spot-on, and you don't really know where you're making your money (or incurring losses) within your

---

[148] *What Is Cost Accounting*, accountingcoach.com website – Q&A,
http://www.accountingcoach.com/blog/what-is-cost-accounting

company. The Cash Flow/Budget is perfect for that, which makes it even more crucial before then, when you're in the planning stages ... when you're trying to find out if your business idea will even fly. (Cash flow budgeting and cash management are two different things, and each will be explored separately – in this chapter we're going to talk about cash flow budgeting.)

The Cash Flow/Budget is also an important tool for well-capitalized companies, when new and inexperienced business owners assume they can spend lavishly with that pile of money in the bank, with the mistaken belief there will always be plenty of cash. Stories abound, particularly from the go-go start-up days (such as we experienced in the frenzy leading up to the 2000 tech-bubble – and could be happening again now, 17 years later) of young companies leasing expensive office space and furniture that drains the coffers, or providing lavish employee perks that aren't affordable over the long haul. Instead, the focus should be on conservative spending habits, watching every dollar that goes _out_ the door – and just as important, watching every dollar that comes _in_ the door.

(Suggestion: The next time you need office furniture and have the urge to buy the latest design from an expensive supplier, try looking into a surplus office furniture auction. Businesses are constantly moving to new locations, and their existing office furniture just doesn't fit, so they sell like-new furniture for a pittance at auctioneers. The money you save here could likely pay for some much-needed marketing efforts, which will bring in new revenue better than fancy office digs.)

It's every new business owner's dream that customers will begin knocking down the door the minute word gets out about your product or service, but this is rarely the case. The reality is, your revenue projections will almost certainly be optimistic (both timing and amount, which is normal – otherwise, you wouldn't be an entrepreneur) – and your expense estimates will be pessimistic, erring on the low side. Getting a handle on this is the primary purpose of a Cash Flow/Budget, particularly one that presents optimistic, pessimistic, and best case scenarios.

Just so we're on the same page, let me say it again. Creating a Cash Flow/Budget is one of the most important things you'll do _in the run-up to opening your business doors_ – and throughout the subsequent operation of your small business. Without it, you're flying blind; with it you'll feel more comfortable there will be sufficient _positive_ cash flow to keep the doors open. If you don't use this all-important tool, you're faced with an almost sure-fire situation of running out of cash, forcing you to close the doors.

As an aside, the mere mention of the word _budget_ always made me cringe in my early small business days. In _big company_ experiences before my entrepreneur life (including time in the U.S. Air Force), frequent references were made about padding expense budgets _just in case_. And I saw quite a few instances where managers would unnecessarily deplete their budgets in the waning months of a budget year, on the theory of _use it or lose it_ in next year's budget – in my estimation one of the most pernicious things a manager can do to the financial wellbeing of a company.

With this background, I fiercely (and naively) resisted cash flow budgets in my own small company for many years, learning late in the game just how valuable they can be. When I finally accepted them as an intelligent way to actually _manage_ the cash flow and budgeting of my company, I regretted all those early years – and regretted that I didn't have the financial knowledge that can enable much faster growth (not to mention better sleep).

As a start-up, if you're thinking, *"I don't know enough yet about my business to create a Cash Flow/Budget"* – well, rubbish! A Cash Flow/Budget is nothing more than a bunch of guesses and assumptions – that hopefully get better as your experience grows. Put another way, if you can't come up with forecast budget numbers that you can make sense of ... well, you aren't ready to start your business yet.

Creating a Cash Flow/Budget Report. (Note: download the sample Cash Flow/Budget that's described in the preface to this chapter before proceeding.)

Unlike the more standardized financial statements, such as the Balance Sheet and the Income Statement (a.k.a. Profit and Loss Statement, or P&L for short), the combined cash flow and cost accounting report that I recommend – called a Cash Flow/Budget – should be developed long before actual start-up for your company. It can have whatever format you prefer, with a level of information that works best for you. The format I recommend is a hybrid of the Statement of Cash Flow report and a Cash Budget report that you typically see recommended by accountants and business advisors. Since the goal here is to make the Cash Flow/Budget a large segment of a business owner's financial management repertoire, the goal will be to make it relatively easy to load the numbers, easy to understand, and intuitive for day-to-day management by any first-time entrepreneur.

As such, the Cash Flow/Budget report goes well beyond what you normally see in "how to run your start-up business" books and websites. On an everyday basis, the report format is directly valuable to you as a hands-on business owner, although you might also find it valuable for your business banker as part of your monthly financial statements if you have an outstanding bank loan. The report provides ongoing monitoring of all financial aspects of your business, helping you identify your most profitable products and services, the costs of producing those products and services, whether your pricing model is appropriate, how much everything else in your business is costing you, how well you are doing in forecasting business revenue and expenses, and how much money you have in the bank.

The best part of the Cash Flow/Budget is that there's much less highfalutin accounting complexity involved (as there is with the Balance Sheet and Income Statement). It's something any business owner can understand from the get-go – although, it will require a fair amount of detailed number-gathering from you at the outset to create the initial budget numbers. As mentioned above, you are free to customize the Cash Flow/Budget to fit your specific business needs, but to begin, I recommend that you start with the suggested format.

If possible, you'll want to first create this report while your business is in the early planning stages. By doing so, the Excel spreadsheet numbers will be created by you, rather than by your bookkeeper or accountant. After all, you know your products and services better than anyone, what you expect to charge for them, how many/much you hope to sell, and your level of hoped-for growth. It will require you to carefully analyze all of your costs, up front and before you actually start to spend money ... beyond the mere daydreams that got you to this point in the first place. Putting your projected revenue and expense numbers into a spreadsheet allows you to adjust them up and down to see the effect, and enables you to subject your numbers to what-if scenarios. At that point you will not only have these cash flow projections for the start of your operations, but as your business takes shape and you have the first month's sales and expenses, you'll begin having actual numbers to fill in each month. From this you can readily see the effects of missed revenue projections and unexpected expenses, and how this can ripple down to your company's bottom line. As you learn more and more about your business, you can tweak the projections, hopefully making them more reliable as you gain experience of how your revenue and expenses are tracking.

Creating a Cash Flow/Budget spreadsheet. The process is somewhat lengthy, with dozens of revenue/expense details you need to pull out of the air – and the nuts and bolts of it are thoroughly explained in the Template Instructions that accompany the download of the sample spreadsheet. In addition to the blank template, there's also a mock-up spreadsheet for a hypothetical craft brewery start-up company, hopefully providing some real-world-like numbers and assumptions to the cells that help illustrate how it all goes together.

Once you've created your customized Cash Flow/Budget report, how do you get the most from it? The three best ways to use it are:

- For your own understanding of what's necessary to make your company profitable and successful. This tells you which products are the most profitable, and likely the most important for your success. This is a day-to-day type of spreadsheet – not that you'll necessarily look at it every day, but it gives you real operating information about how your business needs to perform this week, this month, and this quarter. It can provide insight into how and where you need to cut expenses, and depending on how you use it, to shorten production and process cycles.

  (Note: the Template Instructions contain at least a dozen ways that you can use the Cash Flow/Budget spreadsheet to plan "what-if" scenarios, and this is where a major value of the spreadsheet comes in.)

- For your managers, to be able to see exactly where and how their contributions are affecting the business, not only for revenue, but for expenses they can control. Assuming you're OK with sharing these numbers with a subset of your employees (highly recommended), a 1-2 hour monthly meeting is all it should take to go over the report, illustrating to you and your managers how well your goals have been met for the previous month – whether you're on track year-to-date, and revenue/expense goals that are necessary in the months ahead.
- For year-to-year budgeting. Towards the end of the calendar year, the current year's numbers will be invaluable for producing next year's Cash Flow/Budget. In fact, a good suggestion is to add another column in each month's section, with the actual number from the same month a year ago. That way, you can see, year-over-year, if – and how much – your business is growing and how well you're controlling costs. I like to keep the same spreadsheet from year to year, naming each worksheet with the year, and that way when I'm using the actual Excel spreadsheet I can quickly compare data from one year to the next.

Some business owners might feel uncomfortable sharing certain data fields with managers – such as salary figures, cash in the bank, line of credit balances. Removing these cells from the spreadsheet will skew the results, so a good way to prevent them from appearing in shared meeting printed copies is to temporarily change the font color in these cells to "paper white" and even though the numbers are still there in the actual spreadsheet, they will appear as blank cells in the printed report. You can also ask that copies be returned to you at the close of the meeting so they can be shredded for confidentiality.

Let's get started. Begin by creating a couple of lists, preferably in a quick and dirty spreadsheet that isn't necessarily connected to our budget spreadsheet.

- The first list identifies every product and service in your business that will provide revenue. This should lead to some serious and realistic thinking about pricing for each product and service. You'll then need to estimate (again, as realistically as you can) how much of each product or service you'll sell, month-by-month, throughout the next year. For the first-time entrepreneur, much of this analysis might very well addle your brain, as it will seem like too much guesswork, but if you can't come up with numbers that you feel able to justify, well, you're frankly not ready to start your business.

- The second list identifies every expense you expect in the first year of business, the month that you expect it to fall in, and the amount you want to budget for each expense. This includes recurring expenses for product materials, production costs, rent, salary and wages, taxes, administrative costs, travel and entertainment ... anything you'll be writing a check for or charging to your company credit card. As you're compiling this list, separate the expenses that are _directly related_ to the production of each product and/or service from the first list (for developing what's known as a "cost of sales" section of the budget).

As you plug the product-by-product revenue numbers into the spreadsheet, followed by the associated expenses, you'll begin to see what each product costs to produce, giving you the _gross profit margin_ you'll earn from each product. In so doing, you'll also begin to develop an understanding of which products are more vital to your success, and which ones might be a real drain on that success. (This exercise will illustrate to you the importance – and difference between – the terms _gross and net profit margin_.)

To make certain you fully understand that, stop and think about this for a second – if Product A is producing a 75% gross profit margin, while Product B is only producing a 40% gross profit margin, an obvious deduction is that you might want to concentrate more of your efforts on either selling more of Product A, or figuring out ways to improve Product B's gross profit margin (by lowering its cost of production, increasing sales of it, or raising prices). As you begin to play with the numbers (again, keeping it as realistic as you can), this cost of sales analysis might illustrate there's nothing you can do to make a profit on some product or service – and the last thing you can afford is to find that, the more you sell of a product, the more loss it is for you.

As you progress deeper into the spreadsheet numbers – to the sales, marketing, and administrative costs (known as G&A, for General and Administrative expenses), you'll now see if your overall gross profit margins are high enough to cover your general operating costs – and this gives you your _net profit_ – which is now getting pretty close to telling you how much money the business is really putting into your pocket.

If you're wondering what percentage of gross or net profit margins you should be shooting for ... well, there's no right answer. Two companies in the same industry, with similar products or services, might have significantly different gross and net profits. There are just too many variables for each company to have one right number. Your goal here is to determine the numbers *for your particular company*, use those numbers to determine if your company is *making it* (i.e., successful to the extent necessary for you), and to then work towards a capability to increase the numbers – at least at the very bottom line level (overall profitability). Tracking both net and gross profit is very important, so they should go into the separate spreadsheet you develop for keeping track of your other business metrics.

Sounds simple, huh? If it does, you're ready to download and begin filling in the spreadsheet template for the Cash Flow/Budget.

Bedrock of accounting – cash or accrual, and tax returns

Before we proceed to the more formalized set of financial statements, some basic accounting background is necessary – and you'll quickly see why preparing these reports should be left to your bookkeeper or outside accountant (and why more effort is necessary to really understand them to become useful). The big problem for the non-accountant, new business owner is gaining an understanding of a dozen intertwined concepts, with terminology that isn't intuitive.

Choosing your tax year. The first concept we'll look at is choosing your business' *tax year*. Non-business people are often confused by this because there's no such thing as choosing a tax year for your personal taxes – by definition the calendar year is your tax year, and that's just the way it is. And if your small business is structured so that income and expenses flow through to you, as the individual (as in a sole proprietorship, partnership, an S-Corp, or an LLC taxed as a sole proprietorship), the IRS requires that you select calendar year as your tax year. Otherwise, you're free to select any month-end as your tax year, at which point you then file your business taxes for all business operations in the preceding 12 months.[149] Some seasonal businesses prefer this, as their taxes then follow the flow of the business. Unless you have a really good reason to choose a month-end *other than* December for your tax year, don't do it – it will seriously complicate your business life, and remember, you're in business to keep the business going and growing, not to make it more complicated.

Asset depreciation and expensing. The next concept (and arguably much more important) is *asset depreciation*, because it figures prominently into the basic concepts of business accounting – a method that we'll discuss in just a bit for recording your income and expenses, called *cash basis* versus *accrual basis*. As we'll see, each business gets to choose which method to use (within accepted guidelines), primarily differing in the *timing* of when financial transactions are credited as income or debited as expenses. We'll briefly touch on a third method – *tax basis* – which is just cash or accrual basis with a twist.

An asset, by the way, can be either a tangible asset, like a piece of equipment that you purchase, or intangible, such as a copyright, patent, or computer software. It can also be a prepaid amount, let's say for a year's worth of business insurance, or a service contract, declining in value each month as the asset is used up.

---

[149] Caron Beesley, *Calendar or Fiscal? Which Tax Year is Right for your Small Business?*, SBA blog – Managing a Business, January 7, 2013, https://www.sba.gov/blogs/calendar-or-fiscal-which-tax-year-right-your-small-business

Depreciation (in the accounting sense) is technically defined as "a method of allocating the cost of a tangible asset over its useful life ... businesses depreciate long-term assets for both tax and accounting purposes".[150] Put another way, the purpose of depreciation is to match the purchase cost of an asset with the income that the asset helps the company to earn.

Expensing an item that you've purchased means that you deduct the full cost of purchase from your business income on your accounting books at the time of purchase. This is also known as *writing it off*.

Depreciation is a hard concept for most small business owners to fully understand and appreciate. It is considered a *non-cash expense* in your business, and as such doesn't directly affect your revenue or expenses to actually operate your business. Depreciation does, though, have a significant effect on your financial statements, improving or reducing how well your business *looks* from a financial health standpoint. It can also have significant tax effects. So it's a financial aspect that a small business owner must learn about, to consider when purchasing depreciable items for your business, and to understand how it can affect you financially.

As a business owner you can choose to depreciate a capital item over time, or expense it all at once – and you're allowed to depreciate it even if you haven't fully paid for it yet (i.e., you're paying it off on time). You cannot depreciate leased or rented assets – but if you purchase an asset and lease or rent it to someone else, you can depreciate it as *your* asset (because you're the one who bought it). Assets that can be depreciated are generally considered those that are income-producing or are used in your business to produce income. If you have assets that are used for both business and personal, only the business portion can be depreciated (such as a vehicle that you use personally, as well as for business). Inventory, while it's listed as an asset on your financial statements, cannot be depreciated since it was made or purchased by your company and is being held for sale to a customer (and therefore, is not used in the course of your business).

Which is better – fast or slow depreciation? Your choice of depreciating or expensing an asset can have significant tax and profit/loss implications for your business, and your overall profit or loss that's offset by the depreciation is an important consideration. If the asset is being depreciated, speed is also important. In simple terms, the faster you can depreciate something, the better it *usually* is for tax reasons – you have more money in your pocket, as you're able to deduct the depreciated cost from your income sooner rather than later.

Your depreciation methodology also has to be weighed against the value the asset adds to your company's net worth in your financial books, as each dollar you write off decreases your company's current net worth by that much (in accounting parlance, it decreases the *book value* of your company by that amount) – and therefore, slower depreciation helps make your balance sheet look better because the value of the asset "stays on your books" longer. This is why it's a good idea for you (and your bookkeeper to have an annual discussion with your tax accountant about how you expect to handle depreciation in the coming year.

Small, short-life purchases (such as office supplies and other expendables that don't have an expected lifespan of more than a year) are immediately expensed. You don't really have a choice in this ... being short-life items, there's no justifiable reason to depreciate them.

---

[150] *Definition of Depreciation*, Investopedia, http://www.investopedia.com/terms/d/depreciation.asp

Longer-life assets (that typically cost more than $100), such as equipment, commercial buildings, office furniture, computers, and autos to name a few, will probably have to depreciate as an expense over multiple years on your financial statements (and on your tax return).[151] This is also known as *capitalizing*, as the *depreciated value* of the asset will be reported on your books – and the longer the capitalized asset remains on your books, the higher your company's total assets will be. And as we'll see in a bit, higher total assets help your company have a higher net worth (total assets minus total liabilities equals net worth) – which is a metric that helps you, as a business owner, as well as your bank and outside investors, know the health of your business.

For depreciation purposes, long-term assets fall into two categories:

- The first is real estate – buildings, property improvements. Land that you own can never be depreciated, as it's not an asset that wears out or reaches the end of its useful life. If you purchase real estate that includes both the land and a building, you can only depreciate the fair market value of the building, but not the land. The cost of equipment used to create property improvements also cannot be depreciated.
- The second is pretty much all other assets – including equipment or machinery used in your business, computers and software purchased for use on the computers, furniture, fixtures, vehicles, and intangible assets such as patents or copyrights *that you've purchased*, etc.

For tax purposes, the IRS has different time periods and rules under which each asset category can be depreciated. Real estate is depreciated over 25 years; all other assets will generally be depreciated over what is considered each asset's useful life – the time period in which the asset gets *used up*, loses its value, wears out, or becomes obsolete.

The basic methodology for depreciating uses the following parameters:

- For buildings and capital improvements, the standard depreciation period is 25 years; for capital improvements it can be 10, 15, or 20 years.
- For all the rest, you can use one of several depreciation methods, such as straight-line or accelerated (where more losses are ascribed at the beginning than in later years), and others that are allowed or prescribed by IRS rules. Examples of accelerated depreciation are declining balance, sum of the year's digit depreciation, double-declining balance, and several others that are allowable by the IRS.
- The initial value of the asset (presumably assets that initially cost more than $100). This is a primary test for a depreciable asset, but not the only one.
- A piece of equipment used in the business is a depreciable asset, and maintenance of that equipment can also be depreciable. For example, you can purchase a machine for $45,000 and depreciate it. You can later spend $16,000 to repair that piece of equipment, and that amount too can be depreciated.
- The useful life of the asset. The useful life is the reasonable time the asset can be used to generate income for the company or benefit the company. It doesn't necessarily refer to the actual time the asset might last, and could be affected by technology changes and other factors.

---

[151] *A Brief Overview of Depreciation*, IRS, http://www.irs.gov/Businesses/Small-Businesses-&-Self-Employed/A-Brief-Overview-of-Depreciation

- The time period the IRS allows you to depreciate.[152] The list is so complicated that careful reading of the referenced IRS publication is necessary – but more importantly, use a tax accountant who really knows the business. In general, here's the gist of it:
  - Three years for property such as farm equipment that's used *over the road*, manufacturing tools, and others
  - Five years for computers, office equipment, research and experimentation equipment, farm animals, cars and light trucks, alternative energy equipment (solar, geothermal, wind power), and equipment and furnishings used in a residential rental property
  - Seven years for office furniture, appliances, agricultural machinery, and others
  - Ten years for most water vessels used in business, single purpose agricultural and horticulture equipment, trees or vines bearing fruits or nuts, and smart electric grid equipment
- The residual value of the asset at the end of the useful life (assuming it has one), which is calculated into the amount that can be depreciated using the straight-line method (but not accelerated).

Here's a simple example of depreciation, using 5-year depreciation for the computer and office equipment that you purchased to start up your business. Assume the total value of the equipment purchased was $25,000. You figure the residual value will be $5,000 at the end of five years. You record the equipment as a capital asset worth $25,000 on your financial books, leaving you with a depreciable value of $20,000 over the five years. You depreciate the value by $4,000 each year (1/5th of $20,000), whereby the equipment value reaches $5,000 on your accounting books at the end of the fifth year. By that point in time, the *book value* shown on your Balance Sheet for your company will also have decreased (depreciated) by the entire $20,000. Over that time period, the equipment theoretically helped you generate revenue, but it also provided you with a tax deduction of $4,000 each year, applied against your profits for the year. And from a tax standpoint, you were able to deduct the depreciation amount from the revenue generated in each of those years.

Faster or slower depreciation can either help or hurt your tax liability, depending on your gross revenue each year that you apply the tax deduction. If your gross profit is high in the year you purchase the asset, it might be more advantageous to accelerate deductions. If your gross profit is low, and/or it will take time for the asset to really begin generating gross profit for you, slower depreciation could be better. Discussions with your tax advisor about revenue growth versus asset depreciation can be crucial for you.

Where this gets more complicated is the various rules you have to abide by in (a) whether you must expense or capitalize an asset purchase, and (b) determining the number of years over which you can depreciate an asset. Some of the rules are dictated by the IRS; others are dictated by GAAP standards.

Oops! Now I've mentioned GAAP, so it needs a brief explanation. This acronym, pronounced "gap", stands for Generally Accepted Accounting Principles, and is nothing more than a set of

---

[152] *Figuring Depreciation Under MACRS*, IRS website, publication 946, https://www.irs.gov/publications/p946/ch04.html

commonly accepted accounting standards that have been established by a national policy board known as FASB – an acronym for Financial Accounting Standards Board, and pronounced "fas-bee". (GAAP will be discussed more thoroughly in a later section of this chapter.)

Our example above ($20,000 over five years) is known as *straight-line depreciation*, the simplest GAAP method and the most common for small businesses. Other methods are *units of production* (UOP), *sum of the years' digits* method, and the most aggressive method is known as *declining balance* – all of which are too complicated for our purposes here.[153]

By contrast, the IRS has its own depreciation methods for most items, the two most common being the *Accelerated Cost Recovery System* (ACRS), and *Modified Accelerated Cost Recovery System* (MACRS)[154] – both of which use IRS-defined *declining* percentages. The IRS also allows the *amortization* method, which is similar to straight-line depreciation for certain assets.

So, with two different ruling authorities on depreciation, which should you use? Let's look at the typical solution.

The best of both worlds for depreciation – two sets of books. Wow! That almost sounds like cooking the books, but it's not. Many (most?) businesses keep two sets of books, and it's perfectly legal and proper. You can keep one set of books for tax purposes – how you report your finances to the IRS and other taxing authorities, and from which you pay your taxes. The other set of books is for your general accounting requirements – for your use in managing your business, plus what you report to the bank on your profit/loss, and what you show investors and other outside sources. Each set of books can use a different set of depreciation methods.

For example, GAAP rules used for your general accounting books might dictate that you use a specific time period for certain categories of asset, such as matching it to the useful life of the asset, spreading the cost that you incurred this year over several years. By contrast, the tax code might allow a special accelerated depreciation, and taking the deduction sooner rather than later might save dollars on this year's taxes.

It's imperative that your bookkeeper discuss the advantages and disadvantages for both sets of books with your tax accountant. It's imperative that you also participate in the discussion, as this not only affects your actual bottom-line dollars in your pocket, but also a huge effect on how your business looks to a banker deciding whether to grant you a loan or line of credit.

And that brings us to the promised *bedrock of accounting* – the <u>basis</u> you choose to credit income and debit expenses in your accounting system.

<u>Cash basis.</u> Many small businesses choose cash basis – for several reasons, but usually because the typical small business owner doesn't have an accounting background, and cash basis (in some situations) seems more intuitive when your revenue and expenses are based on actual cash-in and cash-out (i.e., you don't deal with invoices for either sales or expenses).

---

[153] Keela Helstrom, *GAAP Depreciation Methods*, Houston Chronical (Chron), http://smallbusiness.chron.com/gaap-depreciation-methods-55425.html

[154] *How To Depreciate Property*, IRS information Publication 4562 for Form 946, http://www.irs.gov/pub/irs-pdf/i4562.pdf

With cash basis, income is booked to the accounting system on the day money is actually handed to you, or when a credit card payment is received. If your company is dealing with revenue and expense invoices, income in a cash basis business is booked to the accounting system when an accounts receivable invoice is *actually paid*, rather than when you close a sale, and not when an invoice is sent out at the time of a sale. Expenses are booked when cash or a check is *actually written* to pay for something your company purchased (and not when you received the bill for it). Everything I just wrote in this paragraph can easily go in one ear and out the other for a typical first-time small business entrepreneur, so examples should help explain it.

Example #1. Let's say you have a small software company and you sell a copy of your software product today. The customer has paid the entire amount for it at the time it was ordered. In a cash basis business, you will book the sale today, since you received the payment today.

On the expense side of it, you stop by your local computer retailer and purchase a laptop to use in your business, paying for it with a company check. You'd book the expense today, as it's when you actually paid the expense. Or, if a vendor delivered raw materials that you'll use in a production process, and you write a check on the spot to pay for them, the expense is booked today.

These examples are typical of a cash-based business, and are quite easy to grasp the concepts. But as we'll see in the next example, it isn't always this intuitive.

Example #2. Again, assume your company is on a cash basis accounting system – and so we book revenue/expenses when cash comes in or goes out the door. If you sell a product to a customer in June for $1,000 and have a signed purchase order or contract for it at that time, you don't book it until you actually receive the check from the customer, which may be July or August. Likewise, if your company purchases a new computer on a company credit card for $1,000 in June, but you don't write the check for the credit card payment until July, the expense isn't booked until July.

In this example, it's no longer so intuitive. Granted, the money for the sale hits your checking account at the same time you book the sale, and the money that you actually pay for the computer goes out of your checking account at the same time you book the expense – but neither matches with your *expectations* of the money coming in at the time you closed the sale, nor your *obligation* to pay the bill at the time you order the computer. It does match, though, what's actually happening in your business checking account, and that's why it's called cash basis accounting. A similar downside is, if you make a sale in December that you don't get paid for until January, you won't get the benefit of booking the revenue until the next year. If you make a purchase in December that you don't pay for until January, you won't get the benefit of the business expense in the year you purchased it, but rather, next year.

Accrual basis. All medium-to-large businesses, particularly publicly-traded companies – and many, many small businesses – use the accrual method because accountants, savvy business owners, analysts and investors feel this method more accurately reflects the financial health of the business.

While it doesn't seem like it, the accrual basis actually matches better with what's going on in your company – although with a bunch of caveats. Technically, with accrual basis, you can book the revenue when a sale is made, or when the product/service is delivered, without regard to when the actual money is received. Likewise, on the expense side, the expense is booked when a goods and services invoice is received, _or_ the goods or services themselves are received, regardless of when you pay for them.

At face value, this timing seems well and good ... but hold on a minute. We just said that you would book a sale when you have the contractual event of the sale – this is true, but it isn't always that simple. With cash basis, the event that triggered booking to the accounting system was clear and distinct – it was when the money was received into your checking account, and when money went out of your checking account. With accrual basis, on both revenue and expenses, there are further rules you have to abide by (note the word _or_ in the revenue/expense definitions in the previous paragraph). Let's look at some examples to better understand the rules.

Example #1. If you close a deal in June with a customer to sell them 5,000 widgets, but you don't actually deliver the widgets until July, you can't book it as a sale until you've delivered in July; likewise, if you book a $10,000 consulting contract with a customer in June, but your work on the project is 1/5th per month starting in June, you can only book 1/5th of the contract in June and then the percentage completed in each following month that you perform work. Similarly, if you purchase a quantity of production resources under a single contract, but only 1/5th of the resources are delivered each month, you can only book 1/5th of the expense each month, and only on the percentage of the resource's income value received each month.

Let's delve into the consulting contract from the previous paragraph. Sure, you got the customer to agree to a full $10,000 contract that is to last for five months, so presumably the customer is expecting you to invoice at each month's end for the work performed to date, and so your invoice to the customer and the amount you book should be the same. But what if the customer tells you to invoice for the full $10,000 at the signing of the contract, but you're still doing 1/5th of the work each month – well, each month you can only book an amount equal to the work you did, even though the full contract amount is sitting in your business checking account.

The more you think about it, the more the accrual method makes sense – but you have to be more careful in following the _revenue/expense recognition rules_. And for many companies, questions continue over time about whether the revenue/expense recognition rules are being followed correctly and consistently. Revenue recognition can have a very large effect on your profitability, and therefore the taxes you pay, and whether your company looks fiscally sound on your financial statements. (It can also lead to big fights between you and your tax accountant, where each of you have different ideas for the acceptable revenue recognition rules that your business operates under – see Example #2).

A lot of firms that are required to file financial statements (by the Securities and Exchange Commission, investors, or financial institutions) find themselves in trouble, getting caught up in booking irregularities – which often involves revenue/expense recognition problems. In a small business, you have quite a bit of leeway here, as you won't be required by law or regulation to file financial statements (unless the IRS decides you're fiddling your books to escape taxes). But if you have outstanding debt with your bank and they are requesting monthly financial statements, you'll find yourself answering questions early on about how you are booking revenue and expenses. Likewise, down the road when you initiate a sale of your company, one of the very big items in the buyer's due diligence will be your revenue/expense recognition standards, and if things aren't found to be on the up-and-up, it could kill your deal. The advice from your bookkeeper or outside accountant goes a long way here towards making sure things are done correctly.

Example #2. My company's software had an annual maintenance *package* the customer would almost always purchase, at an additional annual price of 15% of the software's purchase price. We received the entire maintenance amount at the beginning of the *maintenance* year, but by GAAP accrual basis accounting rules we could only recognize 1/12th of the revenue each month as the year progressed. We had the money in the bank and we could spend it in any way we wished, but for accounting purposes (i.e., profitability that we could report to our bank), it didn't show up on our accounting books until it was officially recognized. (This was one reason my company was frequently outside of our loan covenants – our *actual* money in the bank indicated better company health than our accrual-basis revenue, yet our covenants (i.e., our ability to repay our loan) were based on the latter. It's one of those situations where the small business owner has to understand this *stuff*, allowing you to argue to your benefit when dealing with people who don't really understand your company's finances.)

Tax basis. Just like you do each year as an individual, your business must file annual tax returns, and IRS requirements might force you to alter some of your accounting numbers for your filing.

You'll have to declare your accounting basis the first time you file an IRS tax return for your new business (at the end of your first tax year). It's one of the first questions asked on IRS Schedule C, Profit or Loss From Business[155] – and the choices are: cash, accrual, or other (it implies at the top that this form is just for sole proprietorships, but it's also for an LLC and others).

The IRS doesn't care which method you use – *you just have to be consistent from year to year with what you've declared*. From your first business tax year on, you must continue to use the same accounting basis unless you file a Form 3115 to request a change with the IRS (and at that point, it gets really complicated to adjust for the current year how your income/expense numbers are to be applied).

Essentially, tax basis is the same as either cash or accrual basis (i.e., whichever one you elect), but with some minor differences – mostly in the way the IRS allows you to handle asset depreciation. Also, tax basis does not conform to GAAP accounting rules, which isn't a problem for small businesses without outside requirements to be in GAAP compliance, or who might not want to spend the money to have an accounting system based on GAAP. (Many banks and investors accept tax basis accounting.)

Suffice it to say here that tax basis, for both depreciation and inventory, must follow the rules spelled out by the IRS; whereas GAAP follows its own set of rules established by FASB. For example, GAAP depreciation is also known as *book* depreciation, and the number of years over which you depreciate an asset can be very different than for tax basis. Another example, assume that you're keeping two sets of financial books, one tax basis for the IRS and one GAAP for the bank. If you decide that the $25,000 computer and office equipment really only have a useful life

---

[155] *Profit or Loss From Business*, IRS Form 1040, Schedule C, http://www.irs.gov/pub/irs-pdf/f1040sc.pdf

of three years, but the IRS requires you to depreciate it at five years, you can certainly use your own useful life time period for your GAAP books, but then pay your taxes based on the IRS rules. This accelerated time period means you are taking more depreciation (i.e., lowering the value) of your equipment in the first few years of the equipment's life span and less depreciation in later years – effectively saving you some tax money in the early years but costing more in taxes in the later years. This might actually be more beneficial – tax-wise – if your company is highly profitable. In some situations, the IRS rules might allow for immediate expensing at the time of purchase for tax preparation, whereas on your financial books you're using some other GAAP-based depreciation method.

All of this is extremely complicated, and that's why doing your own business taxes should not be attempted by the uninitiated.

Owner's equity and tax basis in a business. Now let's look at an entirely different use of the word "basis" – as in *tax basis* – and how it affects the business owner's equity interest from a tax standpoint in your financial statements. I know, I know . . . we've already used the term tax basis in another context, but here we have it again, with a totally different meaning – and in fact, most accountants refer to it *cost basis*, or *adjusted basis*, or simply *basis*. Whatever you call it, it's an important concept that will likely confuse the small business owner for the life of the business – and it will need to be explained to you multiple times by your bookkeeper.

Here's the gist of it. You might very well own 100% of your company, giving you total control over everything the company does. But from a *tax standpoint* the IRS considers your tax basis in determining how you calculate depreciation or tax loses – and therefore, how you calculate something that, to me, has always been pretty arcane – *owner's equity*. This concept of tax basis can have a significant effect on the *value* of your business ownership, or owner's equity, as reported on your Balance Sheet financial statement.

As listed on your company's Balance Sheet, the owner's equity (the purported dollar amount of the business that you own) is a running calculation of:

- How much cash and non-cash property you contributed to the company when it was founded. Over time, the value of the non-cash property raises and lowers – added to when there are any capital improvements to the property, and subtracted from as the property depreciates.[156] (Since much of this is made up of non-cash property – property that's also in the depreciation process – here's where the concept of owner's equity is really squishy, and why it's not well understood by non-accounting types.)

- Reductions equal to the sum of owner withdrawals or dividends from the business.

- Additions equal to the sum of all retained earnings (which is net income that hasn't been withdrawn or paid out in dividends). A net loss will result in a reduction of retained earnings (equal to the dollar amount of the net loss.

- The owner's equity interest dollar amount at the end of your business' tax year is your tax basis in the company for all tax considerations.

---

[156] At any point in time, the value of each capital asset will usually not be equal to the current fair market value of the asset.

That last bullet is where all this is relevant to our discussion here. Where tax basis trips up (and confuses) many small business owners is at tax calculation time at the end of each tax year, and also several years down the road when your taxes are calculated *on the sale of your business*. The rules on *how* tax basis works – and *where* it works (on the business' tax return or on the owner's individual return) – is based on the type of business entity (partnership, LLC taxed as a partnership, S-Corp, or C-Corp), and those rule details are outside the scope of this book. Therefore, we'll only discuss it in general terms here.

Simply put, in any given year's annual tax returns, the maximum amount you can deduct for losses cannot exceed your *tax basis* in the business (i.e., your owner's equity). Any loss over and above that amount can be carried forward to future years – which means that you don't necessarily get to deduct losses to the full extent of the actual dollar loss *in the year in which the loss occurred* – which can result in higher taxes this year. On the whole, though, this is a good thing as you don't lose the tax value of the loss that you weren't allowed to deduct – in future years, the loss can carry-forward to offset profits in those years.

In case that didn't make sense, let's word it a bit differently. Let's say you had a particularly bad business year this year, and for tax purposes it would be advantageous to write all of it off in one year. By tax basis rules, though, you can only deduct the loss this year to the extent of your current tax basis in the company. You'll still get to carry the remainder of the loss forward to future years, but it might be *this* year that's important for maximum tax benefits. Tough luck – your tax basis at the end of the tax year controls it. You'll understand the pain of this when you look at your year-end tax return, not understanding why you owe taxes when you just know you had a large tax loss to write-off – and your tax accountant responds with, "yes, but you didn't have enough *basis* in the company to offset your profit with all of the loss you incurred".

Financial statements

Assuming your start-up business is successful and growing, at some point in your new business owner life you'll meet face-to-face with the Holy Grail of business management – the two financial statements known as the Balance Sheet and the Income Statement (the latter also known as the Profit & Loss Statement, and colloquially as the P&L).

If you've taken some college accounting or business classes you might be somewhat familiar with these reports, but if not they will likely be total Greek to you (particularly the Balance Sheet). So, as usual, you'd probably do an internet search to find a website that explains them – and that's where your head gets wrapped around an axle. Virtually every internet source assumes you're trying to understand the financial statements for a Fortune 500 company, which are *very* different from those of a small business. They'll contain many extra data fields that pertain to aspects of large publicly-traded companies, but which are not seen in the average small business financial reports– not to mention a dazzling list of footnotes that have no relevance to a small business situation.

In short, a description of the analysis required of financial statements for a small business owner – to use these reports to assist in day-to-day operations of a small business – will take some real digging from internet search results. Don't waste your time on it. The following discussion, along with a bit of tutorial assistance from your bookkeeper or accountant, should give you enough knowledge to understand your small business financial statements.

Reading the Balance Sheet

(Note: A proper Balance Sheet is too large to be included in this book. There's a Preface at the beginning of this chapter describing how to download a sample Balance Sheet that you can follow as we discuss how to read this important financial statement.)

The Balance Sheet pairs with the Income Statement (also called the Profit and Loss Statement, or P&L for short – and that's what we'll call it from now on in this book) as the two most widely-referenced financial statements about your business. Your Balance Sheet is also known as a Statement of Financial Position, but that's far too wordy. It would be nice if there was an acronym for the Balance Sheet, but talking BS with your banker doesn't sound good, and no one would figure out what an SFP is, so we just call it a Balance Sheet.

In this book, we won't cover how to create a Balance Sheet – that's more the purview of your bookkeeper or accountant, and results from financial data that's been accumulated from the day your business opened. Instead, we'll focus on how to read and interpret a small business Balance Sheet, and how it can help you understand the financial health of your company.[157 and 158]

The Balance Sheet is a dated report, a snapshot in time of the company's financial status, typically the last day of the month, quarter, or year. Along with your Income Statement, the information in the Balance Sheet can be used to solve many financial ratios that you, your banker, and investors will be looking at.

The Balance Sheet provides a broad overview of your company's financial status:

- what your company owns – this is your Assets.
- what your company owes – this is your Liabilities.
- your company's net worth – this is your Owner's Equity. (This is the amount you'd be left with if all of your assets were converted to cash and your liabilities were paid off – and in that sense, it's the amount that you actually *own* with the business. But, this is not the amount you'd sell the business for if a buyer came along – that's a whole different story.)

Based on this, the Balance Sheet's main focus is to solve the following equation:

Assets = Liabilities + Owner's Equity

It's called a Balance Sheet for one reason – by definition, the number on the left side of the equal sign must equal (or balance with) the sum of the two numbers on the right side of the equal sign. (This is the result of an accounting practice known as *double-entry* bookkeeping, where each entry in the accounting system has equal and opposite effects in at least two different accounts, thus balancing the accounts with each other.)

---

[157] Andrew Youderian, *How to Read a Balance Sheet (The Non-Boring Version)*, ecommercefuel blog, October 17, 2013, http://www.ecommercefuel.com/how-to-read-a-balance-sheet/
[158] Kristin Ewald, *How To Read a Balance Sheet*, QuickBooks Resource Center, http://quickbooks.intuit.com/r/money/how-to-read-a-balance-sheet/

Assume the following definitions for the above equation, <u>each based on the date of the Balance Sheet being reported</u> (and you should reference the downloaded sample Balance Sheet to follow along with this):

- Assets are the financial engine that you use to run your business, and allow you to pay operating costs. The standard format for assets shown in a Balance Sheet is to list them in the order of how *liquid* they are – how quickly they can be turned into cash (in order of quickest to slowest). Assets are of two types: current and non-current.
  - Current assets are those with a life span of one year or less, and only include those that can be readily converted into cash. This includes cash in the bank, petty cash, security deposits or prepaid expenses, cash equivalents (Treasury Notes, equities the company owns), outstanding accounts receivable (money owed to you), the total value of product inventory, and any credit you might have extended to customers.

    Prepaid expenses are expenses that have been paid in advance, or any payments you've made where the underlying benefit or service has not been used up. Since they represent cash-on-hand that you would otherwise have in the bank at this moment, the *unearned* amount of each is a component of the company's assets. An example might be business or company insurance that's paid in advance (i.e., for the next six months), and you've recently made that payment. Since you haven't *used* those six months of insurance coverage, it is a prepaid expense.

  - Non-current assets (also known as fixed assets) are those with a life span greater than a year, which won't be turned into cash for at least that time period. This includes such tangible assets as equipment, office furniture, computers, leased assets, and importantly, assets that you've purchased with loans. Non-tangible assets such as goodwill, copyrights, or patents that your company holds can also be included – with very specific rules (such as a GAAP requirement that they be <u>purchased</u> non-tangible assets, not internally created).[159] (This is a strange rule to me – as an example, the value of a patent that you purchase is included, but a patent for something you've internally developed isn't. Go figure.)

    As discussed in the previous section, depreciation is subtracted from these assets, accounting for the declining value of the asset over time. For clarity, the depreciation for all capital assets is often maintained separately, and appears on the Balance Sheet as a single line item called *accumulated depreciation*.

  - Liabilities are the current and future financial obligations (debts) your company owes to someone else. As with assets, liabilities are usually grouped in the report as near-term and long-term.
    - Near-term liabilities include a bank line of credit balance, credit card balances, the total of your accounts payable, local, state and federal taxes that are due (but not yet paid), short-term fixed asset leases (less than one year remaining on the lease), wages payable (but not yet paid), and rent or property mortgage payments due.

---

[159] *How do intangible assets appear on a balance sheet?*, Investopedia, http://www.investopedia.com/ask/answers/013015/how-do-intangible-assets-appear-balance-sheet.asp

- o Long-term liabilities include the total of accrued (but not yet paid) severance and vacation wages for employees, long-term fixed asset leases (more than one year remaining). (As your company grows and gets older, this number can be a gulper.)

- o In some situations, unearned revenue can be a very large liability number. This could be a situation where a customer has paid up front for a service or product that will be delivered later. (In my own company, a very high percentage of our revenue was from software maintenance contracts, paid at the beginning of the contract year, but we were only allowed to *recognize* it on our Balance Sheet at the rate of $1/12^{th}$ each month. Each month, the total unearned revenue would quickly become the single biggest number in our Liabilities column, and even though the money was safely deposited in the bank and we operated profitably with it, it made our financial health look terrible. As a result, our bank had a difficult time creating line of credit loan covenants that were appropriate for our particular business.)

  A significant percentage of today's software (such as Microsoft Office 365) is sold on a subscription service basis, with a one-year subscription period. At the beginning of the period, the entire paid amount would be unearned income, which then reduces month-by-month for each monthly Balance Sheet that's created. Another example might be the obligation to ship products or provide services in the future to someone who has contributed to your crowdsourcing campaign.

- o Owner's equity (also known as *book value*) is the total amount of the business assets that you own, free and clear. (In a corporation, or a publicly-traded company, this is typically listed as *stockholders* or *shareholders* equity.) Theoretically, this is the value if you sold all of the company's assets and paid all of its liabilities, and is calculated from data within the company's accounting system, including:

  - o the net earnings in the most recent period (the last month if it's a month-end Balance Sheet, for example, or the last quarter, or the whole year)

  - o retained earnings, which is the sum of all previous net earnings (after taxes) that have been retained inside the company and have not been paid out as dividends to the owner

  - o the value of all investments to the company (which is heavily influenced by your tax basis in the company – as discussed earlier)

  Mathematically, owner's equity could be calculated simply as Assets minus Liabilities (by simply moving Liabilities to the left side of the equation above). This isn't how it is done by real-world accountants, though, as standard accounting practices utilize double-entry bookkeeping. By keeping a running calculation of owner's equity separately, you can double-check that your accounting ledgers are accurately maintained (and therefore, will balance).

Useful information from a Balance Sheet. From a small business owner's practical perspective, looking at the numbers in a single Balance Sheet is usually not very instructive – and it most certainly doesn't give you much to go on in day-to-day management of your company.

Most often, a Balance Sheet includes comparative numbers, such as previous and current year in side-by-side columns, or month-to-date-last-year compared to month-to-date-this year – or just as useful, by comparing two or more separately-produced Balance Sheets, looking at them side-by-side. With this comparison, you can see if your company, from one period to the next, is heading in a positive or negative direction.

Where you can get led astray is by thinking you should compare your financials to those of "*other companies in your industry*", or "*your peers*", which is commonly suggested in accounting books, business books, and internet articles. Rubbish! And not because the suggestion itself is inherently bad, but because you won't *find* any useful Balance Sheets *for comparison*. If you're reading this book, by definition you're a small business owner, and the fact is, *you won't find* a Balance Sheet from any other small business, whether it's in your business category or not. All of these businesses will be closely held (meaning privately-owned, just like yours), and this information is virtually always proprietary by the other business owner. Just try calling up your favorite competitor (or even a small business that isn't a competitor) and ask for their Balance Sheet, and you'll almost certainly be told what to do with your request. No small business owner is going to hand this information out, and if they have an ounce of sense in their head, they won't be posting their financial statements on a social media page (but I'm sure lots of people do these days).

Sure, searching around on the internet, you can find a Balance Sheet for virtually any publicly-traded company, and undoubtedly for some in your industry category (or close to it). But if you're a small craft brewery, comparing your Balance Sheet to any large, publicly-traded brewery will have no basis in reality. It's not that the magnitude of the numbers being so different makes it useless (i.e., the fact that your company is maybe in the thousands or tens of thousands of dollars, whereas the publicly-traded company is in the millions or hundreds of millions) – no, it's the fact that the economies of scale are so different, their manufacturing process, their sales and distribution methods, and their entire business model is so different from yours.

Where the Balance Sheet *can* be valuable for a small business owner is twofold:

- comparing this month's Balance Sheet to last month's, or this month's to the same month a year ago, or this year's to last year
- it's one of the two primary sources of information for a myriad of ratios that financial whizzes love to use (and track) when trying to interpret how well you're running your business (the other being the P&L).

So, as a rule, don't bother comparing your Balance Sheet to those of large, publicly-traded companies, and don't compare your financial ratios to those of other companies.

These other aspects of the Balance Sheet will give you an idea of how your business is doing.

- **Total Assets.** As you see your Total Assets grow from one period to the next, coupled with how well you expect your company to do in the near/far term based on the Cash Flow/Budget spreadsheet, you begin to have a very real basis for the level of business growth that you can afford to pay for.

  If your Total Assets are growing, on average, by x-percentage, and your Cash Flow/Budget shows that net profitability for next year is on track, you'll have much more confidence that you can afford to purchase the new whizz-bang piece of equipment that can produce more revenue, or that you can afford to hire the sales staff necessary to move into a new territory, or perhaps develop an entirely new product to expand your revenue base.

That same justification can be used in a business loan application, showing that you have the wherewithal to repay the loan. (This same type of analysis and conclusion can also be drawn from a figure known as EBITDA, which we'll explore shortly. Whether you use Total Assets or EBITDA, the Cash Flow/Budget will also be important for future projections.)

- **Accounts Receivable.** On a day-to-day basis (rather than just the day when a monthly, quarterly, or annual Balance Sheet is produced), your AR total is a really good number to know (assuming your business issues an invoice on each sale – if not, read below).

In my own software business, I queried my office bookkeeper at least once a week about our current AR total – because it told me the number of dollars that were likely to be received in the next month. As our business grew, so did the AR number, but having it in my head on a regular basis gave me a single metric that told me how we were doing at any point in time. I also asked how much of the AR number was due to late invoice payments, how much was due in before the next payroll, and how much wouldn't be due in for a month. If, as an example, the typical AR number this year was $300,000, I also knew it was enough to support the collateral requirement for our revolving line of credit used to fund day-to-day working expenses.

If your business is more cash-based – or better stated, a business where you sell products or services and receive payment at the same time as you deliver – you can still use your daily sales numbers to review your financial status. For example, if your business normally takes in sales of $1,000/day – and you're able to achieve profitability from that – each day that you take in at least that amount is a good day (and obviously days with fewer sales aren't so good). To minimize surprises at the end of the month, keeping a running tally of sales dollars each day will give you something akin to an Accounts Receivable number at the end of the month.

It's worth stating here that if your business uses the accrual method of accounting, your total AR (that's listed on the Balance Sheet) does not include portions of *pre-paid* sales that are being booked to your accounting system on a month-to-month basis. Rather, pre-paid sales will show on your statements as unearned revenue. AR specifically means money that is still owed to the company at the point in time of the Balance Sheet.

- **Inventory.** For a retail business (or any business that manufactures a product to be sold) inventory can be an important – yet complicated – topic.

By itself, inventory doesn't tell you a lot (other than to compare it month-to-month, quarter-to-quarter, and year-to-year). For comparison, you need multiple columns in your Balance Sheet that provide last month, last quarter, last year, or even average inventory figures. As an example, if inventory from quarter-to-quarter is growing, yet revenue in the same comparative periods isn't, this could be an indication that you're not managing your inventory well enough.

Looked at another way, inventory might not be a good item on the *plus side* of your Balance Sheet (remember, it's current assets that can be readily converted to cash) – particularly if you're in a down business cycle and you're having trouble selling your products. When that happens you might not only have to discount your inventory to make sales, but also discount its value from your Balance Sheet.

From a tax standpoint, how you manage your inventory should be discussed with your accountant, to make some choices that are important to the IRS on your tax filings (in this context, we're talking about how you _value_ inventory on your financial statements, and not how you physically manage it). To make life simpler, when you choose your bookkeeping and accounting software you should consider how well it handles various inventory factors related to your business.[160]

Since inventory is a component of your company's assets, its valuation is important in figuring cost of sales, and therefore on the amount of income earned – which subsequently determines the amount of taxes you'll pay. From the outset, you'll need to pick an inventory calculation method, and then stick with it.[161]

o   If the number of product units sold (i.e., your unit of sales) is very small (or very expensive per unit of sale), you can choose the _specific identification method_ of inventory control. If your inventory is controlled by serial numbers, you'll almost certainly use this method. With the specific identification method, you account for each individual unit of inventory from the moment it is received (or created), until the moment it is shipped (or sold) to a customer. This includes the original cost to you for that specific unit, as well as the specific income you receive from it at time of sale. This method is not practical when unit numbers are high (or unit cost is small), and it doesn't work well when you purchase inventory material that is broken down into smaller units and individually sold (for example, a large roll of carpet that you then sell as smaller pieces).

o   If your raw material costs or unit costs of source inventory are increasing before inventory units are sold, you'll need to choose between LIFO (last in, first out), FIFO (first in, first out), and FILO (first in, last out). Generally, a LIFO method will result in lower reported profits, and therefore lower income taxes. If it's easy in your particular business to account for your inventory units with this method, it's probably the preferred one to use. If not, the IRS allows a modification to LIFO called _dollar value LIFO_ whereby you apply price indexes to the inventory costs (you should be talking to your accountant before choosing this).

o   For some retail businesses, two aspects of inventory – _inventory on hand_ and _available inventory_ – don't affect your financial statements, and generally don't have any effect on income taxes. The two concepts sound alike, but at any point in time, inventory on hand may be quite a different number than available inventory.[162]

---

[160] _Inventory tracking and cost accounting_, QuickBooks FAQ, QuickBooks Learn and Support Home Page, https://community.intuit.com/questions/1192206-inventory-tracking-and-cost-accounting

[161] _Inventory and Cost of Goods Sold_, Accounting Coach, http://www.accountingcoach.com/inventory-and-cost-of-goods-sold/explanation/5

[162] _What's the Difference Between On Hand (Shelf) and Available (Store) Inventory?_, bizelo blog, August 10, 2012, http://blog.bizelo.com/blog/2012/08/10/whats-the-difference-between-on-hand-shelf-and-available-store-inventory/

Inventory on hand is the actual amount of product in your warehouse or storage facility. Even if you've committed to sell one or more units of that inventory, if you haven't yet shipped it to the purchaser, it is still recorded as on hand to your accounting system. If large quantities of inventory are on hand, it can have a negative effect on your tax liability for an accounting period.

Available inventory is the quantity of inventory that is actually available for sale – and generally goes down with each unit that you sell (at the time you sell it, assuming it doesn't languish for very long between sale and shipping). You might have inventory units set aside that are not available for sale (for whatever reason).

These two concepts can be useful from strictly a cost accounting perspective, so therefore, are valuable to you from a business management point of view.

o   At the very least, you should familiarize yourself with IRS rules and regulations, as it will give you a good idea of the data needed to track inventory as part of your cost of sales calculations. [163 and 164]

Reading the Income Statement (P&L)

(Note: A proper Income Statement is too large to be included in this book. There's a Preface at the beginning of this chapter describing how to download a sample Income Statement that you can follow as we discuss how to read this important financial statement.)

The Income Statement pairs with the Balance Sheet as the two most widely-referenced financial reports about your business. The Income Statement is also known as a Profit & Loss Statement, commonly called the P&L. Because P&L is so much easier to say and write, from this point on we'll refer to it as P&L in this book.

Unlike the Balance Sheet, which shows the company's financial health at a particular _moment in time_, the P&L gives a snapshot of a _period of time_ in the company's operations. It typically covers the previous month, the previous quarter, or year to date (YTD). The Cash Flow/Budget Report is also based on a time period, and shows detailed down-in-the-trenches type of data, including both forward projections and also backwards actual data. But the P&L is more of an overall summary of the operating income and expense items in your company's operations. [165]

Much like your Balance Sheet, the P&L can be used to solve many of the financial ratios that your banker and investors will be looking at – but it's also very valuable to you as the business owner, giving you a standardized set of values that you can use comparatively, or just for one-time.

---

[163] _Inventory – Manufacturing Tax Tips_, IRS, http://www.irs.gov/Businesses/Small-Businesses-&-Self-Employed/Inventory-Manufacturing-Tax-Tips

[164] _How To Figure Cost of Goods Sold_, IRS Publication 334, http://www.irs.gov/publications/p334/ch06.html

[165] _Understanding Where You Stand: A Simple Guide To Your Company's Financial Statements_, Illinois Small Business Development Center, https://www.wbdc.org/wp-content/uploads/2016/06/Understanding-Your-Business-Financial-Statements.pdf. This guide, in PDF format, is also useful for understanding your Balance Sheet, as well as a basic Cash Flow Statement.

In this book, we won't cover how to create a P&L – that's more the work of your bookkeeper or accountant (although, if you've created the Cash Flow/Budget during your start-up efforts, you have most of the elements that make up the P&L). Instead, we'll focus here on the background behind some of the data, and how it can help you understand the financial health of your company.

The main focus of the P&L is how much income (revenue), and how many expenses you've had during the reporting period. Subtracting expenses from income gives you your Net Income for the period. Positive Net Income during the period is your Profit, and Negative Income is your Loss – hence, the term Profit and Loss Statement: Essentially, the P&L is solving the following equation

$$\text{Income - Expenses = Net Income}$$

P&L Details. The sample downloaded P&L shows its typical format and content. In many situations, an abbreviated form of the P&L is used, with each category of data listed as a single line item, showing a total for the time period. You would most likely format it this way, for example, when sending it to the bank for monthly financial statements to support a loan. For internal purposes, you might want to expand each category, listing each product/service that you sell, along with the cost of sales for each product/service, interspersed with the income numbers. This way, you can more readily see Gross Profit for each product/service, or you can choose to keep that level of detail only on your Cash Flow/Budget Report. Your choice. (Large publicly-traded corporations are required to follow specific rules about Financial Statement reporting, but for a small business, these reports are primarily for your use in managing your company, so you have plenty of latitude in the level of detail).

Assume the following definitions, each based on the time period of the P&L statement being reported.

o **Income** – also known as Net Sales, or Revenue, is listed at the top. Income is often listed as a single line item, showing the total revenue that was actually booked during the time period of the P&L. So, a month-end P&L would show the total revenue added to your company's accounting system as sales during the preceding month.

   Notice we're using the term *booked* which doesn't necessarily mean the actual number of dollars that flowed into the company's checking account.

   If your company's bookkeeping system is based on the cash method of accounting, then yes, *booked* is essentially the number of dollars you've collected and deposited into the checking account in the P&L period.

   If you're using the accrual method of accounting, booked is the dollar value of all sales completed during the month, regardless of how much money was actually deposited to the checking account. With accrual, the booked value also includes the accrued revenue from longer-term contracts that are collected in advance but proportionate amounts are accrued to your income on a month-to-month basis (for example, an annual subscription sale of your software, actually received at the beginning of the sale year, but proportionately accrued monthly to your accounting system).

- o Immediately below Income is **Cost of Sales** (COS), also known as Cost of Goods Sold (COGS).[166] In this book, we'll use the term Cost of Sales (COS). In simple terms, this is a dollar value representing the total cost of direct expenses that went into producing the Income number right above it. Included in the direct expenses are all material costs used in production, production salaries, and product shipping and transportation costs. This number should include salaries of all production staff.
- o Subtracting total Cost of Sales from Income gives you the **Gross Profit** (or Loss) for the period. In most P&L statements, the Gross Profit is listed as both a dollar value and a percentage – known as your Gross Profit Margin. Gross profit margin is a percentage of Gross Profit divided by Income, then subtracted from 100%.
- o Total **Sales & Marketing** (also known as Selling Expenses) identifies all direct sales and marketing expenses necessary to sell the company's products and services – including salaries of sales and marketing staff, overhead expenses to support sales efforts (tradeshows, visiting customer sites, producing printed marketing materials), advertising, and website maintenance.
- o **General & Administrative Expenses** (also known as G&A) includes all staff/management salaries, and all day-to-day expenses necessary to operate your business (rent, utilities, bank fees, office supplies, phones, professional services, business taxes, and insurance costs). One category in particular, Miscellaneous Expenses, can be a sign of expenses that are swept under the carpet, or may simply represent an uncategorized expense that has not yet grown to the point where it should be separately categorized.
- o **Operating Profit** (or Loss) – also known as Operating Income. This line shows what your profit or loss is from actual operations within your company ... your so-called core business activities. It does not include profit/loss from the company's investments, interest earnings, or taxes.

  As we'll see in a bit, EBITDA (which stands for *earnings before interest, taxes, depreciation, and amortization* and is pronounced "e-bit-da") is one of the much-ballyhooed numbers that banks and investors sling around. The Operating Profit line in your P&L gives you the EBIT portion of EBITDA.

- o **Non-operating income and expenses**, such as investment income, interest income and expenses from outside loans the company has extended (i.e., that are not part of the business), and income taxes paid.
- o **Net Profit** (or Loss) – also known as Net Income, but also known as your **Bottom Line** – is your overall profit after all expenses have been paid.

---

[166] Sean Ross, *What's the difference between cost of goods sold (COGS) and cost of sales?*, Investopedia online, http://www.investopedia.com/ask/answers/112614/whats-difference-between-cost-goods-sold-cogs-and-cost-sales.asp. The two terms are essentially used interchangeably, and mean the same thing. Some accounting types prefer Cost of Goods Sold for financial statements that report on a lot of physical products sold, and use Cost of Sales for service-oriented businesses. Both terms represent the cost to a business to purchase a good or service to be sold to customers. There are no hard and fast rules for which expenses can/cannot be included in Cost of Sales, although the IRS does have some rules, and IRS publication 334, *Tax Guide for Small Businesses* covers the deductions in detail. It can be downloaded at https://www.irs.gov/pub/irs-pdf/p334.pdf.

Ever wonder where the well-known expression *bottom line* comes from? Well, simply because it's usually the last line in a P&L statement, and that bottom line reflects how much you made in the P&L reporting period, after all expenses have been subtracted from all income.

So, *improving your bottom line* means that your Net Profit in this reporting period has increased from a previous reporting period, possibly as the result of increased revenue, or cutting costs. Either way it typically means better profitability. But don't necessarily pat yourself on the back if your bottom line is better one quarter than another – it could simply be due to seasonal business changes, and nothing to do with anything you've done to improve it.

Looking at one set of P&L numbers isn't all that valuable, other than to give you a single data point ... but looking at comparative P&L statements of your small business can tell you which way your numbers are trending.

Your bookkeeper or accountant will probably give you comparative P&L numbers (as well as comparative Balance Sheet numbers) in your monthly, quarterly, or annual P&L. *For your own analysis, a good suggestion is to create a spreadsheet that lets you see all of the numbers, side-by-side, starting from the month you open your business doors.* That way, you can crunch the numbers any way you wish, allowing you to spot trends and to see areas where your business is doing better or worse.

I know, I know, you're supposed to have your nose to the grindstone in building your business – but if you aren't also keeping a close eye on these *financials* (as they're known colloquially), you won't know how to make the best decisions to help your company grow. Remember I stated earlier that luck has little to do with the success of your business? Spotting and taking advantage of opportunities, serendipitous or otherwise, is key to your success. Using your business' financial information wisely is the first step in taking advantage.

Useful information from a P&L From a small business owner's practical perspective, looking at the numbers in a single P&L is usually not very instructive – and it most certainly doesn't give you much to go on in day-to-day management of your company.

For the first-time small business owner, the P&L is probably easier to understand then a Balance Sheet – because it contains data that is closely aligned with your actual company operations, and much of it is also contained in your Cash Flow/Budget spreadsheet. Like the Balance Sheet, though, it's also the primary information source for a myriad of ratios that financial whizzes love to use (and track) when trying to interpret how well you're running your business. We'll see several of these ratios in a bit.

Here are some suggestions and aspects of the P&L that provide the most useful information about your business.

- Include percentages, not just dollar numbers. If your bookkeeper isn't including percentages already, have them added to every line (at least, at the main category line) of your P&L. This gives you a more descriptive picture of each category, and enables you to export the percentages to various types of graphs to make it even easier to understand.

- Add comparative numbers and percentages. Knowing each number is valuable in itself, but knowing how this month's (quarter's, or year's) number compares with last month (quarter or year) is much more instructive – showing you whether revenue is growing in parallel with expenses, whether revenue, cost of sales, or expenses are getting skewed, or whether you're getting more efficient (revenue increases while expenses decrease).

- For example, if income (revenue) has grown from last year's 30% to this year's 40% ... well, you've achieved a significant year-over-year sales gain. If that translates to a 15% Gross Profit gain from last year, you must also be getting your expenses under better control.

- Do not include non-cash expenses – such as depreciation, amortization, and depletion – in the P&L for your small business, at least not for the P&L version that you (the business owner) see. Another non-cash example is a *write-down* or a *write-off*. Big, publicly-traded companies include these to lower their net income, and thereby reduce taxes. Small businesses do that also, but frankly, on the P&L that you need to look at for day-to-day running of your business, they just confuse the issue. The P&L is trying to show you the actual operating profitability for your company, so you're better off removing these non-cash items – but have your bookkeeper/accountant include them as necessary for financial statements sent to the bank or used for tax calculations.

So, how do these non-cash expenses (depreciation, amortization, and depletion) affect your P&L?[167] At your discretion, they can be moved to a subsequent P&L, adding these expenses that you've previously paid for into some future net income. It's sort of an artificial inflation of your revenue for the P&L period that you're now looking at. It's all perfectly aboveboard, but for a lay person operating a small business, it can be very misleading.

Write-Down's and Write-Off's. Have you ever read business articles about a well-known company that's *taking "a charge"* for something or other? For example, in Summer 2015, the business press had a headline, *"Microsoft cuts 7,800 more jobs, takes $8B charge in retreat from Windows Phone ambitions"*.[168] What in the world does this mean? Did Microsoft just lose $8B in real money during the past month, quarter, or year? Where on their financial statements will this $8B occur? Did it just destroy or improve Microsoft's bottom line? And finally, why do I care?

The article further explains in its opening paragraph: *"Microsoft this morning confirmed that it will be cutting 7,800 additional jobs, primarily in its Windows Phone business, and taking a $7.6 billion charge related to its acquisition of Nokia's smartphone division, plus a restructuring charge of another $750 million to $850 million."*

---

[167] *Are depreciation, depletion and amortization similar?*, Accountingcoach.com Q&A, http://www.accountingcoach.com/blog/are-depreciation-depletion-and-amortization-similar
[168] Todd Bishop, *Microsoft cuts 7,800 more jobs, takes $8B charge in retreat from Windows Phone ambitions*, GeekWire, July 8, 2015, http://www.geekwire.com/2015/microsoft-cuts-7800-more-jobs-takes-8b-charge-in-blow-to-windows-phone/

Ahhh, so this charge is related to the Nokia acquisition that occurred ... hmmm, in April, 2014 ... and Microsoft is taking this action in their financial statements over a year later??? Well, that certainly didn't answer the questions. Investopedia explains this in their definition of *cash charge*.[169] To paraphrase, it's typically a one-time dollar amount that a firm charges against its earnings (revenue) on its Income Statement, "as part of a plan to downsize or to improve company efficiency", and as a way of reducing net income (which can reduce taxes). Any particular cash charge is not expected to occur more than once, and if it does, it may signal that the company is fiddling the books (for example, writing down excess inventory each month). Additionally, the company can record the charge as an extraordinary cash charge on the Balance Sheet. So, basically Microsoft is *writing off* their earlier purchase of Nokia, and is essentially now calling it a failed acquisition.

An interesting question is, why take the charge now? Well, these big companies that spend huge efforts *managing their investors* (i.e., their stock price), getting their financial statements to look their best for investors is a big deal. *Making the numbers* can have a huge effect on stock price, so they choose the best time from that standpoint to take the charge.

As a small business owner, all of this artificial effort might make sense between your bookkeeper and tax accountant in your financial statements presented to the bank, or used in calculating your taxes, but for the most part it doesn't help you in day-to-day business operations – unless, of course, you have plans to be a business financier, in which case you're no longer a small business owner.

- Digging into your cash flow. The P&L doesn't necessarily show you what's happening with actual cash, which is the real engine that drives profitability, and where you can go with the company. In other words, you want to see cold, hard cash flowing into your bank account in a reasonable fashion with regard to your profitability. So, in analyzing your P&L, you need to cross-reference it with your Cash Flow/Budget report (for equal time periods), as profit is shown in the P&L and actual cash flow is shown in the Cash Flow/Budget report. In simple terms, if your profit is increasing a lot faster than your cash flow, that may indicate that the "quality" of the profit isn't all that good – and maybe you should be looking into the underlying cause.

  Here are some ideas for digging deeper into areas of your cash flow that might be raising questions:[170 and 171]

  o Look into your AR collections to see if you are extending too much credit to customers. If you're letting customers slide on paying you, it's going to be a hit to your cash flow. All the while an invoice is aging, or the deadbeat customer isn't paying the chits you're extending, your business is humming along (maybe stumbling along) on revenue it could use for its continuing operations.

---

[169] *Cash Charge*, Investopedia, http://www.investopedia.com/terms/c/cashcharge.asp?layout=infini&v=3A
[170] Norm Brodsky, *How to Fix Cash-Flow Problems*, Inc. online, May 1, 2009, http://www.inc.com/magazine/20090501/street-smarts-how-to-fix-cash-flow-problems.html
[171] Matt Quin, *How to Understand an Income Statement*, Inc. online, July 1, 2010, http://www.inc.com/guides/2010/06/how-to-understand-an-income-statement.html

o Are you getting stuck with a bunch of bad debt? Do you have AR invoices that you're having to actually write off? Are credit card or check-writing customers getting the goods without actually paying for them, leaving you holding the bag? If so, this is a hit to your cash flow.

o Is your inventory growing? Perhaps you're producing goods too efficiently or at too rapid a pace, and the extra production means you're paying for more raw materials or products, which is now noticeably tying up your cash flow. Or, your sales may be in a slump, but you haven't yet noticed it. Time to cut back on production, as it's creating a hit to your cash flow.

o Is inventory being sold out the back door without your knowledge? Are your cash management controls working properly?

o Are your profit margins high enough? Almost all of the margin percentages in your P&L are unique to your particular business, and you can't tell which might be out of whack by the time-honored (and much touted) advice given for large, publicly-traded corporations – by comparing them to similar businesses in the same category. As mentioned several times now, your small business margins won't compare one way or another with those of similar large businesses (the economies of scale will be different, and you simply won't have the same business model), nor will you be able to get your hands on profit margin amounts from other small, privately-held businesses (just as you shouldn't be handing out this information when another small business owner comes calling on you – and it doesn't make sense to be touting this kind of information through your social media accounts).

The solution is that you need to know enough about *your* P&L margin percentages so that you can tell when they're out of whack. The only way to do that is by creating your own database (i.e., a spreadsheet) that you keep tucked in your back pocket, with comparative numbers from your company's financial statements – numbers that go all the way back to the first day you opened for business.

When analyzing these profit margin numbers and percentages, you also need to know what's behind the numbers. Are your fully-burdened employee costs (wages, employment taxes, benefits, etc.) costing far more than you expected? Did you really screw up this year on the new commission plan you're paying your sales people, resulting in every sale they make being a loss for you – but proverbially, you're going to make up for it in volume? Is the advertising campaign too costly for the sales it's bringing in? Did you purchase new equipment that's too large, or too costly, to achieve profitability on the product in the near term (or maybe, ever)? Did you set pricing too low, or offer too many discounts on the pricing, on the premise that you'll do *anything* to increase revenue, without really understanding what it would do to your margins? Are you pushing credit card sales at the expense of cash (or debit) sales, not fully understanding how much the credit card merchant fees are?

As a small business owner, you're probably the only person in your company who can make this analysis, and after that, you're the only person who can begin the process of digging the company out of the hole. The key to this analysis is a solid understanding how your business works – and recognizing that the phrase "cash is king" really refers to your cash flow.

- Understand the sales-to-payment process and when actual hard cash _from a sale_ flows into your company – not just how cash flow appears on your Cash Flow/Budget report, but the cycle time in which you close a sale to when the actual cash is received.

  It's easier to see this cycle in a company operating on a cash accounting basis, and more difficult if you're on an accrual basis. In a cash-basis company, you'll mostly receive cash for a sale when the sale is recorded on the company's books. The income number that you see on your P&L likely correlates very closely to actual cash received.

  But in an accrual-basis company, with an invoice-driven system after sales are closed, a lot of variables need to be factored in. The most important factor in understanding this might be your revenue recognition policies. For example, prepaid sales are only booked to revenue when the product or service is delivered. So multiple-fill orders paid for in advance only appear as revenue when each part of the order is filled. Maintenance or subscription contracts that are paid upfront are typically booked month-by-month, or year-by-year. In these examples, the actual cash might be in the bank near the time of pre-pay – which means you might have already spent the money when you see it in the Revenue category on the P&L, but you won't see that actual revenue in your Cash Flow/Budget Report. For one-time sales, the revenue is booked at the time the sale closes, but your payment terms dictate when the actual money hits your bank account – which might be 30, 40, or more days later than reported on the P&L (maybe showing up on the next month's P&L).

  But revenue isn't the only part of it. With accrual-basis accounting, your expenses are also booked when you commit to the expense (or when you receive the expensed item), so you actually pay cash out of your bank account 30 or more days after it's booked to your P&L. For your pre-paid expenses, such as insurance, which is paid ahead of time for six months or a year, the money will be spent long before it hits your P&L.

  To resolve this, it's a really good idea to have your bookkeeper convert your accrual-basis P&L to a cash-basis P&L just for your own day-to-day use – where the conversion isn't something _you_ want to be doing personally, but the bookkeeper can do it without much trouble (your accounting software probably has a built-in function for this). This doesn't change the fact that your accounting system is accrual-based – it just gives you an alternative P&L to help you better understand your business.

- **Free Cash Flow (FCF) and Free Cash Flow From Operating Activities (CFO).** Even though Free Cash Flow isn't part of the day-to-day cash flow topics I've covered above, I've included a discussion about them (and the following topic, EBITDA) here because they are metrics that help define your company's financial health. FCF and EBITDA are most commonly used by an outside person – maybe an investor, or maybe a potential buyer of your company – who uses them to value your company for that purpose. You may still want to be familiar with them, but they aren't values that help your day-to-day running of the business.

  Free cash flow is the actual cash that your small business has available (or is able to generate) after you've spent all the money necessary to maintain or expand what is commonly known as your "asset base".[172] The FCF number is interesting to investors because it tells them how much money your company has to "pursue opportunities that enhance investor value", or to put it more greedily, how much profit they can pull out of your company. Since FCF is really outside the scope of this book, you can read more about this in the Investopedia article at http://www.investopedia.com/terms/f/freecashflow.asp.

- **EBITDA.** An acronym that stands for *earnings before interest, taxes, depreciation, and amortization*, this financial metric is used by investors and bankers to gauge how profitable your company is. For most small business owners, the metric is quite squishy, and you might be just as well advised to use Operating Profit from your P&L as the metric of choice. Nevertheless, the following discussion will explain what EBITDA is, and how it is derived.

One big problem with EBITDA is a lack of legal requirement to include it anywhere as an actual line item in a company's financial statements. Therefore, the calculation method used for EBITDA can be changed at each company's whim and situation. Another problem is that it includes non-cash expenses (which we recommended above not to include in your business owner version of the P&L statement). Also, some P&Ls don't include a line for business income taxes, as the specific tax amount for a given P&L period won't be calculated until after year-end – so many don't include taxes in their EBITDA calculation. Are you starting to see why this number is squishy?

Having said that, here are two calculations for EBITDA:

EBITDA = Net Income + Interest + Taxes + Depreciation + Amortization[173]

EBITDA = Operating Income + Depreciation + Amortization[174]

Which to use? Well, take your pick, as they both produce the same result for EBITDA even though they look quite different (the difference being that Operating Income already includes Interest and Taxes, so it's already the EBIT part of EBITDA). In reality, the best one to use depends on which line items your P&L has.

Before we leave this discussion, let's get some definitions straightened out in the terms that you see above. *Income* is the same as *profit*, so Net Income can equally be labeled as Net Profit, and Operating Income might be labeled as Net Profit on your P&L. And for some reason, people who deal in big-company financials tend to use the word *earnings*, whereas small business owners tend to prefer *profit*.

---

[172] As defined by Investopedia.com, your asset base consists of all of your company's assets that give value to your company – but only your owned value of the asset (i.e., minus any liabilities that you have – such as a loan, or pledged collateral value – on the asset). Since assets can increase or decrease in value (through depreciation, for example), your asset value on any set of assets can go up or down.

[173] *EBITDA - Earnings Before Interest, Taxes, Depreciation and Amortization*, Investopedia website, http://www.investopedia.com/terms/e/ebitda.asp?layout=infini&v=3A

[174] *Earnings Before Interest, Tax, Depreciation and Amortization (EBITDA)*, InvestingAnswers website, http://www.investinganswers.com/financial-dictionary/financial-statement-analysis/earnings-interest-tax-depreciation-and-amortizatio

Now, can we at least determine what EBITDA is supposed to be telling you? Sure – it's a way to evaluate your company's financial performance without including any financing and accounting decisions, or your tax consequences. The problem is, what's a good number? Again, comparing it to big, publicly-traded companies in your industry won't tell you anything, and trying to find out the EBITDA of your closest competitor will be impossible. My suggestion is to simply use Operating Profit from your P&L, comparing it from one P&L to the next (and keeping it as a line item in your database of financial numbers).

When will EBITDA become important for you? Well, most importantly, when you get ready to sell your company. If you hire an investment banker to find a buyer for your company, the first question asked will be, "what is your company's EBITDA?" You can bet the banker will have EBITDA numbers memorized for all businesses that are similar to yours, and how yours stack up will determine how your company can be "positioned" in the marketplace. The potential buyers of your company will also know referential EBITDA numbers for companies such as yours, and this will be the "currency" in which they think about how good your company would be to acquire.

What is the *quality* of your financial statements? Anyone from the outside (banker, bonding company, tax authority, investor, potential buyer) looking at your company's financial statements will want to know the answer to that question. (The financial statements referenced here are the Balance Sheet, the P&L, and if you prepare one, the Statement of Cash Flows. Your Cash Flow/Budget is not included here, as it is considered to be an internal-use-only document.)

But what do we mean by quality? Let's say you submit your résumé to a potential employer and say, "trust me, I put together all of this information and you don't need to verify any of it", the reader isn't going to put a lot of faith in its accuracy. If you included with that résumé a certification from a reputable *résumé-checking* firm that everything listed is accurate, then that raises the quality level. Well, you get the picture.....

The four categories of financial statement quality are listed here from lowest- to highest-quality – and importantly, lowest- to highest-cost:

- **Company-prepared financial statements.** These are internally prepared, typically by your accounting system, and the financial data going into them has not been validated at all by an outside authority (such as a CPA).

  Company-prepared are the least expensive financial statements to produce. No matter how good and thoroughly prepared they are, and no matter how much you claim them to be accurate, they won't be considered as anything more than your internal management information reports. For small businesses who don't have anyone outside the business demanding anything more, internally-prepared financial statements are just fine – assuming you (as the business owner) feel comfortable with not having things looked over to see if everything seems OK.

- **Compiled financial statements.** Compiled financial statements have been created by an outside accountant, *using* company-prepared financial statements. In standard practice, the accountant doesn't verify the accuracy of any data contained in the financial statements you provide, but instead, ensures that the *look and feel* conforms to the financial statement organizational standards dictated by GAAP. The accountant does not trace any transactions through the system, or for that matter, doesn't look at the accounting system at all to determine if the processes conform to GAAP. As a result, the outside accounting firm will not be able to certify anything about the *numbers* within the financial statements, other than that they conform by organization and look and feel to GAAP standards.

From a cost-to-produce standpoint, compiled financial statements will cost the time and effort required by the accounting firm. Depending on the size of your business (and therefore, the complexity of your financial statements), a compilation might cost in the low thousands of dollars, possibly as little as $1,000. Figure you are getting what you paid for (and some might call this lipstick on a pig).

It's fair to say that a majority of small businesses get by for years on compiled financial statements, and only graduate to the next level when some outside force (for example, a banker reviewing you for a loan) requires more. Oftentimes, even your banker will accept compiled financial statements, knowing this is what you can afford.

- **Reviewed financial statements.** These begin as compiled financial statements (i.e., created by an outside accountant from company-prepared financials), with a few added checks and balances.

  This typically involves an accountant spending some onsite time at your company, perhaps for several days (again, depending on how complex your accounting process is). The accountant doing the onsite review of your accounting process won't necessarily be a CPA, and might be a staff accountant, but the accountant issuing the review statement will be a CPA (which is important, as the hourly charge for the two are (and should be) very different.

  By GAAP review standards, the following types of review should be performed:[175]

  o   A discussion with the company's internal bookkeeping and accounting staff, to determine the accounting practices and principles used to maintain the books.

  o   The process by which financial transactions are recorded in the books.

  o   Obtaining written assurance from the company executives/owners of accuracy and completeness of all financial information given to the accountant, as well as a check on oversight of the accounting process by management.

  o   A discussion about management oversight of checks and balances to ensure that fraud isn't happening.

  o   A check of *significant events*, past, present, or future, that might affect the financial system.

  o   Running the numbers – specifically financial ratios and other analytical procedures – to determine if results meet expectations, or are plausible.

As a result of the review process, the CPA will issue a statement (perhaps titled Independent Accountant's Review Report), first identifying the process and review criteria that was used, and then issuing a Limited Assurance statement, typically worded as such ...

---

[175] *Audit, Review and Compilation: How CPA Reports Differ*, Gelman, Rosenberg & Freedman, http://www.grfcpa.com/media/AuditReviewCompiliationWhitePaper.pdf

"we are not aware of any material modifications that should be made to the accompanying financial statements in order for them to be in conformity with GAAP".

Given the amount of outside accounting time, effort, and responsibility to perform a financial statement review, costs will be considerably higher than for a set of compiled financial statements. It's hard to pin down the cost, as it depends on company size and complexity, and how well your company's books are maintained. Suffice it to say that reviewed financial statements are not worth it, unless there is some outside requirement, or possibly if you (as the business owner) want to spend the money to know that your bookkeeping and accounting staff are performing up to snuff (and that you aren't being cheated).

Often the bank granting your line of credit will require reviewed financial statements.

- **Audited financial statements.** This is the highest level of quality you can produce for your financial statements. It is a significant step up from reviewed financials, and requires *a lot of work*, not only for the outside accounting firm, but also for your internal bookkeeping and accounting staff.

  In addition to everything done in a review process, an audit will also include:

  o A more thorough investigation of overall company operations, financial reporting, and information about fraud and errors.

  o Checking regulatory guidelines to determine if recorded transactions are handled correctly (such as revenue recognition, accounts receivable and payable management, depreciation calculations, inventory control and calculations).

  o Checking a random number of financial transactions with outside third parties to determine proper handling.

  When the audit process is complete, the CPA will issue one of three opinions: unqualified, qualified, or adverse.

  o An unqualified opinion is the one you most want – stating that *"yes, in my opinion, the statements do present fairly"* all that they represent.

  o A qualified opinion is not quite as good, and generally means there isn't a clear *"yes"* to the opinion – something isn't quite understood for whatever reason, or information is missing, but the level of these anomalies isn't considered insurmountable.

  o An adverse opinion is the worst, and definitely not something you want. It could be that fraud was detected in your books, or some other significant irregularity in accounting practices was identified (possibly incorrect revenue recognition, miscounted inventory, or the like). If someone requires you to furnish audited financials and you get this opinion, your best course of action is (if possible) to take your lumps, and modify whatever is causing this opinion.

  Don't assume that you can hide behind a second (maybe shifty) accountant who will gloss over problems, as present and former accounting firms are required to communicate about previous audited financial statement opinions, and if this opinion becomes known, the accounting firm issuing an incorrect opinion on egregious grounds can lose its certification.

The cost of audited financials is normally beyond the budget of most small businesses. They will be required if your company goes public. Until then, very few firms (let alone bankers and everyday investors) sniffing around to buy or merge with your company will require audited financials,

Financial ratios

Business analysts use dozens of financial ratios (brief formulas) to analyze the financial health of a business.[176] There are so many ratios floating around that entire books are written on this one topic (go to amazon.com and type in "financial ratios") – you could easily spend hours each day just running these numbers – *and not running your business*.

My suggestion is, run a few of the ratios (about the number you can count on one hand) and let your business banker who is overseeing your bank loan run all the numbers he/she wants each month when you submit your financial statements – and if they see any they don't like, you'll be hearing from them. There's no question, if the bank starts to feel uncomfortable about your ability to repay your loan, you'll be getting a call or e-mail asking what's going on. But the odds are, you already know this from your day-to-day sense of things – orders are down, inventories are too high, customers aren't paying on time, you're worried about making payroll and paying bills. What you need to develop for yourself is an *intuitive sense* of how things are going.

The terminology in many of the ratios can be confusing, not the least of which is that people (and companies) use different *values* in their calculations. In other situations, different formulas are used, but the ratio is still named the same.

The other problem is understanding the difference between the term *ratio* and *margin*.

By definition, ratio means the *"quantitative relation between two amounts, showing the number of times one value contains or is contained within the other"*. This implies that the formula for each ratio consists of one number (or the result of a calculation) divided by another.

By definition, margin means *"the amount by which one number exceeds or falls short of another number"*.

So, what's meant by a term such as *gross profit margin ratio*? Is it a margin or is it a ratio? Is it a number or a percentage? The only answer is that it depends – and you'll just have to follow the formula. Sorry, but there's not much you can do when the rest of the world is so inconsistent.

Here's a small handful of ratios that you might want to track, just so you can better see the specifics of what is changing in your business.

Debt-to-Equity Ratio. Sometimes it's simply known as the *debt ratio*, or *D/E ratio*.

- **What it tells you:** In highfalutin official language, this ratio estimates a company's financial leverage, indicating the proportion of equity and debt used to finance its assets. In

---

[176] *Analyzing Your Financial Ratios*, Branch Banking and Trust Company (BB&T) website, http://www.bbt.com/bbtdotcom/business/small-business-resource-center/growing-a-business/financial-ratios.page

more simple terms, it indicates the level of debt you've taken on, either in regular day-to-day operations, or in financing your growth.

You can bet this is a ratio your banker (or whoever you've borrowed from) will be looking at, and it's a good one for you to know as well.

- **The formula is:**

$$\text{Debt-to-Equity Ratio} = \text{Total Liabilities} / \text{Owner's Equity}$$

Note: If you want to show the Debt-to-Equity result as a percentage (which some companies do in their annual statements), multiply the resulting number by 100 and then add the %-sign to it.

- **Data comes from:** the Balance Sheet.

- **Example:** Using our example downloaded Balance Sheet, our Debt-to-Equity Ratio at this point in time is (typically expressed as a percentage):

$$\$14,240 / \$36,460$$

Our example Debt-to-Equity ratio is: .39

o **What's a good number:** Consider this statement:

> *"Debt-to-equity ratio is a key financial ratio, used as a standard for judging a company's financial standing. It is also a measure of a company's ability to repay its obligations.   If the ratio is increasing, the company is being financed by creditors rather than from its own financial sources which may be a dangerous trend.   Lenders and investors usually prefer low debt-to-equity ratios because their interests are better protected in the event of a business decline.   Thus, companies with high debt-to-equity ratios may not be able to attract additional lending capital."* [177]

So, a low D/E ratio is better than a high D/E ratio. Getting back to the question ... is the one shown here a good debt-to-equity ratio? Search all you want on the internet and you're not likely to find anything that tells you what a good debt-to-equity ratio is for a company like yours. The fact is, your company's debt-to-equity ratio *is what it is* at the particular point in time you pull the numbers from a Balance Sheet, and the best thing you can do is watch for trends, by using your growing database of financial ratios (you *have* bought into doing this, haven't you?).

The pundits (who are mostly looking at financials for large, publicly-traded companies) tell you to look at the ratio for other companies in your industry. Yeah, sure, your competitor (also a small business) on the other side of town is hardly likely to open the financial books to tell you their debt-to-equity number. So let's go about it a different way. We're a craft brewery – how do we stack up against the big breweries? Well, you can do a search on "anheuser-busch debt-to-equity ratio", and it appears their historical ratio runs around 1 – which tells me nothing about our .39. Maybe looking at a smaller brewery might be better – so a search on Redhook Ale Brewery comes up at .24. Then we spot Boston Beer

---

[177] *Debt-to-Equity Ratio*, ReadyRatios website,
http://www.readyratios.com/reference/debt/debt_to_equity_ratio.html

Company at .32. So, at least from the smaller breweries, it looks like our .39 is in the ballpark – at least in relation to two medium-sized breweries.

But don't expect to compare your numbers with other very large businesses, particularly in other industries. If you look at the aircraft manufacturing business – an industry that requires huge sums of money and lots of debt to finance next-generation airplanes that are capital-intensive to develop – Boeing comes in right now at 2.27, whereas Lockheed Martin is a (comparatively) whopping 4.41, and Northrop Grumman is at .37.[178] The point is, it can be very misleading to gauge your company against others, particularly if they're in a different industry, or of a different size.

o **How often to monitor:** This ratio should be tracked monthly, quarterly and annually, with the result stored in your financial ratio database.

Is this really giving us compelling insight, though, that makes it the key financial ratio we need to keep our eye on? Could be, but what we'll need to do is watch our own company's debt-to-equity ratio _trend over time_. Is it going up (which means we're starting to carry more debt), or going down (which could mean we are paying down our debt, or aren't taking advantage of _debt spending_ that might help us grow the company). For that, you need to graph it to visually show trends. And that will be your best indicator of how well you're doing – but only over a period of time.

Quick Ratio. Also known as the _liquidity ratio_, or the _acid test ratio_, or the _quick asset ratio_.

- **What it tells you:** This ratio presents a clue to short-term liquidity, by measuring a company's short-term debts against its most liquid assets. In this context, liquidity means how quickly assets can be turned to cash. Since stored-up inventory might be overvalued on the financial books, and/or hard to peddle under many circumstances, it's removed from the asset pool for this calculation.

- **The formula is:**

    Quick Ratio = (Current Assets - Inventory) / Current Liabilities

o **Data comes from:** the Balance Sheet.

o **Example:** Using our example downloaded Balance Sheet (all of our listed liabilities fall in the current liability category), our Quick Ratio at this point in time is:

    ($29,200 - $1,200) / $14,240

    Our example Quick ratio is: 1.96.

o **What's a good number:** An internet search indicates that a quick ratio of 2.1 is considered good (or a standard) – so I'd say our 1.96 is pretty close to that.

o **How often to monitor:** Since a large part of current assets is cash in the bank (and cash equivalents plus receivables), your quick ratio can take a dive in short order if your sales drop (reduced sales reduce your AR balance as you continue to burn through cash). So this is obviously a ratio you'd want to monitor on a regular basis. And again, you should keep

---

[178] Shubh Datta, _Are Boeing's Plans Too Ambitious?_, The Motley Fool, May 1, 2012, http://www.fool.com/investing/general/2012/05/01/are-boeings-plans-too-ambitious.aspx

an historical record that shows the trending of this ratio and how much it moves up or down from one reporting period (or calculation point) to the next.

Current Ratio. Also known as the *cash asset ratio*, or the *cash ratio*.

- o **What it tells you:** This calculation provides an estimation of your ability to pay back short-term obligations (just a different word for liabilities).

- o **The formula is:**

    Current Ratio = Current Assets / Current Liabilities

- o **Data comes from:** the Balance Sheet

- o **Example:** Using our example downloaded Balance Sheet (all of our listed liabilities fall in the current liability category), our Current Ratio at this point in time is:

    $29,200 / $14,240

    Our example Current Ratio is: 2.03

- o **What's a good number:** Again the pundits tell us, "*A higher current ratio indicates a better capability of a company to pay back its debts*" – but it begs the question, is our 2.03 high or low?

    A group of small investors who write for a website called trendshare.org,[179] go on to say, "*A good Current Ratio is at least 1 ... which indicates that your business hasn't taken on more short-term obligations than it can afford if everything went wrong tomorrow ... a current ratio of 2 is really good; it's the sign of a very healthy company*".

    So, that's encouraging, as our hypothetical craft brewing company falls right on that *really good* number. For a further sanity check, the Current Ratio for Boston Beer Company at the time of this writing is 2.45, and that too is in line with our number.

    Described another way, a ratio below 1 raises a warning sign as to whether the company is able to pay its short term obligations on time. At the first sign of trending below 1, start looking at what's causing it and what you can do to improve it. On the other hand, if all other signs of your company are good, and this ratio stays low over time, it might just be a characteristic of your business, where you have to operate at high debt levels (and in that case, if you're outside your bank loan covenants, you need to discuss it with your business banker).

- o **How often to monitor:** This ratio should be tracked monthly or quarterly, the result stored in your financial ratio database, and graphed to show it visually.

Gross Profit on Net Sales Ratio. This ratio goes by a bunch of names, and it's one whose terminology is often confusing. The ratio is also known as the *Gross Margin Ratio*, the *Gross*

---

[179] *What is the Current Ratio and Why Does It Matter?*, January 29, 2015, https://trendshare.org/how-to-invest/what-is-the-current-ratio-and-why-does-it-matter

Profit Margin, or the *Gross Profit Percentage* (which is the name we use on the Cash Flow/Budget template).

- **What it tells you:** This ratio essentially answers the question of whether your average markup on goods sold is enough to cover the cost to produce them. This is similar to a ratio that's calculated on our suggested Cash Flow/Budget, but at individual product sales levels.

  Another good way of looking at the importance of this ratio is ... it tells you how much you can discount without taking a loss.

- **The formula is:**

  Gross Profit on Net Sales Ratio = (Revenue - Cost of Sales) / Revenue

- **Data comes from:** P&L (also one of the standard calculations in our Cash Flow/Budget template). The calculation can be based on your total net sales or individual product (if they are broken out with both sales numbers and Cost of Sales in your Cash Flow/Budget).

  Note: This is a ratio where many people (companies) can't seem to get the terminology right. Sometimes you'll see Revenue referred to as Net Sales – and that's very confusing, as normally, Revenue minus Cost of Sales already equals Net Sales, but their formula then subtracts out Cost of Sales.

  In this context, Revenue is just another name for Gross Sales. The term Gross Sales might be used when sales for multiple products are listed, and when combined together the total becomes Gross Sales. Gross sales can also be thought of as sales numbers before any deductions are made.

  Also, to smooth out the result for this calculation, an average on the Revenue/COS might be used (although this isn't often done). For example, for a single month calculation, the Revenue and COS from last month and this month are added together, then divided by two. For a year-end or YTD calculation, the Revenue/COS for the appropriate months is added together, then divided by the appropriate number of months.

- **Example:** For this, we'll use our downloaded sample Cash Flow/Budget report for our craft brewery company. Assume we have sales for three beer types broken out in the report, with revenue (sales) for the month of $9,563, and $1,440, and $5,436, and with Cost of Sales (for the overall group) of $6,712. The total revenue is $16,439.

$$\frac{\$16,439 \ - \ \$6,712}{\$16,439}$$

<u>Our example Gross Profit on Net Sales is 59%.</u>

- **What's a good number:** If it produces a negative number, you're losing money – which you obviously don't want. If it's at (or near) zero, you're breaking even. If it's positive, you're making a profit. <u>Keep in mind that this is your Gross Profit before Sales & Marketing and General & Administrative expenses have been subtracted out</u> (i.e., this isn't Net Profit). It's only telling you the profit margin at the production level, giving you information to help determine if your prices are high enough, or if your costs to produce the goods are too high. To put it another way, if you can't get your product pricing or production costs under control, you certainly can't make up for it elsewhere on your financial statements.

This metric varies greatly from business to business, product to product, even within the same industry. There are just too many variables for each company's sales – who is discounting when the other isn't, who is negotiating better vendor deals, and a host of other factors. This is also a metric that you need to calculate when you analyze your monthly financial statements (P&L and/or Cash Flow/Budget), store in your ratio database, and watch for trends about your own business – particularly a downward trend, which often signals even lower profitability in future.

o **How often to monitor:** Monthly, quarterly, YTD, and annually. This should be a calculation in your Cash Flow/Budget spreadsheet, and as you (or your bookkeeper) fill in the sales and expense numbers each month, the spreadsheet will automatically calculate this.

Accounts Receivable Turnover Ratio.

o **What it tells you:** This is a useful ratio for any business that invoices customers for products sold or services rendered (as opposed to a cash-based business that receives payment at the time of sale). It indicates your ability to collect payments from your *credit* customers (where credit means the length of time a customer is given to pay an invoice, such as a term of "net 30 days"). Essentially, the more times receivables turn over during the year, the shorter the time between the sale and collecting the money for the sale.

c **The formula is:**

$$\text{Average AR Turnover} = \text{Revenue} / \text{Average AR Balance}$$

o **Data comes from:** P&L or Cash Flow Budget for Revenue; Balance Sheet for determining the average AR Balance (which must be calculated first)

Notes: Revenue should only include those sales that are done on a credit basis (i.e., an invoice has been issued). If you have any sales that are paid at time of sale, subtract them out of revenue before use in this formula.

The reporting period that you are calculating for is important in developing the numbers. If this is an end-of-year (or trailing 12 months') calculation, use the year-end number (or add up the monthly revenue for the trailing 12 months) for revenue; for quarterly, use the quarter-end or trailing 3 months' total; for monthly, use the previous month. For the *average* AR, use the same logic as for the various revenue periods, and then divide it by the number of months in the period before using it in the formula.

o **Example:** Our example brew pub business is a cash-only business, so this ratio isn't relative to it. Instead, let's just use some sample numbers for illustration purposes.

Let's assume that on our year end financial statements we have total revenue for the year at $2,000,000 (keeping our numbers simple for calculations). From the Balance Sheet for December and each of the preceding 11 months, summing them all up we get a total AR balance of $1,320,000; dividing that number by 12, we get an *average* AR of $120,000.

$$16.667 - \$2,000,000 / \$120,000$$

Our example Average Accounts Receivable (AR) Turnover Ratio is 16.667.

Note: you might have expected the *total* AR balance (used in calculating the average AR) to equal the total revenue for the same period. There's no reason it couldn't, but also no reason it *has* to. If your invoice payment net due period (your credit period to your customer) is 30 days, some will pay in, say, 25 days, while others might pay in 35 days (or even wilder swings). The AR numbers you're using here are specifically end-of-period numbers, and you have no way to *see* what's happening within the period.

o **What's a good number:** Essentially, the higher the ratio, the faster your collections; but if it's too high, it might mean your credit is too tight, which can result in loss of customers; too low and it can mean your sales are sliding.

But so far that answer doesn't tell me much – I need to know more detail. OK, by taking the ratio calculation one step further and dividing the answer into the number of days in the period (365 days in this example), you get the **average collection days per invoice**.

In our above example, we calculated an AR Turnover Ratio of 17 (rounded up). If we divide that into 365 days, we get 21 (and some change) – which tells us that our average invoice collection length is about 21 days.

The closer your actual collection is to your invoice credit terms, the more you're getting your money on time (and if it's lower than your credit terms, that's even better). If, in our example above, our net payment period on invoices is 30 days, we're collecting most of our invoices upwards of nine days ahead of that – which is pretty good. If we were above 30, it becomes "less good", and maybe we should put some effort into collecting invoices faster.

Keep in mind, by invoicing customers you are extending free credit during this invoice pay period, and while it's something you might have to do as a business, it's costing you money you could be using for other business purposes, so you need to keep it as short as possible.

o **How often to monitor:** Quarterly, year-end, and trailing 12 months give you the best information – of those three, year-end and trailing 12 months are better. The latter, though, means that you need to be in business for at least a year before it's possible. But during that first year, you can always calculate it at the end of the first quarter, then end of six months, end of nine months, followed by your year-end number. Just make sure you use the correct divisor to calculate the average AR number.

Calculating this ratio each month probably isn't valuable, as that time period is likely to be the same as your invoice period (i.e., net 30 days).

Inventory Turnover Ratio. Inventory turnover is also known as *Inventory Turns, Merchandise Turnover, Stock-Turn, Stock Turns, Turns,* and *Stock Turnover.*

o **What it tells you:** As the word *turnover* implies, this ratio tells you the number of times, on average, your inventory is sold and replaced over a period of time. In accounting parlance, this ratio tells you the liquidity of your inventory – in other words, how quickly you are turning over your goods for sale into cash.

Sure, you say, I can tell that just by looking at the stuff on my shelves in the back room – but this doesn't show the information in a quantifiable metric that you can monitor for trends. (Or to write about in your "*how are we doing report*" to your business banker when asked to explain some other financial information that might be starting to look pear-shaped. Don't forget that when you're carrying debt from the bank, your business banker is now sort of a partner in your business, and that's another person you need to keep happy and informed.)

In a small business, turning over the stuff you make for sale is critical to your business success. If you find the inventory of stuff is piling up on the shelves because you're concentrating too much on production and not enough on getting more sales, you have a problem. As a small business, you can dig a financial hole in no time if you don't get an immediate focus on sales (or in cutting production). Yet many small business owners are more enamored with the stuff they create and build, but just aren't cut out to be sales gurus – and at the same time can't get interested in the business side of keeping the doors open. On the flip side, some business owners may be so focused on sales that they don't keep an eye on their inventory numbers, leading to sales they can't fill This ratio can help with both sides of that coin.

o   The formula is:

Inventory Turnover Ratio = Cost of Sales / Average Inventory

Note: The formula for calculating the Inventory Turnover Ratio can be slightly different in each reference source you look at. The above formula is the one this book recommends (to illustrate this, a Wikipedia article on Inventory Turnover[180] has a mind-numbing number of formulas for Inventory Turnover).

o   **Data comes from:** P&L or Cash Flow/Budget for Cost of Sales; the Balance Sheet for Inventory (which must be calculated first).

Note: The reporting period that you are calculating for is important in developing the numbers. For an end-of-year (or trailing 12 months) calculation, use the year-end number (or add up the monthly number for the trailing 12 months) for Cost of Sales; for quarterly, use the quarter-end or trailing 3 months' total; for monthly, use the previous month. For the average Inventory, use the same logic as for the various COS periods, and then divide it by the number of months in the period before using it in the formula.

Ideally, it would be best to calculate this ratio for each product category in your P&L or Cash Flow/Budget. However, you might not have individual Cost of Sales numbers for each product, since breaking out raw material costs at that detail level might not be feasible. Just keep in mind then, if you calculate on overall inventory, you might have one production category that is over-stocked or obsolete, obscuring the location where your inventory problems are.

Also, unless you have sophisticated inventory management practices or software, you might not be able to know your inventory data on a month-by-month basis, forcing you to only perform this ratio calculation annually when you take official stock inventory.

Lastly, the granularity of the numbers used in your calculation is important, so that's why you should use an average inventory number – as levels of inventory can fluctuate dramatically during the time period of the calculation, or from one time period to the next. For example, for your year-end calculation, you might be carrying excess inventory for

---

[180] *Inventory Turnover*, Wikipedia, https://en.wikipedia.org/wiki/Inventory_turnover

several months, then sell a lot of inventory just before the end of the year (seasonal sales, for example) – and your turnover ratio won't show that you've had excess inventory for a long period leading up to that. Averaging helps smooth that out.

- o **Example:** We don't have multiple monthly or year-end Balance Sheet and P&L statements to use for this calculation, so we'll assume this is a trailing 12-month calculation – and let's say it's being done after our June (month-end) financial statements are produced. We add up our total Cost of Sales on the June P&L, plus each of the preceding 11 month P&Ls (May-this-year, going backwards through July-last year) and get $200,000 (keeping our numbers simple for calculations). From the Balance Sheet for June and each of the preceding 11 months, we get a total 12-month COS of $144,000; dividing that number by 12, we get an *average* Inventory value of $4,000.

$$3 = \$12,000 \ / \ \$4,000$$

<u>Our example Average Inventory Turnover Ratio is 3.</u>

- o **What's a good number:** Essentially, the higher the ratio, the more times during the period that you've turned over your inventory; the lower the ratio, the less times you've turned it over. But too high can also be problematic, so you need to find your company's sweet spot.

  Too low can indicate poor sales or excess inventory, which can lead to revenue problems if the inventory becomes obsolete (through product upgrades or new, better products that you introduce). On the other hand, you may be intentionally building up inventory due to expected material shortages, higher material prices, or for a seasonal selling period.

  Too high also presents analysis challenges. It could (in the ideal world) be due to strong sales that continue to deplete your inventories – but if that's carried to the extreme, it can result in losing future sales if you can't satisfy customer demand. It could also be, though, that you are buying material in small quantities, causing your COS of sales to be higher than necessary.

  Some financial analysts suggest that if you multiply your inventory turnover ratio by your gross profit margin percentage and the answer is greater than 100, your average inventory turnover *isn't* too high.

  There's a wealth of information about analysis of this ratio if you search on "*what is a good inventory turnover ratio*".[181]

- o **How often to monitor:** Quarterly, year-end, and trailing 12 months give you the best information – of those three periods, year-end and trailing 12 months are better. The latter, though, means that you need to be in business for at least a year before it's possible. But during that first year, you can always calculate it at the end of the first quarter, then end of six months, end of nine months, followed by your year-end number. Just make sure you use the correct divisor to calculate the average inventory number.

---

[181] *Inventory Turnover Formula | Stock Turnover Ratio*, Accounting Tools online, http://www.accountingtools.com/inventory-turnover-ratio

More resources for financial ratios. The financial ratios highlighted above barely scratch the surface. Many others won't be relevant to your particular business and situation, many are too arcane and esoteric to be of much value – and might only be of value for an avid numbers wonk. And in a small business, someone of that focus isn't keeping an eye on the important stuff – running the company. If you want more ratios to look at, do a search on *small business best financial ratios*", and you'll get all the hits you can stand.

Chapter 6   Hiring (and Firing) Employees and Work Rules

"Recently, I was asked if I was going to fire an employee who made a mistake that cost the company $600,000. No, I replied, I just spent $600,000 training him. Why would I want somebody else to hire his experience?"
Thomas Watson Sr. founder and CEO from 1914 to 1956 of IBM

Adding new employees – interviewing and hiring

<u>**As far as you can take it alone.**</u> You've created this tiny start-up company all by yourself, you are Employee #1, and except for the unpaid help of your spouse or a friend, you've been running the show all on your own. All business decisions made so far have been on your back, and you have no one to answer to for any bad decisions.

But now, just as you're starting to see a bit of light at the end of the tunnel, you've run out of bandwidth, or more likely, several areas of business management that you have no experience whatsoever in need expansion. Besides that, you're about to run out of gas – frazzled and burned-out by all the work you're putting in. And ... (because you thought you had the bull by the tail and were spending too much on luxuries), you've only managed to salt away a small amount of money in the company checking account. How do you grow this company? More importantly, how do you grow it *right*?

When you add Employee #2, then #3, and so on, you're heading up (or down) a rocky and risky slope that can either take your company to new heights, or open one can of worms after another. At this early business stage, you're doubling, tripling, quadrupling your company's size with each new employee ... and the corresponding headaches might increase exponentially. Worse, each new person could be working in an area that you know absolutely nothing about, so you not only have challenges in even hiring the right person(s), but also in managing them. Also, adding just a handful of employees might not sound like much, but it begins to set the most significant company policy and practice precedents you'll likely *ever* have. And the problem is, you're pretty much on your own to make sure you get them right ... all the while that you're stretched to your limits with the day-to-day alligators snapping at you. This could easily be the most dangerous period of your young business' life.

The precedents you set here can haunt your company (and you) for years if they aren't established carefully. And when you're a new and inexperienced business owner, researching and thinking them through can be challenging. This includes employee hiring practices, salary and payroll policies, employee communication issues, benefit policies, workplace policies, new tax issues, new business development issues, creating a corporate culture ... the list could go on and on.

Granted, you don't have to resolve every one of these in great detail right now, but you'd better start thinking about them from the moment you make the decision to hire the first employee. If you don't, precedents you set can come back to bite you if they're left to drift sideways. At the very least, read through the next chapters so that you'll have an idea of things to start thinking about.

W-2 Employees or 1099 contractors? This seems to be one of those curve-shaped questions that swing back and forth, where one decade both employers and employees clamor for the idea of 1099 contractors, and the next decade the pendulum swings back to W-2 employees. Starting in 2015 we seemed to be moving towards the latter, to some degree the result of federal, state, and local governments cracking down on *misclassification* of workers, and also due to contractor lawsuits demanding employee benefits. If you currently favor hiring independent contractors, make sure your situation is on the legal side of the issue, as it can be very costly if you're not. The rules on it *are not always absolutely clear*, and that can lead to judgmental decisions that might not go in your favor. Tread very carefully on this issue.

An article in the Entrepreneur online website reports that fully one third of companies audited for potential misclassification of employees *fail the audit*, and the IRS found an astonishing 46% of independent contractors misclassified. [182]

Simply put, many employees starting to work for a small business actually want to be classified as a 1099 independent contractor. The typical reason is, they figure the small business isn't going to shower them with lots of good benefits (such as 401(k) plans, health insurance, good vacation time, maternity leave, etc.), so why not work as a self-employed contractor and have as many tax benefits as possible on their own. When a big company, let's say a Microsoft, wants to hire you and tells you they'll only bring you on as an independent contractor, you'd be missing out on all of the great benefits that regular employees are getting, so it's not such a good deal in that case.

Why does all of this about contractor/employee status matter to the IRS and state agencies? The official IRS and U.S. Treasury Department statistics on the issue are very old (the last study was done in 1984, with a new study supposedly due out in 2015 – no sign of it yet), but the data suggests that misclassification of employees as independent contractors costs state and federal agencies upwards of $70B (yes, that's 70 *billion* dollars) in unpaid employment taxes. [183] Obviously, it's easy to see why a lot of employers and employees prefer the independent contractor route, and why government finance agencies prefer the employee route.

The worst of it is, if an audit goes against you, the penalties can be severe, not only from the IRS but also from state regulatory agencies, particularly if the misclassification is deemed *willful disregard* – with penalties ranging from $5,000–$25,000 *per misclassified employee*. In some

---

[182] Rebecca Cenni, *W-2 or 1099? Why It Pays to Classify Your Employees Correctly*, Entrepreneur online, May 13, 2015,
http://www.entrepreneur.com/article/246139?utm_source=feedburner&utm_medium=feed&utm_campaign=Feed%3A+entrepreneur%2Flatest+%28Entrepreneur%29

[183] American Bar Association newsletter, July 2011,
http://www.americanbar.org/newsletter/publications/youraba/201107article05.html

states you may also be blacklisted from state contracting bids.[184] On the IRS side, not only will you be liable for paying all back *employment taxes*, but you'll also be assessed stiff penalties (an additional percentage of the tax) – even if the IRS finds that you unintentionally misclassified.

How do they catch you? Pretty simple: the IRS requires that you (as the employer) file a Form 1099-MISC on each independent contractor that you hire during the year in order to report the amounts paid to that independent contractor. The IRS simply looks for tax filers who have a single 1099-MISC – which indicates they only worked for one company during the year, and that's a good sign the individual is really an employee of the company that issued the 1099-MISC. Another red flag is individuals who received both a W-2 and a 1099-MISC from the same company during the tax year, a likely situation for someone who has been doing employee-type work, then switches to an independent contractor doing the same work.

The Entrepreneur website also mentions that independent contractors and so-called *temporary employees* who are disgruntled from having been misclassified – more common now than ever – are filing lawsuits to gain employee status, and that this is one of the hottest areas in employment litigation. So if you think the fines mentioned above are steep, imagine what your legal fees could be if you step into this type of mess.

So, what's the difference between an employee and an independent contractor? Sometimes it's a fine line, and one that's open to interpretation. Straight from the horse's mouth (if I can describe the IRS that way): *"The general rule is that an individual is an independent contractor if the payer has the right to control or direct only the result of the work and not what will be done and how it will be done"*.[185] Well, that's vague enough to drive a truck through – but it's the single rule that most employers/employees hang their 1099 versus W-2 hat on.

The IRS goes on to say: *"you are not an independent contractor if you perform services that can be controlled by an employer (what will be done and how it will be done)"*. This applies even if you are given freedom of action. What matters is that the employer has the legal right to control the details of how the services are performed. If an employer-employee relationship exists (regardless of what the relationship is called), you are not an independent contractor.

If you're still confused, you're not alone, and now you can see why I mentioned above that this is an area that's oftentimes ripe for interpretation. (For an interesting example of how even large companies – such as FedEx Ground – get it wrong according to the IRS, go to the later section on Overtime and Compensatory Pay to read a *very* costly ruling.)

To determine how to classify those working for you, you should evaluate any work position you're trying to fill with something called the "Darden factors" – the name of which derives from a 1992 U.S. Supreme Court Decision called *Nationwide Mutual Insurance Co. v. Darden*, 503 U.S. 318 (1992) ... aaaahhhh, I can see your eyelids drooping already, but wait, *this issue actually starts to make sense here*. The Darden factors have been quite clearly spelled out as 12

---

[184] *Employee Misclassification – Be Careful!*, Autopaychecks, Inc. blog, August, 2013, http://autopaychecks.com/2013/08/29/autopaychecks-blog-august-2013-employee-misclassification-be-careful/
[185] *Independent Contractor Defined*, http://www.irs.gov/Businesses/Small-Businesses-&-Self-Employed/Independent-Contractor-Defined

cons.derations, _any_ of which could be seen as being for or against an individual's classification as an independent contractor, on the Frequently Asked Questions (FAQ) page of the U.S. Department of Labor (DOL) website.[186] (Note – the IRS now considers that if any of the factors below are true, they figure the worker is to be considered an employee. That's pretty clear.)

Here's a list of the 12 so-called Darden factors, and you can find the background on each at the footnoted DOL FAQ website:

- The contractor's right to control when, where, and how the individual performs the job.
- The skill required for the job.
- The source of the instrumentalities and tools.
- The location of work.
- The duration of the relationship between the parties.
- Whether the contractor has the right to assign additional projects to the individual.
- The extent of the individual's discretion over when and how long to work.
- The method of payment.
- The contractor's role in hiring and paying assistants.
- Whether the individual's work is part of the regular business of the contractor.
- Whether the contractor is in business.
- The provision of employee benefits to the individual.

The DOL website FAQ page that details the Darden factors ends with a suggestion for what the employer should do after the analysis (_How do I apply the Darden factors?_): "_If, after analyzing all the Darden factors, the contractor determines that the individual is an "independent contractor" and not an employee, it need not include the individual in its AAP_ [Affirmative Action Plan]. _The contractor should document the analysis it used to come to this conclusion and retain this documentation as an employment record. OFCCP_ [Office of Federal Contract Compliance Programs] _may conduct its own Darden analysis during a compliance evaluation of the contractor and make the final determination as to whether an individual is properly classified as an independent contractor or other nonemployee, giving due consideration to the contractor's reasoning for its classification decision._"

(The above quote is referring to employers who are federal government contractors, as the question that prompted it came from an employer specifically asking it with respect to the Federal Contract Compliance Program, and not as a private employer. Nevertheless, it's pretty apparent from the Department of Labor response that it would be considered the same regardless.)

So here's the important part. As mentioned in the quote, you (the employer) should document the analysis you used in analyzing each of the above factors, date, _and retain_ this documentation as an employment/contractor record. Then, if it's ever raised as an issue, this is your defense document that might help you successfully argue your case. Without this, your only hope is that

---

[186] _Employer-Employee Relationship_, http://www.dol.gov/ofccp/regs/compliance/faqs/Employer-Employee_Relationship.html

you can talk your way out of it with the government agency that questions it. Putting this another way, arguing your way out of it at the time it's challenged isn't going to help your case.

An overall recommendation might be, if in doubt, treat the individual as an employee. Later, if you lose an audit with the taxing authorities, anything you saved by granting independent contractor status will be more than lost in back taxes, fines, and accounting and legal fees that you'll then be stuck with. It just isn't worth it.

Hiring that first employee. Seems easy, huh? Take out an advertisement with an online job placement service, interview a few people, and away you go. Hold on, though, as there's a lot that goes along with this process, and before you're finished and know all the ramifications, you'll wish you had prior experience working in a personnel office or HR department.

Anyone who's watched their 401(k) yo-yo'ing up and down the past several years (2009–2015) has almost certainly figured out that a good portion of it was due to the monthly *jobs report*, the much-anticipated figure from the federal Bureau of Labor Statistics that tells us how many jobs have been created across America in the previous month (due to the massive number of jobs lost during the 2007–2009 recession, this has been a highly-watched figure in the news, indicating how well the economic recovery is doing).[187] Did you ever wonder how these figures for the number of new jobs created was derived? Well, wonder no more. When you begin hiring employees for your new company, _you_ explicitly become the source of that information.

Whether that first employee is you (if you have a corporation) or your #2 employee for that first real expansion, you have a bit of bureaucratic work to do. If you're new to this, start with the Small Business Administration (SBA) website page that outlines the steps you need to take to "Hire and Retain Employees".[188] It will list all of the steps you need to take, and all of the forms identified can be easily downloaded by searching on the form name or number.

Here are your first steps before hiring the first employee:

- Get an Employer Identification Number (EIN) from the IRS (if you have a bank account, you almost certainly already have an EIN assigned). This is also known as your Employer Tax ID, and it's similar to your personal Social Security number (it's a unique 9-digit number, but in a different format from an SSN). While the primary purpose of an EIN is for employment tax reporting, it's also used for identification of your business – for example, an EIN is required whenever you open a bank account – and it remains with you throughout the life of your company. You can apply online for your federal tax ID, which is the easiest way to do it.[189]

- Set up the processes you'll need to withhold federal and state employment (Social Security and Medicare) and income taxes. This includes:

---

[187] Officially, the report is the Employment Situation Summary, issued the first Friday of each month by the U.S. Department of Labor's Bureau of Labor Statistics, with a summary of employment across America. It can be found at http://www.bls.gov/news.release/empsit.nr0.htm

[188] *Hire and Retain Employees*, SBA, https://www.sba.gov/content/hire-your-first-employee. Another good SBA site is at https://www.sba.gov/content/employment-and-labor-law

[189] *Federal Tax ID/EIN Application*, IRS Form SS-4, IRS website, https://www.irs.gov/businesses/small-businesses-self-employed/apply-for-an-employer-identification-number-ein-online

- o Document the process. This is important for several reasons. You don't want to reinvent the process each time you hire an employee. You need to be certain that you consistently set up each employee's personnel file, and this is the start of it. Whoever takes over this process will need to know how it works.

- o Each new employee (including you if you are being treated as an employee, such as in a corporation, or an LLC being taxed as a corporation) must fill out a W-4 form – the Employee's Withholding Allowance Certificate – that is used to calculate the amount of withholding tax to be withheld from the employee's paycheck. Usually withholding is based on the employee's number of family members, but an employee may choose to use a higher number if there's a wish to have more withheld.

- o At year's end (no later than January 31), you are required to issue a W-2 Wage and Tax Statement to the employee (and submit it to the Social Security Administration, who will also forward the information to the IRS as a double check against what the employee reports). This form identifies all wages and tax withholding by your company for each individual employee.

- o Create a payroll system, even if it's a rudimentary one.[190] As the SBA website blog sagely advises at the outset, *"Whether you have one employee or 50, setting up a payroll system not only streamlines your ability to stay on top of your legal and regulatory responsibilities as an employer, it can also save you time and help protect you from incurring costly IRS penalties"*. The list of 10 important steps outlined on this website are all good, and should be followed (only three were highlighted here). According to Inc.com, *"the IRS typically penalizes one out of every three business owners for payroll errors"*.[191]

- Registering with and reporting to your state's new hire program. (This is where the federal labor statistics are derived that give the new employee numbers each month.) Rules and procedures are different for each state, so find the details for your state at http://www.dol.gov/whd/contacts/state_of.htm. (This Department of Labor website page has a link for every state's Wage and Hour Division Labor Office.)

- Your state's business licensing agency might also require you to update your business license, indicating that you now have employees working for your company. For example, in my state (Washington), you're required to file a new Business License Application if you want to hire employees for the first time.[192] To ensure you're in compliance, check with your state's business license website page.

- Obtain workers' compensation insurance, either with a commercial policy or through your state's Workers' Compensation Insurance Program (as a small business, don't even think about the concept of self-insuring, as you won't qualify). Known simply as Workers' Comp in everyday language, this insurance provides wage replacement and medical

---

[190] Starting and Managing, Managing a Business, https://www.sba.gov/managing-business/running-business/managing-business-finances-accounting/10-steps-setting-payroll-system
[191] Issie Lapowsky, *How to Choose a Payroll Service*, Inc.com bookkeeping track, http://www.inc.com/guides/2010/05/choosing-a-payroll-service.html
[192] State of Washington, Business Licensing Service, *Add Employees*, http://bls.dor.wa.gov/addemployees.aspx

benefits to employees injured in the course of employment. It's administered by the U.S. Department of Labor.[193]

- Within three days of hiring each new employee, you must verify the eligibility of the employee to work in the United States, and then fill out a Form I-9 – Employment Eligibility Verification.[194] You keep the form in your personnel files only (i.e., you do not submit it to the government), but you must produce it if requested by Immigration and Customs Enforcement (ICE). Once you have the completed I-9 form in hand, you can access and use the online E-Verify service at the U.S. Citizenship and Immigration Services (USCIS) website (at http://www.uscis.gov/e-verify).

  Important note: It is recommended that you keep I-9 forms for *all* employees in a single file (rather than in each employee's personnel file), so that if ICE (or some other government agency) asks to see it, you can just produce the I-9 and not risk having the employee's entire personnel file handed over (you don't want them snooping around in data they have no business seeing).

- Establish a location within your workplace where you can display all posters and notices that inform your employees of their rights, and your responsibilities as an employer, under state and federal labor laws. At the earliest stages of your new company, this seems like a do-nothing requirement, but as you grow larger and have an employee break or lunch room, this is the perfect place for it. An even better place is an employee-access-only *intranet* website, where employees can sign in and access various types of company and employment information. In the meantime, a good recommendation is to have a file of these and make sure each new employee is given easy access to the file during the initial hiring process. Another recommendation is to have each new employee sign or initial a statement that they've had access to this file. Links to many of the notices and posters can be found at http://www.dol.gov/whd/resources/posters.htm (many of them will not apply to your company, so read through the list and download only the ones that are applicable).

Job Postings and Candidate Interviews. Before you start the hiring process, the questions you need to think about are manifold. Luckily, good websites can assist with several of the areas, so make sure you're creative in searches to find best practice advice (try searching on "employer job interview questions"). A word of caution, though, most of the hits from this search will focus on the prospective new *employee's point of view*, so drill down far enough to find the right questions.

- How will you search out new employees? Will you advertise on monster.com, recruiter.com, or one of the other worldwide internet sites? Will you use a paid recruiter? If you only want local job applicants, consider an advertisement in your local newspaper? By all means, look for websites that help you with "best practices advice for job postings".[195]

---

[193] For more information, see http://www.dol.gov/dol/topic/workcomp/

[194] Department of Homeland Security, U.S. Citizenship and Immigration Services, Form I-9, Employment Verification, https://www.uscis.gov/i-9

[195] *Recruiting Ideas: How to Find Good Hourly Employees*, monster.com, http://hiring.monster.com/hr/hr-best-practices/small-business/hiring-process/find-good-employees.aspx

If you use an international internet site, expect a lot of responses, but they'll come from all over – which is OK if you are planning a stay-put employee who will work remotely. But if you only want local responses, it's going to eat up a fair amount of effort to weed out the distant responders.

If you decide to use a recruiter (and have never done so before), ask lots of questions about cost, how they search for candidates, and what your recourse is for an employee hired through them who doesn't work out (typically a guarantee that refunds part of the recruitment fee). Will the contract arrangement be on a contingent, retained, or contract basis? If it's a contingent fee arrangement, you pay nothing up front, but the recruiter is likely to work hard and fast (but not necessarily smart) so that their fee is earned quicker. With a retained basis, you pay a deposit (typically $1/3^{rd}$), then another $1/3^{rd}$ at a pre-determined point in the process, and the final $1/3^{rd}$ when a candidate is hired. On a contract basis, the recruiter is paid hourly, and it's up to you to keep the costs under control. The overall fee is typically negotiated at 25%–35% of the candidate's first year's salary. **Important:** Make certain you thoroughly discuss the candidate's first year salary components and how that is factored into the recruiter's fee, particularly if the new hire is expected to have a bonus, or work on commission (the agreement might spell out that the fee includes them in the salary).

- Have you read the legal do's and don'ts of job postings?[196] Odds are, at this stage of your business you won't be on any legal beagle's radar screen, or have the feds knocking on your door. Nevertheless, the last thing you want is a disgruntled job seeker turning you in as a way of getting back at you when things don't go well.

- Are new employees going to work at a brick-and-mortar facility where your business is based? Will they work from home? Do they need to be physically in the same town as your business (to attend meetings, planning sessions)? Are you willing to pay relocation costs? Are you willing to pay travel costs if they have to commute? Your job posting should identify any of these factors.

- Should you hire friends and family? An important corollary to that is, are you prepared to *fire* (or discipline) friends and family if they don't work out? You can bet family and friends will come out of the woodwork, thinking they have an inside track or thinking you owe it to them, even if they don't have the experience or knowledge you're looking for. If you decide to hire family members, don't underestimate the challenges you'll face from other employees when charges of nepotism surface.

---

[196] The Immigration and Nationality Act of the United Stated Department of Justice prohibits a job posting that treats "individuals differently because they are, or are not, U.S. citizens or work authorized individuals. U.S. citizens, asylees, refugees, recent permanent residents and temporary residents are protected from citizenship status discrimination. Employers may not reject valid employment eligibility documents or require more or different documents on the basis of a person's national origin or citizenship status." You may not specify any of the following: "Only U.S. Citizens", "Citizenship requirement", "Only U.S. Citizens or Green Card Holders", "H-1Bs Only", "Must have a U.S. Passport", "Must have a green card". *Best Practices for Online Job Postings*, United States Department of Justice website, http://www.justice.gov/crt/about/osc/htm/best_practices.php

- If new employees work from home offices and need office equipment, who will own their home office equipment? Are you willing to pay for it, plus pay to have it set up? Don't underestimate the challenges and difficulties with this. Everyone has a different skill level in setting up a business-level home network, and troubleshooting their problems can eat up lots of time and resources. You'll likely get pushback from techy new-home-based employees who think they know more than you about their (and your) system's network security. They'll prefer to use their favorite system software – i.e., they might have an aversion to anything related to Microsoft software, or Mac software, your internet browser standard, or your preferred system security software. The more tech-oriented your company is, the more problems you'll have in this area.

Are you prepared for a possible deluge of responses from your posting? It could easily number in the hundreds (maybe thousands), and it's surprising how much time it eats up to wade through all of them. Expect lots of responses from people who are _way_ overqualified – typically looking for a temporary job while they continue to search for the real job they'd like to have.

> *"Hire character. Train skill."*
> Peter Schultz, founder and director GNF

Reading résumés and setting up interviews. If submitting a résumé (also known as a CV, for Curricula Vitae) is important for your job applicants, specify that requirement in your job posting, and then set aside enough time to wade through the pile you'll receive. Receiving 50–100 résumés from a published job posting isn't unusual, and from some of the large online posting sites don't be surprised to receive 150 résumés or applicants. That seems incredibly daunting, but once you've gone through a few you'll find it quite easy to spot the really good, the merely good, the not so good, and the really bad.

The first task is whittling the pile down to a manageable number (let's say, 15–20) for further review. That makes it easy to keep your head around the special qualities you find in some, and help you build a *preference pile*. From that second review, further narrow the selection down to maybe ten of the *best candidates so far*. At this point you could communicate back to each of them that they are under consideration and you'd like to schedule phone interviews – and state a day/time for them to choose from. From this, you should be able to identify five or six that you'd really like to interview in person, and let them know they've made the final cut. And importantly, have an e-mail response – individually addressed – to each of the best candidates so far, telling them they might hear further from you if a final job offer isn't accepted from the ones you're interviewing face-to-face (it's a common sense courtesy, letting them know you're an honorable person – and company – and not leave them on the hook wondering if you'll contact them again).

Résumé lies. In your résumé analysis, look for telltale signs that the person is either hiding something or is lying on their résumé. If the job position requires (or would be expected to require) a college degree, but they don't list a degree, assume they're hiding the fact they don't have one. If details look scant in their previous employment history, they're either hiding something or are lying about it. You don't need to necessarily pitch these into the round file right away, but annotate them for further review in the event they get through the initial whittling-down process. Note gaps in employment dates on their résumé, and if they get to further review, make sure you follow up on those by asking about them. If they look over-qualified, be suspicious they might be looking for a temporary job, spending time on your nickel doing their next job search, and won't be with you long (I had an ex-bank branch president send in a résumé for a bookkeeper position that I was advertising – duh!). A lot of this subterfuge can be brought to light in the interview, or in the post-interview reference and background checking, but as you figure out ways to spot it up front, it can save you extra work later.

According to a recent survey by careerbuilder.com, here are the most common résumé lies:[197]

- Embellished skill set – 57%
- Embellished responsibilities – 55%
- Dates of employment – 42%
- Job title – 34%
- Academic degree – 33%
- Companies worked for – 26%
- Accolades/awards – 18%

Surprisingly, one falsehood that isn't in the list but should be is inflating past salary (maybe because salary is usually not contained in a résumé, but rather, is stated verbally in the job interview). Whichever, it's easy to state a figure that's 10%, 15%, maybe 20% higher than it actually was, and almost certainly you'll ever know. It's a question not likely to be asked in post-interview calls with previous employers, and even if asked you won't get a response. The problem is, if you feel you need to match (or exceed) whatever number they put down, it goes straight to your bottom line, and you've just been hoodwinked.

Can you believe it? There are even websites such as www.careerexcuse.com that will create fake job references, including anything from an associate degree to a doctorate degree to a fellowship.[198]

Phone interviews. Don't be afraid to do phone interviews, which are a very time-effective way to narrow the search when you have too many promising résumés, but not enough time to interview all of the candidates. One word of caution – in doing phone interviews, it's important to work from a script that you've prepared ahead of time, keep the interview on task, and have a good idea ahead of time about what you are trying to accomplish from it – and by all means, take notes of responses. You could easily find you still have the same number of applicants as before if you aren't sure what and how to weed out and identify top candidates from this process.

Face-to-face interviewing. Many start-up business owners have never interviewed prospective new employees before. It sounds easy as 1…2…3, but it isn't. Sure, you've probably

---

[197] *Fifty-eight Percent of Employers Have Caught a Lie on a Résumé, According to a New CareerBuilder Survey*, careerbuilder online, August 7, 2014, http://www.careerbuilder.com/share/aboutus/pressreleasesdetail.aspx?sd=8%2F7%2F2014&id=pr837&ed=12%2F31%2F2014

[198] Alice Gomstyn, *Faking Job References for a Price*, ABC News online, August 26, 2009, http://abcnews.go.com/Business/fake-job-references-real-jobs/story?id=8401993

interviewed for a job or two of your own, but you were on the other side of the desk, not inside the head of interviewer, and you were probably too nervous to even remember much about it – other than that it either landed you a job or put you back out on the street.

For face-to-face interviews, block out time for them as your schedule allows, but fit them into the shortest possible overall time period. No matter what, your head is going to spin by the fourth or fifth interview (maybe sooner), so allow time after each interview to make notes, get your head cleared (and your bladder), and mentally ready for the next one. In other words, don't schedule hour-long interviews, on the hour every hour, for a whole morning or afternoon, as it doesn't allow for an interview to run long, it doesn't give you any time to jot notes, and it doesn't give you enough time to mentally prepare for the next interview.

If I'd known in those early days of my company what I've since learned about conducting job interviews, it would have been a huge help. I spent far too much time talking and not enough time listening – telling the prospect what our company was like and why they should come to work for us. As a start-up, I really felt that I had to sell my company's good points, rather than asking them to sell me on why I should offer them a position. That left little time to ask them probing questions about the value they could bring to my company, and why they were qualified for the position I had open. Don't fall into this trap – give the interview candidate an overview of what you're looking for, and then spend the bulk of the interview finding out about them. If you hire the person, they'll have plenty of time afterwards to learn all the in's and out's of your company.

This advice doesn't hold true when you're trying to land a senior executive from the hottest company around – which will obviously be a relationship sell, where you might need this particular person more than they need you. In this case you'll need to spend a lot of time talking about how wonderful your company and its prospects are. This type of interview might start off with a social focus – maybe a breakfast or dinner meeting just to break the ice – and then at the next step move towards a more formal interview. It might even involve one or more written exchanges, where you each tout your benefits to the other, and cautiously begin to lay out the entire package of expectations and offerings.

Interview questions

Questions you should ask in a job interview. It's obvious that this topic is very intertwined with your particular company and the specific job you're trying to fill. An expansive list of questions or topics could be given here, but none might be relevant to your actual situation. Also, if you do a Google search on "best interview questions to ask", most hits will center on questions a job *applicant* should ask the interviewer (which is totally irrelevant for our discussion here). Even the hits that are on the mark are based on personal opinions of the person writing the website page. Sure, they could get your thinking started, but for the most part they won't help all that much.[199]

---

[199] For an interesting list to ponder, try *33 Questions Employers Ask At Interviews*, careerrealism online, June 9, 2014, http://www.careerrealism.com/questions-employers-ask-interview/

Instead, this is an area where you should probably sit back on your own, think for a long while before you begin the interview process, and then build your own list that you will use for every job candidate in a particular applicant round (obviously it will result in a different list for each position that you subsequently interview for). Consider these aspects:

- Develop your own idea of what you need to learn from the applicant that would make you feel good that he or she fits the job you're trying to fill – and helps you articulate the exact description of the job itself – i.e., what is the job description?

- From that, you can then jot down the qualifications a successful applicant needs to best fulfill that job. For example, if you are looking for a software documentation specialist, do you need someone who has a background in hardcopy documentation for a large software product, or someone who is more adept at creating online help documentation (there's quite a difference in skill set between the two). If you're looking for a field person to add to your landscape contracting business, is your primary need for someone who can correctly plant trees and shrubs, or is it someone who can lay brick and tile? If you're hiring a production manager for your up-and-coming craft beer brewery, what aspect of the production do you need help in? If you're looking for a sales person, do you want someone with mostly cold-calling experience, or someone who is really trained and experienced at relationship selling?

- What level of experience are you looking for? Are you looking for someone with minimal experience in your particular industry, but with some general background – allowing you to *bring them along* with your methodology, grow with your company, and make a career out of it? Or are you looking for someone who already has vast experience, someone who can teach you a thing or two to help you grow your business – but who might be looking for a short-term job until they can find the job they really want? The latter idea touches on the question of over-qualified – such as hiring a person with experience as a CFO (Chief Financial Officer) of a larger company as your bookkeeper, thinking they will have all the experience in the world about setting up your financial system, but who then spends all their time looking for another job and not doing the job you're paying them for. Either side of this question could be a good or bad thing, depending on your needs and where you plan to go with this new hire – and only you can answer that.

- Can you articulate exactly what the job entails, and will you know if the candidate can perform those functions? Once you have the bullet points plotted out for your job description, go through a mental walkthrough of how to discuss this, and what questions you will need to ask the candidate about their experience in meeting them. Assuming you're allocating roughly an hour for each interview, this needs to be carefully thought out ahead of time. It will hopefully be the *meat* of your interview time, so I'd recommend planning 30 minutes for it. If it's any longer, you'll probably run out of time, or run over your allotted time.

This point is trickier than you think, since you might be hiring someone for a position that you have little or no knowledge of how that position really works. Sure, you might have been doing all the sales and marketing work up to this point, but do you really know enough about what a sales or marketing _expert_ does to even know what you want the new hire to do? After all, the reason you're hiring them is for their expertise – expertise that you don't have – so how do you gauge whether they honestly know what they're doing, whether they're BS'ing you in the hopes of learning on the job, or will they turn out to be the greatest thing since sliced bread? Oftentimes you're forced to take a leap of faith, and when you do, your choice can turn out to be a crapshoot – so be prepared for having to correct for it down the road ... and you might find yourself having to get rid of the person ("*sorry, just didn't work out*") and have to start the hiring process all over again.

- What level of gung-ho-ness are you looking for? Do you need someone who works well from 9–5 and then goes home, or do you need the type of person who will be thinking about how to help build your company, giving you 18 hours a day when you're paying for eight? You certainly don't want to ask specific questions about this, but there are ways you can talk around it, getting the person to volunteer what you need to know.

- What are your work rules? If you're comfortable with the person working from their own home office, you need to know – ahead of time – the boundaries you'll accept, including the facilities you'll provide, what is expected of the employee, whether some level of in-office time is required for certain days or hours of the week. If you expect the candidate to travel often to another work site, you need to be able to articulate this clearly and in detail.

  If you aren't wild about (or won't accept) a new employee who has tattoos or piercings, you should know your opinion ahead of time and be ready for how you'll handle it.[200] For example, you *are allowed* by law to decide *not* to hire someone based on having body art – but you *are not allowed* to fire someone if they have it, so you are required to make the decision at the time of hiring.

- What are you willing to pay? This is usually a difficult issue on both sides of the table – for the interviewer and the applicant. Both want to play this negotiation close to the vest, so you need to know ahead of time exactly how you're going to broach the topic. If you're a decent business owner, you don't want to low-ball your new hire or they'll be looking for another job as soon as they figure it out. If you offer too high, you've put money on the table that you didn't need to, affecting your bottom line. What you need is a way to open the discussion so that neither of you walk away without some negotiating. My preference at time of interview would be to simply ask the candidate, "What are your salary expectations?" – and then leave the discussion at that. By doing so, you aren't actually negotiating a salary in the initial interview, and maybe not even in the second interview – but rather, just getting the topic out in the open. Leave the serious salary discussion for job offer time, once you've settled on a narrow band of candidates – which isn't easy to do, so think about it ahead of time.

Questions you *can't* (or *shouldn't*) ask in a job interview.[201] If you're a novice interviewer, it would seem that any question you want to ask is fair game, but that can land you in a heap of

---

[200] Jay P. Whickson, *Workplace Discrimination on Tattoos & Piercings*, Chron online, undated, http://smallbusiness.chron.com/workplace-discrimination-tattoos-piercings-16708.html

[201] *30 Interview Questions You Can't Ask*, HR World online, undated, http://www.hrworld.com/features/30-interview-questions-111507/. Another good list is at *Managing Illegal Interview Questions*, at timesunion.com, http://blog.timesunion.com/careers/managing-illegal-interview-questions/957/. Both of these lists are much longer than included here, so consult them for a comprehensive list before you do your first job interview.

trouble. Some questions are just inappropriate to ask, others are downright illegal, while still others have right and wrong ways to ask. You need to have these boundaries firmly in mind _before_ you start the interview so that you don't go down a path that leads to problems. Here are some do's and don'ts:

- *How old are you?* A big no-no, as it can raise the specter of age discrimination, particularly if the person appears to be nearing retirement age (and you select someone younger instead of that person). Obviously some jobs require a young person to be of a certain age, so to determine if they are legally old enough to do the job you're hiring for, you're allowed to ask, "Are you over the age of 18?" (or whatever the requirement is). If the reason behind your curiosity is to determine the candidate's level of maturity, you can find that out in lots of other ways (how they respond to other questions, their demeanor). If you do ask this question (and others that follow below), document it – word-for-word – in your interview notes and store it away if questions are later asked about it.

- *How much longer do you plan to work before you retire?* Again, a claim of age discrimination can bite you on this one, so don't go there _at all_.

- *Are you a U.S. citizen?* Worded like that, stay away, as _this one is actually illegal_. And that's strange too, because upon hiring you are then legally required to determine the person's legal situation with respect to being in the U.S. So, what you need to ask is, "Are you authorized to work in the U.S.?" and from that you find out what you need to know. If there is a specific reason that U.S. citizenship is required (such as a high-security clearance that only a U.S. citizen can get), you need to state that ahead of time in the job posting.

- *What is your native tongue?* That one too seems like a no-brainer – as a way for you to determine if a person has, let's say, English language fluency – but it flunks on the issue of ethnicity and country of origin. What you can ask is, "What languages do you speak, read, and write?" and you're in the clear (importantly, note plural in the word "languages"). Don't ask any questions related to the candidate's ancestry, such as Native American, African American, or any other race-related question – for obvious racial discrimination reasons.

- *What religion do you practice?* Absolutely _no_ religion-related questions. If your business is faith-based, whether you can ask questions on this topic is an ongoing discussion,[202] so read the footnoted references below, or do a Google search on "job interview questions allowed for faith-based businesses".

- *Are you pregnant?* Nope, don't ask it. You also can't ask if the person _plans_ to become pregnant, as both of these are considered discriminatory. If you ask, and then don't hire the person if they respond yes to either question, they can hit you with a discrimination lawsuit.[203] Instead, you can ask the person what their long-term career goals are, and if

---

[202] *Hiring Law for Groups Following a Higher Law: Faith-Based Hiring and the Obama Administration*, Pew Research Center online, http://www.pewforum.org/2009/01/30/hiring-law-for-groups-following-a-higher-law-faith-based-hiring-and-the-obama-administration/

[203] A costly lesson. An employer in Florida was hit with a $100K settlement after rescinding a verbal job offer for a woman who called up after her interview to ask further questions about the company's maternity benefits – and in the process admitted she was pregnant. Within minutes of the call the offer was rescinded, with the statement, "we need to have someone in the position long term". A discrimination lawsuit was filed by the EEOC on behalf of the woman under the Pregnancy Discrimination Act (PDA).

they mention that raising a family figures prominently in it, well, you have your answer. If the reason for asking this has to do with your curiosity about the person working well with kids in the new daycare center that you operate, that's a relevant line of thought, but the way to ask it is, "What is your experience with x-age group?"

Along that same line, don't ask if the candidate can get a babysitter on short notice for business travel or overtime requirements. Instead, mention that the job requires overtime or travel, and ask if this would be a problem for them. If they know they can't get a babysitter, they'll most likely mention it.

- Don't ask anything about where a person lives. In your mind you might be asking just to find out if the person's commute is reasonable, or to gauge whether you think they'll be at work on time – or even something as simple as whether there are public transportation services available – but it could also be construed as helping you create a discriminatory basis, such as coming from a neighborhood that's heavily populated by a specific ethnic or social class.
- Don't ask about a person's health or sickness background, other than asking to explain gaps in work periods due to long-term sick leave.
- Don't ask *anything* about a person's credit, including whether they've ever filed for bankruptcy, what their credit score is, or if they're able to obtain a credit card. Instead, at some point in the interview state: "We run credit checks on all of our potential new employees, and this is a standard practice that everyone must accept as a condition for hire". And once you say that the first time, you have to make certain you then run credit checks on *every* new hire, and not just the ones you might be worried about – and here's the law – you then must keep records of each credit check and they have to be stored in a locked file cabinet that is accessible to only one person who is responsible for personnel issues.
- Military service. If it's listed in the job history section of the applicant's résumé, you can ask what they did in the military, and about their training and education; if it's not listed, don't even ask if they were in the military. It's OK for you to mention that your company fully supports a Hire Veteran program, and from that it's likely you'll get quite a bit of information offered up from a veteran candidate.

If the candidate's résumé indicates military service, but doesn't mention the type of discharge, do not ask about it. Unless, of course, you are a federal government contractor and need to know this for work requirements (in which case, you are allowed to ask about military service and discharge type).

If the candidate's résumé indicates he or she is in the Reserves or National Guard, do not ask about any future deployments. Do not ask about any type of disability from military

---

For details, go to http://hrdailyadvisor.blr.com/2017/05/24/smoking-gun-managers-e-mail-maternity-leave-costs-employer-100k/?source=HAC&effort=44&utm_source=BLR&utm_medium=Email&utm_campaign=HRDAEmail&spMailingID=11107715&spUserID=MTg2NjgxMDIwNzIyS0&spJobID=1162170976&spReportId=MTE2MjE3MDk3NgS2.

service, particularly anything related to PTSD or having received any injuries (mental or physical) during service.

- Don't ask *anything* about criminal history, including felonies or misdemeanors. Again, all you can say is, "We run background checks on all of our potential new employees to check for felonies and misdemeanors, and that is a standard practice that everyone must accept as a condition for hire". Again, though, once you say this the first time, you have to run background checks as a standard practice for all subsequent new hires. Chances are, once you say this, the candidate being interviewed will volunteer the information. The ruling on this has lots of twisty turns, so if you're thinking about running background checks, consult an HR attorney or specialist to get full details.

(Besides the question being offensive, the statistics behind it are staggering. In 2012 (the most recent year for these statistics), the entire voting age population in the United States is 235 million – which closely tracks with the total number of people who might be looking for work. Of those, reportedly "70 million Americans have criminal histories that can limit their job opportunities or shut them out of work altogether"[204] – *essentially a third of American adults*.)

- *Do you have any disabilities that would prevent you from doing this job?* Don't touch any aspect of this with a 10′ pole, as the Americans with Disabilities Act (ADA) provides protection for people with disabilities. An extensive discussion of the ADA and small business can be found in Chapter 9. In brief, though, to see if your business is covered by ADA regulations, check out the section titled *Who Is Covered By The ADA?* in the publication, *ADA Update: A Primer For Small Business*, published by the U.S. Department of Justice. You can find it online at http://www.ada.gov/regs2010/smallbusiness/smallbusprimer2010.htm.

If any disability would prevent an applicant from doing the job you're hiring for, you must state specific requirements in the job description – *before any interviews*. For example, if the applicant must have 20/20 corrected vision, or must be able to lift 50 lb. sacks of flour, or must be able to type 110 words/minute, or have good communications skills, that requirement must be listed in the job description. And if any candidate fails to meet those requirements, you must document that as the reason to deny employment, and *not* because they have a disability.

At-will employment

Every U.S. state, except Montana,[205] has adopted labor law called at-will employment. This means that an employer can terminate an employee without what's known as *for cause* – meaning a person can be fired for any reason (and a reason doesn't have to be stated at time of firing),

---

[204] The Editorial Board, *A Criminal Record and a Fair Shot at a Job*, The New York Times Editorial Page, November 11, 2015, http://www.nytimes.com/2015/11/11/opinion/a-criminal-record-and-a-fair-shot-at-a-job.html?&moduleDetail=section-news-0&action=click&contentCollection=Opinion&region=Footer&module=MoreInSection&version=WhatsNext&contentID=WhatsNext&pgtype=article

[205] In Montana, the at-will concept only applies during an initial probationary period.

provided the termination isn't due to illegal reasons (discrimination, for example). *But, like a lot of other employment situations, an at-will employer must still be very careful in what is said at job interviews, at time of hiring, during employment, and at termination to stay out of possible trouble with an at-will firing.*

In general, you are considered to be an at-will employer by default, and you can strengthen this by clearly <u>making a statement that the employee will be an at-will employee during the employment interview,</u> or in any employment documents the employee signs at time of hiring. Nevertheless, you can easily turn an at-will situation into one that isn't at-will if you make statements *at any time*, such as, "oh, you'll always have a home here", or "we only fire for not meeting our performance standards". Similarly, if you've asked an employee to sign any type of employment agreement that promises or alludes to job security, you've given up your employer at-will rights for that employee.

Having said all that, it must be understood there are caveats to the at-will doctrine. These include discrimination, and retaliation for a legally-protected action (such as whistleblowing, refusing to do an illegal action, workplace investigation, among others).[206] Also, quite a few states (well over a majority, in fact) have enacted specific exceptions, including Public Policy Exemptions, Implied Contract Exemptions, Covenant of Good Faith Exemptions – so, again, make certain where your state stands on this issue before terminating an employee.[207] This is also why it's a good idea to discuss any employee firing that you're contemplating with your HR attorney – *and have the discussion before you do the firing* – this talk can be invaluable about what you can, should, and can't say during the firing process.

Past employment competitive information. If the person being interviewed is coming from a competitor, particularly if the interviewee may have proprietary information from a previous employer, make certain you brief them on exactly what they can and cannot do with respect to that information (and consult the outside HR attorney you should have in your back pocket by this time). If they have internal (and proprietary) product knowledge, make certain this information doesn't find its way into your products, or in any aspect of the development of your products. If they have sales knowledge, be very careful to let them know that using it in a way that can get you sued by the competitor will not be tolerated – and in fact, will be a cause for termination. Also, determine if the interviewee has any previous Employment or Termination Agreement terms that you should be aware of, and again, advise in no uncertain terms that violating any of them on your behalf is absolutely unacceptable and will not be tolerated.

When you first hear of all the proprietary goodies this prospective employee can bring to you, you'll probably have drool running down your chin. But common sense, personal morality, business morality, your corporate culture, and most importantly, the future of your company should immediately enter the picture. Violating any of this can jeopardize your company to the point of ruination.

---

[206] Bridget Miller, *What Does At-Will Employment Really Mean?*, HR Daily Advisor, May 1, 2014, http://hrdailyadvisor.blr.com/2014/05/01/what-does-at-will-employment-really-mean/

[207] *What States Are At-Will? List of At-Will Employment States*, RocketLawyer, https://www.rocketlawyer.com/article/what-states-are-at-will-employment-states-ps.rl. Note that the list of states in each exception are those that *do not have* the modifying exceptions to at-will law.

My experience. I once hired a guy who worked for a competitor – and I mean a competitor who was right in our face, day in and day out. He had exactly the right skills that I needed, and he was reputedly very good at his job. Because of this, I had received detailed instructions from our outside corporate HR legal advisor about exactly what I needed to do to keep our company in the clear. Unknown to me, though, on the day this guy exited from his previous employer, all the time he was sitting in his exit interview (across the desk from his manager, with his company laptop sitting on his lap), he was apparently preparing an e-mail with a large number of attachments that had *a lot* of serious proprietary information about his employer's product that competed directly with some of our products. At one point the manager asked him what he was doing, and he said, "nothing". Suspecting something, she asked him to immediately hand over the laptop and he refused. By the end of the interview, he had sent out the e-mail, and then handed over his laptop. Forensic tests conducted on the laptop by his former employer showed that he had sent the e-mail to himself at a private e-mail address, *and cc'd it directly to me*. Luckily, I never received it (and he apparently never received it at home as well), as the size of the e-mail attachments exceeded his mailbox limit.

When we hired this employee, we went to great lengths to advise him that bringing any proprietary information with him was strictly forbidden, and he assured us everything was clean. But several months after the hiring, my company received a subpoena (as part of a lawsuit against him), demanding that *every* computer within our company that might have any correspondence with this new employee be turned over to a forensic testing company for analysis (because of this new employee's position within our company, that would essentially have been every computer in our entire company – which would have shut us down). This was the very first I'd heard of the situation – and I only know the details now because the conversation quotes from his exit interview were explicitly described in the subpoena I received. You can bet this new employee didn't last at my company, but it sure left us with some tense moments, and an expensive lesson!

Post-interview résumé checking

You've just completed a grueling round of interviews, maybe even a batch of second interviews, and you're zeroing in on your preferred candidate. Getting to this point has been exhausting, and your primary thought is to get it over with so you can move on. My best advice is, don't cut corners now that you're this far, and don't believe everything you've read in the stellar résumés, nor with everything you've been told in face-to-face and phone interviews.

Before you make a job offer, you should check references, check school and diploma claims, check legal immigration paperwork, and check anything else that's possible about the résumé and interview details – *and if you've made it a standard company hiring policy*, do your background checks on criminal record and financial status (see the next section for why I highlighted the company policy phrase). It's the only way you'll find out if the person you're hiring is really the person they say they are.

Previous employment – checking résumé information. The first big recommendation is to ensure you call the immediate supervisor or manager that the candidate reported to – and if the candidate's résumé doesn't list that person, ask for it. If you reach a personnel staff member on your call, it's likely all they can respond with is verification of employment dates, and whether the person is eligible for rehire (it's a cover-your-butt situation, where companies are worried about being sued for making statements about an ex-employee). You may get the same type of response, though, from a direct-report manager, as many have been advised by their personnel or legal departments to be spartan with subjective comments. Try anyway, as how they give their response is sometimes ′nuff said!

Personal references can be problematic, as it's hard to believe a candidate would list a personal reference who doesn't give a glowing report. It's possible, though, that a personal reference could lead to another, then another – and somewhere along the line (if you're really on a hunt to close on some bit of information), you might just get some unexpected information.

Here's a pretty good list of questions to ask previous coworkers or manager/supervisors:[208]

1. Verify the candidate's dates of employment, title, and role.

2. Is the candidate eligible for rehire? Why or why not? What was his/her reason for leaving?

3. Determine the candidate's advancement in the company; did he/she receive any promotions or demotions, or did he/she remain in the same role throughout his/her tenure?

4. What was the candidate's beginning and ending salary? How often did the candidate receive salary increases? (You probably won't get anything on this question.)

5. What kind of duties and responsibilities were assigned to the candidate? Did he/she complete them satisfactorily? Did he/she go above and beyond what was required without being asked?

6. What were the candidate's strengths as an employee? Would you describe him/her as a hard worker?

7. Ask the reference to evaluate the employee's performance with regard to the tasks likely to be assigned in the new position.

8. Was the employee punctual? Were there any issues with tardiness or absenteeism?

9. Did the employee get along well with his/her peers? With managers? With customers?

10. Is there anything else I should consider before I hire this candidate?

This is a very extensive list, and unless you get an out-of-the-ordinary previous manager, you won't get this much time for the reference call – but you might with a previous coworker. Since selling my company, I've been called well over a dozen times to provide employee references, and the questions I've been asked mirror the ones given here. Although my attorney would probably advise otherwise, I was OK with giving honest and truthful answers to each of the questions (although I typically didn't have exact employment dates and salary amounts in my head).

Education records verification. When checking with educational institutions to verify résumé claims, ask for the school's records department and provide the candidate's social security number. Simply request the year the candidate attended classes and the graduation date. If a graduation date cannot be given, that's a red flag that you should follow up on – specifically by getting back to the candidate, asking to explain the discrepancy, and provide follow-up proof.

---

[208] *Checking References: Top 10 Questions To Ask*, Hcareers online, August 7, 2014, http://www.hcareers.com/us/resourcecenter/tabid/306/articleid/298/default.aspx

The onus to comply is on the candidate, and if they want the job, they'll either produce valid documentation or come clean on the lie.

Social media check. These days it's very common for employers to check a candidate's social and professional profiles on LinkedIn, Facebook and Twitter. But beware of making this check, because once it's known by others in your company that you do this, it can kill your level of trust, not only in the eyes of the applicant, but also other employees. And you're also on somewhat shaky legal grounds. Doing the check itself isn't illegal, but doing so may give you knowledge of the person's protected characteristics – maybe their religion, maybe their sexual orientation – stuff that would not be apparent from a résumé, so this opens you up to potential discrimination cases that could be avoided entirely. So unless you've been given a specific tip to check something on an employee's social media page, consider steering clear of it.

Should you do background checks? This seems like an easy question. Who wouldn't want to know that every employee being hired is squeaky clean? The real answer is ... it depends ... on several things, none of which help you towards a definitive answer.

If you believe everything you read on the internet, you'd conclude you're a fool if you don't run background checks on every new hire – but then, quite a few of these website recommendations are written by people who work for companies performing background checks as a business and they have a biased opinion based on wanting to sell you something. Quite a few are written by freelance magazine or blog contributors who seem to have been influenced by background check companies who are using PR firms to create dire warnings about the subject – and who very likely have never actually run a business and had to make the decision on whether to run background checks (or pay for them). Even the SBA recommends that background checks be done – but who's to say that the person writing an article such as this has any real experience with running a small business, or has direct knowledge of the hundreds of dollars that might be spent on *each* background check?

One internet writer advises, "Conventional wisdom says employers should run background checks on all potential new hires. The thinking: If you don't do your due diligence, you could wind up with a problem employee — or worse". But when specifically asked if background checks are absolutely necessary, the writer continues with, "It depends on the job position, the company, and the broader industry ... but in many cases the answer is: No, they are not. You just want to make sure that they're not an ax-murderer and they are who they say they are". And he goes on to say that just a basic criminal background check can cost between $20 to $100 per hire – and it can rise quickly if you're doing checks in multiple states or doing more thorough background checks.[209]

In my own situation, owning a small company that never exceeded 83 employees in its 30+ years – and had a couple hundred total employees pass through during that time – I never did any background checks. Overall, I had exactly one new hire candidate whose prior misdeeds might have come to light in a background check (the bookkeeper candidate mentioned later in this section), but I would have learned about that in any case if I'd simply checked her previous employer references, and that doesn't fall in the category of background checks. Since I owned a

---

[209] Kevin Casey, *Are Background Checks Worth the Cost?*, Intuit QuickBooks blog, July 30, 2013, http://quickbooks.intuit.com/r/employees/are-background-checks-worth-the-cost/.

small mainframe software development company (which is a relatively close-knit niche community), the vast majority of my new employees were recommended by current staff members, some were from current customers, and many I knew personally from my years of experience. In these situations, highly valued personal references took the place of any need to do background checks.

Yes, the statistics bandied about on the internet indicate that as many as two-thirds of all companies conduct background checks. Supposedly, and presumably in support of running background checks, an AARP study has shown that it can cost you as much as 50% of the employee's first year salary (in turnover costs) if you have to fire them after they were hired – and the firing offense could have been identified with a background check.[210]

Personally, I think the number of companies that perform background checks is far below the number listed, and of those who do, they're being conducted on only certain categories of employees within a company – mainly employee candidates who are in sensitive positions, positions where failing to pick up a criminal conviction can wreak real havoc on a company. Another example might be a situation where you're hiring someone who will be driving on official business and you fail to discover that the person has a half dozen DUI convictions in their past – and if that person has a DUI accident while on the job, your company might be sued for negligent "hiring and retention".[211]

Having said that, there are quite a few companies and organizations where state and federal laws *mandate* background checks. According to the federal Office of the Inspector General memorandum on state requirements for conducting background checks on employees who work in "home health agencies" (a.k.a. HHA),[212] 41 of 50 states surveyed require HHAs to conduct background checks on prospective employees, and several more plan to do so in the near future. So, if your new small business has anything to do with home healthcare or long-term healthcare, you need to check with your state health and welfare department for rules concerning this. Interestingly, state laws are considerably more lax on background check requirements for home day care facilities,[213] yet in my state (Washington), businesses in the trucking industry are required to perform background checks. To find out about your state, go to the home page of your state's primary government website and search on "background checks" – and hopefully your state will detail their requirements for small business.

If you decide to do background checks, a difficult question becomes: who should do them? Outside firm costs are high, plus you have to put in quite a bit of effort to find one that does a

---

[210] *What Are The Costs of Employee Turnover?*, AARP online, April 14, 2011, http://www.aarp.org/work/employee-benefits/info-04-2011/what-are-the-costs-associated-with-employee-turnover.html

[211] *What is Negligent Hiring and Retention?*, HG.org, http://www.hg.org/article.asp?id=31800.

[212] Office of Inspector General, Department of Health and Human Services, *State Requirements for Conducting Background Checks on Home Health Agency Employees*, May 29, 2014. As of this writing, the following states require employment background checks: AK, AL, AR, AZ, CA, CO, CT, DC, DE, FL, GA, HI, IA, ID, IL, IN, KS, KY, LA, MA, MD, ME, MI, MN, MO, MS, MT, NC, ND, NE, NH, NJ, NM, NV, NY, OH, OK, OR, PA, RI, SC, SD, TN, TX, UT, VA, VT, WA, WI, WV, WY

[213] For more information, go to http://childcareaware.org/families/health-and-safety-in-child-care/background-checks-what-you-need-to-know/

good job. If you try to save money by doing it in-house, the costs and risks can be even greater. Anyone who's ever tried to locate even an address and phone number of someone through the internet knows that your search pulls up dozens of scammers – again, firms that are just trying to wheedle some money out of you, with limited results.

The other big problem is, how do you stay within the law? Most states require that you inform the candidate ahead of time that you're doing a background check, and get a signed release from the candidate. You must then give the candidate a copy of the report (so corrections or explanations can be made if necessary), and you must follow strict privacy procedures for filing these reports (and if you throw them away you're in even deeper trouble).[214]

As I said at the outset, this discussion likely won't provide definitive guidance on whether to conduct background checks. There's no question they can be a valuable tool to weed out unsavory types who can cause great harm, but the whole process is fraught with problems.

My example – a candidate with an embezzlement background. In the very early stages of my company (and importantly, when I was under a crush of operational details to keep things afloat), I had just finished a very tiring round of interviews for a replacement bookkeeper. At the end of a half dozen interviews, I had identified a candidate who was at the top of my list after a second interview. According to her résumé, she was currently working at a nearby city government in their accounting department, and her education and experience perfectly fit my requirements. Quite stupidly and without thinking it through, I jumped the gun at the end of the second interview, openly hinting that she was my choice, and she could expect a formal employment offer after the weekend.

By chance, the next day I happened to run into a friend who consulted with this particular city government and I casually asked if he knew her. What a response I got! "Man, don't you read the newspapers or listen to the news?" he blurted out. "She's under indictment for embezzlement, and is expected to be charged this coming week!" I admitted that, no, I'd been traveling almost constantly up to that point, and local news just wasn't on my radar at the moment.

My cardinal sin, though, was that I hadn't even checked her previous employer reference – the manager she had worked for at the city government. So, first thing Monday morning I called the reference number listed on her résumé. At the outset I gave my reason for calling, and before I could say anything more the person on the other end broke in and said she'd have to transfer my call. A moment later, a person came on the line, identifying herself as the city attorney (which instantly raised my eyebrows). I again explained the purpose of my call, and was quickly told, "I'm sorry, I can't say anything at this time." My immediate response was, "Well, thank you very much, you already have!" To which she then stammered, "Ah, uh, no, I didn't mean to tell you *anything* you wanted to know." My response was, "Well, thanks, but you did". I rang off, and almost immediately called the candidate to tell her I'd filled the position with someone else.

---

[214] Mikal E. Belicove, *The 10 Dos and Don'ts of Conducting Employee Background Checks*, Forbes online, October 12, 2012, http://www.forbes.com/sites/mikalbelicove/2012/10/26/the-10-dos-and-donts-o-conducting-employee-background-checks/

At this point, my concern was whether I had already said _anything_ to the applicant that might give her grounds for false offers of employment. In the end, I decided she already had more problems than she could handle, and this would be the least of them. I had dodged a bullet – but not from anything brilliant on my part.

The moral is, it's better to check this stuff ahead of time, rather than later – maybe after the person does even more damage to your own company. Sure, you're legally in the right to later fire a person for lying on their résumé or application, but the overall costs are unreasonably high.

Making the job offer and salary negotiations

How to make the job offer. Finally, you've reached a decision on the candidate you want to hire! Now you have to get them to accept your offer – and the critical part is, before they accept an offer somewhere else. It's time to close the deal.

Following are several basic tips on how to accomplish the task:

- _Make the offer as soon as you've decided._ You'll have no idea how many other companies this candidate is interviewing with, _and the last thing you want is to lose out to another company (perhaps your competitor) who moved faster._

- _Don't notify other candidates until/unless your preferred candidate accepts._ Your second-in-line candidate might be waiting for word from you before accepting another position – and if you go off half-cocked you could then lose Candidate #2 if Candidate #1 doesn't accept (or you can't come to terms on, let's say, salary negotiation).

- _Start the offer process with a phone call._ Don't send an e-mail. Make the call before you begin preparing the official offer letter (assuming the position requires that level of protocol). This way you can show your enthusiasm for your hoped-for new employee, and also be able to gauge right away the candidate's enthusiasm.

- _Be as enthusiastic as you can._ Tell the candidate he/she was the first choice out of _x_- résumés, and how you think he/she will be perfect for your company's needs.

- _Outline the company's benefit package._ Assuming you aren't lowballing employees on benefits, this is your chance to highlight how good your company is to work for. As a small business, you'll find it's already tough enough to get good employees – employees with experience, and employees who will stay with you over the long haul, through thick and thin. A good benefits package is one way to attract them. If you offer a 401(k) plan, talk it up. With the Affordable Care Act, even businesses with fewer than 25 employees can get pretty good deals on employee health care insurance (which wasn't previously the case) – and it's a good way for you to get your own health insurance inexpensively too – and it's an excellent way to attract good employees. Discuss vacation benefits, family leave, and any other benefit that makes your company look really good.

- _Get a commitment._ It might be worded as: "If we were to extend you an employment offer that looked like this, would you be interested in joining us?" You might get an immediate verbal acceptance of your offer, or the candidate might ask to think it over. If you don't get an immediate acceptance, at least ask what the candidate thinks so far – and from that you should be able to gauge if it's being seriously considered. If there's any pushback, this is the time to ask "why" questions and attempt to allay any fears or concerns.

- *In salary negotiation, be fair to the candidate.* Never offer less than what the previous job paid (unless there are extenuating circumstances), and figure you'll have to top the previous salary by at least 10% (otherwise, why would the person jump ship?). And don't lowball on the salary – i.e., don't pick the employee up on the cheap just because you can. Once this is discovered, the new employee will resent it every time their paycheck is received.

- *Follow up immediately with an offer letter.* This can be either an e-mail or snail mail – and do this regardless of whether the candidate gave you a positive response to your verbal offer. This way, the candidate is given a second chance to review the offer, which increases the odds of acceptance (also starts to create the paper trail of their employment) – *and it forces the candidate to reach a decision.* Include all details about the job – job title, base salary, bonuses, benefits, vacation, holidays, perks, etc.

Negotiating salary. Establishing a salary structure or pay structure for new employees can be crucial, and you have to think it through very carefully ahead of time. Odds are, some of your first employees will be hired into positions that you have no experience with, and no information about. All of your past personal experience might be in very different disciplines, and with very different types of salary structures than you're familiar with (e.g., you've only been hourly and now you're hiring someone who will be salaried, or more difficult, on a commission basis).

Here are some things to consider:

- What is the typical salary range for the type of person you're hiring? With today's internet, with information on anything and everything, this sounds like an easy one to answer, but believe me, it isn't. A search might pull up many sites that sound exactly like what you want, but can easily lead you down a wrong path.

  For example, try www.salary.com. You want to find the typical salary for a software documentation specialist, so enter that in their search window and it brings up a dozen or so position types with that overall job category. Click on the one that's appropriate to see a nationwide median salary, plus a bell curve graph showing 10%, 25%, 75%, and 90% percentiles. You can also enter your address or ZIP code to narrow the salary range to your location, and you can get lots more detail with the Refine By buttons. So far, so good. Alas, after you enter in a few job descriptions as you play around, you find this site primarily wants money from you before they'll give you much data.

  So now try another one: www.payscale.com – and it too primarily wants to *sell* software that allows access to a veritable promised wealth of information in the cloud.

  Turns out, few sites are going to give you much information for free. Nevertheless, by hook or by crook, your task is to find this information.
  - Monster.com will help you with lots of job posting information, but not salary.
  - LinkedIn.com doesn't help.
  - Indeed.com has a Salaries link at the bottom of their home page that lets you search by job title and ZIP code, giving you a couple of graph types with a bit of salary information.
  - Simplyhired.com seems of no help.

- o Glassdoor.com has salary information by clicking on the Salaries tab above the job title that you fill in.
- o Idealist.com, a job posting site for nonprofit jobs, provides some salary information.

- One important thing to remember is, once you've set someone's salary level, you can't correct it later if you've made a mistake. Set it too high and they'll want similar pay increases to what everyone else is getting, even if they are at the top of the salary scale for what you feel the position is worth.

Set it too low (i.e., get an employee on the cheap), and you could later wish you hadn't.

My personal experience with this. Early in my professional career I left the U.S. Air Force after eight years, with some very good experience in my career field. On my résumé I listed my current military salary, and had no way of knowing what typical salaries were for equivalent civilian positions (this was 1974, long before the internet). I accepted a position at a very large Fortune 500 company, in a mainframe computer department with about 20 staff members, all doing the exact same job as me – and I had no way of knowing their salaries. Two years after joining, a co-worker set a sealed box on a filing cabinet in his cubicle, then spread the word that everyone was free to drop two pieces of paper into a slit in the top of the box – one containing their name and the other containing their salary. Virtually everyone in the group did, and a few days later the coworker distributed a paper containing an alphabetical list of names, and an ascending list of salaries (i.e., there was no correlation between names and salaries). To my astonishment, my salary was at the bottom of the list, and not by just a bit, but by a huge amount (*like 60% of the next higher salary*). The long-time manager who hired me had hired every other person in our group, so he knew full well that he'd lowballed me. I completely lost respect for that manager, and from that day forward about 50% of my efforts were directed towards getting out of that company, and within a year I founded my first small business. The year before that, I had been awarded the group's Employee of the Year. Never again would I put my heart and soul into that company.

- A corollary to that problem is – ever-widening salary ranges for same/similar job categories as new employees join. An example probably explains it best. You decide that your salary range for software developers is $50–65K. You hire your first developer at $55K, and both of you are happy. A year later you need a second developer – but the hotshot you really want for the important upcoming project is demanding $75K, because he claims it's just above what he's getting now. This is outside of your range, but you feel this guy has the exact skills you need, so you cave in. Even with a small annual raise after a year, your original developer is maybe up to $57–$60K. Both employees are happy – for now – but you're beginning to hear rumors through the grapevine that Employee #1 feels he's doing as good a job as Employee #2 and is getting shafted, leading you to believe there's been some salary discussion.

Don't think the word won't get around about salaries among your employees. It will, *and there's nothing you can do about it.* Lots of companies, big and small, in plain language and in obfuscated prose, try to bar employees from discussing salaries, even threatening termination. But in fact, any attempt to do so can run afoul of a federal labor law that's been on the books since 1935 prohibiting companies from banning workplace discussions of "things that matter to you at work", <u>including salary</u>.[215]

- Instead of raises, consider giving bonuses whenever possible. This allows you to keep actual salary amounts in line with your budget, and at your discretion you can reward the top performers (or the low-salary people) with whatever level of bonus you feel is appropriate. You can also be discriminatory with bonuses, awarding them for particular merit. But be careful, as bonus amounts will almost certainly be discussed and, again, you don't want unhappy people from casual talk at the water cooler.

Overtime and compensatory time off

We probably all know what overtime pay and compensatory time off is. What might not be known are the actual rules about each, the pros and cons, and what to look for from a legal standpoint.

First, staying on the right side of the law. In Chapter 9, we'll discuss the broader labor law issues embodied in a U.S. Department of Labor law called the Federal Labor Standards Act (FLSA). Here we'll just discuss the aspects that apply to overtime pay versus compensatory time off, whether FLSA overtime laws apply to your company, and if so, which of your employees are covered by them.

So, is your small business covered by the FLSA? Many laws governing business operations use minimum employee numbers to determine whether laws apply to small businesses (such as fewer than 15 employees and you're exempt). The FLSA has small business limits as well, but with a very different metric – it establishes the bar for applicability at "any business whose annual sales total more than $500,000", *or any business engaged in interstate commerce*. This would not only exempt a good many mom-and-pop shops in the country, but also many newly-created small businesses.

But whoa! Don't let your first glance convince you that your small business is off the hook. Even if your company is below the FLSA minimums, many state, county, and municipal governments have their own employee labor laws with lower employee count or annual sales metrics for exemption, pulling in a lot of small businesses that would otherwise be exempt. For example, some states set the gross receipts bar at $150,000 total annual sales. Others set it at 10 employees. The rules are all across the board.

More importantly, consider the second interstate commerce clause above. If you look it up, the standard accepted definition is something like, "interstate commerce means any work involving or related to the movement of persons or things (including intangibles, such as information) across state lines or from foreign countries". Fair enough, but, you say, this doesn't apply to my little stamp collecting business. Well, think again.

Over the years various courts have narrowed the interpretation of what constitutes interstate commerce, to the point that virtually all small businesses are scooped under coverage of FLSA

---

[215] Tom Driesbach, *'Pay Secrecy' Policies At Work: Often Illegal, And Misunderstood*, NPR online, April 13, 2014, http://www.npr.org/2014/04/13/301989789/pay-secrecy-policies-at-work-often-illegal-and-misunderstood. The law is the National Labor Relations Act of 1935.

rules, particularly on wages and how they are paid. But more than that, "courts have ruled that companies that regularly use the U.S. mail to send or receive letters to and from other states are engaged in interstate commerce ... even the fact that employees use company telephones or computers to place or accept interstate business calls or take orders has subjected an employer to the FLSA".[216] So your stamp collecting business buys and sells stamps, and you purchased one last week over the internet from another shop like yours in another state, and the week before that you sold a stamp to a shop in still another state. In all likelihood, you'd be considered to be involved in interstate commerce.

Nevertheless, some firms _are_ exempt (small farms, for example), but given how expensive it would be to fight your exemption status _after the fact_, you'd be well advised to research your situation earlier rather than later.

Exempt vs non-exempt employees. Another significant factor in who is covered by FLSA wage and overtime rules is an individual employee status known as "exempt" versus "non-exempt".[217] Every employee in your company is either exempt or non-exempt, and it's imperative you know and understand the rules about this.

As you might expect, _an exempt employee is one who isn't covered by FLSA_. Within a company a broad swath of employees may fall into the exempt bucket – including salaried employees if they meet certain kinds of work requirements, executives, professionals, highly-compensated employees (currently $23,660/year or $455/week, scheduled to go to $50,440/year, or $970/week on December 1, 2016, and automatically adjusting upward every three years after that – but this may be thrown out the window by the new federal Administration and Congress that's in power). Exempt also includes outside sales people, certain highly-skilled computer workers (software developers, systems analysts), independent contractors, and a slew of "miscellaneous" workers.

Therefore, _the rules of the FLSA apply to all non-exempt employees_ – in other words, the workers who are not exempt from FLSA rules.

Overtime. One of the principle results of the FLSA was the establishment of the 40-hour work week.[218] The FLSA accomplished this not by mandating a maximum of 40 hours in the work week, but rather, by simply requiring payment of 1½ times the worker's regular hourly wage for all hours worked over 40 within a consecutive 7-day period (and is commonly known "time-and-a-half"). As you'd expect, many states have their own rules about overtime, such as a California rule that requires overtime pay for all worked hours over 8 in a given day, regardless of total hours in the week. In other states, you might be entitled to overtime pay under federal FLSA law, but are considered exempt under state law, or vice-versa. The overtime premium pay applies to non-exempt workers, and not exempt workers, who are not entitled to coverage after working more than 40 hours (supposedly, it's factored into higher pay for exempt workers).

---

[216] Barbara Kate Repa, _Who is Covered by the Fair Labor Standards Act?_, Nolo.com, http://www.nolo.com/legal-encyclopedia/free-books/employee-rights-book/chapter2-2.html

[217] Barbara Kate Repa, ibid.

[218] Keep in mind that the FLSA, written and implemented in 1938 during the Roosevelt administration, was an outgrowth of industrial worker abuse resulting from the tight labor market following the Great Depression. Major corporations had few restrictions on how many hours they could force people to work, what they paid for that work, and there was no lower limit on worker age.

Where overtime goes wrong. Whether by accident or through unscrupulous means, not paying overtime when you're supposed to not only dumps you in hot water, but it could cost you far more than if you'd paid the overtime. The three most common violations of overtime rules – which can be caused intentionally, or by accidental or careless handling of the issue – are:

- short-changing an employee's hours worked
- short-changing an employee's hourly wage
- classifying non-exempt employees as exempt

Whether accidental or intentional, each of these adds up to wage theft – which is simply wrong and should never happen. Wage theft might seem like an overly harsh term, but when an employee is legally entitled to receive pay for a job worked, depriving the employee of any part of it can't be called anything but theft. (OK, OK, if it's the result of a truly accidental reason – and ignorance of the law isn't accidental – then some slack might be cut, but in that case, you have some making up to do.)

More often than not, violations are simply due to greed on the part of the business owner. Here's a challenge: do a search on "*mystate* overtime abuse violators", and you'll almost certainly find _well-known businesses in your area_ who have been found in violation of this. According to published reports,[219] the number of unpaid overtime claims is sharply on the rise across the nation, and speculation is that more and more employers are feeling they'll never be caught. But with all the talk these days about raising the minimum wage, and how difficult it is to make ends meet in today's economy, you can bet your workers will be all over the issue if you try to sneak through a violation.

Short-changing hours worked and pay amounts. A McDonalds franchisee in New York, Michigan, and California was named in a class action lawsuit because workers weren't credited time worked for "counting their register before and after work", and because timecards were altered. As a result, workers weren't paid overtime they were entitled to.[220]

In a particularly audacious case, the franchise owner of six Papa John's outlets in the New York City boroughs was not only ordered in 2015 to pay $510,000 in back pay and fines for "stolen wages" as the result of "rounding down to the nearest whole hour each employee's workweek", but also received 60 days of jail time.[221] In another incident, the well-known restaurant chain, Houlihan's, has a franchise group in New Jersey and New York that is being sued by the Department of Labor, alleging that worker's tips of at least $40K were pocketed, didn't pay workers for all the hours they worked, and overcharged workers for meals they ate on the job – among other allegations against FLSA rules.[222]

---

[219] Steven Greenhouse, *More Workers Are Claiming 'Wage Theft'*, The New York Times, August 31, 2014, http://www.nytimes.com/2014/09/01/business/more-workers-are-claiming-wage-theft.html?_r=0

[220] Dave Jamieson, *New York Settles With McDonald's Restaurants In Wage Theft Investigation*, Huffpost Business web site, March 17, 2014, http://www.huffingtonpost.com/2014/03/17/mcdonalds-wage-theft_n_4981336.html

[221] Kate Taylor, *Papa John's Franchisee to Pay Employees $460,000 for Wage Theft*, Entrepreneur online, July 16, 2015, http://www.entrepreneur.com/article/248495

[222] Mary Beth Quirk, *Restaurant Group Behind 17 N.J. Houlihan's Sued For Allegedly Pocketing Workers' Tips*, Not Paying Overtime, Consumerist online, October 2, 2015,

And the problem isn't just in the restaurant business. A couple working for a janitorial subcontractor that cleans Regal Cinemas at L.A. Live worked 11-hour night shifts, seven days a week for more than six years. Throughout that time they received regular $700 paychecks every two weeks – that's roughly 308 hours a month, at about $2.27/hour take-home pay.[223]

Working "off the clock". FLSA considers job-related work that an employee is asked to do "off the clock" to be "potentially compensable", such as "taking work home, job-related telephone calls at home or outside of work, working through lunch, working before or after a regular shift starts, taking care of work-related equipment and job-related volunteer work". The key factor in the term *potentially* is whether the employer required the work, and knew (or should have known) that the employee was doing it.[224]

For an example of working off the clock, consider this. In several class action lawsuits filed in various states, the highly-acclaimed clothing department store chain, Nordstrom, is alleged to have refused paying minimum wages to commissioned sales clerks unless they "exceeded minimum commission for the pay period". A decade earlier (1993), Nordstrom agreed to settle another lawsuit over unpaid overtime (for $20M in back wages), after years of requiring employees to work off the clock, such as writing personal thank-you notes to customers, delivering merchandise – all of this on their own time, at no pay. For the Washington State employees (where Nordstrom is headquartered), the company was also found to have been calculating overtime pay incorrectly – on the basis of base pay, rather than average pay.

Classifying non-exempt employees as exempt. While the classification rules are quite specific in many cases, they aren't in other situations – and as a result, you might be forgiven (sympathetically, but not legally) if you get this wrong. For example, you might have an IT person on your payroll who seems to fit right into the exempt rule – but a regulator's interpretation might be very different from yours.

Nevertheless, a lot of businesses intentionally misclassify workers specifically to get around overtime rules, but some also do so by significantly misinterpreting the employee/contractor rules from how the IRS views it. In California, FedEx Ground settled a long-running dispute over its classification of drivers as independent contractors. Through the classification, not only did this save a bundle of employee taxes for FedEx, but it also allowed them to "shift to its drivers the costs of FedEx branded trucks, FedEx branded uniforms, FedEx scanners, fuel, maintenance, insurance, and more. Drivers were not provided pay for missed meals, rest periods, or overtime compensation".[225] Note that last item – overtime compensation. FedEx subsequently lost a similar lawsuit (which went all the way to the Kansas Supreme Court, followed by an appeal that

---

http://consumerist.com/2015/10/02/restaurant-group-behind-17-n-j-houlihans-sued-for-allegedly-pocketing-workers-tips-failing-to-pay-overtime/

[223] Chris Kirkham, *Few wage theft victims ever get their back pay*, Los Angeles Times, September 4, 2015, http://www.latimes.com/business/la-fi-wage-theft-20150904-story.html

[224] *FLSA Overtime*, Chamberlain, Kaufman and Jones, http://www.flsa.com/overtime.html

[225] Robert W. Wood, *FedEx Settles Independent Contractor Mislabeling Case For $228 Million*, Forbes online, June 16, 2015, http://www.forbes.com/sites/robertwood/2015/06/16/fedex-settles-driver-mislabeling-case-for-228-million/#2715e4857a0b2a8a50ef5f5a

was heard by the U.S. Court of Appeal), again with a significant factor being nonpayment of overtime pay, where drivers were routinely required to work 10-hour shifts, but paid for eight.

Compensatory time off (a.k.a. comp time). For both the small business and employee, there may be situations where comp time seems like a better alternative to overtime pay. The company may be strapped for cash, but needs some extra manpower to get through a big project. The employee may need additional time off later, rather than a fatter paycheck now – and in fact, may even request comp time in lieu of overtime pay. Tough luck, though. The FLSA allows comp time for non-exempt employees *only when they work for "government agencies"* – including federal, state, county, or city. In other words, even if employer and employee both agree comp time is the way to go, the FLSA doesn't allow it for non-exempt workers.[226]

With that said, there is one exception to the "no comp time off" rule for non-exempt employees under FLSA control – and it has to do with the length of your standard pay period. Also, your state may have exceptions for non-exempt workers, allowing comp time off under certain narrowly-defined circumstances, which falls under the category of "other" compensatory time off – and your state may have rules that block these exceptions too. Here are the two circumstances:

- When an employee works more than 8 hours in a given day, but not over 40 in the overall work week – and assuming the state doesn't have a daily overtime rule (such as California) – the employer can negotiate comp time with the employee. The FLSA doesn't address this, so it's based on whether your state has a rule against it.

- Assume your standard pay period is every two weeks, and an employee works more than 40 hours in the first week of the pay period, comp time could be taken in the second week of the pay period to offset it. Big note of caution: When "other" comp time replaces overtime pay, it must be at the 1.5 times rate (i.e., time-and-half). For example, if an employee works 45 hours in the first week of an 80-hour pay period, 7.5 hours would be the computed comp time for the second week (5 times 1½), so the maximum hours the employee could work in the second week would be 32.5 in order to be within FLSA law – and of course, *the employee gets paid for the entire 80-hour work period*.[227]

Comp time is allowed for exempt workers, and since it's not an FLSA-regulated scheme, it's up to the employer to develop a comp time policy. Establishing a comp plan policy (or a paid overtime policy) for exempt employees is considered somewhat risky, though, as the legal

---

[226] In the past couple of years, a hotly-debated, highly partisan bill, titled the Working Families Flexibility Act, has been approved in the U.S. House of Representatives, but not passed in the Senate, loosening FLSA rules to allow comp time instead of overtime pay for non-exempt workers. One side considers it "worker-friendly legislation"; the other side argues it would be ripe for abuse, might not (in fact) be an option for employees, allowing employers to push workers to work overtime at no out-of-pocket cost to the employer. It's also argued that passage of the legislation would have a large effect on the 40-hour work week, the foundation of the FLSA. Source: Dave Jamieson, *Working Families Flexibility Act Passes House Over Opposition Of Democrats, Labor*, Huffpost Politics online, May 9, 2013, http://www.huffingtonpost.com/2013/05/08/working-families-flexibility-act-passes_n_3231385.html

[227] Jay Norman, *When can you give comp time instead of paying overtime?*, HR Insights, October 18, 2013, http://www.bizjournals.com/bizjournals/how-to/human-resources/2013/10/can-comp-time-off-be-provided-instead.html?page=all

beagles might consider an employee in this situation to be a misclassified non-exempt employee. It's advisable to talk this over with your business attorney or HR specialist for advice. Some considerations for this type of comp plan policy are:

- Will comp time be granted on a pro rata hourly basis (i.e., one hour of comp time for one extra hour of work), or on the standard 1½ times rate used in paid overtime with non-exempt employees?

- Is the company policy written as an *obligation* to grant comp time for extra hours worked (which might be one of the triggers for misclassification mentioned above)?

- Who will authorize comp time – the exempt employee's immediate supervisor?

- What procedures and documentation will be followed to ensure that comp time matches actual extra hours worked (and vice-versa)? (The reason for this, plus the next consideration, is that often exempt employees work extra hours, which the company (management) really appreciated at the time, but then the subsequent comp time is regretted (and resented) by the company (management) when it's time to take it. The chances of this happening are reduced if it's required for comp time to closely follow the extra hours.)

- How soon does comp time have to follow extra hours worked? What safeguards will be written into the policy so that claims of "undue disruption" to work production won't push earned comp time further into the future?

- Write up the comp time policy and put it into the employee handbook. To start, run a sample policy past your attorney or HR specialist, rather than writing one from scratch (and paying for writing the complete draft of it).[228]

Employment and intellectual property agreements

These two agreements (or rolled into one) might seem to be too highfalutin for your new small business. At first glance, you might figure you don't have any intellectual property to worry about, and your work agreement with your first employees isn't complicated enough to warrant an actual signed agreement, but in all likelihood, thinking like this could be a big mistake. If you're going to survive in the marketplace, you'll need product and service angles that differentiate you from the competition. You'll develop processes and techniques that create a leg up for your business.

In Chapter 12 we cover quite a bit of ground on a company's intellectual property rights, including an example about a secret sandwich sauce called Nunya Sauce, where "nunya" stands for "nunya bidness". The owners of that street food cart company obviously spent considerable time and resources developing this sauce that makes the food they sell very special. It stands to reason that it's important for their employees to keep the ingredients secret.

---

[228] *Compensatory Time Off Policy: Private-Sector, Exempt Employees*, July 9, 2014, https://www.shrm.org/resourcesandtools/tools-and-samples/policies/pages/cms_021284.aspx

You might not have a plan on Day One of your new business to create an equivalent to Nunya Sauce for whatever product or service you're creating, but down the road you almost certainly will. For that reason, it's imperative that, before you hire your first employee, spend a bit of time creating a template for the employment and intellectual property information agreement that you'll use, and make sure everyone signs one as part of their employment on day one.

Like a prenuptial agreement, asking for it afterwards usually doesn't work well. If a prospective employee wants to come to work for you, odds are they'll be agreeable to the sometimes touchy terms of an employment and intellectual property agreement – and that's when you have the leverage to insist on it – but after they've worked for you for some time, trying to ram through some of the necessary terms might not fly. The trick is to have a template agreement ahead of time – one that's been checked out by your legal counsel, who is most likely serving as your HR advisor at the start-up stage. (In my own company, and for reasons that are irrelevant to this discussion, I had about five software developers on staff before I implemented employment and intellectual property agreements. I managed to get them to sign the standard agreement, but it wasn't easy, and I'm sure in their minds it was a snake oil situation.)

Typically, employment agreements are not a one-size-fits-all situation, so you need to think ahead about the type/level of people you're going to hire early on, and whether you'll require an employment agreement with every one of them. It's not uncommon for small businesses to have employment and intellectual property agreements only for key employees, or employees who have special knowledge about the business and its products, where you would be harmed if this information was to be leaked or given to a competitor. Even so, if you have, let's say, an administrative person who is normally involved in routine day-to-day operations, but who fills in at a critical position (maybe when you go on vacation) and is then required to know some proprietary information, that person should sign an employment agreement that protects your intellectual property (IP, also known as trade secrets, or simply *company proprietary*). Another example is, the primary job of the front desk person might be to answer phones, but this same person is often tasked to work on customer mailings, and almost any company would consider their customer list to be company proprietary. And don't forget your very best friend that you hire today might decide in the future to leave, either to join a competitor or start his/her own company that competes with you, and if you've spelled out your rights from the outset in an employment or intellectual property agreement, you later have a legal leg to stand on if you need to restrict the damage that person can do to you.

Many new business owners fail to recognize the importance of the company's IP, and the damage it can do to the business if this information ends up in the hands of a competitor. And it doesn't have to be top secret patentable information to be harmful to you. It could just be a unique process that you use, or a small manufacturing technique that you've developed – anything that has given you an edge on the competition can be considered your company's proprietary information. You deserve to have it protected, and it's up to you whether to include IP clauses in your employment agreement, or if the wording of it is substantial enough to warrant a separate Intellectual Property Agreement.

Even the most junior employee on your staff, or the employee who seems to have the least access to proprietary information might actually have valuable proprietary information – and that's your customer information. A *non-solicitation covenant* in your employment agreement is the best way to ensure that an employee doesn't solicit customers or clients of your company after they terminate their employment with you. For some reason, a lot of departing employees feel this information is in the public domain, or they feel, "hey, I put in a lot of effort to get these customers for you, so I consider them to be mine too" – but then, they put in that effort while taking a salary from you, so the information about these customers belongs to you, not them. This clause alone might be a good argument for having an employment agreement with every employee you ever hire.

What does an employment agreement include? At the very least, it spells out the terms of employment, including date of hire, position hired for, wages and salary information (including bonuses and commissions), type of employment (full-time, part-time, casual), location of work, benefits (although this might instead be in your Policy Handbook, except for specifics such as vacation time). It might also include restrictions on outside employment, such as not working for a competitor while they're working for you, or not using your resources and proprietary information while working on outside jobs. As mentioned earlier, it could also include restrictions on use of proprietary and confidential information, and company intellectual property. It might also include termination conditions if applicable. (Make sure you read the earlier discussion on at-will employment status, as it could be affected by employment agreements that you have in place.)

Should you have a non-compete clause with key employees? A lot of fast-growing, highly-competitive, highly-technical business owners say the answer is yes. They feel that employees working for them are developing ideas on their nickel, and therefore the company not only owns those ideas, but the brains where those ideas are stored. There's another side of the coin, though. Granted, you don't want an employee charging off on their own, stealing proprietary information that they blatantly use to develop a competing product that embodies your proprietary information, or stealing your customer list and working them to move your business over to them. But that type of problem can be handled with a separate agreement – called a non-disclosure (a.k.a., NDA for short) – that doesn't try to keep a departing employee from competing in your same business space, provided they don't use your proprietary information.

An interesting case was made in a recent Inc. magazine article,[229] arguing that forcing strict non-compete agreements onto employees can actually stifle creativity and productivity, and results in employees in your company who aren't really the ones you want to have, whereas the ones who won't sign a non-compete agreement are the ones who might be better for you. There's also the problem of enforcement, and what the cost of that is.

For example, if your craft brewing business is taking off and you need a specialist to craft several new brews, this person's knowledge of exactly what goes into those brews will be crucial to you. But if you force that person to sign a non-compete agreement that stipulates he/she cannot work in the craft brewing business for one year after leaving your employ ... well, since that's the livelihood of someone with this specialty, it would make total sense that you might find it very difficult to get a top-of-the-line specialist to work for you.

---

[229] Jeff Haden, *The Case Against Non-Compete Agreements*, Inc. online, November 15, 2013, http://www.inc.com/jeff-haden/non-competes-could-cause-the-death-of-your-business.html

Where to find sample or template employment agreements? At company start-up time, you might feel this is an area where you just don't have any money to spend on outside counsel and advice to create this agreement – and that usually leads to an internet search for something that looks good to you. A quick search turns up several sites that will even assist you in development of a supposed custom agreement that is based on employment law in your state. While these sites might be a good place to start educating yourself on what an employment agreement looks like, keep in mind that the actions of just a single rogue employee – whose actions are not covered by an agreement that you cheaped out on – or some unintended consequences stemming from a misunderstanding that could have been spelled out in an agreement – the cost of this omission could be many, many times the cost of getting good legal and HR advice ahead of time.

Telecommuting and flextime

The debate on telecommuting has been going on for decades. Obviously, working from home is not appropriate for employees whose work requirements make it mandatory for them to be at a specific location (shop clerks, technicians, and consultants who work in the field, manufacturing workers, and the like). But telecommuting can be beneficial for many other types of jobs, including software and website developers, documentation specialists, call center, and technical support staff.

Telecommuting also comes in a variety of flavors, including a simple work-from-home arrangement for employees who otherwise live within commuting distance but who choose telecommuting. Another is *hire in place* employees who likely obtained their skills at another employer and who you elect to have work from their current location (maybe on the other side of the country), to save relocation expenses.

When I first looked into the concept of telecommuting for my own company, my concerns were:

- employees could more easily shirk work time and lower everyone's productivity, by mixing in personal tasks throughout the day when they should be working on company business
- employees are more difficult to manage and communicate with, due to lack of face-to-face interactions between manager and employee
- employees becoming less collaborative and innovative, due to less time *around the water cooler.*

Not only has my own experience now shown just the opposite, but published studies support the same findings.

Here are some pros related to telecommuting:

- *Cost savings on employee workspace.* While this is partially offset by the costs of setting up certain aspects of the employee's home office, it still should be a considerable net savings to the company. The savings can be huge if the entire company uses virtual workspace, as it can totally eliminate the need for the company to have a brick-and-mortar facility just for employees to work in.
- *Elimination of relocation costs at hiring.* I always called this *hiring in place*, as the cost of relocating new employees to my tiny company headquarters could easily cost $10,000–

$20,000 each (or more), and there was just no reason to pay that cost. In my case, for example, software developers can just as easily work from home as at an office desk, and for software sales and support people, it was even better to leave them physically located in the territory they would be selling into and supporting. This doesn't work for every company.

For example, the recent decision by CEO Marissa Mayer of Yahoo, who issued her "returning to the office" memo, with its no more telecommuting mandate. But elsewhere it's a growing trend.

And in late 2016, IBM's Software and Systems unit, as well as their marketing department, are forcing their staffs to come in from the cold (i.e., home) and work at "strategic" office locations scattered around the country – and they are pitching this as a "move to improve productivity, teamwork, and morale".[230]

- *Elimination of commute time.* If you're starting your company in Small Town, USA, far away from the crowded city hubs, this is not much of an argument. But if you're in any of the 146 worst cities in the world for commuting as reported from a study by TomTom,[231] this can be a big deal. Many employees will gladly swap most (maybe even more) of the commute time towards extra time working for you if they could eliminate the frustrating and worthless time spent in traffic jams, particularly if good rapid transit isn't available.

Good employees are often hard to find, and in a growing economy keeping them can be even harder – particularly if they face a grueling commute, or if they have family commitments difficult from working away from home.

For example, my company was located in the Seattle suburbs to the east of the city, and at one point we hired several software developers who worked for the IT division of a bank in downtown Seattle. They had bought or built homes in the suburbs south of Seattle, and because their jobs had been downtown, they had access to reasonable public transit into the city. To get to my company in the suburbs, though, commuting by private vehicle or public transit was very time-consuming. Telecommuting was the only possible way that we could hire these valuable employees.

- *Environmentally better.* Fewer cars on the highways reduce use of nonrenewable resources (gas and oil), cut down on greenhouse gas emissions, and reduce wear and tear on roads and highways.

- *Employee satisfaction, higher productivity, lowered attrition, and improved work/life balance.* It's not intuitive, but allowing employees to work from home some or all of the time actually empowers them and decreases stress, by giving workers increased control over their work/life balance. In U.S. News & World Report, a Stanford University study

---

[230] Shaun Nichols, *Big blues: IBM's remote-worker crackdown is company-wide, including its engineers*, The Register, February 9, 2017, https://www.theregister.co.uk/2017/02/09/ibm_workfromhome_cull_companywide/.

[231] *Measuring Congestion Worldwide*, TomTom Traffic Index, 2014 data, http://www.tomtom.com/en_gb/trafficindex/#/list

found that employees working from home are 13% more efficient than their office counterparts.[232]

- *Likely increased work time from employees.* According to this same U.S. News & World Report, "telecommuters log five to seven more hours per week than non-telecommuters, often working even when they're sick or on vacation".

Here are some cons related to telecommuting:

- *Increased effort to set up home office support systems.* If you've never had employees working at the company's facility, this item is irrelevant. But if you have other workers already working onsite, this cost could be significant. It'll require someone (either an administrative person or the employee himself/herself) who does all the legwork to establish and set up the *working-from-home-capability*, whether it's phone support, IT support, office supplies – and all of this effort will probably occur on your nickel.

  It also depends on whether you choose to have the telecommuting employee work with his/her existing personal systems – which I recommend you seriously analyze before allowing. If you do allow it, you run the risk of employees using software that could be injurious to your business, and you lose control over anti-virus/hacking protection on their system. You also create security risks for you and your customers (consider the many recent incidents of corporate hacking, where it's suspected the hackers wormed their way into large corporate IT centers via backdoor breaches from employee and vendor/employee platforms). A strong word of caution: your business is safer if a work-from-home employee is using home office equipment that you've purchased and installed, as it can then be configured to meet your security needs. If you go this route, make certain your employees adhere to it.

  Chances are, all of this will be a thorn in the side of the work-at-home employees if you take charge as suggested, as the things they like and feel comfortable with won't necessarily match your needs and requirements. For example, the employee might be a total Apple fan, but your entire company runs on Microsoft PC software – and to use everything in place within your company they'll have to use a PC at home. If they prefer an Android phone, but features on an iPhone are necessary for your business, well, you are the one paying for it, so you need to have the employee use what the company requires.

- *Cost and effort to supervise and communicate.* One way or another, you (and your management) have to directly supervise your employees – and that must also include your work-from-home employees. There's an expectation of meeting a *work product* commitment, and that should be defined for all employees. If employees are hanging too much around the proverbial water cooler at work, they can also be doing the same when working from home (or out doing personal errands and such without you knowing about it). You need to have controls in place that give you confidence you're getting a day's work for a day's pay.

---

[232] Michael Boyer O'Leary, *Telecommuting Can Boost Productivity and Job Performance*, U.S. News & World Report, March 15, 2013, http://www.usnews.com/opinion/articles/2013/03/15/telecommuting-can-bcost-productivity-and-job-performance

Just as importantly, you need to establish effective communication rules with your work-from-home employees, as there will almost certainly be requirements for you, other employees, or even customers to be able to reach these employees. If the phone rings off the hook every time anyone attempts to reach them, or if e-mails and messages go unanswered for hours at a time – well, you have a problem. In my own company, almost all of our software developers worked from home, and our lead software development manager established a requirement that if any developer was to be away from his/her desk for longer than 5 minutes, a group SMS message was required so that others would know you were not available (I thought this was draconian when I first heard of it, but the developers themselves insisted on it, because it was important for them too if coworkers were in good communication).

And just so this discussion is fair and balanced, also consider that supervising employees is a two-way street, and knowing what they're doing, how they're doing it, and how long it takes them to do it keeps you informed of employees doing an outstanding job, and maybe deserves a pat on the back, a bonus, a promotion, or whatever is appropriate.

- *Lack of camaraderie and company closeness with work-at-home employees.* This would be more of a problem for full-time work-at-home employees – and this was the exact reason given by Marissa Mayer when she ordered all of the work-at-home Yahoo.com employees to now work from corporate offices. Whether this solves a bigger problem than it causes is still a big debate, not only for the company but for the employees as well. In my own company, we found both sides of the situation to be problematic. Some employees opted to work from the office even though they were authorized to work from home; other employees definitely suffered from the isolation of working from home (we had one employee who, the longer he worked from home, the more he was considered an unbearable curmudgeon from many of the staff who had to deal with him). If this proves to be a problem, well, this is just another of the personnel challenges you'll have to fine-tune for your situation.

- *Extra state taxes to worry about.* It should be obvious to every company owner/founder that you'll face tax consequences from the state you're organized in and do business in. But what isn't well known is that companies also face state taxes from states "*they have contact in*" – and this principle is actually derived from wording in the U.S. Constitution.

  The operative words are "contact in" – and while historically most states haven't bothered about this too much, the new computerized world of cross-checking state IT databases allows states to "stretch the limits of traditional taxing principles in order to collect its share of tax revenue".[233]

  In basic terms, what this means is that if you have a work-at-home employee domiciled in a state where you also have customers that you are selling to, the state will very likely know about this from their database cross-checking and will come after you for taxes *on any revenue you derived from that state*. And the trouble is, you have no idea which states are

---

[233] Brendan T. Lund, *Tax Consequences of Telecommuting Employees*, Carr, McClellan website, May 5, 2014, http://www.carr-mcclellan.com/insights/tax-consequences-of-telecommunicating-employees/

aggressive about this, and which states can even figure out that your company has this liability.

So, let's be honest about this. Most companies will simply ignore this, assuming it's up to the individual states to figure out if you owe taxes to them. Your position is, I'm not going to pay any taxes I'm not forced to pay ... let them come after me. Well, when/if they do, it might be a bigger hit up the side of the head than you expected. First of all, you've likely already paid taxes on that revenue in your home state, so now if you pay it in the state demanding it, you'll have to file for a refund from your home state or you'll end up paying double taxes. If the overall amount is worth it to the state, they might send auditors to your doorstep, and get you for every penny of revenue you've earned within the existing statute of limitations. In the worst case, if you're in a due diligence process with an acquiring company (or someone who is getting ready to invest in your company and they want to see if you're *clean*), having a tax liability like this hanging over your head could be a serious red flag.

My advice is, factor this tax situation into your cost analysis when you're deciding to have work-at-home employees that are out-of-state, and in states where you're also doing business. My suggestion would be to do everything possible, including internet searches, for states that are known to be tax-hungry for businesses that have *contact* within their state. According to a 2014 survey by CFO magazine, the states that are most aggressive in this are California, New York, New Jersey, Michigan, and Massachusetts.[234] (And from my own experience, I would add Arizona to that list.)

- *Difficult/costly to include <u>distant</u> work-at-home employees in company-sponsored social activities.* Hosting your employees to periodic or holiday-related after-work socials can be great for team-building and corporate camaraderie. A summer picnic/BBQ works well, a Christmas party in a private dining room at a nice local restaurant is always fun. Anything that gets people out of the work environment for a bit of social contact, particularly among people who don't work together every day can be valuable. It's also a good way to let office-bound workers get to know the work-at-home employees from the area too. But if some of your employees live distant from your office environment, it's hard to include them. Then you have to resort to something that makes them feel a part of the corporate culture. This can be really difficult, and if you aren't careful it can backfire on you.

A real-world example might illustrate it best. We had employees in Australia, the U.K., the Netherlands, and scattered to the four corners of the U.S. and Canada – and our corporate headquarters were in the Seattle area. For the December holiday season one year, we decided to book a festive evening boat cruise around the local waters for our 25 or so local staff, with food and beverages aboard, giving everyone a chance to spend some quality time together. But what to do for the other 40+ employees who couldn't be with us? Our office manager was of British heritage, and a holiday gift basket for each of the distant staff was her idea. She searched out very nice holiday gift baskets, and arranged to have them sent to arrive on the same day as our cruise. To our surprise, word trickled back to us that many of

---

[234] Edward Teach, *Taxing Issues: Discretionary authority, economic nexus, and the taxing of services loom large in the state tax landscape*, CFO magazine, April 7, 2014, http://ww2.cfo.com/tax/2014/04/taxing-issues/

the distant employees were offended by this – not just unhappy, mind you, but actually offended – as they perceived the holiday baskets to be inferior to a *lavish* cruise (their words), even though the actual cost per/person of the gift basket was actually higher than we'd spent on the local employees. Flying everyone to Seattle, paying hotel costs, and losing productivity for the travel time would have been prohibitive, particularly since we had just hosted an all-hands product/sales meeting a couple of months earlier (and it was not a good business idea to schedule this around the holiday season). And even though the work-at-home staff were living a life they really enjoyed, they resented the out-of-office time we'd carved out for our HQ staff. Go figure.

- *Lowered opportunity for promotion and choice assignments.* According to the U.S. News & World Report article referenced earlier, researchers at Stanford University found that employees working from home, even though they are more productive, are also promoted less. In fact, after the Stanford study ended, half of the workers who worked from home returned to working at the office – and they were the ones who performed badly when working from home (couldn't manage their own time, needed more supervision, needed other employee communication and collaboration) – or they discovered there was less opportunity for advancement.

Flextime is a very different kettle of fish from telecommuting. For the most part, the term refers to offering a flexible work time arrangement for your employees, enabling them to choose their work hours, rather than strictly adhering to a 9-to-5 type of schedule. Your flextime plan could, though, include a combination of flextime and working from home, allowing employees to set their own schedule, as well as working part of some (or all) days at home. It could also include longer work days, providing a 4-day workweek, rather than five. One fairly common rule in many companies is that everyone must work a *core time*. Oftentimes, a company's flextime rules are not documented in a formal plan, potentially resulting in even more flexibility if managers want to bend the rules a bit.

While the statistics are rather old (2004), the U.S. Department of Labor, Bureau of Labor Statistics estimates that upwards of 30% of American employees work under some form of flextime rules.[235] These numbers were relatively unchanged from the last reported statistics in 1999, so it could very well be that this phenomenon has reached a plateau, or by now the numbers are even higher.

As with telecommuting, there are pros and cons, not only for you as the employer, but for the employee. The pros include:

- *Employees love it.* Flextime helps to create a better work/life balance, and improves company loyalty. A working couple with kids might have to drop the kids off at school, or pick them up from school, at hours that don't match the standard corporate 9-to-5 schedule. An employee might find that working in the office a half day from 9:30AM–3:30PM, then work at home between 8:00PM–10:00PM after the kids are put to bed is a perfect combination of flex time and telecommuting. As a result of this accommodation, you (as the employer) might find that employee retention and employee satisfaction yields superb

---

[235] *Workers on Flexible and Shift Schedules in 2004 Summary*, U.S. Department of Labor, Bureau of Labor Statistics, July 1, 2005, http://www.bls.gov/news.release/flex.nr0.htm

productivity results. Still other employees have personal metabolic and brain functioning systems that result in better work efforts (i.e., productivity) if they arrive late and leave late, or arrive early and leave early (just be cautious of the employee who wants to arrive late ... and leave early to make up for it).

- *The environment, community, and employee love the difference it makes in lowering traffic congestion.* Getting single driver commuters back and forth to work at non-rush hour can be a huge savings for everyone, not just the individual employee. The commute might be absolutely hellish at 8:45AM and 5:15PM, but a dream trip at 9:45AM and 6:15PM.

- *Productivity can actually increase.* Since employees are often motivated by factors other than money, it can be argued that increased employee satisfaction as a result of flextime is a leading cause of employee productivity increases.

- *Better business access to/by customers.* By proactively managing flextime schedules (i.e., jockeying employees towards flextime hours that can also benefit the company), you can increase business hours in situations where it's important to be open for business. This can be especially valuable for companies that operate across time zones, where it's important to be accessible by customers (or far away employees) for more hours than just a regular 9-to-5 in your local time zone.

The cons include:

- *Employees feel isolated.* The employee working the flex hours, plus other employees on the team, might feel that there's not enough face-to-face working relationship, resulting in a loss of camaraderie.

- *Communication challenges.* Scheduling meetings, presentations, and team events might be very difficult when schedules across several flextime employees don't align. One way to alleviate this to some degree is to have an agreement with each flextime employee who needs to attend a meeting or presentation during hours he/she won't be in the office that they attend by teleconference or web conference if possible – in other words, the employee needs to be as flexible as the company is.

- *Work habits might suffer.* Some employees won't work well with this type of arrangement, requiring a more structured schedule to keep them on task and to stay motivated. Temptations to pop down to the store three times a day, without making up for it with a longer work day could become the norm for someone who doesn't feel the office-instilled code of conduct for how to put in a day's work for a day's pay. This could be particularly troublesome for an employee who doesn't like what he/she is doing in the first place and, finding that someone isn't looking over their shoulder at work, could take advantage of it.

- *The company goals might suffer.* The company itself might not work well with this type of arrangement in some situations. It's counter-productive to have happier employees if the result is their team is sometimes understaffed, killing any productivity gains you might get from flextime. (Think about how you, as a customer, would feel when you call customer support and hear the almost-every-time message, "due to increased call volumes, your wait time might be longer than expected" – and then you find out this occurs every single day due to half the support staff not having shown up for work yet.)

- *Employees resent each other.* Friction can be generated by employees whose job functions won't permit flextime, resulting in a feeling that the flextime employees are getting better treatment. This can be a totally unintended consequence, even leading to some employees not supporting their coworkers to the extent they should, or in the worst instances, sabotaging other employee's work.

Before you rush into OK'ing flextime for your workers, you need to carefully think it through for each category and type of worker. If you don't, and you implement flextime willy-nilly, without the plan being fully understood by both management and employees, you'll end up accomplishing what the naysayers believe – a plan that doesn't work. For each employee on flextime, it's important that the employee and his/her manager agree on the tasks and job performance expected of the employee, including specifics about how information is to be channeled from the employee to manager, and vice versa. When a task is assigned, agreement by both must be understood (and importantly, documented) – including deadlines, deliverables, accountability, and communication. It should go without saying, but both manager and employee should document and clearly understand the rules of flextime – otherwise, assumptions can lead to unintended consequences.

The bottom line for both telecommuting and flextime is that it has to work for the company if it's going to work at all. As a last example, the hot place at the moment to work in America is Google – voted #1 of the Top Ten U.S. companies with at least 1,000 employees to work for by a CNN Money survey – and while they might have flextime and I'm sure many telecommute, one of the single biggest reasons for their lavish office perks is to keep people working at the office, and not at home.

Company-paid equipment and services

For lots of job positions, work life is just a matter of showing up for work, doing a job that's assigned, and that's that. If you're starting a landscape development company, most of your new hires might be laborers, or you might hire administrative staff who will be using office equipment you'd earlier used yourself.

But if the new hire is your first full-fledged sales person, someone who will actually be out knocking on potential customer doors each day, or someone who is on the road each day sourcing materials, or for that matter, someone who is working from home, you might very well need to furnish equipment and services for them to work with – and doing it with company-supplied equipment and support services can do wonders to make your company appear more professional and larger than it might actually be.

If you cheap out and let your employees use their personal cell phones, with ring tones that don't convey your company image, or they answer it like it's a personal phone, you can easily lose more business than it would cost to present the company image the way you want it. If employees are using their personal e-mail accounts on personal laptops/PCs/tablets/Blackberries, this also doesn't convey to your customers that you have an up-and-coming business, running the risk they'll take their business to a more professionally-run operation. Lastly, if you want your employees to feel good about the company they work for – and take pride in – treat them as if you really value them and give them the tools to do the job in the best way possible.

The downside of this is that it's going to take a level of support you don't currently have, or you can't afford. The opposite side of this argument is: you can't afford *not* to do this. By the time you have employees, you've reached the point where your company is hopefully here to stay, and how your company is perceived can make all the difference in the world in its success.

- **Corporate computers/tablets.** If you provide this level of equipment to an employee, you then have the right to insist on the type of computer, the operating system level that's maintained on it, the internet and network software it will run, what the desktop will look like (if that's important to your company image, for example, while doing customer demos), the type and profile settings for antivirus software to protect your company's data, the type of support software and e-mail system it will run, and anything else that will help standardize this all-important piece of equipment linking your employee(s) not only to you and others in the company, but to your customers and vendors.

  Cyberattacks aren't always pointed at the federal government or major corporations – but more commonly (and more easily) focus on small-medium businesses that don't put enough emphasis to stop the attacks. An online article in Entrepreneur online magazine outlined how a local gang of cyber thieves that recently targeted dozens of small businesses in the Seattle area with a theft that amounted to over $3M in total – and the havoc this wreaked undoubtedly cost the companies far more than that (and note the word *local* – this wasn't a gang of bandits in Russia or China, but was actually located in the same high-rise building as several of the victims).[236]

  A lot of break-ins are due to simple mistakes, such as easily-hacked passwords and unprotected Wi-Fi systems (read the article footnoted above, as it provides several top-notch ideas for better protecting your business' network. The article also stresses that physical break-ins by brazen thieves who scoop up every piece of hardware in sight, and are out the door with it in record time, can be just as damaging). Lastly, create backup processes, and do it in such a way that every computer in your company is fully backed up, with the backups stored where they too won't be compromised.

  If you don't have the in-house expertise to establish best practices for security and backup, spend some time to find a local consultant that you can hire – but make sure you can trust that person – and contract with them on an ongoing basis to set up your initial standards, and to review them periodically to ensure they are still up to date.

- **<u>Smart phones or Blackberry-type devices.</u>** The same advice for computers/tablets holds true for mobile communication devices – if you can afford it, purchase these for your employees who need them. This gives you the flexibility and control necessary to establish standards, not only on the hardware/software they use, but also on the usage by the employee. It doesn't give your company very much professionalism if a private mobile phone is being answered like a private phone, and with ring tones and off-the-wall voicemail greetings that don't reflect the image you want for your company. Most likely, if you supply the communications devices, they will essentially also become the private mobile devices for many employees, which is OK in most situations, provided the employee understands that business use takes priority.

---

[236] John Patrick Pullen, *How to Protect Your Small Business Against a Cyber Attack*, Entrepreneur online, February 27, 2013, http://www.entrepreneur.com/article/225468

Most importantly, you need a company policy in place from the outset on cell phone *usage* – and you need to make certain that everyone is on board with the policy.[237 and 238] Many of the policies you need to consider have nothing to do with who bought or who owns the cell phone – but rather, with general day-to-day cell phone usage and etiquette when employees are at work, at customer sites, or at vendor sites. Stupid-sounding ringtones that interrupt company meetings are one issue; being interrupted in general by cell phone calls, or employees who insist, "Oh, I have to take this call" during a meeting is another issue; loud conversations around the office on a cell phone (and who isn't annoyed by those?) are still another. Texting (particularly sexting) from/to employees is a serious issue, and you need to let everyone know, in no uncertain terms in your policy statements, that you won't tolerate it. Surprisingly, an employee talking about business on a cell phone while driving can make you liable in case of an accident (remember, when lawsuits are filed, everyone in sight is listed on the suit), so an important inclusion in your policy is to completely forbid the use of mobile devices in such situations (and not just talking, but texting, website browsing, and e-mail use).

The two single biggest reasons for owning the mobile devices your employees use are: (1) you have the right to tell the employee that there is no such thing as privacy with regard to information on the phone (including address book, messages, photos, etc.), and (2) you also own the phone number that's tied to the phone. With regard to this, it would be crazy for a terminated employee to be able to walk away with this information, *along with the phone number that customers/prospects/vendors are used to phoning to work with your business.* An employee can't walk away with your company's mailing address – why should they be able to walk away with your company phone numbers? A strong suggestion is to make certain this is understood at the outset when the employee is first given the device, and when it comes time for the exit interview, make certain the phone is handed over – and not wiped clean of any data/information that you own – as part of the termination process. Don't accept excuses about this, such as "geez, this has become my only phone number, and it's the only number that family/friends know to call me on". That may be true, but this is company equipment, company data, and it's important to you.

Once you create this policy, require everyone to sign it as part of their hiring process. That way, no one can later claim that you've implemented after-the-fact policies. Employees can win this claim in court, so don't be caught short with it.

Lastly, make sure someone in your company is keeping track of mobile device charges. If someone is running over their data plans (particularly if it's due to personal use), the extra data charges can become expensive in a hurry. (A lot of these considerations also apply to use of computers/tablets too, so make certain you take that into account when drafting your mobile device policy.)

E-mail accounts. If your company is interested in business professionalism from the outset, creating company-wide e-mail addresses through an e-mail hosting service that matches your

---

[237] J.J. McCorvey, *How To Create A Cell Phone Policy*, Inc. online, February 10, 2010, http://www.inc.com/guides/how-to-create-a-cell-phone-policy.html
[238] *Cell Phone Usage and Policy Guide* (pdf), www.legalzoom.com, http://www.legalzoom.com/download/pdf/cell-phone-usage-policy.pdf

internet domain name is something to seriously consider at the time you first open for business. If your company's domain name is www.turning-ip101.com (which means you own the domain name "turning-ip101", you really should set up e-mail hosting at the company that manages your domain name, so that every e-mail address within your company is *name@turning-ip101.com*. It's surprisingly *inexpensive* to set up, and the extra oomph it gives to your company's professionalism is well worth it. (When I meet someone for the first time, particularly in an out-of-office setting, and if they have an e-mail address such as *name@turning-ip101.com* – and therefore, not a gmail, yahoo, icloud, or such address, you can bet that I'll very soon access that URL – and the owner of that website will have another pair of eyes looking at what they do. Priceless.)

For reasons similar to mobile device usage, having a business e-mail policy is extremely important. Not only can e-mail misuse get you into huge discrimination and harassment problems, but it can also waste valuable company resources, and make your company look stupid and amateurish.[239]

E-mail is the single most common form of business communication, far outpacing snail-mail printed on a piece of corporate letterhead and mailed through USPS as was done 30 years ago. Unfortunately, a huge number of today's e-mail writers most likely grew up with texting, and when they find themselves having to actually *write* to co-workers, vendors, or customers with e-mail or a business letter, they have very little practice in proper writing. The result is that too many of today's people in business write with techniques and styles that worked well in their high school and college days of very casual communication, but these communications don't create high marks for them when they graduate to the working world. Worse, we're far enough into the age now that their managers aren't any better trained, so they see nothing wrong with it. *It's your business*, though, and your communication window creates a large part of how you look and how others respond.

- E-mail is not private, even if you expect or ask it to be. Once you hit the Send button and it's gone off to the ether, you have little control over where it goes next. If the recipient decides that something in its content should be read by someone else, forgetting (or not realizing) that something said elsewhere shouldn't be forwarded – maybe even in another e-mail far down the thread – it's now out in the open before you know it.

- E-mails get *lost* in the Send process, they get sent to the wrong person, and an unintended receiver who is not nicely talked about in the e-mail can be doubly problematic.

- E-mails might not be responded to as quickly as you'd like, and that can raise hackles when one recipient responds in five minutes and another takes two days. (I had a person in my company who felt that business e-mails – as well as business phone calls – were an intrusion on his work day, and he'd let e-mails go unanswered for a couple of days, and send phone calls into voicemail until he got darn good and ready to respond.)

- E-mails don't convey attitude, humor, and meaning nearly as well as face-to-face conversation, so don't substitute e-mail when a phone call might be better. On the other hand, verbal conversations don't document things being said as well as e-mail can, so it's a

---

[239] *Ten things to include in your corporate email policy*, OPSWAT (formerly red earth software), https://www.opswat.com/blog/10-things-include-your-employee-cyber-security-policy

balancing act on which to use (or consider using both, one to better get the point across, and the other to document what you've said).

- If there's the slightest reason that you shouldn't send an e-mail that you've agonized over, either don't send it at all, or wait 24 hours to see if you still feel the same way. I've used this technique for the past dozen years and it's worked pretty well, although all too often I still find myself feeling the same way the next day, sending off an e-mail that I shouldn't have – and most likely wouldn't have if I'd instead gotten a second opinion about whether to send it (which is an even better suggestion).

- E-mail is not considered by many to be a medium where grammar and good writing is necessary. What a mistake! Writing a sloppy e-mail to a coworker can create huge conflict – even more so than a sloppy verbal conversation, as clarification isn't nearly as easy. Writing a sloppy e-mail to a customer not only creates confusion, but it can mark your company as being full of dunderheads. I'm constantly amazed that e-mails aren't spell-checked before sending, and that so little attention is paid to clear and concise writing. Run-together sentences, incorrectly-used words, poor punctuation and grammar, and stream-of-consciousness sentences and paragraphs are endemic. It's even gotten to the point where the incredibly inane use of "like", or "you know", or "I mean" have now crept into business writing.

- E-mail Subjects (titles) are often ill-chosen or omitted, which makes it difficult to judge whether an e-mail should even be opened. On business correspondence, the subject should clearly and succinctly describe what the main, overall message of the e-mail is. For example, if I'm sending an e-mail to a group of employees and the purpose is to announce an all-hands-on-deck meeting, I should say that: "Meeting Notice August 14 – Product Review". It should not be something like, "Be in my office for product review", or worse, simply left blank because you forgot to include a subject. All too often, an e-mail's subject reads like the opening sentence of the e-mail.

- Reply All is used far too often, and with e-mail threads that go on and on, oftentimes with mundane, unnecessary, and off-topic responses. E-mail can clutter up people's work lives to the point where e-mail becomes a turnoff. Caution your employees to only reply to recipients that an e-mail applies to, and clearly point out that automatic use of Reply All can be a huge waste of company time.

Company uniforms and corporate apparel. This might seem like a totally irrelevant topic, but in fact it's quite a common consideration. The term doesn't necessarily apply just to formal apparel that everyone must wear to work every day, but also to logo shirts and pants that employees wear at tradeshows or other corporate events. Corporate apparel could be logo T-shirts or shirts that you'd like your field representatives to wear when visiting customers.

It's a great idea, again giving your company an image of professionalism, and letting current and potential customers know that your business is here to stay. Apparel needn't be costly (but can be if you want to go top drawer), and it's usually fairly inexpensive to create the initial logo setup.

The next time you're out for the evening – at a baseball, football, or soccer game, or at a neighborhood restaurant or bar, note how many people are wearing their company's logo clothing in social settings – and for the most part, they aren't wearing it because they've been told to.

If you have a really good logo design (and you should, as it can make your brand more recognizable than even your company name), plus a good tag line that goes with it, you have a recipe for good logo clothing.

To work best for a small business, bring your employees in on the design, including colors, clothing styles, fabric, and anything else that needs to be decided. If they have buy-in to the process, they are much more likely to wear it.

During some construction at my private residence recently, I was surprised at the number of tradespeople who are now wearing casual company-logo shirts at the job site – the general contractor's foreman, heating and electrical technicians, painting crews, and even landscape contractors. Frankly, I was impressed with those companies.

Whatever the cost, the purchase will almost certainly be on your nickel, and you'll have to plan ahead to establish how much to purchase for each employee, based on their frequency of wear (for example, if most of your tradeshows are three days in length, you might need to plan on three shirts for each employee who attends), and you might also need to pay laundry costs for events in a hotel. If you expect your employees to pay for their own work clothes, this needs to be clearly spelled out in the employment interview, and you should expect some pushback.

Employee layoffs

An employee layoff is often misstated as a firing, so it's going to be discussed first, and firing second. The difference (at least in this book anyway) is that a layoff *is not* because the employee has necessarily done anything wrong, but rather, it's an involuntary termination as a result of a downsizing or retrenching of your business. A firing is typically for some kind of reason (performance, for instance), or it might actually be a *for cause* situation (to be explained in the next section). A layoff is also known as a *reduction in force*, or RIF.

A layoff is typically for one of (at least) three reasons:

- Business losses, when you can no longer afford to keep one or more employees on the payroll without jeopardizing the viability of the business. This is a situation where there's no alternative. A strong suggestion is to recognize the situation sooner rather than later, and cut to the bone if you need the cutbacks to survive.
- Shutting down a department or division within your business, as a result of unprofitability in that area. Keep this in mind – you're in business to make a profit, and that includes not only paying wages and salary to your employees, but to yourself as well – plus keeping your overall company viable. If you have a department or division that just isn't cutting it and you need to jettison it, do so when you know it isn't going to get any better, or it's causing a drain on your other profitability.
- Pruning excess employees as a result of bloating in the hiring process over time. This is a valid reason for layoffs, as you might have estimated certain growth in an area that just didn't pan out, or it could be due to unexpected (or even expected) economies or production improvements. It could have been a situation, in hindsight, where hiring temporary employees might have been a better idea to get you through a short-term production push.

Here's a dubious twist – from an Entrepreneur.com writer who actually touts periodic layoffs as a really good business strategy, cutting (let's say) 10% of the inherent deadwood employees as a way of doing regular, healthy pruning. While the idea might have some merit from a strictly cost-cutting perspective, it certainly isn't going to do employee morale any good. As the author bio at the end of the article states, *"he is now traveling the world seeking new methods of making employees' lives miserable".*[240] You'd do well to stay away from this type of advice (and not hire this person as a consultant).

Whatever the reason, layoffs will be a painful experience, fraught with potential problems, and might have huge morale effects for your company, not only with employees but with customers too. Employees who aren't laid off will be wondering when the next shoe will drop. Customers who hear about it will wonder if your company (and therefore your products and services) are on the way out. So, if it's necessary, you need to do it right. In a small business, both you and the employees probably know each other quite well, things might be like a big family, and each employee you lose might be gut-wrenching.

Here are some considerations:

- Determine if there are alternatives to layoffs.
  - Create inexpensive employee incentives (such as saving their jobs) for implementing cost-saving measures. Oftentimes, employees who know the company is on the ropes – or better, who know their jobs are on the ropes – will come up with some pretty amazing alternatives that can save some or all of the jobs.
  - Cut out the extras and non-essentials. Implement a hiring freeze, stop overtime work, slash bonuses and raises, eliminate unnecessary travel expenses, and cut or eliminate perks. Delay equipment upgrades.
  - If you have any outsourcing costs, consider moving some or all of it back onsite, having existing in-house staff do the work, saving direct out-of-pocket costs.
  - Look at converting some of your staff to a virtual office, allowing you to either reduce or sublet part of your brick-and-mortar space.
  - Cut part-time staff and contractors. You face far fewer legal problems shedding these categories rather than full-time staff, so make the cuts here first.
  - Implement job-sharing. Employees have been known to take a 50% cut if they can job-share, where two employees each work 50% of the time and reduce their individual salaries by half.
  - Consider cutting some of the workweek in non-critical areas (where layoffs would happen anyway) – from five days to four days a week, with a corresponding cut in pay – and that's a 20% savings. Or you could cut hours from eight to seven, with a corresponding reduction in total pay – a 12% savings.
  - Offer longer time off – for example, a three-, four-, or five-week vacation where two weeks are paid. For some, that could even be considered a perk (you never know until

---

[240] Dale M. Galvin, *How To Lay Off Employees*, Entrepreneur.com, October 1, 2001, http://www.entrepreneur.com/article/45392

you ask). You could even offer longer-term unpaid sabbaticals (perhaps as long as a year) – but with a job guarantee when they return (assuming you're still in business).

o   Cut pay and benefits. Before proposing this, look to the top of this list for cuts that will go over much better with the rank and file.

- Before finalizing the layoff list, look around the rest of the company and determine if there are any low-performers who might be better candidates – and particularly if anyone on the targeted list could be a replacement for that position.

- Once the alternatives are exhausted and the decision is made, do it quick and clean. And if possible, lump all of your planned layoffs into one. The sage advice is that it's less demoralizing to the employees to have one big layoff, rather than a layoff in dribs and drabs. If you don't have one big layoff, and particularly if word leaks out (or suspicion builds) that further layoffs are in the pipeline, significant morale issues can arise. It could even result in losing employees that you really want to keep, but lose through fear. If your instinct, though, is to make a smallish cut and then hope to see if it proves to be enough, it really helps to level with the remaining employees at the time of the first layoff, telling them that other cuts might be necessary if the financial situation isn't sufficiently improved by the initial cuts.

- Make sure you follow legal requirements, particularly with regard to discrimination. If you're a very tiny company (less than 15, let's say) you probably don't have any labor laws that concern you, but definitely check with your state's labor website for guidelines. Nevertheless, you still can't discriminate. All it takes is for a couple of laid-off (and disgruntled) employees to file a discrimination claim, and you not only have a financial headache to worry about, but one that can really divert your attentions.

Once you develop your basic plan for how much – and where – the layoffs need to be, and you've identified the likely layoff candidates, write down your plan, the employee's information (age, gender, race, disability, etc.) and then set up a meeting with your outside HR consultant and legal counsel to discuss it. The money spent here will be well worth it.

Check to ensure that you're following the requirements of the Worker Adjustment and Retraining Notification Act (a mouthful just to create the acronym, WARN – a federal law) that requires employers with over 100 employees to give at least 60 days' notice before a mass layoff. Many states have their own version of WARN, and you should know what these are for the state where your business is located, as well as any state where you have an employee

- Common sense says to pick your timing right ... and your message.

Unless business financial requirements give you no option, don't do it on a Friday, or just before a holiday ... particularly a holiday such as Christmas. Don't do it on a Monday morning, particularly after the employee has just weathered a horrible commute to get to work.

The best advice is to schedule layoffs on a Tuesday. It's more compassionate for the employee, giving them the remainder of the week to get some job hunting started. But more importantly (for you), it gives you the rest of the week to better manage the emotions and communications of your remaining employees. On a Friday, they're likely to be talking about it all weekend, Tweeting and posting Facebook comments – and by Monday morning they return angry, and this isn't good.

Your message really should be delivered personally, by the direct manager or supervisor of every employee being laid off. Forget the stupid hire-a-hack character played by George Clooney in *Up In The Air* – that was a totally fictional job description to make the moviegoer understand the type of person who would have such a pathetic personal life. Also forget the movie and newsreel caricature of workers being handed a pink slip as they walked through the factory gates. In today's world the act of laying someone off needs to be done in person, with compassion, and with decency – that is, if you have any business sense about you. Consider that this laid-off employee will almost certainly be focusing on your direct competitors for their next job – and would you rather have an employee who just can't wait to unload all of their pent-up baggage about how rotten your company is, or would you prefer to have this ex-employee feeling like you still have a great company, but financially things didn't work out?

So, exactly what does a layoff really mean – is it a permanent termination, or should it be an expectation that the employee may be *recalled* to work? Well, it's a terminology thing ... and the recall aspect is really associated with a furlough, while a layoff is almost always permanent. With a furlough, employees are typically told that the non-working time period will be such-and-such days, weeks, or months, and during that time they won't be paid. With a layoff, benefits are also stopped, such as medical insurance.

Terminating and Firing employees

As soon as you hire your first employee, you need to begin thinking about what's involved in terminating employees. Not because you'll be hiring and firing in quick succession, but in reality, some employees simply won't work out as expected when you hired them, perhaps lacking the skill set or work habits and ethics you were expecting. Another example is a Jekyll and Hyde type, who interviews very well, then turns into a completely different person after starting work. Perhaps a new hire unexpectedly turns on other employees, creates harassment or discriminatory situations, or offends customers. Maybe the employee steals company-proprietary information or products, embezzles company money, or steals from your customers. While these will be rare, you have to be prepared for them, and when it comes time to terminate an employee you need to know how to do it properly and legally, and to ensure the least amount of future problems as a result. Just as important, employees who terminate voluntarily will require an exit process at some level, depending on the role they played in your company.

The first time you have to fire a new start-up employee is the hardest – even if you've done it a few times in a previous employment. Early employees in a start-up become almost like family, and because you've probably interviewed and hired them personally, you have a lot of vested interest in them. The same will likely be true in reverse, which could make their reaction doubly difficult for the task you face. In any case, it won't be an easy task for anyone – most of all for the employee being terminated, but also for you (or the manager doing it), and for the angst and morale challenges of coworkers.

Here are some tips and information that can help the process, and hopefully lower your risk of a wrongful dismissal lawsuit.

- Involuntary firings usually fall into two categories:
  - o Performance and related problems – such as unsatisfactory performance, insubordination, missing work or showing up late (or at the wrong place), safety violations that might injure the employee or coworkers, poor attitude, creating co-worker problems. For this type of problem, there is oftentimes a long lead-up to the termination, following a course of warnings on deficiencies and an opportunity to improve.
  - o *For cause* reasons – such as theft or embezzlement, product sabotage, fraud and dishonesty, disclosure of company trade secrets or proprietary information, unethical behavior, illegal conduct, violence against others, harassment, bringing weapons to work, violation of work rules, extreme insubordination, records falsification, drug and alcohol use (on or off the job), failing a drug abuse test – even watching pornography while on duty. Some companies also include willful misconduct that is damaging to the company, its reputation, products, services, or customers. These offenses are serious enough that a termination without warning (and on a first offense) is warranted. This list is not exhaustive, and unless you want to limit yourself to a specific list, an attorney might advise additional causes that are possible. Generally speaking, an employee fired for cause will not be eligible for unemployment compensation – but again, you should check with your HR attorney or the Department of Labor in your state.

- **Document and discuss performance or employee conduct (or misconduct) problems.** If the problems are performance-related, create a process to document the problems and to give guidance for how to improve. Identify whether problems are due to sloppy work standards, failure to meet deadlines, or inappropriate customer communications or dealings.

  If the problems are employee conduct (or misconduct) or behavior (such as inappropriate customer communications or actions, or dealings with coworkers), establish the boundaries that are acceptable.

  Unless you're an employer who happens to think that regular employee performance reviews are the greatest thing since sliced bread, you probably don't do them in your company – which makes it imperative that you (and your managers) buckle down and have appropriate talks with employees who aren't performing to company standards. It's also important that you document each of these talks, clearing laying out your expectations, identifying what needs to change going forward, and mentioning that failure to meet these expectations will have consequences. An extemporaneous signed and dated copy of the notes from each talk should be kept in the employee's personnel file in the event a future termination is warranted.

  Before reaching a firing decision, make a clear evaluation of whether the employee's performance or transgressions have reached the level of firing – as opposed to moving the employee to another position, demoting the employee, or providing additional training and/or on-the-job support. It could very well be that the employee is still right for your company, but is in the wrong position – and if that's the case you can avoid a termination.

- *For cause* **terminations.** The term *for cause* is widely used, but often not defined – at least, not clearly and thoroughly, and not in the important places (i.e., employment contracts). It can also be a very hazy concept. Some define it simply as "sufficient reason to justify job termination". Others define it as termination of an employee, "at any time, without notice, and for any cause, good or bad, or for no cause at all". Others simply figure they know it when they see it. Gee, that's helpful, isn't it?

  Most often, *for cause* terminations are for the more egregious violations, but they can also be for performance and behavior problems (when defined). Where they most often cause termination problems – or more specifically, financial problems for the employer following a *for cause* termination – is with employment agreements where the company's definition of *for cause* hasn't been clearly defined, or is too narrowly defined.

  An example of a *for cause* problem might be a company that lists conviction or a guilty plea for a crime of moral turpitude as a *for cause* reason for termination – which then leaves the company in a real lurch if the employee is arrested for such a crime (but conviction requires a long time), or is acquitted for lack of evidence, but everyone still suspects the person did it. The company's own definition of *for cause* stops them from firing the person, but if they try to fire the employee, the employee may sue – but who knows who will win; a dizzying amount of effort and turmoil to sort out may be required, and all the while the company is mired in the turmoil.

  In many senior executive employment agreements, involuntary termination – with or without cause – before the end of the agreement term typically provides for lucrative severance packages – for instance, when a company's owners or Board of Directors wish to get rid of an executive just because they don't like the job he/she is doing, but don't have real cause to do it. The severance package in that instance might consist of a gazillion stock options, or a year's salary (or more), or an earned but unpaid bonus. It should be pointed out here that contract wording of this type also removes the *at-will* nature of the employee's firing status, as it essentially ties the company's hands in termination only at the end of the contract period, or if they pay out the huge severance earlier. (And this isn't only done in big companies – if a small business is growing and needs the expertise of some savvy hotshot, this could be a show-stopper for a candidate if you don't agree to include it.)

  A real-world example might illustrate it better.[241] In early 2012, Yahoo hired a new CEO, Scott Thompson. Within a few months of his hiring, an activist Yahoo investor (Dan Loeb) published a letter noting that a Yahoo filing to the SEC (a legal document) stated that Thompson "holds a Bachelor's degree in accounting and computer science from Stonehill College", and the letter questioned whether this was an embellishment. When asked about it, Stonehill College responded that only a degree in accounting was granted (and

---

[241] There are dozens of references for this. To delve more thoroughly into it, simply search on "Yahoo Thompson for cause", or look through the references at the end of the Wikipedia article titled *Scott Thompson (businessman)*, at https://en.wikipedia.org/wiki/Scott_Thompson_%28businessman%29. Another thorough article is by James B. Stewart, *In the Undoing of a C.E.O, a Puzzle*, New York Times – Business Day, May 18, 2012, http://www.nytimes.com/2012/05/19/business/the-undoing-of-scott-thompson-at-yahoo-common-sense.html

supposedly, the college didn't even have a computer science degree program at the time). Press reports then stated that Yahoo was planning to fire Thompson "for cause" as a result of this apparent lying (embellishment, or whatever you want to call it) – which, if they had gone through with it could have seriously put the brakes on Thompson's career future. Many behind-the-scenes twisty turns followed over the ensuing week, and on May 15, 2012, CNN Money announced that "Scott Thompson 'resigned' from his post as Yahoo's CEO in the wake of his résumé-embellishing scandal, and he'll receive no severance". Nevertheless, after a mere five months on the job, Thompson walked away with the $7 million in cash and stock that he received at his time of hiring. As part of termination negotiations, though, he forfeited "all outstanding but not fully vested stock, plus "other plans and arrangements". It's not been released exactly how much this fiasco cost Yahoo, or how much Thompson gained from his short employment.[242]

So, if your company plans to have wording about *for cause* termination in its employee handbook, or stated in employment agreements, a lot of thought and research should go into it. Otherwise, you are leaving yourself open to potential problems later on.

- **Make sure you're on the right side of the law.** First and foremost, you want to avoid future legal problems as a result of a termination, particularly a wrongful termination lawsuit. Leading up to the termination, get HR and legal advice about what you're planning, and determine that what you are contemplating is legal and that you are using good judgment. Here are some thoughts:

  o Make certain you have the facts. Unless you've caught the person red-handed with indisputable evidence, it's always possible that another employee is actually the wrongdoer, shoving blame onto a coworker to hide their own blame. The facts might not stand up after an investigation is done. Any of these will likely cause you more harm than good if you rush to judgment.

    (By the way, the problems noted here also apply to an employee accused of performance and behavior problems, as it's not uncommon for an employee (or group of employees) to cause problems concerning a coworker, particularly when existing performance ranking systems might affect salary advances or promotions.)

  o For performance or behavior problems, be sure you've established the basis for this. The types of behavior in this category have all been upheld in court cases over the years. If you've documented the specifics of how, when, where, and why the employee has failed, assuming you've followed the guidelines of warning/opportunities leading up to the firing, you shouldn't have a problem.

  o When evaluating the employee's poor performance or behavior problems, look for potential extenuating circumstances – such as an abusive manager, or unfair treatment by a manager or coworkers. Ensure the problem isn't the result of sexual harassment, racial harassment, religious harassment, or illegal retaliation for exercising legal rights in the workplace.

---

[242] Julianne Pepitone, *Ousted Yahoo CEO will get no severance*, CNN Money, May 15, 2012, http://money.cnn.com/2012/05/14/technology/yahoo-ceo-no-severance/

o   Establish whether your performance and behavior criteria are consistently applied across all employees. Even if you have an employee handbook statement that your policies and actions will be uniformly and consistently applied, the reality is that executives and managers make exceptions to the rules all the time, trying to do good deeds, typically out of concern for the employee, or concern for the company. Sometimes, it's felt that a benefit can be gained for your company by breaking the rules in favor of a wrongdoer – for example, a person is critical to a project that has a tight deadline, or the person's knowledge is critical to a direction the company is heading. Any time this happens, if a terminated employee is treated differently and you haven't made the same (or similar) accommodations for other employees, they may have a legal leg to stand on if they file a wrongful dismissal lawsuit.[243]

o   If your company has 15 or more employees, several factors cannot be any part of your firing decision, including age (if the person is at least 40), pregnancy (or a medical condition related to pregnancy or childbirth), gender, genetic information, sexual orientation, religion, whistle-blowing, taking time off for a medical or military leave, or garnishment of wages by a creditor. State discrimination laws often vary from the federal ADA, and it's important that you research laws in the state where your company is located or where the employee resides.[244]

o   If the employee has an employment contract, you'll want advice on how/whether you can terminate without tripping a costly clause in the agreement (or whether it's better to take the financial hit). If the employment contract has a length term that hasn't yet expired, you may be faced with a legal challenge for an expensive severance package, which will be costly to defend, or you'll likely have to resort to arbitration that might only result in a minor reduction in severance. (Once you've faced this issue the first time, you'll have a completely different perspective on employment agreements.)

o   Discuss exactly how to conduct the actual firing – how to keep an emotional lid on it, how to defuse it if that should be necessary, what to say and not say.

o   Discuss what should be done in the exit interview, including any release forms that you'll expect to be signed in meeting the conditions of the termination. The attorney should advise you on some do's and don'ts with regard to company equipment (home office computers and peripherals, communications devices, software, and such).

o   The HR person should be able to tell you what's required with respect to COBRA health insurance as a bridge for the employee before they find a new job. Also find out

---

[243] *Supreme Court Reaches Decision in Raytheon Co. v. Hernandez ADA Case*, Southeast ADA Center, December 5, 2003, http://www.adasoutheast.org/news/articles.php?id=4100. This article describes an interesting legal case that went all the way to the Supreme Court, with the plaintiff (Hernandez) claiming that Raytheon had not acted consistently in applying their re-hire policy. As it turns out, the Supreme Court ruled in favor of Raytheon, but it illustrates how dangerous it can be if a company doesn't maintain consistency in HR policies.

[244] For example, in Washington State, the Washington Law Against Discrimination (WLAD) applies to companies that have eight or more employees. Source: Disability Rights Washington, http://www.hum.wa.gov/employment.

how to handle any of your benefits packages, particularly the employee's 401(k) account, and their accrued vacation and sick leave.

o   If there's any possibility the employee will owe money to the company (previously overpaid, paid in advance, paying back for damaged company equipment, or failure to return company equipment upon termination), the inevitable question will come up – can you withhold money from the employee's final paycheck? The most likely answer is that you can't, but in some situations the answer is yes, and they are very dependent on state law. Laws vary from state to state, so make sure you find out exactly what your state allows (or doesn't allow) from your HR person or legal counsel.

- **Decision time.** Before delving into the details of this, let's get one big don't in the open – *do not fire an employee on the spot* … unless, that is, the actions are so egregious that your best course of action is immediate removal of the employee from the workplace.

  When you've reached the decision that termination is inevitable, start the process, but don't rush into it before you know exactly how you'll carry it out, where you'll do it, what you'll say, and who you'll have as a third party in the termination meeting. Accept that the employee might not take it well, there might be argumentative words from the employee, it will likely be emotional – and you need to be ready for it, with words already thought out.

  As an alternative to firing, you might want to discuss with the employee the option of voluntarily resigning in lieu of a firing. This option is often easier and smoother for all parties – it saves you (or your manager) the task of firing, it allows the employee to save face and not have a firing for cause in their employment record, and it very likely reduces the morale hit to co-workers and other employees. If this is the route taken, be careful of how you do it – and again, consult your attorney before going through with it. Later, the employee could regret the decision and want to sue you for *forcing the situation* or some other claim. For this reason, you should get a signed release statement from the employee before the termination stating a waiver of future legal action. Don't forget, if you are ever asked for an employment reference and you say, "I'd never hire this person again", it could trigger this regret, so it should be one of your considerations. If you say this – and don't have a release statement from the employee, they might claim defamation of character.

  But assuming you're going ahead with the termination, determine if the employee will be expected to remain for a severance or turnover period (probably better not to, unless it's a mutual parting of the ways), and assuming not, be ready for the employee to walk out the door for the last time at the end of the exit interview. Have a final paycheck already made out, including a possible severance package that you decide on (and assuming it's agreed to). Also, have all of the release forms that need to be signed (*including acknowledgement of any Non-Disclosure Agreement*, and if appropriate, the terms under which the employee accepts the severance package (abiding by the NDA, no malicious swipes at your company – either verbally, in writing, or on social media).

- **Secure your company and employees.** No matter how much the employee might be directly responsible for losing his/her job, and no matter how much you and the employee might be like family you will almost certainly now be the enemy, and neither you nor the company will be high on the favorites list. It's imperative that you do everything you can to keep the termination meeting on an even keel, but you never know how the employee is going to react. Here are some things to protect against:

o   From the moment the termination decision is made, nothing should be said to anyone in the company who doesn't have an absolute need to know. At least one person among the bookkeeping staff will have to know, as a final paycheck needs to be cut, termination paperwork has to be created, and final employee benefits have to be established.

o   If your company has a computer system and the employee being terminated has access to it, consider whether access to it should be shut off *at the beginning of the termination meeting* – and that way, the employee cannot return to his/her desk immediately after the termination to delete or trash anything. If you go this route, someone on your IT staff will need to be in the know of the upcoming termination. It might also be critical to secure the e-mail account *at the same time*, removing the employee's access to ensure that (a) company data isn't sent out, and (b) e-mails aren't wiped clean. This last, though, raises the question of whether you should allow the employee to send a final e-mail goodbye to friends and co-workers. If you do, be very careful, as it can lead to more being said than necessary or appropriate. A suggestion might be to have someone sitting with the employee during the writing and sending to ensure this doesn't happen – and make it clear that this is simply following protocol.

o   Expect there might be problems after a firing. If there's any indication that things might turn nasty after a firing (and even if there isn't), research and think through ways to keep everyone safe and secure. A firing can be one of the worst-ever experiences for an employee, and it's hard to know how they will react. It's always better to be safe than sorry.

o   After the employee has departed for the last time, make a *low-key* company announcement that so-and-so is no longer with the company, and therefore should no longer have access to the company, the company's products, and the company's data. It doesn't need to be to the entire company, but instead, may be to a select group. Some of the terminated employee's best friends might also be current employees, so it will be a good idea to keep your ears and eyes to the ground in case of negative reactions to the termination.

- **Doing the termination.**[245] Here are some do's and don'ts:

o   Firing someone is emotional, both for the manager as well as the employee. It's imperative that it be done face-to-face, and by the direct manager or supervisor of the employee.

o   Respect the privacy and confidentiality of the employee, by doing it in a private place.

---

[245] *Issues To Consider In Firing An Employee*, Stone Business Law, P.C., http://www.stonebusinesslaw.com/resource/general-business-law/issues-consider-firing-employee. This website page isn't offering legal advice on how to fire an employee, but rather, some common sense ideas for how to make an employee firing go better – for all parties. It's worth reading.

- o Tell the employee directly and unequivocally of the termination. Don't leave it ambiguous, and don't say it in such a way that it will lead to an argumentative situation.
- o Have a letter prepared, outlining the termination, that you will hand to the employee, or will be read to the employee. Having this in writing ensures that what needs to be said is actually said, and it gives you the time to think it through ahead of time.
- o If possible, have two people in the room, but only one person talking – the other to take detailed notes.
- o Make sure that whatever is said in the termination is respectful, tactful, and considerate. If you are insulting or disagreeable, the odds of future legal action increase.
- o Have a final paycheck and benefits statement prepared. If this isn't possible, tell the employee when and how it will be delivered.
- o Don't draw out the process. It's in no one's interests to make it any longer than necessary.

Chapter 7 Employee Benefits

"It's about getting the best people, retaining them, nurturing a creative environment and helping to find a way to innovate."
Marissa Mayer, President and CEO, Yahoo!

Your employee benefit package(s)

Employee benefits might seem like a luxury you can't afford when your business is young and short on cash. But here are three ways to look at their value:

- when you need to hire the best employees away from other companies (particularly competitors), your benefit package could very well make a difference in their decision
- the corollary to this is, when your competitors are trying to hire away your employees, your benefit package could be a deciding factor in not jumping ship (or vice-versa)
- benefits granted to your employees should also be taken by yourself, so assuming they are tax deductible benefits to the business, you should also get the benefits at a pre-tax or group cost.

When it comes to their total compensation package, most employees are quick to figure out the value that working for your company brings to their lives. And while salary is a big factor, the benefits you provide to them can be significant, not only in the actual money they bring home in the paycheck, but also in the peace of mind your benefits bring.

In most small companies the employee benefit package usually grows with the business. Obviously, when you're the only employee of the company, you'll implement those benefits that are valuable to you – and you might initiate some that you'll want to drop when you hire your first employee (so think about that when the time comes to hire, as it may be difficult to have discriminatory benefits, and worse, it will set you up as a lousy employer if it's later found out that you're taking benefits for yourself that aren't offered to employees).

The key is to add to your available employee benefits as you grow the business, and as your financial cushion enables it. The more generous you are, the more your employees will want to join your company – and importantly, remain with your company. A strong word of caution, though – don't set up Google-type benefits or benefits you can't afford unless you have a billion dollars in the bank. You don't need breakfast and lunch bars, in-house daycare centers, and fitness gyms to attract really good employees (you only do that when you're in a competitive situation and have lots of money to burn through).

Employee benefits come in two categories, mandatory and optional. They can also be categorized by the size of your company – typically referred to as a small business. Let's look at the permutations.

Small business definition. Many people assume that, by government definition, a small business has no more than 50 employees. If that definition was ever true across the board, it definitely isn't true today. As a rule, the number is considerably higher, or is based on average annual receipts,[246] rather than a simple number of employees. Further, employee number and revenue limits are based on industry groups, as defined by a code known as the North American Industry Classification System (NAICS),[247] and those numbers frequently change. For many businesses, the maximum employee number to be a small business is as high as 500, and/or the gross revenue might be in the millions of dollars.

This definition can be important to you for a variety of reasons: (a) determining if your company is eligible for government contracting possibilities and other government programs, (b) if you're looking for an SBA-guaranteed loan, (c) whether certain employee benefit requirements apply to your business, (d) and whether certain federal and state employment rules apply to you.

Mandatory employee benefits

These are government-mandated benefits, either at the federal or state level – and while they might not seem like an employee benefit (but rather, an employee right or a civic duty), they are nevertheless a benefit that employees should recognize as such.

These benefits include:

- **Employer portion of Social Security and Medicare taxes** (also known as FICA taxes) – a federal requirement. The FICA employer portion amounts to slightly more than 7.5 % over and above the employee's salary (up to dollar limits) that the employee would otherwise have to pay. (This also applies to employees that you hire in a sole proprietorship and an LLC that is not taxed as a corporation, but not for the owner (or member if it's an LLC taxed as a sole proprietorship), as they are not considered employees in this type of business structure and directly and personally pay their entire FICA taxes.)

- **Unemployment tax, worker's compensation (and possibly, disability) insurance** – state requirements for all businesses.[248] Again, most employees wouldn't think of these as a benefit. After all, many people in today's world think that anything called a tax can't possibly provide any benefit to them. That is, until they become unemployed and want to

---

[246] The SBA defines average annual receipts as "total income" (or "gross income") plus "cost of goods sold" as these terms are defined and reported on Internal Revenue Service (IRS) tax return forms. For more information on this, refer to U.S. GPO, Code of Federal Regulations, Title 13 §121.104, *How does SBA calculate annual receipts?*, August 13, 2015, http://www.ecfr.gov/cgi-bin/text-idx?SID=f6205cdcbdc1228a0466ae4ce359255f&mc=true&node=se13.1.121_1104&rgn=div8

[247] *Summary of Size Standards by Industry Sector*, SBA article, 7/14/2014, https://www.sba.gov/content/summary-size-standards-industry-sector

[248] *Determine your state tax obligation*, SBA article, https://www.sba.gov/content/learn-about-your-state-and-local-tax-obligations

draw unemployment benefits, or get hurt on the job and want to receive wage and medical benefits, or suffer a disability that makes it impossible to work in their core skill set.

A handful of states (or territories) require employers to provide "partial wage replacement" to eligible employees for *non-work-related* sickness or injury. They are: California, Hawaii, New Jersey, New York, Puerto Rico, and Rhode Island. [249]

- **Premium-Only-Plans (POP).** A POP is one type of benefit plan offered in a so-called Cafeteria Plan. State law in about a dozen states requires businesses (under certain circumstances) to establish a POP, and most other states have similar laws under consideration.[250] Cafeteria Plans and POP are described later in this chapter.

- **Jury duty** – federal and state requirements for all businesses. This is another tough one, primarily because of its possible duration. Federal and state law "prohibits employers from discharging an employee who takes leave to serve on a jury, as well as other forms of reprisals". [251]

Some states (such as Oregon) go beyond that, ruling that "employers with ten or more employees cannot stop providing health, disability, life or other insurance coverage for an employee during times the employee serves or is scheduled to serve on a jury". Most states do not require employee compensation be paid during jury duty, although a few are more demanding. Colorado, for one, requires that "all regularly employed trial or grand jurors must be paid their regular wages by their employer – up to $50 per day unless mutually agreed otherwise by the employer and employee –for the first three days of jury service or any part of a day", but backs off on this if the company can prove it would be a financial hardship.

So, what's the right thing to do? Given that you're unlikely to have anything like a well-thought-out policy on this in the early days of your company (and most likely won't have a Policy Handbook yet), the best thing might be to take it on a case-by-case basis (documenting it as such so you aren't establishing a precedent that can come back later to bite you). Keep in mind the number of vagaries surrounding jury duty: (1) the employee won't have a clue this is coming up in their life until the notice arrives in the mail one day, (2) no one knows whether they'll just sit at the courthouse for three days and never get picked for a jury, and (3) if they are picked for a jury, won't know if it will be for 3 days, 3 weeks, or 3 months. It's highly unlikely during the hiring process that an employee will pick your company over another based on jury duty benefits, but if the employee ever gets stuck on a two-week jury trial and their only income is the small amount paid by the court, they might not be all that happy with your benefits package if you stiff them.

Jury service is a civic duty, and since my preference would be to have the very best jurors deciding my fate if I was ever faced with a jury trial, my recommendation is to pay full

---

[249] Megan Sullivan, *Guide to Employee Benefits for Small Business*, Intuit QuickBooks, June 25, 2014, http://quickbooks.intuit.com/r/healthcare-and-benefits/guide-employee-benefits-small-business

[250] Rick Lindquist, *Small Business Employee Benefits and HR Blog*, ZaneBenefits, http://www.zanebenefits.com/blog/bid/97332/FAQ-What-is-a-Section-125-POP-Premium-Only-Plan

[251] *Jury Duty Leave Laws by State*, Business Owner's Toolkit, http://www.bizfilings.com/toolkit/sbg/office-hr/managing-the-workplace/jury-duty.aspx. The site contains a map, with links by state that briefly give each state's position on jury duty leave.

wages to employees for their jury service (which is what I did with my own company – and the total number of times it arose could be counted on one hand).

- **Employees serving on military duty (reserve and active duty)** – a federal requirement, for all business sizes. All employers are required to grant military leave to any employee (except a temporary employee) who is called to active duty military service or reserve duty (including national guard encampments, maneuvers, drills, training, or other duty), regardless of how long the employee has been with the company or the employee's probationary/permanent status.[252]

As a private employer, you are not required to provide compensation for military leave, but you may, by agreement with the employee. If you provide compensation, the amount can be whatever you negotiate, including picking up the difference between full-time pay and the military pay amount.

You are not allowed to *require* the employee to use accrued vacation or sick leave during their military leave, although the employee can choose to do so if you are not otherwise paying compensation.

Upon return from military service (and this could be problematic for small businesses), you must reinstate the employee to the position (or a similar position) held at the time of departure. This could result in displacing another employee you brought into the position, so it would be wise to ensure that the fill-in employee knows of this requirement from the outset.

Due to the large number of military reservists called up for war duty in the last decade, and because of the extended duration of these call-ups, the SBA created a loan program called Military Reservist Economic Injury Disaster Loan (MREIDL). It's available to small businesses only, providing operating capital funds due to an essential employee who was called up for active duty as a military reservist.[253] There are very detailed eligibility requirements, and you'll have to jump through a lot of hoops, but when you're on the ropes having lost a key employee for a year (or so), this could be a life saver for your business.

- **Family and medical leave benefits** – a federal requirement, but only for certain aspects of leave, and only for employers with more than 50 employees (or public agencies and elementary and secondary schools), and if the employee is eligible. Only leave benefits that fall under the Family and Medical Leave Act of 1993 (FMLA)[254] are mandatory, and as you can imagine – since it's a federal program – the do's and don'ts are complex. The footnoted reference is a very clearly-written guide (in PDF format) that clarifies the rules.

---

[252] *Military Leave Laws for Employees*, BizFilings, http://www.bizfilings.com/toolkit/sbg/office-hr/managing-the-workplace/military-leave-laws-for-employees.aspx
[253] *Fact Sheet: Military Economic Injury Loans*, SBA article, https://www.sba.gov/content/fact-sheet-about-us-small-business-administration-military-reservist-economic-injury-disaster-loan-program
[254] *The Employee's Guide to the Family and Medical Leave Act*, United States Department of Labor, http://www.dol.gov/whd/fmla/employeeguide.pdf . At the beginning of this booklet is a flowchart that clearly identifies eligible employers and employees.

Optional employee benefits

Being optional, the following benefits are those that you can select based on their affordability, or whether they are appropriate for how you want to run your company. They should be chosen with care, as they are similar to salary, in the sense that once an employee has them, it will not be easy to take away any part of them. There are so many possible benefits you can add to your employee package that it's hard to know where to start. So, let's begin with the big one (but by no means the easiest one to get your arms around) – health care insurance.

Health care insurance

Yes, this is the big one – providing health care insurance, <u>including dental care, vision care, and possibly mental health care,</u> for your employees – even if the employee is required to pay a portion of the premium. It's the single biggest benefit you can provide, and while you might think you can't afford it, you really should consider it. Chances are you can.

And consider this – according to a 2016 survey on the value of workplace benefits,[255] *"workers overwhelmingly consider health insurance to be the most important workplace benefit when considering whether to stay in a current job or choose a new job"*.

One of the best provisions of the Affordable Care Act (ACA, a.k.a. Obamacare) is the financial assistance provided to small businesses, particularly businesses with fewer than 25 employees. The current status of the Affordable Care Act is in doubt as this update is being completed, with attempt after attempt by the Republican-controlled Congress and Administration to repeal and replace it. When this effort was defeated, there were still many changes that have destabilized the ACA to the point that it could wreak serious havoc on the viability and affordability of universal health care. Changes in Medicaid funding to the States could seriously alter financial assistance, and this in turn could undermine the state-run health care exchanges and cause health insurers to flee the states they operate in. Right now (late summer, 2017), it far too early to know what the final outcome will be, making it difficult to know if some of the information in this section will remain as stated (see an important update at the footnote below[256]).

As of now, though, several small business programs are provided by the Affordable Care Act – one for self-employed, another for fewer than 25 employees,[257] one for 25–50 employees, and still another for over 50 employees ... plus there are varying rules that apply to companies up to 100 employees, so make sure you check out all of the links at the SBA site. Also, if you have

---

[255] Paul Fronstin and Lisa Greenwald, *Value of Workplace Benefits: Findings from the 2016 Health and Voluntary Workplace Benefits Survey*, Employee Benefits Research Institute (EBRI) Notes article, https://www.ebri.org/pdf/notespdf/EBRI_Notes_v38no5_WBS.18Apr17.pdf.

[256] As of August 24, 2017, and importantly after Repeal and Replace failed, according to a report in U.S. News and World Report (https://www.usnews.com/news/national-news/articles/2017-08-24/last-bare-county-in-us-to-have-obamacare-coverage-in-2018), "every county in the United States is expected to have at least one health insurer offering coverage through the Affordable Care Act's exchanges in 2018".

[257] *Employers with Fewer Than 25 Employees*, SBA Health Care website article, https://www.sba.gov/sites/default/files/files/ACA_101_Deck_-_October_2015.pdf

both full and part-time employees, you need to know the rules for calculating "full-time equivalent" employees.[258]

With so many programs, the intricacies for each are far too detailed for this book (not to mention still too fluid as the Affordable Care Act continues to settle in), so we'll only scratch the surface here (and provide links to study it further). Suffice it to say that this program has finally made it possible for even the smallest of small businesses to offer this type of benefit at an affordable cost, without being jerked around by the health insurance companies as businesses were 15–20 years ago (due to pre-existing conditions, upwards of 35% annual premium increases, having to search high and low for "groups" you could join that enabled you to even purchase reasonable cost insurance, etc.).

After reading through the program details appropriate for your company size, one suggestion is to consider using a health care *advisor* – and that doesn't mean a health insurance company *agent*, as that category of person works for a specific insurance company. A health care advisor is independent, not aligned with any particular insurance company, and will be able to steer you to the best plan for your specific situation. And they get paid by the health insurance company you choose, so the advisor doesn't cost you anything out of pocket (that doesn't mean the advisor isn't getting a better pay-off from one health insurance company over another, so this is a question you should ask).

Assuming you're at the start-up stage, the best place to begin is with the "fewer than 25 employees" information, to find the best options through the SHOP Marketplace (Small Business Health Options Program).[259] While the SHOP Marketplace is available to businesses up to 50 employees, if you're under 25 employees it also provides a tax credit of up to 50% of your annual employee coverage premiums. To qualify for this tax credit, you need to purchase your employee's coverage through the SHOP Marketplace, you must be paying at least 50% of your employee's premium amount, and your *average* employee annual salary must be $50,000 or less. (According to the web site it gets even better – if you have fewer than 10 employees and their average annual salaries are less than $25,000, you can obtain an even larger tax credit – but don't count on this, as repeated calculations for various employee numbers and annual salaries resulted in an exact 50% tax credit.)[260]

However, if you are the sole proprietor who has no employees (other than you and possibly a spouse) – you are not eligible for the SHOP Marketplace, and you must purchase your health insurance through the regular HealthCare.gov website as an individual subscriber.

In all states, you (the employer) can offer only one SHOP health plan to your employees – and your choice is either a Bronze, Silver, Gold, or Platinum plan. Each plan determines the premium amount and the total out-of-pocket expenses each employee would have to pay over the year. The plans range from covering 60% of the total cost of care (with the employee paying 40%) for

---

[258] *Full-time Equivalent (FTE) Employee Calculator*, HealthCare.gov, https://www.healthcare.gov/shop-calculators-fte/

[259] *Overview of the SHOP Marketplace*, https://www.healthcare.gov/small-businesses/provide-shop-coverage/shop-marketplace-overview/

[260] *SHOP Tax Credit Estimator*, HealthCare.gov, Small Business tab, https://www.healthcare.gov/shop-calculators-taxcredit/#results

Bronze, to 90% of the total cost of care (with the employee paying 10%) for Platinum. If you elect to add a dental plan (and doing so would be a huge benefit for your employees), the plans typically cover between 70–80% of the total care cost.

Once a plan *level* is selected, you can then begin to shop for an actual insurance plan. To begin, go to the HealthCare.gov web site page titled *"How to enroll in the SHOP Marketplace"*[261] and then follow the detailed instructions found there. It will instruct you to create a profile and asks you to select the state where your business resides. From there it will direct you to your state's marketplace, or to the federal marketplace set up for your state. You then provide information about your company, upload your employee data for each employee you plan to cover, and you'll be given a price quote for the insurance premiums.

Before you go to all this work, you can also check out average health insurance costs in your state, at a site that provides average premiums for the small group market, state-by-state.[262]

- **Vision care insurance.** Vision insurance generally isn't covered under the Affordable Care Act. However, pediatric vision care *is* a required benefit in all plans that qualify as "minimum essential coverage" – it's called "vision health", and is part of the Essential Health Benefit (EHB).[263]

  The basic EHB coverage is for kids under 19, and includes an annual exam, both eyeglasses and frames, and contact lenses instead of glasses.

  If a vision plan is part of the plan chosen for your company, the employee can use an ACA benefit called "cost assistance". For 2017 (and presumably in later years too), the ACA provides three types of cost assistance: Premium Tax Credits, Cost Sharing Reduction Subsides, and Medicaid/CHIP.[264]

  Adults (i.e., your employees and their spouses) can purchase vision insurance either through a standalone plan (purchased directly through a private health insurer), or a federal or state Marketplace plan. Tax credits can be used, and/or cost assistance can be applied for with the premiums of a Marketplace plan (but not if it's a standalone plan).

  Lots of other rules and conditions apply, so check with the ACA website (and www.obamacarefacts.com) for more details.

- **COBRA insurance.** If your business grows to more than 20 employees and has created a group health insurance plan, you need to be aware of COBRA insurance and your obligations under it (make sure you read all the way through this, as there may be requirements for company size less than 20 employees).[265]

---

[261] *How to offer employee health insurance using the SHOP Marketplace*, HealthCare.gov, https://www.healthcare.gov/small-businesses/provide-shop-coverage/enroll-in-shop/

[262] *State average premiums for the small group market*, Small Business Majority, http://healthcoverageguide.org/helpful-tools/charts/state-average-premiums-for-the-small-group-market/

[263] *Affordable Care Act Vision Coverage*, ObamaCare Facts, http://obamacarefacts.com/vision-insurance/

[264] ObamaCare Cost Assistance for 2017 Plans, https://obamacarefacts.com/obamacare-cost-assistance-for-2017-plans/.

[265] *COBRA FAQs*, COBRAinsurance.com, http://ww1.cobrainsurance.com/cobra_faq/#What%20triggers%20the%20obligation%20to%20offer%20COBRA%20coverage

COBRA (the Consolidated Omnibus Budget Reconciliation Act of 1985) requires most employers with group health plans to assist employees with temporarily continuing their health care coverage under their employer's plan if it would otherwise cease due to termination, layoff, or other change in employment status (assuming the employee health plan is covered by COBRA). The employee's health insurance coverage is typically allowed to continue for up to 18 months under COBRA, with the employee paying the monthly premiums.

While COBRA is a federal requirement, many states have enacted their own "mini-COBRA" laws, aimed at small businesses with 2–19 employees.[266] While the rules vary in each state, they basically mirror the federal COBRA intent. Do a search on "*yourstate* COBRA".

When an employee terminates for almost any reason, the employer is obligated to offer COBRA coverage (except *possibly* a "gross misconduct" reason – which is considered more serious than a "for cause" termination described earlier).[267] If the employee elects to use COBRA, the employer files the necessary paperwork, bills the terminated employee for the premium and pays it along with the company's regular insurance premium.

This is listed as an employee benefit, and it is a benefit in the sense of continuing to provide health insurance to an employee who has been terminated, but it's actually something you (as an employer) are required by law to do, and certainly won't be a benefit that you'll tout in your new employee offer letter.

Cafeteria plan

A cafeteria plan is a wonderful and inexpensive employer-sponsored benefit that you can offer to your employees. It's so-named because that's the name it goes by in IRS Section 125 of the Internal Revenue Code that defines how it is to work – and because it allows the employee to pick and choose which medical and dependent care expenses to cover by contributing pre-tax dollars from their paychecks.[268 and 269]

---

[266] Gloria Ju, *Health Care Continuation Coverage (Mini-COBRA) Laws by State*, http://www.xperthr.com/quick-reference/health-care-continuation-coverage-mini-cobra-laws-by-state/16579/

[267] *COBRA Exception For Gross Misconduct*, Explanation letter from GrayRobinson attorneys, May 28, 2010, http://www.gray-robinson.com/Elerts/100528_Employee_Benefits_COBRA_Exception_for_Gross_Misconduct.pdf. Note the Conclusion paragraph that mentions this court ruling was in Massachusetts, and courts in other states might decide otherwise – making this information strictly informational, and you should not rely on it.

[268] *FAQs for government entities regarding Cafeteria Plans*, IRS website, January 6, 2015, https://www.irs.gov/Government-Entities/Federal,-State-&-Local-Governments/FAQs-for-government-entities-regarding-Cafeteria-Plans

[269] To read more about an IRS Section 125 Cafeteria Plan, do an internet search on "*Section 125 Cafeteria Plan*", or download the IRS PDF that describes the plan, at https://www.irs.gov/pub/irs-drop/n-05-42.pdf .

Who can participate in a cafeteria plan?[270] Generally, any person classified as an employee can participate. The big question is whether company *owners* can participate, and that is determined by your company's structure and whether the IRS views the owners as employees.

- o If your company is a sole-proprietorship, or any kind of partnership, the owner is considered by the IRS to be self-employed and therefore cannot participate in a cafeteria plan (unless certain conditions are met and the plan is offered as an after-tax benefit, which loses much of its financial advantage).
- o If your company is an LLC, but taxed as a partnership, the members of the LLC are considered self-employed by the IRS and cannot participate in a cafeteria plan (except in the condition noted above).
- o If your company is an LLC, but taxed as a corporation, the members are considered employees by the IRS, so they can participate in a cafeteria plan.
- o If your company is a corporation (either C-Corp or S-Corp), all corporate executives are considered employees by the IRS and can participate in a cafeteria plan. Shareholders who do not work for the corporation as an employee cannot participate.

Is a cafeteria plan required? As of 2016, about a dozen states have passed legislation *requiring* employers under specified circumstances to offer at least the Premium-Only-Plan (POP) described below. To find out if your state is one of them (and to see what other health insurance-related tax provisions might apply in your state), go to *Summary of State Tax Provisions Relating to Health Insurance*, at http://healthcoverageguide.org/states/summary-of-state-tax-provisions-relating-to-health-insurance/.

How does a cafeteria plan work?
- • There are two types of plans an employer can set up – and a cafeteria plan can include either or both of these:
  - o **Premium-Only-Plan (POP).** With a POP, you (the employer) determine the "qualified benefits" that the cafeteria plan can provide – namely a list of insurance. This allows for *employee-paid premiums* of certain IRS-defined insurance plans to be paid with pre-tax dollars. The premiums can only be for employer-offered insurance, including:
    - ▪ Health insurance (but not on a plan for individual health insurance offered through an Individual Exchange, *but it can be if the plan is through a SHOP exchange – which is beneficial to small businesses*)[271]
    - ▪ Prescription insurance
    - ▪ Vision insurance

---

[270] *May owners of an LLC (usually called "LLC members") participate in the LLC's medical or cafeteria plan and receive employer HSA contributions?*, American Benefits Group, December, 2015, https://www.amben.com/article/items/may-owners-of-an-llc-usually-called-llc-members-participate-in-the-llcs-medical-or-cafeteria-plan-and-receive-employer-hsa-contr.html

[271] For more information about health insurance and references to learn more about it, refer to the earlier section on health insurance and the Affordable Care Act. For more information on health care exchanges: *Overview of the SHOP Marketplace*, https://www.healthcare.gov/small-businesses/provide-shop-coverage/shop-marketplace-overview/

- Disability insurance
- Employee group term life insurance
- Cancer insurance
- Medicare supplemental insurance
- Hospital indemnity insurance
- Accident insurance

o **Flexible Spending Account (FSA).** An FSA is much less restrictive than a POP, allowing the employee to decide which areas of health care, child care, or dependent care they are already spending money on, and then setting aside pre-tax dollars in the cafeteria plan to cover it. The expenses can be any of the following (but aren't restricted to this. (Important: see the Wikipedia article, Cafeteria Plan, for an amazing list, at https://en.wikipedia.org/wiki/Cafeteria_plan.)

- Out-of-pocket health care costs, such as copays, co-insurances, deductibles, dental work, eyeglasses and/or contact lenses, orthodontia, and other medical, dental, vision, and hearing products and services.

- Dependent care costs, such as childcare away from home or in your home (baby sitters or nannies), before- and after-school programs, summer day camps, adult daycare. (Expenses that cannot be paid from an FSA include kindergarten, private school tuition, educational classes, and overnight camps.)

- Employee transit and parking costs. Up to $2,550 (for plan years beginning in 2015) can be contributed by the employee to pay for transit costs to/from home to the workplace, and/or private vehicle parking while at work.

- Both of these plan types are employer-sponsored, which means that you (the employer) create the plan through an IRS pre-approved provider. Once you select your provider and decide which type(s) of plan you'd like to have, you then authorize the provider to set up the plan and file necessary paperwork on your behalf with the IRS. After that, any employee in your company can sign up to participate in the plan.

- IRS Section 125 specifically prohibits any cafeteria plan from providing deferred compensation, and an employer is prohibited from operating "in a manner that enables employees to defer compensation" (this can be a serious downside for employees being able to fully utilize a Section 125 cafeteria plan, so make sure this is well understood). In other words, a cafeteria plan is not allowed to "carry over unused elective contributions or plan benefits (e.g., accident or health plan coverage) from one plan year to another". A cafeteria plan is also not allowed to permit participants "to use contributions for one plan year to purchase a benefit that will be provided in a subsequent plan year". The basic purpose of the cafeteria plan under Section 125 does, however, inherently create a short-term deferred compensation for employee contributions, but only for a "short, limited period" within a single plan year. The only other allowances to the deferred compensation rules are described in the next paragraph.

- A cafeteria plan is set up on a plan year basis, oftentimes calendar year, but it could be on the company's health insurance plan year. Grace periods, typically 75 days at the end of the plan year, allow employees to *use up* remaining funds from last year's plan. In addition, participants have a 90-day *run-out* period where they can submit reimbursement requests for expenses that occur in the grace period. After that, any remaining employee funds are returned <u>to the employer</u> (a use-it-or-lose-it type of thing – but don't forget, the taxes saved by the employee might offset this – but in any case, it means an employee needs to evaluate their anticipated costs for the year very carefully).

- Once the plan is up and running, each employee who wants to participate registers with the plan (through paperwork from the provider). Based on calculated costs paid from the cafeteria plan, the employee specifies how much money to set aside in the plan. Each payroll period, a *slice* of the set-aside money (by dividing the total amount by the number of payroll periods) will be deducted – before taxes – from the employee's paycheck and is *deposited* in the employee's account within the cafeteria plan (in actual fact, the money is deposited in a trust account in the employee's name and set up by the provider). It is then paid out to the employee when reimbursement *invoices* are received and accepted from the employee. It's important to take note of the amount of employer accounting/HR effort this will require, and the cost of that is borne by you, the employer.

- The employer's cost for establishing the plan is a one-time set-up fee (typically $700-$1,000), plus a <u>*monthly*</u> participant fee for continued administration of the plan (usually $4.00–$10.00 per participant). Some plan providers also charge for *communication materials* – including brochures and explanatory documents that are used to pitch the idea to your employees, plus they might charge for enrollment meetings, where a specialist from the provider comes to one or more of your company locations to hold discussions with your employees about the benefits. These latter two fees can add up quickly, so negotiate and keep an eye on them so they don't balloon on you.

- There are tax benefits to the company in setting up a cafeteria plan – namely reduced FICA, FUTA, SUTA, and Worker's Compensation taxes on participating employees – *which can almost completely offset the employer costs of setting up and running the plan.*

- Employee tax benefits with a cafeteria plan can be huge if properly planned and handled. Depending on tax bracket, an employee can save up to 40% on the premiums and health/dependent care dollars currently being spent.

Drawbacks to a cafeteria plan (for both employer and employee).

- Cafeteria plans are qualified, non-discriminatory employee benefit plans, so a discrimination test (most likely done by the provider) must be met, based on the elections of the participants, combined with any contributions by the employer. Another way of saying this is that a plan cannot be set up (or continue to run) that favors highly-compensated employees – and if the plan is found to be discriminatory, the company's highly-compensated employees will lose their tax benefits from the plan (but non-highly compensated employees will not).

- An employee can spend up to the total elected amount of the plan before the amount has been paid in through payroll deduction, and can then terminate employment. <u>The employer is on the hook for the cost.</u> An example – an employee elects $1,500, then has medical treatment that isn't covered under insurance (let's say, laser eye surgery), claims the entire amount against his/her cafeteria plan and gets reimbursed for it, then terminates from the company before sufficient paycheck deductions have been taken to fully fund the account.

The employer has no recourse, and the company is stuck, having to pay the difference between the employee's contributions to the plan to date and the amount paid out for the expenses.

- IRS requires a *use it or lose it* rule at the end of the plan year (which is typically calendar year). The onus is on the employee to plan ahead how much their medical and dependent care costs will be, and if at the end of the year they haven't spent all of the amount they elected to have set aside in the cafeteria plan, *the remaining money is forfeited – to the employer*, who can use the money (for example) to make up for other participants who departed the plan through termination with disbursements that exceeded their plan contributions.

Time off from work (vacation, holidays, sick leave, family leave)

"All work and no play makes Jack a dull boy" is a well-known proverb that dates back to a Victorian novel of the late 19th Century – but it also has a place in small business employee management. The 40-hour work week is all well and good, and in fact, lots of people work far more than that, but there are times in our lives when we each need to get away from work, perhaps while recuperating from illness, caring for a family member, adding to the family with a childbirth or adoption, grieving for a lost loved one, or just re-charging life's batteries. If all an employee ever has is a 2-day weekend, every single week of the year, the proverbial Jack wouldn't just become a dull boy – he'd be looking for other work.

Generally speaking, all of these forms of employee leave are optional (except for a growing number of places where mandatory paid sick leave is enforced). Nevertheless, all of these personal and family leave types are becoming more prevalent, and if you hope to attract employees who are already working for another company, offering these benefits will be important in getting new employees to sign on.

This is not a trivial part of your new business owner decision-making – it's near the top of the most important employee benefit categories that you'll face. If you hope to attract employees who are already working for another company, offering these time off benefits will be important in getting new employees to sign on.

When you're a 1-person company you obviously won't need to worry much about this – you'll take off whatever time the business can afford – and if the business can't afford it, you'll work when you're sick (up to a point), and you'll forego vacations if you have to.

But *before* you hire your first employee, carve out some time to at least think about the first three types of leave – holidays, vacation, and sick leave. If you don't bring it up in the job interview, the candidate(s) you're interviewing will, so you need to be ready for it – and an off-the-top-of-the-head response can set a precedent you can't easily get out of, and trying to be the nice guy without running the numbers can cost money you can't afford.

Study the critical aspects of your business, figuring out how you'll be able to accomplish certain tasks when people are off (either on paid or unpaid leave), whether you'll need to hire temp workers in their absence, or how you'll shift other workers around. Run some scenarios on your Cash Flow/Budget template to see how it affects your cost of sales.

Sure, it's going to cost you money – lots of it in fact, but it's money well spent, mainly in terms of having employees who want to work for you and help you build your company. The problem is that employees might be away from work at inconvenient times for the company, leaving you short-staffed at the worst possible time. Most businesses tout that "our employees are our greatest asset", and if that's really true, you'll create the environment where employee time off isn't a burden to your business, but instead, a reward for a job well done.

Holidays

This topic seems like a no-brainer and easy to establish, but when you get down to the details, it isn't so easy at all. In fact, it will be more difficult than you ever thought possible, and a policy that you will have to consider every year (since many holidays fall on different days of the week and month each year).

In addition to affordability, your business will likely dictate whether you need to be open for business on holidays, and if so, which ones, who will work them, and what your employee pay practices will be.

Before you can establish an employee holiday plan, you first have to know what your company's needs are for closing or staying open during holidays. If you're in the retail or storefront business and everyone around you (plus your competition) is open or closed, you probably need to follow their lead. If you're in the online business, particularly if any of your business comes from international customers, you'll most likely need to remain open for business. If you're a vendor to a larger business and they remain open or closed, you may need to follow their lead and be open when they're open. Certain industries traditionally tie some of the year's biggest bargain sales to holidays, and they could be boom or bust days for your business.

Also, you need to determine which holidays are important to your business, and which you will observe. That too seems like a simple decision, but try an internet search on *"U.S. public holidays"* and you'll be faced with more decision-making than you ever thought possible. You'll find there are public holidays, bank holidays, federal holidays, U.S. holidays, and less-than-national holidays that are observed only in certain states.

What's the rest of the business community doing? According to a 2014 survey by the Society for Human Resources Management (SHRM)[272], 90% of U.S. businesses will observe (by closing) on the following days:

- New Year's Day (January 1)
- Memorial Day (near the end of May)
- Independence Day (July 4)
- Labor Day (early in September)
- Thanksgiving Day (late in November)
- Christmas Day (December 25)

---

[272] *SHRM 2014 Holiday Schedules*, Society for Human Resources Management, October 15, 2013, https://www.shrm.org/hr-today/trends-and-forecasting/research-and-surveys/pages/2014holidayschedules.aspx

You'll notice that Columbus Day (September 12) is not on the list, nor is Martin Luther King Jr. Day (mid-January), President's Day (mid-February), and Veteran's Day (November 11). These are all considered second-tier holidays, and it's up to each company to decide whether to observe them Something like two-thirds of all businesses are closed on "Black Friday" – the Friday after Thanksgiving, primarily to give employees a 4-day holiday. Another option at some companies is to give each employee their birthday off – or in some cases simply a floating holiday on the day of each employee's choosing (and if you go this route, you need someone in authority to monitor and manage it).

So, after sorting through that, what's your holiday policy for employees? By law, you're not obligated (as an employer) to give employees holiday time off, nor are you required to compensate employees if you do give them time off on holidays that you recognize. Both of these are benefits that you have the *option* to provide. But just because you're not obligated isn't a good reason to ignore the observance of holidays, and to not compensate your employees – and to do so would put you at great risk of showing your employees that you're a stingy and uncaring employer. At the very least – and if you do have good business reasons to be open for business on some or all of the popular holidays, you could allow your employees to take off another day of their choosing, with pay, as compensatory time off – and maybe even with extra pay if they work it (such as time-and-a-half, double-time, or even triple-time in some situations). Another option is to run a skeleton crew on holidays, maybe alternating from holiday to holiday with employees who are required to work.

Example of *stingy*. A small building trades company that works in residential construction observes a typical number of public holidays throughout the year, but doesn't compensate employees for the holidays until they've worked for the company for at least a year. Since that mostly impacts younger (and therefore lower income) employees, several of them actively promote in-home work with the company's customers on holidays so that they don't take the paycheck hit. The company isn't violating any employment rules, either state or federal, but the overall impact on the employee's salary could easily be $1,000–$1,500 if an employee who really needs the money doesn't find customers who can/will accept work on holidays. Besides just being plain tough for the employee, *it's very possibly enough money for an employee to keep an eye out for another job to jump to*, and every time an employee does, it defeats the business decision not to give the holiday off with pay. Personally, I think it's cheap (and uncaring to the employee) on the part of the business owner.

Vacation

After health care, vacation time is the next most important benefit for most employees. It seems like an expensive benefit – paying someone when they're off on a family camping trip – but the wise thing is to not look at it that way. First of all, employee wages are already wages factored into your Cash Flow/Budget, so it's not as if you're paying for expenses that you'd not otherwise be paying (unless, of course, you have to pay a temp worker to fill in during an absence). Second, the benefits *to your company* when everyone is taking their accrued vacation time are just about as high as they are to the employee – raising morale, regaining energy.

At the same time, when you're a very small business (just a handful of employees, or maybe just one or two besides yourself), even one employee away on holiday can constitute a huge percentage of your workforce. The impact this can have on your business is something you need to be aware of and plan for in advance.

Here are several considerations and planning ideas:

- Decide what your company motives are for providing vacation time. It's obviously a benefit to the employee, but important company factors could be to create a rewards structure, a morale booster, or to be competitive for hiring employees. There's no right or wrong basis here – it's just what you think is important to your company.

- Establish a starting point and accrual schedule for vacation for full-time employees. Many companies establish a plan that gives 10 days after one year of service, and an additional vacation day for each year after that. Some older line companies set it at 2 weeks for the first five years of service, then three after 10 years, four after 15, and so on – but employees these days might feel this is a bit stingy. Others simply set it at two weeks for all employees, and that's that. (1099 contractors have to be factored into this as well, but since you won't be paying them for time not worked, it's just a scheduling consideration.)

- How to account for accrual and usage of vacation time? The worst thing you can do is let each employee keep his/her own records – it just won't work, and *you'll be very sorry for this in the future.* When you're really small (if you can count the total number of employees on two hands), it's easy enough to do this yourself, or to assign it to a trusted employee (or your outside bookkeeper if you want to pay the expense) – and if you do, make sure it's in a spreadsheet that can accurately record it, and can be kept up to date at least every pay period. Once you're beyond the capability of manual management of this, you'll need to look into a software package, one that will handle all types of employee leave.[273] However you do it, though, don't set it up so that an individual can fiddle the numbers – if it can be fiddled, someone will. And once it's not up to date and accurate, it's a he-said/she-said situation that can turn nasty.

- Establish some basic rules for how much (or how little) vacation your employees can take at one time. As a small company, you'll likely be impacted more by vacationing employees than a large company will, so you need to lay down the rules sooner, rather than later. Will you allow half-day increments of use? Will you require employees to take no less than a week at a time? Will you have a limit on maximum time taken at once? (It defeats the purpose if an employee saves up, then takes 8 weeks of vacation all at once, leaving you in a lurch for such a long time.)

- Scheduling for your business needs. How far in advance does an employee have to give notice of a vacation request? How will you settle conflicts between business needs? How will you settle conflicts with other employee requests (for example, two employees in the same department, one who has to cover for the other, and both want time off at the same time)?

- How much vacation time can an employee carry over from year to year? Will you establish a use-it-or-lose-it rule (which will not be popular, but possibly necessary)? With many employees, this is a significant problem, as you'll find individuals who have no interest in

---

[273] *Top Attendance Tracking Software Products*, Capterra, http://www.capterra.com/attendance-tracking-software/

taking vacation time off (or who can't afford the money to actually go on vacation), and before you know it someone has accrued five years of vacation – and you now face the problem described in the next paragraph. Establish the accrual rules early on, as once an employee goes beyond what you can afford, it's too late.

- What will you do about accrued vacation time when an employee terminates? Most employers would voluntarily pay for all accrued vacation at regular pay rates, and if you're thinking otherwise, you should check state law, as many (most?) states have laws that require it, considering it a form of wages. You'll want to consider this carefully when you establish your accrual policy, as the employee who doesn't seem to want to take vacation on a regular basis can accrue so much that it becomes a financial burden if/when that employee terminates.   When money is tight, the last thing you want is the cost of replacing an employee, and at the same time paying out a possible employee severance, and accrued sick leave and vacation time that breaks the bank.

All of the above considerations should illustrate that getting a handle on *your vacation policy needs to be done before hiring the first employee*. More importantly, the rules you establish cannot be left to verbal understandings – they must get into a written format, which could be one of the first building blocks for your first employee handbook – the employee benefit section. As stated at the outset, vacation time is very likely your second most important employee benefit, and you need to get it right.

Sick leave

A handful of states (and individual cities) require *paid* sick leave, including California, Connecticut, Massachusetts, and Oregon (beginning in 2016). As of this writing, 20 cities across the country now require it (the number is growing each year), and one county (Montgomery County, MD). If your business is headquartered in any of these locales (or if you have employees based there), it's important that you carefully check out the do's and don'ts, as each location has different rules.[274]

For example, California and Oregon law requires it for all businesses, regardless of size; Connecticut requires it only if your business has more than 50 employees; Massachusetts requires it if your business has more than 11 employees; the District of Columbia requires it for all businesses, regardless of size, and in addition to sick leave, it also applies to "employees for their own or a family member's illness, or for reasons relating to domestic violence or sexual abuse"; the City and County of San Francisco is basically the same as for the state, but with expansion of the details; Seattle law requires it only if your business has more than 4 employees. The list is in flux, so as a small business owner you need to check your city, county, and state law requirements.

---

[274] *Overview of Paid Sick Time Laws in the United States*, A Better Balance, The Work and Family Legal Center, November 12, 2015, http://www.abetterbalance.org/web/images/stories/Documents/sickdays/factsheet/PSDchart.pdf. At the end of the document is a list of links to the city, county, and state websites that detail the paid sick time requirement for each location.

Elsewhere, paid sick leave is optional (and covered in an earlier section), but the reality is you need to have a policy that includes it in some form. You're asking for trouble if your employees feel the need to come to work sick, risking the spread of their illness to everyone else at work. Likewise, if an employee has a sick child who needs at stay at home, the employee needs to be with that child, and if they can't afford to because they'd lose a day's pay, you don't have a productive and satisfied employee.

Once you implement a paid sick leave policy, you also need to establish several rules to govern and manage it.

- What will the accrual policy be? The most typical is either one hour of paid sick leave for every 30 hours worked, which works out to approximately 8 days of sick leave for a year of full-time work. Some employers provide one hour for every 40 hours, or 7 days a year.

- How to account for accrual and usage of sick leave? Same problem and solution as for vacation time mentioned above – make sure you have a procedure, *and don't let each employee keep their own records*.

- What happens to accrued sick leave at year's end, and if it can be carried over, how much can be carried over? When an employee terminates, will you pay them for their accrued sick leave? Unlike vacation time, this one is not mandated by law.

- What constitutes acceptable absence for sick leave? Most (many?) employers allow sick leave not only for the employee's sickness, but also for illness of immediate family members, and while caring for elderly parents. The more liberal you are with this aspect, the more it goes to gaining loyal employees ... employees who will want to stick with you when the hard times come.

- What will you do if some employees seem to be taking more than usual Friday or Monday days off for sick leave – treating their sick leave as an extension of weekends or paid vacation time? If you don't stay on top of this, it results in lost productivity to you, but also in lowered employee morale as other employees figure out what the slackard is doing (and they *will* figure it out). At the very least, require employees to call in every day they are sick, and it's not unreasonable to require a doctor's note for serious illnesses. Monitor patterns of sick leave usage.

Paid Family Leave (Maternity, paternity, nursing mother, and caregiver)

In most states right now, this is a tough one for a small business, particularly a very small business, as it's a policy that tests your mettle as a compassionate employer, one who cares about the company's employees, and one who wants to do the right thing – yet having so few employees to get the job done.

As a new entrepreneur, make sure you keep your nose and ears to the ground about the changing nationwide attitudes concerning companies, even ultra-small businesses, being required to offer *paid* family leave for a variety of reasons. When the topic rises to the level of being specifically mentioned in the President's 2015 State of the Union address, and when serious public money (from the Department of Labor) is given to the states to fund it, you can bet the issue will get even hotter in future years.

As of 1993, the federal Family and Medical Leave Act required employers to offer 12 weeks of _unpaid_ leave – but this is such an inadequate requirement that it places the U.S. dead last among developed countries in this regard.[275] Besides, there are many loopholes that leave employees uncovered, including a requirement that companies under 50 employees are not covered. It's been estimated that 40% of the nation's workers are not covered under the act. Besides the unpaid protection given by this act, it's estimated that only 13% of private sector workers in the United States have any kind of _paid_ family leave. Compare this to the U.K., where there's a national law providing a whopping 52 weeks of _paid_ maternity/paternity leave (it isn't mandatory that all of it is taken, except for the first two weeks – and it's paid for by a nationwide program). Or the rest of Europe, where it's typically 3+ months of leave, and it's paid, usually at 100%.

As of July, 2017, there are five states that have mandated _paid_ family leave, including California, New Jersey, Rhode Island, New York (to be effective in 2018), Washington State, and the District of Columbia (to be effective in 2020) – and as many as 20 additional states are considering it.[276] Each state has its own set-up and rules for benefits, and here are some highlights:

- California – in effect since 2002, the California Paid Family Leave (PFL) program provides up to six weeks of "partial pay to employees who need to take time off from work to care for a seriously ill family member (child, parent, parent-in-law, grandparent, grandchild, sibling, spouse, or registered domestic partner, or to bond with a new child (including newly fostered or adopted children)". There are more details, rules, and eligibility requirements at http://www.edd.ca.gov/Disability/About_PFL.htm.

- New Jersey – the New Jersey Family Leave Insurance (FLI) program is not actually a "leave" program, but rather, a wage replacement (effectively an insurance program, similar to unemployment) administered through the State's Temporary Disability Benefits program within the Department of Labor and Workforce Development. It provides a payable benefit for up to six weeks to "bond with a newborn or newly adopted child or to provide care for a seriously ill family member". The program is funded 100% by the employer based on payroll. There are more details, rules, and eligibility requirements at http://lwd.dol.state.nj.us/labor/fli/fliindex.html.

- Rhode Island – the Rhode Island Parental and Family Medical Leave Act was created in 2014, providing for up to 13 weeks of continuous leave in any two year period, with at least four weeks of it paid leave at 60% – paid from a fund that's paid into by a mandated employee payroll deduction of 1.2%. The maximum benefit paid out is about $800 per week, and even part-time workers are eligible for the benefit. The plan allows for care of a newborn, adopted, or foster child, a seriously ill child, a parent, a spouse, a domestic partner, a parent-in-law, or grandparent.

- New York – to be implemented on January 1, 2018, the New York State Paid Family Leave Program "will provide New Yorkers job-protected, paid leave to bond with a new

---

[275] Rita Rubin, _U.S. Dead Last Among Developed Countries When It Comes To Paid Maternity Leave_, Forbes, April 6, 2016.

[276] Clare O'Connor, _As NY And SF Pass Paid Family Leave, These 20 States Could Be Next_, Forbes, April 6, 2016

child, care for a loved one with a serious health condition or to help relieve family pressures when someone is called to active military service".[277] The program will be phased in over four years, providing for 8 weeks of paid leave in 2018, 10 weeks in 2019-2020, and 12 weeks in 2021. Paid family leave for military service is unique among the current states offering the benefit, enabling "loved ones to spend time with those called to active military service and alleviates the pressure of working and caring for a child while a loved one is away".

- Washington (State) – to become effective in 2020, providing 12 weeks of paid leave time for the birth or adoption of a child, or for a serious medical condition of a worker's family member (an additional two weeks are granted in the event of a serious health condition with a pregnancy). The state's new plan is right now considered the most generous in the nation, where "both employers and employees pay into the system, and weekly benefits are calculated based on a percentage of the employee's wages and the state's weekly average wage — which is currently $1,082 — though the weekly amount paid out would be capped at $1,000 a week. Workers who earn less than the state average would get 90 percent of their income. Employees must work at least 820 hours before qualifying for the benefit". As an example of the cost, "an employee who makes $50,000 a year would pay $2.42 a week, while their employer would pay $1.42 a week, for a weekly benefit of about $703".

- District of Columbia – the D.C. Universal Paid Family Leave Amendment Act of 2016 provides "workers in Washington, D.C. with eight weeks of paid leave to care for a new child, six weeks of paid leave to care for a sick family member and two weeks of paid leave for a personal illness. To qualify, a worker need only be employed by a private employer in D.C. Residents of other states with jobs in D.C. will be eligible for the benefit. The program is to be funded by a new payroll tax on employers of 0.62%. D.C. employers will begin paying this new tax by July 1, 2019, and employees will be able to access the new benefit beginning July 1, 2020".[278]

In addition to these government initiatives, several large corporations have recently jumped on the bandwagon, with Netflix leading the way with an announcement of *unlimited* paid maternity/paternity leave, in an incredibly flexible plan. Other large companies are beginning to follow suit, including Google (18 weeks' maternity and 12 weeks' paternity), Facebook (17 weeks), Bank of America (12 weeks), and Microsoft (which increased its paid maternity leave to 20 weeks).

So, if you're not located in one of the mandates paid family leave areas, what's a very small start-up company to do? Well, you'd better be creative if you're looking to attract top talent (male or female), particularly talent that currently works for a company that has a good, paid maternity/paternity plan ... and the potential employee is looking down the road to the time of starting a family. You'll be on the short end of the stick if you aren't progressive in your policy.

---

[277] *New York State Paid Family Leave Program*, New York .gov website, https://www.ny.gov/programs/new-york-state-paid-family-leave.

[278] Guy Brenner and Ryan Hutzler, D.C. Universal Paid Family Leave Law Now In Effect, Proskauer: Law and Workplace, April 12, 2017, http://www.lawandtheworkplace.com/2017/04/d-c-universal-paid-family-leave-law-now-in-effect/.

And if you already have an employee with a good marketable skill who is starting to think about a family – and assuming they're planning ahead – you could lose that person to a company that has a better plan than you have. For that category of employee, the beginning of today's new normal could be problematic for you.

And while we're on the topic, don't forget to think about the *nursing mother* situation. At least there's a bit of federal law behind this issue (U.S. Department of Labor, as a result of the Affordable Care Act in 2010). The law requires employers *"to provide reasonable break time for an employee to express breast milk for her nursing child for one year after the child's birth each time such employee has need to express the milk. Employers are not required to compensate employees for such time. Employers are also required to provide a place, other than a bathroom, that is shielded from view and free from intrusion from coworkers and the public, which may be used by an employee to express breast milk."*

My example. The first maternity leave situation in my company occurred with our Financial Controller – when the senior management person who headed up our accounting department became pregnant. By this time, our company was well-established and growing, and after a lot of consideration, we granted a six-week paid maternity leave – which was very progressive at the time. To our surprise, after being on leave for three weeks following the baby's birth (and frankly yearning at times for work and the office culture of adult conversation) she privately approached me with a proposal – would I agree to letting her finish the second half of her maternity leave by returning to work half time, bringing the baby to work on the 2½ days each week that she'd be in the office. It would thereby stretch the overall maternity leave to nine weeks, essentially giving her nine weeks of leave. Because she was breast feeding the baby, she'd need to bring a breast milk pump to work. She had a private corner office next door to mine, with blinds on the exterior and interior windows that could be drawn for privacy. It seemed like a win-win situation for her and the company, and I readily agreed. It went well, even to the point of it being written up as a great work/life balance idea in the Seattle Times when a local reporter got wind of it. A year later, though, when a second female employee told us she was pregnant, she requested the same accommodation – but unfortunately, she was a cubicle worker, and at the time we didn't have a single vacant office in our workplace where she could express breast milk for the baby – and to my chagrin, we had to tell her it wasn't possible. The earlier experiment – that seemed so *right* at the time – had created a precedent that came back to haunt us. Luckily, the second employee was understanding.

Important. As my personal example above illustrates, and with all types of leave, make certain your policies are consistent across each category of employee (salaried, hourly, management, technical, administrative). If they aren't applied equally, you could be in for discrimination claims, and they can become costly very quickly. Also, if someone has earned time off, you'll very likely be on the wrong side of the law if you don't honor it.

Retirement plans – 401(k)

When your new business is in the start-up phase, the last thing you'll be thinking about is retiring employees (including, most likely, yourself). You should be, though, for two reasons:

- You (and most importantly, your employees) are never too young to be thinking about how much money will be required for retirement
- And even if you aren't thinking about it, your employees will be

The quality of your retirement plan will be a big factor in attracting (and keeping) good employees. Like other employee benefits, this is one that you need to give a lot of thought to, as a mistake up front is not only difficult to fix later on, but it can be costly (such as matching funds).

There are two major types of plans, and because their names are similar it's difficult to keep them straight. Here's a good way to think of them: the one with the word *benefit* in it means you're paying for the pension; the one with the word *contribution* in it means the employee is contributing to his/her own pension. Can you guess which one is better for you as a new entrepreneur?

In discussing retirement plans, one term you'll often hear is ERISA (pronounced *"ear-issa"*, the Employee Retirement Income Security Act of 1974). ERISA is a federal law, created by the U.S. Department of Labor, setting minimum standards under which retirement plans in private industry must operate. ERISA does not require any employer to create a retirement plan, but if one is created, ERISA rules control many aspects of the plan.[279]

Defined Benefit Pension Plan. There's only one suggestion on this – *stay away from it!* *(But it might pay to read all the way through this discussion for one potentially valuable situation.)*

You'd have to be living in a cave not to hear about the disastrous financial woes of large legacy companies over the past couple of decades due to their defined benefit pension plans, not to mention a surprising number of city and state governments going bankrupt over their underfunded pension plans. As Wikipedia defines it,[280] a defined benefit pension plan is one in which an employer "promises a specified monthly benefit on retirement that is predetermined by a formula based on the employee's earnings history, tenure of service and age, rather than depending directly on individual investment returns".

Imagine a small business owner trying to forecast years in advance what it will take to fund a pension plan, not knowing what actual employee salaries will be during the years making up the earnings history, plus having no idea how long these employees will live after retirement. And then a global financial crisis like 2007–2009 hits, or some other bump in the road strikes your profitability – and you're in for a disaster, not only with your company, but also with your employees, who were counting on financial security promises that you now can't keep up with.

In an earlier era these plans were fine for the likes of IBM, General Motors, Boeing, and other big Fortune 500 companies, but in today's world they are turning out to be a huge pension disaster for millions of people.[281] It's no wonder these major companies and local governments are shedding their plans – and if they are, it's a good indication you should stay away too.

---

[279] *What is ERISA – Frequently Asked Questions*, United Stated Department of Labor, http://webapps.dol.gov/dolfaq/go-dol-faq.asp?faqid=225

[280] *Defined benefit pension plan*, Wikipedia, https://en.wikipedia.org/wiki/Defined_benefit_pension_plan

[281] According to *The 10 Biggest Failed Pension Plans*, U.S. News and World Report, August 23, 2010, the largest defined benefit pension plan failures were all big airlines, very large steel companies, and one auto

<u>My example of setting up a Defined Benefit Pension Plan.</u> Having just described how horrible a defined benefit pension plan is, it might be very valuable in one situation: in a 1-person company that you expect to remain as such, at least for the foreseeable future. For several years my company had remained just a single employee – me – and I was growing revenue by leaps and bounds as I built up more and more customers. I also had few ways to shield the company's revenue from taxes, until one day a pension plan manager suggested I look into a defined benefit pension plan. Unlike a defined contribution plan (such as a 401(k) that we'll discuss next), a defined benefit plan allows the company to contribute much larger amounts – an annual amount up to the employee's annual salary (maximum $210,000/year). Wow! That meant my company (owned solely by me, and I was the only employee) could stash away far more than a 401(k) – currently $18,000 – in pre-tax dollars. Because it's a complicated plan, I paid quite a bit to set it up, but for the benefits it gave me, it was well worth it. A few years later, I started adding employees to my company, and before long they were clamoring for a 401(k) plan. As the new 401(k) plan was initiated, I terminated the defined benefit pension plan and rolled all of the money in it over to an IRA, ending further defined benefit contributions. During the time I had the defined benefit pension plan, it was well worth the cost to set up, and provided a huge boost for stashing a large amount of pre-tax cash into a pension plan – a boost that no other plan could provide .

Defined contribution pension plan. With this type of retirement plan, today's contribution to the plan is the most important aspect, and the contribution can be either by the employer (optional) or the employee (or both). Inside the plan, an account is set up for each participating employee and the money contributed to that account is held specifically for the benefit of that employee.

The downside of a defined contribution pension plan is that, while the money being contributed to the plan is known at the time of contribution, the eventual pension yield from the plan cannot be known. Typically the money in each employee's account is invested in mutual funds, usually with the employee having some level of control over the investment strategy (but only for his/her own account – i.e., risk-averse, high-yield, etc.). If the investments don't do well, that's the risk the employee takes, and the plan might yield an inadequate pension at the time of retirement (for example, many defined contribution pension plans were down by as much as 50% during the 2007–2009 global financial crises). As a "plan sponsor", the employer retains a certain amount of fiduciary responsibility – based on the level of control that the sponsor carries over the plan.

- **401(k) Plan and the various IRAs.** The plan most people are familiar with is the 401(k) plan (named after subsection 401(k) of the IRS code). 401(k)s are established by the employer (the costs will be discussed in a bit), and participation by each employee is optional.

  By IRS definition, a 401(k) plan is considered to be a qualified profit sharing plan. The word *profit* in it is a bit of a misnomer, as typically, the primary share of the money contributed to each employee's account is directly from the employee's pre-tax paycheck.

---

parts manufacturer, dumped $27B of total pension claims across a half-million vested participants onto the Pension Benefit Guarantee Corporation (PBGC), an agency of the U.S. federal government. Source: http://money.usnews.com/money/blogs/planning-to-retire/2010/08/23/the-10-biggest-failed-pension-plans

If the employer elects to contribute, either by matching some or all of the employee's contribution or by a non-elective contribution to the plan – only then is the money actually from the company's profit. This fact doesn't change the goodness or badness of a 401(k), but rather just sets the record straight on how this type of retirement plan works.

There are several types of 401(k) plans – enough, in fact, to make your head spin, and you definitely need someone keeping score as you read this and research the types (after all, it's a government program, and they are trying hard not to force everyone into a one-size-fits-all concept):

- A traditional 401(k), where the employee and employer can each contribute to the plan (in any combination). [282] Employee contributions are tax-deferred until withdrawal; employer contributions are treated as a tax deduction. Employer contributions can be either (a) matching to the employee's contribution, (b) or contributions of a set percentage of each employee's compensation. The maximum allowable contribution from employer/employee combined is $18,000 in 2017 (same as in 2015 and 2016), often (but not always) rising annually for cost-of-living increases. Employee loans from a participant's account are allowed, under very stringent rules.

  A vesting schedule for *employer* contributions is allowed, creating a forfeiture if the employee doesn't remain with the company through the vesting period. Specific non-discrimination tests must be made each year by the employer, to ensure that plan contributions meet strict IRS non-discrimination requirements, and in particular, don't favor highly compensated employees in the company.

- Safe Harbor 401(k), a plan that is almost identical to a traditional 401(k), with the two major exceptions being (a) a requirement of 100% immediate vesting of employer contributions, and (b) no requirement for annual non-discrimination testing (thereby allowing certain types of discrimination in favor of highly compensated employees). Employee loans from a participant's account are allowed.

- SIMPLE 401(k) and SIMPLE IRA – you'd think these are named Simple because they're easy to set up and manage (and they are!), but SIMPLE is actually an acronym for Savings Incentive Match Plans for Employees. The two are almost identical, with the only difference being whether the employer can set up additional pension plans across the company – a SIMPLE 401(k) can have an addition pension plan for other employees who don't qualify for this one; a SIMPLE IRA cannot have any other plans within the company. The plans are easily adopted just by filing either IRS Form 5304-Simple or 5305-Simple. [283]

  A Simple 401(k) or Simple IRA is allowed for companies with fewer than 100 employees. With either type, an employee can contribute to his/her plan. Unlike other plans, the employer is required to contribute either (a) a matching contribution of up to 3% of the employee's compensation, or (b) a non-elective contribution of 2% of each eligible

---

[282] Other employer-provided defined-contribution plans include 403(b) plans for nonprofit institutions, and 457(b) plans for governmental employers.

[283] *Choosing a Retirement Plan: SIMPLE IRA Plan*, IRS website, http://www.irs.gov/Retirement-Plans/Choosing-a-Retirement-Plan-SIMPLE-IRA-Plan

employee's total compensation (up to a salary limit specified by the IRS). All contributions vest 100% immediately, and the employee has ownership of all money in his/her plan.

Pros and cons:

- easy to create the plan, simply by filing an IRS form
- participant loans are not allowed (this could be a big negative), no discrimination tests are required (which means discrimination is allowed), contributions are not as flexible as with other plans, and it has lower contribution limits than other plans

- SEP IRA (or Simplified Employee Pension IRA) – a retirement plan that an employer or self-employed individual can set up, with each employee having an individual IRA account at a financial institution. A business of any size can set up a SEP IRA. All contributions by the employer are voluntary, and vest 100% immediately. The IRA owner (employee) directs the investments. It's very similar to a traditional IRA, following all of the investment, distribution, and rollover rules.[284] Employee loans from a participant account are not allowed.

How to set up a 401(k) plan? If you wish to set up the paperwork yourself for your company's 401(k) plan, you certainly can. A good place to start is at the IRS home page for retirement plan tax guidance,[285] and from there you can slide into an oblivion of sheer bureaucratic tangle, with dozens of links to various aspects of the process to follow. Another good resource is the SBA website, where the place to start is their blog post about planning and managing a retirement plan.[286] Better yet, the U.S. Department of Labor website has an excellent 401(k) page that provides a detailed bullet list of why you should establish a 401(k) plan, how to establish one, and how to manage the plan – including an extensive resource link list for additional information. You could easily spend two weeks of full-time research on the internet sites available, and you'd wind up being the most educated small business owner in the country on 401(k) topics (not a good idea).

Unless this happens to be your professional specialty, your time and effort is probably better spent on building your business and making a profit – and hiring a professional to advise you – and once your decisions are made, to have that professional set up your plan. Unlike your other professional services fees (attorney and tax advisor) for your many other business decisions, your best 401(k) advisor will likely be from the financial institution where you set up the plan.

- **Cost to set up and maintain a 401(k) plan.** Assuming you use a financial institution advisor who will subsequently administer your plan, there will likely be just a small upfront charge for their services – something on the order of $500–$1,500 for a very small business. Ongoing fees (monthly or annual) to manage your overall account should run around $200–$1,000 per year. Shop around for a management company geared to small

---

[284] *Simplified Employee Pension Plan (SEP)*, IRS website, http://www.irs.gov/Retirement-Plans/Plan-Sponsor/Simplified-Employee-Pension-Plan-%28SEP%29

[285] *Tax Information for Retirement Plans*, IRS website, http://www.irs.gov/Retirement-Plans

[286] Caron Beesley, *Planning and Managing a Business Retirement Plan – Government eTools That Can Help*, SBA blot – Managing a Business, October 17, 2012, https://www.sba.gov/blogs/planning-and-managing-business-retirement-plan-government-etools-can-help

businesses, as some prefer to work only with large companies (where the dollar amounts in every aspect are larger, resulting in fees to a small business that might be too high).

Make sure you ask about *all of the fees*, and not just the initial setup fees, as the ongoing fees to manage your account can be steep if not negotiated. Ask how each fee is calculated – for example, is the annual management fee based on the total dollar amount invested in the plan, the overall number of employees in your company, or the number of 401(k) participants? (Generally, the latter is preferable, but run the numbers to be sure.) Ask for a written fee schedule – *and make sure it clearly states that the listed fees are the only ones you'll ever be charged*. Otherwise, you might be in for a surprise if the management company charges you for every new employee who joins the plan or existing participants who exit the plan, or charges to prepare tax filing paperwork, or charges to do discrimination tests on your behalf.

Very importantly, ask about all fees the <u>individual</u> participant accounts will be charged, including investment transaction fees, mutual fund buying/selling load fees, 12B-1 fees,[287] and any other administrative or management fee that is specifically charged inside the participant's account. This information is not only important in the management company decision-making process, but this fee schedule should also be clearly documented in the participant packet prepared for your employees.

- **Employer tax deductions.** Before we talk about tax deductions, let's first mention a tax *credit* that might make the setup costs of a 401(k) free to you. If you have fewer than 10 employees, and you're setting up your company's first 401(k) plan, you most likely qualify for a tax credit of up to $500 in each of the first three years that your plan operates. How does it work? You report the total setup fee, plus the annual administration charges for management of your plan, and your tax credit is equal to 50% of that total amount – up to a maximum of $1,500, spread over three years.

  Now for tax deductions. All of your expenses in setting up and managing your company's 401(k) program are tax-deductible as a business expense. It shouldn't surprise you that all employee salary amounts that are designated as employee contributions are also tax-deductible (the same way all employee salary is deductible). All employer matching contributions are also tax-deductible.

- **Employee participation and discrimination tests.** It might not seem that it makes any difference to you (as an employer) if employees don't participate as much as you thought they would when your plan was first set up. It does, though, if your plan has discrimination test requirements to determine if the plan is "top-heavy" towards highly compensated employees (which usually includes you, as the owner).

  By IRS definition, a top-heavy plan is one where, on the last day of a plan year, the total dollar value of all plan accounts <u>for owners and managers</u> is more than 60% of the total

---

[287] "An annual marketing or distribution fee on a mutual fund. The 12b-1 fee is considered an operational expense and, as such, is included in a fund's expense ratio. It is generally between 0.25–1% (the maximum allowed) of a fund's net assets. The fee gets its name from a section in the Investment Company Act of 1940. Source: *12B-1 Fee*, Investopedia, http://www.investopedia.com/terms/1/12b-1fees.asp

dollar value of all plan accounts. If your plan fails the discrimination test (and most plans do fail at first calculation), IRS rules force you to either make a "non-elective" employer contribution to the plan for all non-highly compensated employees (ouch!), to whatever extent it takes to pass the discrimination test,[288 and 289] or the highly-compensated employees in the plan will have some percentage of their employee contributions returned as taxable wages, with the result they'll likely pay more in income taxes. In the most extreme instance, if the employer doesn't fix the discrimination test failure in the IRS-specified timeframe, the plan's qualified status could be taken away, resulting in all money in the plan being returned to the participants – as taxable income.

Whew! That's some heavy medicine, and a pretty powerful incentive for you to make special efforts for maximum participation – not only in the number of employees who participate, but the dollar amount they contribute – *particularly by non-highly compensated employees*.[290] Making sure you do the lengthy and complicated calculations and determinations in the discrimination tests is also important, and is a good reason to have your plan administrator do it for you as part of their paid service.

So what are some good ways to get employees to participate (particularly non-highly compensated employees)? Communicate ... communicate ... communicate – and when you can afford it, establish some level of contribution matching. See the section below about how to effectively communicate to your employees, not only what the plan is all about, but how important it is for each employee to participate.

- **Employer matching contributions.** Hey, I'm already paying more than I can afford in employee wages – how in the world can I possible add employer contributions to a 401(k) plan???

  That's a really good question, and one that only you can provide the answer to, knowing the financial situation of your company. The simple answer is, you can do several things to make it affordable – and in so doing, significantly increase the perceived value of your company's benefit package, and thereby increase employee morale, job satisfaction, and the ability to attract higher quality employees (not to mention, retaining current employees who might be tempted to jump to a competitor).

  To see what it might cost you for a 20% employer-matched contributions assume the following hypothetical situation (and keeping the arithmetic simple):

  - Your company currently has five total employees.

---

[288] *401(k) Plan Fix-It Guide - The plan failed the 401(k) ADP and ACP nondiscrimination tests*, IRS Topics for Retirement Plans, http://www.irs.gov/Retirement-Plans/401k-Plan-Fix-It-Guide-The-Plan-Failed-The-401k-ADP-and-ACP-Nondiscrimination-Tests

[289] *Understanding 401(k) ADP and ACP Testing*, Dyatech Insights newsletter, February 2008, http://www.dyatech.com/pdf/February_2008.pdf

[290] By IRS definition, a highly compensated employee is anyone who owns more than 5% of the company in any given year, or paid more than $120,000 for calendar year 2015 (it typically rises each year), and in a group comprised of the highest-paid 20% of employees of the company. Source: *IRS Announces 2015 Pension Plan Limitations*, IRS website, October 23, 2014, http://www.irs.gov/uac/Newsroom/IRS-Announces-2015-Pension-Plan-Limitations-1

- The maximum contribution amount for 2017 is $18,000.

- You have a traditional 401(k) plan, so therefore, a discrimination test is required (but not factored into this example, as it isn't the point of the example – nevertheless, it's very likely a plan with these numbers would fail the test, and a fix would have to be applied).

- You are employee #1, and being the 100% owner, by definition you are a highly compensated employee (identified as HCE in the example below). You decide you'd like to contribute 10% of your salary to the 401(k) plan, limited to the maximum amount if necessary).

- There is one other highly-compensated employee (a manager, let's say), who decides to contribute 8% of salary.

- There are three non-highly-compensated employees, and because of their lower salary they each can afford a 5% contribution.

- The 20% employer matching contribution is then calculated for each employee, and the total for each employee's account contribution is shown in the right-hand column.

Employee Contribution Percentage	Salary	Employee Contribution	Employer Contribution	Total Contribution
Employee #1 (HCE) - 10%	$50,000	$5,000	$1,000	$6,000
Employee #2 (HCE) - 8%	$35,000	$2,800	$560	$3,360
Employee #3 (non-HCE) - 5%	$20,000	$1,000	$200	$1,200
Employee #4 (non-HCE) - 5%	$18,000	$900	$180	$1,080
Employee #5 (non-HCE) - 5%	$18,000	$900	$180	$1,080
Plan total:	$141,000	$10,600		$12,720
If you provide an employer match of 20% (or $1 for every $5 the employee contributes), it will cost you:		$2,120		

Result: In this example, our annual wage total of all five employees is $141,000. The total matching cost to you is $2,120 – which is less than a 1% increase to your total salary costs. Granted, it's $2,120 that isn't going directly to your company's bottom line (i.e., profitability), but having a 401(k) plan – particularly one where the 20% employer matching contribution benefit can be touted – could be well worth it to bring in top-notch employees (at hiring time, make sure you tout the 20% matching employer contribution, *but don't do the math as shown here* ... let them figure it out, as a 20% employer matching contribution will be seen as a *really* good benefit amount – and frankly, it is).

Also, note that almost half of the total employer match is going right into your own pocket, since you're making the largest employee contribution, and the matching employer contributions apply to your account as well as all other employees.

Be very careful not to decide on a matching contribution formula if you don't fully understand the consequences. For example, if you search the internet on "employer matching contributions for 401(k) plans", it might pull up an article[291] that suggests "a common formula is to match 50% of employee contributions up to the first 6% of salary". At first glance, the numbers sound really good – and it's easy to see that matching 50% rather than 20% would sound so good to your employees. Using our same example as above would change the numbers to:

Employee Contribution Percentage	Salary	Employee Contribution	Employer Contribution	Employee Account
Employee #1 (HCE) - 10%	$50,000	$5,000	$2,500	$7,500
Employee #2 (HCE) - 8%	$35,000	$2,800	$1,400	$4,200
Employee #3 (non-HCE) - 5%	$20,000	$1,000	$500	$1,500
Employee #4 (non-HCE) - 5%	$18,000	$900	$450	$1,350
Employee #5 (non-HCE) - 5%	$18,000	$900	$450	$1,350
Plan total:	$141,000	$10,600		$15,900
If you provide a 50% employer match, up to an employee's contribution of 6% of their salary, it will cost you:			$5,300	

Result: For the very same employees, this matching formula will cost you over 2½ times as much – a whopping $5,300! As before, almost half of it, though, is going into the owner's account, but it's still money that has to be coughed up. (Keep in mind, this example would fail the IRS discrimination test for high-compensated employees, so depending on how it was fixed, it could either raise or lower the higher cost to the employer.)

To afford an employer matching contribution, you could factor in the salary offerings that you make (but again, don't mention this fact), or you could factor it into your product/service pricing structure. The odds are, the increased employee satisfaction will more than pay for this in higher revenue and more employee productivity gains.

Since any amount of employer matching contributions is essentially a form of profit-sharing, you should also make it known right up front that each year's contribution percentage will be based on the previous year's profitability, which can go up one year and down the next (or the match could be dropped completely in some years). Employees will understand that you're going to have differing levels of profitability from year to year, and you might have varying profit numbers that, simply put, need to go into company expansion (or into your own pocket for that matter, or the pockets of your investors if you have any), so don't feel obligated to dole out your hard-earned profitability to employees – unless you actually have the profitability. It's all a balance that you must achieve, with benefits to attract top-flight employees on the one hand, and deciding that the profits need to (or must) go elsewhere.

---

[291] Ashlea Ebeling, *The Big 401(k) Match Mistake*, Forbes/Investing, January 13, 2102, http://www.forbes.com/sites/ashleaebeling/2012/01/13/the-big-401k-match-mistake/. And note, this article is referring to matching contribution mistakes *by the employee*, not the employer!

- **Employee loans from their 401(k) account.** Assuming your company's 401(k) plan documents allow it, employee participant loans are allowed by IRS rules, with very specific and strict guidelines (participant loans are not allowed with SEP and Simple 401(k)s and IRAs).

  If you want your company's 401(k) plan to allow loans, you must write that into the plan document (yes, you must have a plan document created for your specific plan), including procedures for how a participant can apply for the loan, maximum loan amounts that will be allowed, and repayment requirements. And obviously, this is one more accounting/HR bit of work that adds to your overhead costs of the plan.

  According to the IRS, "Repayment of the loan must occur within 5 years, and payments must be made in substantially equal payments that include principal and interest and that are paid at least quarterly". The maximum that can be borrowed from any participant's 401(k) account is 50% of the *participant's* account balance, up to a maximum of $50,000.

  If employment is terminated, it's likely the employee will have to repay the entire loan balance within 60 days of termination, and if that isn't possible, the IRS will categorize the loan as a distribution, applying the 10% early withdrawal tax penalty. (This is a big gotcha for employees, but for you it actually helps create a golden handcuff that will keep the employee with you, so make sure you advise the employee on this when they talk with you about taking out a plan loan.)

  Many financial advisors believe that borrowing from a 401(k) account is the worst possible thing an employee can do – after all, borrowing from retirement assets (if the participant cannot repay the loan) puts the retirement nest egg in jeopardy. So, while you might think you're doing your employees a favor in providing for plan loans, think long and hard about this supposed benefit before writing it into the plan documents. Your employees will probably really like the ability to take loans ... until, that is, a disaster hits one of the participants – and the last thing you want is a participant accusing you of violating fiduciary responsibility if it's believed you (as plan sponsor) crossed some line of prudence in accepting the participant's loan application.

- **Distributions upon retirement and employee terminations.** When an employee terminates or retires, your plan documents must spell out what happens to the participant's (employee's) plan account. This issue is too complex for this book, and *you'll want the advice of your company's benefit plan advisor at the time you're first setting up the plan* (so that you'll know what to expect). Basically, though, the options include leaving the participant's money in the plan, cashing the employee's account out, rolling the participant's account to an IRA, purchasing an annuity, or taking installment distributions.[292]

- **Fiduciary responsibility.** When setting up a 401(k) plan, the high-falutin words, *fiduciary responsibility*, bestow a legal responsibility to you towards the plan itself, as well as to the participants in the plan, making you the adult in the room concerning trust and respect for

---

[292] *Distribution options, Smart401(k)*, http://www.smart401k.com/Content/retail/resource-center/strategy/distribution-options

the participants in the plan. Specifically, with respect to the 401(k) plan, the IRS expects you to:[293]

- act solely in the interest of the participants and their beneficiaries (don't forget, you're also a participant, so you're acting on your behalf in that respect also);

- act for the exclusive purpose of providing benefits to workers participating in the plan and their beneficiaries, and defraying reasonable expenses of the plan;

- carry out duties with the care, skill, prudence, and diligence of a prudent person familiar with the matters;

- follow the plan documents; and

- diversify plan investments.

This all seems like pretty vague stuff, but in fact, it can be a blessing or a curse, depending on the situation. So, if you pull some stunt with your plan that is obviously over the line and warrants action against you (such as stealing from the plan, flouting IRS rules, not correcting plan mistakes when the IRS says you must), you could be up against a judgment that you failed your fiduciary responsibility.

Along the way (and as clearly spelled out by the IRS), there are ways you can limit your liability. First of all, document all of your decisions about how the plan is to be run, the processes behind which you operate the plan – and most important of all, don't get yourself involved in investment decisions concerning participant accounts (and keep this documentation in the plan files). Set your plan up so that the participants have the lion's share of investment decisions within their own accounts, even though this allows the risk-taking decisions to be given to people who might understand the consequences of their decisions (but after all, once the money is in their account, it's their decision to make). Most of all, lay out your rationale for all decisions you make concerning the plan. Lastly, consider hiring a plan advisor who will handle most of the functions that take on fiduciary responsibility, and take out a fidelity bond to cover fraud and dishonesty by any of your employees who are handling plan funds.

- **Communicating the plan to your employees.** As the founder/owner of the company, one of the hats you absolutely must wear is that of Chief Communicator, or Chief Morale Officer, or Chief Company Booster, or whatever you want to think of the job as – and this is particularly important with respect to your company's 401(k) plan. You need to be comfortable with the idea of communicating – either in writing or verbally – with your employees on a regular basis, starting with the day you establish the plan, and continuing through the coming months and years. My recommendation is to communicate both ways, but particularly with written memos, in-house newsletter articles, on the intranet side of your company's website, and as part of each new-employee's new-hire packet – allowing them to read it at their leisure.

---

[293] *Retirement Plan Fiduciary Responsibilities*, IRS website, http://www.irs.gov/Retirement-Plans/Retirement-Plan-Fiduciary-Responsibilities

Encourage everyone to participate, and suggest they participate financially to the maximum contribution amount. You might be surprised to see that higher wage earners participate far more than lower wage earners – but then the reality hits you of which type of employee can best afford to participate. It's an unfortunate fact of life, but it's typically the ones who will need retirement income the most are the ones who can least afford to stash money away today for their retirement. This creates a good argument for establishing an employer matching contribution, which will hopefully entice low wage earners to participate.

You certainly don't want to present the problem as "*all of you non-participating, non-highly compensated employees are really messing up the discrimination tests for us highly-compensated people who want to stash away as much money as we can in the 401(k) plan*". No, instead you need to be a bit of a parental financial coach, frequently putting good words around several common reasons why people don't participate in 401(k) plans:

- Not aware of what it will take at a given stage of working life to achieve a comfortable retirement (and therefore, "we'll work on it later")
- Not aware of the plan's existence, or if they are, haven't a clue what a 401(k) is
- Weren't coached on the plan's availability and benefits at initial time of employment, or when the first available enrollment period came around
- Too busy paying for *now* things, such as a new house, new car, having a family, or taking splashy vacations
- Everyday expenses are such that it's just not possible to be funding a retirement plan
- Aren't aware that participant's assets in the plan can be tapped (as a loan) for buying a home, paying for college expenses, or in an emergency
- Not aware of employer matching contributions – even if it's only a dime or a quarter on a dollar
- Intimidated by how a 401(k) plan works, and feel they don't know enough about financial planning to make wise investment decisions
- Already contributing to an IRA account that was rolled over from a previous employer (and therefore, don't know how much better a 401(k) plan is)
- And importantly, do a browser search on "*how to communicate the importance of 401(k) contributions*" and you'll come up with a dozen hits that provide even more ideas.

If you commit to communicating about all of the above points, you could easily write a monthly or quarterly companywide newsletter blurb on each of the topics mentioned above (plus several more), keeping each of the topics in the forefront of employee's thinking.

The more open and upfront you are about your 401(k) plan to your employees, the more they will appreciate this valuable benefit your company is providing – a benefit that's far greater than from individual participation in any type of IRA.

Have a 401(k) packet available for each employee – and make it part of their new-hire information. Much of the packet can be professionally-prepared literature from the plan advisor company, but make sure you preface it with your own written statement – a statement clearly explaining the value of this benefit that you've elected to provide. By all means, don't make promises you can't keep, <u>don't offer *any* investment advice</u>, and stay away from any mention of expected investment returns. But you can certainly say that your 401(k) plan is each employee's best option for having a comfortable and secure retirement. ***Do not* make any promises about future employer matching contributions, even if you plan to possibly add this at some time.** Leave that to the future, after you have a better idea how much each employee's participation would cost if you decide to match contributions.

Stock options, restricted stock, and phantom stock

Stock ownership in your company is possible only if it a corporation – either C-Corp or S-Corp – and cannot be done in any other type of business entity (and that's one of the important reasons why phantom stock is discussed here – it isn't restricted to corporations). This is an area, though, you don't want to do anything about until you have serious and significant discussions with your legal counsel and tax advisor ... and your business development advisor if you have one. Simply put, stock options, and stock grants (and from a financial standpoint, phantom stock) are situations where you are giving away part of your company, and it isn't something you should do lightly. Under a wide range of circumstances, though, these benefits can also be highly valuable. *Tread carefully.*

Here is some basic information about stock options and restricted stock, including some differences, some pros and cons, and a little bit about how they are set up:

What are stock options? In our context here, a stock option is a right, granted by you (the company owner) to an employee, giving that employee the right (but not the obligation) to purchase one or more shares of your corporation (known as *exercising* the option) at a specified price (called the *grant* or *strike* price), within a certain period or on a specific date.[294]

Stock options are generally granted to top management and key employees, either as an incentive for performance, or as a golden handcuff to keep these important employees in your employ. However, you can make stock option grants as broadly-based across the company as you wish, provided you follow your *plan* rules.

Yes, you need a stock option plan in place for your corporation before you can grant stock options. There are many complexities in how a plan is administered, and to keep you on the right side of corporate oversight regulations, you are required to have a stock option plan. It will need to be drawn up by an attorney who is well-versed on the topic, and you need to have someone in your company who is competent to administer it (such as your internal bookkeeper or accountant). There are two types of plans, called Qualified and Non-Qualified.[295] For reasons too complicated for discussion here, Non-Qualified plans are more common, mainly because of fewer restrictions and differences in tax rules. In any case, if you go this route, don't cheap out

---

[294] *Stock Option*, Investopedia, http://www.investopedia.com/terms/s/stockoption.asp. There's also a good overall discussion about stock options at the Investopedia page, http://www.investopedia.com/university/employee-stock-options-eso/eso1.asp
[295] *Qualified versus Non-Qualified Stock Option Plans*, Diffen.com, http://www.diffen.com/difference/Qualified_vs_Non-qualified_Stock_Options

on analysis of the option plan – read as much as you can about it before you make any decisions, and be sure you obtain good legal/tax advice, as partial ownership of your company is at stake here (and once it's in someone else's hands, it's hard to get back).

Stock options are often a way to create higher value compensation for your employees, when, at the same time, you need to hang onto every penny of cash possible to meet the growing needs of your company. How well this works depends on how good your sales and communication skills are about your company's future, and whether the employees feel that forgoing some amount of current salary is worth it for the potential upside of the stock options. (For quite a few years, many early Microsoft employees (before its IPO in 1986) felt their stock options wouldn't even buy a Starbucks latte; at the IPO, these stock options created something like 1,500 millionaires in one single day – but that was an extraordinary event.) Put another way, creating a stock option plan hopefully gives the employees a tangible stake in increasing the value of your company, and at some point, they *might* (emphasis on might) benefit from that increased value.

Each stock option grant will identify a strike price – typically a discounted price that each option share will cost at exercise time (maybe not so much of a discount now, but hopefully it will be at exercise time). The challenge with setting the strike price is that your company is closely held (meaning that you, and maybe a few others, are the only shareholder(s), and valuing this type of company is very difficult without going through the major expense of obtaining a professional valuation (which is probably cost-prohibitive for something like setting up a stock option plan, not to mention each time you later decide to issue further stock options).

Another important aspect of stock options is the vesting period. Since you're trying to achieve some type of behavioral result with your stock options – such as retaining valuable employees – this is most easily done by assigning a vesting schedule to your options. Establishing this schedule (and you almost certainly want one) is strictly at your discretion, and usually defines a time period that must elapse before the employee can exercise the option, or the schedule may state that a performance goal must be met before the option can be exercised.

Since your corporation is closely held, there isn't a *market* for the employee to either exercise his or her stock options or to sell stock options, so the options remain as just that – an option to purchase the shares when/if an event such as an IPO or merger/acquisition occurs (remember, this book is not about a company that has skyrocketed to an IPO, so it's still small – most likely at the start-up phase – and you are the primary shareholder). Essentially, this restriction creates the golden handcuff, keeping the employee *locked into* your company until the vesting requirement is met – and even beyond that, to the *event* timeframe. This is why it's extremely important for you to carefully craft the vesting schedule <u>with each instance</u> of granting stock options.

An important part of the stock option plan document, as well as the individual options agreement that accompanies each option grant, is clearly defined exercising rights if the employee terminates employment. Since your primary purpose in creating a stock option plan is to keep valuable employees from departing, the last thing you want is for them to terminate, walking away with shares in your company that they've exercised. Once the vesting period is met, any employee who has been granted options can exercise some or all of them simply by ponying up the number of dollars equal to the strike price multiplied by the number of shares they want to exercise. Throughout the time your company is closely held and private, most likely employees won't exercise their options, as they would almost certainly still be tiny minority shareholders, which wouldn't give them any real power over day-to-day company decisions. Also, exercising the options requires a cash outlay, and financially it's likely more valuable to keep the options until an event occurs that makes exercising a good thing (and it might be an event where a cashless transaction is possible, so there wouldn't be any money out of pocket).

For vested stock options that have been exercised (i.e., the employee now actually owns stock in your company), you can also create a restriction agreement forcing the employee to sell their stock back to you if they leave the company. This helps you control the stock, keeping it from falling into the hands of someone you don't want to own it (i.e., which could otherwise happen if an ex-employee goes to work for a competitor but still holds stock in your company). (Note, this restriction is irrelevant for granted, but not exercised options, as they automatically disappear when an employee terminates.)

Big caution! Before the preceding paragraphs convince you that stock options are the way to go, your tax advisor will (or should) explain that IRS rules introduced in 2006 require the company to *expense* (in the accounting sense) the value of your stock options at the time they are granted (this charge was the result of option valuation abuses leading up to bursting of the dot-com bubble in 1999). Let's suffice it to say that the challenges created in this new expensing requirement should convince you to put any thought on hold about creating a stock option plan very soon after starting up your business. You'd be far better off spending the large amount of money and effort in building your company first, and letting stock options percolate to the top at a much later stage. Therefore, we'll hold off further discussion of this topic – but if you want to study it a bit further now, there's a good write-up of it in Investopedia's article on Options Basics.[296]

How do stock options really work, and how do I understand them? Let's look at a hypothetical picture of the possible upside of stock options (and this is all made-up numbers). Let's say you are Bill Gates (Microsoft co-founder), and the year is 1980 – a handful of years after Microsoft launched, and six years before its IPO. It's the go-go years of Microsoft's early growth, and the window of opportunity is at that time, the potential for high growth is good, but cash on hand is tight for fueling that growth. To meet your commitment to build a new operating system for IBM's yet-to-be-announced PC, you need to hire a large team of software engineers. But the current wage for this skill set is beyond your means, because it's taking every penny you have to build the other aspects of your company infrastructure. At the same time, you need these software engineers to work 14, 16, 18 hour days to meet your aggressive schedule.[297]

You (Bill Gates) are the consummate salesman, your salary offer is 20% below the going wage, so you sweeten the offer with a signing bonus of 10,000 stock options. Over the coming years, every member of this team works like hell, and every year each member receives an additional 15,000 stock options. By the time of the IPO, each software engineer has amassed 100,000 stock options, at an average strike price of $25. On that day, half of the software team is worn out, they've had several good years of their life sucked out of them, and they decide to cash in the

---

[296] Rick Wayman, *The Controversy Over Option Expensing*, Investopedia, http://www.investopedia.com/articles/analyst/092502.asp

[297] Remember, the numbers and facts here are purely hypothetical, and Bill might dispute every single one of them in the example. It's just for illustration's sake.

100,000 stock options they've amassed and live the easy life from this point on. The other half are getting a second wind, and want to ride this as far as they can. Let's see how the two halves fare.

Here's the arithmetic for the first half: Let's say Microsoft's share value on IPO day is $50 – and remember, your average strike price was $25. We'll discuss this as a "cashless" exercise, as in fact, we can make the mechanics of it work this way in the real world. You (the employee with the stock options) have an overall exercise price of $2,500,000 (100,000 options * $25 strike price = $2,500,000). The total IPO value of your options is $5,000,000 (100,000 options * $50 IPO share price = $5,000,000). In this cashless deal, your overall strike price would be subtracted out, and you'd pocket a cool $2,500,000 (the difference between your overall strike price and the overall IPO price of your 100,000 shares). Not bad, considering that you gave up 20% of your otherwise-expected salary – let's say it "cost" you $10,000/year in lost salary for six years, or $60,000 ... and you got back $2.5M in exchange for it. Nope, not bad at all, and that's a hypothetical example how 1,500 real-life millionaires were created from the Microsoft IPO in 1986.

But wait, don't forget that a bunch of hold-off software engineers stayed with the company beyond the IPO, hoping to see even better glory days a further few years down the road. For comparison purposes, let's ignore any additional stock options this group might have gained in those years, and just look at how things would be for them with regard to the original 1980–1986 stock options. By the end of 1992 (six years after IPO), some from that second half decide to throw in the towel, sell their original 100,000 shares, and retire to the easy life. By this time, Microsoft's NASDAQ share price had been ever-increasing – so much so that it had gone through two 2:1 stock splits, and two 3:2 stock splits. Just from the stock splits, the 100,000 original shares have now become equal to 675,000 shares, and the adjusted share price is now around $85/share. If we do the same math as before, but with these new numbers, the employee would walk away with a whopping $55 million. (And don't forget, in this calculation we ignored the additional stock options the employee might have earned in the subsequent six-year period, which could easily double, triple this number.)

I'd say both employee stock option groups got what they wanted. Some who cashed out early used their money to start their own companies, which may have netted them as much (or more) than the eventual payout to the engineers who stuck with the company.

Talk about *upside* for a bunch of employees! And in both situations, these stock options cost Bill Gates $0 out of pocket for issuing them – well, that's not entirely true, as it reduced his eventual value in the company by that amount, but when he's sitting on $55 billion from his own share valuation, what's a few million between friends? The benefit for Bill Gates? He got that team of software engineers at a cost he could afford, and he created the advanced operating system software that propelled Microsoft to what it is today.

What is Restricted Stock? This relatively new version of stock-based incentives has gained significant popularity over stock option plans in many companies. Restricted stock can be either actual company stock that is granted (not a stock option, but an actual grant of stock), or compensation that is valued-based on your company's stock value. In both cases, it isn't immediately given to the employee, but instead, the employee receives it according to a vesting and/or distribution plan. Upon completing the performance goals established with the grant, or when the employee reaches a specified period of time (known as the vesting period) with the company, the stock or compensation is then given to the employee.

Since the mid-2000s, Restricted Stock (and its cousin, Restricted Stock Units, known as RSUs) have become more popular than stock options due to accounting rule changes in how corporations are required to treat stock options for tax purposes. Stock options are required to be expensed by the company at time of issuance (which is an immediate hit to your Balance Sheet, whereas restricted stock is expensed when the vesting requirements are met, and is taxed to the individual in the tax year that vesting occurs.

Generally, restricted stock does not have the potential upside for the grantee that stock options have. At the same time, though, an employee with restricted stock fares better than with stock options if the company's value goes down between the time of the grant and the end of the vesting period. Both restricted stock and stock options can create multi-millionaires, but for a wildly successful company like Microsoft in those days, the value of *multi* would be very different.

Big caution. The rules governing most aspects of restricted stock, particularly income tax treatment, require fairly accurate knowledge of the company's *fair market value* (i.e., the share price value), not only at the time the restricted stock is granted, but also at the time it vests. As we earlier saw with stock options, during your early start-up days (and all the way through to some milestone event, such as an IPO or a merger/acquisition), fair market value is not only very difficult to ascertain in a closely-held company, but it can be costly to obtain every time a restricted stock event occurs (and the valuation won't necessarily be very accurate). For that reason, restricted stock can be difficult and expensive to administer, not only for the company, but for the employee who is receiving it.

As I said earlier for stock options, this challenge and expense should convince you to put thoughts on hold about issuing restricted stock any time soon after opening your business doors as a start-up. You'd be far better off spending the large amount of money and effort in building your company first, and letting restricted stock grants begin to factor into your employee compensation plan at a much later stage. Therefore, we'll hold off further discussion of this topic – but if you want to study it a bit further now, there's a good write-up of it in Investopedia's article on Options and Futures.[298]

Is Phantom Stock the way to go? The use of phantom stock avoids many of the complicated legal and tax issues of stock options and restricted stock. It also removes the risk a start-up company owner faces with having additional shareholders.

A phantom stock grant is simply a contract between you (the company owner) and an employee to pay a bonus amount (in dollars), at some point in the future (vesting time), based on the value those phantom stock shares would be worth at that time. Granted, this still requires a share valuation when determining the phantom stock value, but this can be done through a mechanism written into the grant that doesn't require an expensive outside appraiser to value the company.

---

[298] Mark P. Cussen, *How Restricted Stock and RSUs Are Taxed*, Investopedia, http://www.investopedia.com/articles/tax/09/restricted-stock-tax.asp?performancelayout=true

This works particularly well if the vesting time is simply a number of years in the future, where there isn't a specific event (such as an acquisition) that creates an actual valuation. If the vesting does specify an acquisition or IPO event, then it will be easy to divide the company's total real shares into the acquisition value to determine the share price value – and from that the value of the phantom stock grant can be easily calculated.

The benefit of phantom stock is when it's tied to verifiable company performance goals, giving the employee "a way to share a stake in the business while avoiding the need to invest cash or suffer taxable income",[299] which is a significant drawback to stock options or restricted stock grants.

Better than a cash bonus for performance up to now, a phantom stock grant rewards the employee for increasing the value of the company in the future. This provides the golden handcuffs that help ensure the employee will remain with your company until vested. (Although, if another company wants your employee badly enough, they could buy him/her out of it by offering a signing bonus that's greater than your phantom stock grant is worth – but that's always your challenge in determining how to maintain total employee compensation that entices them to stay with you.)

The tax consequences of a phantom stock plan work just like a cash bonus – it remains non-taxable until the cash payout is made, so the cash is taxable to the employee as ordinary income, and the company gets the standard salary deduction at the time it is actually paid out.

Big caution. While a phantom stock plan doesn't require your company to have a formal written plan to use the concept, you still need to be careful in how you structure it. If you intend the phantom stock plan to benefit most or all of your employees across the company (as a way of profit-sharing, for example), you may find yourself in trouble, as the U.S. Department of Labor (who oversees company retirement plans) might decide that your informal phantom stock plan is really a "de facto ERISA plan"[300] – the Employee Retirement Income Security Act of 1974. If you structure your phantom stock plan to benefit a limited number of employees (such as critical executives or high-level managers), you most likely avoid these issues.

And just like stock options and stock grants, don't even think about creating a phantom stock plan until you have decided how much of your company to give to others, whether paid in actual stock or as compensation. While phantom stock doesn't really give true ownership rights, it does create a monetary promise that commits you in the future to paying out profits. Know your goal in how much you hope to achieve in your company's growth, or in achieving your exit strategy, and plan so that the amount you have to distribute when reaching that goal doesn't diminish it.

My example. I had an S-Corp, with about 50 total employees at the time. I had reached the point where I began to think seriously about my exit strategy. But, in researching it (my plan was an acquisition by a larger company), I realized my company wasn't yet large enough (in terms of annual revenue and profitability) to attract a serious buyer, requiring some rapid growth to get

---

[299] David King, *Why Phantom Stock Can Be Better Than Real Stock*, Forbes online, October 15, 2013, http://www.forbes.com/sites/dking/2013/10/15/why-phantom-stock-can-be-better-than-real-stock/
[300] *Phantom Stock and Stock Appreciation Rights (SARs)*, NCEO – The National Center For Employee Ownership, https://www.nceo.org/articles/phantom-stock-appreciation-rights-sars

there. I knew my company was never headed for an IPO (too small of a growth rate, too little industry buzz for the niche I was in), but I figured it could command a good price in a merger or acquisition.

To accomplish the necessary growth, I'd have to hang onto every possible penny in order to launch such a growth strategy. And I felt one of the best ways to do this would be to create a Non-Qualified Stock Option Plan to hold down the highly-compensated salary growth. It was also not long after the Microsoft IPO that was so lucrative for employees, and I hoped this success would rub off on my situation.

Given the amount of time and legal effort that went into creating it, I'm sure the plan cost several thousand dollars to set up (most likely in the neighborhood of $10–15K at a minimum). And this doesn't begin to account for the hours and hours of my time spent on it – time that could have been spent, very possibly more profitably, on solving challenges that would actually grow the business. But lots of business literature was hyping how companies were squeezing huge productivity gains from employees (while paying substandard salaries) with stock option plans.

I needed to ramp up my growth rate (annual revenue) to 35% *year over year*, and create a situation where that was sustainable. This would require more software products, and bigger feature sets on existing software products. And to sell all of that I needed a substantially larger sales and marketing capability. All of which costs money – and I needed somewhere to get it.

Our outside attorney drafted the plan documents, including a raft of restrictions that ensured any exercised options granted through the plan would remain in the hands of current employees (or be sold back to the company upon termination). We had an all-hands-on-deck company meeting to announce the new plan, and granted our first-ever variable amounts of stock to every employee, with the intention of making the granting options every year. It was clearly outlined, not only in the plan documents, but in everything we said to the employees, that it was a discretionary plan, based on each individual's performance and their overall value to the company.

What we didn't anticipate was the lack of employee understanding of the overall concept of stock options (even though it was explained multiple times), not to mention a grasp of how corporate shareholding itself worked. For example, three or four years into the plan, we needed to increase the total number of outstanding corporate shares – going from a current 1 million shares to 10 million shares of overall corporate stock. At the same time, the intent was to *not* dilute anyone's current number of option shares – so rather than just issuing 9 million more shares (which *would* have seriously diluted everyone's options), we did a 1:10 *reverse stock split* (a one-for-ten exchange, in simple parlance, essentially *multiplying* everyone's option share numbers by 10, including my own. The effect would be to increase the total number of shares to 10 million – and thereby kept everyone in the exact same *percentage* of total company ownership if they exercised their options. Well, at an explanatory meeting one senior manager strenuously objected, saying that this was all a scam – snake oil on my part – to *dilute* everyone's option shares to 1/10th of what they previously were – *which was the exact opposite of what we were doing*. Nothing I said would change his mind.

(If this sounds like snake oil to you too, consider this (using numbers that are easy to calculate):

- Assume a company has a total of 1,000 shares and the share value is somehow determined (or guessed) to be $100/share

- The company would be valued at $100,000   ($100 x 1,000 = $100,000)

- If we increase the total number of shares through a 1:10 reverse stock split, there would now be 10,000 shares, but because the company itself hasn't changed in value, the share price would be divided by 10, making each share now worth $10. The company would still be valued at $100,000   ($10 x 10,000 = $100,000)

- If an employee had 10 shares before the split, the value at $100/share would be worth $1,000.   ($100 x 10 = $1,000)

- With the split, their number of shares would increase to 100, and with the new share price of $10, the total of their shares would still be valued at $1,000.

                ($10 x 100 = $1,000)

So _after_ the split is the same as before the split. The trouble is, most (maybe many) people in your stock option plan will not have been through the exercise before.

The bigger problem with our stock option plan, though, was _apathy_ by many of the employees about the value these stock options actually added to their lives. Seeing this happen was a total shock to me. Surprisingly, the apathy was most apparent among our highly-paid software developers, where I hoped to keep salaries about 15–20% lower than the industry standard, yet still entice them into thinking of half-days as 12 hours, in order to achieve a much greater company growth (i.e., value to them). Because the company itself was looked upon as a bit of a plodder in the software world – meaning that a mainframe company lacked the pizazz of the dot-com companies that were exploding at the time – it just didn't seem like anything of consequence would ever happen to our company – and therefore, the stock options were treated by several as pretty much worthless.

Besides, many of the developers were older than me – in fact, many were near normal retirement age, and they figured their working life would be over before I'd sell the company or have any other kind of event that might pay off for them. Nosiree – even after I passed out stock options, they still wanted absolute top dollar salaries, and if I didn't pay it, they'd find work elsewhere (or wouldn't join our company in the first place).

In the end, the stock option plan didn't do what it was supposed to do –maintain more retained earnings within the company, allowing us to expand and grow. I still gave out stock options, but over time only about 10% of the share option numbers I had planned when I set up the stock option plan. As a result, the company didn't grow as much as I'd hoped, and the employees didn't get the touted payout that I'd originally forecast. We both lost on this deal – which gets back to the point, the most important aspect of getting a stock option plan to work well is to communicate – over, and over … and over again.

Chapter 8   Corporate Mission Statement, Culture, Ethics

"If every day at work feels like a Friday, then you are doing what you were meant to do."

Alan W. Kennedy, The Alpha Strategies, Understanding Strategy, Risk, and Values in Any Organization

Mission Statement (a.k.a. About Us)

Your company's Mission Statement can be likened to a company founder's 1-minute elevator speech, and should be readable in about that amount of time (or a bit more if you prefer) – signaling to your customers, employees, business partners, and suppliers what your business is all about – your business goals, objectives, and philosophies. It describes your products and services, and the marketplace you're in. It should also capture the mood and spirit that you want your company to convey. In writing your Mission Statement, don't be boxed into the stodgy format and layout that legacy companies have used for decades – with bulleted lists of one-line platitudes that quickly put the reader to sleep – or worse, stilted words that are copied from someone else's Mission Statement.

These days, the sky is the limit, where the most-read version of the Mission Statement is on the company's website, headlined with a couple-paragraph Company Overview, and followed by a bit longer statement (maybe a couple of paragraphs) of what this means to the customer, the suppliers, and the employees. For many new start-ups, it's written in a chatty tone, maybe spunky and with lots of pizzazz, but certainly positive and forward-looking about where your company is going and how it's going to get there. Often, it's not even identified as a Mission Statement, but simply is the *About Us* page on your website. And even better, the words are frequently accented by photos and graphics that help to tell the story.

A Mission Statement is actually difficult to write – precisely because it needs to be brief and to the point – and must say so many things in so few words. For many writers, it's easier to explain things with lots of words, and multiple paragraphs. But boiling it down to something that can be read in 30 seconds can bring on writer's panic. Today's world, though, is a lot less static than it was just a few short years ago – when the Mission Statement was often etched into a large acrylic Plexiglass plaque mounted and displayed on your company's wall just inside the entrance door.

In today's electronic form, the words and images can be changed as you improve on it, and no one's the wiser if today's version is better and more effective than last year's.

Some suggest keeping your Mission Statement short and sweet, including this advice from Richard Branson, founder of Virgin Group, which is made up of over 400 companies:

"Brevity is certainly key, so try using Twitter's 140-character template when you're drafting your inspirational message. You need to explain your company's purpose and outline expectations for internal and external clients alike. Make it unique to your company, make it memorable, keep it real and, just for fun, imagine it on the bottom of a coat of arms."

Writing your company's Mission Statement. It's often better to start with a company-wide brainstorming session, where you ask everyone to write their version of what they think the company's statement of mission should be. This gets the juices flowing from multiple directions, bringing out many more perceptions of what the company is all about – in other words, how others think it should be perceived, not only from the outside, but from the inside as well.

However you go about the task of writing your Mission Statement, here are the four fundamental elements that it needs to address:[301]

- What do we do?
- How do we do it?
- Whom do we do it for?
- What value are we bringing?

Example #1. See if you agree that the following Mission Statement answers these questions (and be sure to go to the About Us page on the company's website to see the powerful graphics that go with it, at https://www.adafruit.com/about):

Adafruit was founded in 2005 by MIT engineer, Limor "Ladyada" Fried. Her goal was to create the best place online for learning electronics and making the best designed products for makers of all ages and skill levels. Adafruit has grown to over 50 employees in the heart of NYC with a 15,000+ sq ft. factory. Adafruit has expanded offerings to include tools, equipment and electronics that Limor personally selects, tests and approves before going into the Adafruit store. Limor was the first female engineer on the cover of WIRED magazine and was recently awarded Entrepreneur magazine's Entrepreneur of the year. Ladyada is on the NYC Industrial Business Advisory Council. In 2014 Adafruit was ranked #11 in the top 20 USA manufacturing companies and #1 in New York City by Inc. 5000 "fastest growing private companies". Adafruit is a 100% woman owned company."

Example #2. Here's another example to whet your appetite (pun intended), not only for some good transplanted Hawaiian street food, but for a great Our Story write-up on the website for Seattle's Marination – a food truck start-up that now includes a couple of brick-and-mortar restaurants serving Hawaiian-type food. It's too long to print here, so you'll just have to go to their website, at http://marinationmobile.com/our-story/.

---

[301] Patrick Hull, *Answer 4 Questions to Get a Great Mission Statement*, Forbes online, Jan 10, 2013, http://www.forbes.com/sites/patrickhull/2013/01/10/answer-4-questions-to-get-a-great-mission-statement/

Example #3. And nothing says you can't slip a video into your website Mission Statement, as the husband/wife founders of MOD Pizza have done. If all goes right for them, their made-on-demand (MOD) pizza idea just might take the world by storm – and their text/video "We Are Mod" story definitely answers the above questions. You can see it and read it at http://modpizza.com/we-are-mod/.

All three of these examples capture the spirit and vibes of their founders/owners, whether you're a customer or employee.

Whatever you do, don't create a copycat Mission Statement from a stodgy old legacy company, with nothing but a bulleted list of tired old clichés, bad grammar, or vague and hokey claims to be superior, have excellence in everything you do, ... whatever. For example, Dell Computer makes me want to turn the page with statements like, "Commit to substance; Grow with clarity, "Delivering results that make a positive difference", "Leading with openness and optimism", "Winning with integrity", and finally, "Support positive growth; Watch the world thrive". (Interestingly, they haven't gotten this right through several iterations at Dell – if you do a browser search on "bad corporate mission statements", Dell comes up in the hits quite often, and over the years descriptions of their mission/value statements have gone from "none to be found" to "super-boring", to "say nothing".)

And then there's McDonalds, an iconic company, and one of the most recognizable brands in the world. But compare their Mission Statement (taken directly from their website) to any of the examples above:

> *McDonald's brand mission is to be our customers' favorite place and way to eat. Our worldwide operations are aligned around a global strategy called the Plan to Win, which center on an exceptional customer experience – People, Products, Place, Price and Promotion. We are committed to continuously improving our operations and enhancing our customers' experience.*

Yup, McDonald's official Mission Statement is a real inspirational zinger, packing customers in the door and attracting employees from all over ... not! Definitely written by a committee, and never tested among employees or in the marketplace to see if it conveyed the image the company should be projecting. A global strategy called the "Plan to Win" ... come on. But, having said that, take a look at McDonald's "Our Company" page at http://www.aboutmcdonalds.com/mcd/our_company/our-ambition.html, and yes, they got it right in this iteration. This is really what a company's Mission Statement should be all about.

"You have to be a place that's more than a paycheck for people."
Rick Federico, CEO, P.F. Chang's

Growing your corporate culture

If you specifically set out to create a corporate culture in your new start-up, a culture might not be created at all, or the culture won't develop into what you were looking for. For many start-up business owners, just trying to objectively describe *what* you want your corporate culture to be is a challenge – you'll know it when you see it, but describing how some other company got there, or identifying how you're going to get there and what you want to be isn't so easy.

The culture that's instilled in your company could come from the top (but not always). In some companies, culture develops from a particular mix of people that you employ and the sum of all the paths they've taken to get where they are. Whatever it is, it shouldn't be accidental, and it should have a positive effect on how you win over customers, how well you develop and produce your products, and how much your employees enjoy coming to work. Oftentimes, though, it *is* somewhat accidental (and not always for the best), and it results over time from the "cumulative traits of the people the company hires".[302]

The large, established brand name companies that really do it well have been at it a long time – think Apple, Southwest Airlines, Four Seasons Hotels, Nordstrom, REI – and while you can study them for examples of their corporate culture, what works for another company might not be right for you, and it very well may be unattainable for you. At Apple, the Steve Jobs mania for getting the last design detail of each product exactly right was paramount. At Southwest Airlines, the personality of founder Herb Kelleher came through in the zany antics and fun-in-the-sky atmosphere that he created. For Four Seasons Hotels and Nordstrom, it's developing each employee's passion for impeccable customer service. And at REI, the mantra is to have employees with a "deep passion for the outdoors and to help others explore it".

Some culture coaches advocate getting your first start-up product right, and then use that to help identify the basic attributes of the culture you'll develop. Others suggest waiting until you hire your first employee team, and then collectively brainstorm. Another suggests that you actually designate someone on your management team to oversee how the culture is rolled out, and ensure that it's taken seriously. If you have to hire a consultant to help, you'll probably never get the culture that *works for you, and the employees that you hire*.

If you haven't already, by the time your company grows and you're starting to hire more people, you'll definitely want to have serious ideas in your head about several culture aspects that you want your company to have – and then factor those into your hiring decisions. If you want your corporate culture to be a significant part of your start-up's everyday life, you'll really want high buy-in towards your company, and compatibility with everyone that you hire. At the beginning, you (as business owner) are likely personally handling all new employment recruiting, but when you advance to the point that managers who work for you are doing much of the hiring, you'll need to ensure they too have this level of focus.

Example: in my own company, my highly-trusted office manager had a really good head about almost all aspects of our business, but for several years when she hired office staff she gravitated towards the *lost cat* type of person (sometimes hiring because they needed a job, not because they had the skill set we really needed). This resulted in some pretty dreadful front-office people that all other employees greeted first thing on coming to work, and who were the first impression when customers called in for support. It took considerable effort to change that hiring perspective, even though she knew in her head the type of person that really fit our culture best – and who had the skill set most important for us.

---

[302] *Definition of Corporate Culture*, Investopedia, http://www.investopedia.com/terms/c/corporate-culture.asp

What benefits are there for a good corporate culture?[303]

- Helps in recruiting new employees. Unless your company is hidden behind a brick wall, the word will get out about how good your company is to work for. Business magazines and local newspaper articles frequently list the "Top 25 Places to Work", and if your employees feel your start-up should be one of them, they'll suggest and vote yours onto the list. Being able to point to that in job interviews not only brings better talent to your doorstep, but it very well may also require you to pay less than top dollar to attract them.

- Helps identify which potential employees will fit during the recruiting process. If teamwork is important for accomplishing your company's goals, the questions and discussions during interviews should be directed towards that goal. If, by choice or not, your company environment is a pressure-cooker (that's obviously a culture trait), people you're hiring should be aware of that, and be up to it to survive.

- Builds employee morale, which enhances employee productivity. When employees have really bought into the company they work for, they put their heart and soul into it, often far in excess of how much their paycheck motivates them. When they do this, their productivity increases, their cost control towards your bottom line increases, and customer satisfaction increases. Easy question – if everyone at Apple absolutely hated the pressure-cooker environment at work, do you think we'd have anything like today's Apple products?

- Employees going *with* you, not *against* you. The business world changes, and directions you're going today might be very different tomorrow. A product design that looked really good at the beginning might turn out to be all wrong when customers don't accept it; serious competition might unexpectedly smack you at the worst possible moment; a global recession might hit when you least expect it; and a thousand other possibilities could occur – all of which could require a major change of direction for your business. If your employees hated to work there anyway, they'd be out the door the moment they get a whiff of disaster. If they absolutely love the place as a result of its culture, and think there's no better place in the world to work, they are likely to stick with you, and they'll be a huge asset in helping you steer a course to recovery.

- A corollary to the previous benefit – employee loyalty. Retaining good employees is crucial to your start-up success, and you'll only retain employees who are satisfied with the place they work. When employees are personally invested in the company they work for, they feel like they're part of a team, with a feeling of concern about the overall success of the company, and not so much just their own personal accomplishments.

- Benefits to your supply chain at the front end, and to your customers at the back end. The corporate culture that your company practices – and outwardly projects in all directions outside its environment – has a direct effect on how well your suppliers work with you (including deals they'll offer you), and the interest level your customers will have in purchasing products and services from you. As a start-up company, you'll naturally face obstacles from both directions as a result of being an unknown, but if the culture is starting to spread about your company, your employees, and your products, it can significantly help break the ice.

---

[303] Barry Phegan, Ph.D, *The Benefits of a Good Organization Culture*, companyculture.com, http://companyculture.com/141-the-benefits-of-a-good-organization-culture/

- When it comes time to sell your company (or, for that matter, to buy another company to expand). Almost every company touts the line that their employees are their single biggest asset – and if true that can add a huge number of dollars to your company's value when a merger/acquisition partner comes along. The largest factor in making those employees so valuable is the corporate culture they work in. If the culture stinks, many might jump ship the moment the first rumor is out (and believe me, it's hard to keep the genie in the bottle). If your company is the buyer, having a well-respected corporate culture to point to can be huge in winning over the bought-out employees when they join you.

So, what is corporate culture?

- We all know that every company has a culture, but even within your own company you (and your employees) might not be able to describe it. Apple has a much-touted corporate culture, but can you put it into words?
- Spoken and unspoken beliefs – often called the "company's core values" – that identify the shared values and norms between employees and the owner(s). Companies often have a written set of Core Values,[304] and these are not just hidden away in an Employee Handbook that no one looks at after initial hiring – but rather, are prominently displayed on the company's public website for all to see (not just current employees, but also employees-to-be, outside suppliers, customers, and competitors). Core values are often included in the company's Mission Statement, in company communications, company literature, on plaques on the company's walls, and will be mentioned as often as possible by company management.
- The latitude each employee has in decision-making, developing and acting on new ideas, and personal expression – allowing the employee to feel empowered. The result is usually an organization where employees are highly committed to collective objectives.
- The behaviors that determine how a company's employees and management interact and handle outside transactions. Put simply, "Culture tells us what to do when the CEO leaves the room, which is of course most of the time", say Frances Frei and Anne Morriss in a Harvard Business Review article.[305] As the authors put it, "culture guides discretionary behavior and it picks up where the employee handbook leaves off".

  Take this well-known example from 1994, as described by Snopes.com (also published in Newsweek in 1989), which supposedly happened in Anchorage AK: "*About a dozen years earlier, a guy walked into a retail business that had formerly housed a tire company – but had been turned into a Nordstrom department store. He walked up to the tire counter, put the tires down, and asked for his money back. The clerk, who'd been working there for all of two weeks, saw the price on the side of the tires, reached into the cash register, and handed the man $145.*" According to Nordstrom company lore, the story is true, and is constantly repeated as being absolutely true – even by a

---

[304] You can see Twitter's Core Values at http://genius.com/Twitter-core-values-annotated, and the company is ranked at 4.5 on a scale of 1–5 for culture and values by its employees – considered "the tops" across the U.S.

[305] Frances Frei and Anne Morriss, *Culture Takes Over When the CEO Leaves the Room*, Harvard Business Review, May 10, 2012, https://hbr.org/2012/05/culture-takes-over-when-the-ce

member of the Nordstrom family – although parts of the story just don't add up on close scrutiny. Even if the story is an urban legend, no one can dispute it's a great legend for illustrating the company's focus on service.

Corporate culture isn't something you can write about in the opening page(s) of your employee handbook, leave it at that, and expect it to catch hold. It's also not something you can instill in rah-rah speeches when you're whipping up employee enthusiasm for what you're trying to accomplish. Much of your corporate culture will come from leading by example, not only by you as the founder, but also in the actions of your managers. If you're seen as the owner or manager who lavishly throws money around, it's hard to instill frugality among your employees (and keep them happy and ready to go all out for you). If it's known that you cheat on travel expenses, it's hard to blame employees who do the same. If employees hear you berate customers behind the customer's back, the employees can only assume this behavior is acceptable. So, trying to develop a *do as I say, not as I do* approach to creating a corporate culture can only end in failure – for your company and your employees.

Your best bet is to begin thinking about the company values and beliefs you subscribe to no later than the day you open for business, even if you're the only employee. Jot down notes about it as your day-to-day business builds. These notes should cover: (a) the values you'd like to instill in your company; (b) characteristics of how you will treat your employees in various situations – and just as importantly, how you want them to treat you; (c) and how you want to establish relationships with your customers. As you continue to formulate your own unique culture, these notes can guide you in the early employee hiring process, and help you build consistent ways of doing business. In doing this, think long and hard about how you will write this message and get it across to everyone who will read it.

Sometimes the culture is all about the company, and not the employee. Microsoft, Apple, and Amazon probably wouldn't be where they are today if not for their corporate culture – and if you can believe the press reports about employee stress, employee workloads, and a somewhat dog-eat-dog environment, you might come away with the opinion that the corporate culture has little to do with the employee, but more to do with raising the company to new heights, maybe even *at the expense of the employee*.

In the long-ago days of Microsoft's explosive growth, stories abounded of employees who worked 15–18 hours at a stretch, then bedded down on a cot next to their desk to start the next day. Employees openly talked about being burned up and spit out, all for the sake of getting the latest product out the door, or testing the next software release and getting it ready for delivery. Some (maybe most) thrived in the pressure-cooker environment, turning a lot of them into millionaires when they realized their stock options; others were churned out the door, knowing there were a dozen more waiting outside for every one that departed. A corporate culture created this, but was it good for the employee, or just for Microsoft? I think both.

As vaunted as the culture is at Apple, it apparently has its corporate culture detractors too. Ex-employees of Apple (who can now talk about it – the first rule of Apple is, don't talk about

Apple[306]) says the secretive culture at Apple teaches you that "you are part of something bigger than you", which suggests that an individual is subservient to the company's well-being, that when Steve Jobs was still alive, projects that you worked on (and that he was interested in) were given top priority, but things didn't get done if he wasn't involved. Another ex-employee said that the work environment was awful as a result of strictly one-way communication, (with the suggestion to guess which direction that was), but in defense of the company, exclaimed that the food in the employee cafeterias was wonderful. Walk into any Apple retail store (which is about the only place you can actually meet Apple employees), and it's hard to believe the employee enthusiasm for the job they're doing.

In one of the most widely-read (and hotly disputed) exposés about the supposed corporate culture evils at Amazon,[307] a New York Times article uncovered a punishing workplace, where the founder and CEO (Jeff Bezos) has an obsession for telling people how to behave, confrontational bluntness, and a workplace totally driven by metrics (measuring and profiting from the results) – although Bezos disputes it and remarked that this isn't the Amazon he knows. One ex-Amazon employee quoted in the article, Bo Olson, reported that "nearly every person I worked with, I saw cry at their desk" over the savageness meted out in book review meetings. Along the growth path, Amazon developed its fourteen articles of faith[308] – which are not vague philosophical platitudes, but actually rules that describe how employees should behave. These rules are not casually inserted in the opening paragraph of the employee handbook, but instead, inscribed on laminated cards that are handed out to each new employee on their first day at work – and who are then quizzed to recite the rules several days later. Not used only at hiring, though, the rules are constantly discussed in meetings, and even by the employees themselves on their time off (and the real converts teach them to their children, as if they are a guiding principle of life). It's hard to believe that Amazon would be at the highest levels of retail sales (plus everything else they are involved with) if there wasn't another side to this story – one that describes people who are really happy working at Amazon, and believe in what they are doing.

> *"Real integrity is doing the right thing, knowing that nobody's going to know whether you did it or not."*
> Oprah Winfrey

Business Code of Ethics

Your business Code of Ethics is the third cornerstone on which to build your business. Like the tenets that make up your corporate Mission Statement and culture beliefs, you need to establish your ethics by clearly spelling them out to all employees (executives, managers, and staff), then

---

[306] Jim Edwards, *What Apple Employees Say About The Company's Internal Corporate Culture*, businessinsider.com, October 9, 2013, http://www.businessinsider.com/what-apple-employees-say-about-the-companys-internal-corporate-culture-2013-10

[307] Jodi Kantor and David Streithfeld, *Inside Amazon: Wrestling Big Ideas in a Bruising Workplace*, New York Times, August 15, 2015, http://www.nytimes.com/2015/08/16/technology/inside-amazon-wrestling-big-ideas-in-a-bruising-workplace.html?_r=0

[308] *Our Leadership Principles*, www.amazon.jobs/principles

practice what you preach, *and don't just preach them once*. Your business Code of Ethics also provides a main foundation of your company's mission and culture.

For most small businesses, a business Code of Ethics isn't something you put in writing in the early days of the company's existence. In fact, for a start-up, an early *written* Code of Ethics should be ranked no higher than 2 on a scale of 1–10 (with 1 being the lowest), unless of course, you suddenly find yourself with lots of free time during a transcontinental flight. Instead, it should be something that you jot down, bit by bit, as you develop thoughts and beliefs about how your company's employees (including you) should comport themselves in every aspect of business.

That doesn't mean you should undervalue a Code of Ethics – it's just that in the first few years of any new start-up, you would do better to formulate a Code of Ethics *in the back of your mind* (or in notes), live and operate by them on a day-to-day basis, communicating them to employees in small doses as statements and messages of how you want your company to *behave*. When you feel comfortable the Code of Ethics can actually be articulated in a written policy, only then should you add it to the company's policy for all employees to read. Just don't wait too long to get it started, as the beliefs and actions behind it need to be in practice from the start.

That advice might sound a bit wish-washy and contradictory, but in the very early time of your start-up, you're not likely to know enough about your business ethics to be able to write them down. You probably won't have a company policy manual yet, because you're scrambling and clawing to keep your business afloat, you're already wearing a dozen manager's hats, and you need to stay focused on your goals.

Nevertheless, this early time in your business life is when you need to begin *thinking* about your business Code of Ethics – gathering your own collection of values, principles, and practices that you believe in. Getting these ideas in mind will not only help to outline your business culture as your company grows, but will also provide talking and writing points as you communicate with your initial employees. From that modest beginning, you'll have a clearer idea of the boundaries you feel comfortable operating in, and so will your employees. From there, it should be easier to create the ethical atmosphere that you want for your company.

Most importantly – and this is true from the very first day that you open the doors – you need to watch carefully that your business ethics are adhered to, and if they aren't, or if there are even whisperings that they aren't, jump in immediately to investigate and take action. I know from personal experience that if you don't, you'll have sent a signal that you condone the behavior – and it will spread like wildfire. Not only will the perpetrators continue their behavior, but others who watched or heard about it will know the true situation.

Why should you have a code of business ethics? First of all, it illustrates to your employees, customers, and vendors that you value honesty and integrity in the way you run your business. Most importantly, though, it helps you and your employees make difficult decisions when you find yourself in a gray area. Like all companies, your new business is made up of human beings, and we all make transgressions at one time or another in our business life. Without a Code of Ethics that helps define when employee behavior has crossed the line, everyone will assume that poor behavior must be OK, and it will be repeated.

In addition, having a defined code of business ethics:

- creates increased employee morale
- attracts customers who prefer to do business with an ethical provider
- increases customer loyalty
- enhances your corporate reputation
- decreases negative press and customer backlash from doing the *wrong* thing
- reduces the odds of getting into legal or financial challenges due to unethical behavior

Your business ethics begin with you, the owner and founder. Many times, the technical or product knowledge base that allows you to start your own business comes from the work you did for previous employers. That's good, and you have the right to put your knowledge to work as an entrepreneur – but you need to follow the same business ethics that you expect of your own employees. If you stole proprietary information from your previous employer(s) and are surreptitiously using it now in your own business, it probably won't stay secret for long. If your employees learn (or suspect) that you've done this, anything and everything you might do to establish good business ethics could fail completely. In the case of ethics, no one is going to buy an argument of *do as I say, not as I do.*

Living up to your business ethics. A company's business culture isn't just created from a policy manual – but rather, springs from the actions and statements of its leaders. Your business ethics make up a large part of your company culture, and you need to walk the talk every day in order to instill the ethics with employees, and also to ensure they are adhered to.

Writing a policy manual, splashing it all over the walls of your business, or creating a website page that touts your ethics can be a good idea, but if you don't follow through to ensure enforcement – particularly for those who should be setting the example – it isn't worth the time you spend on it. Here's a good example of what I mean.

I visited Walmart headquarters in Bentonville, AR in the early 2000s to present a marketing pitch to their mainframe software group. I was led by a security escort along a long hallway whose walls were filled with corporate ethics slogans, including names of employees who were currently serving in the Iraq war. At the time, the company's website State of Ethics page listed a "5th Guiding Principle" that was "*Respect and encourage diversity, and never discriminate against anyone*". This display of good *family* values is enough to give anyone a warm and fuzzy feeling.

Yet not long after that visit, Walmart found itself battling a gender discrimination lawsuit that ended up at the U.S. Supreme Court. The suit claimed that something like 80% of Walmart's hourly jobs were held by women, but only 33% of all management positions within the company were women.[309] Incredibly, the company's argument to the court showed that female employees earned only 85–95% of what their male colleagues earned – *and their lawyers touted the goodness of that by pointing to the U.S. at large, where women only earn 77% of what men earn* – as if their slightly better statistic somehow excuses it. The suit also claims that "a store executive gave approval to hold management meetings at Hooters, the restaurant chain with scantily-clad waitresses".[310] Walmart even stated that "any unequal treatment was at the local

---

[309] As argued in the gender bias class action lawsuit before the Supreme Court in 2011.
[310] Fortune Magazine, April 4, 2011, *Wal-Mart's Gender Bias Case: What's At Stake?*, http://management.fortune.cnn.com/2011/04/04/wal-marts-gender-bias-case-whats-at-stake/

level and not initiated at the corporate level". Hells bells! How can the world's largest company (at the time) claim to have ethics <u>standards</u> if they only apply to the corporate level, and not at the local level where 99% of their employees work?

Frankly, with statements and behavior like that, this is an unconscionable *lack* of corporate ethics. Interestingly, now on the Walmart Global Ethics Office website, (https://www.walmartethics.com/home.aspx?LangType=1033), you'll see a link to a 38-page PDF document titled Statement of Ethics, fresh up on the website at the time this was written. It'll be interesting to see if the company actually performs to their ethics standards this time around.

So, the point is, no matter how large or small your company, you can tout your corporate ethics all you want in policy handbooks, or slap slogans and stickers up on the office walls, but if you don't walk the talk, you really aren't living by your own corporate ethics – and you obviously aren't enforcing them throughout the organization.

<u>Problem # 1.</u> Here's a common rub. If you, the founder and chief boss, know the Code of Ethics that you want for your company, but don't require managers and employees at all levels to live up to them, well then, <u>you simply don't have a business Code of Ethics</u>. Along with your written and spoken communiques about ethics, you also need to instill an ingrained sense of perspective that *actions have consequences* – and let it be known that actions cannot be swept under the carpet (which can often be a lot more convenient, at least for the short term). If someone oversteps the ethics boundaries, it needs to be handled promptly and appropriately. A record of the transgression must be made, either in the employee's personnel file (preferred) or in a company database that's maintained specifically for this (more on this in a bit). If this practice had been incorporated at Walmart, it's hard to see how the argument about any offenses being *local* could have been deemed acceptable.

<u>Problem #2.</u> Another common rub – and especially in a small company – is that an ethics offender might be considered too much of a golden boy (i.e., too valuable to the company's future), or too nice of a guy, or too much of a friend. If any of these considerations get in the way of resolving an infraction, with the thought that doing so might risk negative consequences, believe me, you've started down a slippery slope – and I know, because I let this happen several times in my own company – and learned it was not the right thing to do.

If you're like me, tackling this type of problem is very difficult, involving personal, face-to-face confrontation to expose the facts, implementing the consequences at a later time will be even more difficult. Likely there's another side to the story (or at the very least, a claim to another side), or mitigating facts that you're not aware of. Claims of impropriety could, in fact, turn out to be totally baseless, in which case you still have damage control to attend to. But regardless, it has to be confronted.

<u>Problem #3.</u> The slippery-slope of business ethics – also known as "moral disengagement". Odds are, your company isn't headed towards an infamous Bernie Madoff $18B Ponzi scheme that fleeced hundreds of unsuspecting investors. According to good 'ole trusted Bernie, here's

what got it all started for him (as reported in a Bloomberg Business article[311]): "Well, you know what happens is, it starts out with you taking a little bit, maybe a few hundred, a few thousand. You get comfortable with that, and before you know it, it snowballs into something big." I'm sure the bookkeeper candidate I almost hired (discussed in Chapter 6) didn't start her embezzlement at a local city government with a large-scale plan in mind either – rather, she was later deemed to be a shopaholic with credit cards max'd out that she couldn't pay down, who then pocketed a relatively small amount from the city's cash drawer at first, planning to pay it back from her next paycheck ... but then it happened again and again ... and soon she was in over her head. On this topic, the researchers in the Bloomberg Business article suggest one very important rule about ethics breaches – "quickly condemn even small lapses before they compound", as they may very well lead to more serious ones if you don't.

Define business ethics. Your company's business ethics define the moral code upon which all of your business decisions and practices are based. It's basically your *right and wrong* weathervane for how your company operates – and it not only defines behavior within the company, but it also forms the basis for how others see your company – and therefore, whether prospective employees want to join your company and customers want to buy from you.

Business ethics are made up of the following:[312]

- **Honesty.** This isn't something you tout from the highest nearby mountain. Instead, it comes from your actions – paying your bills and your employees on time and fairly, treating your customers fairly in the products or services you provide or contracts you sign, paying your taxes, and meeting all of your other obligations as a business. By contrast, <u>*not*</u> doing any or all of these things shows that you are failing your corporate responsibilities, creating a climate of mistrust, and possibly creating legal issues.

- **Integrity and keeping your promises.** Integrity isn't just another word that means honesty. For example, you may not be acting dishonestly when blinded by the money in a deal, resulting in a situation that's really good for you, but not so good for other stakeholders – but those stakeholders will surely see it, and you'll lose integrity in their eyes. Other examples occur when you've made commitments to customers, but then fail to meet those commitments – and if you don't act to mitigate those failures to your customer's satisfaction, your integrity will slip in their eyes. To maintain a high degree of integrity, you must be seen as honest to a fault. Not accepting responsibility if you fail to meet a commitment, and then not admitting your failure, shows a lack of integrity.

- **Loyalty and fairness.** Loyalty is a many-faceted street, each one linked with your company – between your company and its employees, your suppliers, and your customers. In addition, there's a loyalty requirement between you and your company. While you should never place loyalty above your other principles (and it should never be used for unethical purposes), your loyalty to each of these entities should be a guiding moral compass, giving you a high road to operate from.

---

[311] Cory Weinberg, *When Tiny Fibs Create Big Risks for Businesses*, BloombergBusiness, June 26, 2014, http://www.bloomberg.com/bw/articles/2014-06-26/how-telling-little-lies-eventually-leads-to-major-ethical-breaches.
[312] Travis Bennett, *12 Business Ethics Examples*, udemy blog, April 4, 2014, https://blog.udemy.com/business-ethics-examples/

If your business is driven strictly by self-interest, where you aren't trying to reach a win/win situation that benefits not only your company but all of your company's stakeholders, you might reach for short-term success at the expense of greater long-term gain.

- **Trust, respect, and caring.** Respect for your employees, as well as your customers, is just plain good business, and is a foundation of business ethics.

  When your employees know you value their contributions, they're more likely to rebuff a competitor who approaches them with a job offer. When you are flexible and demonstrate empathy with employees and their individual needs, they have even more reason to stick with you, thick or thin, even if a competitor offers a higher wage. (This is one of the surprising areas where employees aren't just looking for the highest-possible salary or wage – they're often looking for a stable place to work, where they are valued, where their work is valued, and where they are treated well.)

  The same applies with customers, and it can give you a decided edge over competitors who are trying to beat you with a better price point. Trust can lead to more repeat business, which usually carries a much higher profit margin than having to find new customers.

  Horrendous example.[313] In October, 2014, 250 Walt Disney World information technology employees were suddenly called in for a meeting – thinking they had done such a good job they were going to receive bonuses – only to be handed pink slips, and were then required to train their foreign outsourced replacements before they exited. Several major American corporations are exploiting loopholes in the federal H-1B temporary visa program – which was specifically "intended for foreigners with advanced science or computer skills *to fill discrete positions when American workers with those skills **cannot be found**". These loopholes actually *eliminate* higher-paid American workers in favor of unskilled foreigners from places like India. It's a shameful practice, and one that can destroy any trust and respect the company might have previously had, not only with employees, but also with customers.

- **Not just inside your company.** Your Code of Ethics should extend to partnerships, suppliers, and outsourced organizations as well, so make sure they are included in your policy, and then incorporate into your agreements or work definitions with them. Your company's integrity goes out the window, for example, if you outsource some of your production to overseas vendors, then find they are running sweatshops that you didn't check into ahead of time, or keep from happening.[314]

Writing your business Code of Ethics. As stated before, the early days of your start-up probably aren't the time when you should write and formalize your Code of Ethics. But – and this is a big but – you should be formulating your business ethics in your head throughout all of

---

[313] Julia Preston, *Pink Slips at Disney. But First, Training Foreign Replacements*, The New York Times, June 3, 2015, http://www.nytimes.com/2015/06/04/us/last-task-after-layoff-at-disney-train-foreign-replacements.html.

[314] Daniel Viederman, *Overseas Sweatshops Are a U.S. Responsibility*, Bloomberg Business – The Debate Room, https://d2ct263enury6r.cloudfront.net/RUcOjiA6ztdbFJc03c4ocqr5ZpjQkSusWyUg4ICXqx1sZSh0.pdf

your early business dealings, making notes to later incorporate into your company's documented code. For the time being, act ethically with your customers, with your suppliers, and with your employees as you begin to grow. And when new employees are hired, at the very least you need to verbally convey what is expected of them in this context, and what the ramifications are if your expectations aren't met.

At some point, you need to force yourself to tackle laying out your company's Code of Ethics, but the big question will be, how and where should it be documented? For maximum buy-in, consider involving two or three other senior employees to help write the code and complete the rollout. During the process, consult with all of your employees, encouraging them to provide not only input for creating the code, but also feedback when it's all written. Some people may hesitate to offer input during face-to-face meetings with other employees, so also provide an anonymous way for them to submit ideas. Others may feel this entire process is a total waste of time ("just let me get back to my job – that's all I care about, and it's what you're paying me for"), and for those you might need to think ahead of time of ways to get everyone motivated to participate.

During the writing process, determine who will be the future "compliance officer", and also who will update the code as necessary, and who will handle any ethics transgressions that are reported. This person should be committed to the company and its Code of Ethics, and should be seen as a figure of authority within the company (and very likely is you, the founder and owner, at least in the early days).

For the actual writing process, don't waste your time trying to write it yourself from scratch – and don't waste your money hiring an attorney to do it for you (a lawyer isn't typically an ethics specialist, although you might want to run your finished product by your attorney to check legality). Your best bet is to find samples of current Code of Ethics documents that closely match your ideals, then *massage those examples to be yours*.

Here are some considerations before you lay pen to paper (or ... fingers to the keyboard):

- Where will your Code of Ethics reside, who is the audience, what will you call it, and how will you get people to read it?

  There are three obvious audiences: customers, employees, and vendors. Each audience has a different reason for reading it, so you may want to create three similar, but slightly different versions.

  o The customer version could be on your website, possibly as an adjunct to the About Us page. Likely, you'll abbreviate the employee version to create this. Basically, you're trying to convey to your customers the values that drive every aspect of your business decisions, such as how you treat your customers, employees, the environment (if applicable), and that all business dealings will be honest and with integrity.

  o For employees, the best location might be the beginning section of the Employee Handbook, and would be the most detailed version of the three. It would spell out the company's core ethics principles – how customers should be treated, how the company will treat employees, how all employees should treat all other employees, and how vendors and suppliers should be treated. If appropriate, environmental issues will be covered. It will cover the company's expectations about all aspects of business practices. (Your company probably won't be ready for something this substantial for a long time, but for ideas to consider, read the excellent 32-page PDF file *Business Ethics and Compliance* that Starbucks and every employee is expected to live by.[315])

- o For suppliers and vendors, this version is your method for announcing your company's business ethics that you expect them to comply with if they want to do business with your company. This may seem presumptuous on your part, but assuming you (as the business owner) truly want to conduct all aspects of your business in the manner spelled out in the customer and employee ethics guidelines above, this is the only way you can get it across. It should be written as a signed addendum to your vendor agreement (or work order, or whatever paperwork establishes your vendor/supplier relationship). It should be detailed enough to clearly identify their compliance requirements, and the consequences of noncompliance.

- Coordinate the contents of the Code of Ethics, Mission Statement, and Employee Handbook, and ensure their consistency. For example, if your Mission Statement mentions that a goal of your company is to always practice sustainability with its products, this should also be a part of your Code of Ethics. Assuming you want your Code of Ethics to stress respect for the individual, this also factors into the integrity aspect of your Mission Statement.

- Write your Code of Ethics in plain, simple language (applying that to the other two documents as well). Make it user-friendly, in clear unambiguous language that everyone can easily understand.

- Include expectations wherever possible, citing examples of specific unethical behavior that is not acceptable – but if you include examples, make certain it clearly states these are examples only, and aren't to be considered definitive.

- How will you get employees to read it and comply? This probably presents the single biggest challenge. A boilerplate employee Code of Ethics you find on the internet will be skimmed at best when an employee is first hired, and then never looked at again. Assuming you're a new business owner who really cares about this, you need to incorporate aspects of this into every company communication that you develop. Here are some ideas:

- o First, when you get the Code of Ethics down in writing, ensure that every employee has read it, understands it, and knows they are expected to comply with it. Preferably, the document will be handed to all new employees, along with a signed Acceptance form to be returned to their personal file when it's been read. For current employees, you need to create *an event* to discuss its introduction – preferably a company-wide meeting or all-company teleconference. A much less effective way to introduce the Code of Ethics is via a newsletter or company-wide e-mail (due to the number of employees who feel they are simply too busy to read it).

---

[315] Business Ethics and Compliance. The Starbucks website page introducing the program is at http://www.starbucks.com/about-us/company-information/business-ethics-and-compliance. The PDF file that fully describes the program can be downloaded in several languages from links at the bottom of the website page.

- o   Regular company communications are the backbone of how you should be motivating your employees. Incorporating ethics into regular meetings or training sessions is a great way to communicate these ideas. The owner of a local software company conducts a morning 10-minute yoga session for her nine employees, which could be a good time to slip in some aspect of company culture or business ethics. A Monday morning all-hands company meeting might have a standing agenda item that covers this. A weekly TGIF beer/wine get-together could begin with a serious 5-6 minute time to get a point across. A big customer sale announcement e-mail to all employees – a good thing in itself – could also include a few words of wisdom. As Chief Communicator, these are all things you could be doing to help build your company's culture, and instilling a Code of Ethics and company mission fits right in with that.

Here are some resources to look at:

- Inc. Magazine online, *Business Ethics: Sample Policies*.[316] This article quotes sample policy statements from Levi Strauss & Co., and Northern Networks Corporation (formerly Northern Telecom, known as Nortel, a multinational telecommunications company). They are both brief, to the point, and can be a good place to start.
- Codes of Ethics Collection, housed at the online site for the Illinois Institute of Technology.[317] A seemingly overwhelming collection of over 1,000 codes of ethics, categorized into dozens of professional groupings – allowing you to browse the collection by any trade, or one that closely matches your business operations. For example, enter "software" in the search window (above the professional categories list), and it displays 77 search hits to select from.
- The Ethics & Compliance Initiative (ECI) website[318] has an excellent toolkit page that walks you through the process of writing an ethical code of conduct, including tips and techniques. It also includes lists of code provisions for you to consider.
- If you don't find something that provides workable examples for you, try a browser search on "business code of ethics examples", and you'll almost certainly find several good examples. (Buyer beware: Any time you are searching for something like this, you'll likely get a hit for a website called www.biztree.com, and as you'd expect, they have a sample Code of Ethics among their 1,800+ business templates. This service costs $200 to access, arguably a pittance compared to the cost of a lawyer. However, you don't need to spend *anything* to get samples from real companies that you can massage to make your own, and you'll still want your attorney to look your finished product over anyway.)

---

[316] *Business Ethics: Sample Policies*, October 20, 2000, http://www.inc.com/articles/2000/10/14404.html
[317] *Center For The Study Of Ethics In The Professions*, Illinois Institute of Technology, http://ethics.iit.edu/cseplibrary
[318] *Ethics & Compliance Toolkit*, Ethics & Compliance Initiative, https://www.ethics.org/resources/free-toolkit

Chapter 9   Policies – Labor Rules, Discrimination, and Harassment

"I strongly believe that you can't win in the marketplace unless you win first in the workplace. If you don't have a winning culture inside, it's hard to compete in the very tough world outside."
Douglas Conant, former CEO of Campbell Soups, and author

Workplace labor rules, and discrimination and harassment policies are separated here from all other company policies, primarily due to the overly large impact they can have on your business operations. If you make a misstep in your employee benefits package, or you fail to incorporate some detail in your company's travel policies ... well, that's correctable. But if you open the mail one day to find a letter from a federal or state agency about a labor law violation, or a discrimination or harassment claim against your company – your world could suddenly go topsy-turvy.

You, the new small business owner, must understand the implications of federal and state laws that you must follow. No one said starting a small business is easy, or that you get to do exactly what you want every single minute of your new business life. Establishing labor policies and enforcing harassment and discrimination policies – and then abiding by them – is one of the toughest areas you'll have.

As a rule, the federal and state agencies aren't looking too closely at your small business if you have fewer than 15 employees. Certain rules and requirements, however, apply to companies as small as one employee, *and you'd better know which those are*. Also, as your business grows, it's pretty easy to reach the magic 15 employees without even thinking about this threshhold.

Most importantly, many (if not most or all) of the requirements relating to labor laws and discrimination and harassment are things that are simply *right* for your company, and as such, they will play a big role in the company culture that you want to create and the business ethics you want to follow. Therefore, while they are two really big deals that carry a lot of weight in your employee handbook (when you're ready to create it), they also need to be solidly implemented in your everyday company practices from the moment your business starts up.

Who sets legal policy for labor laws and discrimination and harassment claims? Several federal and state agencies are charged with regulating and enforcing rules and laws that protect small business employees, and they take quite a positive stance about doing that.

At the federal level, the five you need to be most concerned about are:

- The **National Labor Relations Board** (NLRB), which interprets and enforces the National Labor Relations Act.
- The **Federal Labor Standards Act** (FLSA), which establishes minimum wage, overtime pay, recordkeeping of employee hours and pay, and youth employment standards.
- The **Equal Employment Opportunity Commission** (EEOC) is the primary creator and enforcer of almost all discrimination and harassment policies in every aspect of employment.
- The **Americans With Disabilities Act** (**ADA**), a civil rights law enacted in 1990 that falls under the Civil Rights Division of the U.S. Department of Justice, but is enforced by the EEOC. Title I of the ADA is concerned with employment as it relates to disabled people.
- The **Occupational Safety and Health Administration** (OSHA) establishes and enforces compliance with workplace safety and health standards.

Many states have similar agencies, with similar names, and with rules that often go beyond those at the federal level – or enforce compliance for smaller businesses than the federal agencies. As a general rule, federal always takes precedence over state, but the detail and granularity at the state level can be finer and have other nuances.

- In my state (Washington), when I bring up www.wa.gov, then enter a search on "labor laws". I get an Access Washington page that provides a long list of *Labor & Industry, Washington State* hits that will take me anywhere and everywhere within the state government's website that has anything to do with labor laws for companies doing business within the state. If I want to know about *workplace rights*, or what my requirements are if I want to hire a teen, or fair labor standards, or breaks and meal periods ... I can find it. Try a similar search for your state.
- If your business is in California, do a search on "California labor laws" and you'll get a hit on a state (i.e., ca.gov) with an FAQ page for *California Department of Industrial Relations*. There, you'll find just everything about labor laws that California adds to the federal requirements.
- Almost any state you plug in will produce something similar.

What if you just lie low on the horizon – will any of these agencies catch you? The fact is, the odds are low that any of these organizations, federal or state, will find you on their own – you are likely too small potatoes and there are just too many businesses like this for the meager resources of the government agencies. No, it will likely be an employee (or someone who knows your company) who alerts a federal or state agency to a violation on your part, potentially resulting in a heavy slap up the side of your head. Or, computer cross-referencing available with today's databases could trip you up. Or, just a coincidental stumbling upon your company as some other aspect of governmental process is going on.

Worse, if you just decide to ignore all of this – maybe because you're up to your waist in snapping alligators while trying to keep your business afloat, or maybe you just don't give a hoot about it ... well, you do so at your own peril. If you're less than a decent human being, you could end up building the kind of business you really don't want, treating people unfairly, making people miserable with their jobs, and your company will likely become one of the small business statistics that isn't around at the end of five years (or less).

Instead, let's assume you have a good moral backbone, and like many new small business owners, you really do care about your employees, you're starting a company for the long haul, and you want to sleep at night because you're doing the right thing – then you've already made a great leap towards business success.

Let's look at how labor, equal opportunity, and safety laws affect you.

The NLRB and your workplace

National Labor Relations Board (NLRB). The NLRB has long had rules defining illegal or prohibited employer conduct towards employees, most of it contained in Section 7 and 8 of the National Labor Relations Act (NLRA, originating way back in 1935). Much of the long history of the NLRB is associated with labor unions and the employee's right to collective bargaining – which was an outgrowth of years of serious labor unrest in the United States after WWI. Back then major (and violent) labor strikes were sweeping through the automotive industry, the meat packing industry, the transportation industry, and among agricultural workers, as a result of appalling working conditions, lack of employment opportunities, income inequality, and low wages. Across the U.S., there were 2,000 strikes in 1934 alone.[319]

While the NLRB still focuses primarily on ensuring worker's rights to organize and decide whether to have unions as their bargaining representative, it is also the ruling agency on such questions as Facebook "Like" issues (i.e., whether employees have the right to post them), and whether student/athletes should be paid based on employee status, and whether a company's employee dress code is legal. Overall, the major scope of their labor rulings has become pretty broad, and much of it is focused toward today's world.[320]

For example, in early 2015, the NLRB signaled their active interest in employee handbooks, issuing a lengthy memorandum by the organization's General Counsel that outlines several areas that the NLRB is on the lookout for.[321] Essentially, the memorandum puts employers, *big and small*, on notice that the NLRB will not tolerate employee handbook rules, no matter how well-intentioned, "that would inhibit employees from engaging in activities protected by the Act" (the NLRA). The 30-page memorandum then provides real-life examples of handbook rules that

---

[319] By comparison, across the U.S. in 2016, there were a total of 15 major work stoppages, and in the lowest-ever year – 2009 – there were 5. Source: *Table 1: Work stoppages involving 1,000 or more workers, 1947-2016*, Bureau of Labor Statistics, https://www.bls.gov/news.release/wkstp.t01.htm

[320] *Analysis, resources and commentary on developments in traditional labor law*, McGuireWoods Labor Relations Today, http://www.laborrelationstoday.com/articles/nlrb/. This interesting blog contains an archive of NLRB cases, compiled from the NLRB RSS feed and categorized month-by-month. You can scroll back in time to find older posts. This blog probably isn't all that valuable to the typical small business owner, but if you are researching (for example) federal agency opinions on classification of workers as 1099 contractors, you could search on that ("1099 contractors") and find every NLRB ruling on it (in an earlier discussion on that – Chapter 6 – we focused only on what the IRS thinks of it – here is what federal labor law people have to say about it).

[321] Richard F. Griffith, Jr., General Counsel, *Report of the General Counsel Concerning Employer Rules, Memorandum GC 15-04*, March 18, 2015, http://apps.nlrb.gov/link/document.aspx/09031d4581b37135

unlawfully violate NLRA rules, then explains the NLRB's reasoning, and finally, includes modified employee handbook wording that was found to be acceptable.

As explained earlier, NLRA Section 7 gives employees the right "to discuss wages, hours, and other terms and conditions of employment with fellow employees, as well as with nonemployees, such as union representatives".[322] Often, employee handbooks flatly state that this type of information is confidential, and caution that such discussions (even among employees) will result in disciplinary action. In fact, the NLRA memorandum states that if employees even "reasonably understand" that such prohibitions exist, the company would be in violation. The memorandum goes on to clearly state that an employer has every right to demand restrictions of valid company confidential information, but that it must be carefully worded. Forty+ years ago, old-line legacy companies (such as IBM and Boeing) commonly had workplace rules that prohibited any discussion of wages, making it a cause for dismissal. That rule hasn't been allowed for a long time now, but nevertheless, it's still a holdover in many companies.

One example of unlawful confidentiality wording concerns a company rule not "to discuss customer or employee information outside of work, including phone numbers and addresses". On the face of it, this seems perfectly reasonable, but the memorandum concluded that this wording is unlawfully overbroad with regard to "employee information", in that it makes a blanket ban on discussion of contact information "without regard for how employees obtain that information". While this may seem a picky interpretation of the words, in the hands of a skilled lawyer, it can make a huge difference in the outcome of a legal case. Similar examples are given that relate to discussion of wages, hours, workplace complaints, and terms and conditions of employment among employees – "as well as with nonemployees, such as union representatives."

The memorandum's Section B addresses illegal employee handbook rules that prohibit employees from criticizing their employer's labor practices, even if done so in a public forum (including Facebook or Twitter posts, for example).

Section C then gets to the origins of much of the NLRB's focus – handbook rules that might be construed as preventing employee discussions on forming a union. Interesting, this section goes so far as to state: "although employers have a legitimate and substantial interest in maintaining a harassment-free workplace, anti-harassment rules cannot be so broad that employees would reasonably read them as prohibiting vigorous debate or intemperate comments regarding Section 7-protected subjects ", again providing several examples of lawful or unlawful wording. Further along this line, the NLRB cautions that even though many states have "at-will employment", employees still have the right to collectively bargain and participate in concerted activities to improve working conditions – and attempts to terminate employees under at-will provisions will be considered unlawful.

Section D covers an area that is the bane of many employers – company media policies that restrict employees from communicating "with the news media, government agencies, and other third parties about wages, benefits, and other terms and conditions of employment". In careful reading of the memorandum, it's not that restricting such communications is unlawful in itself – but it has to be very carefully worded to be a lawful restriction.

---

[322] *Employee Rights – Rights We Protect*, National Labor Relations Board, https://www.nlrb.gov/rights-we-protect/employee-rights

Section E covers what would seem at first glance to be a perfectly acceptable employee handbook restriction – on employee use of company logos, copyrights, or trademarks. Legal use would obviously be anywhere an employee uses them for legitimate company business, and it would seem fair that employees can't use them for their own purposes outside of the company. But, as the NLRB memorandum points out, "handbook rules cannot prohibit employees' fair protected use of that property ... on picket signs, leaflets, and other protest material". And in a slant towards today's world, it also isn't allowed to have a blanket policy such as "Do not use any Company logos, trademarks, graphics, or advertising materials in social media".

Further sections cover handbook rules that restrict photography and recording on company premises – which in today's world of ubiquitous cell phone photos/videos, could put a chill on employees recording unlawful practices – and policies on not showing up for work, or engaging in conflict of interest activities.

All in all, this memorandum leaves one with the impression that no small business employer will have the legal background to craft an employee handbook whose wording can stand up to the scrutiny implied from this memorandum – and the only way you can do it properly is to have a fully trained HR attorney draft it from inception, or that attorney scrutinize with a fine tooth comb the handbook that you create. That's not exactly true, but it does imply that you need to be very careful with your research and your writing.

The FLSA and your workplace

Federal Labor Standards Act (FLSA).   The FLSA, Wage and Hour Division, an organization within the U.S. Department of Labor, is responsible for defining and enforcing labor laws that set minimum wages, overtime pay, employee hours and pay recordkeeping, and youth employment standards. The FLSA also provides guidance and compliance assistance to employers. As such it has created a 20-page publication on Labor Standards Information for New and Small Businesses,[323] written in a Q&A format to give small business owners the information they need to comply with the laws and regulations of the federal Department of Labor. (Importantly, see the section on exempt versus non-exempt employees and the "highly compensated" salary limits that affect overtime pay requirements in Chapter 6.)

Specifically, the FLSA is concerned with employers meeting the requirements of:

- minimum age, maximum work hours, overtime requirements, allowable occupations for youth 14 or 15 years old, and bans on employment in certain hazardous occupations for anyone under 18 years old
- the Family and Medical Leave Act (discussed earlier in Chapter 7)
- fiduciary, disclosure, and reporting by employers who offer pension and welfare benefits to employees under the Employee Retirement Income Security Act (ERISA)
- the employee garnishment limitations specified in the Consumer Protection Act

---

[323] *Labor Standards Information for New and Small Businesses, WH Publication 1482*, U.S. Department of Labor, December 2012, http://www.dol.gov/whd/regs/compliance/NewBus3.pdf

- employee wage and benefit protection by contractors and subcontractors on federally financed and assisted construction and services projects, as specified by the Davis-Bacon and McNamara-O'Hara acts
- worker protection under the Migrant and Seasonal Agricultural Worker Protection Act (MSPA), and field sanitation and labor camp provisions established by OSHA
- restrictions on employer use of polygraph (lie detector) tests for pre-employment screening or on current employees
- returning veterans who served in the armed forces, as administered by the Veteran's Employment and Training Service (VETS)
- and 180 other federal laws, some of which apply to small businesses.

One valuable feature of the publication is a resources guide that cuts across many federal agencies, providing website addresses and phone numbers where small businesses can go for help with questions. It also attempts to link small business owners with state and local laws, including a link to a Department of Labor page in each state.[324]

On the FLSA website, a very useful FAQ provides much greater detail, but is organized in more user-friendly topic areas.[325] For example, there's a link simply titled *Women,* which answers questions about female-related issues in the workplace, particularly pregnancy and newborn child care leave, affordable child care, domestic violence, and how to develop work skills.

Besides the Federal Labor and Standards Act, every state has an equivalent labor policy agency that sets standards at the state level, including the minimum wage law for all employers in the state (or employers from another state who have employees domiciled in their state). Besides minimum wage, employee work rules can vary greatly from state to state (and from the federal standards), so you really need to be up on this for your situation.

In addition, local work rules can apply – particularly in cities such as New York City, San Francisco, and Seattle – and the laws across the country are changing fast, so staying up to date is important (to get the latest, search on "*yourcity local labor laws*"). A good place to start researching your state's FLSA rules is a very useful section called *Wage and Hour Laws by State*, at http://www.nolo.com/legal-encyclopedia/fair-pay (scroll down to that heading) [326]. The site provides an FAQ about each state, along with links to the labor law website for the state government itself.

In summary, for new small business owners, the responsibility toward these labor laws results in further required reading that you can find on the FLSA website, particularly at the link for the above-mentioned FAQ. It's also where you should look for answers whenever you are contemplating employee policies affected by these areas.

---

[324] *State Labor Offices,* www.dol.gov/whd/contacts/state_of.htm
[325] *Frequently Asked Questions,* U.S. Department of Labor, http://webapps.dol.gov/dolfaq/dolfaq.asp
[326] Another good state-by-state resource is at: *Overtime & Minimum Wage Laws: State By State,* Wage/Advocates, http://wageadvocates.com/overtime-pay-laws/overtime-wage-laws-state-by-state/

The EEOC and your workplace

Equal Employment Opportunity Commission (EEOC). The EEOC was created as part of the Civil Rights Act of 1964, establishing workplace rules – particularly regarding discrimination of all kinds – and encouraging/requiring these rules to be placed in employee handbooks and posted in employee bulletins. According to the EEOC, "Most employers with at least 15 employees are covered by EEOC laws (20 employees in age discrimination cases). Most labor unions and employment agencies are also covered".[327]

States also have their own discrimination and harassment laws,[328] including employee-boundary applicability limits (as low as one employee in many states). You would do well to check the laws in the state your business is registered in, *as well as any state where you have employees domiciled.*

There are differences between discrimination and harassment, and we'll discuss separately the definition of each. Your processes and procedures once a claim of discrimination or harassment is known are similar, and we'll cover that as a single topic following the definition.

What behavior is considered discriminatory? Quite a few practices have been identified as discriminatory and legally prohibited. In general, the rules intend to protect employees from discrimination on the basis of:

- Age
- Disability (including disability leave)
- Equal Pay/Compensation
- Genetic Information
- Harassment (sexual or otherwise)
- National Origin (including birthplace, ancestry, culture, or linguistic characteristics common to a specific ethnic group)
- Pregnancy
- Race/Color
- Religion
- Retaliation
- Sex (gender and sexual orientation)

The rules also include workplace actions that demonstrate discriminatory *bias* in the following work-related activities:[329]

- recruiting workers and posting job openings; testing, training and apprenticeship programs
- hiring and/or firing employees (including not hiring a woman because she's pregnant at interview time, or fearing she could later become pregnant)
- promotions, transfers, assigning and classifying employees

---

[327] *Overview*, U.S. Equal Employment Opportunity Commission, http://www.eeoc.gov/eeoc/index.cfm

[328] *State Laws Prohibiting Discrimination and Harassment*, Nolo online, http://www.nolo.com/legal-encyclopedia/workplace-rights

[329] *Prohibited Employment Policies/Practices*, U.S. Equal Employment Opportunity Commission, http://www.eeoc.gov/laws/practices/index.cfm. This is a very good place to start your research on the actual EEOC rules that employers must abide by.

- recalling and laying off workers
- disability leave
- dispensing fringe benefits
- retirement

What constitutes harassment? In the words of the EEOC, here is the definition of workplace harassment:

"Harassment is unwelcome conduct that is based on race, color, religion, sex (including pregnancy), national origin, age (40 or older), disability or genetic information. Harassment becomes unlawful where 1) enduring the offensive conduct becomes a condition of continued employment, or 2) the conduct is severe or pervasive enough to create a work environment that a reasonable person would consider intimidating, hostile, or abusive. Anti-discrimination laws also prohibit harassment against individuals in retaliation for filing a discrimination charge, testifying, or participating in any way in an investigation, proceeding, or lawsuit under these laws; or opposing employment practices that they reasonably believe discriminate against individuals, in violation of these laws."

Harassment is based on two categories – "quid pro quo harassment" (Latin for "something for something", or "this for that"), or hostile workplace harassment.

Quid pro quo harassment is most often thought of as sexual harassment, but it also legally encompasses unwelcome behavior of a religious nature. Both usually occur when the offending individual makes (or hints at) an employment decision as a way to get an employee to commit to sexual or religious activity (yes, it seems a bit strange that sexual and religious activity are the _only_ two types of quid pro quo harassment the EEOC worries about, but that's how it is right now). For example:

- An employment candidate is interviewing for a job. At the close of the interview the male interviewer places his hand on the female candidate's knee. The candidate objects or pushes the hand away. The interviewer says, "Don't you want this job?" – implying that the candidate must accept this sexual advance to get the job. This has definite connotations of the movie director's couch, but that certainly isn't the only place this type of behavior exists.
- This exact example could substitute a requirement that the applicant has to join the interviewer's religion (or religious beliefs) in some way.
- A supervisor (who could be you) offers preferential treatment, a promotion (or denial of promotion), demotion, or possible termination, based on whether the employee accepts sexual or religion demands.

Hostile workplace harassment usually involves "unwelcome conduct of supervisors, co-workers, customers, contractors, or anyone else the victim interacts with on the job" and is defined with these key words: behavior "which renders the workplace atmosphere intimidating, hostile, or offensive" (EEOC's words[330]). Hostile workplace harassment may include harassment of a

---

[330] *What Do I Need To Know About ... Workplace Harassment*, United States Department of Labor website, Civil Rights Center, http://www.dol.gov/oasam/programs/crc/2011-workplace-harassment.htm

sexual or religious nature, but it is harassment without a quid pro quo aspect. Hostile workplace harassment includes (but isn't limited to) these types of behavior:

- Unwelcome physical contact or verbal statements or advances; frequently situations between a manager and subordinate, where there's also an implied (or stated) threat of retribution if the employee doesn't comply. These actions don't have to be sexual in nature, but instead could be threatening or hostile.

  Just as often, harassment occurs between employees of similar levels, where persistent attempts reach the level that are considered harassment. Asking a co-worker once for a date wouldn't be construed as harassment – depending on how it was asked – but asking several more times when it's been clearly responded to negatively could be.

  Seemingly innocent (wink ... wink) actions on the part of a manager towards a subordinate can also be construed as unwelcome. For example, a senior male manager praises a female employee who works directly for him, then walks around her desk to plant an overly generous kiss on her cheek ... and it's received as unwelcome.

  Another example: two co-workers on a company business trip, both married, with spouses at home, staying at the same hotel where a company function is held. In the elevator at the end of the evening, the male co-worker clasps the female co-worker's hand in his and amorously invites her to his hotel room. This isn't harassment if it began mutually, but if not, it's definitely an unwelcome advance.

- Invading someone's physical space. Most people have a natural sense of appropriate physical distance and stay outside others' personal space. But some people deliberately invade the space as a means to dominate or intimidate.

  Some people may unintentionally enter another's personal space due to poor social skills, inadequate personal boundaries, or lack of awareness of the other person's comfort zone. Some cultures have fundamentally different personal space boundaries than others, possibly as a result of population densities.

  The person being offended may feel harassed and make a complaint – a complaint that definitely needs to be addressed, either simply with a sideline conversation with the offender (if it's unintentional), or with consequences if it's done intentionally. The complaint definitely needs to be documented in the offender's personnel file, as a reference in case it happens again.

- Bullying.[331] This form of harassment includes threatening behavior, gestures, or actions. It often includes intimidation, humiliation, aggressive behavior, sabotage and verbal abuse. Bullying can include sabotage that destroys work in progress, or prevents work from being done. Not surprisingly, a large number of bullying instances are done by bosses or people in charge. Over a quarter of workers have experienced bullying in their workplace. Nevertheless, it can also be done at equal co-worker levels, maybe as a way of jockeying for position or promotion. It really doesn't matter who is doing it to whom, though – if it's bullying, it's wrong.

---

[331] *The WBI Definition of Workplace Bullying*, Workplace Bullying Institute, http://www.workplacebullying.org/individuals/problem/definition/

Because this form of harassment is prevalent, be sure that references to workplace bullying are included in your employee handbook, and just as importantly, that you and your managers be on the lookout for it (and also, make certain you're not one of the bosses doing it). It's also important to watch for incidents that are just a euphemism for bullying, such as incivility and disrespect, people who are considered to be *difficult to work with*, and ill treatment of others – these are typically bullying by another (incorrect) name.

- Damaging personal property. An example might be someone smashing an item on your desk because they're mad at you.

- Offensive gestures and/or statements.

- Possession or display of derogatory pictures or other graphic materials.

- Sending inappropriate electronic text or graphics via e-mail or other electronic means. Today's press and social media are full of examples of this type of offensive behavior, which cannot be tolerated in the workplace, even if between two consenting adults.

  Almost all of us know someone who sends unsolicited racist jokes, cartoons, sayings, or links to websites that contain inappropriate material. Other offenders send out-of-bounds political propaganda and attacks that could be considered offensive by a recipient. (As an example, an otherwise straitlaced guy in my company – with two kids of his own, no less – developed a long-running collection of *dead baby jokes*, prattling these off to other office people, many of whom had kids.)

- Here's the catch-all – any other offensive or demeaning act directed at someone because of his or her sex, race, color, religion, national origin, age, disability or other legally protected status.

What Constitutes Prohibited Inappropriate Conduct? Some of this definition falls in the category of behavior that isn't necessarily illegal, but that could be included in your Code of Ethics. This list is meant only to provide some examples of inappropriate behavior and is not a complete list. By all means, search the hundreds of websites that can be found on the internet to see if others fall within your value system.

In general terms, inappropriate conduct is anything that falls in the category of verbal or physical conduct towards an individual containing the use of:

- Epithets
- Innuendos
- Threats, insults, and slurs
- Name-calling
- Negative stereotyping
- Jokes, pranks, or other bantering comments
- Foul language

The key to many of the above situations is to recognize when comments are simply playful, inoffensive joking around between two people – two guys hurling joking low-level insults at each other over their football picks, versus one of the guys telling a female co-worker, "my God, you're tarted up today!" Everyone has to draw a hard line on which side of the fence these are on

– and if it's offensive or hurtful *to the recipient*, it needs to be stopped. In other situations, not even a single offense is acceptable and it must be dealt with.

Quid pro quo or hostile environment harassment of/by vendors, customers, or customer employees. This is also known as "third-party harassment".[332]

Some people may think harassment is restricted to employees within your own company – but it isn't. Any time your employees interact with people outside your company, you could have claims of harassment arise – and the claims could be instigated from either side. Wherever and however it arises, you need to be aware of the potential problem, including procedures for documenting it and taking actions to stop it. If you don't, your company can be held liable, just as it is for similar behavior between company employees.

Protecting your business against discrimination or harassment claims. It is better for your business, and far cheaper, to never get your company into any form of discrimination or harassment claim. Once a claim has been leveled at you (i.e., your company) or an official claim filed with the EEOC, you're headed down an expensive path that's fraught with danger. Any claims that become known to your employees will likely be a morale destroyer in many ways. Claims are very disruptive, because it shifts your focus, and could potentially completely derail your company. Doing everything possible to stay away from these kinds of claims is a far better path to take.

Here are several specific things you can do to lessen the possibility of a claim:

- **Educate all employees – managers included – on the rules.** The above definitions of identifiable discrimination and harassment practices are daunting on their own, but that's before you even get to the specifics of exactly what constitutes discrimination or harassment in each area.

  For example, what is age discrimination? By EEOC definition,[333] age discrimination "involves treating someone (an applicant or employee) less favorably because of his or her age".

  OK, so to test you, here's an example. You openly choose to hire someone for a particular position who is 30 years old, rather than someone 22 years old – and do so because you prefer the maturity of a 30-year old. Are you guilty of age discrimination? The correct answer: no – and you wouldn't be regardless of which one you hired in this example. The Age Discrimination in Employment Act (ADEA) only forbids age discrimination against people who are age 40 or older.[334]

  Another example: You have two *equally* qualified job candidates, one 50 years old and the other 35 years old. Do you *have* to choose the 50-year old candidate to be free of any claim

---

[332] Lisa Guerin, *Third-Party Sexual Harassment,* Employment LawFirms, NOLO website, http://www.employmentlawfirms.com/resources/employment/workplace-safety-health/what-third-party-sexual-harassment
[333] *Age Discrimination*, U.S. Equal Employment Opportunity Commission, http://www.eeoc.gov/laws/types/age.cfm
[334] Although some states set a lower limit on age discrimination. It's the federal EEOC that sets the limit at 40.

that you're discriminating based on age? Well, interestingly, no, you don't. The 50-year-old candidate could grumble loudly when turned down, and could actually file a claim that you've discriminated based on age – that's their right based on the law. But if, in your thorough interview process you found the 50-year old to be argumentative and seemingly not interested in being a team player (whereas the 35-year old exhibited none of that), you can choose the 35-year old based on that preference – but you'd better document it in detail at the time of your decision (and *don't* wait to document it when a claim is made). In this example, you need to *extemporaneously* document something to the effect that, in your judgment, both candidates were equally qualified *technically* (or in their skill set as it relates to the actual job performance), but not equal in temperament or their ability to get along. Without that documentation, anything you say in court or a deposition is likely to be treated as hearsay.

Could you, or any manager in your company who is in a hiring position, have recognized the nuances of these examples and responded correctly? Not very likely. By the way, if the two candidates, 35 and 50 years old, *weren't equally qualified*, you can also choose based on better qualification – but again, if you choose the under-40 candidate you'd better document that.

Another question – what constitutes equal pay or compensation discrimination? Again by EEOC definition,[335] The Equal Pay Act (EPA) "requires that men and women in the same workplace be given equal pay for equal work". This quote is taken directly from Title VII of the Civil Rights Act of 1964, a federal law that encompasses employers in every state. However, pay differentials are permitted when based on seniority, merit, quantity or quality of production, or a factor other than sex. These are known as *affirmative defenses*, and it is the employer's burden to prove that they apply. [336]

So, let's test your knowledge again. Your office manager hires a female receptionist with light clerical requirements at near-minimum wage (let's say, $9.50/hour, or $19,760/year). Another manager in the marketing department hires a male for clerical work gathering sales leads and assisting with phone calls setting up tradeshow events – and pays him $12.00/hour, or $25,000/year. Is this (a) in the same workplace, and (b) equal work? Yes, it's the same workplace, even though not the same department. Based on the skills requirement, yes, odds are the female receptionist has a valid claim for wage discrimination, since the example refers to initial hiring wages, and it would be hard to argue there is a skill difference. As the EEOC EPA further points out, the jobs need not be identical to be considered "equal work", but rather, the skill (measured by experience, ability, education, and training) required to perform the job is what settles the issue.

Again, would you (or both of your managers in the above example) have the necessary knowledge of equal pay/compensation discrimination to keep you on the right side of the

---

[335] *Equal Pay/Compensation Discrimination*, U.S. Equal Employment Opportunity Commission, http://www.eeoc.gov/laws/types/equalcompensation.cfm
[336] *Facts About Equal Pay and Compensation Discrimination*, U.S. Equal Employment Opportunity Commission, http://www.eeoc.gov/eeoc/publications/fs-epa.cfm

law? Not very likely. *(By the way, a small business that isn't otherwise covered by EEOC laws is subject to the Equal Pay Act.)*

What makes the equal pay law so challenging for a small business is that, with so few employees, it's likely that everyone does multiple things in their day-to-day jobs, with varying skill requirements, and so it's difficult to define "equal work". Nevertheless, in the case of the two new hires in the example above, if the male in the marketing department is also expected to have skills to update the company website (assuming those skills are higher than those typically required for a receptionist), that fact should be documented as the basis for a salary difference.

Unfortunately, the EEOC hasn't done a very good job of providing helpful education and training for small business owners. Starting at the home page of their website (www.eeoc.com), there are no links to any training courses that an employer or manager can go to – only links to the actual do's and don'ts of the various types of discrimination. The EEOC website lists an EEOC Training Institute (https://eeotraining.eeoc.gov/profile/web/index.cfm?PKWebId=0x2547b105), with a listing of seminars for the public. A self-study course, or a series of webinars would be great, but there just aren't any, at least not directly from the EEOC. One bright spot was finding an EEOC website page that lists Small Business Liaisons in over 50 major cities, identifying a specific person's name and phone number that you can call for EEOC compliance questions in specific workplace situations – but that assumes you know which questions to ask, which isn't the same as a focused training session.

- **Awareness.** You, your managers, and your employees all need to know their rights and responsibilities regarding best workplace practices to prevent discrimination. And like so many other aspects of good leadership, it starts with you – actions that you take, establishing awareness through company memos and newsletters, placing EEOC posters where workers and managers can see them, and developing an employee handbook that clearly spells out company ethics.

  This certainly shouldn't be demagoguery, and needn't be something you're on a mission about (and in fact, it could be *ineffective* if you are). You just need to incorporate as much awareness as possible into the way you want the business to be run, and into the company culture. Every company should have a weekly staff meeting, and hopefully a separate manager's meeting. Always scheduling a brief topic on some aspect of discrimination or harassment prevention would be an excellent idea – particularly given how easy the topic can be to discuss, compared to how damaging even a single discrimination/harassment incident can be.

- **Follow your workplace policies.** Whether you have an employee handbook or just a bunch of ad hoc policies, make sure that you (and everyone in the company) consistently follow the policies – to ensure that you do what you say you will do.

  If you have a progressive discipline policy for discrimination, adhere to it regardless of who the offender is, and how important he/she is to your company. You might have a mid-level manager who is responsible for bringing in 1/3rd of your entire company's annual revenue, but another manager – and this one just happens to be a minority – yet you ignore complaints that the hotshot is riding roughshod over employees and you don't impose any disciplinary action, yet you discipline the minority manager. You've left yourself open to a discrimination complaint.

Remember that the primary characteristic of discrimination is treating people differently even though they are in similar situations and are performing their jobs consistently well. If you don't follow policies consistently, applying them the same way to all employees, you can land in hot water. If for any reason you have to deviate from a policy, make sure to jot a note about the deviation, and file it with your other non-discriminating recordkeeping.

- **Take all discrimination complaints – even verbal – seriously.** You not only have a legal obligation to do so, but this is also your first hint of a potential future complaint that could go straight to the EEOC. If anyone in your company is found to have swept a complaint under the carpet, not only a formal complaint, but also informal scuttlebutt of a complaint, this is serious business, and it's a serious violation. It should be clearly stated in your employee handbook that this won't be tolerated, and ignoring it should be treated as seriously as the complaint itself. Perhaps a formal complaint wasn't filed because the person felt uncomfortable making the complaint, and didn't want to go on record about it. It should be clearly stated in your employee handbook that this won't be tolerated, and it should be treated as seriously as well. As the business owner, you should make it well known that filing a complaint will not result in retribution, and that people should feel safe in doing so. You should also make it known that the complainant's identity will be protected if at all possible (based on the situation, of course). Most of all, make sure that everyone in the company knows that complaints, even talk, will be taken seriously.

Even if a complaint turns out to be non-discriminatory or non-harassing, and doesn't reach a sustained level, it may still be an indication of insensitive behavior – and this can lead to employees believing they are victims of discrimination or harassment, which can be just as damaging for morale, productivity, and company goals. It is therefore critical that you take all claims and talk seriously, and make corrections as necessary.

Here's a good list of _what not to do_ with employee complaints:[337]

- o Joke about the incident with others
- o Rush to judgment and take sides
- o Fire the complainer
- o Text, e-mail, use social networking or otherwise discuss the complaint with others
- o Ignore the complainer in meetings, in e-mails and during office activities

Yet, according to the article referenced above, these exact behaviors are done all too often, and each of them indicate a serious lack of sensitivity towards the complainer, as well as not taking discriminatory behavior seriously. Anyone caught doing this should have disciplinary action taken towards them – and if you don't, your company could be found at fault when/if the complaint goes further.

---

[337] Rebecca R. Hastings, _What Not To Do With Employee Complaints_, SHRM online, January 26, 2011, https://www.shrm.org/resourcesandtools/hr-topics/employee-relations/pages/whatnottodo.aspx

- **Pay particular attention to mid-level managers.** In most companies, the mid-level managers are the biggest hirers and firers of employees, so it stands to reason they are the ones in your company that you face the greatest risk of discrimination from (and don't forget, you, as the business owner, also fall in this category in many ways).[338] For this reason, you need to ensure they aren't singling out workers for unfair treatment, either by the manager or other workers. At your regular manager's meetings (yes, you should have them), make certain you add an agenda topic each time that reminds mid-level managers of their responsibilities, including not only being impartial, but *appearing* to be impartial as well.

  Take note of which manager(s) receives more complaints, or which is more talked about with regard to unfair behavior, and then have a talk with that manager to determine if a problem exists that needs to be corrected. Keep in mind that if a complaint is lodged with the EEOC, the complaint will be against your company *first*, and the manager *second* – so it's extremely important that you nip any bad behavior in the bud right from the start. By the time you hear from the EEOC, the problem is a long way down the pike. For that reason, if and when you have both mid-level and high-level managers, make sure that you also instill the latter with the importance of this, as the mid-level managers will then be reporting to them at this point.

- **Keep good records.** The importance of this cannot be overstated. If the EEOC enters the picture with an investigation as a result of a claim being filed, one of the first things they'll ask for is a complete set of the incident records (assuming you're already aware of a problem). Your recordkeeping could be your best form of protection if an employee (or employee candidate) complains about you or anyone in your company, and in the worst case, it could substantially help you in the event of a lawsuit.

  Importantly, keep notes of job interviews – particularly reasons why you chose one person over another, comments about candidates from other employees who might have been involved in the decision, and also about new-employee salary decisions. When firing someone, make certain that full details of why the firing was done are written and filed with the employee's personnel records (which need to be kept). When promoting one employee instead of another, make notes about that, particularly why that person was selected and not the other. When making employee assignments, jot a note about it with regard to *any* aspects that might later come up in a discrimination claim.

  If you have an employee who just can't seem to follow the rules, make sure you create a paper trail of attempts to correct this employee's behavior. If, after multiple offenses you end up having to fire this employee, and the employee subsequently files an *unlawful* discrimination complaint with the EEOC, they'll ask for records of how you tried to work with this employee to correct the behavior. If you've correctly maintained your company's at-will status, you can certainly fire an employee for no stated reason, but it could lead you to a discrimination charge – and not having a paper trail will make your job much harder.

---

[338] *Protecting Your Business Against Discrimination Claims*, Wolf, Baldwin & Associates, P.C., http://www.wolfbaldwin.com/Small-Business-Articles/Protecting-Your-Business-Against-Discrimination-Claims.shtml

Doing all of this recordkeeping might not be intuitive, and it's a pain in the patoot – but the alternative is an even bigger pain. For example, when you (or a manager) are in the interview process for a new employee, a myriad of other things are spinning in your head, but for your own future protection, you need to do sufficient recordkeeping so that a future discrimination investigation finds you did the right thing. This should be one of those topics in your weekly manager's meeting, keeping this towards the front of your manager's thinking.

- **As you grow, be aware of policy change requirements.** When you're a 3-person company, your *legal* obligations concerning discrimination might be different in some areas than after you reach 15 employees (don't forget, though – the *moral* obligation is the same whether you have one or fifteen employees). As you grow, a periodic review of your policies is important anyway, but to protect your company from discrimination claims you should also review your policies from state and federal EEOC requirements (a good person to perform this review is the administrative person you've chosen to maintain personnel records), because there may have been regulatory changes. If this review results in any policy changes, you'll need to notify all employees about the changes. This includes employee contracts as well as your employee handbook, so make sure you review all that are relevant.

- **Adopt a zero-tolerance policy and/or open-door policy.** Either or both of these should be written into your ad-hoc policies, or formalized in your employee handbook – written as part of your anti-discrimination and anti-harassment policy. These are important to your company not only because they are right and fair, but also because they can be part of a potential future defense that you had appropriate measures in place to prevent and correct discrimination or harassment situations from occurring.

If you seriously commit to these policies, they can lead to better employee satisfaction and reduce your risk of discrimination and harassment claims.

They are tough to implement, as the number of people you're relying on increases as your company grows, and any one of them can fail to adhere to it – but ultimately it's your company that is liable.

A word of caution: these can backfire on you if you don't totally commit to enforcing these policies – and failure to do so can itself lead to a discrimination claim.

They are each pretty self-explanatory. Zero-tolerance means that you will evenhandedly investigate and take appropriate action for every instance of discrimination or harassment that is brought to your attention, or to the attention of your managers. If one person gets away with an infraction of discrimination or harassment, but another employee is sanctioned or fired, the latter will have a valid complaint to file against you.

Open door means that employees can bring complaints about co-workers and managers to upper-level management without fear of retaliation. If employees feel they have no one to talk to about discrimination or harassment situations, they are more likely to file an official complaint, when in fact, it could have been resolved by having someone in authority to discuss it with so that action can be taken if appropriate.

Documenting and investigating a discrimination or harassment claim. The trouble with many of the discrimination and harassment issues is that there might not be third-party witnesses around to verify them. By their very nature, these offenses usually happen when two people are alone, making them he said/she said situations, without corroborating witnesses or evidence to back up a claim. Therefore it's incumbent on you (as the employer) to understand what constitutes discrimination or harassment, and to be ready to handle an investigation – and to be ready to take any actions necessary to stop it. Not doing so is a sure recipe for landing your company in hot water, including an investigation from the outside, possibly legal action against your company, and a fine that could jeopardize your business.

As a small business employer, odds are that a discrimination or harassment claim might be made against actions you've taken as the employer, which creates a totally different situation than a claim between employees in your company, or against/by outsiders and your employees. They are such different situations that covering them separately is necessary.

Employee-against-employer claim. First, a few words about employee discrimination or harassment claims aimed specifically about your own behavior (as the employer). Unless your company has already reached the size where you've created an HR/personnel organization, it's somewhat unlikely an employee will step forward to personally and directly charge you with discrimination or harassment (unless, of course, they're announcing that they've already filed a claim with federal or state authorities). Sometimes an employee will have the moxie to stand up to his/her boss and tell the person he's doing something that's not only wrong, but illegal. More likely, the employee will take his/her complaint to a trusted employee of your company (a manager, your accountant or bookkeeper), who is now approaching you with the news.

What should you do? Well, the obvious answer is, take it seriously! The reality of the situation, though, is that *if you are knowingly guilty of this*, it's likely you have the moral turpitude of a slimeball and the odds are you'll either deny it outright, sweep it under the carpet by simply ignoring it, fire the employee, attempt to pay the person off to keep quiet, or make the situation worse by creating an even more hostile environment for the employee. If any of these are the route you take, you deserve any sanctions or penalties that later come down the pike – and hopefully, the employee will press the claim against you (and win). Assuming you're a decent human being, though, you might learn from the experience that you have a serious problem, and rectify the situation – knowing that it's rightfully going to get you in a lot of hot water.

The other possibility is that *you're not guilty* of the claim, and maybe there's some ulterior motive for the employee's behavior in creating the claim. After all, you have every *innocent-until-proven-guilty* right as any other employee, so the allegation should be investigated in exactly the same way as it would be against any other employee.

Co-worker-against-manager/co-worker claim. First, we'll examine the process and procedures you should set up for discrimination or harassment claims between one employee and another (manager against employee, or co-worker against co-worker).

(Claims made by or against an outside vendor/customer against one of your employees is just as important – and if you don't treat them seriously, you can be held liable. The difference is, you don't have the same authority to investigate the outside vendor/customer environment as you do with your own employee. You certainly, though, have the responsibility to notify an appropriate person at the outside vendor, or discuss it directly with the customer. Other than that, you should investigate it as if it was a violation completely within your own company.)

Upon hearing of a discrimination or harassment claim:

- Don't waste any time, or make any attempts to sweep the allegations under the carpet. It could be interpreted as a sign that you aren't taking it seriously. Evidence could be lost or destroyed, and further discrimination or harassment could occur.

- Take the complaint seriously and listen carefully to the accuser.

- Keep it confidential. It might be impossible to keep it completely confidential, as the investigation will include others who might be witnesses. It can be very damaging to company morale if rumors sweep through your company.

- Do not retaliate against the accuser – and do not allow any retaliation against the accuser. Treat the accuser as the victim of the situation, and don't shoot the messenger. The odds are, the accuser doesn't want to be in this situation, and shouldn't be made to feel the problem is his or hers.

- Thoroughly investigate the allegations, including an examination of what occurred, when and where it occurred, exactly what was said and done, and whether there were witnesses. Determine if evidence exists that might corroborate the allegations – this could include e-mails, timecards, schedules, and notes from meetings. Interview anyone who might have knowledge of the incident(s).

- Consider hiring a third-party investigator, such as a certified HR consultant, or your corporate attorney – but if you do, get someone who specializes in employee discrimination and harassment claims. This could be especially important if the claim has become public, if it's against a high-ranking individual in the company, or if the charges might be considered criminal.

- Throughout the investigation, document everything possible, including all steps you've taken, notes of interviews, files of any evidence, your findings from the investigation, and any discipline. These documents will be very important if the employee files a claim with the EEOC, who will request them when beginning their investigation. Additionally, without this documentation, you could be on shaky ground, especially if you later need to terminate the accused employee.

"Remedies" for discrimination or harassment. If your investigation concludes that the accused did indeed discriminate or create a hostile work environment, the action you take is up to you – and the word used to describe it is always "appropriate". In other words, neither the federal or state EEOC commissions dictate what your action should be, but they suggest that it be commensurate with the offending deed. That leaves you with a lot of latitude, presumably ranging from a "good talking to", and/or notes in the person's personnel file, transfer to a different part of the company ... all the way to termination. Since discrimination and harassment come in so many flavors, it would be very difficult to list what your actions will be in an employee handbook – and in fact, it would be inappropriate to do so.

A big concern is what the legal actions against your company might be. The EEOC website[339] describes in very general terms the "remedies" – that's what they call the action they'll take if your company is found to be guilty and liable – and they include compensatory, punitive, and "liquidated" monetary damages. The amounts listed can be seriously damaging, particularly to a small business that usually doesn't have a large bank account balance anyway. (Interestingly, the website specifically lists remedies for discrimination offenses, with no mention of harassment – and a search doesn't locate any – but a comment buried on the EEOC website states that the remedies listed for discrimination are the same for harassment.)

In addition to monetary remedies, an employee can also bring a lawsuit directly against you (your company) for discrimination or harassment. Before the lawsuit will be accepted by the court, a "Charge of Discrimination" (which also includes harassment[340]) must first be filed with the EEOC, who decides to investigate the claim or not. If a lawsuit is filed, you will have no choice but to defend it (or accept it and reach a settlement).

Disciplining a *false* accuser of a discrimination or harassment claim. This is a weird situation, but one you need to be aware of. Any number of events or situations around your company can lead to disgruntled employees, including employees who *have it in* for another employee, or against you, your company, an outside vendor, or a customer. Possibly an employee who knows he/she is about to be disciplined or terminated, and decides to create a smokescreen – or maybe even a delaying tactic – by creating a false discrimination or harassment claim, thereby paralyzing the employer for taking the planned action. It could even be an employee who's trying to use the claim for monetary gain – basically shaking you down for a possible payoff to drop the claim.

Even if you suspect it's a false claim at the time it's brought to you, take the claim seriously and treat it exactly as you would any other discrimination or harassment claim. If your investigation reaches a conclusion that the claim is false (and here is where you need to be *more certain of your facts* than otherwise), you not only need to discipline the false accuser, but also repair any damage the accusation has done to the accused, as well as to your company, other employees, customers, and vendors. Worse, you are setting yourself up for a potential follow-on claim of retaliation, which can be really damaging to you if it should be upheld. Retaliation claims can be extremely costly – and risky – to defend.

(By the way, the preceding paragraph recommended that you investigate *all* claims brought to your attention – even if you suspect it is a false claim. The courts have determined that an internal company investigation – even if alongside an EEOC investigation – cannot be considered retaliatory, as the employer must be free to investigate any and all discrimination or harassment claims, so as not to be seen as indifferent.)

Consider this. Filing a discrimination or harassment claim is considered *protected activity* by the claimant through EEOC laws (both federal and state – i.e., these are EEOC words). That makes any decision by you that it's a false claim doubly difficult – you're basically dammed if you do and damned if you don't in terms of how you proceed. There are no *light accusations* of

---

[339] *Remedies for Employment Discrimination*, EEOC website, http://www.eeoc.gov/employees/remedies.cfm

[340] *Harassment*, EEOC website, http://www.eeoc.gov/laws/types/harassment.cfm

discrimination or harassment – and since you are duty-bound as an employer to handle each accusation thoroughly and fairly, let the facts and evidence lead you where they will, and then make an honest decision that conforms to those facts and evidence.

So, now the big question – can you discipline a claimant for false claim of discrimination or harassment? The answer is a definite yes. The fact that it is *protected activity* does not insulate an employee from discipline. Throughout your investigation, if you have any suspicion that the claim is false, you can certainly pursue that angle as well. Nevertheless, having filed the claim and gaining the *protected activity* status, the claimant has won an important right in the process ... namely to give the claimant protection against retaliation even if it is proven beyond a doubt that the claim was false.

Hmmm ... *you can discipline ... but you can't retaliate* – and how is anyone supposed to know the difference? Hardly seems right and fair, you say? Well, a good portion of the American business world would probably agree with you, but the courts that have upheld this ruling have the upper hand ... so if you fire or otherwise discipline an employee for a false discrimination or harassment claim – the seriousness of which would certainly be a disciplinary act in any other situation – you do so at your own peril. *If you think you want to head down this route, don't do it before getting really good legal advice.*

At the first hint that a discrimination or harassment claim smells fishy, make sure you research everything you can after searching on "employees who make false discrimination or harassment claims". The fact is, you've just landed between a rock and a hard place.

The ADA and your workplace

The Americans With Disabilities Act (ADA). The ADA was created and signed into law in 1990, and is one of America's most comprehensive pieces of civil rights legislation for persons with disabilities. Those protected by the ADA "have a disability, which is ... a physical or mental impairment that substantially limits one or more major life activities, a person who has a history or record of such an impairment, or a person who is perceived by others as having such an impairment". The ADA does not specifically name all of the impairments that are covered.

How does the ADA protect? In their own words:

> "*The ADA ... prohibits discrimination and guarantees that people with disabilities have the same opportunities as everyone else to participate in the mainstream of American life -- to enjoy employment opportunities, to purchase goods and services, and to participate in State and local government programs and services. Modeled after the Civil Rights Act of 1964, which prohibits discrimination on the basis of race, color, religion, sex, or national origin – and Section 504 of the Rehabilitation Act of 1973 – the ADA is an "equal opportunity" law for people with disabilities.*"

How does the ADA affect a small business? Some portions of ADA have exemptions for businesses with fewer than 15 employers, but other areas – those providing products and service to the public – *apply to businesses of all sizes*. As with other federal statutes, many states provide their own extended versions of the federal ADA, and not just in the specific provisions concerning discrimination, but even in the definition of "disabled". To locate the specific statewide provisions enacted in your state, search on "*yourstate ada*".

Title I of the federal Act applies to small businesses *with more than 15 employees*, and specifically relates to equal rights *in all employment areas* for employees (e.g., application, hiring, firing, advancement, job training, etc.), including both applicants and current employees.

Title III applies to businesses *of all sizes* (plus non-profits), prohibits discrimination against customers with disabilities, and requires businesses to provide accommodations that improve accessibility and participation for disabled customers.

Availability of relevant and easily-readable information about the ADA regulations. It's unlikely any small business entrepreneur is going to read the entire text of the Act – it runs hundreds of pages, and is written in such bureaucratic legalese that only an attorney or HR professional can fathom it – and that goes for the state versions as well.[341] Luckily, a wealth of "technical assistance materials" has been created, some of it in general information booklet format, many in the form of FAQs, and some in video format. The relevant materials for small business owners are available at ada.gov:

- Title I: http://www.ada.gov/ada_title_I.htm.
- Title III: http://www.ada.gov/ta-pubs-pg2.htm#titleiii, but links to the various Title III publications are buried at this website page, so scroll down to the heading, *Title III: Materials Specifically For Businesses and Non-Profits.*

Title I. This section of the ADA mandates that employers (with more than 15 employees):

> *"provide qualified individuals with disabilities an equal opportunity to benefit from the full range of employment-related opportunities available to others. For example, it prohibits discrimination in recruitment, hiring, promotions, training, pay, social activities, and other privileges of employment. It restricts questions that can be asked about an applicant's disability before a job offer is made, and it requires that employers make reasonable accommodation to the known physical or mental limitations of otherwise qualified individuals with disabilities, unless it results in undue hardship".*[342]

So, what does that mean to a small business employer? If two candidates for a job are being evaluated and one does, and one doesn't, have a disability, does the ADA require the employer to hire the person with the disability? No – the wording clearly states, "provide ... an equal opportunity". This means then, that the employer is free to choose the *best qualified candidate*, and if that candidate happens to be disabled, the candidate cannot be discriminated against as a result of the disability. In fact, the ADA doesn't require an employer to "give preference" to a disabled candidate – but rather, to just give them an equal chance against a non-disabled candidate.[343]

---

[341] *Americans With Disabilities Act of 1990* (full text, with all amendments to date), ADA.gov website, http://www.ada.gov/pubs/adastatute08.htm

[342] *A Guide To Disability Rights Laws*, ada.gov website, July 2009 (with all following amendments), http://www.ada.gov/cguide.htm

[343] The preference factor has one exception – as defined by Section 503 of the Rehabilitation Act (RA) – covering employers who are federal contractors or subcontractors. The aim of Section 503 is to increase the *known* (versus unknown) employment rate of people with disabilities compared to others, by ensuring "that federal contractors include disability in their strategies around recruitment and hiring". To this end,

During the interview process, it also restricts the type of questions that can be asked of the candidate – specifically, an employer is not allowed to ask the candidate if he/she has a disability. What can be asked, though, is whether the candidate, having read the posted job description can satisfy all of the requirements of the job. Therefore, if the job being filled requires lifting 20 lb. sacks of flour all day long, and an applicant can't perform that level of physical activity, it would be their responsibility to say so in response to this question (and hopefully, from your posted job description, wouldn't have applied in the first place, knowing he/she isn't qualified).

The same type of rules apply for existing workers in your business. When you have a disabled worker, you cannot discriminate in promotions, salary, benefits, training, or any of the other business areas listed above.

But back to the ADA mandate above for an additional clarification. What is the ADA definition of a disability? Well, that's a tough one, as even the ADA clearly acknowledges that their rules don't list or identify every disability. By ADA definition:

> *"An individual is considered to have a "disability" if s/he has a physical or mental impairment that substantially limits one or more major life activities, has a record of such an impairment, or is regarded as having such an impairment. Persons discriminated against because they have a known association or relationship with an individual with a disability also are protected".*

Whew! No wonder something like 50 million Americans are reported (by the ADA itself) to fall in this category. And no wonder the ADA rules and regulations are so relevant to a small business entrepreneur. This description is not only broad and inclusive, but it contains some very real gotcha's that can trip you up. You are prohibited from asking about disabilities, either before or after employment begins, yet you are supposed to have job descriptions in your new job postings that enable a candidate to know if they qualify for the job or not, particularly on the "mental impairment" side of it. Also, the rule that any person who has a "known association or relationship with an individual with a disability" cannot be discriminated against could leave the employer open to claims even when none actually exist.

Lastly, there's the question of "a physical or mental impairment that *substantially* limits one or more major life activities", and "*reasonable* accommodation ... unless it results in *undue* hardship". The words "substantially, "reasonable", and "undue", by their very definition, are subjective words, and what's substantial, reasonable, or undue to one person might not be to another. You are still at risk of a discrimination claim unless you document the relevant background behind any of your actions and decisions, so that they can be used as explanation if a claim arises. It may not result in a decision in your favor, but it should be a factor taken into consideration.

Title III. This section of the ADA prohibits any business (*of any size*) to exclude:

Section 503 encourages these employers to "invite applicants to voluntarily self-identify as a person with a disability", as a way to develop better data about workers with disabilities. More specifically, Section 503 actually requires employers with more than 50 employees, and who have federal contracts or subcontracts of $50,000+ must have an affirmative action plan for hiring employees with disabilities. For more information about this, see *Section 503 of the Rehabilitation Act New Rules: Fact Sheet*, ADA National Network, 2015, https://adata.org/factsheet/section-503.

"people with disabilities from everyday activities, such as buying an item at the store, watching a movie in a theater, enjoying a meal at a local restaurant, exercising at the local health club or having the car serviced at a local garage".

One of the difficulties in understanding Title III is the terminology (as it also was in Title I). Keep these definitions (in ADA words) in mind:

- o "public accommodations" are "private businesses that provide goods or services to the public".

    There are 12 business categories covered under the term "public accommodation", and they encompass businesses such as restaurants and bars, retail stores and shops, service establishments, hotels, theaters, private schools, recreation and convention centers (sports stadiums and fitness clubs), doctors' offices, homeless shelters, private transportation services and transportation depots, zoos, funeral homes, day care centers. In other words, nearly all types of private businesses that serve the public are included in the categories, regardless of size.

    So, if you own, operate, lease, or lease to a business that serves the public, you are covered by the ADA and must comply, not only for existing facilities, but also for facilities that are altered, and new facilities that are constructed. *Existing facilities are not exempted by grandfather provisions that are often granted by building code officials.*

- o "private entities" and "public entities". A private entity is a private business – simple as that. A public entity is a state and local government facility, which is covered by a different area of the ADA.

What type of "public accommodations" might be required? The challenge here is you can't easily access a list of requirements directly from the agencies that enforce ADA compliance. Working with the U.S. Department of Justice, the Small Business Administration has created an *ADA Guide For Small Businesses*, a 19-page booklet that explains a smidgeon of ADA requirements, along with several examples to illustrate the types of accommodations a small business entrepreneur might be faced with.[344] If you serve the public in your business, this is a good place to start.

What will these accommodations cost, and what if I can't afford them? For large corporations, it's apparent from the language of the Act that everything they do in the future, plus everything that currently exists has to be made compliant, and with no fiddling around. Luckily for small businesses, the enforcers of the ADA recognize that small business owners don't have bags of money to throw around, and they seem pretty accommodating. To that end, "the ADA has requirements for existing facilities built before 1993 that are less strict than for ones built after early 1993 or modified after early 1992".

They also recognize that making a small business facility fully accessible might not be feasible, and the situation can be negotiated so that "accessibility is improved" without excessive expenses

---

[344] *ADA Guide For Small Businesses,* Small Business Administration booklet in cooperation with the U.S. Department of Justice, http://www.ada.gov/smbusgd.pdf

that could financially harm the business. Explained another way, when profits are down, removing access barriers can be delayed, and when profits are back up, there will be expectations to make some improvements. *Another factor to consider is, if you're in leased facilities the onus on getting the improvements completed can be with the landlord.*

Additionally, the ADA rules provide for tax credits to offset accessibility improvements (which should not be confused with a tax deduction – a tax credit is subtracted directly from your bottom line tax owed). This is available for businesses with less than $1M in previous year's revenue and with fewer than 30 employees.

OSHA and your workplace

Occupational Safety and Health Administration (OSHA). Unlike the NLRB, OSHA hasn't issued any memorandums or public pronouncements that identify employee handbook policies and rules that go against OSHA guidelines and regulations. Many employee handbooks simply contain a statement that the company is committed to a safe and healthy work environment – one that is free of safety hazards that might harm employees.

The flip side is that if you don't maintain that type of safe environment, you could be investigated by OSHA. Your employee handbook cannot prohibit an employee from filing a complaint with OSHA, or requesting an OSHA investigation – *nor can it prohibit disclosing or discussing workplace conditions with nonemployees from the outside.* It's against the law to "fire, demote, transfer, or discriminate in any way against a worker for filing a complaint – so again, establishing an employee handbook rule that makes a complaint to OSHA an actionable offense will be unlawful".[345] In fact, you might hear from OSHA without ever knowing that it was one of your employees who turned you in, as a complainant has the right to request anonymity.

OK, so you're thinking that your business has no real occupational safety and health concerns. You'd be surprised – and it would be a rare business indeed if that were true. If you have any type of premises that employees work in, you almost certainly have multiple factors to consider.

For example, take electrical wall outlets at employee workstations – seems innocent enough. But what if an employee adds one or more power strips to an electrical outlet, then loads it up with too many electrical gadgets, overloading the circuit that feeds the outlet (and if you have five workstations with outlets on that same circuit, what if those employees overload too). It's a recipe for starting a fire, and if you've overlooked the situation you may have an OSHA problem on your hands.

Another example. Let's assume you start up a small window-washing or painting company – both of which frequently use ladders. You supply your crews with 10′ step ladders they carry on their trucks. You don't provide any training, and don't make any rules for the workers with guidelines on how high to safely climb the ladder. Then you (as the owner of the business) bid a job that obviously requires the painter or window washer to reach higher than is possible from the maximum safe height of the ladder – and someone falls. You very well may have an OSHA investigation on your hands.

---

[345] *OSHA – How To File A Safety and Health Complaint,*
https://www.osha.gov/as/opa/worker/complain.html

Or, you decide to open an auto repair shop, but because automobile engines these days are so high-tech, you decide to specialize in repairs that are low-tech. Your shop does brake and clutch jobs (among other things), but you're not aware that OSHA has a rule governing such repairs – due to the likelihood of asbestos in the brake and clutch linings. If you do over five of either type per week, you must use one of two authorized practices to mitigate ingestion of asbestos fibers – a *negative-pressure enclosure/HEPA Vacuum System method*, or a *low pressure/wet cleaning method*. Even if your shop does fewer than five per week, you must still use a *wet wipe method*. Essentially, you're just a small business, operating by the seat of your pants, and you don't think you have any liabilities. One of your workers, though, ends up with health issues and it's diagnosed as mesothelioma – and sues your company for damages. Even if this worst circumstance doesn't happen – let's just say that an employee figures out that your workplace isn't operating up to proper safety standards and decides to call the local OSHA office to ask for a workplace review – then you still have serious safety and health problems on your hands.[346]

So, what should you do to ensure compliance with OSHA?

First, download and read the OSHA Small Business Handbook.[347] It's "not a legal interpretation of the provisions of the Act" (the Occupational Safety and Health Act of 1970 – known simply as "the Act"), but rather, recommendations based on federal standards for generally accepted safety and health practices. In addition, at least 24 states operate their own OSHA-approved safety and health programs, and while they may have different rules in some circumstances, they are not permitted by the Act to be less than the federal standards.

Second, get a copy of the *required* OSHA workplace safety and health poster and post it where employees will most likely read it at your business. To obtain a free printed copy of the poster, go to https://www.osha.gov/Publications/poster.html to order or download it.

Third, using the recommendations found on page 13 of the OSHA Small Business Handbook , identify those that are appropriate for your business. Then develop a plan for safety and health management at your place of business. It may sound hokey for a small business that seemingly has no obvious sources of safety and health issues, but even if that's true, no business is free from circumstances and events beyond your control (floods, fire, earthquakes, a car smashing into your premise ... the list would have no end).

---

[346] *Occupational Exposure: Auto Mechanics*, Asbestos.com, http://www.asbestos.com/occupations/auto-mechanics.php.
[347] *Small Business Handbook*, Occupational Safety and Health Administration, https://www.osha.gov/Publications/smallbusiness/small-business.pdf

Chapter 10 Basic Company Policies

"If your company has a clean-desk policy, the company is nuts, and you're nuts to stay there."

Tom Peters, business management consultant
and author of In Search of Excellence

Operational policies

Ground rules must be laid to identify customer care rules, company business hours, employee working hours, workplace rules, employee schedules, employee payroll routines, use of company equipment, expense accounting, and a myriad other details that arise day-by-day. Earlier chapters provide lots of pros and cons about each of these. When it's just you and a handful of other employees that you've brought on board, operational policies can be handled very casually, and although they may still lead to costly disputes later on, odds are good that you can fly under the radar for most of them. At some point these rules will be ready for creation of a formal Operating Manual, particularly for outward-looking policies – i.e., those that deal with situations outside your company, such as customers. Others, specifically relating to inward policies are better suited for inclusion in your Employee Handbook. We'll cover just a few of them here.

The key to success with these rules is having documentation about each, if nothing more than background notes that you first stuff away in a document file on your laptop, so that when a problem or question is raised, you have contemporaneous thinking that backs up how you arrived at your decision. For example, if you've casually established an overtime policy for extra hours worked, you need evidence (in writing) that it was actually agreed upon between you and the employee (and that it meets FLSA requirements, as discussed in the previous chapter). If you've agreed to provide a company-paid cell phone, but stipulated that everything stored on the phone is owned by the company, and that the phone – *including its assigned phone number* – is to be returned at the end of employment, you'd better have a record of that agreement, created at the time the agreement was reached. If you've cut some special salary deal contingent on performance, it should not be a verbal agreement, but rather, a written and signed agreement that's made at the time it was originally reached.

It obviously doesn't make sense to have dozens of individual agreements *for each employee*. So unless an agreement is specific to one employee, it's better to standardize your policies, write them up, and have them in an employee handbook – but only after carefully reading the section in Chapter 9 with its warnings about following the guidelines of the National Labor Relations Board in what you can/can't say in an employee handbook. From a practical standpoint, though, and notwithstanding the cautions in that section, it would be foolhardy for you to operate your business without an employee handbook – at least for getting the basic standards down in writing for how you expect your employees to work on your behalf.

In this chapter we'll just scratch the surface of employee policies, covering a few of the most important ones.

> *"Your most unhappy customers are your greatest source of learning."*
> Bill Gates, co-founder, Microsoft

Refund and dissatisfied customer policies. Virtually every business faces the possibility that a customer will not like whatever they purchased from you and wants to either return it or get a refund. No matter how good your customer service policies are, you'll also have an unsatisfied customer at one time or another. It's just the nature of business. The challenge is, how to establish upfront policies that are fair, and that you can afford. No matter how much you inherently think "I'm the good guy and I'll always do right by the customer", it's imperative to remember that you're a small business, and can't absorb losses as easily as a large business can. To put it another way, you don't have the deep pockets that larger businesses will have.

Your first task is to establish your policies before the question arises for the first time, and have it clearly displayed (or noted) for customers to see at the time of purchase. This means posted on the commerce section of your website (if you do e-commerce business), or on store signage. Your return/refund policy could be printed right on the purchase receipt, or you could attach a separate return/refund policy to the purchase receipt.

The notice should state the time period that a return must be made, the documentation that must accompany it and the condition it must be returned in, and how a return will be made (replacement goods or service, or money returned to the purchasing credit card (never refund cash, and never without a purchase receipt). Decide in your own mind whether you will accept refunds for any reason, or only for what you consider a valid reason – and how firmly you will stand by that decision, or will you capitulate if it's a known good customer. Consider that your employees might be the company's face on a return/refund transaction, and therefore, are you creating a policy that will provide a fair working environment for you employees (i.e., asking your employees to face a situation that you would be unwilling to face yourself).

For some businesses, the return window of time can be critical, so don't just automatically set it at the standard 30-day default. Think carefully about how it can affect your particular business. With today's busy customers, many returns can stretch out to your maximum limit, and by the time you get some returns, the *season* for the goods might be over – and you're stuck and can't resell them. It's your business, so if a 10-day return window works best for you, or if a no-return/exchange-only policy works best, say so and stick with it.

Make certain your employees who deal with customers are well-versed in your return policy – before they are involved in their very first sale. Instruct them in how consistent you expect them to be in managing returns, and how they should escalate any problems that arise.

A more challenging aspect of this is training employees to deal with customers in handling confrontational situations. Whether it's over the phone, via a chat line, or face-to-face, knowing how to diffuse a situation is far better than letting a customer's frustration escalate the situation until it's out of control. Some employees may already have this skill, but others might naturally be more hot-headed and happy to escalate rather than diffuse. It's your customer, so the onus is on you to ensure all customer contacts are handled the way you want them to be.

If your returned goods are shipped back to you, how will you control shipping, and who will pay the additional shipping costs? If your rules are vague or nonexistent, you could wind up paying the cost, wiping out any profit on the sale. This can be especially painful if the shipping address is remote or rural, with high shipping costs, and you didn't think about that ahead of time.

When returns are made, try to find out the reason behind the return. Establish a mechanism to document the reasons, and if patterns can be identified, they provide valuable feedback for future products – thereby avoiding the same returns in the future. A lot of returned goods are due to poorly described offerings, which is particularly true for e-commerce sales. If your primary focus is pushing more sales at the expense of product descriptions, assume you're going to get a lot more returns, which defeats your original purpose.

Unfortunately, the overall area of customer service is outside the scope of this book, so you'd be wise to make follow-up internet searches (or get your hands on customer service books) for additional policy aspects.

Time-off policies. The following policies will rear their head the moment you have your first employee, and you need to get an early cut at them. Since several of them might have vesting time periods, or accrual considerations, it's not enough to just settle on *how much*, but also *how* you'll maintain recordkeeping for them. This will force you to develop at least a rudimentary personnel system, and that requires effort on your part, or an office manager if you have one.

Note: there's a thorough discussion about the pros and cons of these benefit-category policies in Chapter 7, Employee Benefits. For the next several operational policies, this is just a reminder to get the policies thought out and formalized.

- **Vacation and sick leave policy.** This is often a topic that new, first-time business owners fail to think about ahead of time. You definitely don't want the first thoughts about your vacation and sick leave policy to pop up in the middle of your first hiring interview (i.e., when the prospective employee asks what your policy is). Since they are both precedent-setting policies, you want to have them thought out and documented *before* that first interview.

  While your vacation policy is strictly an optional benefit, in practice it's essentially mandatory and you won't have employees for long if they don't see any vacation time on the horizon.

  Sick leave has long been a policy that small businesses don't often consider (or feel they can't afford), forcing employees to take unpaid leave when they are too sick to work – which means you'll have sick employees on the job, spreading illness to others (including customers) because they can't afford to take time off without pay.

- **Holiday policy.** Questions about your holiday policy will also arise when hiring your first employee (or shortly thereafter, when the first holiday rolls around), and you need to be ready for it. What will be your company's open/closed policy for holidays? If you're open, what is your policy on employees who have to work? What will you pay? If employees do not work on holidays, will they be paid regular salary? This set of questions is something you should think seriously about, and consider including some (all) of your employees in the discussion.

  And don't forget to evaluate the holiday list each year – preferably a couple of months before the start of the year – since several holidays (such as New Year's Day, 4th of July, and Christmas) change days of the week each year. You'll also need to decide whether the Friday before (or the Monday after) a holiday that falls on a weekend will be observed as the holiday (or not at all if you're a Scrooge), and whether the Friday after Thanksgiving will be a business day or a holiday. This is a surprisingly thorny set of questions, and you need to have a grasp on the issue ahead of time. Keep in mind that many people plan their time off from work far in advance, so you'll get questions about this earlier than you'd expect.

- **Family leave policy.** As an employer, you never know when this policy question will crop up. A new employee could have a death in the family the week after starting work, or you could find out a month after hiring a new employee that a baby is on the way – and what is your policy going to be?

Expense accounting. All valid business expenses, including travel expenses, are tax-deductible against your company's revenue – but *valid* is the operative word. Your bookkeeper or accountant will determine which expenses are valid business deductions, so make that determination part of your policy documentation. Getting employees to properly report those expenses is also something that needs to be documented. If you repay employees for their home office expenses, you need to document that the expenses are required to operate your business, and develop a procedure for the employee to report those expenses.

If an employee meets with current and prospective customers, not only does the expense reporting need to be documented in a procedure, but it would also be prudent to have some guidelines written up about types and amounts that are appropriate. Most businesses don't approve of 3-martini lunches, and evenings out at a club that specializes in pole dancing. So if that's the case, you'll be wise to mention it.

Travel expenses – quite a bit about the mechanics of travel expense reporting was discussed in Chapter 3 on recordkeeping suggestions. The do's and don'ts should also be documented in your policies, getting the point across that any employee who incurs a reportable travel expense is responsible for submitting a timely expense report – and that just handing in a credit card receipt isn't sufficient documentation, neither for your business justification of it, but also for satisfying the IRS. You need to let all employees who travel know that there will be consequences for not filing an expense report in a timely manner – and don't underestimate the importance of this, as employees generally don't step up to this requirement on their own.

Travel policies

Most small businesses will, at one time or another, have a need for business travel. Travel could range from a once-a-year-trip to a tradeshow, to almost daily travel that becomes a way of life for the employee. Travel could be as simple as loading up the truck to haul your wares to an exhibition of some sort, or it could be multi-week jaunts with customer stops all over the world. Whatever it is, and however much money it involves, you'll certainly want to treat the costs as business expenses that can be deducted against business revenue at tax time.

This is a prime area where you might feel comfortable straddling the line of correctness, but keep in mind the IRS will dig deep into travel expenses if they decide to audit, so be very careful to pick your comfort zone (i.e., whether you want to sleep at night). Likewise, it's an area where some employees might assume they can wheedle a few extra bucks out of you if they fudge expense reports, so make certain you pay close attention to the details on how all of this is accounted for. In one way or another, *all of this involves your money*, so don't be afraid to make the rules and then enforce them.

Expense travel style – guidelines for air, hotel, car reservations, and taxi services. How *you* travel can influence how your employees travel (or would like to travel). If they see you traveling first class and they're in coach, there will be resentment (I'm not saying it isn't possible to do this – just be sensitive to the potential problems if you do). So determine right up front if your company will have a class structure with regard to this, or if it will be egalitarian.

Are you aware of the actual cost difference in coach class airfare, versus business class or first class, particularly for international travel? Do you know the difference in hotel rates between a Hampton Inn or Residence Inn, a Marriott or Hilton hotel, and a Four Seasons or Carlton hotel? Do you know the daily price difference between renting a Hertz everyday economy or midsize car and a "Prestige Collection" car? Are you aware of the many add-on charges for car rentals – for example, an additional $16/day for a car with GPS, and should your employees waive the additional insurance (that's possibly covered by your company credit card)? Do you know the pros and cons of your employees having an open-ended expense account versus a per diem allowance for meals and incidental expenses? Hopefully, before settling on any travel expense policies, you'll have traveled enough to know these differences in detail. Travel expenses are very likely money from your bottom line that's going out the door, so this is an area you should be personally involved in decision-making and oversight.

But let's start at the beginning.

Who will make travel reservations? Ask this question of any employee and the answer you'd get is to let the employee do it. Before you go that route, consider it very carefully. This decision can cost you lots of employee time and extra company expense, so make sure you think it through long and hard before settling on the answer.

- Do you want your employees to spend company time being their own travel agent? If a professional travel agent (who uses sophisticated travel software every day) charges $25–$75 to book a business trip, it's very likely that booking will save you more than that over the cost of your employee doing it. And don't forget the time factor of your employee – if it takes them 15 minutes to discuss a specific trip with a travel agent, versus two hours of employee time fiddling around with a glitchy online tool, that's time on the clock they're spending – and it's not the job you hired them for.

- Do you want your employees making travel arrangements that get them the most airline/hotel perks and awards, or do you want what's financially best for your company and customer? Flying from Seattle to New York might be $50 cheaper on, let's say, United than on Delta, but if your employee is working his/her butt off to make Delta's Medallion Elite status, guess which airline will be chosen by the employee? If the upcoming customer visit has a Hilton just a block away, but a Marriott five miles away and requires a car rental – and the employee is two nights away from the Marriott Platinum Rewards level – guess which hotel will be booked if the employee has any say? Multiply the dollar differences, times how many employees you have traveling, times how many business trips your employees take, and this is the direct out-of-pocket costs to your company's bottom line if you don't get this right.

- You might have some employees who are great at booking their own travel, and others who make a total mess of it. Having a one-size-fits-all policy might not please everyone, but if you decide before you hire your first employee, then include that in whatever employee handbook or set of rules that each employee accepts at time of hiring. That way, you aren't changing rules midstream. This doesn't seem like such a big deal, but many employees somehow feel it's a perk to book their own travel – and if that's taken away later, rather than never being allowed, it can be problematic.

- Travel research by your travel agent can be significantly better than amateur research – better routing, better pricing, fewer screw-ups, better fallback support if there *is* a screw-up, more visibility on how to reach an employee in the event of problems, and very importantly, the booking can almost always be faster (particularly if the employee is doing it on company time). Good travel agents have lots of other clients providing feedback, and they typically have other travel agents in the office to collaborate with.

- If you choose to use a travel agent for the whole company, you can usually negotiate an arrangement with the agent so that you aren't nickeled and dimed. In my own company, I used one travel agent exclusively for the first two years – I was the only employee – and when I hired my first employee, I required that the same agent be used ... and it remained that way for the next 75 or so employees and 25 years. Because all of my employees booked through the same agency, we were not charged a per-ticket fee, so our prices were never more than we could get anywhere else – and were often less.[348]

- Having a companywide travel agent means that you have a single agent/company who knows your company's travel policies, sticks to them, and reports back to you if you have an offending employee (make certain you tell the travel agent you want that feedback). The travel agent will have a profile of your travel preferences, including which airlines you prefer to fly (assuming the price is the same), your typical flight time preferences, what seat you prefer, what hotel in each city you prefer, and all of the details of your car rental preferences.

---

[348] Larry Olmstead, *Why You Need A Travel Agent*, Forbes online, January 20, 2012, http://www.forbes.com/sites/larryolmsted/2012/01/20/why-you-need-a-travel-agent-part-1 /

Oftentimes, this means that you (or an employee) can call up and say, "I need to be in San Francisco on Sunday night, return late on Wednesday afternoon, usual hotel, and I don't need a car rental for this trip". Try doing this yourself online – the 5-minute call to the travel agent will be $1/10^{th}$ the time to do it online yourself. If an employee travels to a location that another employee has been to previously, the travel agent can also reference that information.

- Employees will argue that your company can establish profile requirements that online booking agencies (such as Expedia or booking.com) will hold bookings to – for example, not allowing first class travel, or not booking concierge-level hotel rooms. That may be true, but those profiles are very loose and lax, with loopholes your employees can slip through with ease. Besides (and as an example), booking a full price airline ticket in order to get a better frequent flyer upgrade option, or to gain more frequent flyer miles, can easily cost you as much as a first class ticket, so they're staying within the *profile requirements*, but totally defeating your basic cost-saving goals. With a travel agent – i.e., a real human – who makes the reservations for your employees, you can ensure that all of your cost-saving goals are adhered to.

- Travel agents know _all_ the ins and outs of fare types – all of those fare codes that you see on ticket stubs and reservations – defining whether the ticket is refundable, nonrefundable under any circumstances, nonrefundable but can be exchanged for a future ticket, and on and on. A good travel agent can also work some magic when an unexpected trip change or cancellation comes up, and that magic probably won't be nearly as possible with employee-booked travel. The travel agent should be given guidelines on the types of fare classes to use, and that can be huge in controlling costs.

- If travel problems occur during a trip, the travel agent is indispensable for getting the traveler out of a jam – much more so than with an online booking site, or booking directly with the airline. Make certain your travel agency provides their emergency contact information to every employee traveler, including off-hours support – and also make sure that information is in the hands of back-home office support personnel, as they might need to reach an employee during travel times, or assist with problems.

- Travel agents provide complete itineraries of a trip, including airline information (even multi-airline reservations), hotel information, car rental information, the cost breakdown, and all of the traveler information – and all in one format. They can shoot it to you in electronic form for easy reference.

  Sure, if you book airfare yourself on Expedia, for example, you get an itinerary e-mailed after you've completed your reservations. But what if you then booked a hotel through Trivago, and then found the best car rental rate by booking directly with the rental company? You now have multiple itineraries, each in a separate e-mail. This wide disparity of information is difficult enough for the traveler to keep track of ... and impossible for your office back home to get a handle on (or even have access to).

- When you have multiple employees traveling to the same location – for example, to a tradeshow or convention – the benefits of a travel agent multiply, since just one person is working on all of it at the same time, rather than each employee spending online time. In my own small company, we had a traveling tradeshow booth for conventions and provided technical tradeshow speakers to a half-dozen shows each year, with upwards of 10 people in attendance at each – and often arriving from all over the country. Granted, the travel agent had to work on different flights for each person, but could book multiple rooms in the same hotel, with the same keystrokes necessary for a single room. Local transportation was a lot easier to coordinate (and a lot cheaper) with one person doing the arrangements. Having one point of contact, our office knew exactly how to contact any employee outside of tradeshow hours. And it was a huge benefit in managing overall travel costs, particularly important since these travel expenses were all on our nickel.

- Employee online-booked travel is significantly more difficult for multi-leg journeys, let's say, if you're going to New York, then to Atlanta, then Washington, D.C., then Los Angeles, and then back home through San Francisco. Using an online service, you can have multi-leg reservations, but the complexity of doing so, and the individual training required to successfully book it just doesn't make sense. During the trip, if you have just one problem along the way, the complexity of getting it smoothed out is excruciating. Dog-leg routing is also very difficult, as are out-and-back round trips with return points different than the original destination point (i.e., fly to New York, take the train to Washington, D.C., and fly home from Washington, D.C., producing a gap between NY and DC). For a travel agent, this is all duck soup because of their reservation system software.

- Southwest Airlines was a long time holdout on allowing travel agents to book flights on their airline. That has changed, provided the travel agent/agency has a "Travel Agency Certificate" on file with the airline. Nevertheless, Southwest Airlines does not allow online booking sites such as Orbitz, Travelocity, Priceline, Expedia, and others to participate in travel searches – it is the only U.S. air carrier that does not "syndicate" its fare system to these search sites. Supposedly, by not allowing third-party booking sites, it allows them to "keep their fares lower, and they have better control over the customer experience" (these are their words, and almost certainly have little actual fact, so take it with a grain of salt).

In my own company, the decision to use a designated travel agent was totally a no-brainer ... but nevertheless, one or two employees grumbled about it constantly. The fact of the matter was that it was my privately-owned company's money they were traveling on, and I had every right to set the rules and expectations. Every employee had the right to make their own travel arrangements when traveling on personal business – but guess what? – almost all of them used our company travel agent even for their personal travel ... they found it easier and better.

What to do about frequent traveler accounts? The easy and best answer is, nothing. Whatever points/miles the employees can accrue, so much the better for them. It's their bum that sat in the airline seat, it's the employee who had to be away from family and friends to do business on your company's behalf – and provided all of the cautions above are considered, this is a good employee perk that doesn't cost the employer anything.

Long ago (1990s), some companies took the stance that frequent traveler points/miles earned while on business travel belonged to the company,[349] and required employees to sign over miles

---

[349] Adam Bryant, *Earning It: In This Buyback, the Stock Is Your Frequent-Flier Mileage*, The New York Times, December 10, 1995, http://www.nytimes.com/1995/12/10/business/earning-it-in-this-buyback-the-stock-is-your-frequent-flier-mileage.html

from their personal account to the company, either for their own future company business travel, or worse yet, for another employee's travel. It takes an incredible bean counter mentality to think that's right. It was a very unpopular idea twenty years ago, and one that you don't want to even consider.

Assuming you buy that argument, frequent traveler programs have nevertheless opened the door for a potential employee conflict of interest. The programs aren't known as "loyalty programs" for nothing – they are specifically designed to create loyalty in their frequent travelers. So for many employees, if deciding between a less-expensive airline ticket and the employee using their preferred frequent traveler program, guess which they'll choose? It takes a pretty straitlaced employee to opt on their own for saving the company money (particularly if a customer contract is paying for it). That's one of the biggest and best arguments in requiring travel to be booked through the company's travel agent.

Your company has a potential way to benefit from this too, and we'll explore that in the next topic.

Business account credit cards for employee business travel. Most likely when your first employee is scheduled to depart on business travel, it will become obvious that your employees need a way to pay for expenses during their trips. Providing corporate credit cards to your employees might seem like an unnecessary luxury, and it might seem like a terrible financial risk, but the fact is, you don't really have much choice. Sure, if you (the owner) are going to accompany every employee who travels, you can pay for their expenses on your card, but that soon becomes impractical.

Expecting your employees to put your company's travel expenses on their personal credit cards is totally unacceptable for many reasons. The employee might not have sufficient credit available on their cards – and damage deposits required on hotel and car rentals can easily put them over the top of their credit limit, without them even realizing it. Plus, they need to pay down their personal credit card accounts on a completely different timeframe than you're set up to deal with. You'd be mixing _your_ business expenses with _their_ personal money – just think about the rigmarole of vetting their expense reports with their personal credit card statements. Lastly, it isn't professional and businesslike, and besides, it just isn't fair to ask that of your employees.

The simple fact is that if your employees need to pay for airfare, hotel rooms, car rentals, and other business expenses to travel for your company, they need a business credit card, and you need to step up to the plate. Besides, none of these three travel industry types accept cash, and for hotels and car rental agencies, they additionally have damage and no-show deposits that are required to be on a credit card.

Once you make the decision, you'll almost certainly want to standardize cards across all of your employees. That leads to the question of which brand of credit card is overall best for your company. The choices will make your head spin, but you'll probably winnow it down to basic criteria discussed below. Unless your mind is already made up on a preferred card, your best bet is to research the latest offerings with available websites that have comparison tools – such as www.comparecards.com, www.cardhub.com/best-credit-cards (this one is particularly good if award perks are important to you, as it breaks the cards out by category), www.creditcards.com, www.creditkarma.com, www.nerdwallet.com, or www.reviews.com/business-credit-cards. If you

are interested in a credit card that awards the best airline mileage perks, try
http://viewfromthewing.boardingarea.com/best-credit-card-offers/.

Here are several considerations you should take into account when selecting a business credit card for employees:

- **Charge card vs. credit card.** These two terms are often used interchangeably, but in fact they are significantly different. With a charge card (such as the standard American Express card), you use the card just as you would a credit card, but the *total amount* charged during the card's statement cycle is due on the following payment date – and the card does not have a credit limit. By contrast, with a credit card, you can either pay the full amount due at the end of the monthly cycle, or make a minimum payment and let the rest roll over to a revolving credit balance. When a credit card limit is reached, no further charges can be made over the limit.

  In fact, a charge card account *does* have an internal credit limit, based on your previous spending habits, and you often aren't told what that limit is. When the limit is reached, the charge card company will contact you to find out if all is financially OK, and for reassurance that you're going to make the necessary payment – and they may not allow further charges until you've made a payment that satisfies them. You need to stay on top of this, as the card might be denied when an employee is trying to check into a hotel 3,000 miles away from the office.

  Because a charge card requires full payment each month, there is no interest rate associated with the card, but a penalty will be assessed if you don't pay the balance on time. A charge card typically carries a higher annual fee, because the card company isn't relying on interest charges from unpaid balances. A higher initial fee will usually be assessed when taking out a charge card, and a higher merchant fee will usually be assessed for a charge card. For that reason, some merchants won't accept charge cards.

  The two types of cards have minor differences with respect to your company's credit score and credit rating. Because a charge card doesn't have a preset spending limit, it usually requires a higher credit rating than a run-of-the-mill credit card. But because a charge card doesn't provide you with actual credit, it doesn't help build a better credit score or credit history (except to flag whether you pay on time or not). As a result, any balance you carry on a charge card isn't treated as debt when your company's debt-to-available-credit is calculated.

  The two charge cards most in use are American Express and Diners Club International (this latter card was essentially gone from the market for many years, but as of 2014 is back – although it's really a MasterCard in disguise).

  VISA and MasterCard are the two dominant credit card issuers, but each has dozens of variations to choose from, all sponsored by banks or other financial institutions. Most link with additional partners (airlines, hotels, you name it) in providing award perks.

- **Annual fees.** Annual fees range from $0 to hundreds of dollars. Make sure you read the fine print on this, as many offering a low initial fee jump to a hefty annual fee after the first year. The average annual fee for an everyday VISA or MasterCard is around $50/year, so make sure you multiply this by the number of cards you'll need, not only now, but in future years. (In my own company of 80 people, we had around 60 employees who were frequent travelers and carried the American Express Business Gold Card, where today's annual fee is $175 – for a total annual cost of $10,500 – at the time, though, it was only $50/year, or a *mere* $3,000.)

- **Piercing the corporate veil ... again.** If your company is structured as an LLC or corporation, where the single biggest benefit is your limitation of liability, protection from the financial liability again goes out the window with corporate credit cards. In signing the agreement for a corporate credit/charge card program, a non-negotiable clause you'll be signing is a personal commitment to pay all charge amounts if your company isn't able or willing to. So you're personally on the hook if you simply can't pay down the credit charges, even if an employee decides to skip town and move out of the country.

- In my company, where we had two dozen traveling employees at any given moment, our corporate American Express balance every month was over $100,000, due and payable in full 30 days after each statement date. That was a huge nut to crack for the company, but it was also something that kept me awake at night if I knew the company was having cash problems. This additional personal risk factor made it doubly important to keep a close eye on travel costs, even if a customer was paying for the travel, as the credit card payment was typically due before we were paid by the customer.

- **Interest rate on revolving credit.** Similar to annual fees, low introductory interest rates are offered by many card issuers to sucker you in, then they jack up rates after the first year to what could almost be called usurious rates. (In fact, credit card interest rates are typically far higher than many state's usury law maximum limit for non-credit card loans – which, for example, is 12% in Washington state[350]). Incredibly, usury laws generally do not apply to retail credit cards, especially if the issuing company is headquartered in a state that does not have a defined maximum interest rate limit, or has a ridiculously high percentage. So guess where the credit card issuers are headquartered?

- Protections afforded by the card. Some cards provide rental car insurance that cover damage and injuries better than a personal policy provides. Others provide life insurance for the traveler when the purchase for the travel is booked on the card. Some offer extra traveler insurance for unexpected events, such as last-minute cancellations, lost or damaged luggage. If your employees (or you) are traveling a lot, these protections can be valuable.

  One time I had a checked suitcase stolen from the baggage carousel, and when I tallied up the personal items lost with it, their value was far higher than the airline would pay – and every additional dollar of the value was covered by my corporate American Express card.

- **Airline or hotel affiliations with credit card companies.** Card perks (cash back, loyalty program miles/points) with branded credit cards are well-known these days, but as a business owner, you should be aware of significant ramifications. The airline/hotel affiliation awards mileage or points to the card owner (note I didn't say the card holder), such as a United Airlines Chase VISA that awards Mileage Plus miles for charges on the

---

[350] *Usury Law*, Washington State Department of Financial Institutions, 2014, http://dfi.wa.gov/financial-education/information/usury-law. To find your state's usury law limits, go to http://www.lendingkarma.com/content/state-usury-laws-legal-interest-rates/

card. As suggested above, employees are getting the direct airline, hotel, and car rental mileage/points on their personal frequent traveler accounts, so, you want to ensure that the additional business credit card miles/points accrue to the primary master account (controlled by you). So in selecting a credit card company, make sure it has a corporate account capability, sign up each employee's card, and make sure the points can be consolidated to a single account, where these perks are available for however you wish to use them.

The perks available in this category are too numerous to mention in detail, plus they change so fast, it would take a serious credit card or travel blog to keep up with them.

Here's an example, though, of how perks can work to your benefit. In my own company, we selected the American Express Corporate Gold Card for each employee's travel card. When our accounting department enrolled each new traveling employee for their corporate Amex card, they also registered that card in a corporate version of the Amex Membership Miles program. The miles in that program were privately owned by my company, justified (in my mind) on the basis of my personal guarantee for payment of the entire account if the company defaulted on it for any reason. With 60+ employees traveling a lot, this added up to about a million miles each year, and the company took good advantage of it to pay for my travel when it wasn't paid for by a customer contract. The employees were aware of it, they were aware of the reason for it, and I never heard a whisper of complaint about it. Also, each employee got to keep their own airline and hotel mileage/points, which is what they really wanted.

- **Foreign transaction fees.** If you have employees traveling internationally, these fees can quickly add up, and based on how much it could amount to overall should be a definite factor in your card choice. The fees are typically 2% of the entire transaction amount (some are as high as 2.7%), which can add up to hundreds of dollars if there are lots of charges on a trip. Elite or prestige cards often waive foreign transaction fees, but usually charge a higher annual fee.
- **Prestige of the card company.** This might matter to an employee handing his/her card across the counter to a hotel reception clerk, but that should not be your consideration. It's customers you want to impress, not vendors, and you hardly ever show your corporate credit cards to customers. The card companies will often use this in their advertising, but there are much better reasons to consider one card issuer over another.

Overall, a business credit card account is a good thing for your company to have. Whether you have traveling employees or not, there will be numerous other times that you'll need to use the card for payment. It provides a good paper trail of business expenses, and a great way to ensure personal finances aren't commingled with business.

Lastly, the credit card account will be in your company's name, but each employee's card will have their individual name on the card. The monthly statement will be sent directly to your business address – an aggregate statement that includes the charges against every card. This provides a cross-reference for your bookkeeping staff to correlate charges against expense reports. It's also an important way to ensure an employee isn't embezzling from you by using a personal card and passing fraudulent or incorrect charges on to you.

Set a strict rule – *no* **use of a company credit card for personal charges –** *period.* This should be an ironclad rule, and one with serious sanctions if anyone violates it. Sure, you might excuse (one time) an employee who claims to use a company card accidentally – making the excuse, "gee, I just grabbed the wrong card from my wallet", but the odds are, the person's personal card(s) were max'ed out at the time, and they figured this would be an easy way to cover it in the short term. My suggestion is, don't buy it.

My example. After an international business trip, one of my company's technical staff stopped by our accountant's office to alert her to a charge that would show up on the next corporate American Express statement – and that it should be moved over and charged to him as a cash expense for the trip. He explained that it was *accidentally* charged to the company American Express card by mistake and asked that it be charged against his cash allowance for the trip when it arrived. She took him at his word, but then when the statement arrived she found the charge was listed to the "Happy Time Escort Service". She was pretty naïve about it, and when I came into the office that morning she asked if I knew what an escort service was. It was known that the guy's wife handled all the money and bill payments in their family, and if he'd used his personal credit card he would have been found out when the next statement was received.

Use of personal vehicle for business travel. This one is pretty straightforward. For any business travel that must be done with an employee's personal car, require the employee to submit an expense report, claiming the number of miles driven, and then reimburse using the current IRS mileage rate allowance. The rate allowed by the IRS changes every year, so look it up on the internet each year, and get a memo out to all employees on the new rate for the year. For 2017, the rate is $.535/mile (down from $.54/mile in 2016) – so you can see that the rate actually goes up and down from year to year.

In my company, we had a frequent traveling employee who owned his own small plane, and he actually made it a condition of his employment with us that he be allowed to fly to customer locations (within a certain radius of his home base). I was extremely leery of it at first, but after thoroughly checking it out we decided to allow it. Our attorney and insurance agent advised that we require him to add our company as a named insured to his aircraft liability insurance, which didn't cost him (or us) anything, and it was easy to do. He paid for all aircraft expenses (fuel, parking ramp fees, and obviously, maintenance), and claimed his flight miles as if they were highway miles by car, and we paid accordingly. In a dozen years that he worked for us, there was never a problem.

Airport shuttle services and airport parking. This doesn't seem like an expense that should need to be covered in a travel expense policy, but if you don't get a handle on it, the costs can be high – and many employees will opt for whatever is easiest for them, regardless of what it costs you. There isn't a one-size fits all solution for how your employees will get to/from the airport, either at their home end of the trip, or in the city they're heading to. This also isn't something a travel agent will book for your employees, and whichever your employees choose, they'll expect you to pay for it. So, you'll probably need to establish a somewhat flexible policy, and then have your bookkeeper monitor it for abuse.

Every city is obviously different, every airport is different, and the distance from each employee's residence to the airport is different. Most medium-to-large cities have an airport shuttle van service, where the ride pick-up/drop-off can be at home or at a nearby hotel. On average, the one-way, 1-person charge in a shared van service is likely to be $17-$25, so this might add up to a total of around $50 for the total on both ends of a trip.

By contrast, an employee parking their car at the *on-airport parking garage* can run from $25-$35 *per day*, making the parking cost for a week-long trip around $175. Big difference!

An employee parking their car at an *off-airport parking lot* (and using a discount coupon that's always available for the asking), the same week-long trip would cost around $75. It's a bit more than a shuttle service, but within reasonable range, so these should be your two policy standards that employees are required to use.

So, what's the best policy option for the airport/hotel transfer at the customer end of the trip? Again, it depends on which airport and city. The costs are all over the map, and you should look carefully at it when more is known about the cities your employees will travel to. Here are some examples just to get an idea.

- Denver – (DEN) the airport is 25 miles outside the city, and taking a taxi to/from the airport and the city is at least $55, whereas a SuperShuttle is around $22. There's no possibility for any type of light rail transportation.
- Chicago – (ORD) the main airport (O'Hare) is under 20 miles from downtown. At $5, taking the 'L' (which is short for the Elevated Train, and officially it's the Blue Line) to/from O'Hare and downtown Chicago is the cheapest, easiest, and fastest way to get there – but the downsides are, you have to schlepp luggage on and off the train, plus it dumps you at a train station, and from there you likely have to take a taxi. One alternative is by taxi, and the cost would typically be around $40-$50 + tip, and the other is a shared-ride shuttle service, at around $35 each way.
- San Francisco – (SFO) the main airport is about 20 miles from downtown. Three options: BART train service, taxi, and airport shuttle. A *round trip* BART purchase-ahead voucher costs $20, and this is by far the most economical option – but again, the downtown termination is at a BART station, and from there to a hotel is either by walking or taxi. Taking a taxi will run about $45 each way, so a round trip will be upwards of $100. An airport shared-ride shuttle service will be under $20 each way.
- New York – (JFK, LGA, EWA) JFK has become mostly an international airport, LaGuardia is the closest airport to Midtown and Upper Manhattan, and Newark (NJ) is closest to Lower Manhattan. The airline your employees fly in or out of will likely determine which airport is used. Subway, taxi, shuttle, and private hire cars are available for all three airports, and the options and cost are so varied that you should look at https://www.tripadvisor.com/Travel-g60763-s301/New-York-City:New-York:Arriving.And.Departing.html for details.

Paying for pets during employee business travel. This one might come as a shock, but it's not uncommon for employees to insist the company pay for boarding their pets during business trips – the argument being that the company needs the employee to travel, so therefore it should be responsible for out-of-pocket costs they incur with it. Don't buy it. A word of caution, though – any employee who feels unjustly treated by this rule will likely be the one who fiddles their expenses in other ways to make up for it.

Some employees feel they can only travel if their pet goes with them. That's OK, but don't accept extra hotel charges for pet sanitizing or cleaning, or additional pet charges with the airline. Also, most car rental companies don't allow pets in their cars, so the employee is violating their rules if they disobey it.

Accompanied pets on airline travel also incur costs – either in-cabin or in the baggage area – and if you don't have procedures and rules in place, the cost of this can readily be hidden in the overall ticket price. While the additional pet cost will be separated out on the flight itinerary, it would be easy for the employee to list the overall airline cost on the expense report (including the traveling pet), and if the bookkeeper isn't checking the itinerary for hidden costs, this can go unnoticed – at a typical cost of $100 each way on the ticket.

Per diem or expense account for meals and incidentals during business travel? This decision can be complicated – not to mention messy – in several ways.

A big travel expense question you'll face is how your company will pay for meals an employee eats "on the road" – meals they would otherwise be eating anyway, but where eating at home could be purchased at lower cost. It's also relevant to all the little cash costs that add up during a business trip – hotel doorman/bellhop tips, the taxi ride across town to meet with a client (now it's often charged to a company credit card), an Uber/Lyft account or public transportation charges, and laundry and dry cleaning.

It's hard to locate good information on which of these travel expense methods to use. You can find pros and cons of each, but it basically comes down to your company's situation. Of the few statistics available, most companies use a combination of actual travel cost method for some items (air fare, hotel, car rental), and a per diem for others (meals, incidentals).

Expense Account. When you give an employee an expense account for travel, even if you establish some fairly detailed rules, you're basically giving them carte blanche to spend your money any way they see fit. Odds are, you'll have some employees who are as spend thrift with your money as they are with their own – and you'll have other employees who have no problem spending your money with abandon.

Sure, you can write all the guidelines you want on expense account charges, but you'll almost certainly see an uptick in the number of business lunches and dinners where clients are wined and dined, and where the employee is actually getting really good meals that aren't of very much business value – with the employee basically dining on much better meals than you'd like to be paying for. Hotel minibar charges will start to show up on expense reports. You'll see the employee becoming the extravagant tipper they'd like to be (but otherwise can't afford). They'll begin to prefer a town car for airport-to-hotel trips rather than a plebian taxi or light rail. Rather than pack a few more day-to-day clothes into a bag that might have to be checked, you'll find more and more hotel laundry and dry cleaning charges. These extras can easily add several hundreds of dollars to a trip – and it's coming out of your pocket.

Unless you want to spend a lot of your time (or your bookkeeper's time) poring over expense reports to validate expense account charges, or worse, dealing with a growing number of invalid charges, and facing confrontations with employees who are abusing it, you'd do well to avoid expense accounts.

Per diem. With a per diem (which is Latin for "each day") the employee travels on a meal and incidental expense *allowance*, meaning it's a set dollar amount the employee receives for each day of travel, and they can choose how to spend it on meals and incidental out-of-pocket cash expenses.

The best way to make this work is to have an actual expense account allowance for the major expenses – airline, hotel (including WiFi charges), personal car mileage allowance, taxi or car rental, bellman/doorman tips, airport shuttle services. Then the per diem will cover expenses that the employee would have at home, but that cost more when away – such as meals, snacks and cold drinks from vending machines or minibar, hotel laundry services, etc.

To be fair about travel cost differences from city to city, the per diem amount can differ from location to location and country to country. In my company, we used a couple of different per diem rate guides, and on the internet today you can find one that fits your requirements. Just be careful which guide you use – if it says anything about government employee per diem rates, stay away from it, as the rates are astonishingly low (plus they tend to include hotel costs in the bundle). If it's from an upscale source – such as Travel + Leisure magazine from American Express – it will probably include all daily costs for the employee in a given city, including high-cost hotel rates – and it will completely ignore the less-traveled places your employees might be going to.

For my own company, we used a per diem guide that made sense for the areas we were traveling to – not high enough that our employees could live high on the hog, but not so low that they'd starve (and knowing they would be paying for food costs back home anyway, so this was meant to cover the *differences* in cost).

Interestingly, how our employees used their per diem ranged all over the map. Word got back on a couple of them that they ate breakfast, lunch, and dinner at McDonalds, easily pocketing over half of their per diem – effectively a salary boost for them, but not very nutritional. We had one instructor who packed *a week's worth* of tuna fish salad sandwiches in a cold pack and flew off to New York City – with just the clothes on his back and his guitar under his arm (it's amazing he didn't get ptomaine poisoning from the sandwiches – and we ended up sacking him for a bunch of other stupid things).

Cash advances for business trips. Employees shouldn't be required to front the cash expenses – such as all meal costs – while on a business trip. For a 5-day trip, that could easily cost $500, and many people don't have that kind of cash lying around. You can solve that by giving a cash advance check to each employee before they set off on a trip. The advance would simply be your daily per diem amount multiplied by the number of days of the trip. At the end of the trip, the employee would reconcile the cash advance with actual cash expense account items (tips, taxi, etc.) and per diem on his/her expense report, and if their cash expenses were valid and over the per diem amount they'd either get a check for the difference, or the debit carried forward to their next trip advance.

Filing expense reports. Everyone – including you, the owner – must be required to turn in an expense report *for every trip* – and your policy should be that it must be filed within one or two days of returning from a trip (which, I can assure you, will be like pulling teeth). Without this documentation, business expense deductions for the travel costs cannot be declared – and many traveling employees aren't too concerned about this hammer over your head.

Expense report filing should never be allowed to be sloughed off, because that invites after-the-fact creation of expenses that never occurred – plus in some cases you can't invoice if it's a customer-paid expense. Employees should be encouraged to fill them out on the trip home, with accompanying receipts, and have them ready to hand in the first day back at work. If not, you're setting yourself up for a problem that can be costly.

Nowadays on the internet or in smartphone apps, you can find any number of software programs for expense reporting, and if you go that route you need to pick one that's right for your company – now and for the longer term. As in other situations discussed in this book, at the Capterra website page on Top Expense Report Software Products (http://www.capterra.com/expense-report-software/), you can research dozens of products available. What you won't readily find, though, is easy-to-compare pricing information in relation to feature requirements for your situation.

For example, with one top-rated product, Certify Travel Expense Management, you either need to speak directly with a sales representative to get pricing, or you need to sign up for a 15-day free trial period. If you dig through the details of the payment expected at the end of the trial period you'll discover that the software cost is $8/month/user – which can add up pretty fast. If you only have one or two people in your company who are traveling, spending $200/year isn't much, but once you get up to 10 traveling employees you're now spending $1,000/year. On the other hand, if you integrate this software with your accounting software, plus other cool features it could have, you might conclude that it's a real bargain compared to every traveler filling out forms, submitting them, and then having a bookkeeper manually enter the data into the accounting system.

Your expense reporting guidelines can help you sleep better at night, knowing that you aren't being bamboozled by one or more sharpie employees who want to take you to the cleaners, and figure the best way to do it is with some fiddled expense charges. With all else you have going on as an entrepreneur, you don't need to lose sleep at night over this.

Company-paid memberships to airline lounges. Most companies don't provide employees with memberships to airline lounges as a benefit, even to very frequent travelers – unless, of course, the company is large enough that it can throw a lot of business towards the airline and gets the membership at a discount.

First, those memberships are not valid, deductible business expenses to the IRS – some people claim they've managed to get it accepted, even on a tax audit – but it might depend how thorough the person conducting the audit is. TurboTax (from Quickbooks) says it isn't accepted by the IRS: "Some business expenses are not deductible under any circumstances: Dues to business, social, athletic, luncheon, sporting, airline, and hotel clubs".[351]

Second, it can quickly become quite expensive, at maybe $500/year per employee (United Club, AA Admiral's, Delta Sky Club, and Alaska Airlines are all within striking range of $500 each).

---

[351] *Valuable Business Tax Deductions*, a downloadable PDF, http://wbarlincpa.com/wp-content/uploads/2015/02/Tax_Deductions_Businesses.pdf

There's no question, airline lounges can be a quiet, comfortable refuge from the hordes of travelers at the gate, but if your employees want the comfort of these lounges, they can pay for them with airlines miles or out of their own pocket.

Staying in hotel "concierge-level" rooms. Many business category hotels (Hilton, Marriott, Westin, and a dozen others) have special member-type floors, where guests receive extra perks – such as a morning continental breakfast, happy hour glasses of wine and appies, free newspapers, free WiFi, all in a comfortable lounge. They also provide a cachet for the traveler too, since they typically require a special key card for access to the floor, or to the lounge – and for some people, they indicate "I've arrived".

Employees love the concierge-level rooms, since the free breakfast means more cash that's not coming out of their per diem. Free drinks in the evening mean they also aren't hitting the hotel room minibar at their expense.

Whether these rooms are worth it isn't the question here. The question is: can your small business budget afford it? Each night's room charge for a concierge floor versus a standard room can easily cost $25–$50 – yes, that's *each night's* extra cost – and if you're paying for the employee's travel expenses (rather than charging it off to a customer), that amount is coming right off your bottom line.

Which brings us back to the question of who is making travel arrangements in your company. If your employees have talked you into letting them make the reservations, it will be very difficult for you (or for your bookkeeper, for that matter) to know if they've booked into a concierge-level room or a standard room. If all travel reservations are done by a travel agent, it's easy to establish a policy with the agent that use of hotel concierge-level rooms is strictly forbidden, unless personally approved by you.

If your employees really want to stay in a concierge-level room (let's say, when they are traveling with their spouse and want a little extra luxury), they can always pay the difference, or they can use their hotel's frequent guest points to upgrade to that room. There's really no reason you should pay for it. (A challenge will be to pick up on an employee who decides to upgrade to a concierge-level room upon arrival, since the difference in nightly cost won't be known by your accounting office.)

Mixing personal travel with business travel. Having a spouse or companion along to share travel makes any trip more enjoyable, especially if the travel location is a desirable vacation destination, and a few extra days are tacked on. That's all good, creating happier employees and making it easier for them to agree to travel – but you need to have rules in place on how travel costs will be handled. This area is rife with opportunities for abuse, and one where you need to set guidelines with your travel agent, the employee who is traveling, and with the bookkeeper who needs to scrutinize the expense report.

For air travel, the employee obviously pays for the spouse's ticket, but your rule (which employees and your travel agent need to be aware of) should specify that the spouse's ticket be charged to a personal credit card. Employees may want to use 2-for-1 airline ticket deals, which often require that a *full* price ticket be purchased in order to get the free one. Obviously, the traveling employee will be on the paid ticket, but that ticket may be much more expensive than the discounted ticket that would have been purchased otherwise. This can easily cost you $200-

$500 more than the lowest coach fare, and you shouldn't be paying for it as part of your employee's spouse traveling for free. Your travel agent should handle these situations on a case-by-case basis, and alert you of the situation for decision-making on how you want to handle it.

Hotels sometimes charge more for two people in a room. Aside from the traveling employee, the only other person who might notice this would be the travel agent (who should notify your bookkeeper when this occurs, for appropriate handling of the expense report). A more expensive room (such as a king bed room, or concierge-level room) may be requested. The chosen hotel might be where the fun part of the trip is planned, possibly resulting in higher costs.

Extra days on the trip should be closely monitored from the expense report. If the normal business portion of the trip is scheduled for Monday–Wednesday, with travel out on Sunday and return on Wednesday, the reported expenses should only be covered for that time period, and the employee should pay for anything else. In this case, though, the downside for the company is that some of the expenses will be charged to the company credit card (extra hotel and car rental days, for example), which means the amounts will have to be collected from the employee, with credit card payment covered by the company until that happens.

So, what appears at first glance to be a great win-win situation for the company and employee is actually a situation fraught with potential problems – problems that you need to get a handle on with guidelines before the first such trip comes up.

Chapter 11   Developing Your Employee Handbook

"Large or small, our actions forge our futures and hopefully inspire others along the way."
Howard Schultz, Executive Chairman of Starbucks

As you're working hard to make your new start-up company viable as a bona fide business venture, don't rush to create a formal employee handbook to contain your policies. The things you get wrong can be as dangerous as the ones you're trying to control, so you'll want to work on the handbook when you've learned more about your business operations. For now, give the following discussion a good study so that you know what your areas of concern should be – so that as you're getting your company past the early growth stage, you aren't tumbling into any of these pitfalls. Later, when it's time to actually create your employee handbook of policies and expectations, you'll have a better chance of getting it right.

It goes without saying (or should) that an employee handbook isn't required until you have ... well, um, employees. In some business structures – a corporation, for example, or an LLC that has elected to be taxed as a corporation – you, the founder, will be the company's first employee – so you'll fit that definition from the get-go. And while you might think that you, as the owner, don't have to abide by official policies, you'd better get used to the idea very early – if for no other reason than to keep from establishing precedents that might make life difficult for you when you have additional employees. More importantly, though, you'll need to have several policies fleshed out before you place the ad to begin hiring your first new employee.

At first you can just write them down on ad hoc pages that you hand to your newly-hired first real employee, and include along with it an acknowledgement by that employee when hired. Some policies could be verbal. The acknowledgement can then go into the employee's personnel file (which you're about to create). This not only gets you off to a reasonably good start, but can potentially save you a lot of grief later on.

Research for your employee handbook

Some HR experts advise that you use caution when writing an employee handbook and policy statements, keeping various parts of them intentionally vague, and containing general statements to avoid implied contractual commitments. And that you should always make explicit statements within the text that you reserve the right to alter, amend, or change any handbook policy, at any time and for any reason. (See the section on *at-will* employment in Chapter 6 for specific details on this concern.)

Check your state and local labor laws. Before you settle on your employee policies, it's important to verify they are in compliance with state and local law – and for that you need to do several internet searches to find applicable law.

The first search should be: *"yourstate employee labor law".* Not all states are created equally, though, so you need to be careful about the hits you get. To avoid the clutter of commercial sites that are trying to sell you consulting services for creating an employee handbook, or an expensive online template that you can create a handbook from, concentrate on hits that have a URL qualifier of .gov. At those sites, you can browse all you like, right at the source where your state's labor rules are written and enforced. You might expect to find a bunch of government legalese, but quite the contrary – many states have created easy-to-read English language definitions of labor law, or FAQ pages.

Some examples of a few representative states:

- a search on *"washington state employee labor law"*[352] brings up "Workplace Rights – Washington Department of Labor and Industries" – at http://www.lni.wa.gov/workplacerights/, and from there a page of links to comprehensive rules or policies for employees working in the state. Each link takes the reader to a simple language definition, with a few FAQS to clarify details.
- a search on *"illinois employee labor law"* brings up "Laws and Rules – State of Illinois", at https://www.illinois.gov/idol/Laws-Rules/Pages/default.aspx, and again, there's a long list of links to the labor laws and rules for the state.
- a search on *"california employee labor law"*, a near-top hit is "Frequently Asked Questions – California Department of Industrial Relations", at http://www.dir.ca.gov/dlse/dlse-faqs.htm and – each link directs to narrowed-down FAQS specifically about a topic.
- a search on *"wyoming employee labor law"*, a non-.gov hit has a heading of *Labor Standards – Wyoming Department of Workforce Services* at a .org URL - http://wyomingworkforce.org/businesses/labor/. It is an official website of a state agency, and has a link at the top of the Home Page to Employers/Businesses where you'll find all of the state's labor policies and rules.
- for the state that's rated the "most entrepreneurial state" – partly on survey results that factored in "helpful government websites to cut red tape" – a search on *"arizona employee labor law"* turns up a mishmash of hits, only one of which is state government agency (.gov) related, and it's a terse 5-page PDF, promisingly titled *Arizona State Senate Issue Brief – Labor Employment Laws'* (at a download address of http://www.azleg.gov/briefs/Senate/labor%20employment%20laws.pdf), but it's actually quite lacking. (And maybe that's the point – it's popular for employers because it has few employee labor laws to contend with.)

---

[352] I added the word 'state' in this particular search because most browsers will confuse Washington State with Washington, D.C.. In all other states, it's better to leave off the word "state", as it leads the browser to think you're looking for labor law for that state's government employees.

- even Alaska (our least populous state) yields several .gov hits on a search for "*alaska employee labor law*", _including a few that will get you waylaid_ (so don't go there). The best hit is an 86-page PDF titled *Employment Practices and Working Conditions – Wage and Hour Administration, Pamphlet 100.* And while it's written in actual statute language, you can use an alphabetical index at the back to locate any topic.

Another good source for early start-up browsing on employee policies is the SBA page on employee handbooks at https://www.sba.gov/content/employee-handbooks. While it's not written as a how-to guide for actually writing an employee handbook, nor does it have detailed topics and content for the handbook, it's a good overview of the types of policies and procedures you should be thinking about when you're starting your business.

Keeping up with labor law changes. As soon as you hire your first employee, it's incumbent on you to stay up to date on local, state, and federal labor law changes. Many states and local governments are in the process of major changes that you need to be aware of. Minimum wage laws are a hot topic of discussion (*as of this writing, California, Arizona, Washington – in all nineteen states have increased their minimum wage above the federal limit of $7.25/hour[353]*). Paid sick leave and paid/unpaid minimum maternity leave are two others. "Just-in-time" scheduling, creating havoc with employee's lives, is also being looked at. As a new business owner, you need to keep your ear to the ground on these topics and learn how they are going to affect your business. Most of these topics are covered in local news, so watching your local TV news, or subscribing to your local business journal publication could be important.[354]

Finally, get your hands on at least one sample employee handbook. A search on "sample employee handbook" will find a dozen commercial firms that want to sell you a handbook or handbook template (they aren't worth it).

Check federal labor laws. Once you've thoroughly checked your state's requirements, your next search should be for federal labor laws that can affect your employee handbook. Most small business owners never expect to find themselves in trouble with federal regulators – how in the world would they even _find you_ when there are 5 million small businesses in America? But remember, if the feds do hear about you, it's most likely the result of a disgruntled employee, or even a competitor who doesn't play fair.

Your best source for that is the National Labor Relations Board (NLRB), and several website references were provided in Chapter 9.

---

[353] *State Minimum Wages | 2017 Minimum Wage by State*, National Conference of State Legislatures (NCSL), 1/5/2017, http://www.ncsl.org/research/labor-and-employment/state-minimum-wage-chart.aspx.
[354] American City Business Journal (ACBJ) has pretty much rolled up the local business journal marketplace across the U.S. Their publications, known collectively as The Business Journals, include 64 – and counting – of the largest metropolitan areas in the country, providing local business news in each area. The home page for ACBJ is www.bizjournals.com. A list of the cities and metropolitan areas they cover is at https://secure.bizjournals.com/subscribe?csrc=6311. (Your local publication is also a very good place to have your business written up, particularly if your potential customers might also be reading the journal. Your local business journal is likely on the lookout for small business to highlight.)

Creating an employee handbook

At some point as your business grows, you'll find it's appropriate to formalize an employee handbook. There's no right time for this, but given how litigious our society is, the earlier you can do it the better. As soon as you have employees – and no employee handbook – the odds grow that you'll find your company in some sort of dispute, maybe with an employee who makes a claim against something you've done (or not done). The longer you have a haphazard set of company policies, the more likely you are to lose in a dispute. Additionally, having these policies codified (and presumably well-written) will likely increase your company morale, as well as employee confidence that your company is a good one to work for. It also gives employees a better sense of their rights and responsibilities.

Whenever you decide is the right time, the importance is in getting it right, not half-right. You need to ensure that the handbook maintains your status as an at-will employer. It should also help to define employee classification, such as full-time, part-time, seasonal, and exempt/non-exempt employees.

A reasonable assumption is that you won't implement your first employee handbook until after you have some number of employees (you almost certainly have too much to do in getting your business up and running before that time, and besides, you probably don't know enough about how to write it and what it should include until then). That assumption affects how you will implement it, as there will likely be some ad hoc policies and practices that existing employees are already operating under, and you'll want to start new employees beyond this point on the first day with the handbook policies.

Who will oversee responsibility of the handbook? Chances are that you don't have an official HR person at this stage. If you have an in-house bookkeeper/accountant, that person is likely the official record-keeper for the company, with a secure (i.e., locked) office or file cabinet where personnel records are kept. This person should be your first choice for overseeing the handbook, or maybe even the person overseeing the writing of the handbook. This is not a trivial decision, as the details of how the handbook gets distributed, how you've accounted for receipt-of-handbook documentation, and a slew of details about how you format any disclaimers or important topics, all require you to handle this carefully.

The big problem for employee handbooks is ... getting employees to read them. They are usually tomes of at least 30–40 pages, full of do's and don'ts, a dry list of all company benefits for employees, and in general, not as interesting to read as the latest hot novel to hit the bookstores. At the same time, neither party (employer or employee) wants to be surprised – for example, an employee finds out later rather than earlier that some verbal suggestion or promise isn't really true, or the employer learns that no one is aware of a particular company requirement.

The supposed solution to this is having each employee acknowledge initial receipt (and reading!) of the employee handbook upon hiring or when it's first introduced, and just as importantly, acknowledging that they have received and read any additions or changes subsequently made to the handbook. Not surprising, this acknowledgement is the part *not done* most often, maybe because it requires a lot of follow-up, resulting in many policies that are difficult or impossible to enforce if it comes to a legal situation where lawyers start to chip away at your legal grounds. More on this in a minute.

<u>What published format should the handbook have?</u> Important questions to resolve are how to disseminate your employee handbook, and where to keep the official copy, and how to manage future updates. If you're of the old-school mindset, a printed copy will work just fine, handed out to every employee. If you're high-tech, it could be an electronic copy on your company's secure intranet (that requires employee sign-in to access).

As mentioned above, the typical employee handbook runs at least 30–40 pages, so if you're planning a printed version, be prepared to print one for every employee, decide how it will be distributed, and how you'll know it's been received and read. Advance of this, it's very important to resolve your plans for handling future updates to the employee copies as they are completed in the master copy of the handbook. You could have nicely bound copies made at your local printer, or a 3-ring binder – but again, think about how it will get updated in future. Some employees will be diligent in filing updates; others will throw updates onto stacks of other papers, never to see the light of day again. If the updates have to be filed at the back, plan on them possibly never being read again (resulting in the original version being considered in force). Some of today's workers have an aversion to reading anything printed on a piece of paper, so that could be another consideration.

An electronic copy of the handbook, either a shared copy that everyone can look at on the company intranet or an employee-protected area of the web site, or distributed individually as an e-mail attachment, works equally well. As an economical matter, an electronic handbook copy is certainly cheaper than printed copies, for both the original and for subsequent updates.

However, a practical problem with an electronic version could rear its ugly head in the midst of a legal dispute and could cost you huge amounts of money – and the more money at risk, the more likely a lawyer will be looking for angles such as this. The problem has to do with how you highlight important disclaimers and other information in the handbook, and whether that highlighting shows up in all situations where an employee might be reading the handbook. For example, you might use colored font in either an electronic copy or a printed color-copy version – but what if you send it to employees in electronic form and the employee prints it in black and white ... the colored highlighting disappears. Or, in your electronic copy you use highlighting tricks for really important things – such as flashing fonts or symbols – and this doesn't show up in a printed copy that someone might read.

What type of situations – i.e., disclaimers or important information – are we talking about? Primarily, those concerned with at-will employment and implied employment contract litigation. With either one, you can lose your rights as an employer to deal with employees as necessary. Nobody wants to fire an employee for no good reason, but there might be times when you have a good reason, but don't have the accepted documentation, or know there are financial difficulties looming and you have no choice.

Every state in the U.S. (except Montana) presumes an employer is an at-will employer, and it's incumbent on you to clearly spell that out in all written documents or verbal statements between you and the employee relating to employee status. When I say "clearly spell that out", I mean that you should take great pains to state this in employment contracts and in your employee handbook (and by all means, don't make statements such as, "oh, you have a job here for life" – as that can be considered a promise). In your employee handbook, don't bury the at-will statement in a paragraph that no one is going to read – instead, highlight it in colored or bold font, surround it with a box, repeat it multiple times in appropriate areas, and make sure it isn't ambiguous. When it comes to a legal challenge, how specific and pointedly you state this to employees, the more likely it's going to stand up to the challenge. By all means, read up on this to get more details – it's *that* important for you.[355]

Planning guidelines for introducing your employment handbook:

- Communicating it to your employees. Every company has some preferred methods of communicating important business information – your style of doing things, your workplace and employee structure will be a factor, your company geographic issues, and how the handbook will be disseminated might dictate it. Whatever communication method you choose, make sure it's done in such a way that everyone sits up and takes notice and is primed to read it. You could do it by e-mail, cc'ing every employee in the company; it could be at your regular Monday morning meeting; posting it in the employee break room; or mailing to employee home addresses – or any combination of these, so long as it will reach everyone to let them know there is a call to action (which is, reading it and signing the acknowledgement when it arrives).

- In the communication, clearly lay out when the policy handbook will become the "law of the land". You might discuss particularly important new or changed policies in the handbook (and if appropriate, any grandfathering provisions), and how the handbook policies differ from today's – shall we say – ad hoc company policies.

- State when and how the handbook will be distributed, and stress the importance of reading the handbook in its entirety, as it will be the official source for the policy details.

- Clearly note the employee acknowledgement requirements, and have a policy statement that covers employees who don't (or won't) read and sign whatever acknowledgement plan you've settled on – and just so you don't forget it in future, have the statement include the same actions for any handbook changes that come down the pike later.

- You'll likely win points if you stress that the handbook is in no way intended to be punitive in any regard, but rather, informative as to what is expected of each employee – and importantly, what each employee can expect of the company. Try to portray it as a beneficial new step forward for the company, showing everyone that they are valued employees, and that the intent of the handbook is to more clearly spell out policies that were previously word-of-mouth, or ad hoc.

- If there are any new and significant policies – or benefits, for example – that will have transitioning issues, get those out in the open. This could include changes in carryover policies – such as comp time, sick or vacation leave, or *clearing of the slate* issues such as attendance.

- Include a disclaimer statement (which you'll also want to have in the handbook itself) that reserves the right to change policies at any time, with or without notice. And here's where you also want to include a statement that employment with your company is at-will (as described by the labor laws of your state – and states where employees are domiciled), and that the handbook does not constitute an employment contract of any kind (this is such

---

[355] Lisa Gueren, *Employment At-Will: What Does It Mean?*, Nolo online, http://www.nolo.com/legal-encyclopedia/employment-at-will-definition-30022.html

important legalese stuff that you want to make certain it's been reviewed by an attorney or certified HR person).

- Last, but certainly not least, ensure that nothing you say – verbally or in writing – makes any reference that would suggest limiting of employee rights as defined by the NLRB, such as the right to join a labor union, discuss salaries, and discuss work-related issues that affect employees.

Acknowledgement of company policies by employees. It is in your best interest to obtain a written acknowledgment from each employee whenever he or she receives a copy of the handbook, and to file the acknowledgment in the employee's personnel file as proof the handbook was properly distributed. Most importantly, this also shifts the responsibility for knowing the policies outlined in the handbook onto the employee. Because you're also going to include (aren't you?) the at-will and "no contract" language in the acknowledgement form, this will also demonstrate that the employee understands this situation.

Sometimes misguided employees will refuse to sign the handbook acknowledgement form, on the mistaken assumption that refusing to sign will mean they cannot be held accountable for *not* following and complying with policies and procedures in the handbook. This is not true, as the acknowledgement simply documents that they have received the handbook, and in itself does not legally commit them to abide by it (check this statement out with your attorney or HR specialist to ensure its validity in your circumstance). The fact is, their continued employment is conditioned on their compliance with the handbook – and this is strengthened by your continued standing as an at-will employer. If an employee refuses to sign, you can have a witness affirm that the employee received the handbook but refused to sign – and the witness then signs the acknowledgement form. Another option is to have the employee write on the form that he/she has refused to sign – illustrating that the employee was given the opportunity to sign. Frankly, this is a really strange situation, and it very likely means that you have other problems with the employee, and maybe those problems need to be checked out first.

You can find any number of handbook acknowledgement forms on the internet – search on *"employee handbook acknowledgement"*. Make sure you get a signed acknowledgement from every employee, not only for receipt of the initial handbook, but for every revision.

Managing employee handbook revisions. It's imperative that you establish – right from the start – procedures for changing existing policies and adding new ones. A "change" page that notes every update to the document is an extremely good idea, providing the date of the change, briefly annotating what the policy was before and after – and then filing a before/after image of the change in your recordkeeping file(s) for the handbook. This will take care of your historical change management, giving you a way to identify when and how change came about (which might also be a good thing to note on the change page).

At the same time, develop a plan for how you will introduce changes to the employee's copy, and how you will communicate the change to all employees (including their acknowledgement).

Chapter 12   Intellectual Property Rights

"People have to respect intellectual property"
Coco Lee, Hong Kong-born, American-raised
songwriter, record producer, dancer, and actress

Non-disclosure agreements

If your company has any proprietary information that would (or could) be damaging if leaked, or became known outside your company, you need to have non-disclosure agreements (NDA) in place with every employee who has access to that information. As discussed in Chapter 6, the likelihood that your company has valuable proprietary information is greater than you might imagine.

If your pricing structure is strictly between you and your customers, having someone leak your price sheet to a competitor can be damaging. You might have published prices, but negotiate hefty discounts to various customers ... and for varying reasons, and any discounts given are proprietary to your business. You have a right to identify it as such in your NDA.

If your customer and prospect list is disclosed to a competitor, they not only know your existing customer to go after for swap-out business, but also now have knowledge of potential new customers they weren't previously aware of.

If you've developed a process that enables you to manufacture your product less expensively or better than your competitor, or if you use a unique ingredient in your production, this can very definitely be considered proprietary information. It might not be a patentable process (or it might not justify the cost of a patent), but nevertheless, it can be claimed as proprietary information or company secrets.

It could be the key ingredient that gives your top-selling sauce its highly sought-after pizazz (and that you sell by the dozen over the counter in your café) – and every single employee who knows what it is – even in the accounting department where the invoice for purchasing raw materials – could be privy to this proprietary information.

Here's an example. In Chapter 8 we briefly discussed a small Seattle food purveyor, Marination, that serves Korean-Hawaiian street food. Several of their menu items are slathered with a sauce – it's really special and they call it Nunya Sauce. They also sell Nunya Sauce by the jar in their online store, and in the product description it lists soy, mayonnaise, and garlic – with a mention that the sauce gets its product name from the remaining "secret ingredients". As the owner of Marination explains in a press interview, Nunya is short for "nunya bidness". You can bet that every back office employee involved in producing and packaging this sauce – or has any association whatsoever with it – has signed an NDA.

There are literally dozens of things like this that make your business unique from your competitors, and you have every right to consider information about it to be proprietary to your company. You can craft an NDA covering every single detail that you want to keep confidential – but you risk the possibility of missing one or more crucial details, or additional details need to be added to the agreement as time goes by. So an alternative is to draft a broad definition of confidential information that covers virtually all inside company information an employee learns about that is not *publicly available* (and the last two words there are important).

To protect this proprietary information, it's incumbent on you to require employees to sign an NDA (a.k.a. Confidentiality Agreement, but that doesn't have the easy-to-remember acronym as NDA). The key decision is to determine exactly which employees must sign an NDA, and to make this a requirement at time of hiring. At first glance, you might think that only your key employees should sign, but don't forget that even staff level employees have intimate knowledge of who your customers are, what your prices are, what your processes are, and a myriad of other details about how you run your business.

You can find template NDAs all over the internet, but remember this – the cost of hiring an attorney to write an NDA template that's tailored for your business is inexpensive compared to the dollar value of a gaping hole that a cheap'ed-out agreement could cost you.

Post-employment agreements. Trying to push an NDA onto employees after they've been with you for a year or so smells fishy, and besides, by then, you lack leverage to get them to sign. It can be done, but typically requires some sort of consideration – a promotion or raise, a bonus check ... whatever works, based on how important it is for the agreement to be signed. If a post-employment agreement is signed, it's as binding as a pre-employment agreement.

Does an NDA zip the lips of an employee after termination? Yes, you can draft an agreement that binds the employee for a specified period of time after employment terminates – or you can even make it indefinite. Make certain this is specifically covered at the time of the employee's termination exit interview – any later and your recourse diminishes.

Consequences for breach of confidentiality. The most obvious consequence is termination – and this could be enforced even if the employee hasn't signed an NDA – for example, if a piece of information is known inside the company to be confidential and an employee discloses it, the employee can be liable for the disclosure. In addition, the employee could be sued, and if the suit is successful, the employee could be liable for monetary damages. If the information is disclosed to a competitor, loss of market share can be claimed, and the damages owed by the employee could be significantly greater. This is an area you really want to discuss with your attorney – and the best time to do it is *before* the problem arises.

Protecting your intellectual property – patents, trademarks, and copyrights

Intellectual property (IP) – particularly IP that you've assiduously protected, can be very valuable to your company. It can be an extremely valuable aspect of your sales and marketing success, it can be very valuable in keeping competitors at bay, and most important, it can significantly increase the value of your company when/if you decide to sell it.

Patents, trademarks, and copyrights on IP can be a multi-way street – they can protect you from someone else profiting from what you've developed, but if you aren't careful, they can also put you on a road to financial ruin. If you're getting ready to develop a technique or process that could lead to significant IP for your company, take the time and spend the money to check how clean it is against existing registered patents or trademarks.

Copyrights are a different breed, as current copyright law allows works to be legally copyrighted even if the copyright has not been registered – but you still need to make a concerted effort to search for existing copyrights.

It can be nasty to be down a development or marketing path – and worse, to the point of completed sales – and then find yourself in a patent, trademark, or copyright dispute with someone who beat you to it. If it's the latter situation, you could be slapped with a cease-and-desist demand; then when it's sorted out, you could be forced to pay very large sums of money to right the situation. In the former situation, if you can't find a non-infringing workaround, you might have no choice but to pay a license fee, or drop your idea altogether. Either way, odds are it could have been determined in advance, at much less cost than when you're further down the road.

You can do some of the upfront legwork yourself, by spending time on the U.S. Patent and Trademark Office (USPTO) website (https://www.uspto.gov/). First, click on the link for Patents or Trademarks, then click on the Search tab, where you'll find search instructions. My money would be on hiring a patent attorney to do the search, as they usually have better search tools (Lexis/Nexis, for example), and typically some trained staff paralegals who know how to do fast and efficient searches.

Is your intellectual property patentable? The USPTO has a clearly-written definition of what inventions are patentable – but it's difficult to determine in advance if your invention fits the definition. In simple terms, you can patent anything that is *"new, non-obvious, and useful"*, provided it falls within one of the following four categories:

- process
- machine
- article of manufacture
- composition of matter

And you must be able to describe your invention in detail, in terms that would enable someone "of ordinary skill in the art to make or use the invention".

Simple, huh? Well, yes, until you start reading the mass of information behind these "simple" rules established by the USPTO – with a lot of the basic rules over three centuries old. For example, their document describing the nitty-gritty details just for "patentability" is 240+ pages (in PDF format, which of course you can download if you wish) – *and this is just for computer-related patents!*

Common sense says that anything as complicated as patent writing and application submission is best left to experts. Working with a patent attorney to prepare, file, and monitor the process of a patent application can cost (at a minimum) somewhere between $5,000–$10,000, however, this may be some of the best money you'll spend as an entrepreneur. As a small business owner, this probably seems like a huge amount of money, but in the scheme of things it isn't very much, and if it can keep competitors from copying whatever new *thing* you've patented, it could be a drop in the bucket.

The ins and outs of patents are best left to a professional – and I can assure you, even with an attorney you'll have your hands full with assistance in writing the description, creating diagrams, and reviewing this quite long document.

Submit your patent application, and then wait ... and wait ... and wait.

Finally, your patent is issued – in my case shown in the sidebar, it was almost exactly three years from the date submitted.

Critical aspects of filing your patent application.

Timing is of the utmost importance in obtaining a patent for your invention. Here are the key dates you need to know with respect to filing a patent application:

- **Patent application date** (or filing date). Of all the dates that are relevant to your patent, none is as important as this one.

  As soon as you receive notice of your patent filing date, you can begin using the notation, "Patent Pending", with all sales and marketing literature or product distribution paraphernalia. This notation serves notice to your product's potential *infringers* of your patent that they may be liable for damages (including back-royalties), or seizure and injunction *once the patent is issued*.

  Patent Pending is actually a legal term, and you can only use it if you have received notice from the USPTO of your patent application. Using the term without it is considered a "deceptive act", and a fine can be levied for every such offense (in the case of

---

**Patents by Inventor
Ronald K. Ferguson**

Patent title: Reorganization and repair of an ICF catalog while open and in-use in a digital data storage system
Patent number: 7158999
Abstract: MVS mainframe computer systems employ the ICF (Integrated Catalog Facility) catalog environment to manage numerous data sets. To provide 24×7 availability of those data sets, the BCS (250,270) must be re-organized while leaving the catalog open to access by applications. To perform a re-org while open, a data CI correlation table (500) is constructed (314) and used to lay the data CIs into a backup file in logical order (316), so that they can be loaded into the new BCS (324) without sorting, thereby reducing downtime. Additionally, if the BCS is damaged during normal operation, repair of the structure must also be performed to ensure that correct access is maintained to all data that is cataloged in the BCS. Throughout the re-org process, structural integrity checks are performed on the data and index component of the BCS, and if errors are encountered, they can be repaired.

Type: Grant
Filed: February 20, 2004
Issued: January 2, 2007
Assignee: Mainstar Software Corporation
Inventors: Richard G. Pace, Martin K. Hasegawa, Ronald K. Ferguson

---

a product, every copy of the product can be considered an offense, so the fine can add up very quickly). This can be important to know, as you might have an unscrupulous competitor who is doing everything possible to get the best of you, including listing a patent pending when, in fact, there *is* no pending patent application.

Since patent law in the U.S. (plus Europe, and a bunch of other places) is based on first-file date, if two competing entities file a patent application for the same invention on different dates/times, the earlier date/time will have priority – and will be the only application allowed through the entire examination process for issuance of a patent (and this is where the importance of a possible provisional application can be important).

The patent filing date is also important in the context of a "provisional patent application filing" – which is a very specialized circumstance, and for this you are really advised to get a patent attorney.

- **Patent expiration date.** In almost all situations, your patent expires 20 years from the filing date. Note, this is from the *filing date*, not the issue date.
- **Patent publication date.** There are actually two patent issued dates, and you need to be careful which one you are referring to.

The first (and more traditional one) is the day exactly 18 months after your patent application's official filing date, and marks the date your <u>application</u> is published in the USPTO *Gazette*.

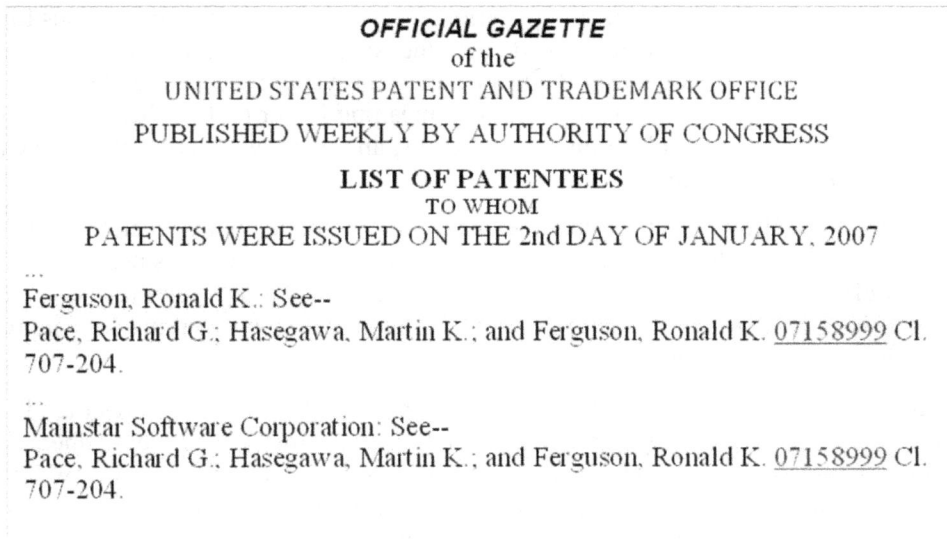

OFFICIAL GAZETTE
of the
UNITED STATES PATENT AND TRADEMARK OFFICE

PUBLISHED WEEKLY BY AUTHORITY OF CONGRESS

LIST OF PATENTEES
TO WHOM
PATENTS WERE ISSUED ON THE 2nd DAY OF JANUARY, 2007

...
Ferguson, Ronald K.: See--
Pace, Richard G.; Hasegawa, Martin K.; and Ferguson, Ronald K. <u>07158999</u> Cl. 707-204.

...
Mainstar Software Corporation: See--
Pace, Richard G.; Hasegawa, Martin K.; and Ferguson, Ronald K. <u>07158999</u> Cl. 707-204.

The second important date is when your patent is issued or granted. The implication of the *first* publication date is that anyone who looks up your patent application can see the details of your patent, such as how it works, how it is created, and what it can be used for. This seems dangerous, and in some ways it is, as anyone who now wants to *get around* your patent technology knows the details of what you've developed, and they can attempt to engineer workarounds that don't infringe.

If your patent description was written carefully enough, it's possible you have *invented* the only reasonable or practical way to accomplish it, and anyone who attempts a workaround will know what they are up against. It may be more advantageous for them to negotiate a licensing agreement with you, assuming you're willing to grant one (which could be lucrative, as it might result in a royalty to you for every copy of their product that's sold).

- **The patent issue date** (also known as the "grant date", or the "day of grant"). This is the big day you've waited for – the notice that USPTO has actually granted you a patent. This can easily be three or four years after your original patent filing date, and by now you've probably forgotten all the hard work you did in getting this patent – which is OK, since the protection for your invention actually began from the filing date. The importance of this date is that you can now begin to actually enforce your patent, and not just *threaten* to enforce it. The details on this are in the next section.

Getting the details right. Your patent is only as good as the information you put into it. Unless you've already filed for a dozen patents and have a good understanding of the patent process, you probably don't know how important it is to get right.

- Patent "claims" are the arcane part of a patent application that are guaranteed to make your head hurt as they are being written, and are the make-or-break details that will ultimately determine the success of your application – and later, will determine how well your patent stands up to infringement actions (and getting these claims exactly right is why it's really advisable to have an experienced patent attorney drive your patent application process).

There are three main parts of the patent application that you'll most likely be responsible for writing – at least the draft – of the actual text part: the Abstract, the Description, and the Claims. Of these, the claims are by far the most important, yet are the least understood by the average Joe Blow. Words with a common English meaning in our real world can take on specific legal meanings that aren't intuitive or obvious, and that's where the experience of your patent attorney is invaluable.

Being an average Joe Blow, when I wrote the basic text for my patent application, I first sat down for several hours with our patent attorney and we discussed what was necessary for the abstract and definition. When I'd finished writing these, we had a few more discussions to get them just right, particularly the detail level of the diagrams he'd asked me to write for the description, but otherwise it was a straightforward writing task.

When it came to writing the claims, though, we went back-and-forth more times than I could count. It was obvious the attorney had a really good idea of how the patent examiners think, and how they interpret the words within your claims. In the end, I let the attorney write the claims, and I verified them for technical accuracy. Luckily, my attorney had a bit of a software background, so he was a quick study on the highly technical aspects of what my invention was doing, and which parts of the process were important to the task.

In concept, the claims seem straightforward enough – "they serve the practical purpose of defining the elements that are protected ... [and] the claims are the pieces that are targeted in invalidity searches, to prove that they existed previously"[356]. In other words, the claims are the basic pieces of your invention that make it new, unique, and non-obvious (the three fundamental requirements for granting a patent), and therefore, if anyone wants to challenge your patent, they will try to disprove any or all of the three – and will cleverly try to pick

---

[356] Excerpt from Article One Partners website, Patent Claims, http://learn.articleonepartners.com/patent-claims/

apart the legal meaning of various words in your claims to their advantage. This is what often makes the claims section of a patent so crucial.

Importance of patents. The obvious and primary reason to patent an invention is to protect valuable intellectual property – potentially intellectual property that's cost you a lot of time, most likely a lot of money, and also very likely, a lot of blood, sweat, and tears.

A brief study of my patent might help put this in context. In the early 2000s, my company already had a software product on the market that was beginning to get some sales traction, not only in the U.S., but in other parts of the Western World. It was the fastest growing product in our small portfolio of products, and sales for it were approaching 40% of our overall revenue – which meant it was becoming vitally important to us.

We were soon locked in mortal combat, though, with an upstart software company that had the technical capability to develop a competing product, and once they did, they were willing to play any sort of clean or dirty tricks to win over market share (keep in mind, the worldwide mainframe software market for this type of product is in the hundreds of copies, so it's quite a thin market). It was imperative that we develop a slam-dunk addition to our product – an additional feature the competition couldn't quickly and easily add to their product.

In absolute secrecy, we launched a development effort for a product feature that would be highly sought-after by almost every mainframe computer user in the world, but which almost no one thought was possible (and even our own software developers were highly skeptical of being able to pull it off). The development proved successful, and knowing that our competitor could, by hook or by crook, duplicate our development once the overall concept was revealed – and worse, the only way they could do it was with under-the-covers techniques the same as we had used.

While development was still underway, we began a parallel patent application process. Once submitted, we still had to maintain absolute secrecy until the official application filing date. Immediately after that we trumpeted to the world what we had accomplished, and developed an entire marketing strategy for the product around that new feature.

In the end, this patent – which cost around $10,000 to obtain – paid for itself many times over, not only in product sales revenue, but in the company's later valuation for acquisition.

Enforcing patents. This is a two-way street – the first being the enforcement of a patent that you own, and the second is a claim that you've infringed someone else's patent. We'll have a brief look at both.

Let's look first at protecting your own patent. In the USPTO's own words, the specific purpose of a patent is "*a grant to the patentee ... of the right to exclude others from making, using, offering for sale, or selling the invention throughout the United States or importing the invention into the United States, and, if the invention is a process, of the right to exclude others from using, offering for sale or selling throughout the United States, or importing into the United States, products made by that process*".[357] In other words, a patent gives an inventor the right to exclude

---

[357] Excerpt from U.S. Patent Office website, Patent Laws, 35 U.S.C. 154(a)(1) Contents and term of patent; provisional rights, http://www.uspto.gov/web/offices/pac/mpep/mpep-9015-appx-1.html#al_d1fbe1_19854_1ee

or prevent others from using the patented invention – the right to enforce the patent if infringement occurs.

The operative words, though, are that a patent gives an inventor "the right ... to exclude or prevent". If you suspect someone of infringing your patent, the responsibility is yours to follow up, demand that they cease, and possibly either pay royalties on sales already completed and going forward, or negotiate with you for a license to use your patent property or process. The U.S. Patent and Trade Office will essentially provide little or no support in this, as it's not their responsibility, or even in their government agency charter.

By all accounts, pressing an infringement claim is a complicated business. Almost certainly, the first thing you'll want to do is hire an attorney who is experienced in patent law, and most likely, not just one who is conversant in patent law itself, but also in pursuing patent infringement claims.

But first, how do you even know if someone is infringing your patent? If your patent was a U.S.-only scope, someone in a foreign country could copy your invention with total impunity, provided they don't try to import it into the U.S. Even if the infringement is within the geographic scope of your patent rights, if you aren't watching your competitors like a hawk, they could use your invention without you even finding out. Depending on what your invention is, it could be incorporated into a finished product (or used in a different enough process) that even your best attempts to keep an eye out might fail. The worst situation could be that someone might be suspected of infringing – but who actually isn't, and might have found a workaround of your claims – and you go off on an expensive and distracting wild goose chase to stop it, only to find out that you haven't a case.

Who's Name Is On The Patent? Put more simply (and more accurate legally), who owns the patent rights to an invention? This could be very important to you in the future, either positively or negatively – and careful advance planning can ensure it isn't the latter.

If you are the sole inventor, or you are the single employee in your company, and you file and are awarded the patent, then not only will your name be on the patent, but you'll also own the rights to the patent (assuming, of course, that your application lists your name as inventor).

Patent rights can be assigned, either ahead of time with a "pre-invention assignment", or after the fact with a signed agreement. Either way, the individual inventor(s) name that was filled in on the original patent application will forever be the name on the patent when you search for it, even though another individual or company now owns the patent rights. When patent ownership rights change, the patent owner should, but is not required by law, to notify the USPTO Assignment Services Division by filing a Recordation Cover Sheet, either by hardcover submission, or through their online system (Electronic Patent Assignment System, or EPAS).[358]

---

[358] As a result of Executive Action by President Obama in June, 2013, the USPTO has issued "a draft rule to ensure patent owners accurately record and regularly update ownership information when they are involved in proceedings before the USPTO. This effort is aimed at improving the quality of patents issued, enhancing competition, facilitating technology transfer, and making it harder to hide abusive litigation tactics behind shell companies [my emphasis]. After receiving input from the public, the USPTO aims to issue a final rule in the coming months." Source: *FACT SHEET - Executive Actions: Answering the President's Call to Strengthen Our Patent System and Foster Innovation*, February 20, 2014,

When someone other than yourself – and possibly multiple people – is involved in creating a patented invention, all names can be listed on the patent application, and unless there is an ownership assignment, they will generally own the patent rights. Here's where your careful pre-planning comes in.

When an employee creates an invention while employed, the employee owns the patent rights to the invention, unless there was an employment agreement that assigned invention rights, or unless the employee was specifically hired (even without an employment agreement) for their inventing skills or to create the invention. A third situation is called a "shop right", where an employee may hold rights to the invention under patent, but because the employer provided, let's say, salary, work time, materials, tools, and a workplace, the employer gains a "shop right" to use the patented invention on a non-exclusive, non-assignable, royalty-free basis – even if the employee later assigns or sells the patent rights. All of this is murky, though, and not the best situation to find yourself, regardless of whether you're the employer or employee.

In the case of my patent mentioned above, the original patent holders include me and two of our software developers who wrote the bulk of the code, so our patent can be located within the USPTO data base by any of our names. Since the patent was assigned to our company (Mainstar Software Corporation) – through employment agreements – the company name is also listed as a "patentee" through the assignment, and the patent can be located on a search by company name. All three of us had Confidentiality Agreements with my company, and that agreement stipulated that any patents rights would be assigned to the company. When the company was subsequently sold, the patent rights then transferred to the company that purchased my company. Nevertheless, our individual names and my company's name will forever be in the patent file at the U.S. Patent and Trademark Office.

Trademarks. We've all seen the tiny ® symbol following product names. The letter R simply means "registered", and this symbol denotes a _registered_ trademark – i.e., registered with the USPTO. Similarly, the ™ symbol that you often see means only that someone _claims_ their word or symbol is a trademark, but most likely hasn't registered it.

By USPTO definition, "A trademark is a word, phrase, symbol, and/or design that identifies and distinguishes the source of the goods of one party from those of others. A service mark is a word, phrase, symbol, and/or design that identifies and distinguishes the source of a service rather than goods. The term "trademark" is often used to refer to both trademarks and service marks".[359] Unlike a patent that has a lifespan of 20 years, a trademark is perpetual – as long, that is, as you continue to use the trademark.

By registering a trademark with USPTO, you are serving notice that you own the mark, and that you have the exclusive right – nationwide – to use the mark in connection with the goods or services _associated with the mark._ Even if you don't register a trademark with the USPTO, you can still claim a trademark merely by using a trademark in the marketplace – but this type of

---

http://www.whitehouse.gov/the-press-office/2014/02/20/fact-sheet-executive-actions-answering-president-s-call-strengthen-our-p. You can read more about this draft rule at http://www.uspto.gov/patents/init_events/attributable_ownership.jsp

[359] Definition excerpted from www.uspto.gov, Trademark, Patent, or Copyright? http://www.uspto.gov/trademarks/basics/definitions.jsp

"local" trademark is conferred by state law, and it wouldn't prohibit someone from having their own similar or same trademark in some other part of the country.

A trademark does not give you exclusivity, in that it doesn't restrict someone from using your word, phrase, or symbol with goods and services that are not similar to yours – they just can't use a similar trademark with similar goods or services. Trademark infringement occurs when someone else's use of a trademark would likely cause confusion about the source of goods or services in the mind of consumers.

The words above, "associated with the mark", are in italics, as they are the operative words in the rights of a trademark. So what's in a word? Obviously, the word "apple" is not trademarked – and cannot be – primarily because you can't trademark a "generic" word that would prevent someone from describing a similar product. But, when Apple Computer (now Apple Inc.) was founded, and the corporate name became a trademarked name (along with trademarking the bite-out-of-the-apple logo), there was no inherent problem in using the word "apple" in the company name and trademarking it, as Apple Computer didn't sell the fruit called an apple. What the trademark did, though, was create a dispute with another trademarked corporate name, Apple Corps Ltd, founded about nine years earlier by The Beatles as their multimedia company. That dispute was settled with a payment (reputed to be $80M) with Apple Computer agreeing to stay out of the music business. So that left the world with three (or more) things that were all called "apple" – a generic name for a fruit, a music company, and a computer company. In 2003, though, when Apple Inc. launched iTunes, they crossed the music line, creating another dispute – one that for years kept all Beatles songs from being sold on iTunes – which was finally settled just recently behind closed doors (and it's why you can now purchase songs by The Beatles on iTunes). Interestingly, Apple Inc. now owns the trademark outright, and has licensed it to Apple Corps *for specific use,* but presumably just in the music business. The fruit called an apple is not infringing and has never infringed on the trademark in any way.

As with patents, a trademark is only as good as your efforts to enforce it. If you don't, you run the risk of your trademark becoming generic, and then anyone can use it. This is why the term "aspirin", originally trademarked by Bayer, is now generic (but only in the U.S. – it's still a trademarked name in Canada and Europe). Kleenex is still a recognized and official registered trademark, but it's used by consumers as if it's generic (i.e., we all say Kleenex in everyday speech to refer to any brand of tissue, but another company that sells tissue could not use Kleenex in their product name). Reputedly, The Boeing Company objects to any use of the word "boeing" used in a generic sense – as in "fly a boeing" even if the actual airplane happens to be an Airbus – as they don't want any association with their famous jetliner product to become generic.

Chapter 13   Get Started!

> *"Sustaining a successful business is a hell of a lot of work, and staying hungry is half the battle."*
>
> *Wendy Tan White, co-founder and CEO of MoonFruit*

Only <u>you</u> know if it's the right time to start a business

Starting a small business is a personal decision, and by its nature a decision that only you can make. As this chapter's quote says, it "is a hell of a lot of work", and it takes a huge amount of commitment, stick-to-itiveness, and the right kind of perspective about your priorities. You can ask friends and family for their opinion, but they cannot know your level of commitment to it, they won't know if it's truly right for you, and if *you're* right for it.

The simple truth is, there's no inherent right or wrong time to start a business. The more accurate questions are, is it the right time to start <u>*your*</u> business, do you have the right product or service, are you in the right place at the right time for this to be successful, and do you have the right business plan to make it happen?

Since the dot-com bubble burst (in the years between 2000 – 2016), an average of 500,000 new small businesses have opened their doors <u>*each year.*</u>[360] That's a pretty staggering number. If you assume equal start-up rates in each of our 50 states, that's 10,000 new businesses every year, in each and every state! But the better news is, around 50% of those businesses will still be around five years after their start. Your mission, should you wish to accept it, is to be one of the 250,000 businesses from your start-up year who are still operating five years on.

> *"Decisiveness is one of the most important characteristics of an entrepreneur."*
>
> *Mark Suster, 2x entrepreneur turned VC*

Here's how to get started

There's no question about it – the information in this book is daunting, complex, and will keep you awake at night if you worry about it. The truth is, you don't have to know the details of all of this information on the day you open your business doors. <u>*You just need to know it when you need to know it*</u> – and that means having an understanding of when that time is, and where to find the information . . . sort of like *just-in-time knowledge* that will keep you from making large and costly mistakes at the worst possible time.

---

[360] *Statistics of U.S. Businesses*, U.S. Census Bureau, https://www.census.gov/programs-surveys/susb.html

Importantly, it isn't hard to start your own small business, and it's something anyone with a strong desire, a good business plan, and who is willing to work hard can do. The biggest challenge is to buckle down, do the necessary planning, sort out your life choices – _make the decision_ – and get on with it!

There's no way to know the statistics of businesses that _aren't_ started as a result of indecision – what we can call _deciding not to start a business by not deciding_ – and therefore, reaching the decision by simply not doing anything. You might call this type of decision-maker the antithesis of an entrepreneur – frozen by fear of not making the right decision, fear of failure, fear of not being up to the task, fear of financial ruin … the list could go on ad infinitum. The trouble with this is, it's not an explicit decision, where you can say, _"this_ is what I've decided". (As we'll see in a bit, an even worse aspect of this is, you finally make a decision to start your company, but then continue to dither away in all of the important decisions you'll need to be made in building the business.)

There are lots of decisions

Some are big, some are small, you'll have dozens before start-up day, and thousands of decisions after you open. As a small business entrepreneur you can't get away from them. They inundate your daily life, and sometimes you just wish they'd all go away. Get past that feeling – they'll forever be a part of your life, so just get used to it.

The first key to successful decision-making is decisiveness. It's an incredibly important and unavoidable aspect of being a successful entrepreneur, so much so that there's no way around it. Most decisions will have to be based on less than complete information, so a quick decision, with little looking back to second-guess it, is the way to go. Because of that, figure that not all of your decisions will be right – maybe if three/fourths of them are right it's a good record – and you just have to move on. When mistakes crop up in your decisions, admit them as soon as you recognize them, correct course if necessary, and learn from them. In fact, some entrepreneur coaches suggest that if you're not wrong enough, well, you're not trying hard enough.

The second key is, as a small business founder you need to get a lot done, and dithering can seriously slow that down – to the point where business opportunities go by the wayside, competitors jump in ahead of you, employees lose focus, and decision requirements pile up on you.

Throughout this book were hundreds, maybe thousands, of decision points that you'll be faced with. Once you make that first gigantic one – to start up a small business in the first place – you ll be inundated with all the decisions that follow. Should my company be an LLC or a corporation? Should I have co-founders? What should the company name be? What logo design do I like best? What domain name will work best? In setting up the data in the Cash Flow/Budget spreadsheet you'll probably have a hundred decisions. Choosing your professional consultants – legal, accounting and taxes, banking, HR – could eat up an inordinate amount of time in reaching decisions.

In short, you can easily become paralyzed with the glut of decisions if you let it happen. Keep this thought in mind – _don't let it happen_! If there's anything you learn during your early start-up days, one of them should be fast and decisive decision-making. But – and this is a very large _but_

– this suggestion does not recommend zero analysis! It recommended that you quickly gather up all of the information at hand, recognize the information (or angles) that you don't have information on, and then make the most instinctive decision you can.

While we're on the topic of this, an even greater load of decisions will hit you square in the forehead *after* start-up. Customers will add complexity to the importance of your decisions. Financial challenges will add to the critical nature of the decisions. Employees will add to the directions you're going to be pulled. Company policies and benefit packages will add dramatically to the level of detail you need to be involved in. It will go on and on, and you'd better get used to it in order to succeed.

Entrepreneurs and personality types

Psychological coaches often try to identify personality types in people across an organization or small business – analytical, drivers, expressives, and amiables – and most people will fall into one or more of the categories. As a small business founder, knowing where you fit can help you understand how you make decisions, knowing the background on your focus in getting the job done, identifying your communication skills as introverted or extroverted, and recognizing whether you'll go out of your way to be non-confrontational or if you tend towards abrasiveness.[361]

In my own company we experienced a time where the company seemed to be heading off the rails – employees were at each other's throats, and several things just seemed to be going wrong. We brought in a psychological coach for once-a-week, half-day counseling sessions. In one of the sessions we were told to self-identify as one of the four personality types and then each stand inside a large circle on the floor with the personality type written in chalk – and if anyone felt they really fit in between two types they should position in between the two corresponding circles. Once everyone located the circle (or near circle) that best fit their own definition, our coach then guided us through a non-threatening and amicable group discussion about each person, with the aim of finding out if others felt each of us had chosen the right personality type. Interestingly, the group itself was in total agreement with each person's self-assessment.

Only two of us were in the drivers group – me (as the company founder) and our Software Development Manager (who was a former small business owner before joining our company). Some of the characteristics of the driver personality group are:

- A *take control* type, one who looks for opportunities to be in charge, and doesn't like situations where there's no say in decisions
- Establishes goals and gets things done
- Lacks patience in the details that aren't related to goals being focused on
- Can be aggressive, arrogant, or standoffish in the heat of the moment, and lacks patience with people seen as being in the way

This isn't to suggest that only a driver personality type can be a good entrepreneur – any of the four types can succeed, but they will each have to succeed in different ways. They will most likely choose different categories of small business to be in. They will each interact differently

---

[361] *Personality Types*, persuasive.net, http://persuasive.net/personality-types-analytical/

with other employees and customers. They will operate on different time scales and levels of urgency in reaching goals. They will operate differently in stress conditions, such as financial hard times or serious competitive situations.

Along this line of discussion, there's a fascinating book titled *Heart, Smarts, Guts, and Luck*[362] that delves into questions of personality types that make good entrepreneurs. According to the authors, all of the personality traits listed in the book's title "are the defining traits of great entrepreneurs" – not so much being combined in a single individual, but rather, which of the four traits is *dominant* in the entrepreneur. Better yet, the author's primary purpose is to see exactly what it is about each of the traits that translates into good entrepreneurial skills or mindsets.

Heart-dominant entrepreneurs have an overriding passion and purpose, most likely about their enthusiasm for the business idea, but also about becoming a business owner. This type of person is so confident the idea will work that rational arguments to the contrary might be dismissed.

The *Smarts-dominant* entrepreneur is highly rational, believing their business idea will work because of the facts they've collected. This person is intent on creating the business after doing a lot of analysis, not only business analysis, but also product, customer, and vendor analysis. There are multiple dimensions of Smarts – where some entrepreneurs excel in Book Smarts, others have lots of People Smarts or Creative Smarts, and there's also Street Smarts. Whatever it is, fundamentally the Smarts-dominant entrepreneur has gained their wide knowledge of the business idea or product/service from a source like this, and they are driven to get the business going. This person also does the most behind-the-scenes research in order to build the business case for their particular model. The book cites Jeff Bezos, founder of Amazon, who didn't create an online purveyor of food or liquor (for example), but rather books, having concluded from his research that this was the best business model to go after.

A *Guts-dominant* entrepreneur is just that . . . gutsy, and rearing to head off onto something new – and is a risk-taker. The guts-dominated arena is shared by two types – (1) the people who thrive on risk and seek it out, getting an emotional high on the risk itself, and (2) those who are risk tolerant, content to take calculated risks when they believe the odds are in their favor – the so-called *risk-tolerators*. An interesting aspect of the latter is their ability to make gutsy decisions to initiate the business decision in the first place, and then have more guts to make it all work.

Fourth is the *Luck-dominant* entrepreneur – several times described as a misnomer earlier in this book, with the author's belief that luck isn't what makes a good entrepreneur, but rather, the ability to recognize a serendipitous situation – good or bad – analyze it to see how it can benefit the situation, and then act decisively on it.

The authors of *Hearts, Smarts, Guts, and Luck*, lump the human characteristic of *optimism* into the Guts-dominant category, and here I tend to disagree. Instead, I would spread the optimism trait across all four personality types – and in fact, optimism might be the overarching personality trait of a good entrepreneur – and without a huge amount of optimism a wannabe-entrepreneur with all the heart, smarts, guts and luck in the world would have a hard time succeeding.

---

[362] Anthony K. Tjan, Richard J. Harrington, Tsun-Yan Hsien, *Heart, Smarts, Guts, and Luck*, Harvard Business Review Press, 2012, available at https://www.amazon.com/dp/B008O7DJT0/ref=dp-kindle-recirect?_encoding=UTF8&btkr=1

Optimism brings out a *positive attitude*, particularly during initial analysis of critical decisions. If every decision point starts with an instant negative analysis – finding all the reasons why it *can't* be done – the chances reduce significantly that a positive decision will be made – when maybe one is warranted. Instead, an optimist starts the analysis with, "hmm, this seems like a good idea . . . let's first see what the positive aspects of it are" – initially looking for all the reasons *to do* it, and then analyzing the drawbacks after gaining the initial enthusiasm. The benefit with this latter method is a greater likelihood of reaching a favorable decision – but it can also lead to a hasty decision that isn't well thought out.

> *"The important thing is to not stop questioning.*
> *Curiosity has its own reason for existing."*
> Albert Einstein

Intellectual curiosity. The granddaddy trait of almost all really good entrepreneurs is curiosity. When you're curious your mind is open to new ideas ... new ideas create opportunities … and the opportunities create possibilities. Curious entrepreneurs never take the status quo for granted. They ask questions relentlessly. They read for the sake of learning. They see learning as something fun. And they use that learning in new and exciting ways.

When you're looking at everything around you with a curious perspective, it's a wonderful catalyst for finding new solutions to customer's problems, identifying better ways to do things, whether it's an innovative new way to market a product, seeking out new pricing points to increase profitability, or better ways to get your products in customer's hands.

Is a curious mind something you have to be born with? For some it is. For others I think it can be learned – or at least, evolved. Growing up I can't remember very much curiosity in my own thinking, particularly compared to others that I read about.[363] Not long after I started my company, something about the process seemed to spark a curiosity in my thinking that has lasted several decades, and if anything it's getting stronger, not weaker. It seems as if the more I know, the more I want to know.[364]

---

[363] Joe Hagan, *Nathan Myhrvold: How a Geek Grills a Burger*, Men's Journal, http://www.mensjournal.com/magazine/nathan-myhrvold-how-a-geek-grills-a-burger-20121119. Former Microsoft CTO, extraordinary entrepreneur, and almost impossible to understand how fertile this guy's mind is until you read this article. While he was obviously born with an incredibly curious mind, it also helps to have boundless money to help it along. Nevertheless, this is an article worth reading.

[364] Interestingly, I think teaching and writing had a lot to do with it. Most of my adult life was spent teaching professional adult education classes, or giving marketing presentations in front of potential customer audiences. Knowing that you can get questions from any direction, plus knowing that you'd better sound as if you know what you're talking about, makes you constantly on the hunt for more information. Frankly, any person who subscribes to the expression "Those who can do; those who can't teach" should be forced to stand up – multiple times – in front of an audience of 300 and make a presentation about exactly what they do for a living. They wouldn't ever say that again. The same goes for writing – particularly technical writing – which forces one to know a topic much more than someone who merely "does" what you're writing about.

So much for the "why" of curiosity. What about the "how"? Since curiosity is best satisfied by reading and observing, it's also the best way to build one's interest in it. There's very little of intellectual value that one can learn from reality television, or for that matter, with virtually any of the sitcoms, game shows, or so-called dramas on today's commercial TV channels (not to mention talk radio of almost any persuasion). But if you instead focus more on the "non-fiction" side of TV and radio, you can hardly go wrong. The same is true with reading – stay away from the pulp fiction, romance novels, and fanfiction, and stick with a bit more serious non-fiction. Additionally, decent newspapers and magazines can help a lot – for suggestions, try The New York Times, The Wall Street Journal, The Washington Post, the New Yorker magazine, The Economist, and your local business journal (all of which you can subscribe to digital versions that aren't expensive). Forget about their political persuasions (small business is bipartisan), and just delve into the knowledge each of these sources can bring to you – and you'll be surprised at how many directions this new-found knowledge can help your business.

An important third element of curiosity is asking questions. It's not only a way to learn, but also a way to endear you to customers – and they should be the source of your product and service ideas. The most direct benefit is when you're asking questions that are directly business related, about ways that your products or services could help the customer, but even more generally, such as challenges the customer has that really need a fix or better solution. Don't forget, though, that the success of asking questions is – drum roll, please – to listen to the answers. I think many entrepreneurs don't listen to others enough, and that's not a good recipe for success.

"The way to get started is to quit talking and begin doing."
Walt Disney

How do I take the plunge?

Once you have the basic business idea plotted out on the back of the proverbial cocktail napkin, it's time for the first concrete steps to be taken. Here are some ideas, not listed in any particular order of sequence that you need to follow.

- Research your barriers to entry (briefly discussed in Chapter 2). The barriers could be financial, infrastructure, and scope. If you're undercapitalized and don't have the capability to raise the capital, you have a barrier that won't let you successfully start a small business that requires a lot of initial capital. If you've just thought up an idea for a best-selling iPhone app that no one has thought of, well, the infrastructure is already there for you to plug into. If you've dreamed up a product idea the world has never seen before and will have to be convinced they really need it, well, the task to do that might be outside the range of a small business.

  So, your task is to start with a serious reality check, to determine if your business idea is doable, affordable, and with a reasonable chance for success and profitability.

- Build a Cash Flow/Budget spreadsheet (discussed in detail in Chapter 5). It may seem counter intuitive for this to be one of the earliest tasks in your new business planning stages, but whether you have sufficient money to initially get the venture off the ground – and then lead it to success – is predicated on whether you have the necessary capitalization. Using the downloadable Cash Flow/Budget spreadsheet template you can take the first baby steps for laying out the financial analysis that will determine if your business idea has the necessary legs to survive (instructions for downloading at the front of Chapter 5). It's been mentioned several times in this book that small business failure is due to lack of business experience, poor planning, wrong timing, bad product idea – and each of the reasons has statistical basic – but the simple fact is, whatever the underlying factors are, the actual reason you'll fail is because you run out of money.

The Cash Flow/Budget spreadsheet is designed to let you see those problems ahead of time – hopefully far enough ahead to switch course, switch strategy . . . switch whatever is necessary to ward off disaster. But at the very early stages, its biggest benefit is to let you see if you can even launch.

- Get your business planning started (notice I didn't say *plan*, but rather, *planning*). This is internal-use only planning, preferably using a spreadsheet to lay out every task you'll need to complete for launch. As the days, weeks, months go by, plot your progress. Identify critical path tasks (i.e., tasks that must be completed that impact other tasks in the schedule).

  This planning will include a decision about your business structure (sole proprietor, LLC, corporation), naming your business and creating its online presence, arranging for operating facilities, production planning and capacity (logistics), inventory control, order and sales fulfillment, how you'll process customer payments (cash, credit card and online payments), initial bookkeeping, legal and tax advice, additional staff requirements – building to a hundred more decision points that will be unique to your particular business.

  (Here's where reading this book from cover to cover comes in very handy, as it will help you lay out a comprehensive list of all the things you need to worry about during the run-up to launch day and beyond.)

- Very importantly, your planning should determine whether your proposed business is scalable. The term scaling is often misunderstood by the new small business owner – where it's thought to mean the growth of your business simply by increasing your revenue – without concentrating on how to gain that increase without an equal (or greater) increase in expenses. *Scaling in this context refers to your ability to increase revenue without increasing resource costs* (or increasing resource costs at a lesser rate). Put another way, if you simply increase revenue as the same rate as your expenses increase, you haven't increased your profitability. But if you can increase your revenue by, let's say, 20%, but only increase your expenses by 10%, your profitability will sharply increase.

- As you work towards the launch date, create a second planning spreadsheet that details your sales and marketing efforts beyond your Grand Opening day. One of the worst mistakes a new small business owner can make is to assume that business generated in the days (weeks, months?) leading up to Grand Opening will carry over to sustaining business beyond that. Once you open for business, all of your operating expenses kick in and if you don't have continued revenue gains, you can run out of operating capital very quickly. The first few months of your small business life is going to test your sales and marketing mettle to the ultimate. Unexpected hiccups during that time will only make it worse. That's what you should be planning for, and that's what you should be gaining experience to handle.

- If your operating budget (from the Cash Flow/Budget spreadsheet) indicates you might have (or might be close to) cash shortfalls *anytime* in the run-up to opening day, and continuing to the end of the first year, you should strongly consider a start-up loan. As discussed in Chapter 4, bank loans for start-up operating capital will be difficult to obtain unless you apply for an SBA-guaranteed loan. Now is a good time for this, as the SBA is eager to guarantee loans for small business start-ups, and that makes banks more eager to lend.

  Important reminder: Don't wait until you're in dire financial straits to apply for a loan, as you'll significantly *decrease* your odds of being approved for it. It might cost you a few more bucks in interest, but taking out a loan *before you need it* is a lot better than waiting until it's too late. If you follow this advice, make sure you are creative in how you "sell" the bank on your need for the loan, your level of collateral for the loan, and what you'll do with the loan proceeds (i.e., if you tell the bank you need $100,000 for equipment purchases plus operating capital, but you then show the bank you already have more than $100,000 in your bank account, your banker will likely wonder why you need the loan).

- In putting your loan application package together, formalize your business planning into a structured business plan – preferably not more than 15 pages – that you will submit to your best-choice banks that specialize in SBA-guaranteed loans. (Remember to identify at least three SBA-preferred lending banks and apply to all three at (or near) the same time, increasing your odds of getting loan approval as quickly as possible.) Keep the business plan succinct, focused, well written (get a business advisor to review it for you), and *don't* repeat multiple times what you need to say to the banker. By this point, you should have expanded your Cash Flow/Budget spreadsheet for the entire first full year of operation – condense the information in it to a single page (maybe by condensing 12 months of columns into 4 quarterly columns) and include it in your business plan.

Step out of the airplane and begin assembling the parachute.

As the Nike slogan says, ***"Just do it!"***

Let's keep talking …

In her book, *Lean In*, Sheryl Sandberg ended with something that I too think is very important. My goal is for this book to not be the end of the conversation about how to be a successful small business entrepreneur, but rather, the beginning.

I've created a website to accompany this book, www.turning-ip101.com, where I have a blog that will continue my side of the conversation. I hope to write about small business areas that didn't fit in this book (and will possibly help create a Part 2 to this book). I'll have a dozen categories of blog posts, plus real-life success stories of small businesses to promote the idea that success can promote further success.

I also plan to update this book on an annual basis, incorporating new and updated information as it's available.

Acknowledgments

Writing this book was a solo effort – but learning everything necessary to write it required a cast of thousands, including all of the employees in my own successful small business, the employees in our alliance partners, our vendors, and of course, our customers.

In nearly 30 years as founder, CEO, and President of my company – and of course, starting out for the first few years as Chief of Everything – I learned firsthand everything discussed in this book. Much of it was from mistakes I made, primarily because I didn't have a book such as this to consult along the way – and of course, it was before the days of the internet.

During the first phase of my company – the software education phase – I taught upwards of 800 five-day classes, at least 600 of them on the same topic, a very esoteric aspect of the IBM mainframe operating system that's now known generically as a "driver". At first blush, this would seem to be a mind-numbing way to build a career, but the amazing thing was, this not only allowed me to learn and understand this particular topic in minute detail, but it also taught me a huge amount about the elementary nature of teaching in itself, plus a large amount about human nature.

As a result of those really gratifying years as an adult education teacher and small business owner, I deeply appreciate everything these people helped to *teach me*.

For a few years after selling my company I often thought about writing a business memoir, a rollicking escapade of the ups and downs I'd faced dozens of times in my business life. I even spent countless hours writing lengthy drafts of that memoir, but discarded them each time with the realization that few would want to read it, and so it would mostly be a vanity book.

But then I learned that a niece and nephew, Kim and Barry, living in Spokane where I grew up, were hoping to start a microbrewery after years of home brewing for fun in the garage. Knowing only the barest of details of my own business experience, they wrote to me asking for advice on whether their proposed small business should be structured as a sole proprietorship, LLC, or corporation. One question led to another – such as how to locate a small business attorney, and behind-the-scenes analysis of brew pub property sites for lease – and when they applied for their (successful) SBA-backed start-up loan I was listed in the business plan as one of their business advisors.

The experience with Kim and Barry convinced me that my years as a small business owner provided a wealth of insight that could be useful to other would-be entrepreneurs, and so I decided to write this latest variation – a resource and planning guide for entrepreneurs who are thinking about starting a small business. My own experience certainly didn't equip me to counsel high flying entrepreneurs like the Mark Zuckerberg's of the IPO world, so that isn't the audience I set out to write this book for. Instead, it's the other 99.9% of the world's entrepreneurs who want to own their own business as a lifestyle choice – but who don't have the experience to just jump out of the airplane and get that parachute put together in the few minutes before the ground comes up at them.

As the manuscript neared the end point, Dave Roeser – a longtime software developer in my company – took on the task of reviewing the draft, and gave me valuable insight into areas where I went off track, didn't explain things well, or was just plain full of it.

Having learned long ago that I can say in 50 words what any other writer can say in 20, I knew the book needed a copy editor. I chose Anne Goldenberger, who was a wonderful copy editor for our software user guides in my old company. I knew that Anne could turn my mangled sentences into readable prose, and in several back-and-forth iterations she did a magnificent job on that. (I also learned that Anne disagrees with my plan to revolutionize the use of periods and commas outside quotation marks, as you'll see throughout this book, and my apologies to Anne for that one source of discontent.)

And lastly, I'd like to thank my wife, Kathryn Parks – who not only tolerated the days . . . and days . . . and days that I was hunched over my PC working on the research for this book – and also provided great insight and humor, and corrected many of my misremembered business life memories. In addition to providing boundless support during this project, she's my best friend, closest advisor – and importantly, my business partner and co-founder of our company.

Index

[i] Casey Coombs, Amazon CEO Jeff Bezos' shadow advisors have gone on to big things, Puget Sound Business Journal, March, 17, 2017, http://www.bizjournals.com/seattle/news/2017/03/17/amazon-ceo-jeff-bezos-shadow-advisors-big-things.html?ana=e_ph_prem&u=ZjsyWY2Pva46UGJhB%2FG%2BwQ08ea75f4&t=1489768538&j=77674741

www.ingramcontent.com/pod-product-compliance
Lightning Source LLC
Chambersburg PA
CBHW080323270326
41927CB00014B/3079